Lecture Notes in Computer Sci

Commenced Publication in 1973
Founding and Former Series Editors:
Gerhard Goos, Juris Hartmanis, and Jan van Leeuwen

Editorial Board

Ching-Hsien Hsu   Xuanhua Shi
Valentina Salapura (Eds.)

Network and Parallel Computing

11th IFIP WG 10.3 International Conference, NPC 2014
Ilan, Taiwan, September 18-20, 2014
Proceedings

 Springer

Volume Editors

Ching-Hsien Hsu
Chung Hua University
707, Sec. 2, WuFu Rd., Hsinchu, 30012, Taiwan
E-mail: chh@chu.edu.tw

Xuanhua Shi
Huazhong University of Science and Technology
1037#, Luoyu Road, Wuhan, 430074, China
E-mail: xhshi@hust.edu.cn

Valentina Salapura
IBM Thomas J. Watson Research Center
1101 Kitchawan Rd., Yorktown Heights, NY 10598, USA
E-mail: salapura@us.ibm.com

ISSN 0302-9743   e-ISSN 1611-3349
ISBN 978-3-662-44916-5   e-ISBN 978-3-662-44917-2
DOI 10.1007/978-3-662-44917-2
Springer Heidelberg New York Dordrecht London

Library of Congress Control Number: 2014948554

LNCS Sublibrary: SL 1 – Theoretical Computer Science and General Issues

Typesetting: Camera-ready by author, data conversion by Scientific Publishing Services, Chennai, India

Printed on acid-free paper

Springer is part of Springer Science+Business Media (www.springer.com)

Preface

This volume contains the proceedings of NPC 2014, the 11th IFIP International Conference on Network and Parallel Computing, which was held in Yilan, Taiwan, during September 18–20, 2014.

NPC is recognized as the main regular event of the world that covers many dimensions of network and parallel computing, including architectures, systems, algorithms, and applications. NPC 2014 is intended to play an important role for researchers and industry practitioners to exchange information regarding advancements in the state of art and practice of IT-driven services and applications, as well as to identify emerging research topics and define the future directions of network and parallel computing.

This year, the technical program of NPC 2014 drew from a large number of submissions: 196 papers submitted from 42 countries representing four regions - Asia Pacific, Europe, North, and South America. In the first stage, all papers submitted were screened for their relevance and general submission requirements. These manuscripts then underwent a rigorous peer-review process with at least three reviewers, coordinated by the international Program Committee. The Program Committee accepted 42 papers for presentation and included in the main proceedings, resulting in an acceptance rate of 21.4%. We believe that this volume not only presents novel and interesting ideas but will also stimulate future research in the area of NPC. To encourage and promote the work presented at NPC 2014, we are delighted to inform the authors that some of the papers will be accepted in special issues of International Journal of Parallel Programming. The journal has played a prominent role in promoting the development and use of network and parallel computing.

Organization of conferences with a large number of submissions requires a lot of hard work and dedication from many people. First of all, we would like to thank the Steering Committee chair, Dr. Kemal Ebcioglu, Prof. Hai Jin, and Prof. Zhiwei Xu; the general chairs, Prof. Wen-Mei Hwu and Prof. Kun-Ming Yu, for nourishing the conference and guiding its course. We are grateful to the publicity chair, Dr. Erik Altman for his excellent job in publicizing the conference. Thanks also go to Prof. Xuanhua Shi for his help with the conference proceedings and a lot of detailed work, which facilitated the overall process of publication. We wish to thank the authors for submitting high quality papers that contributed to the conference technical program. We wish to express our deepest gratitude to all Program Committee members and external reviewers for their excellent job in the paper review process. Without their help, this program would not have been be possible. We appreciate the participation of the keynote speakers, Dr. Michael Gschwind and Dr. Yunquan Zhang; their speeches greatly benefited the audience. Special thanks go to the entire Local Arrangement Committee, Prof. Chang-Wu Yu, Liwen Chang, and Ya-Hui (Batty) Hsu for their help in making the conference a wonderful success. We take this opportunity to thank all the presenters, session chairs and participants for their presence at the conference, many of whom traveled long distances to attend this conference and make their valuable contributions. Last but not least, we would like to express our gratitude to all the organizations that supported our efforts to bring the conference to fruition. We are grateful to Springer for publishing these proceedings.

We are proud to have the authors sharing their research with you, fellow members of the technical community, through NPC 2014 and these proceedings. We hope that you enjoy the NPC 2014 proceedings, as much as we do. Welcome again!

September 2014

Valentina Salapura
Robert Hsu

Organization

General Chair

Wen-Mei Hwu   University of Illinois at Urbana-Champaign, USA

Kun-Ming Yu   Chung Hua University, Taiwan

Program Chair

Valentina Salapura   IBM Research, USA

Robert C.H. Hsu   Chung Hua University, Taiwan

Award Chair

Barbara Chapman   University of Houston, USA

Cho-Li Wang   Hong Kong University, Hong Kong

Publication Chair

Xuanhua Shi   HUST, China

Fuu-Cheng Jiang   Tunghai University, Taiwan

Registration Chair

Chang-Wu Yu   Chung Hua University, Taiwan

Local Arrangement Chair

Cho-Chin Lin   National Ilan University, Taiwan

Publicity Chair

Erik Altman   Thomas J. Watson Research Center, USA

Daqiang Zhang   Tongji University, China

Advisory Committee

Ruay-Shiung Chang   National Dong Hua University, Taiwan

Ce-Kuen Shieh   National Cheng Kung University, Taiwan

Timothy K. Shih   National Central University, Taiwan
Pen-Chung Yew   University of Minnesota, USA

Steering Committee

Kemal Ebcioglu   Global Supercomputing, USA (Chair)
Hai Jin   Huazhong University of Science and
                                     Technology, China
Chen Ding   University of Rochester, USA
Jack Dongarra   University of Tennessee, USA
Guangrong Gao   University of Delaware, USA
Daniel Reed   University of Iowa, USA
Zhiwei Xu   Institue of Computing Technology, China
Yoichi Muraoka   Waseda University, Japan
Jean-Luc Gaudiot   University of California at Irvine, USA
Guojie Li   The Institute of Computing Technology, China
Viktor Prasanna   University of Southern California, USA
Weisong Shi   Wayne State University, USA
Tony Hey   Microsoft, USA

Technical Program Committee

Erik Altman   IBM Research, USA
Bin Bao   Qualcomm, USA
Greg Byrd   NCSU, USA
Mehmet Balman   VMware R&D and Lawrence Berkeley National
                                     Laboratory, USA
Alessio Botta   University of Napoli, Italy
Suren Byna   Lawrence Berkeley National Lab, USA
Jose-Maria Cela   BSC, Spain
Hsi-Ya Chang   National Center for High-performance
                                     Computing, Taiwan
Shin-Ming Cheng   National Taiwan University of Science and
                                     Technology, Taiwan
Thomas M. Chen   City University London, UK
I-Hsin Chung   IBM Research, USA
Luiz DeRose   Cray Inc., USA
Zhihui Du   Tsinghua University, China
Binzhang Fu   Chinese Academy of Sciences, China
Franz Franchetti   CMU, USA
Thomas Gschwind   IBM Research, Switzerland
Georgi Gaydadjiev   Chalmers, Sweden
Esa Hyytiä   Aalto University, Finland
Engin Ipek   University of Rochester, USA
Shadi Ibrahim   Inria Rennes - Bretagne Atlantique, France

Table of Contents

Systems, Networks and Architectures

Parallel and Multi-Core Technologies

Virtualization and Cloud Computing Technologies

Applications of Parallel and Distributed Computing

I/O, File Systems, and Data Management

Poster Sessions

Routing and Wavelength Assignment for Exchanged Hypercubes in Linear Array Optical Networks

Yu-Liang Liu[*]

Department of Computer Science and Information Engineering, Aletheia University, No.32, Zhenli St., Danshui Dist., New Taipei City 25103, Taiwan
au4377@au.edu.tw

Abstract. The exchanged hypercube, denoted by EH(s, t), is a new interconnection network obtained by systematically removing links from the hypercube, while preserves many appealing properties. This paper addresses the routing and wavelength assignment for realizing exchanged hypercubes communication patterns on linear array WDM optical networks. By using congestion estimation, we derive a lower bound of the minimum number of required wavelengths, and propose an optimal wavelength assignment algorithm that uses 2^{s+t-1} + $\lfloor 2^t/3 \rfloor$ wavelengths.

Keywords: WDM optical networks, Routing and wavelength assignment, Exchanged hypercube, Linear array, Congestion.

1 Introduction

In a wavelength division multiplexing (WDM for short) optical network, the bandwidth in optical fiber is partitioned into multiple virtual channels, in which different stream of data can be transmitted simultaneously using separate virtual channels. In this context, a virtual channel corresponds to a wavelength. In general, a WDM optical network consists of routing nodes interconnected by point-to-point fiber links. To achieve all-optical communication without optoelectrical conversions at intermediate nodes, end-to-end lightpaths are usually set up between each pair of source-destination nodes. A connection or a lightpath in a WDM optical network is an ordered pair of nodes (S, D) corresponding to transmission of a packet from source node S to destination node D.

The primary issue for WDM optical networks is to select a proper path and wavelength satisfying the *wavelength-continuity constraint and the distinct wavelength constraint* for each connection of a given communication pattern so that the number of used wavelengths is minimized [12-15]. Up to now, there have been some works about routing and wavelength assignments in optical networks [3-5,8,12-14].

The exchanged hypercube is a link-diluted variation of the hypercube nework, proposed by Loh et al [9], with numerous desirable properties, such as lower diameter and better cost effectiveness. Some related works on exchange hypercubes, such as the domination number [6], the connectivity [10], the super connectivity [11], and fault-tolerance measures [7] have been investigated.

C.-H. Hsu et al. (Eds.): NPC 2014, LNCS 8707, pp. 1–9, 2014.

The rest of this paper is organized as follows. In Section 2, we introduce some preliminaries of exchanged hypercubes and the congestion of embedding schemes. In Section 3, a lower bound of the number of required wavelengths for realizing exchanged hypercubes communication patterns on linear arrays is obtained. In Section 4, we propose an embedding scheme and an optimal wavelength assignment algorithm. Finally, we conclude the paper in Section 5.

2   Preliminaries

In this section, we introduce some preliminaries of exchanged hypercubes and the congestion of embedding schemes.

2.1   The Exchanged Hypercube

Let n be a positive integer. The n-dimensional hypercube (or n-cube for short) Q_n is the graph with vertex set $\{0, 1\}^n$. Two vertices (strings) u and v in Q_n are adjacent if and only if they differ in exactly one coordinate. Let $H(u, v)$ denote the Hamming distance between u and v, namely the number of coordinates in which u and v are different. Thus two vertices u and v in Q_n are adjacent if and only if $H(u, v) = 1$.

Let $k > 1$ and $u = u_{k-1} \ldots u_0 \in \{0, 1\}^n$ be a binary string. We use $u_{j:i}$ to denote the substring $u_j u_{j-1} \ldots u_i$ of u for $0 \leq i \leq j < k$.

Definition 2.1 ([9]). The vertex set V of exchanged hypercube EH(s, t) is the set $\{u_{s+t} u_{s+t-1} \ldots u_0 \mid u_i \in \{0, 1\}$ for $0 \leq i \leq s+t\}$.

Let $u = u_{s+t} \ldots u_0$ and $v = v_{s+t} \ldots v_0$ be two vertices in EH(s, t). There is an edge (u, v) in EH(s, t) if and only if (u, v) is in one of the following sets:

$E_1 = \{(u, v) \mid u_0 \neq v_0, u_i = v_i$ for $0 \leq i \leq s+t \}$.

$E_2 = \{(u, v) \mid u_0 = v_0 = 1, H(u, v) = 1$ with $u_i \neq v_i$ for some $1 \leq i \leq t \}$, and

$E_3 = \{(u, v) \mid u_0 = v_0 = 0, H(u, v) = 1$ with $u_i \neq v_i$ for some $t+1 \leq i \leq s+t \}$.

Let $EH_i(s, t)$ be the subgraph of EH(s, t) induced by the edges in E_i for $i \in \{1, 2, 3\}$. Clearly, EH(s, t) contains 2^{s+t+1} nodes and is a spanning subgraph of hypercube Q_{s+t+1}. For $u \in V(EH(s, t))$, if $u_0 = 0$, then the degree of u is $s+1$; otherwise, the degree of u is $t+1$. Fig. 1 depicts EH(1, 2) which is a spanning subgraph of Q_4. An edge with a label i for $i \in \{1, 2, 3\}$ is in edge set E_i. We can see that each node u in EH(1, 2) with $u_0 = 0$ is of degree 2 and all the other nodes are of degree 3.

Lemma 2.2 ([9]). **EH(s, t) is isomorphic to EH(t, s).**

By Lemma 2.2, hereafter, we may assume without loss of generality that $s \leq t$.

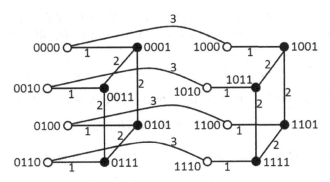

Fig. 1. An exchange hypercube EH(1, 2)

Proposition 2.3 ([6]). $EH_2(s, t)$ (respectively, $EH_3(s, t)$) contains 2^s (respectively, 2^t) copies of Q_t (respectively, Q_s) in which any two distinct copies of Q_t (respectively, Q_s) are disjoint. Moreover, $EH_1(s, t)$ forms a perfect matching between nodes in $EH_2(s, t)$ and $EH_3(s, t)$.

Denote by $Q_t^{u_{s+t:t+1}}$ for the Q_t in $EH_2(s, t)$ in which all vertices $u \in Q_t$ have the same bits in $u_{s+t:t+1}$. Similarly, $Q_s^{u_{t:1}}$ denotes those Q_s in $EH_3(s, t)$ for all vertices $u \in Q_s$ having the same bits in $u_{t:1}$. For brevity, $Q_t^{u_{s+t:t+1}}$ and $Q_s^{u_{t:1}}$ are also denoted by Q_t^x and Q_s^y, respectively, where x and y are the decimal values of $u_{s+t:t+1}$ and $u_{t:1}$, respectively. Fig. 2(a) and (b) show the two subgraphs $EH_2(1,2)$ and $EH_3(1, 2)$, respectively. Note that $EH_2(1, 2)$ contains Q_2^0 and Q_2^1 while $EH_3(1, 2)$ contains Q_1^0, Q_1^1, $Q2_1$, and Q_1^3.

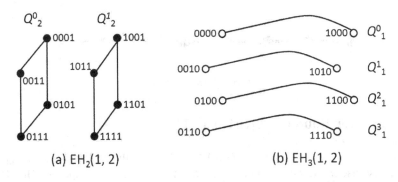

(a) $EH_2(1, 2)$ (b) $EH_3(1, 2)$

Fig. 2. The two subgraphs of EH(1, 2)

2.2   The Congestion

Let $G = (V_1, E_1)$ be the guest graph and $H = (V_2, E_2)$ the host graph, where $|V_1| = |V_2|$. An embedding scheme of G in H is an ordered pair $\Phi = (\Psi, \Omega)$, where Ψ is a bijection from V_1 to V_2, Ω is a mapping from E_1 to a set of paths in H such that, for every edge $e = (u, v) \in E_1$, there is a path $\Omega(e)$ from $\Psi(u)$ to $\Psi(v)$ in H.

Definition 2.4. The congestion of an edge $e \in E_2$ under embedding scheme Φ of G in H, denoted by $c_e(G, H, \Phi, e)$, is the number of paths $\Omega(e')$ for all $e' \in E_1$ passing through e, namely,

$$c_e(G, H, \Phi, e) = |\{e' : e \in E(\Omega(e')), e' \in E_1 \text{ and } e \in E_2\}|$$

The congestion of G in H under Φ, denoted by $c_p(G, H, \Phi)$, is defined as:

$$c_p(G, H, \Phi) = \max_{e \in E_2} c_e(G, H, \Phi, e)$$

The congestion of G in H under Φ, denoted by $c_g(G, H)$, is defined as:

$$c_g(G, H, \Phi) = \min_{\Phi} c_p(G, H, \Phi)$$

Let $\lambda(G, H)$ stand for the number of required wavelengths for realizing communication pattern G on WMN optical network H by embedding scheme Φ. Lemma 2.5 shows that $c_g(G, H)$ is a lower bound of $\lambda_\Phi(G, H)$.

Lemma 2.5 ([1, 3, 12]). $\lambda_\Phi(G, H) \geq c_g(G, H)$.

In this paper, we consider that the guest graph is EH(s, t) and the host graph is a linear array L_n, where $n = s+t+1$ and L_n is a path of 2^n nodes. We label the nodes (respectively, the edges) in L_n from 1 to 2^n (respectively, from e_1 to e_{2^n-1}) in consecutive order. For example, a linear array L_3 is shown in Fig. 3. Given an embedding scheme, each node u in $V(\text{EH}(s, t))$ will be assigned a distinct number in $\{1,\ldots,2^n\}$. The node assigned number i is then embedded to the node i in L_n.

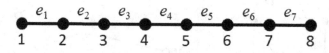

Fig. 3. A linear array L_3

3   A Lower Bound of $\lambda_\Phi(\text{EH(s,t)}, L_n)$

If $u = u_{s+t} \ldots u_{t+1} u_t \ldots u_1 u_0$ is a node in Q^i_t ($0 \leq i \leq 2^{s-1}$) and the decimal value of $u_{t:1}$ is j, then we also use $q^{i,j}_t$ to denote node u. Let R^i_t stand for the subgraph of EH(s, t) induced by the nodes in Q^i_t and all nodes in EH_1 adjacent to some vertex in Q^i_t.

Lemma 3.1. The congestion of embedding the nodes in Q^i_t to a linear subarray L_t of L_n is $2^t + \lfloor 2^t/3 \rfloor$.

Property 3.2. If Φ is an optimal embedding scheme, then Φ will embed nodes in a subgraph of EH(s, t), which is isomorphic to R^i_t, to nodes $1, 2, \ldots 2^{t+1}$ of L_n.

Lemma 3.3. $\max\limits_{e_i;1\le i\le 2^{t+1}} \min\limits_{\Phi}\{c_e(EH(s,t),L_n,\Phi,e_i)\} \ge 2^{s+t-1} + \lfloor 2^t/3 \rfloor$.

Theorem 3.4. $c_g(EH(s,t),L_n) \ge 2^{s+t-1} + \lfloor 2^t/3 \rfloor$.

Lemma 3.5. The number of required wavelengths to realize EH(s, t) communication patterns on linear array L_n is not less than $2^{s+t-1} + \lfloor 2^t/3 \rfloor$.

Proof. By Lemma 2.5 and Theorem 3.4, the lemma is thus proved.
Q.E.D.

4 Optimal Wavelength Assignment for Realizing EH(s, t) on L_n

In this section, we first derive an embedding scheme, and then describe a routing and wavelength assignment algorithm. Let $u = u_{s+t}...u_{t+1}u_t...u_1u_0$ be a node in $V(EH(s, t))$. We partition $V(EH(s, t))$ into eight disjoint subsets as follows:

$S_1 = \{u : u_{t+1} = 0; u_1 = 0 \text{ and } u_0 = 1\}$,
$S_2 = \{u : u_{t+1} = 0; u_1 = 1 \text{ and } u_0 = 1\}$,
$S_3 = \{u : u_{t+1} = 1; u_1 = 0 \text{ and } u_0 = 1\}$,
$S_4 = \{u : u_{t+1} = 1; u_1 = 1 \text{ and } u_0 = 1\}$,
$S_5 = \{u : u_{t+1} = 0; u_1 = 0 \text{ and } u_0 = 0\}$,
$S_6 = \{u : u_{t+1} = 1; u_1 = 0 \text{ and } u_0 = 0\}$,
$S_7 = \{u : u_{t+1} = 0; u_1 = 1 \text{ and } u_0 = 0\}$, and
$S_8 = \{u : u_{t+1} = 1; u_1 = 1 \text{ and } u_0 = 0\}$.

Clearly, the subgraph induced by S_i ($1 \le i \le 4$) comprises 2^{s-1} disjoint $(t-1)$-cubes, and the subgraph induced by S_i ($5 \le i \le 8$) comprises 2^{t-1} disjoint $(s-1)$-cubes. If $s > 2$ for the subgraph induced by S_m ($1 \le m \le 4$), we denote the $(t-1)$-cube by $Q^{m,i}_{t-1}$ where i ($0 \le i \le 2^{s-1}-1$) is the decimal value of $u_{s+t:t+2}$, and the node u in $Q^{m,i}_{t-1}$ is represented by $q^{m,i,j}_{t-1}$, where j ($0 \le j \le 2^{t-1}-1$) is the decimal value of $u_{t:2}$. Otherwise, if $s = 1$, the $(t-1)$-cube is denoted by $Q^{m,0}_{t-1}$, and the node u in $Q^{m,0}_{t-1}$ is denoted by $q^{m,0,j}_{t-1}$, where j ($0 \le i \le 2^{t-1}-1$) is the decimal value of $u_{t:2}$.

Similarly, if $s > 2$, for the subgraph induced by S_m ($5 \le m \le 8$), we denote the $(s-1)$-cube by $Q^{m,i}_{s-1}$, where i ($0 \le i \le 2^{t-1}-1$) is the decimal value of $u_{t:2}$, and the node in $Q^{m,i}_{s-1}$ is represented by $q^{m,i,j}_{s-1}$, where j ($0 \le j \le 2^{s-1}-1$) is the decimal value of $u_{s+t:t+2}$. Otherwise if $s = 1$, the 0-cube with decimal value i ($0 \le i \le 2^{t-1}-1$) in substring $u_{t:2}$ is denoted as $Q^{m,i}_0$, and the only node in $Q^{m,i}_0$ is enoted as $q^{m,i,j}_0$.

Let $u^i = u^i_{s+t}...u^i_{t+1}u^i_t...u^i_1u^i_0$ be a node in S_i ($1 \le i \le 8$), and let $v = v_{s+t-3}...v_{t+1}v_t...v_1v_0$ be a binary string of length $s + t - 2$ with decimal value x ($0 \le x \le 2^{s+t-2}-1$). If $s > 2$, then let $u^i_{s+t:t+2} = v_{s+t-3:t-1}$ and $u^i_{t:2} = v_{t-2:0}$; otherwise, for the case $s = 1$, let $u^i_{t:2} = v_{t-2:0}$. We can find that the nodes u_i ($1 \le i \le 8$) form two reversed direction cycles, denoted by $cycle_1(x)$ and $cycle_2(x)$, respectively. Fig. 4 shows the two reversed direction cycles.

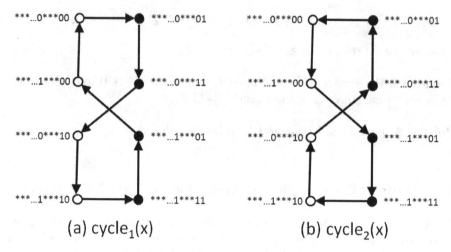

(a) cycle₁(x)   **(b) cycle₂(x)**

Fig. 4. Two reversed direction cycles in EH(s, t)

An embedding scheme α, which assign numbers to the nodes in EH(s, t), is shown in Table 1.

Table 1. An embedding scheme α

Embedding scheme α
Input: An exchange hypercube EH(s, t).
Output: The assigned number $NUM(u)$, $u \in V(EH(s, t))$.
begin
Step 1. Set k = 1;
Step 2. For each node $u \in$ EH(s, t), set $NUM(u) = $ NULL;
Step 3. For $m = 1$ to 4
For $i = 0$ to 2^{s-1}-1
For $j = 0$ to 2^{t-1}-1
$NUM(q^{m,i,j}_{t-1}) = k$;
$k = k + 1$;
Step 4. For $m = 5$ to 8
For $i = 0$ to 2^{t-1}-1
For $j = 0$ to 2^{s-1}-1
$NUM(q^{m,i,j}_{s-1}) = k$;
$k = k + 1$;
end

Property 4.1. In the embedding scheme α, if x ≠ y or $m_1 \neq m_2$ or $i_1 \neq i_2$, then the nodes in $Q^{m1,i1}_{x-1}$ and the nodes in $Q^{m2,i2}_{y-1}$ are embedded into two disjoint linear subarrays of L_n.

Proof. This property is clear from the embedding scheme α.   □

Fig. 5 shows the numbers assigned to the nodes in EH(1,2) by the embedding scheme α.

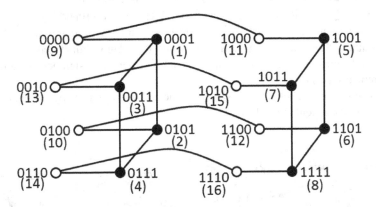

Fig. 5. The numbers assigned to nodes in EH(1, 2)

A routing and wavelength assignment algorithm β for realizing EH(s, t) communication patterns on L_n is shown Table 2.

Table 2. A routing and wavelength assignment algorithm β

Routing and wavelength assignment algorithm β
Input: An exchange hypercube EH(s, t), and the assigned number $NUM(u)$, $u \in V(EH(s, t))$.
Output: The assigned number $NUM(u)$, $u \in V(EH(s, t))$.

begin
 Step 1. For x = 0 to $2^{s+t-2}-1$
       assign 1 unused wavelength to link e in $cycle_1(x)$;
       assign 1 unused wavelength to link e in $cycle_2(x)$;
 Step 2. For m = 1 to 4
     For i = 0 to $2^{s-1}-1$
       Call Algorithm 1 in [3] to assign wavelengths to links in $Q^{m,i}_{t-1}$.
 Step 2. For m = 5 to 8
     For i = 0 to $2^{t-1}-1$
       Call Algorithm 1 in [3] to assign wavelengths to links in $Q^{m,i}_{s-1}$.
 end

Theorem 4.2. The optimal number of required wavelengths to realize EH(s, t) communication patterns on L_n is $2^{s+t-1}+\lfloor 2^t/3 \rfloor$.

Proof. It is clear that Algorithm β considers all links in EH(s, t). In Step 1, we have that links on 2^{s+t-1} directed cycles are assigned wavelengths, and links on each directed cycle are assigned 1 unused wavelength. Hence, 2^{s+t-1} wavelengths are assigned in this step. In Step 2 (respectively, Step 3), Algorithm 1 is invoked to assign wavelengths to links in $Q^{m,i}_{t-1}$ (respectively, $Q^{m,i}_{s-1}$). According to the results in [3], it follows that $\lfloor 2^t/3 \rfloor$ (respectively $\lfloor 2^s/3 \rfloor$) wavelengths are required for each $Q^{m,i}_{t-1}$ (respectively, $Q^{m,i}_{s-1}$) in Step 2 (respectively, Step 3). By Property 4.1, the wavelengths assigned to links in each $Q^{m,i}_{s-1}$ and $Q^{m,i}_{t-1}$ can be reused, and hence, Steps 2 and 3 require $\lfloor 2^t/3 \rfloor$ wavelengths. It is obvious that Algorithm β requires $2^{s+t-1} + \lfloor 2^t/3 \rfloor$ wavelengths. By Lemma 3.5, an optimal wavelength assignment is achieved. This completes the proof.

Fig. 6 shows the wavelengths assigned to the links in EH(1, 2) by the routing and wavelength assignment algorithm β.

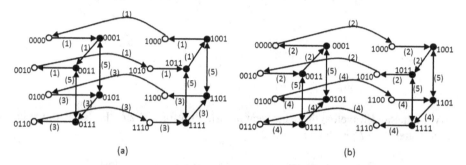

Fig. 6. The wavelengths assigned to links in EH(1, 2)

5   Concluding Remarks

In this paper, we study the optimal wavelength assignment for realizing the exchanged hypercube EH(s, t) communication patterns on linear array WDM optical network L_n by proving that $c_g(EH(s, t), L_n) \geq 2^{s+t-1} + \lfloor 2^t/3 \rfloor$. We also design an embedding scheme and a routing and wavelength assignment algorithm which assigns the optimal number of wavelengths.

For the case when $s = t$, the exchanged hypercube is reduce to the dual-cubes [16], and $2^{2s-1} + \lfloor 2^s/3 \rfloor$ wavelengths are required when the guest network is the dual-cube. For a future research, it is worthwhile to parallelize the wavelength assignment algorithm proposed in this paper, and consider the routing and wavelengths assignment issues for other types of communication patterns, such as, crossed cubes, twisted cubes, recursive circulants, etc.

References

1. Beauquier, B., Bermond, J.C., Gargano, L., Hell, P., Prennes, S., Vaccaro, U.: Graph problems arising from wavelength routing in all optical networks. In: Proceedings of the Second Workshop in Optics and Computer Science, pp. 76–84 (1997)

2. Bezrukov, S., Chavez, J., Harper, L., Rottger, M., Schroeder, U.P.: The congestion of n-cube layout on a rectangular grid. Discrete Mathematics 213(1-3), 13–19 (2000)
3. Chen, Y., Shen, H.: Routing and wavelength assignment for hypercube in array-based WDM optical networks. Journal of Parallel and Distributed Computing 70, 59–68 (2010)
4. Chen, Y., Shen, H., Liu, F.: Wavelength assignment for realizing parallel FFT on regular optical networks. Journal of Supercomputing 36, 3–16 (2006)
5. Chen, Y., Shen, H., Zhang, H.: Wavelength assignment for directional hypercube communications on a class of WDM optical networks. In: Proceedings of International Conference on Parallel Processing, pp. 288–595 (2007)
6. Klav_zar, S., Ma, M.: The domination number of exchanged hypercubes. Information Processing Letters 114, 159–162 (2014)
7. Li, X.J., Xu, J.M.: Generalized measures of fault tolerance in exchanged hypercubes. Information Processing Letters 113, 533–537 (2013)
8. Libeskind-Hadas, R., Melhem, R.G.: Multicast routing and wavelength assignment in multihop optical networks. IEEE/ACM Transactions on Networking 10(5), 621–629 (2002)
9. Loh, P.K.K., Hsu, W.J., Pan, Y.: The exchanged hypercube. IEEE Transactions on Parallel and Distributed Systems 16(9), 866–874 (2005)
10. Ma, M.: The connectivity of exchanged hypercubes, Discrete Mathematics. Algorithms and Applications 2(2), 51–57 (2010)
11. Ma, M., Zhu, L.: The super connectivity of exchanged hypercubes. Information Processing Letters 111, 360–364 (2011)
12. Yu, C., Yang, X., Yang, L., Zhang, J.: Routing and wavelength assignment for 3-aryn-cube in array-based optical network. Information Processing Letters 112, 252–256 (2012)
13. Yu, C., Yang, X., Yang, L., Zhang, J.: Routing and wavelength assignment for 3-ary n-cube communication patterns in linear array optical networks for n communication rounds. Information Processing Letters 113, 677–680 (2013)
14. Yuan, X., Melhem, R.: Optimal routing and channel assignments for hypercube communication on optical mesh-like processor arrays. In: Proceedings of The Fifth International Conference on Massively Parallel Processing, pp. 76–84 (1998)
15. Zang, H., Jue, J.P., Bukherjee, B.: A review of routing and wavelength assignment approaches for wavelength-routed optical networks. Optical Network Magazine 1(1), 47–60 (2000)
16. Li, Y., Peng, S., Chu, W.: Efficient collective communications in dual-cube. Journal of Supercomputing 28, 71–90 (2004)

Page Classifier and Placer: A Scheme
of Managing Hybrid Caches

Xin Yu[1], Xuanhua Shi[1], Hai Jin[1], Xiaofei Liao[1], Song Wu[1], and Xiaoming Li[2]

[1] Services Computing Technology and System Lab
Cluster and Grid Computing Lab
School of Computer Science and Technology
Huazhong University of Science and Technology,Wuhan, 430074, China
xhshi@hust.edu.cn
[2] Department of ECE, University of Delaware, Newark, DE, USA

Abstract. Hybrid cache architecture (HCA), which uses two or more cache hierarchy designs in a processor, may outperform traditional cache architectures because no single memory technology can deliver the optimal power, performance and density at the same time. The general HCA scheme has also been proposed to manage cache regions that have different usage patterns. However previous HCA management schemes control data placement at cache set level and are oblivious to software's different power and performance characteristics in different hardware cache regions. This hardware-only approach may lead to performance loss and may fail to guarantee quality of service. We propose a new HCA approach that enables OS to be aware of underlying hybrid cache architecture and to control data placement, at OS page level, onto difference cache regions. Our approach employs a light-weighted hardware profiler to monitor cache behaviors at OS page level and to capture the hot pages. With this knowledge, OS will be able to dynamically select different cache placement policies to optimize placement of data to achieve higher performance, lower power consumption and better quality of service. Our simulation experiments demonstrate that the proposed hybrid HCA achieves 7.8% performance improvement on a dual-core system compared to a traditional SRAM-only cache architecture and at the same time reduces area cost.

Keywords: hybrid cache, page coloring, multi-core.

1 Introduction

Cache is widely used in todays computers to mend the ever-increasing speed gap between processor core and main memory. Emerging memory technologies have demonstrated significantly different properties in density, speed, power consumption, reliability features, and scalability. Table 1 summarizes the important characteristics of four memory technologies: SRAM, Phase-change RAM (PRAM) [4,6], embedded Dynamic RAM (eDRAM), and Magnetic RAM (MRAM) [5].

C.-H. Hsu et al. (Eds.): NPC 2014, LNCS 8707, pp. 10–22, 2014.

Table 1. Characteristic comparison of different memory technologies

Features	SRAM	eDRAM	MRAM	PRAM
Density	Low	High	High	Very high
Speed	Very fast	Fast	Fast read; Slow write	Slow read; Very slow write
Dynamic Power	Low	Medium	Low read; High write	Medium read; High write
Leak Power	High	Medium	Low	Low
Non-volatile	NO	NO	Yes	Yes
Scalability	Yes	Yes	Yes	Yes

Hybrid Cache Architecture (HCA) has been proposed to take advantage of multiple memory technologies [4–6] in one cache. However, the existing HCA management schemes control data placement at cache set level and hide from software the knowledge about differences in power and performance characteristics of hardware cache regions. This hardware-only approach may lead to performance loss and loss of quality of service.

To address the shortcomings of existing HCA management schemes, we propose a new approach which makes operating system (OS) be aware of the underlying HCA architecture and enables OS to customize data placement in HCA and focus on using our proposed HCA technology to improve the throughput of multicore systems.

This paper makes the following contributions:

- We extend the page coloring capability in OS with a novel awareness of L2 cache access patterns and program behavior. In particular, our technique for the first time dynamically manages hybrid cache at page level through page migration and optimize migration policy to amortize the performance overhead.
- We propose a hardware-assisted mechanism page classifier to monitor the patterns of L2 cache accesses from each core at page granularity. The page classifier could not only monitor L2 accesses but also capture hot pages.
- We propose an effective heuristic to decide when and how to migrate hot pages in or out of fast regions, so as to make full use of HCAs large capability and high access speed at the same time.

2 Proposed Scheme

We assume the shared L2 is divided into a fast region and a slow region. The heterogeneous cache placement is only possible if we can monitor the access frequency of cache blocks and dynamically adjust placement of cache blocks. We propose a hardware-assist software-controlled hybrid mechanism to address the two challenges.

2.1   Page Coloring

Traditionally, the intersection of page number bits and L2 index bits are used as the page color bits, as shown in Fig.1. OS has control over these bits. We choose certain subset of those bits to identify different cache regions, which is called hybrid bits. Thus, when a page is migrated to specified page with certain hybrid bits, its data would be accessed in that cache region. In this study, we assume the size of a page is 4KB and the size of L2 is 128KB. Consequently there are six page color bits in the cache subsystem used by this work, as shown in Fig.1. As the ratio of fast region to slow region is 1:3, the first two bits of page color bits are referred to hybrid bits.

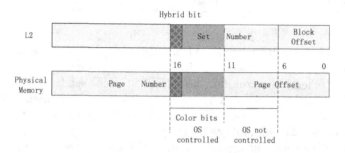

Fig. 1. Page coloring bits and hybrid bits

2.2   Page Classifier

In this study, we enhance L2 cache with a new module: a page classifier. The page classifier is composed of two parts, named Sampler and Mature/Nursery. Mature/Nursery counts the number of L2 access of every page. To reduce the power overhead of the added components, a L2 access filter Sampler is designed and controls how often L2 accesses are counted.

Mature/Nursery classifies the L2 access pattern at page level. They are counter caches. Every block records the access behavior of one page. Its data could include read counter, write counter and total access counter. As it is indexed via physical page number, its tag is the segment of page number.

As what they are called, pages access pattern would be initially recorded in Nursery. When one page becomes relatively hot, its block would be exchanged into Mature. To archive this purpose, Mature and Nursery are designed to have the same cache sets. Block swap happens between the same cache set of Mature and Nursery. As a result, a new L2 access is firstly recorded in Nursery. When the page has more and more L2 accesses, which is higher than other blocks, it would be swapped into Mature. We set a swapping frequency for this progress to avoid block jitters. The access to L2 cache and the access to Mature/nursery are parallel. If the access is a L1 cache miss, the physical address is sent to L2 cache module. If the access to Mature/Nursery is a hit, the read or write counter is increased by one. If it is a miss, the block with least number of accesses (LATBlock) in Nursery would be replaced and the counter would be reset to one.

We exchange blocks between Mature and Nursery periodically. OS compares the blocks of biggest number of accesses in Nursery, named MATBlock, with LATBlock in Mature. If the former is bigger, swapping would happen. After swapping, MAT in Nursery and LAT in Mature both need to update.

2.3   Page Placer

The page placer is designed to determine where and when to migrate a candidate page to a new physical page. Os would scan Mature to find hot pages still in slow region and scan Nursery to find not-hot pages still in fast region periodically.

When choosing page migration destination, we need to specify its page color. We take a round-robin policy in allocating physical pages, to make virtual pages distributed evenly among different colors in memory. This round-robin process of assigning page number is not only used by the page migration process, but also adopted in the allocation of physical pages for virtual pages. In this study, two registers are provided to assist this progress, which record next page color (NPC) for each region. After one page is allocated, the value of next page color would be increased by one; when it reaches the last page color of one region, it would reset to zero. To adapt this policy, traditional buddy system algorithm for managing free page frames is slightly modified: choosing appropriate bulks of page frames for migration destination. For example, we assume 27 pages need to be migrated to fast region. OS would search the list of blocks for buddy system to find groups of 32 contiguous page frames. It would start to allocate page from the page color recorded in NPC register of fast region and allocate 27 pages. After page allocation, the register would add 27 accordingly.

To reduce page migration cost, one simple yet effective approach is to decide the migration time separately for hot pages and not-hot pages. For hot pages, page fault is triggered and the page would be copied to its destination page at once, and thus its blocks are updated to fast region of L2 immediately. As most part of its data has already been in L2, the copy process costs little time. However, not-hot pages is to keep in a drowsy mode: they are invalided and written back into swapping area of the disk in migration period; only when its data is accessed, it writes into its destination page frame. Thus its data would not pollute fast region because they avoid being swapped in and out of L2 frequently. As a result, those policies make page migration damage the performance of the applications slightly.

To reduce migration cost further, not only migration frequency is controlled, but also hot page threshold (HotThreshold) is set. As the analysis above, pages in Mature, which relatively hotter than pages of the same set in Nursery are unnecessarily globally hottest. Therefore HotThreshold is set. There is a formula to describe the relationship of system parameters and estimate an approximate yet reasonable value for HotThreshold:

$$HotThreshold = \frac{MigrCycle \times IPC \times Ratio}{CapabilityMN} \times Multiplier \qquad (1)$$

In Eq. 1, *IPC* is the number of instructions per cycle of the running programs, *MigrCycle* is the page migration cycle, *CapabilityMN* is the total entry number of Mature and Nursery, *Ratio* represents the average times of L2 cache access per instruction, and Multipliecr represents the ratio of HotThredhold to the average times of L2 accesses per page. In this formula, HotThreshold varies directly with *MigrCycle*. As *IPC* and *Ratio* are the characteristics of the programs, we only change *Multiplier* to adjust the ratio of hot pages and set it as 10 in this work. In order to dynamically reflect the L2 access pattern of one page, all counters in Mature/Nursery are aged by right shift by one bit at the end of migration period.

3   Methodology

In this section, we describe our simulation methodology.

3.1   System Configuration

We choose the simulation parameters based on the related studies [4–6,9,12], and we use the typical density, latency, and energy numbers for the three memory technologies, which are calculated using CACTI 6.0 [8]. We scale these parameters to 65nm technology as described in [1]. We use the same cache parameters as described in [11], which are shown in Table 2.

Table 2. Four memory technology parameters

Cache	Normal Density	Latency (cycles)	Dynamic energy (nJ)	Static power (W)
SRAM (1MB)	1	8	0.388	1.36
eDRAM (4MB)	4	24	0.72	0.4

We choose Zesto [7] as our base simulator, which is a cycle-level x86 processor simulator publicly available for academic use. We augment its cache part to study the proposed hybrid cache management scheme. Our system configuration is summarized in Table 3.

Table 3. System configuration

Processor	3000MHz, out of order, (8 way issues), core number depends on design
L1	32KB DL1, 32KB IL2, 64B8way, 8bank, (1 R/W port)
L2 (LLC)	shared LLC64B, 16way, 16 bank, latency and capability depends on design
Memory	400 cycle latency, (memory contr. vs. core speed 1:2),page size:4KB

3.2 Workload

We choose SPEC CPU 2006 as the benchmarks to run on the simulated system. In order to run on multi-core simulated by Zesto, we use a program, *zesto-eio*, provided by Zesto to generate *eio* files and we got 21 *eio* files successfully out of total 29 benchmarks shown in Table 4. After a warm-up period simulation of 100 million instructions, we simulate the system cycle-by-cycle for 100 million instructions and collect the simulation results.

Table 4. Workloads

Benchmarks	Applications
Spec CINT2006	400.perlbench, 401.bzip2, 403.gcc, 429.mcf, 445.gobmk, 456.hmmer, 458.sjeng, 462.libquantum, 464.h264ref Spec
CFP2006	410.bwaves, 433.milc, 434.zeusmp, 435.gromacs, 436.cactusADM, 437.leslie3d, 444.namd, 447.dealII, 450.soplex, 453.povray, 465.tonto, 470.lbm

3.3 Design Methodology

To take advantage of separate characteristics of different memory technologies, we present the hybrid cache subsystem. To compare the performance of the hybrid cache scenario and pure-SRAM cache scenario, we assume that the chip area is the same for all the design cases.

Before we introduce the design methodology, we define the division of tasks between the hardware part (the page classifier) and the software part (the page placer in OS). The hardware part is responsible for profile cache access behaviors of programs. It records how many times a virtual page accesses the L2 and filters the hot page. In this process it does not care the L2 architecture, no matter it is homogeneous like pure-SRAM cache, or it is heterogeneous, such as hybrid cache consisted of SRAM and eDRAM, or it is consisted of SRAM and MRAM, even consisted of eDRAM and MRAM. This means that the design of hardware part is not affected by L2 architecture. OS is the only part that should be aware of L2 architecture. Thus it could re-adjust which part of L2 could be accessed by one virtual page, according to the attributes of different RAM technologies. By simply configuring and taking advantage of those attributes in the page placer algorithm, OS could optimize performance of L2 architecture. As analyzed above, the hardware part is aware of software behaviors and the software part is aware of the hardwares attribution. The unique combination of the two-way awareness enables OS to control the behaviors of cache access without complex hardware design.

Therefore, this design is almost agnostic to the design of HCA (hybrid cache architecture), which makes it scalable for different HCAs. The porting to different HCAs is merely to change the configuration in the page placer algorithm. To improve scalability, this design adopts a simple but efficient way and demonstrates that this hardware-software combined design could work very well for HCA. The advantage can be fully illustrated with a small scale system: dual core and 2MB L2 on CMP, rather than on prevalent larger scale systems.

The design of HCA also follows this simple but efficient methodology. The quickest SRAM and slowest eDRAM are used, to illustrate that even in such radical combinations, our technique can perform well.

There are clear benefits of such hybrid cache design: (1) The new memory technology has a much higher density than traditional SRAM technology, which increases the effective cache size under the same chip area constraint. (2) Performance can be improved by keeping hot cache lines which are accessed relatively most frequently in fast regions and place not so hot cache lines in slow regions. (3) This hardware-software combined design has simplified the process of making OS aware of L2 behavior and controlling it, and is scalable for different HCAs. (4) Flexible and tunable page placing strategies become possible and promising.

4   Result

In this section, we present experimental results of HCA.

4.1   General Evaluation

We assume the total size of the hybrid cache is 2MB, and the size ratio of SRAM and eDRAM is 1: 3. Under the same area constraint, we should study 0.875 MB SRAM as control set. To avoid complicated indexing schemes which are often associated with odd-sized caches, we construct 0.5 MB and 1MB SRAM instead to approach the performance of 0.875 MB SRAM , shown as *Conf.1* and *Conf.2*.

Table 5. Four sets of cache L2 parameters

	L2 parameters
Conf.1	512KB SRAM-only (8 cycles)
Conf.2	1MB SRAM-only (8 cycles)
Conf.3	Fast region: 512KB SRAM (8 cycles); Slow region: 1.5MB eDRAM (24 cycles)

4.2   Results of Page Classifier

To check whether page classifier can pick out the hot pages effectively, we analyze the ratio of the access number of identified hot pages to the total L2 access number. As shown in Fig.2, the ratio is over 0.8 for more than half of benchmarks, and the average rate is over 0.6. The results proves that 1) majority of L2 cache accesses are belong to very small set of pages, and 2) the page classifier does a good job to identify these hot pages.

4.3   Results on Single-Core

First, we apply the page placer to HCA. We name HCA architecture with OS Cache Management as HCACM and HCA refers to the common HCA without OS cache management. Fig.3 compares the performance of HCACM and HCA, and shows that the average IPC improvement is only 1%.

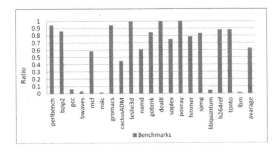

Fig. 2. Ratio of hot page L2 access number to total L2 access number

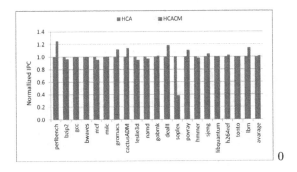

Fig. 3. Comparison of normalized IPC between HCA enabled cache management and not enabled cache management

To find out why this page placer does not work well, we compare the L2 miss rate between HCA and HCACM in Fig.4. We can see that the benchmarks can be divided into three categories: 1) the hot pages have high access frequency and the page placer improves the L2 access performance, such as *perlbench, gromacs, cactusADM*; 2) the hot pages have high access frequency, but their performance almost stays the same, or even degrades, such as *mcf, namd, soplex,* and *hmmer*; 3) page classifier is not so useful for them, the hot page access frequency is lower than normal and the performance nearly stays the same, for example *gcc, bwaves, milc, libquatum.*

The analysis of the results above is consistent with the benchmarks L2 access behavior. The first category of benchmarks are memory-latency sensitive and has small working set, therefore benefiting more from our policy that hot pages are all placed in fast region. The second category of benchmarks has a larger working set that cannot wholly fit in to fast region. Therefore the total L2 miss rate increases much when putting all hot pages in fast region, which could offset performance improvement from low latency, or even hurts the performance. The last category of benchmarks is non-memory sensitive, so they almost stay the same no matter we apply cache management or not.

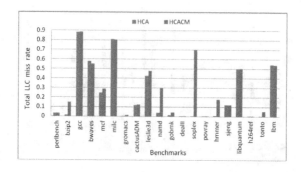

Fig. 4. Comparison of total L2 miss rate between HCA and HCACM

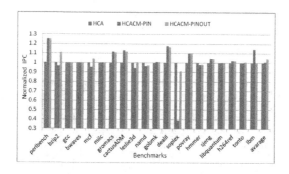

Fig. 5. Comparison of normalized IPC between HCA, HCACM with migration policy PIN and HCACM with migration policy PINOUT

To make page placer perform better in HCA, we focus on the first two categories of benchmarks and pursue a better policy to place hot pages. To resolve the problem, the page placer not only migrates hot pages into fast region but also migrates some out of fast region when its L2 miss rate is high in fast region than slow region by 10% margin. To distinguish between the new policy and the former one, we call the new policy PINOUT and the former one PIN. We compare the two policies in HCA, and the results are shown in Fig.5.

In Fig.5, we can see the following: 1) the average performance improvement for policy PINOUT for all the 20 benchmarks is about 7.6% over policy PIN, 4.2% over HCA; 2) The performance of the second category of benchmarks with policy PINPOUT increases 27.7% over policy PIN. But the performance of the first category decreases slightly, because they have small working set and do not benefit from large capability.

We compare the HCACM-PINOUT (HCACM with migration policy PINOUT) with SRAM with two configurations (*Conf.1* and *Conf.2* in Table 5), and the results are shown in Fig.6. We can see that the average IPC of HCACM-PINOUT is 9.5% higher than that of 512 KB SRAM and 5.8% higher than that of 1MB SRAM. Especially for *bzip2*, *mcf*, and *soplex*, the IPC is more

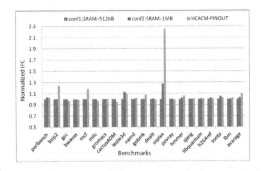

Fig. 6. Comparison of normalized IPC between *Conf.1*, *Conf.2* and HCACM with migration policy PINOUT

than 10% higher than 512KB SRAM. It is worth noting that although cache area used by HCACM-PINOUT is smaller than that of a 1MB SRAM L2 cache, it performs much better than 1MB SRAM L2 cache. This confirms that not only short latency but also large capability bring good performance for HCA when reasonable management is applied.

4.4 Results on Dual-Core

We also apply this mechanism to dual-core system, and we run eight sets of benchmarks, shown in Table 6, on dual-core system with different L2 cache configurations and management policies.

We first run those benchmark sets on dual-core system with policy PIN. The IPC results illustrate that the overall performance decrease a little as shown in Fig.7(a) (the numbers of 1-8 refer to the sets of benchmarks, and 9 refers to the average IPC of all the sets).

The PIN policy on dual cores has similar problem with that on single core, which is proven by the comparing the total L2 miss rate between HCA and HCA-PIN in Fig.7(b). Multiprogram has aggravated the competition in L2 and lead to high cache jitter except set 2 and 6, which are more latency-insensitive than capacity-insensitive.

To solve the cache jitter, we constrain that a candidate hot page could migrate only if its miss rate is lower than a specified miss rate threshold. We call this policy PINTD and run a series of experiments with it. We compare the IPCs

Table 6. Eight sets of benchmarks on dual-core system

Num.	Benchmarks	Num.	Benchmarks
1	gcc+bwaves	5	povray+hmmer
2	gromacs+cactusADM	6	sjeng+libquantum
3	leslie3d+namd	7	h264ref+tonto
4	gobmk+dealII	8	lbm+soplex

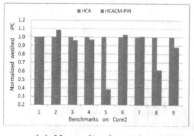 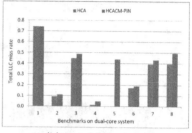

(a) Normalized weighted IPC   (b) Total L2 miss rate

Fig. 7. Sets of benchmarks running on dual-core system

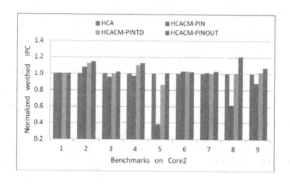

Fig. 8. Normalized weighted IPC of sets of benchmarks running on dual-core system

for HCA, HCACM-PIN, HCACM-PINTD, and HCACM-PINOUT, and get the results in Fig.8. The HCACM-PINOUT refers to the results that we apply policy PINOUT based on PINTD. From Fig.8, we can see the followings: 1) the average performance improvement of HCACM-PINTD is just about 1.6% compared with PIN; 2) The average weighted performance improvement for PINOUT is 13.5% over PIN, 7.2% over HCA, 14.9% over *Conf.1*, 7.8% over *Conf.2*. Sets with higher cache miss rate could benefit more from HCACM-PINOUT. For 2, 4 and 8, they achieve over 10% improvement compared to HCA, especially for set 8 with about 21% improvement. Although set 5 is not suitable for HCA cache management, PINOUT could eliminate the bad effects of cache management. Above all, the page placer which works with policy PINOUT could handle HCA cache management well.

5   Related Work

In recent years, substantial research effort has been dedicated to intelligently manage hybrid cache at fine granularity.

There are many different hybrid cache studies for CMPs. Sun et al. [10] propose two architectural techniques: read-preemptive write buffer and

SRAM-MRAM hybrid L2 cache to mitigate the long latency and high energy of MRAM when writing. Wu et al. [11] , discuss and evaluate two types of hybrid cache architectures, and propose HCA management scheme to control data placement at cache set level and hide from software the differences in power and performance characteristics of hardware cache regions.

Managing shared cache in CMPs, at both finer and coarser granularity has been widely studied [3], but few are applied to hybrid cache management. This method requires complex search to per-core private tag arrays that must be kept coherent, which adds extra design and hardware cost and some performance lost.To avoid the aforementioned problems, many other works manage shared caches in CMPs at page granularity. Chaudhuri et al. [2] have devised OS support mechanism to allow page placement policies in NUMA systems. Awasthi et al [1] extend that concept with new mechanisms that allow the hardware and OS to dynamically manage cache capacity per thread as well as optimize placement of data shared by multiple threads.

In this work, we apply page coloring approach to overcome the shortcomings of existing HCA management schemes. Our key innovation is the introduction of a light-weighted hardware mechanism added to HCA to identify and collect cache behavior of hot OS pages.

6 Conclusion and Future Work

In this paper, we presented a hybrid cache architecture to construct on-chip cache hierarchies with different memory technologies. We proposed a light-weighted hardware mechanism to let OS be aware of underline hybrid cache architecture and studied page placer mechanism to control data placement onto difference cache regions at OS page level.

Overall, we showed the potential benefits of applying hybrid caches to improve the cache subsystem performance with OS-aware cache management. As an initial study, we have mainly presented page-level cache management. In future work, if the extra hardware mapping layer is employed, the granularity of classification and placement can be arbitrary.

Acknowledgments. This work is supported by the NSFC under grants No. 61370104 and No.61133008, National Science and Technology Pillar Program under grant 2012BAH14F02, MOE-Intel Special Research Fund of Information Technology under grant MOE-INTEL-2012-01, and Chinese Universities Scientific Fund under grant No. 2014TS008.

References

1. Awasthi, M., Sudan, K., Balasubramonian, R., Carter, J.: Dynamic hardware-assisted software-controlled page placement to manage capacity allocation and sharing within large caches. In: Proceedings of IEEE 15th International Symposium on High Performance Computer Architecture (HPCA 2009), pp. 250–261. IEEE (2009)

2. Chaudhuri, M.: Pagenuca: Selected policies for page-grain locality management in large shared chip-multiprocessor caches. In: Proceedings of IEEE 15th International Symposium on High Performance Computer Architecture (HPCA 2009), pp. 227–238. IEEE (2009)

3. Chishti, Z., Powell, M.D., Vijaykumar, T.: Distance associativity for high-performance energy-efficient non-uniform cache architectures. In: Proceedings of 36th Annual IEEE/ACM International Symposium on Microarchitecture (MICRO 2003), pp. 55–66. IEEE (2003)

4. Hanzawa, S., Kitai, N., Osada, K., Kotabe, A., Matsui, Y., Matsuzaki, N., Takaura, N., Moniwa, M., Kawahara, T.: A 512kb embedded phase change memory with 416kb/s write throughput at 100μa cell write current. In: Proceedings of IEEE International Solid-State Circuits Conference (ISSCC 2007), pp. 474–616. IEEE (2007)

5. Hosomi, M., Yamagishi, H., Yamamoto, T., Bessho, K., Higo, Y., Yamane, K., Yamada, H., Shoji, M., Hachino, H., Fukumoto, C., Nagao, H., Kano, H.: A novel nonvolatile memory with spin torque transfer magnetization switching: Spin-ram. In: Proceedings of IEEE International Electron Devices Meeting (IEDM 2005), pp. 459–462. IEEE (2005)

6. Lam, C.: Cell design considerations for phase change memory as a universal memory. In: Proceedings of International Symposium on VLSI Technology, Systems and Applications (VLSI-TSA 2008), pp. 132–133. IEEE (2008)

7. Loh, G.H., Subramaniam, S., Xie, Y.: Zesto: A cycle-level simulator for highly detailed microarchitecture exploration. In: Proceedings of IEEE International Symposium on Performance Analysis of Systems and Software (ISPASS 2009), pp. 53–64. IEEE (2009)

8. Muralimanohar, N., Balasubramonian, R., Jouppi, N.P.: Cacti 6.0: A tool to model large caches. HP Laboratories (2009)

9. Pellizzer, F., Pirovano, A., Ottogalli, F., Magistretti, M., Scaravaggi, M., Zuliani, P., Tosi, M., Benvenuti, A., Besana, P., Cadeo, S., Marangon, T., Morandi, R., Piva, R., Spandre, A., Zonca, R., Modelli, A., Varesi, A., Lowrey, T., Lacaita, A., Casagrande, G., Cappelletti, P., Bez, R.: Novel μtrench phase-change memory cell for embedded and stand-alone non-volatile memory applications. In: Proceedings of International Symposium on VLSI Technology, Systems and Applications (VLSI-TSA 2008), pp. 18–19. IEEE (2004)

10. Sun, G., Dong, X., Xie, Y., Li, J., Chen, Y.: A novel architecture of the 3d stacked mram l2 cache for cmps. In: Proceedings of IEEE 15th International Symposium on High Performance Computer Architecture (HPCA 2009), pp. 239–249. IEEE (2009)

11. Wu, X., Li, J., Zhang, L., Speight, E., Rajamony, R., Xie, Y.: Hybrid cache architecture with disparate memory technologies. In: Proceedings of International Symposium on Computer architecture (ISCA 2009), pp. 34–45. ACM (2009)

12. Zhao, W., Belhaire, E., Mistral, Q., Chappert, C., Javerliac, V., Dieny, B., Nicolle, E.: Macro-model of spin-transfer torque based magnetic tunnel junction device for hybrid magnetic-cmos design. In: Proceedings of the 2006 IEEE International Behavioral Modeling and Simulation Workshop (BMSW 2006), pp. 40–43. IEEE (2006)

Temporal-Based Ranking in Heterogeneous Networks

Chen Yu, Ruidan Li, Dezhong Yao, Feng Lu, and Hai Jin

Services Computing Technology and System Lab
Cluster and Grid Computing Lab
School of Computer Science and Technology
Huazhong University of Science and Technology, Wuhan, 430074, China

Abstract. Ranking is a fundamental task for network analysis, bene-fiting to filter and find valuable information. Time information impacts results in content that is sensitive to trends and events ranking. The current ranking either assumes that user's interest and concerns remain static and never change over time or focuses on detecting recency information. Meanwhile most prevalent networks like social network are heterogeneous, that composed of multiple types of node and complex reliance structures. In this paper, we propose a general Temporal based Heterogeneous Ranking (TemporalHeteRank) method. We demonstrate that TemporalHeteRank is suitable for heterogeneous networks on the intuition that there is a mutually information balance relationship between different types of nodes that could be reflected on ranking results. We also explore the impact of node temporal feature in ranking, then we use the node life span by carefully investigating the issues of feasibility and generality. The experimental results on sina weibo ranking prove the effectiveness of our proposed approach.

Keywords: Heterogeneous Networks, Heterogeneous Ranking, Diverse Rank, Information Flow Propagation, Hotspot Detection.

1 Introduction

In recent years, the rapid development and flexible application of networks have revolutionized the way people discover, share, and these rapid changes simultaneously have a serious effect like massive data generated. Those enormous amount of data lead to find the information of user's interest is extremely difficult, making the network analysis techniques emerged. Ranking as one of these is becoming a burning topic gradually, serving to Internet researchers and academics. The common practice is the graph based ranking [1][2]. However, those approaches either assumed that user's interest and concerns remain static and never change over time [3][4] or focused on detecting recency sensitive information [5][6][7]. Simple aggregation and recency extraction can overshadow the temporal trends that could potentially provide valuable signals for better ordering of information, while lots of demands are not satisfied yet like the temporal based rules.

C.-H. Hsu et al. (Eds.): NPC 2014, LNCS 8707, pp. 23–34, 2014.
© IFIP International Federation for Information Processing 2014

In this paper, we take sina weibo (or weibo) ranking for the instance. Weibo as one of the most popular on-line short message communication platform, provides tremendous information. In particular, it focuses on recent hot-spots since user can express opinions immediately. Due to the highly temporal nature, incorporating time information into weibo ranking is crucial. The conventional approaches of weibo rank are based on content or the interaction of users, such as forwarding, comments and following. They all have several deficiencies. First, the characteristics used to rank are relatively simple that all nodes in the network were regarded as the same type. Second, for the weibo content tend to be over-entertainment, not all the information is valuable. Third, the temporal factor is an important measurement for ranking results. To solve the problems described above, we introduce temporal based heterogeneous ranking, i.e. TemporalHeteRank, by integrating the information flow propagation in heterogeneous linked nodes and the temporal feature of nodes to enhance the precision and contribute to detect the hotspot. To summarize, the contribution of this paper are described as follows:

- We study the ranking on heterogeneous networks, where the network actually contains multiple types of nodes and complex dependence structures.
- Proposing a method to use the information flow propagation of multiple types node to capture the correlation between different types of node.
- Integrating the temporal feature i.e. life span of nodes to explore the effect on the process of ranking.
- Performing experiments on the most prevalent social network, sina weibo, as the ranking application on hotspot detection to demonstrate the feasibility.

The remaining of the paper is organized as follows. We present the related work in Section 2, and introduces the fundamental concept and necessary preliminaries in Section 3. We describe the specific process of TemporalHeteRank in Section 4. We carry out the performance evaluation and application in Section 5, whereas our conclusions are drawn in Section 6.

2   Related Work

The fundamental goal of ranking is to filter and extract most relevant information from tremendous data. Thus, ranking could save users time and find informative content [8][9] simultaneously. However, few studies concentrate on or relevant to the heterogeneous networks ranking problem from the past [1][10] to the current[3][4]. The conventional methods [1][10] are both classical ranking method playing an important role in homogeneous networks. The research of [3] puts forward the Tri-HITS algorithm on tweet ranking by using the cross-link between tweet and web document to construct the heterogeneous network. After that, combing the reliability feature of the web documents and heterogeneous information iteratively propagation to improve the ranking quality. However, ranking tweet without considering the node temporal feature can lead to meaningless and unvalued information. As the tweet may be out of popularity time [11] and the ranking may not satisfy users demand like tracking the news or capturing the hot topics. [4] mainly rank the venues and authors on DBLP network. They proposed the authority ranking principles based on the rules, that if the node highly ranked then the other linked nodes should be ranked higher reciprocally. While the defection is that none temporal information has considered on the rankings In [12], they present supervised mathematical method of transfer learning called "learn to rank" to solve the complex ranking issues on heterogeneous networks, but the label information of dataset which needed in the supervised learning are extremely expensive and difficult to obtain in the real world. Those aforementioned approaches either assumed that user's interest and concerns remain static and never change over time or simple focused on detecting recency-sensitive information[5][6][7], for instance [6] proposed a temporal query model, using temporal features for query performance predict. Also many studies like [11][13][14], they all demonstrate that the popularity and influence of tweet varies over time.

3   Concepts and Preliminaries

3.1   Heterogeneous Information Network

An information network represents an abstraction of the real world, focusing on the nodes and the interactions between the nodes. Formally, [4] define an information network as the directed graph $G = (V, E)$ on $V = \{V_1 \cup \ldots \cup V_N\}$ and $E = \{E_1 \cup \ldots \cup E_M\}$. When the types of nodes $N > 1$ or the types of relationship $M > 1$, the network namely is the heterogeneous information networks. Here we give some networks for example.

1. Sina weibo network [15]. The sina weibo consist of two different types nodes (i.e. weibo and user) and many relationships between different types of nodes. Relationships can emerge in same type like weibo forwarding, and different types like user post weibo (see in Fig.1a).

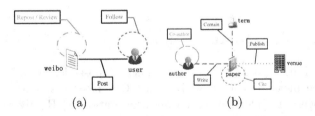

(a)   (b)

Fig. 1. Temporal trend of weibo and DBLP networks

2. DBLP bibliographic network [16]. DBLP contains four types of node, namely papers, authors, terms and venues (conferences or journals). Links exist between authors and papers by the relation of write (or written by), between papers and terms by mention (see in Fig.1b).

Information imbalance exists in heterogeneous linked nodes. Taking weibo and web document for example, weibo possesses the qualities of real-time and massive, whilst the messy weibo makes it uninformative and unreliable. Web could not provide the real time information, but they always come from organizations that reliable inherently. Thus we use the flow propagation to make the information of heterogeneous linked nodes mutually reinforced. The connection of weibo and web document's built through semantic similarity.

The weibo heterogeneous network, defined as graph G inherited from the information network, composes of weibo, web document, and user. Namely $V = \{V_w \cup V_u \cup V_d\}$ and $E = \{E_w \cup E_{wu} \cup E_u \cup E_{wd} \cup E_d\}$.

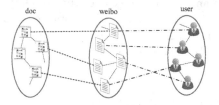

Fig. 2. Weibo heterogeneous network

3.2   Preliminaries

We briefly introduce the work of [2] for the diverse rank in homogeneous networks. Diverse rank or DivRank is a random walk ranking algorithm. In contrast to PageRank, DivRank assumes that the transition probabilities change over time, and the ranking score of nodes varies accordingly. After the z-th iterations, the transition probability matrix M becomes:

$$M(z) = \alpha \cdot M(z-1) \cdot R(z-1) + \frac{(1-\alpha)}{|V|} \cdot E \qquad (1)$$

4   TemporalHeteRank Method

To make the ranking draw attention as much as possible, we define the informative as the measurement of weibo rank. Our basic assumption of ranking is the heterogeneous information flowing propagation: 1) Highly ranked weibo may attract many forwarding amount and reviews generated by highly ranked users, verse vice; 2) Highly ranked weibo aligns with many highly ranked web document content. As the web contains abundant information and comes from formal genre, so it can be used to reinforce the weibo content quality; 3) The recently released weibo should be given the corresponded promotion, as minor forwarding amount and comments that can reveal the process of the information propagation explicitly.

After crawling all the weibo within a specified time window, we first use the weibo forwarding pattern to analyze weibo temporal information. Then we define queries based on the top terms in weibo, and use the Google Search API to retrieve the titles of the top m web for those queries ($m = 5$ for our experiments).

4.1   Ranking the Graph

Life Span Analysis. The life span is an important measurement to evaluate the ranking qualities. Currently there are several approaches to measure the weibo life span, like the temporal variation of hot topic that weibo related to and the weibo forwarding amount. The forwarding can explicitly reflect the information dissemination process, hence we adopt the forwarding to measure the life span. To prove the generality, the life span could be extended to DBLP network [17][18], and we employ the cite amount to analysis the paper temporal trend in Fig.3b.

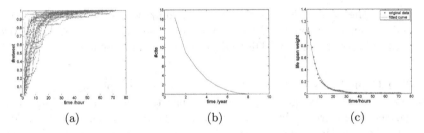

(a)   (b)   (c)

Fig. 3. Temporal trend of weibo and DBLP networks. a) describes thirty weibo's temporal repost; b) shows DBLP's temporal cite amount; c) presents the life span of weibo.

In [11] and [19] they all proved a rule that almost 90% of weibo are rarely forwarded after 72 hours since they are posted. Fig.3a depicts thirty weibo forwarding pattern in 72 hours. It shows that the weibo forwarding amount quickly increases with the time after release but saturates after reaching the time of thirtieth hours after birth and forwarding amount reaches 90% of the total. From the description above we draw a conclusion that weibo forwarding approximates to the sigmoid curve. Then we use the follow function to model the weibo life span:

$$cW_{.t}^{life} = d \cdot \exp^{c-b*t} - a \qquad (2)$$

where $W_{.t}^{life}$ is the weibo life span weight at time t. Parameter a and d are used to convert the horizontal position of curve and the b and c factors are defined to control the decay rate. In Fig. 3c, the simulated trend almost totally overlaps with the dynamic of the real world data forwarding process. The sum of residuals square are all fall below 0.6 in 95% confidential interval.

Initialize Weibo and Web Ranking. As the weibo ranks on multiple topics, so we would like the output keep diversity. DivRank algorithm could achieve diversity by iteratively selecting the most prestigious or popular nodes and continuously updating the transposition probability matrix. At each step, the algorithm updates the dynamical transition matrix Eq.(1). Hence after z-th iterations, the ranking score of weibo and web document become:

$$R(z) = \alpha \cdot [M(z)]^T \cdot R + \frac{(1-\alpha)}{|V|} \cdot E \tag{3}$$

Accordingly the temporal based weibo ranking R^w calculates as $R^w \cdot W^{life}$. The weight of two weibo(or web) w_i and w_j denotes the cosine similarity of them. Each weibo can be treated as a short document, then we employ the TF-IDF method to weight the terms of the weibo words. Each entry of the adjacent matrix M stands for the text similarity of the weibo or web in the graph, and is defined as follows:

$$M_{ij} = \frac{sim(w_i, w_j)}{\sum_k sim(w_i, w_k)}, sim(w_i, w_j) = \frac{\boldsymbol{w_i} \cdot \boldsymbol{w_j}}{\|\boldsymbol{w_i}\| \cdot \|\boldsymbol{w_j}\|} \tag{4}$$

In Eq.(4), the $sim(\cdot)$ denotes the cosine similarity between two weibo (or web) and the $\boldsymbol{w_i}$ represent the TF-IDF vector of the weibo (or webs) w_i. Also TF represents term frequency, IDF said the reciprocal of documents.

Initialize User Ranking. The aforementioned user graph $G_u = (V_u, E_u)$ is a directed and weighted graph. At first we use the following relationship to establish the users graph. When the user u_i follows user u_j, we add a edge (u_i, u_j) to the following adjacent matrix M^{uf}. Thus M^{uf} is defined as follows:

$$M_{ij}^{uf} = \frac{f(u_i, u_j)}{\sum_k f(u_k, u_j)}, f(u_i, u_j) = \begin{cases} 1 & (u_i, u_j) \in E_u \\ 0 & (u_i, u_j) \notin E_u \end{cases} \tag{5}$$

Moreover, we take the credibility of users into consideration, as the prestige is not absolutely coordinate with the credibility. We define the credibility weigh between user u_i and user u_j as M_{ij}^{uc}, according to the number of interactions, for example mentions, reposts and reviews. The creditable weight between two users u_i and u_j is described as follow:

$$M_{ij}^{uc} = \frac{actions\_from\_u_i}{actions\_of\_u_j} \tag{6}$$

Furthermore the users relation matrix M^u becomes $M^{uf} \cdot M^{uc}$. In Eq.(6), $actions \in \{mention, repost, review\}$ represent user interactions with weibo. The $actions\_from\_u_i$ denotes the reciprocal interactions between u_i and u_j. The $action\_of\_u_i$ denotes the alternation of the optional user u_k and u_j. Naturally, we apply DviRank random walk model on user graph using matrix M^u, and compute the ranking score of each user.

4.2 Affinity Matrices

According to the previous description of E_{wd} and E_{wu}, we define two adjacent matrices M^{wd} and M^{wu}. Matrix M^{wd} represents the weight between the weibo and the web documents, and measured by the cosine similarity of document and weibo content.

$$M_{ij}^{wd} = \begin{cases} weight_{ij} & , weight_{ij} > \delta_{wd} \\ 0 & , others \end{cases}, weight_{ij} = \frac{sim(w_i, d_j)}{\sum_k sim(w_i, d_k)} \qquad (7)$$

Matrix M^{wu} represents the weight between weibo and user. We use a set of weibo that a user posts such as w_m in a period of time to compute the cosine similarity with the weibo w_i, if the similarity exceeds the threshold we set the user link to the weibo in M^{wu}.

$$M_{ij}^{wu} = \begin{cases} \max_{sim(w_i, w_k)} w_k & , max_{sim(w_i, w_k)} > \delta_{wu} \\ 0 & , others \end{cases} \qquad (8)$$

w_k in Eq.(8) indicates the element of weibo set that a user posts in a period of time. $sim(\cdot)$ describes the cosine similarity between pairwise weibo.

4.3 Flow Propagation

The tripartite weibo graph comprises three homogeneous graphs and two heterogeneous graphs. The weibo-document denotes the content align inter-relation between the weibo and the web document, and the weibo-user means the implicit relationship between the user and the weibo. Based on the ranking assumptions described at foremost of this section, we use the following iterative information flowing propagation to formulate the procedure:

Step 1. Starting from web document R^d, the update process considers both the last ranking score and the information flow propagation from connected weibo R^w, which can be expressed as:

$$R^d(z+1) = (1 - \lambda_d) \cdot M^d(z) \cdot R^d(z) + \lambda_d \cdot M^{wd} \cdot R^w(z) \qquad (9)$$

Step 2. In the same way, we define the information flow propagation from weibo R^w to user R^u as:

$$R^u(z+1) = (1 - \lambda_u) M^u(z) \cdot R^u(z) + \lambda_u \cdot M^{wu} \cdot R^w(z) \qquad (10)$$

Step 3. Each weibo R^w can be influenced by the information propagation from both web document and user, then compute weibo ranking scores:

$$\begin{aligned} R^w(z+1) = &(1 - \lambda_d - \lambda_u) M^w \cdot R^w(z+1) \\ &+ \lambda_d \cdot M^{dw} R^d(z) + \lambda_u \cdot M^{uw} R^u(z) \end{aligned} \qquad (11)$$

where the parameter λ is to balance the importance of weibo, user, and document. $R^w(z)$, $R^d(z)$ and $R^u(z)$ are the ranking score matrix of weibo, web document and user at z-th iteration. To guarantee the iteration converges, we normalize R^w, R^d and R^u after each iteration using $R(z+1) = R(z+1)/\|R(z+1)\|$. The algorithm typically converges when the difference between the scores computed at two successive iterations for any weibo falls below a threshold ξ (set as 0.001 in our method).

5 Experiment and Application

5.1 Dataset

Sina weibo is the most popular microblogging service in China. The dataset in [20] collected a complete network between 1,700,000 users and all the weibo posted by those users between Jul. 28th, 2012 and Oct. 29th, 2012. We choose the three most popular topics in Aug, 2012 (described in Tab.1) and study how to rank weibo in heterogeneous information network. We also study how life spans of weibo influence the ranking results.

Table 1. Sina Weibo dataset description

Dataset	Users	Follow-relationship	Original-microblogs	Retweets
Sina Weibo	1,776,950	308,489,739	300,000	23,755,810

5.2 Evaluation Metric

For evaluation, we employ two widely used metrics: $MeanAveragePrecision$ (MAP) and $DiscountedCumulativeGain$ (DCG) [21]. In particular, we measure the MAP and DCG on the top-n results, denote as MAP@n and DCG@n respectively. Instead of DCG@n, we adopt $NormalizedDiscountedCumulativeGain$ (NDCG) [22], which is a normalization of DCG in the range [0, 1] calculated as:

$$NDCG@n = \frac{DCG@n}{IDCG@n}, DCG@n = \sum_{i=1}^{n} \frac{2^{rel_i} - 1}{\log_2(i+1)} \tag{12}$$

where IDCG@n is the ideal DCG@n, i.e. the maximum possible DCG value up to the ranking position n. We apply MAP on ranking output under the assumption that the top ranked weibo are more relevant to the hot topic and the rest are less:

$$MAP = \frac{1}{|T|} \sum_{j=1}^{|T|} P_i^j \cdot r_i^j \tag{13}$$

where T represent the topic set. In our experiments we set $n = 5, 10, 25, 50$ i.e. MAP@5, NDCG@10.

5.3   Experiment on Ranking

In our experiment, we primarily show three different kinds of ranking methods in Tab.2 to verify the feasibility.

Table 2. Description of three kinds of analysis method

Methods	Description
1.Weibo-User	Using information propagation between weibo and users purely to rank on weibo-user network
2.Doc-Weibo-User	Ranking by combining the web document and information flow propagation on doc-weibo-user network
3.TemporalHeteRank	Weibo temporal constraint life span included beside information propagation

The Sina Weibo official study points out that there were three drastically discussed topics during August 2012, namely 'Liu Xiang', 'Lin Dan', and 'Diaoyu Islands'. According to the studies, the experiments of ranking falls into two parts: the topic sensitivity and the precision compared with the ground truth ranking. We intuitively rank the topics based on the time it happened. The topic sensitivity is to figure up the text similarity between weibo and topic, and the weibo is much more similar to the higher ranked topic indicates the weibo is relevant to this topic. The relevant is 1 and 0 otherwise, then get the topic sensitivity by MAP. By employing the mutually annotated weibo as the ground truth we use the NDCG to evaluate the precision that compared with the ground truth ranking. Our results are summarized in Figure 4a and 4b. Fig 4a shows the models that elicited above performance. In Figure 4b, it provides results when model performance is evaluated against the gold standard ranking obtained from the weibo network.

Figure 4a shows first method that ranks only on weibo and user perform worst, that implies weibo based on the independent user rank is unable to extract significant information like hot topics for weibo tend inclined to the entertainment. The second performs better than the first. The crucial factor is the information flow propagation between web document and weibo. The results also validate our previous assumptions that making use of web document containing abundant information and formal genre can improve the accuracy of weibo ranking. Comparing with the two methods described above, the TemporalHeteRank i.e. the third indicates the temporal feature of node has great impact on ranking and fully satisfy the demand of topic detection.

We randomly choose weibo from the dataset manually annotated as the ground truth ranking of our reference. Following the annotation guidelines defined by [3], five annotators parallelize each assigned weibo a grade in a 5-star likert scale. When the label difference between annotators is 1, the lower grade is selected. When the label difference is greater than 1, those tweets are re-annotated until the label difference falls below 1. From the Figure 4b, the TemporalHeteRank method constantly performs superior to the other two methods.

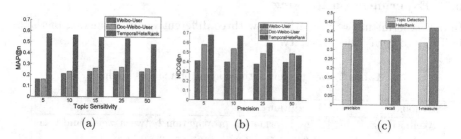

Fig. 4. Describing the MAP and DCG of the three rankings. a) shows topic sensitivity; b) represents precision compared with ground truth; c) denotes the comparison between TemporalHeteRank and topic detection model.

5.4 Experiment on Hotspots Detection Application

As pointed out in the introduction of this paper, the weibo ranking can be applied to hot-spots detection. We compare our approach with the state-of-the-art topic detection model [23]. All the models are subject to use the same dataset and the standard results attested by sina weibo. The detection model (Topic Detection) optimizes the feature selection and weight computation method to filter out those topic-unrelated weibo, and uses a new vector distance calculation method to update the center vector. Fig.4c describes the experimental results on hot-spots detection. The TemporalHeteRank based on information flow propagation and weibo life span consistently outperforms the topic detection model, as the topic detection model never takes the node temporal feature into account. It generates the same hot-spots at any point. Our TemporalHeteRank algorithm models life span regarding the weibo and integrate the information flow propagation to rank. Moreover, it attempts to mine the informative weibo by invoking web document. Both the instances are evaluated by precision, recall rate and F-measure. The data in Fig.4c indicates the hot topics are unexpected and sent by many users from multiple groups, ranking can promote user concern and experience.

6   Conclusion

This paper has investigated the temporal based ranking on the heterogeneous network, and takes the most prevalent sina weibo for the experiments. After crawling the weibo dataset, we analyse the temporal information via weibo forwarding pattern and fit the time-vary life span curve of weibo firstly. Secondly, we use the traditional approaches to filter the noisy weibo and mine the valuable information out from the weibo heterogeneous network. According to the characteristic of entertainment, we improve the ranking precision of weibo resorting to the web thirdly. In fourth step, by adopting the information flowing propagation, the model balance the heterogeneous linked information. Finally, the TemporalHeteRank model integrates temporal weighted ranking results to obtain hotspot of weibo. The proposed TemporalHeteRank method is easy to implement, and the followed experiment shows that it is more efficient and more effective than other conventional methods.

Acknowledgements. The work is partly supported by Technology Innovation Fund of Huazhong University of Sci. and Tech. (No.CXY13Q018) and Ministry of Education and China Mobile Communications Corporation (MoE-CMCC) Research Founding (No.MCM20130382).

References

1. Brin, S., Page, L.: The anatomy of a large-scale hypertextual web search engine. Computer Networks and ISDN Systems 30(1-7), 107–117 (1998)
2. Mei, Q., Guo, J., Radev, D.: Divrank: The interplay of prestige and diversity in information networks. In: Proceedings of the 16th ACM SIGKDD International Conference on Knowledge Discovery and Data Mining, KDD 2010, pp. 1009–1018 (2010)
3. Huang, H., Zubiaga, A., Ji, H., Deng, H., Wang, D., Le, H.K., Abdelzaher, T.F., Han, J., Leung, A., Hancock, J., Voss, C.R.: Tweet ranking based on heterogeneous networks. In: Proceedings of the 24th International Conference on Computational Linguistics, COLING 2012, pp. 1239–1256 (2012)
4. Sun, Y., Han, J.: Mining heterogeneous information networks: a structural analysis approach. SIGKDD Explorations 14(2), 20–28 (2012)
5. Li, X., Croft, W.B.: Time-based language models. In: Proceedings of the 12th ACM International Conference on Information and Knowledge Management, CIKM 2003, pp. 469–475 (2003)
6. Keikha, M., Gerani, S., Crestani, F.: Time-based relevance models. In: Proceedings of the 34th International ACM SIGIR Conference on Research and Development in Information Retrieval, SIGIR 2011, pp. 1087–1088 (2011)
7. Choi, J., Croft, W.B.: Temporal models for microblogs. In: Proceedings of the 21st ACM International Conference on Information and Knowledge Management, CIKM 2012, pp. 2491–2494 (2012)
8. Zhukovskiy, M., Khropov, A., Gusev, G., Serdyukov, P.: Fresh browserank. In: Proceedings of the 36th International ACM SIGIR Conference on Research and Development in Information Retrieval, SIGIR 2013, pp. 1029–1032 (2013)
9. Yan, R., Lapata, M., Li, X.: Tweet recommendation with graph co-ranking. In: Proceedings of the 50th Annual Meeting of the Association for Computational Linguistics, ACL 2012, pp. 516–525 (2012)
10. Kleinberg, J.M.: Authoritative sources in a hyperlinked environment. J. ACM 46(5), 604–632 (1999)
11. Kong, S., Feng, L., Sun, G., Luo, K.: Predicting lifespans of popular tweets in microblog. In: Proceedings of the 35th International ACM SIGIR Conference on Research and Development in Information Retrieval, SIGIR 2012, pp. 1129–1130 (2012)
12. Yang, Z., Tang, J., Li, J.: Learning to rank in heterogeneous network. Sciencepaper Online 4, 273–279 (2011)
13. Cheng, S., Arvanitis, A., Hristidis, V.: How fresh do you want your search results? In: Proceedings of the 22nd ACM International Conference on Conference on Information; Knowledge Management, CIKM 2013, pp. 1271–1280 (2013)

14. Kwak, H., Lee, C., Park, H., Moon, S.: What is twitter, a social network or a news media? In: Proceedings of the 19th International Conference on World Wide Web, WWW 2010, pp. 591–600 (2010)
15. Sina, http://weibo.com
16. Sun, Y., Han, J., Aggarwal, C.C., Chawla, N.V.: When will it happen?: relationship prediction in heterogeneous information networks. In: Proceedings of the 15th ACM International Conference on Web Search and Data Mining, WSDM 2012, pp. 663–672 (2012)
17. Leskovec, J., Kleinberg, J., Faloutsos, C.: Graphs over time: Densification laws, shrinking diameters and possible explanations. In: Proceedings of the 11th ACM SIGKDD International Conference on Knowledge Discovery in Data Mining, KDD 2005, pp. 177–187 (2005)
18. Gehrke, J., Ginsparg, P., Kleinberg, J.: Overview of the 2003 kdd cup. ACM SIGKDD Explorations Newsletter 5(2), 149–151 (2003)
19. Ma, H., Qian, W., Xia, F., He, X., Xu, J., Zhou, A.: Towards modeling popularity of microblogs. Frontiers of Computer Science 7(2), 171–184 (2013)
20. Zhang, J., Liu, B., Tang, J., Chen, T., Li, J.: Social influence locality for modeling retweeting behaviors. In: Proceedings of the 23rd International Joint Conference on Artificial Intelligence, IJCAI 2013, pp. 2761–2767 (2013)
21. Järvelin, K., Kekäläinen, J.: IR evaluation methods for retrieving highly relevant documents. In: Proceedings of the 23rd International ACM SIGIR Conference on Research and Development in Information Retrieval, SIGIR 2000, pp. 41–48 (2000)
22. Järvelin, K., Kekäläinen, J.: Cumulated gain-based evaluation of ir techniques. ACM Trans. Inf. Syst. 20(4), 422–446 (2002)
23. Zhao, X., Zhu, F., Qian, W., Zhou, A.: Impact of multimedia in sina weibo: Popularity and life span. In: Semantic Web and Web Science. Springer Proceedings in Complexity, pp. 55–65 (2013)

Designing Buffer Capacity of Crosspoint-Queued Switch

Guo Chen, Dan Pei*, Youjian Zhao, and Yongqian Sun

Department of Computer Science and Technology, Tsinghua University, Beijing
{chen-g11,sunyq12}@mails.tsinghua.edu.cn,
{peidan,zhaoyoujian}@tsinghua.edu.cn

Abstract. We use both theoretical analysis and simulations to study crosspoint-queued(CQ) buffer size's impact on CQ switch's throughput and delay performance under different traffic models, input loads, and scheduling algorithms. In this paper, 1) we present an exact closed-form formula for the CQ switch's throughput and a non-closed-form but convergent formula for its delay using static non-work-conserving random scheduling algorithms with any given buffer size under independent Bernoulli traffic; 2) we show that the above results can serve as a conservative guidance on deciding the needed buffer size in pure CQ switches using work-conserving algorithms such as random, under independent Bernoulli traffic. Furthermore, our simulation results under real-trace traffic show that simple round-robin and random work-conserving algorithms can achieve quite good throughput and delay performance with feasible crosspoint buffer size. Our work reveals the impact of buffer size on CQ switches' performance and provides a theoretical guidance on designing the buffer size in pure CQ switch, which is an important step towards building ultra-high-speed switching fabrics.

1 Introduction

As content-rich Internet applications such as video streaming, audio streaming, file sharing, live video/voice call, become more and more popular, the demands for higher backbone bandwidth have grown extremely fast. For the increasingly growing link rate, the switching fabric in core routers only has a very short time (e.g 5.12ns for a 64 bytes long packets to be transmitted in a 100Gbps link) to schedule and send out a packet. Thus, how to reduce the scheduling time in switch fabrics becomes a huge challenge. Most of the previous switch fabrics, including input-queued (IQ) switch [1, 2], combined-input-and-crosspoint-queued (CICQ) switch [3, 4] and multi-stage switching fabrics such as [5, 6] allocate major buffers at linecards instead of switch fabrics. To avoid packets conflicting and damaged at the switch fabrics, every scheduling cycle in these approaches mandate a round-trip communication between the linecards and

---

* Corresponding author.

C.-H. Hsu et al. (Eds.): NPC 2014, LNCS 8707, pp. 35–48, 2014.

the switch module, which limits the switching speed. As [7] shows, in order to reduce power consumption, linecards and switch module in modern core routers are often placed in different racks with distance from a few meters to up to 60 meters. Assuming the length of inter-rack cable is 2 meters long and the propagation speed is 2×10^8 m/s [7], the back-of-envelope calculation shows that each scheduling cycle has at least a 20 ns delay caused by round-trip communication, which becomes a bottleneck for a high-speed switch.

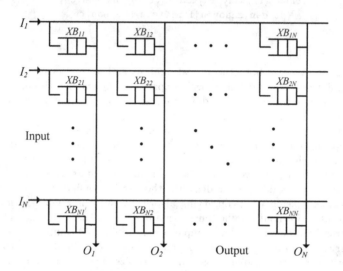

Fig. 1. The CQ switch model

Recently, to overcome above limitations, both academia [8–11] and industry [12] have a growing interest in crosspoint-queued (CQ) switch (illustrated in Fig. 1). Packets are buffered only at each crosspoint using on-chip memory thus switch decision can be made locally by each output scheduler independently, solely based on the conditions of the buffers in the same column as the output scheduler. Therefore, the scheduling algorithms can be made without communications between linecards and switch module, which greatly reduces the scheduling delay.

Although CQ switch was considered to be hard to implement due to the scarcity of on-chip memory many years ago, it has become feasible to implement CQ switch fabrics with large crosspoint buffers by modern technology. Recently, [8] revisited the CQ switch and proved the feasibility using semiconductor integration technology at that time by showing a crosspoint buffer could store over three mega bits packets for a switch with more than a hundred of ports.

Despite the great promise of CQ Switch, there lacks a clear understanding of how to design the crosspoint buffers to meet the switch fabric's overall performance requirement. In this paper, we take a first step towards this direction. We focus on understanding the impact of buffer size on CQ switches' performance, because the on-chip memory resource used by CQ switch for crosspoint buffers is finite and very precious. Previously, [8] presents an accurate analytical model for pure CQ's throughput and delay, assuming a *buffer size of one* and independent and identically distributed (i.i.d.) uniform Bernoulli traffic. However, for larger buffer sizes, the authors introduce only approximate analytical models and simulation results for only throughput. No theoretical or simulating analysis on the switch's average delay has been presented for crosspoint buffer size larger than one. Later on, several papers [9–11] used *simulations* to study pure CQ switch's performance for buffers larger than one under traffic models, such as uniform Bernoulli and bursty.

Compared to these related works, this paper is the first one to provide an *exact* theoretical performance formula for pure CQ switch's *both throughput and delay performance* with buffer size *one and larger* under any independent Bernoulli (both uniform or non-uniform) traffic. The contributions of this paper are summarized as follows:

- To the best of our knowledge, this paper presents the first *exact* closed-form formula of the CQ switch's throughput with any given buffer size, and presents the first *exact* non-closed-form (but convergent) formula of the delay with any buffer size, both under independent Bernoulli traffic using static non-work-conserving random scheduling algorithm.
- Through mathematic proof as well as the comparison between theoretical value and simulation results, we show that theoretical value can serve as a conservative guidance (a loose performance lower bound) for designing buffer sizes of a CQ switch using work-conserving scheduling algorithms.
- Our real-trace simulation results show that with simple work-conserving algorithms, CQ switch is able to reach a very good performance with moderate memory resource consumption, which shows its feasibility in practical use.

Our work reveals the impact of buffer size on CQ switches' performance and provides a theoretical and conservative guidance on deciding the needed buffer size in pure CQ switches, which is an important step towards building ultra-high-speed switching fabrics. Having a better understanding on CQ switches is also an important step towards building multi-stage and multi-plane switching fabrics of large capacity. How to scale up CQ switches to a larger self-sufficient switching fabric is worthy of further studying, which is beyond the scope of this paper.

The rest of this paper is organized as follows. In Section 2, we introduce the CQ switch model and give some necessary definitions and notes. Next, in Section 3, we analyse the throughput and delay performance of CQ switch. We verify our analysis by simulations in Section 4. Finally, we conclude our paper and discuss the future work in Section 5.

2   The Crosspoint-Queued Switch

In this section, we briefly describe the CQ switch model and provide some fundamental definitions used in the rest of our paper.

2.1   The CQ Switch Model

Consider an $N \times N$ CQ switch shown in Fig. 1, the i-th input and i-th output are denoted by I_i and O_i respectively. XB_{ij} represents the crosspoint buffer between I_i and O_j, where $i, j = 1, \ldots, N$. We assume that time is slotted and all the packets are segmented into fixed cells before being sent into the switch, and all the internal and external links of the CQ switch have the same capacity of transferring one cell per time slot. We follow this assumption in the rest of the paper. XB_{ij} has the size of L_{ij} cells.

At the beginning of a time slot, there is one cell or none arriving at each input. If there is a cell arriving at input i heading to the output j at the start of a time slot, it is buffered in XB_{ij} in a first-in-first-out (FIFO) manner if the buffer is not full. The cell will be dropped in the case of that XB_{ij} is full. Within the same slot, the scheduler of each output independently selects one of the buffers in its column according to a certain scheduling algorithm, and sends the head of line (HOL) cells out of the switch through the output if the selected buffer is not empty. If an empty buffer is selected, there will be no cell scheduled out through this output in this time slot. Note that the departure steps at different output schedulers run in parallel.

2.2   Definitions

First we give some definitions that are related to the performance of a switch fabric.

Definition 1. The *throughput* of a switch fabric is the ratio of the amount of cells traversed the switch to the amount of cells arrived at the switch as time goes to infinity. We define TP as the throughput of the switch.

Definition 2. The *loss rate* of a switch fabric is the ratio of the amount of cells dropped by the switch to the amount of cells arrived to the switch as time goes to infinity. We define LR as the loss rate of the switch.

Proposition 1. *For a switch fabric which has finite buffers, the throughput of the switch equals 1 minus the loss rate of the switch, if the average cell arrival rate to the switch is greater than zero.*

Proof. Assume the total buffers of the switch can contain L cells. Let λ denotes the average arrival rate at all the inputs of the switch as time goes to infinity, $L^*(n)$ denotes the total amount of cells in the buffers of the switch at time slot n, hence $L^*(n) \leq L$. We define C_a, C_l, C_t as the total cells arrived, lost and traversed at the switch as time goes to infinity respectively. Obviously, $C_a = \lim_{n \to \infty} \lambda n$, $C_l = \lim_{n \to \infty} \lambda n \cdot LR$, then we have $C_t = \lim_{n \to \infty} (\lambda n - \lambda n \cdot LR - L^*(n))$. Thus, the throughput equals

$$TP = \frac{C_t}{C_a} = \lim_{n \to \infty} \left(1 - LR - \frac{L^*(n)}{\lambda \cdot n}\right) = 1 - LR$$

$\square$

Definition 3. The *delay* of a switch fabric is the average delay of all the packets that traversed the switch as time goes to infinity. We define DL as the delay of the switch.

Then, we give some definitions related to the scheduling algorithms.

Definition 4. A scheduling algorithm is called *work-conserving* if, using this scheduling algorithm, any output of the switch will always be busy if at least one buffer destined to this output is not empty. Otherwise, the scheduling algorithm is called *non-work-conserving*.

Definition 5. A scheduling algorithm is called *static* if the rule of scheduling remains the same regardless of the system's state. Otherwise, it is called *dynamic*.

Definition 6. A static random scheduling algorithm is called *fair* if at each time slot, a column's output scheduler randomly (with the same probability) selects one of the crosspoint to send out its HOL cell.

At the last, we present a definition related to the arrival traffic.

Definition 7. The traffic at an input is said to be *uniform*, if each cell arriving at the input has the equal probability of going to any output of the switch.

3   Performance Analysis with Different Buffer Size

We focus on giving a theoretical throughput and delay calculation expression according to the buffer size in this section.

Consider the CQ switch model shown in Fig. 1. We assume the cell arrivals at each input are governed by independent Bernoulli process and with fixed probability heading to each output. Each output scheduler uses a static non-work-conserving random scheduling algorithm. We use the following notations:

$\rho_i \triangleq$ the Bernoulli parameter of the cell arrival process in input I_i.

$a_{ij}^k \triangleq$ the probability of k cells arrived at XB_{ij} in a given time slot. $k = 0, 1$.

$d_{ij} \triangleq$ the probability of any cell arrived at I_i heading to the output O_j.
  $\sum_{j=1}^{N} d_{ij} = 1$ and $0 \leq d_{ij} \leq 1$ for $i = 1, \ldots, N$.

$s_{ij} \triangleq$ the probability of crosspoint buffer XB_{ij} being selected by output O_j.
  $\sum_{i=1}^{N} s_{ij} = 1$ and $0 < s_{ij} < 1$ for $j = 1, \ldots, N$.

First, we present a formal description of a scheduling cycle in a time slot as follows:

- *Arrival Step:* At the beginning of a time slot, for input i, there exists a probability of ρ_i that one cell will arrive, and a probability of $1 - \rho_i$ that no cell will arrive. The cell arrived at input I_i has the probability of d_{ij} heading to the output O_j. Successive cells and cell arrivals at different inputs are independent.

- *Departure Step:* Within the same slot after the arrival step, each output scheduler picks a crosspoint buffer out of all the buffers in its column with a static non-work-conserving random scheduling algorithm. For output O_j, it selects crosspoint buffer XB_{ij} with the probability of s_{ij}, and schedules the HOL cell out of the switch if the selected buffer is not empty. Otherwise, no cells are transmitted through O_j in this time slot. Each output schedules cells independently and in parallel.

Let L_{ij} denotes the capacity of crosspoint buffer XB_{ij} in cells, we assume that $L_{ij} = L(i, j = 1, 2, \ldots, N)$ for the ease to present. It means that all the crosspoint buffers have the same capacity of L cells. We perform our analysis on a particular crosspoint buffer XB_{ij} without loosing generality.

We assume random variable A_{ij}, A_i, A to be the number of cells arrived to XB_{ij}, input I_i and the whole switch during a given time slot respectively. According to the conditions given above, the value of A_{ij} can only be 0 or 1. Recall that a_{ij}^k denotes the probability that k cells arrive at XB_{ij} in a time slot, then

$$
\begin{aligned}
a_{ij}^0 &= P\{A_{ij} = 0\} = 1 - \rho_i \cdot d_{ij} \\
a_{ij}^1 &= P\{A_{ij} = 1\} = \rho_i \cdot d_{ij} \\
a_{ij}^k &= P\{A_{ij} = k\} = 0 \quad k \neq 0, 1
\end{aligned}
\tag{1}
$$

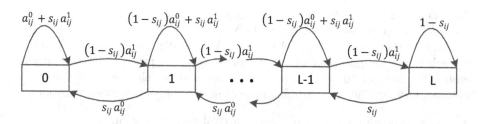

Fig. 2. The Quasi-birth-death state transition diagram for XB_{ij}

We define random variable $Q_{ij}(m)$ as the cells in XB_{ij} at the end of time slot m. According to the conditions stated before, we can find that $Q_{ij}(m)$ can be modeled as a discrete-time Quasi-birth-death process as Fig. 2 shows. The transition diagram can be interpreted as follows:

- The transitions from state l to $l + 1$ mean the probability that there is an arrival at the buffer and the buffer is not selected by the output scheduler.
- Transitions from state l to itself are calculated under 3 different conditions. 1) While $l = 0$, it equals the probability of one arrival and one departure plus with the probability of no arrival. 2) While $l = 1, \ldots, L - 1$, it equals the probability of one arrival and one departure plus with the probability of

no arrival and no departure. 3) While $l = L$, it equals the probability of one arrival and no departure (the cell will be dropped in the arrival step when the buffer is full) plus with the probability of no arrival and no departure.

- Transitions from state l to state $l - 1$ are calculated under 2 different conditions. 1) While $l = 1, \ldots, L - 1$, it equals the probability of no arrival and one departure. 2) While $l = L$, it equals the probability of the buffer being selected (the buffer length will still be L before the departure step begins as the cell will be dropped in the arrival step when the buffer is full).

Let Q_{ij} denotes the steady-state queue length of XB_{ij}, according to the formula of the steady-state probabilities of discrete-time Quasi-birth-death process [13], we can get the stead-state queue length distribution as follows:

$$
\eta_{ij}^0 = \frac{1}{1 + \sum_{l=1}^{L-1} \left(\frac{(1-s_{ij})a_{ij}^1}{s_{ij}a_{ij}^0} \right)^l + a_{ij}^0 \left(\frac{(1-s_{ij})a_{ij}^1}{s_{ij}a_{ij}^0} \right)^L}
$$

$$
\eta_{ij}^l = \eta_{ij}^0 \left(\frac{(1 - s_{ij})a_{ij}^1}{s_{ij}a_{ij}^0} \right)^l , \quad l = 1, \ldots, L - 1 \tag{2}
$$

$$
\eta_{ij}^L = \eta_{ij}^0 a_{ij}^0 \left(\frac{(1 - s_{ij})a_{ij}^1}{s_{ij}a_{ij}^0} \right)^L
$$

where η_{ij}^l defines the steady-state probability of XB_{ij}'s length equals l, i.e $Q_{ij} = l$.

So far, we have derived the steady-state probability distribution of XB_{ij}'s length. Next, we will use these results to analyze the throughput and delay of the CQ switch.

3.1 Throughput Analysis

Obviously, the probability of a cell arrived at XB_{ij} being dropped equals the probability of XB_{ij} being full, i.e., η_{ij}^L for the steady-state.

We define the random variable D_{ij}, D_i and D as the number of cells dropped at XB_{ij}, input I_i and the whole switch during a given time slot at the steady-state. Obviously, D_{ij}, D_i could only be 0 or 1. Then, we can get the probability of a cell arrived at input I_i being dropped in a time slot as

$$
P\{D_i = 1 | A_j = 1\} = \sum_{j=1}^{N} d_{ij}\eta_{ij}^L \tag{3}
$$

The above equation comes from the fact that the probability of a cell arrived at input i being dropped in a given time slot equals the sum of probabilities that a cell arrived at I_i being dropped at any crosspoint buffer of this line.

Further, we have the expectation of the dropped cells at I_i during a time slot as following

$$E(D_i) = \rho_i \cdot P\{D_i = 1 | A_j = 1\} = \rho_i \left(\sum_{j=1}^{N} d_{ij} \eta_{ij}^L \right) \qquad (4)$$

Thus, we get the expectation of dropped cells at the whole switch in a given time slot as

$$E(D) = E(\sum_{i=1}^{N} D_i) = \sum_{i=1}^{N} \rho_i \left(\sum_{j=1}^{N} d_{ij} \eta_{ij}^L \right) \qquad (5)$$

Then, we get the loss rate of the CQ switch as follows

$$LR = \frac{E(D)}{E(A)} = \frac{\sum_{i=1}^{N} \rho_i \left(\sum_{j=1}^{N} d_{ij} \eta_{ij}^L \right)}{\sum_{i=1}^{N} \rho_i} \qquad (6)$$

where random variable A denotes the number of cells arrived at the switch during a time slot and $E(A)$ means the expectation of A.

Therefore, from Proposition 1 we can acquire the closed-form formula of the throughput of the switch as

$$TP = 1 - LR = 1 - \frac{\sum_{i=1}^{N} \rho_i \left(\sum_{j=1}^{N} d_{ij} \eta_{ij}^L \right)}{\sum_{i=1}^{N} \rho_i} \qquad (7)$$

3.2 Delay Analysis

Then, we analyze the average delay of CQ switch. Similarly, we begin with focusing on a certain crosspoint buffer XB_{ij}.

Let random variable W_{ij}, W_i denotes the time slots a cell spent in the steady-state (i.e., *delay*) in XB_{ij} and input I_i respectively. We assume that at the time a cell arriving at XB_{ij}, the buffer length $Q_{ij} = l(0 \leq l < L)$ and the cell has spent n time slots in XB_{ij}. We only consider the delay of a cell while it is not dropped by the switch because the delay of dropped cells is meaningless. Thus, we can have

$$P\{W_{ij} = n | Q_{ij} = l\} = C_n^{n-l} (1 - s_{ij})^{n-l} (s_{ij})^{l+1} \qquad (8)$$

where $n = l, l+1, \ldots, \infty$. This equation denotes that the probability of a cell's delay $W_{ij} = n$ equals the probability of the buffer having been selected l times during n slots to move the cell to the HOL and the buffer being selected after n slots to schedule out the cell.

Thus, the steady-state probability of a cell's delay being n time slots in XB_{ij} equals

$$P\{W_{ij} = n\} = \begin{cases} \sum_{l=0}^{n} \left(\eta_{ij}^l P\{W_{ij} = n | Q_{ij} = l\} \right), & 0 \leq n \leq L-1 \\ \sum_{l=0}^{L-1} \left(\eta_{ij}^l P\{W_{ij} = n | Q_{ij} = l\} \right), & n > L-1 \end{cases} \qquad (9)$$

Using the results of equation (2) and (1), we transform the above equation into

$$P\{W_{ij} = n\} = \begin{cases} \eta_{ij}^0 s_{ij} \left(\frac{1-s_{ij}}{a_{ij}^0}\right)^n, & 0 \le n \le L-1 \\ \eta_{ij}^0 s_{ij}(1-s_{ij})^n \sum_{l=0}^{L-1} \left[C_n^{n-l}\left(\frac{a_{ij}^1}{a_{ij}^0}\right)^l\right], & n > L-1 \end{cases} \quad (10)$$

Then, using the equation above, we can derive the following formula of the mean delay of a cell in XB_{ij} which is not dropped as follows

$$E\{W_{ij}\} = \sum_{n=0}^{\infty} nP\{W_{ij} = n\} \quad (11)$$

Therefore, the mean delay of a cell coming into I_i which is not dropped equals that

$$E\{W_i\} = \sum_{j=1}^{N} d_{ij}E\{W_{ij}\} \quad (12)$$

Thus, we acquire the delay of the switch (i.e the average delay of all the packets that traversed the switch) from the following equation

$$DL = \frac{\sum_{i=1}^{N} \rho_i E\{W_i\}}{(\sum_{i=1}^{N} \rho_i) \cdot TP} \quad (13)$$

Although the above formula of the switch's delay is not closed-form, we have proven its convergency. The proof is omitted here due to the space limitation.

So far, we derive the precise expression of the CQ switch's throughput and delay using static non-work-conserving random scheduling algorithms. Naturally, an appropriate work-conserving scheduling algorithm will lead to a better performance compared to the non-work-conserving random scheduling algorithm that we use, to perform theoretical analysis. Next, we briefly prove that under independent Bernoulli traffic, work-conserving random scheduling (randomly selecting a crosspoint-buffer from all the non-empty ones) performs better than static non-work-conserving random scheduling algorithm both in throughput and average delay.

Theorem 1. *Under same independent Bernoulli traffic, a CQ switch using work-conserving random (WCRand) scheduling algorithm has a higher throughput and lower average delay than using non-work-conserving (nWCRand) fair random scheduling algorithm.*

Proof. Similarly, we could also build a discrete-time Quasi-birth-death diagram for WCRand as Fig. 2 shows. As stated before, for fair nWCRand, we have $s_{ij} = \frac{1}{N}$ in each steady state of queue length. Unlike nWCRand, s_{ij} of WCRand between different states in Fig. 2 are not the same. Let $s'_{ij}(m)$ denotes the probability of crosspoint buffer XB_{ij} being selected by output O_j using WCRand in state m, and $s_{ij}^* = max\{s_{ij}'(m), 0 \leq m \leq L\}$. $\eta_{ij}'^l$ defines the steady-state probability of XB_{ij}'s length equals l using WCRand. Because WCRand randomly selects a crosspoint-buffer from all the non-empty ones in each time slot, we can have

$$s_{ij}^* \geq \frac{1}{N} = s_{ij} \qquad (14)$$

Thus, according to the formula of the steady-state probabilities of discrete-time Quasi-birth-death process, we can get $\eta_{ij}'^L \leq \eta_{ij}^L$. Therefore, it can be derived that WC-Rand has a higher throughput than nWCRand using equation (7). Also, from equation (11-13), we can easily get that WCRand has a lower average delay than nWCRand. $\square$

Similarly, if we use *the frequency of a crosspoint queue being selected by work-conserving Round-Robin (WCRR) algorithm* to approximate *the probability of a crosspoint queue being selected by WCrand algorithm*, we can prove that WCRR also performs better than nWCRand. Furthermore, it is intuitive that longest-queue-first (LQF) scheduling has the highest throughput. A strict proof for these 2 work-conserving algorithms is beyond the scope of this paper. Later, we will show by our simulations that the above theoretical analysis provide an appropriate lower-bound for a CQ switch's performance using work-conserving algorithms.

4   Verification of Analysis and Real Trace Simulations

In this section, we first present simulation results under both uniform and non-uniform Bernoulli traffic to verify our former theoretical analysis in Section 4.1. We consider four scheduling algorithms in our simulations: nWCRand, WCRand, WCRR and LQF. We calculate the theoretical value (TV) of the loss rate and the delay of nWCRand scheduling algorithm, according to the former results we got under both uniform and non-uniform Bernoulli traffic. Various of simulations have been done under different loads and using CQ switches with different port numbers. All these results have verified our former analysis. Due to space limitation, we just present the results of 16×16 CQ under a heavy load of 0.95. Each simulation run was conducted for 10^9 time slots.

Secondly in Section 4.2, we present simulation results of a 16×16 switch fabric under real-trace traffic using the 4 work-conserving scheduling algorithms mentioned above. It's shown that with work-conserving algorithms, the CQ switch is able to reach a good performance with moderate memory resource consumption. Our data consists of two parts from CAIDA [14], 2 1-minute traces from 10Gbps links , one at San Jose and another from Chicago. All the packets are fragmented into 64 bytes long cells before sent into the switch fabric, and the time slot of the switch is set to be 51.2ns according to the transmission time of a cell on a 10Gbps link. We divide a 60 seconds trace into 16 equal size segments for 16 inputs. The destination port of each packet is set as the hash value of destination IP address. The traffic distribution under this situation is not uniform but highly skewed and bursty. We believe this is similar to the real condition of the Internet. Approximately 1.7×10^7 packets with total length of 1.15×10^{10} bytes are sent into the switch fabric during each experimentation. We only present the simulation result of San Jose trace due to space limitation. The results for Chicago trace are similar.

4.1   Verification of Performance Analysis

From Fig. 3 and 4 we can see that, the results of non-work-conserving random scheduling algorithm are almost identical as the theoretical results we derived before, under both uniform and non-uniform traffic. Investigation into the slight difference at the right end of the curves shows that the difference is due to the computer random number generation are not 100% random. Under uniform Bernoulli traffic with heavy input load of 95% as we can see in Fig. 3(a), with crosspoint buffer size of 256 (such buffer size is easy to implement with modern semiconductor technology[8]), the loss rate of nWCRand can be as low as 10^{-7} using the theoretical results we got before. Such a loss rate is good enough for a lot of switch fabrics design and provide loose performance lower bound. Our results also show a simple work-conserving algorithm like Round-robin and Random can reach the same performance with only buffer size of 32 cells, and the theoretical results could serve as a loose performance lower bound for them. Using a more elaborated scheduling algorithm such as LQF, no packets are lost during the 10^{-9} time slots simulation with only buffer size of 16. As for the average delay, our theoretical analysis shows that with buffer size of 64, a CQ switch can have a stable average delay about 10^{-5} seconds using nWCRand, which is shown in Fig. 3(b). While using work-conserving algorithms, the average delay is much lower down to less than 10^{-6} seconds.

Similarly, under non-uniform traffic as shown in Fig. 4, our analytic results are also verified and effectively provide loose performance lower bound to work-conserving algorithms. ω in the picture defines the unbalanced probability (refer

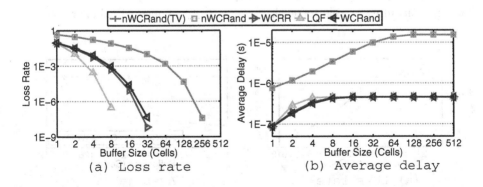

Fig. 3. Loss rate and average delay of a 16×16 CQ switch under uniform Bernoulli traffic with $\rho = 0.95$

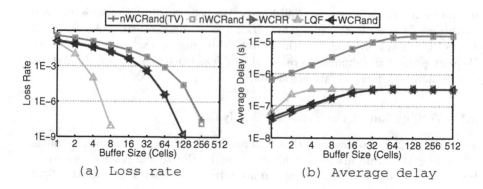

Fig. 4. Loss rate and average delay of a 16×16 CQ switch under non-uniform Bernoulli traffic with $\rho = 0.95$ and $\omega = 0.5$

to [3]) and $\omega = 0.5$ means the traffic is extremely non-uniform. Accordingly, we set the selecting probability parameters of the nWCRand used in this simulation as the same as the load unbalanced probability. The results are very similar to the uniform traffic, except nWCRand and WCRR having a much higher loss rate than uniform traffic because of the blindness to the traffic distribution of their scheduling manner. On the contrary, LQF has the ability to adjust to the imbalance.

4.2 Simulations under Real-Trace

Fig. 5 shows the result of a 16×16 CQ switch under real-trace traffic. The loss rate in Fig. 5(a) refers to the packet loss rate. Once a cell of a packet is dropped, the packet is counted as lost in the switch. We can see that a CQ switch only using crosspoint memory can reach a good performance with simple work-conserving scheduling algorithms. In Fig. 5(a) we can found that the switch can has a loss rate down to 10^{-6} with buffer size of 64 using LQF. A simple Round-robin or Random scheduling is able to reach the same performance with buffer size of

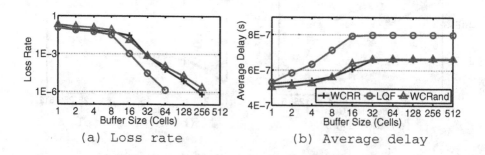

Fig. 5. Loss rate and average delay of a 16×16 CQ switch under real-trace traffic

256, which is totally within the capability of modern chip technology. Also, the delay performance shown in Fig. 5(b) is very good. The delay here refers to the average packet delay. We can see that WCRR and WCRand have a better delay performance than LQF. It's due to that, starvation, which greatly increases the delay, may happen using LQF algorithm.

This result under real-trace traffic demonstrates that a CQ switch with such scale can reach a very good performance with feasible crosspoint buffer size. Thus a self-sufficient CQ switch is exactly suitable for ultra-high-speed link in practical use.

5   Conclusion

This paper reveals the impact of buffer size on CQ switches performance and provides a theoretical guidance on designing the buffer size in pure CQ switch. Also, we show that CQ is a promising building block for high linerate switch fabrics. As a next step, we plan to actually design ultra-high-speed and large-port-number switch fabrics with multi-plane or mutli-stage structure, using CQ as building blocks to scale up. We also plan to design scheduling algorithms with performance better than round-robin algorithm, random or LQF presented in this paper.

Acknowledgment. This work has been supported in part by the National High Technology Research and Development Program of China (863 Program) under Grant No. 2013AA013302, the National Key Basic Research Program of China (973 program) under Grant No. 2013CB329105 and the State Key Program of National Natural Science of China under Grant No. 61233007.

We would like to thank the anonymous reviewers for their valuable comments. We greatly thank Kuan Cheng for his useful discussion on the mathematical demonstration. Also, we thank Zhiyan Zheng for the packet trace of real operational network that he provided us. At last, we thank Juexing Liao for her proofreading on this paper.

References

[1] McKeown, N.: The islip scheduling algorithm for input-queued switches. IEEE/ACM Transactions on Networking 7(2), 188–201 (1999)

[2] Li, Y., Panwar, S., Chao, H.: On the performance of a dual round-robin switch. In: INFOCOM 2001, vol. 3, pp. 1688–1697 (2001)

[3] Rojas-Cessa, R., Oki, E., Jing, Z., Chao, H.: Cixb-1: combined input-one-cell-crosspoint buffered switch. In: HPSR 2001, pp. 324–329 (2001)

[4] He, S.M., Sun, S.T., Guan, H.T., Zheng, Q., Zhao, Y.J., Gao, W.: On guaranteed smooth switching for buffered crossbar switches. IEEE/ACM Transactions on Networking 16(3), 718–731 (2008)

[5] Oki, E., Jing, Z., Rojas-Cessa, R., Chao, H.J.: Concurrent round-robin-based dispatching schemes for clos-network switches. IEEE/ACM Trans. on Networking 10(6), 830–844 (2002)

[6] Iyer, S., Awadallah, A., McKeown, N.: Analysis of a packet switch with memories running slower than the line-rate. In: INFOCOM 2000, vol. 2, pp. 529–537. IEEE (2000)

[7] Abel, F., Minkenberg, C., Iliadis, I., Engbersen, T., Gusat, M., Gramsamer, F., Luijten, R.P.: Design issues in next-generation merchant switch fabrics. IEEE/ACM Trans. Netw. 15(6), 1603–1615 (2007)

[8] Kanizo, Y., Hay, D., Keslassy, I.: The crosspoint-queued switch. In: INFOCOM 2009, pp. 729–737. IEEE (2009)

[9] Radonjic, M., Radusinovic, I.: Impact of scheduling algorithms on performance of crosspoint-queued switch. Annals of Telecommunications - Annales Des Télécommunications 66, 363–376 (2011)

[10] Radusinovic, I., Radonjic, M., Simurina, A., Maljevic, I., Veljovic, Z.: A new analytical model for the cq switch throughput calculation under the bursty traffic. AEU - International Journal of Electronics and Communications 66(12), 1038–1041 (2012)

[11] Cao, Z., Panwar, S.S.: Efficient buffering and scheduling for a single-chip crosspoint-queued switch. In: Proceedings of the Eighth ACM/IEEE Symposium on Architectures for Networking and Communications Systems, ANCS 2012, pp. 111–122. ACM, New York (2012)

[12] Cisco crs carrier routing system 16-slot line card chassis system description. Cisco Systems, Inc. (2012)

[13] Trivedi, K.: Probability and statistics with reliability, queuing, and computer science applications. Wiley, New York (2002)

[14] Anonymized 2013 internet traces, https://data.caida.org/datasets/passive-2013/

Loss-Rate Driven Network Coding for Transmission Control

Chaoyuan Chiang and Yihjia Tsai

Dept. of Computer Science and Information Engineering, Tamkang University
No. 151, Yingzhuan Rd., Tamsui Dist., New Taipei City 251, Taiwan (R.O.C.)
{cory.scorpio,eplusplus}@gmail.com

Abstract. As the growth of network based applications and services, the amount of data transmissions on the network is much more than ever. Transmission control is an important part of the Internet or other computer networks today. Network coding can help to optimize the efficiency of data transmissions by generating the redundant data for error correction. In this paper, we proposed the loss-rate driven coding, LRC, for transmission control. The goal of proposed mechanism is to minimize the coding operations. As a result, the power consumption and computing resource requirement can be reduced. Moreover, the proposed mechanism is compatible with standard TCP and feasible to implement.

Keywords: linear network coding, transmission control, TCP.

1 Introduction

The applications of Internet and other computer networks have become more and more popular recent years. As a result, the amount of data transmissions is growing fast. Transmission control is an important issue for Internet and other computer networks. There are some researches discussed about improving transmission control. We reviewed those works and proposed a new network coding based transmission control mechanism in this paper.

In the OSI model [12], transmission control implements in the transport layer, which is also an important part of Internet and other modern computer networks today. The Transmission Control Protocol, TCP, is one of the most popular transport layer protocols. TCP provides reliable communication for upper layer applications by the acknowledgment mechanism. With acknowledgment mechanism, TCP can detect the segment loss and sense the network condition. Once a segment loosed or timed-out, it represents the network congestion occurred. TCP would control the transmission rate by adjusting the congestion window size to avoid network congestion.

TCP was developed for wired networks at beginning. Wired networks are simple, if the segment loss became often, the network is in congestion. TCP will reduce the transmission rate once congestion occurs. In the modern network

C.-H. Hsu et al. (Eds.): NPC 2014, LNCS 8707, pp. 49–60, 2014.

scenario, more wireless links, more carrier types, more complicated and larger topologies, there are more reasons caused segment loss or time-out, such as interference, fading, or temporary fault in the intermediate network device. The retransmission and congestion window adjustment policy of TCP may decrease the efficiency of transmission. In other words, TCP cannot reach the optimal usage of network throughput in some situations. For this issue, there exist some researches using network coding to improve the usage of network throughput in TCP transmission.

Network coding was first proposed in 2000 [1], which provides solution for optimizing network throughput in wireless networks, such as [6]. The major idea is combining data by XOR operations in broadcasting networks to minimize the amount of transmissions. A branch of network coding is the linear network coding [11]. Linear network coding is often applied in guaranteeing the fairness of peer-to-peer content distribution [2] or generating redundant data for error-correction [16]. The most interesting part of linear network coding is that it can distribute a large content into n pieces equally in logical. For peer-to-peer content distribution, each peer can get the original content by decoding the n received coded pieces. Consider the transmission in lossy networks, if sender divides the data into blocks and transmit in linear coding continuously, receiver can decode and get the original data after receiving any n blocks. The receiver doesnt have to care the order of blocks. The idea above can be applied in TCP with lossy networks. We discussed more about this below in related works.

However, coding takes system resources on the devices. The implementations of linear network coding applied the algebraic operations on Galois Field. The decoding procedure is more complicated than encoding procedure. Minimizing the coded data and reducing the decoding works will have better computing efficiency for the devices. In other words, that would be more friendly to embedded devices with limited system resources. In this paper, we proposed the idea of loss-rate driven coding. We designed a transmission control mechanism, which use network coding as redundancy. The amount of redundancy is related to the sensed loss-rare. In the second section, we reviewed the related works. Then, we proposed our loss-rate driven coding idea in third section, followed by the performance evaluation and conclusions.

2   Related Works

2.1   TCP Congestion Control

The Transmission Control Protocol, TCP, was proposed in [5]. TCP is a widely-used transport layer protocol today. The TCP data unit called segment, the data from upper layer would be divided into segments and transmit. Since the bandwidth of network links and the buffer size of network devices are limited, the packet would be dropped if the data comes faster than the bandwidth of network link. Once packets have been dropped in the lower layer, the transport layer segments would be lost or broken. TCP introduced the acknowledgment mechanism. Sender transmits the segment with sequence number and header checksum. Receiver checks the received segment. If the segment is received correctly, receiver sends an acknowledgement, ACK, to inform the sender. The ACK contains the sequence number of next segment receiver expected. If the segment is lost or incorrect, receiver will repeat the same ACK until received the expected segment correctly. Thus, the completeness of data can be guaranteed.

For higher bandwidth usage, TCP will try to transmit a group of segments continuously, known as congestion window. The amount of segments in the group called window size. The window size will be increased when theres no transmission timed-out or network congestion. TCP will repeat a congestion window until received next correct ACK. Once the transmission timed-out or congestion occurs, TCP will reduce the congestion window size, slow down the transmission rate, to make the segments transmitted correctly.

2.2   Selective ACK

In the TCP congestion window Go-Back-N mechanism, any segment loss or fault will make sender retransmit all the rest segments in the window, some segments will be transmitted more than once, which is not quietly efficiently. The selective ACK, SACK, specified in RFC2018 [10], which allows receiver to ask sender retransmit specified segments.

The SACK scheme solved the redundant retransmission problem. Receiver specified the SACK options in the header of ACK. But there still exist extra costs. Sender takes time and computing resources to process the SACK and retransmit the specified segments.

2.3   Network Coding

Network coding can help to recover the lost segments. There exist some researches applying network coding for peer-to-peer content distribution, such as [2]. The most interesting part of network coding in this field is that data can be uniformly divided into some pieces in logical. That is, if the original divided in to n blocks, any peer can decode and get the original data after collect n coded blocks. This characteristic also can be applied on error correction, such as [16].

The network coded TCP, TCP/NC, was proposed by Sundararajan et al, [13,14,15]. TCP/NC adds a coding layer between IP layer and TCP layer. The coding layer performance the linear network coding operations to encode or decode the segments. Kim et al, [8,9], analyzed TCP/NC and concluded that TCP/NC may have better throughput and better efficiency in lossy networks. The drawback of TCP/NC is the transmission overhead. The segment header of TCP/NC is larger than standard TCP. So the performance of TCP/NC has lower than standard TCP when there is only a few segment loss. Later in 2013, Chan et al. [3] proposed the adaptive network coded TCP. They focus on adjusting the size of coding window according to the loss-rate. That is a quiet good idea, but there is no discuss about the segment header.

In this paper, we improved the efficiency of network coding based redundant mechanism in TCP. Our goal is to minimize the coding operations and get optimal performance. We discussed our idea, including the segment header in the next part below.

3   Loss-Rate Driven Coding

The goal of this research is to minimize the coding operation and coded data. We named it as loss-rate driven coding, LRC. In the following, we use TCP/LRC denotes the proposed mechanism, which combined LRC and TCP. The basic idea LRC is sensing the segment loss rate and using coded segment as redundancy to recover the lost segments. Moreover, the proposed TCP/LRC is compatible with standard TCP. We described the details of our method in the following sub-sections.

3.1   Transmission Model

The sender and receiver both maintain their own coding buffer. The coding buffer is a cyclic queue, called sender queue, Q_S, and receiver queue, Q_R, in sender side and receiver side, respectively. The data came from upper layer would be packed into segments in sender side. Then, the sender would transmit the segment and put a copy into sender queue, Q_S. After received the segment, receiver would put a copy into receiver queue, Q_R, and process the data in the segment for upper layer. For both of Q_S and Q_R, the eldest segment is stored in the first element while the latest segment stored in the last element. In normal condition, Q_S and Q_R will rotate simultaneously with a little delay, like a tape, shown in Fig. 1.

When the network congestion, segment loss or fault occurs, Q_S will rotate faster than Q_R. And some segments in Q_R may not store in right order, shown as Fig. 2. This condition should be fixed. For Q_R, there should be at least one segment in right order. The segments stored in Q_R with the right order are the candidates of coding head. Once sender detects the loss-rate greater than the threshold, sender will pause the processing of new data. Then encode the segments in Q_S into coded segments and transmit. The first segment in Q_S is the coding head. Receiver will receive the coded segments and put them into Q_R until the first segment in Q_R is coding head. That is, the segments stored in the first element of Q_S and Q_R have the same sequence number, shown as Fig. 3. Then, receiver can decode the coded segments in Q_R and get the original data. Thus, Q_S and Q_R become synchronized again and the problem has been fixed.

Fig. 4 is the state diagram of proposed TCP/LRC mechanism. The transmission begins from the starting state, similar to the slow start procedure of standard TCP. The segments will be transmitted in minimal transmission rate, which will be increased each next round. When Q_S is fully-filled, it switches to normal transmission state. Sender will detect segment loss in this state. Once the segment loss exceeded the threshold, it switches to the coding recovery state. In the coding recovery state, sender has paused processing new data, and start

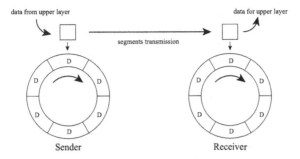

Fig. 1. Both sender and receiver have a cyclic queue with same size, when transmitting under normal condition, the access pointers of two cyclic queue should rotate simultaneously

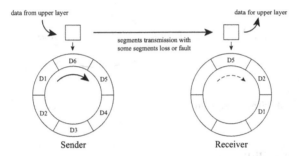

Fig. 2. When segment loss or fault occurs, the access pointer rotation will incompatible, and there may have out-of-ordered segments is receiver's queue

to send the linear combination of the segments in Q_S. Receiver collects the coded segments and performs the decoding procedure. After recovered the lost segments, it switches back to normal transmission state.

3.2 Sensing Segment Loss-Rate

The ACK in standard TCP sends the sequence number of next expected segment. In TCP/LRC, the idea above also works, but with different meaning. Generally, the problem can be fixed by coding if the amount of lost segment is lower than the buffer size. As we discussed above, there should be at least one right-ordered segment in Q_R. But there may have segments not in the right order, which will push the right-ordered segments out of queue. For this condition, TCP/LRC should keep two indicators, the amount of right-ordered segments, R_c, and the amount of out-of-ordered segments, R_g.

Sender calculates R_c and R_g by the ACKs, and keep monitoring the two indicators. If R_c is lower than the last segment of Q_S or R_g is greater than buffer size, the problem cannot be fixed by coding. Such situation should be avoided. If sender detected such situation is going to happen, it will pause processing new data and start sending coded segment.

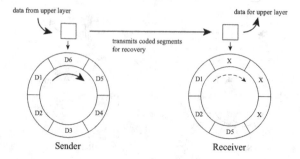

Fig. 3. The amount of lost segments recovered by coded blocks, performing decode operations can get the original segments

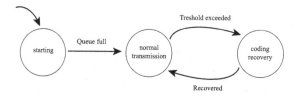

Fig. 4. State diagram of proposed TCP/LRC mechanism

3.3   Segment Format

Considering the compatibility with standard TCP, we use typical TCP segment format. The header is briefly shown as Table [1]. There are nine bits for flags in the TCP header. The three reserved bits generally set to zero in standard TCP. For identification of LRC, we use one of them as flag. We labelled it as COD flag here, which will be used to identify TCP/LRC peer when setting up the connection. If the transmission is in coding recovery state, the COD flag will be set to identify the coding segment.

For the coding segment, we put the additional information in the URG pointer field for generating coding coefficients, which has an introduction in next section. URG mechanism is for urgent data in TCP. When the URG flag is set, it means the data need process quickly, and the URG pointer denotes the position of the urgent data. Thus, receiver can process the segment with higher priority. For the segment lost condition, the urgency is also expired. So here we use the URG point field to transfer additional information in TCP/LRC. When in normal transmission state, the urgent data mechanism is still available.

3.4   Encoding Procedure

Linear network coding performs the algebraic operations in Galois Field. Some researches applied the random linear network coding, which will choose coding coefficients randomly. Random linear network coding can ensure that the linear

Table 1. TCP Segment Header

Bit	Fields		Bit
0	Source port	Destination port	31
32	Sequence number		63
64	Acknowledgment number		95
96	Data offset	Reserved	Flags	Window size	127
128	Checksum	URG pointer	159

combination has a solution. But it will take bandwidth to transmit the coefficients to receivers. In TCP/LRC, we use a hash function, H, to generate the coding coefficients. With the hash function, we only need to put the hash seed in the header. We made TCP/LRC perform the coding operations in $GF(2^8)$. Many researches use $GF(2^8)$ because each number in $GF(2^8)$ is a byte. This makes it feasible for implementation.

When entered the coding recovery state, sender would pick a hash seed, k, for different coded segment. Then get the n code coefficients for n segments, as formula (1). And put the linear combination, X, in the payload of coded segment, as formula (2). The hash seed, k, will filled in the URG pointer field in the segment header. The sequence number of coding head, D_1, will be put in the sequence number field of coded segment. Thus, receiver can identify the coded segments as same group.

$$\{C_1, C_2, \ldots, C_n\} = H(k) \tag{1}$$

$$X = C_1 D_1 + C_2 D_2 + \cdots + C_n D_n = \sum_{i=1}^{n} (C_i D_i) \tag{2}$$

3.5 Decoding Procedure

In linear network coding, n coded segments can be decode and get the original data by the operations in formula (3). In LRC, we hope the amount of coded segments is minimized. When received a coded segment, receiver will unpack it in the buffer and determine whether it has the parts of the coded segment by the coding head number. If receiver already has the uth segment, part of the coded segment X, it will do the operation as formula (4) to remove the uth segment from the coded segment. X' denotes the coded segment without the uth segment and C_u denotes the coding coefficient of X. Because the addition operation in Galois field can be performed by XOR, adding $C_u D_u$ equals to remove it from X. The coding coefficients can be extracted from the hash function, H, with the hash seed in the URG pointer field of the segment header. Receiver also prepares a coding coefficient mask, M, once it received the coded block. The mask, M, is a binary array, or vector, with all zeros. When receiver find out it already has the uth segment, it will also set theu^{th} bit of M to one.

$$
\begin{bmatrix} D_1 \\ \vdots \\ D_n \end{bmatrix} = \begin{bmatrix} C_1^1 \cdots C_n^1 \\ \vdots \ddots \vdots \\ C_1^n \cdots C_n^n \end{bmatrix}^{-1} \times \begin{bmatrix} X_1 \\ \vdots \\ X_n \end{bmatrix} \tag{3}
$$

$$
X' = X + C_u D_u \tag{4}
$$

When there are m zeros in M and receiver has received m coded segments with same coding head, receiver can decode and get the m original segments. Receiver will re-order the coding coefficients, only use the C_i with $M(i)$ is zero. And the size of coefficient matrix in formula (3) will be reduced. Then, receiver can do the decoding operations and get the m original segments.

3.6   Congestion Control

Although network coding can improve the throughput, there still has the bandwidth limit of network link. Transmit the segments too fast will cause network congestion. Standard TCP use the congestion window and ACK for congestion control. When transmitted an amount of segments, TCP will wait for the correct ACK before transmit other segments. TCP/NC adds a new layer between TCP layer and IP layer, so the congestion control is still handling by TCP.

In this paper, LRC also maintains the congestion window mechanism of TCP. After sender transmitted an amount of segments, it would wait for the ACK before continues. When entered the coding recovery state, the congestion window size will be reduced. We are studying for advanced in this issue, to adjust the transmission more accurate by R_c and R_g. This may become our future work.

4   Performance Evaluation

4.1   Theoretical Induction

The first indicator of performance is throughput, which denotes the amount of data can be transmitted per time period. For TCP without SACK, we assumed the average loss probability of each segment is q, and the mean value of window size is w. The Z denotes the expected amount of actual transmitted segments, that is, considered the retransmitted or redundant segments. We calculate the usage of network link like formula (5). According to the Go-Back-N retransmission scheme of TCP, Z will be the equation in formula (6). Our proposed mechanism can reduce Z to Z' shown in formula (7).

$$
\frac{amount \quad of \quad original \quad data}{expected \quad amount \quad of \quad transmission} = \frac{w}{Z} \tag{5}
$$

$$
Z = w + \left(\frac{1+w}{2}\right)\left(1 - (1-q)^w\right) \tag{6}
$$

$$Z' = w(1 + q) \tag{7}$$

Comparing with TCP/NC, our mechanism has no transmission overhead because we use a hash function to generate the coding coefficients. The seed of hash function can be filled in the URG pointer of TCP header. The proposed mechanism does not need extra transmission for coded segments. Moreover, the proposed mechanism will perform coding operations only in necessary condition, the computing overhead and power consumption can be minimized.

For the computing complexity, according to formula (2), the complexity of encoding n segments is $O(n^2)$. This complexity level is similar to some searching and sorting algorithms. So encoding operation is acceptable for most of systems. The decoding operations in formula (3) have a complexity of $O(n^3)$. This is more complicated than most of other operations and is possible to solve by hardware decoding in the future. The proposed LRC mechanism minimized the coding operations, also minimized the extra costs of network coding.

4.2   Packet Loss Model

For the accuracy of simulation, we studied the packet loss model of real computer networks. The packet losses we discuss here are caused by wireless interference or fading, or sporadic fault in the network device, not caused by link failed or network device failed. Hohlfeld et al, [7,4], analyzed the packet loss model by the Gilbert-Elliott Model in Fig. 5, which is inspired by Markov Model. Each of the network links is either in good (G) or bad (B) state. The probability of a correctly-transmitted bit in good state is k, while in bad state is h. On the other hand, the bit error rates in the two states are $1 - k$ and $1 - h$, respectively. In the good state, the probability of switching to bad state is p, staying in good state is $1 - p$. In the bad state, the probability of switching to good state is r, staying in bad state is $1 - r$. These works discussed the packet loss in networks including wireless network and mobile network. We used this model for the simulation network environment.

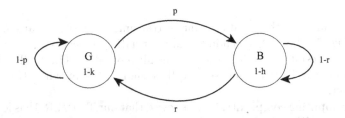

Fig. 5. The Gilber-Elliot Model defines the network link with two states, good (G) state and bad (B) state

4.3 Simulation Results

For simulation, we emulate the lossy network environment by the Gilbert-Elliot
Model. The probability from the good state to the bad state is 0.1, while the
probability from bad state to good state is 0.3. And the bit error rate in the good
state and bad state are 0.000001 and 0.000002 respectively. The content length
is 240,000 bytes while each segment carrying 1200 bytes. There are 200 original
segments in each round. We simulated 20 rounds, after each round, the bit error
rate in both good state and bad state increased 0.000003. We compared the
proposed mechanism, labeled as TCP/LRC here, with TCP/NC and TCP Reno.
Fig. 6 shows the relationship between dropped segments and actual transmitted
segments. As the growth of bit error rate, the amount of dropped segments also
increased after each round. TCP Reno detects segment loss by time-out or triple-
duplicated ACK and discarded the out-of-ordered segments, so the number of
actual transmitted segments was much more than the dropped segments plus
the original segments. TCP/NC and TCP/LRC transmit the linear combination
for the error recovery condition, so the number of actual transmitted segments
equal to the dropped segments plus the original segment.

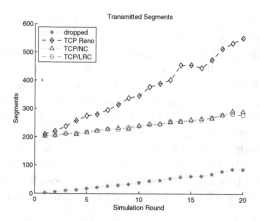

Fig. 6. Comparison of the exact transmitted segments with the bit error rate increased
after each round

We also compared the total amount of transmitted data in transport layer,
shown as Fig. 7. TCP/NC has additional information for network coding in the
segment. As a result, TCP/NC has to transmit more data. Our TCP/LRC just
uses the standard TCP header, so it will be more efficient when transmitting
large content.

For the computing complexity, Fig. 8 showed that our TCP/LRC has less coded
segments than TCP/NC. The encoding and decoding procedure in TCP/LRC is
minimized. This let TCP/LRC can have lower power consumption and lower computing resource requirement.

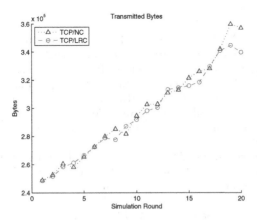

Fig. 7. Comparison of TCP/LRC and TCP/NC by the amount of transmitted data, in bytes

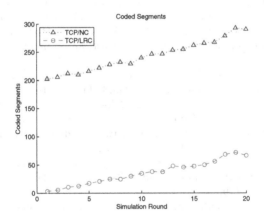

Fig. 8. Comparison of TCP/LRC and TCP/NC by the amount of coded segments

5   Conclusions

In this paper, we proposed the loss-rate driven coding, LRC. And combined LRC with TCP. With this mechanism, the amount of encoding operations and decoding operations can be minimized. The coded segment will be used only if needed. And the amount of decoding operations is also reduced to the actual required amount. Thus, this mechanism will be easier to implement in the embedded systems with limited system resources. We also used the standard TCP segment header in the proposed mechanism. This can let the implement has higher compatibility with standard TCP. For the future works, we are studying about the congestion control issue. With a more accurate congestion control scheme, we hope the throughput could be optimized in the future.

References

1. Ahlswede, R., Cai, N., Li, S.Y., Yeung, R.W.: Network information flow. IEEE Transactions on Information Theory 46, 1204–1216 (2000)
2. Gkantsidis, C., Rodriguez, P.R.: Network coding for large scale content distribution. In: 24th Annual Joint Conference of the IEEE Computer and Communications Societies, Proceedings IEEE (INFOCOM), vol. 4, pp. 2235–2245 (2005)
3. Chan, Y.-C., Hu, Y.-Y.: Adaptive Network Coding Scheme for TCP over Wireless Sensor Networks. International Journal of Computers. Communications and Control 8(6) (2013)
4. Hasslinger, G., Hohlfeld, O.: The Gilbert-Elliott Model for Packet Loss in Real Time Services on the Internet, Measuring. In: 14th GI/ITG Conference on Modelling and Evaluation of Computer and Communication Systems (MMB), pp. 1–15 (2008)
5. Postel, J.: RFC793, Transmission Control Protocol (1981)
6. Katti, S., Rahul, H., Hu, W., Katabi, D., Medard, M., Crowcroft, J.: XORs in the air: practical wireless network coding. IEEE/ACM Trans. Netw. 16(3), 497–510 (2008)
7. Hohlfeld, O.: Stochastic packet loss model to evaluate QoE impairments. PIK-Praxis der Informationsverarbeitung und Kommunikation 32(1), 53–56 (2009)
8. Kim, M., Klein, T., Soljanin, E., Barros, J., Medard, M.: Modeling Network Coded TCP: Analysis of Throughput and Energy Cost, arXiv preprint arXiv:1208.3212 (2012)
9. Kim, M., Medard, M., Barros, J.O.: Modeling network coded TCP throughput: A simple model and its validation. In: Proceedings of the 5th International ICST Conference on Performance Evaluation Methodologies and Tools, pp. 131–140 (2011)
10. Mathis, M., et al.: RFC 2018, Internet Engineering Task Force (IETF) (1996)
11. Li, S.Y., Yeung, R.W., Cai, N.: Linear network coding. IEEE Transactions on Information Theory 49, 371–381 (2003)
12. Stallings, W.: Handbook of computer-communications standards. The open systems interconnection (OSI) model and OSI-related standards, vol. 1. Macmillan Publishing Co., Inc. (1987)
13. Sundararajan, J.K., Jakubczak, S., Medard, M., Mitzenmacher, M., Barros, J.: Interfacing network coding with TCP: an implementation, arXiv preprint arXiv:0908.1564 (2009)
14. Sundararajan, J.K., Shah, D., Medard, M., Jakubczak, S., Mitzenmacher, M., Barros, J.: Network coding meets TCP: Theory and implementation. Proceedings of the IEEE 99(3), 490–512 (2011)
15. Sundararajan, J.K., Shah, D., Medard, M., Mitzenmacher, M., Barros, J.: Network coding meets TCP. IEEE INFOCOM, 280–288 (2009)
16. Zhang, Z.: Linear Network Error Correction Codes in Packet Networks. IEEE Transactions on Information Theory 54, 209–218 (2008)

Multilayer Perceptron and Stacked Autoencoder for Internet Traffic Prediction

Tiago Prado Oliveira, Jamil Salem Barbar, and Alexsandro Santos Soares

Federal University of Uberlândia, Faculty of Computer Science, Uberlândia, Brazil,
tiago_prado@comp.ufu.br, {jamil,alex}@facom.ufu.br

Abstract. Internet traffic prediction is an important task for many applications, such as adaptive applications, congestion control, admission control, anomaly detection and bandwidth allocation. In addition, efficient methods of resource management can be used to gain performance and reduce costs. The popularity of the newest deep learning methods has been increasing in several areas, but there is a lack of studies concerning time series prediction. This paper compares two different artificial neural network approaches for the Internet traffic forecast. One is a Multilayer Perceptron (MLP) and the other is a deep learning Stacked Autoencoder (SAE). It is shown herein how a simpler neural network model, such as the MLP, can work even better than a more complex model, such as the SAE, for Internet traffic prediction.

Keywords: Internet traffic, time series, prediction, forecasting, neural network, machine learning, multilayer perceptron, deep learning, stacked autoencoder.

1 Introduction

Using past observations to predict future network traffic is an important step to understand and control a computer network. Network traffic prediction can be crucial to network providers and computer network management in general. It is of significant interest in several domains, such as adaptive applications, congestion control, admission control and bandwidth allocation.

There are many studies that focus on adaptive and dynamic applications. They usually present some algorithms, that use the traffic load, to dynamically adapt the bandwidth of a certain network component [1][2][3] and improve the Quality of Service (QoS) [4]. Several works have been developed using Artificial Neural Networks (ANN) and they have shown that ANN are a competitive model, overcoming classical regression methods such as ARIMA [5][6][7][8]. Thus, there are works that combine these two factors, therefore producing a a predictive neural network that dynamically allocates the bandwidth in real-time video streams [3].

Initially, the use of neural networks was limited in relation to the number of hidden layers. Neural networks made up of various layers were not used due to the difficulty in training them [9]. However, in 2006, Hinton presented the Deep

C.-H. Hsu et al. (Eds.): NPC 2014, LNCS 8707, pp. 61–71, 2014.

Belief Networks (DBN), with an efficient training method based on a greedy learning algorithm, which trains one layer at a time[10]. Since then, studies have encountered several sets of good results regarding the use of deep learning neural networks. Through these findings this study has as its objective to use the deep learning concept in traffic prediction.

Network traffic is a time series, which is a sequence of data regularly measured at uniform time intervals. For network traffic, these sequential data are the bits transmitted in some network device at a certain period on time. A time series can be a stochastic process or a deterministic one. To predict a time series it is necessary to use mathematical models that truly represent the statistical characteristic of the sampled traffic. The choice of the prediction method must take into account the prediction horizon, computational cost, prediction error and the response time, for adaptive applications that require real-time processing.

This paper analyses two prediction methods that are based on ANN. Evaluations were made comparing Multilayer Perceptron (MLP) and Stacked Autoencoder (SAE). MLP is a feed-forward neural network with multiple layers that uses Backpropagation as supervised training. SAE is a deep learning neural network that uses a greedy algorithm for unsupervised training. The analysis focuses on a short-term forecast and the tests were made using samples of Internet traffic time series, which were obtained on DataMarket database [11].

2 Artificial Neural Networks

Artificial Neural Networks are simple processing structures, which are separated into strongly connected units called artificial neurons (nodes). Neurons are organized into layers, one layer has multiple neurons and any one neural network can have one or more layers, which are defined by the network topology and vary among different network models [12].

Neurons are capable of working in parallel to process data, store experimental knowledge and use this knowledge to infer new data. Each neuron has a synaptic weight, which is responsible for storing the acquired knowledge. Network knowledge is acquired through learning processes (learning algorithm or network training) [12]. In the learning process, the network will be trained to recognize and differentiate the data from a finite set. After learning, the ANN is ready to recognize the patterns in a time series, for example. During the learning process the synaptic weights are modified in an ordered manner until they reach the desired learning. A neural network offers the same functionality as neurons in a human brain for resolving complex problems, such as nonlinearity, high parallelism, robustness, fault tolerance, noise tolerance, adaptability, learning and generalization [5][12].

Deep learning refers to a machine learning method that is based on a neural network model with multiple levels of data representation. Hierarchical levels of representation are organized by abstractions, features or concepts. The higher levels are defined by the lower levels, where the representation of the low-levels may define several different features of the high-levels, this makes the data representation more abstract and nonlinear for the higher levels [9][10]. These hierarchical levels are represented by the layers of the ANN and they allow for the adding of a significant complexity to the prediction model. This complexity is proportional to the number of layers that the neural network has. The neural network depth concerns to the number of composition levels of nonlinear operations learned from trained data, i.e., more layers; more nonlinear and deeper is the ANN.

The main difficulty in using deep neural networks relates to the training phase. Conventional algorithms, like Backpropagation, do not perform well when the neural network has more than three hidden layers [13]. Besides, these conventional algorithms do not optimize the use of more layers and they do not distinguish the data characteristics hierarchically, i.e., the neural network with many layers does not have a better result to that of a neural network with few layers, e.g., shallow neural network with two or three layers [14][15].

3   Review of Literature

Several types of ANN have been studied for network traffic prediction. An advantage of ANN is the response time, i.e., how fast the prediction of future values is made. After the learning process, which is the slowest step in the use of an ANN, the neural network is ready for use, obtaining results very quickly compared to other more complex prediction models as FARIMA [8]. Therefore, ANNs are better at online prediction, obtaining a satisfactory result regarding prediction accuracy and response time [5].

3.1   Multilayer Perceptron and Backpropagation

One of commonest architectures for neural networks is the Multilayer Perceptron. This kind of ANN has one input layer, one or more hidden layers, and an output layer. Best practice suggests one or two hidden layers [14]. This is due to the fact that the same result can be obtained by raising the number of neurons in the hidden layer, rather than increase the number of hidden layers [15].

MLPs are feed-forward networks, where all neurons in the same layer are connected to all neurons of the next layer, yet the neurons in the same layer are not connected to each other. It is called feed-forward because the flow of information goes from the input layer to the output layer. The training algorithm used for MLP is the Backpropagation, which is a supervised learning algorithm, where the MLP learns a desired output from various entry data.

3.2   Stacked Autoencoder and Deep Learning

Stacked Autoencoder is a deep learning neural network built with multiple layers of sparse Autoencoders, in which the output of each layer is connected to the input of the next layer. SAE learning is based on a greedy layer-wise unsupervised training, which trains each Autoencoder independently [16][17][18].

The strength of deep learning is based on the representations learned by the greedy layer-wise unsupervised training algorithm. Furthermore, after a good data representation in each layer is found, the acquired neural network can be used to initialize some new ANN with new synaptic weights. This new initialized neural network can be an MLP, e.g., to start a supervised training if necessary [9]. A lot of papers emphasize the benefits of the greedy layer-wise unsupervised training for deep network initialization [9][10][18][19][20]. Therefore, one of the goals of this paper is to verify if the unsupervised training of deep learning does actually bring advantages over the simpler ANN models.

4   Experiments and Results

The utilized time series data were gathered on DataMarket and created by R. J. Hyndman [11]. The experiments were performed from data collected daily, hourly and at five minute intervals. Altogether, six time series were used, with them being "A-1d", "A-1h", "A-5m", "B-1d", "B-1h" and "B-5m".

These time series used are composed of Internet traffic (in bits) from a private Internet Service Provider (ISP) with centres in 11 European cities. The data corresponds to a transatlantic link and was collected from 06:57 hours on 7 June to 11:17 hours on 31 July 2005. This series was collected at different intervals, resulting in three different time series: "A-1d" is a time series with daily data; "A-1h" is hourly data; "A-5m" contains data collected every five minutes.

The remaining time series are composed of Internet traffic from an ISP, collected in an academic network backbone in the United Kingdom. They were collected from 19 November 2004, at 09:30 hours to 27 January 2005, at 11:11 hours. In the same way, this series was divided into three different time series: "B-1d" is daily data; "B-1h" is hourly data; "B-5m", with data collected at five minute intervals.

The conducted experiments used DeepLearn Toolbox [21], an open source code of different libraries that cover several machine learning and artificial intelligence techniques. Some are, Artificial Neural Networks (ANN), Convolutional Neural Networks (CNN), Stacked Autoencoders (SAE), Convolutional Autoencoders (CAE) and Deep Belief Networks (DBN). The libraries of DeepLearn Toolbox are coded using the MATLAB environment tool.

4.1   Data Normalization

Before training the neural network, it is important to normalize the data [8], in this case, the time series. In addition, for a better calculation and results, the DeepLearn Toolbox requires that the input data are next to zero. Hence, to decrease the time series scale the z-score was used to normalize the data. After that, a sigmoid function was applied, so that the time series values are in the range [0, 1]. The z-score was chosen as through it the data scale are preserved and patterns are not changed.

Table 1. The time interval and size of each time series

Data Set	Time interval	Time Series total size	Training Set size
A-1d	1 day	51	25
A-1h	1 h	1231	615
A-5m	5 min	14772	7386
B-1d	1 day	69	34
B-1h	1 h	1657	828
B-5m	5 min	19888	9944

The original time series is normalized, generating a new normalized time series, which will be used for the training. The range of the 6 time series used varies from 51 values (for the smallest time series, with daily data) to 19888 values(for the largest time series, with data collected at five minute intervals). During the experiments the data range for the training set varied greatly, from 25 values (for the smallest time series) to 9944 values (for the largest time series). The size for the training set was chosen as that of the first half of the time series, the other half of the time series is the test set for evaluating the prediction accuracy. The size of each data set can be seen in Table 1.

4.2 Neural Network Architecture and Topology

For the standard neural network, the MLP was used, with a sigmoid activation function, a low learning rate of 0.01 and Backpropagation as the training algorithm. For the deep learning neural network, the SAE was used, also with sigmoid activation function and a learning rate of 0.01. Higher learning rate accelerates the training, but may generate many oscillations in it, making it harder to reach a low error. On the other hand, a lower learning rate leads to steadier training, however is much slower.

This low value for the learning rate was used because, for our purpose, the training time was not the most important target, in fact, it is the final error achieved by the artificial neural network. Was also tested different ones, such as 0.5, 0.25 and 0.1, yet as expected, the lowest errors were obtained using 0.01 for the learning rate.

The training algorithm of SAE is a greedy algorithm that gives similar weights to similar inputs. Each Autoencoder is trained separately, in a greedy fashion, then it is stacked onto those already trained; thereby, producing a SAE with multiple layers. The greedy training algorithm is used to train unlabeled data, i.e., it does not train the data considering the expected output. On the other hand, for labeled data such as time series, the greedy training is not sufficient and it is used as a pre-training to initialize the neural network weights (instead of a standard random initialization). After that, the Backpropagation algorithm was used as a fine-tuning for the supervised training [9][13][17][18].

Several tests were carried out varying the ANN topology, both in number of neurons per layer as in the number of layers. For the MLP, the best performances

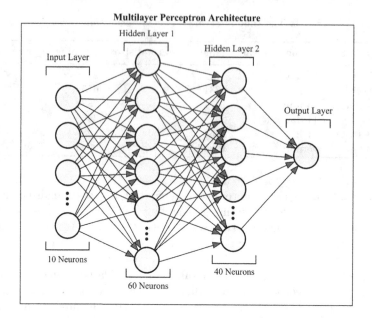

Fig. 1. Neural Network Architecture showing the layers, numbers of each layer and the information feed-forward flow

were obtained with 4 layers, around 10 input neurons, 1 output neuron, 60 and 40 neurons in the hidden layers, respectively, as shown in Fig. 1. It was found that increasing the number of neurons did not result in better performance, the average of Root Mean Square Error (RMSE) was found to be similar. However, for the ANN with 5 or more layers, overly increasing the number of layers was detrimental to performance.

For the SAE, the best results were found with 6 layers, with 20 input neurons, 1 output neuron, 80, 60, 60 and 40 neurons in each of the hidden layers, respectively. Increasing the number of neurons of the SAE did not produce better results; on average the Normalized Root Mean Square Error (NRMSE) was very similar. Similar results were found also with 4 layers, like the MLP, whereas deeper SAE achieved slightly better results. A comparison of the NRMSE of each prediction model will be shown in Table 2.

4.3   Neural Network Training

The neural network training was carried out in a single batch. This way all input data of the training set is trained in a single training epoch, adjusting the weights of the neural network for the entire batch. Tests with more batches (less input data for each training epoch) were also realized and similar error rates were found. Nevertheless, for smaller batches, the training took more time to converge, because a smaller amount of data is trained at each epoch.

The training time is mainly affected by the size of the training set and by the number of neurons of the neural network. The higher the size of the training set and higher the number of neurons, more time is necessary to train the neural network.

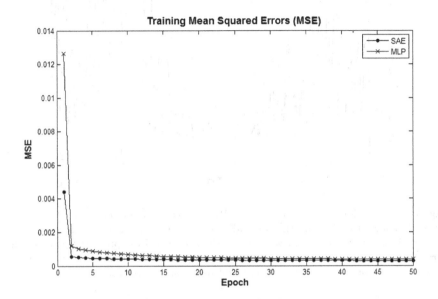

Fig. 2. A MSE comparison of SAE and MLP at each training epoch, for B-5m time series

The MLP training lasted 1000 epochs. The SAE training is separated into two steps. The first one is the unsupervised pre-training, which lasted 900 epochs. The second step is the fine-tuning that uses a supervised training, which lasted 100 epochs. Fig. 2 shows the first 50 training epochs and their respective errors, comparing the fine-tuning training of the SAE with the MLP training. It is possible to observe that, because of the SAE pre-training, the SAE training converges faster than the MLP training. However, more training epochs are enough for them to obtain very similar error rates.

Fig. 3 and Fig. 4 show the time series prediction results for the MLP and SAE, respectively. It is noted that MLP best fits the actual data, nevertheless, both fared well in data generalization. Both, MLP and SAE, learned the time series features and used these features to predict data that are not known a priori.

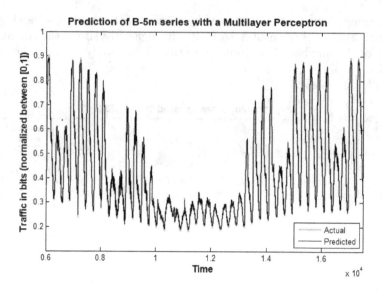

Fig. 3. A prediction comparison of the MLP at each training epoch for B-5m time series. It shows the Actual (the original) time series (represented in grey) and the Predicted one (represented in black). Since the actual and the predicted plot lines are very similar, it is difficult to see the difference with a low scale image. Yet, it is possible to see that the predicted values fit very well to the actual values.

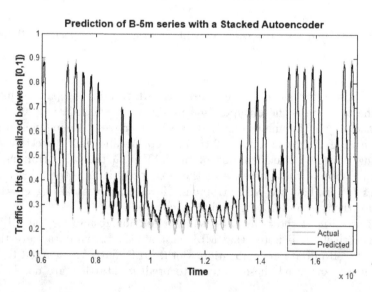

Fig. 4. A prediction comparison of the SAE at each training epoch for B-5m time series. It shows the Actual (the original) time series and the Predicted one. It is noted that the predicted (represented in black) did not fit well from 1×10^4 to 1.4×10^4 period in time, but for the rest of the series the predicted values fit well to the actual values.

4.4 Main Results

The key idea of deep learning is that the depth of the neural network allows learning complexes and nonlinear data [9]. However, the use of SAE for time series prediction was not beneficial, i.e., the pre-training did not bring significant benefits to prediction. The best results for the MLP and SAE with their respective NRMSE are shown in Table 2. Even though the MLP does not have a significant advantage over the SAE, still, the MLP has achieved better results for network traffic prediction.

Table 2. A comparison of Normalized Root Mean Squared Error (NRMSE) results

Data Set	NRMSE	
	MLP	SAE
A-1d	0.1999	0.3660
A-1h	0.0479	0.0756
A-5m	0.0192	0.0222
B-1d	0.1267	0.2155
B-1h	0.0421	0.0556
B-5m	0.0131	0.0184

In the time series prediction, the SAE method has more complexity than the MLP, since it has the extra unsupervised training phase, which initializes the neural network weights for the fine-tuning stage. Even with the additional complexity, the SAE was slightly inferior. Due to this fact, this approach is not recommended for time series prediction.

There are works, in the pattern recognition field, where the use of Autoencoders are advantageous [20], as they are based in unlabeled data. On the other hand, there are works, in time series prediction and labelled data, showing that the Autoencoders approach is worse than classical neural networks [22], such as MLP and Recurrent ANN. Each of these problems has a better method for solving it, so it is important to analyse the entry data type before choosing the most appropriate method to be used.

5 Conslusion

Both types of studied ANN have proven that they are capable of adjusting and predicting network traffic accurately. However, the initialization of the neural network weights through the unsupervised pre-training did not bring an improvement for time series prediction. The result shows that MLP is better than SAE for Internet traffic prediction. In addition, the SAE deep neural network approach reflects on more computational complexity during the training, so the choice of MLP is more advantageous.

The use and importance of deep neural networks is increasing and very good results are achieved in images, audio and video pattern recognition [19][20][23][24]. However, the main learning algorithms for this kind of neural network are unsupervised training algorithms, which use unlabelled data for their training. In contrast, network traffic and time series, in general, are labeled data, requiring an unsupervised pre-training before the actual supervised training as a fine-tuning. Yet, as shown in [24], the DBN and restricted Boltzmann machine (RBM), which are deep learning methods, can be modified to work better with labeled data, i.e., time series data sets.

Future works will focus in other deep learning techniques, like Deep Belief Nets and Continuous Restricted Boltzmann Machine (CRBM) and other models of ANN, such as the Recurrent Neural Network (RNN), with others training algorithms, such as Resilient Backpropagation. Even better results are expected, since they are more optimized for learning sequential and continuous data. Other future works will use the network traffic prediction to create an adaptive bandwidth management tool. This adaptive management tool will first focus on congestion control through bandwidth dynamic allocation, based on the traffic predicted. The objective is to guarantee a better QoS and a fair share of bandwidth allocation for the network devices in a dynamic and adaptive management application.

References

1. Han, M.-S.: Dynamic bandwidth allocation with high utilization for XG-PON. In: 16th International Conference on Advanced Communication Technology (ICACT), pp. 994–997. IEEE (2014)
2. Zhao, H., Niu, W., Qin, Y., Ci, S., Tang, H., Lin, T.: Traffic Load-Based Dynamic Bandwidth Allocation for Balancing the Packet Loss in DiffServ Network. In: 11th International Conference on Computer and Information Science (ICIS), pp. 99–104. IEEE/ACIS (2012)
3. Liang, Y., Han, M.: Dynamic Bandwidth Allocation Based on Online Traffic Prediction for Real-Time MPEG-4 Video Streams. EURASIP Journal on Advances in Signal Processing (2007)
4. Nguyen, T.D., Eido, T., Atmaca, T.: An Enhanced QoS-enabled Dynamic Bandwidth Allocation Mechanism for Ethernet PON. In: International Conference on Emerging Network Intelligence, pp. 135–140. EMERGING (2009)
5. Cortez, P., Rio, M., Rocha, M., Sousa, P.: Multi-scale Internet traffic forecasting using neural networks and time series methods. ExpertSystems: The Journal of Knowledge Engineering 29, 143–155 (2012)
6. Hallas, M., Dorffner, G.: A comparative study of feedforward and recurrent neural networks in time series prediction. In: 14th European Meet. Cybernetics Systems Research, vol. 2, pp. 644–647 (1998)
7. Ding, X., Canu, S., Denoeux, T.: Neural Network Based Models for Forecasting. In: Proceedings of Applied Decision Technologies (ADT 1995), pp. 243–252. Wiley and Sons, Uxbridge (1995)
8. Feng, H., Shu, Y.: Study on network traffic prediction techniques. In: International Conference on Wireless Communications, Networking and Mobile Computing, vol. 2, pp. 1041–1044. WiCOM (2005)

9. Bengio, Y.: Learning deep architectures for AI. Foundations and Trends in Machine Learning 2, 1–127 (2009)
10. Hinton, G.E., Osindero, S., Teh, Y.: A fast learning algorithm for deep belief nets. Neural Comput. 18, 1527–1554 (2006)
11. Hyndman, R.J.: Time Series Data Library, http://data.is/TSDLdemo
12. Haykin, S.: Neural Networks: A Comprehensive Foundation, 2nd edn. Prentice Hall PTR, Upper Saddle River (1998)
13. Erhan, D., Manzagol, P.-A., Bengio, Y., Bengio, S., Vincent, P.: The difficulty of training deep architectures and the effect of unsupervised pre-training. In: Proceedings of The Twelfth International Conference on Artificial Intelligence and Statistics (AISTATS 2009), pp. 153–160 (2009)
14. Villiers, J., Barnard, E.: Backpropagation neural nets with one and two hidden layers. IEEE Transactions on Neural Networks 4, 136–141 (1993)
15. Hornik, K., Stinchcombe, M., White, H.: Multi- layer feedforward networks are universal approximators. Neural Networks 2, 359–366 (1989)
16. Vincent, P., Larochelle, H., Bengio, Y., Manzagol, P.A.: Extracting and Composing Robust Features with Denoising Autoencoders. In: Proceedings of the Twenty-fifth International Conference on Machine Learning (ICML 2008), pp. 1096–1103. ACM, New York (2008)
17. Unsupervised Feature Learning and Deep Learning. Stanford's online wiki. Stacked Autoencoders,
    http://ufldl.stanford.edu/wiki/index.php/Stacked_Autoencoders
18. Bengio, Y., Lamblin, P., Popovici, D., Larochelle, H.: Greedy layer-wise training of deep networks. In: Schlkopf, B., Platt, J., Hoffman, T. (eds.) Advances in Neural Information Processing Systems 19 (NIPS 2006), pp. 153–160. MIT Press (2007)
19. Larochelle, H., Erhan, D., Vincent, P.: Deep learning using robust interdependent codes. In: Dyk, D.V., Welling, M. (eds.) Proceedings of the Twelfth International Conference on Artificial Intelligence and Statistics (AISTATS 2009), vol. 5, pp. 312–319 (2009); Journal of Machine Learning Research - Proceedings Track (2009)
20. Ranzato, M.A., Boureau, Y.-L., LeCun, Y.: Sparse Feature Learning for Deep Belief Networks. In: Platt, J., Koller, D., Singer, Y., Roweis, S. (eds.) Advances in Neural Information Processing Systems 20, pp. 1185–1192. MIT Press, Cambridge (2007)
21. Palm, R.B.: DeepLearnToolbox, a Matlab toolbox for Deep Learning, https://github.com/rasmusbergpalm/DeepLearnToolbox
22. Busseti, E., Osband, I., Wong, S.: Deep Learning for Time Series Modeling. Stanford, CS 229: Machine Learning (2012)
23. Arel, I., Rose, D.C., Karnowski, T.P.: Deep Machine Learning - A New Frontier in Artificial Intelligence Research [research frontier]. IEEE Computational Intelligence Magazine 5, 13–18 (2010)
24. Chao, J., Shen, F., Zhao, J.: Forecasting exchange rate with deep belief networks. In: The 2011 International Joint Conference on Neural Networks (IJCNN), pp. 1259–1266 (2011)

Optimization of Uncore Data Flow on NUMA Platform

Qiuming Luo[1,2], Yuanyuan Zhou[1], Chang Kong[1], Mei Wang[3], and Ye Cai[1,2,*]

[1] Guangdong Province Key Laboratory of Popular High Performance Compters
[2] College of Computer Science and Software Engineering, SZU, China
[3] School of Computer Engineering, Shenzhen Polytechnic, China
{lqm,caiye}@szu.edu.cn, clarkong89@gmail.com

Abstract. Uncore part of the processor has a profound effect, especially in NUMA systems, since it is used to connect cores, last level caches (LLC), on-chip multiple memory controllers (MCs) and high-speed interconnections. In our previous study, we investigated several benchmarks' data flow in Uncore of Intel Westmere microarchitecture and found that the data flow of Global Queue (GQ) and QuickPath Home Logical (QHL) has serious imbalance and congestion problem. This paper, we aims at the problem of entries' low efficiency in GQ and QHL we set up an M/M/3 Queue Model for GQ and QHL's three trackers' data flow, and then design a Dynamic Entries Management (DEM) mechanism which could improve entries' efficiency dramatically. The model is implemented in Matlab to simulate two different data flow pattern. Experiment results shows that DEM mechanism reduces stall cycles of trackers significantly: DEM reduces almost 60% stall cycles under smooth request sequences; DEM mechanism reduces almost 20~30% stall cycles under burst request sequences.

Keywords: NUMA, Uncore, Data flow, DEM.

1 Introduction

The number of processors or cores of PC servers are increasing with the growing demand of performance. The memory conflict becomes more and more serious. Instead of using faster and bigger processor caches, NUMA have solved the memory bandwidth issues to some extent by using asymmetric hierarchical memory model and has become the mainstream of modern server architecture. In a NUMA system, the memory chips are distributed in physics and all this memory shares a global address space. Accessing the remote memory needs processor interconnection technology. There are two main processor interconnection technologies currently. They are, respectively, AMD's HT (Hyper Transport) [2] and Intel's QPI (Quick Path Inter connect) [3]. Obviously, accesses to the local memory are faster than accesses to remote memory, because accesses to remote nodes must traverse the interconnection. Because of this, previous optimization work on NUMA platform often focus on

---

* Corresponding author

C.-H. Hsu et al. (Eds.): NPC 2014, LNCS 8707, pp. 72–83, 2014.

scheduling the process and moving data from remote to local to maximize the local accesses. Some of these are based on performance profile after execution [4][5][6], while others can deal with it during execution dynamically [7][8][9][10][11].

But in recent two years, the studies[12][13][14][15] have shown that microarchitecture have a great effect on optimizing the memory performance on NUMA platforms, even under some circumstance decreasing data locality may procure better performance. In our previous work [14], two 8-way NUMA architectures with different memory subsystems are experimentally analyzed, this two 8-way NUMA systems have diverse memory access feature because of their different microarchitecture. Dashti's work [15] also shows that remote delays are not the most important source of performance overhead, congestion on interconnection links and in MCs can dramatically hurt performance.

In our previous studies [1], we have made deep analyze of the inner architecture of uncore in Westmere processor and explored the data flow of Uncore in NUMA systems and discussed the unbalance and congestion of Uncore traffic, we will describe this later in this article. That unbalance might challenge the fixed entry number of GQ and QHL, which infer a dynamic entries management.

In this paper, we propose DEM (Dynamic Entries Management) mechanism and verified it efficiency by simulating the data flow using Matlab. We conclude that the DEM mechanism improve entries' efficiency dramatically.

The rest of the paper is organized as follows. In section II, we descript uncore modeling. Section III focuses on DEM algorithm description. Section IV presents our experiment results and analysis. Our conclusion is in section V.

2   Unbalance and Congestion of Data Traffic of Uncore

We have used the Intel Westmere as the target NUMA platform. In this section we will introduce the Uncore structure briefly and detail the unbalance and congestion of data traffic of Uncore in Intel "Westmere".

2.1   Microarchitecture of Uncore

Uncore is a term used by Intel to describe the functions of non-in-core parts in a microprocessor. The uncore unit in Intel Westmere is shown in Fig.1. It includes LLC, QPI, QMC and other components. Cache line requests from the local cores or from a remote package or the I/O hub are handled by uncore's GQ. There are 3 trackers in GQ to deal with the requests. One for write requests with 16 entries is called write tracker, the other one is read tracker for read requests with 32 entries, and the last one with 12 entries for other socket requests delivered by the QPI named peer probe tracker. Data access requests that miss the local LLC are sent to the QHL (QPI home logic) unit to retrieve the data. Such requests are speculative by nature, as a hit (m) response to a snoop requests to the other caching agents may return the line more quickly and supersede the request to the local QHL. Again, QHL has 3 queues for requests from local, remote sockets and IOH, and entries for each queue are 24, 16 and 24, respectively.

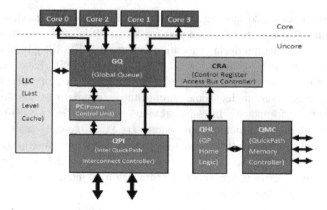

Fig. 1. Details of Westmere Uncore

2.2   Unbalance and Congestion of Data Traffic

In our previous work [1], we used Likwid [18] to measure several hardware performance events which can be classified into two groups: GQ Full and QHL Full, and Full means entries in trackers are used up and new requests should wait for empty entries. We measured the unbalance and congestion of data flow in uncore with using NAS Parallel Benchmark [19] and STREAM Benchmark [20].

After a series of experimental measurements and studies, we found that the unbalance of GQ's and QHL's trackers is serious and the usage rate of entries is low both for GQ and QHL. Such as GQ, Fig.2 shows the unbalance of GQ's three trackers. Each NPB applications run in Class C with 8 threads. We set GQ peer probe tracker's full cycles as 1 and normalized the other trackers' full cycles. Ten is the exponent in Y-axis. The X-axis lists the ten NPB applications. We can see that the unbalance of GQ's three trackers is really serious, the biggest unbalance rate is more than 800 times happened in FT's read and write trackers; the smallest unbalance rate is less than 1/100 times happened in CG's read and write trackers. And similar things happened in QHL.

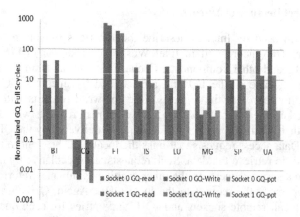

Fig. 2. The unbalance of GQ's three trackers

And also the rate of entries does not match the rate of full cycles of every application because each application's memory access pattern is not the same. As for the congestion of data flow, we found that the Full cycles growth patterns of three trackers were not the same for both GQ and QHL with threads number increase from 2 to 8.

3   Dynamic Entries Management

In this regard, we propose DEM (Dynamic Entries Management) mechanism as shown in Fig.5 and Fig.6, all the entries for the three Tracker are managed uniformly. Compared with FEM (Fixed Entries Management), DEM will improve the efficiency of the usage of the entries and reduce the number of the stall cycles.

3.1   Modeling Trackers of GQ/QHL

The M/M/3 queuing system is a model of the process that customers get service from server desk, the two "M" represents the interval of the customers arrive and the service time needed by customers are exponentially distributed (no memory, random, or Markov property), and the "3" refers to there are three Server Desk. We use the M/M/3 queuing system to simulate the flow of data which go through the GQ or QHL. Both GQ and QHL have three Server Desks to provide services for three Trackers, for GQ, the trackers are Read tracker, Write tracker and Peer Probe tracker. There are Local tracker, Remote tracker and IOH tracker for QHL. The data requests and responses are the customers. Cores, LLC, QPI and QHL will generate customers to GQ. And for QHL, GQ, QPI and QMC will produce customers. Each customer will be stored in an entry through a Tracker, then wait for getting service from one of the three Sever Desks.

In Intel Westmere, the number of entries for each tracker is fixed, as show in Fig.3 and Fig.4. If there is no free entries for one tracker and the newly arriving customers (data requests and responses) who want to enter into that tracker will have to wait. At the same time, the components generate customers have to stall cycles until a new free entry is available, though the other two Trackers might have free entries. We call this FEM mechanism, as Fig.7 shows.

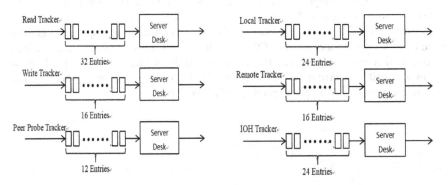

Fig. 3. GQ FEM M/M/3 queuing model   **Fig. 4.** QHL FEM M/M/3 queuing model

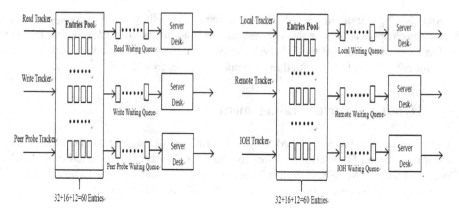

Fig. 5. GQ DEM M/M/3 queuing model   **Fig. 6.** QHL DEM M/M/3 queuing model

3.2   The Implementation of Dynamic Entries Management

In this section we will detail the FEM and DEM algorithm and we take the GQ as an example to illustrate these algorithms. Cores, LLC, QPI and QHL generate data requests or data responses to GQ, we call this a new customers' coming. The customer with different data access type will be stored in free entries through the different tracker. Such the customer with data-read request will go through the Read tracker, and the customer with data-write request will go through the Write tracker. For FEM, the entries divide into three parts according the type of the tracker, the number of entries for read tracker is 32, 16 for write tracker and 12 for peer probe tracker. Therefore, the customers with different type of data access can use the corresponding entries only. For instance, the customer with the type of data read can only be store in one of the 32 entries. All the customers stored in the entries will get service (the data requests or responses will be handled by GQ) from corresponding Server Desk according FIFO. Flow chart of the FEM algorithm is showed as Fig. 7.

   For DEM all the entries are uniform to customer. We treat all the entries as in an entries buffer pool. In order to make the customer get service from the right Server Desk, when a new customer comes, a free entries from the entries poll is assigned to the customer and must mark this assigned entries with the label of the Tracker where the customer from. Then, the customers with the same label form a queue to get the service from Server Desk according FIFO. At the end of the service, the entrie which has been marked must be removed the mark and put back into the entries pool. Flow chart of the FEM algorithm is showed as Fig.8. In this case, just when all the entries in the pool are used up will produce Stall Cycles.

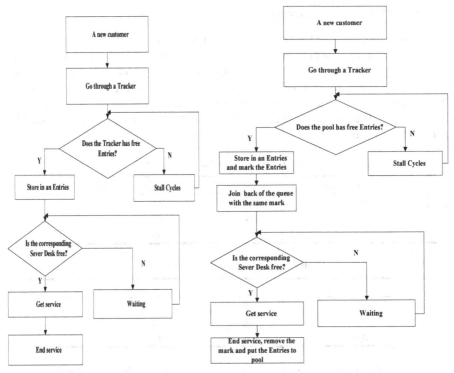

Fig. 7. FEM algorithm   **Fig. 8.** DEM algorithm

4   Experiment Results

We adopt M/M/3 system to simulate the flow of data which through the GQ or QHL by Matlab. We have assumed that the customers arrive according to a Poisson process, which means the interval time of arrival is exponential distribution. The probability density function of exponential distribution is showed in Formulas (1) and the average of probability density function of exponential distribution E[x] =1/λ. We create a parameter **Parameter1** (the value of 1/λ) to represent the average interval time of arrival, the greater of the value of **Parameter1**, the heavier the pressure of the customer's request. So in this simulation, we adjust the customer's request pressure by set the value of **Parameter1**.

$$f(x) = \lambda e^{-\lambda x} . \tag{1}$$

We also assumed that the time each customer gets service is an exponential distribution, we use a similar parameter **Parameter2** to simulate each customer's average service time, we choose a relative middle value 0.6 for **Parameter2**.

In order to make the comprehensive comparison of the FEM and DEM algorithms, we simulate two scenarios. One scenario is that the customers are generated gently, it means the customer's arrival request pressure is relative stable, another scenario is that the customers arrive with burst mode. The following content is the result of the simulation and analysis of the results.

4.1   Smooth Request Sequences

For this scenario, we used two sets of parameters, one for the situation that the customer's arrival request pressure is relative low and the entries for each tracker will not be used up, another for the situation that the request pressure is relative high and the entries for some trackers will be used up (for FEM). The parameters shows in Table 1 and Table 2, where the **Customer Number** represents the number of customers, and **Tracker1**, **Tracker2**, and **Tracker3** represent the three Trackers in GQ or QHL respectively.

Table 1. Parameters of low pressure

	Parameter1	Parameter2	Customer Number
Tracker1	0.5	0.6	200
Tracker2	0.5	0.6	120
Tracker3	0.5	0.6	80

Table 2. Parameters of high pressure

	Parameter1	Parameter2	Customer Number
Tracker1	0.9	0.6	200
Tracker2	0.9	0.6	120
Tracker3	0.9	0.6	80

The result of the simulation about low pressure is showed in Fig.9. We define the time of the customer's arrival with no stall cycles as the theoretical arrival time or the ideal arrival time. In fact, when the entries for customers is used up , the customer will have to stall some cycles and the following customer's arrival time will be pushed back. We define this arrival time as actual arrival time. The X axis is the sequences of the customers; the Y axis is the time of the customer's arrival in cycles. The red curve is the customer's theoretical arrival time; the blue curve is the customer's actual arrival time using FEM and the green curve for using DEM. As the picture shows, the three curves are coincided, therefore we just can see one green curve. That means under low pressure, whether use the FEM or DEM, there is no stall cycles occur and the efficiency of this two arithmetic are the same.

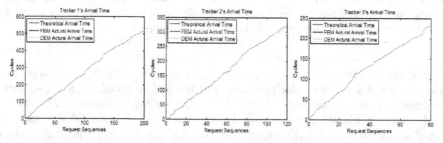

Fig. 9. The time of customer's arrival of the three Trackers under low pressure

Fig.10 shows the results of the simulation about high pressure. We can clearly see that stall cycles occurred for all the three Trackers, because the red curve is lower than other two curves in some time. For Tracker1, both FEM and DEM algorithm can provide enough entries for customers at the beginning, so the green curve covers the blue and red curve in the beginning. Then the blue curve begin to separate upward, this indicates that the entries is slowly be used up with the increase of request of customers and some stall cycles begin to appear for using DEM algorithm. But for FEM, the number of entries for Tracker1 is relative more (32) and it can continue to meet the requests, so the blue curve is coincided with the red curve. With the further increase of the requests of customers, the blue curve begin to separate upward and the growing is faster than green curve. This indicates that DEM algorithm begins to perform better than the FEM algorithm. It is because the other Tracker may have free entries, DEM algorithm can use these free entries for Tracker1. For **Tracker2** and **Tracker3**, because of the entries for them is relative few, the DEM performs decisive advantage over FEM.

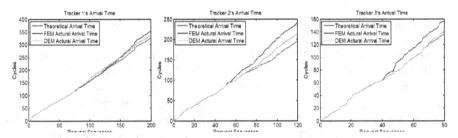

Fig. 10. The time of customer's arrival of the three Trackers under high pressure

We have also counted the average number of stall cycles of each customer of the three Trackers. The result is showed in Fig. 11. Compared with FEM, the DEM reduced the average number of stall cycles by 60 percent.

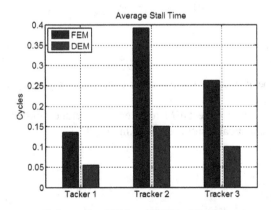

Fig. 11. Average stall time using FEM and DEM of Smooth request sequences

4.2   Burst Request Sequences

We adjusted the **Parameter1** dynamically to simulate the burst scenario. The lowest black arrow in Fig. 12 shows the trend of customers' arrival when we adjust **parameter1** and the number below the black arrow is the size of **parameter1**. Larger **parameter1** indicates the interval of customers' arrival is smaller, so the decreases of the slope of the curves mean burst requests occur. The parameters setting is shows in the table 3.

Table 3. Parameters of burst mode

	Parameter1	Parameter2	Customer Number
Tracker1	0.9（10.0）	0.6	200
Tracker2	0.9（10.0）	0.6	120
Tracker3	0.9（10.0）	0.6	80

Compared with Fig.10 and Fig.12, we can find that the trend of the curves is similar to Fig.12. For **Tracker1**, in the same way as high pressure situation, because the entries of **tracker1** is relative more for FEM, the curve of DEM actual arrival time separated upward later earlier than of FEM. For the three trackers, at the end of the burst, the number of stall cycles of FEM begins to overtake those of DEM. what is different is that the blue curves and green curves separate upward earlier in Fig. 12 than in Fig.10. Such as the **Tracker2**, the blue curve separates almost at 30 cycles, while in Fig.10 it separates almost at 100 cycles. This is because the burst occur at beginning of **Tracker2**, so the entries for Tracker2 is used up rapidly.

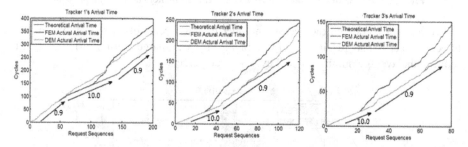

Fig. 12. The time of customer's arrival of the three Trackers under dynamical pressure

For burst mode scenario, the DEM reduced the average number of stall cycles by 20% to 30%. The statistical result is showed in Fig.13.

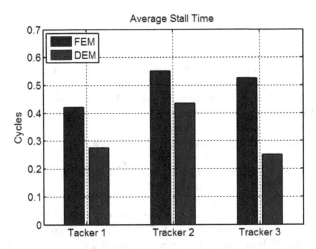

Fig. 13. Average stall time using FEM and DEM of Burst request sequences

5   Conclusion

Uncore component is important for the whole NUMA system, because it is the data transport center. We have found that serious traffic unbalance or congestion happens here when using the current FEM mechanism in our previous studies. In this paper, we proposed DEM mechanism and we used the Matlab to simulate two different data flow pattern of GQ and QHL. According to the experimental results and our analysis , we conclude that the DEM reduce almost 60% stall cycles under smooth request sequences; and reduce almost 20~30% stall cycles under burst request sequences DEM mechanism. Compared with fixed entries number in each tracker, we think that dynamic distributing entries according to each tracker's pressure have more advantages. The DEM could improve entries' usage rate and reduce trackers' stall time, therefore reduce stalling cycles of the preceding out-of-order instruction execution pipeline and improve the performance of the whole NUMA system.

In addition, the implementation of DEM may need some additional hardware to mark the entries and select the entries with the same label to get service by FIFO.

Future work: Our next work is to obtain the memory traces of various multithreaded applications, so we can testify DEM efficiency on "real" memory request sequence other than a Poisson process. Then we are going to design DEM trackers for GQ and QHL in VHDL to verify its functionality and assess its hardware overhead.

Acknowledgement. The research was jointly supported by the following grants: China 863-2012AA010239, NSF-China-61170076, Foundation of Shenzhen City under the numbers JCYJ20120613161137326, JCYJ2012061310222457, and Shenzhen Polytechnic Foundation 601422K20008

References

1. Luo, Q., Kong, C., Zhou, Y., et al.: Understanding the Data Traffic of Uncore in Westmere NUMA Architecture. In: 22th Euromicro International Conference on Parallel, Distributed and Network-Based Processing. IEEE, Turin (2014)
2. Advanced Micro Devices. AMD HyperTransport Technology-based system architecture [EB/OL]. AMD, Sunnyval (May 2002),
   http://www.amd.com/us/Documents/
   AMD_HyperTransport_Technology_based_System_
   Architecture_FINAL2.pdf
3. Maddox, R.A., Singh, G., Safranek, R.J.: A first look at the Intel QuickPath Interconnect [EB/OL]. Intel Corporation, Hillsboto (April 28, 2009),
   http://www.intel.com/intelpress/articles/
   A_First_Look_at_the_Intel(r).QuickPath_Interconnect.pdf
4. Li, H., Tandri, S., Stumm, M., Sevcik, K.C.: Locality and loop scheduling on NUMA multiprocessors. In: International Conference on Parallel Processing (ICPP). IEEE, New York (1993)
5. Marathe, J., Mueller, F.: Hardware profile-guided automatic page placement for ccNUMA systems. In: Proceedings of the eleventh ACM SIGPLAN symposium on Principles and Practice of Parallel Programming (PPoPP). ACM, New York (2006)
6. McCurdy, C., Vetter, J.C.: Memphis: Finding and fixing NUMA-related performance problems on multi-core platforms. In: International Symposium on Performance Analysis of Systems & Software (ISPASS). IEEE, New York (2010)
7. Ogasawara, T.: NUMA-aware memory manager with dominant-thread-based copying GC. In: Proceedings of the 24th ACM SIGPLAN Conference on Object Oriented Programming Systems Languages and Applications (OOPSLA). ACM, New York (2009)
8. Tikir, M.M., Hollingsworth, J.K.: NUMA-aware Java heaps for server applications. In: Proceedings of the 19th IEEE International Parallel and Distributed Processing Symposium (IPDPS). IEEE, Colorado (2005)
9. Tikir, M.M., Hollingsworth, J.K.: Hardware monitors for dynamic page migration. Journal of Parallel and Distributed Computing 68(9), 1186–1200 (2008)
10. Verghese, B., Devine, S., Gupta, A., et al.: Operating system support for improving data locality on CC-NUMA computer servers. In: Proceedings of the Seventh International Conference on Architectural Support for Programming Languages and Operating Systems (ASPLOS). ACM Press, New York (1996)
11. Wilson, K.M., Aglietti, B.B.: Dynamic page placement to improve locality in CC-NUMA multiprocessors for TPC-C. In: Proceedings of the 2001 ACM/IEEE Conference on Supercomputing (SC). ACM/IEEE, New York (2001)
12. Awasthi, M., Nellans, D.W., Sudan, K., et al.: Handling the problems and opportunities posed by multiple on-chip memory controllers. In: 19th International Conference on Parallel Architecture and Compilation Techniques(PACT). ACM, Vienna (2010)
13. Majo, Z., Gross, T.R.: Memory System Performance in a NUMA Multicore Multiprocessor. In: Proceedings of the 4th Annual International Conference on Systems and Storage (SYSTOR). ACM, New York (2011)
14. Luo, Q., Zhou, Y., Kong, C., Liu, G., Cai, Y., Lin, X.-H.: Analyzing the Characteristics of Memory Subsystem on Two different 8-way NUMA Architectures. In: Hsu, C.-H., Li, X., Shi, X., Zheng, R. (eds.) NPC 2013. LNCS, vol. 8147, pp. 155–166. Springer, Heidelberg (2013)

15. Dashti, M., Fedorova, A., Funston, J., Gaud, F., Lachaize, R., Lepers, B., et al.: Traffic management: A holistic approach to memory placement on NUMA systems. In: The 18th International Conference on Architectural Support for Programming Languages and Operating Systems. ACM, Houston (2013)

16. Intel Corporation. Intel 64 and IA-32 Architectures Optimization Reference Manual [EB/OL]. Intel Corporation (April 2010),
    http://www.intel.com/content/dam/doc/manual/
    64-ia-32-architectures-optimization-manual.pdf

17. Yang, R., Antony, J., Rendell, A., Robson, D., Strazdins, P.: Profiling directed NUMA optimization on Linux systems: A case study of the Gaussian computational chemistry code. In: The 25th IEEE International Parallel and Distributed Processing Symposium. IEEE, Anchorage (2011)

18. Treibig, J., Meier, M., Hager, G., Wellein, G.: Poster - LIKWID:Lightweight performance tools. In: The2011 High Performance Computing Networking, Storage and Analysis. ACM, Seattle (2011)

19. NasPrallel Benchmark [CP],
    http://www.nas.nasa.gov/publications/npb.html

20. STREAM Benchmark [CP], http://www.streambench.org/

APP-LRU: A New Page Replacement Method for PCM/DRAM-Based Hybrid Memory Systems

Zhangling Wu[1], Peiquan Jin[1,2], Chengcheng Yang[1], and Lihua Yue[1,2]

[1] School of Computer Science and Technology,
University of Science and Technology of China, Hefei, China
[2] Key Laboratory of Electromagnetic Space Information, Chinese Academy of Sciences, China
jpq@ustc.edu.cn

Abstract. Phase change memory (PCM) has become one of the most promising storage media particularly for memory systems, due to its byte addressability, high access speed, and low energy consumption. In addition, hybrid memory systems involving both PCM and DRAM can utilize the merits of both media and overcome some typical drawbacks of PCM such as high write latency and limited lifecycle. In this paper, we present a novel page replacement algorithm called APP-LRU (*Access-Pattern-prediction-based LRU*) for PCM/DRAM-based hybrid memory systems. APP-LRU aims to reduce writes to PCM while maintaining stable time performance. Particularly, we detect read/write intensity for each page in the memory, and put read-intensive pages into PCM while placing write-intensive pages in DRAM. We conduct trace-driven experiments on six synthetic traces and one real OLTP trace. The results show that our proposal is able to reduce up to 5 times of migrations more than its competitors.

Keywords: Phase change memory, Page replacement policy, Hybrid memory.

1   Introduction

Recently, the big data concept leads to a special focus on the use of main memory. Many researchers propose to use a large main memory to improve the performance of big data processing. However, the increasing capacity of main memory introduces many problems, such as increasing of total costs and energy consumption [1]. Both academia and industries are looking for new greener memory media, among which the Phase Change Memory (PCM) receives much attention [2]. PCM is one type of non-volatile memories, and provides better support for data durability than DRAM does. Further, it differs from other media such as flash memory in that it supports byte addressability. Because of the unique features of PCM, some people argue that PCM may replace DRAM in the future, as shown in Fig. 1(a). However, PCM has some limitations, e.g., high write latency, limited lifecycle, slower access speed than DRAM, etc. Therefore, it is not a feasible design to completely replace DRAM with PCM in current computer architectures.

A more exciting idea is to use both PCM and DRAM to construct hybrid memory systems, so that we can utilize the advantages from both media [2, 3]. PCM has the

C.-H. Hsu et al. (Eds.): NPC 2014, LNCS 8707, pp. 84–95, 2014.

advantages of low energy consumption and high density, and DRAM can afford near-ly unlimited writes. Specially, PCM can be used to expand the capacity of main memory, and DRAM can be used as either a buffer for PCM, as shown in Fig. 1(b) or the secondary main memory like DRAM, as shown in figure 1(c). Presently, both the architectures illustrated in Fig. 1(b) and (c) are hot topics in academia and industries. Many issues need to be further explored, among which the most focused issue is the buffer management schemes for hybrid memory systems involving PCM and DRAM. The biggest challenge for PCM/DRAM hybrid memory systems is that we have to cope with heterogeneous media. Traditional management schemes yield some specific page replacement policies that are designed either for DRAM-only main memory or for the system shown in Fig. 1(b). However, in this paper we focus on the hybrid memory systems with the architecture shown in Fig. 1(c).

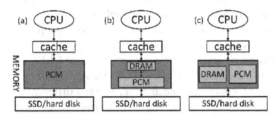

Fig. 1. Architectures of PCM-based memory systems [4]

The objective of this paper is to design an efficient page replacement scheme for PCM/DRAM-based hybrid memory systems as shown in Fig. 1(c). We propose a novel method called APP-LRU (Access-Pattern-Prediction-aware LRU). This method employs an algorithm to predict the access pattern changes and further uses the access patterns to reduce writes to PCM and keep stable time performance for PCM/DRAM-based hybrid memory systems. The main contributions of the paper are summarized as follows:

(1) We present a new page replacement method named APP-LRU for PCM/DRAM-based hybrid memory systems. APP-LRU records the access history of each page using a history table to identify the read and write intensity of pages. As a consequence, read-intensive pages are stored in PCM and write-intensive pages are saved in DRAM. Further, we propose an LRU-based on-demand migration algorithm to move pages between PCM and DRAM. (**Section 3**)

(2) We conduct trace-driven experiments in a simulated PCM/DRAM-based hybrid main memory environment under six synthetic traces and one real OLTP trace, and compare our proposal with several existing methods including LRU, CLOCK-DWF and Hybrid-LRU. The results show that our proposal reduces up to 5 times of total migrations more than its competitors. Meanwhile, it maintains comparable run time in all experiments. (**Section 4**)

2   Related Work

PCM is a kind of alternative memory devices because of its merits such as high densi-ty, low idle energy and so on. However, its limited life and long write latency is the main obstacles when implement traditional main memory management policies on PCM-based memory system.

There are many researches focus on reducing redundant writes to PCM, such as enhancing the fine-grained management approach [2, 3] with a Data Comparison Write (DCW) scheme that utilizes the bit alterability feature of PCM and only updates the changed bits [5-7]. However, these works are towards hardware design, while this paper employs a software-based research to reduce PCM writes. Moreover, Using DRAM to gather data writes are also a commonly used method for reducing the total number of writes to PCM [1, 8-11]. In this method, PCM is used as main memory, and thus we have to cope with heterogeneous memories in such hybrid memory systems. This hybrid architecture brings new challenges to buffer management schemes, because traditional page replacement policies mainly focus on improving hit ratios, while new policies for hybrid memory systems have to consider the unique features of different storage media in addition to keeping high hit ratios.

Recently, several page replacement policies have been proposed for PCM/DRAM-based hybrid memory systems. The page replacement policy denoted as the *"Hybrid-LRU"* method proposed by Hyunchul Seok et al. [10] and CLOCK-DWF proposed by Soyoon Lee et al. [11] are based on hybrid PCM/DRAM main memory. Hybrid-LRU monitors the access information of each page, assigns different weights to read and write operations, and predicts page access patterns. After that, it moves write-intensive data to DRAM and moves read-intensive data to PCM. However, inappropriate placement of a page when it is first read into memory will cause additional migrations between PCM and DRAM. The main idea of CLOCK-DWF is placing pages that are going to be updated to DRAM. If the data to be updated is currently stored in PCM, a migration is triggered to move the data from PCM to DRAM, and if DRAM is full at the same time, cold data stored in DRAM will be migrated to PCM. But CLOCK-DWF may cause a lot of unnecessary data migrations between PCM and DRAM since it often causes migrations if a page to be written is in PCM. As a consequence, both Hybrid-LRU and CLOCK-DWF introduce lots of data migrations between PCM and DRAM. This situation will degrade the overall time performance of buffer management schemes, because many additional CPU and memory operations are introduced.

The LRU approach has been widely used in the buffer management for flash memory based data management [14, 15]. Our work differs from these works in that we are mainly towards the architecture shown in Fig. 1(c). There are also some previous works focusing on hybrid storage systems involving flash memory and magnetic disks [16, 17]. These studies are orthogonal to our work, as we concentrate on the memory layer but they focus on the SSD/disk layer shown in Fig. 1.

3   The APP-LRU Method

In this section, we describe the details of APP-LRU. APP-LRU aims for reducing PCM writes but keeping stable time performance. For a tree-structured index, the leaf nodes receive more updates than the internal nodes do. Generally, file data accesses have certain access patterns. On the other side, the access patterns of data are usually stable during a certain time period [12]. This feature is used in our proposal to improve the performance of buffer management.

The overall architecture of the hybrid memory system that APP-LRU is towards is shown in Fig. 2. APP-LRU maintains three lists including one LRU list and two sub-lists (denote as "*List-PCM*" and "*List-DRAM*"). The LRU list is used to maintain the pages in both PCM and DRAM. A page is put in the MRU position of the LRU list when it is accessed. The structures of both *List-PCM* and *List-DRAM* are shown in Fig. 2. All the pages in *List-PCM* are divided into several groups, so are those pages in *List-DRAM*. The pages in the same group of *List-PCM* have the same local-write counts, and the pages in the same group of *List-DRAM* have the same local-read counts. The local-read (or local-write) count is the number of read (or write) operations aggregated since the page is stored in DRAM (or PCM). For example, if a new page is read from disk to PCM, its local-write count and total read/write count is 0, if a page is migrated from DRAM to PCM, its local-write count is reset to 0, but total read/write count does not change. Different groups are ordered by the local-read/write count of the pages in the groups. The pages in the head group among *List-PCM* (*List-DRAM*) have the maximum write (or read) counts. Whenever a page is read from disk or moved from DRAM to PCM (or from PCM to DRAM), it is placed to the tail of *List-PCM* (or *List-DRAM*). When a DRAM page is read or updated, its group will be changed, either from *List_PCM* to *List_DRAM* or vice versa. Basically, APP-LRU employs two algorithms. One is to predict page access patterns and the other is to perform page replacement and migration. The details are described below.

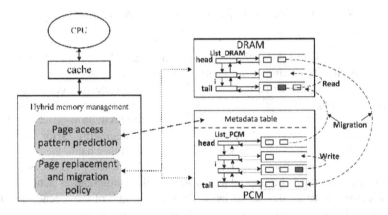

Fig. 2. Overall architecture of hybrid system

3.1 Page Access Pattern Prediction

Unlike DRAM-only memory systems, a hybrid memory system consists of both PCM and DRAM. First, storing data with frequent writes in PCM will introduce the problem of performance degradation, because the write operations to PCM spend much more time than DRAM does. This will also reduce the lifetime of PCM. Second, read and write amplification problems will occur because of data migrations between PCM and DRAM. In order to reduce the number of extra read and write operations caused by migrations, we propose a page access pattern prediction algorithm to predict the future assess patterns of pages.

The basic idea of access pattern prediction is to record the read and write counts for each logical page and then to distinguish read-intensive pages from write-intensive pages. For this purpose, we first maintain some metadata as shown in Fig. 3.

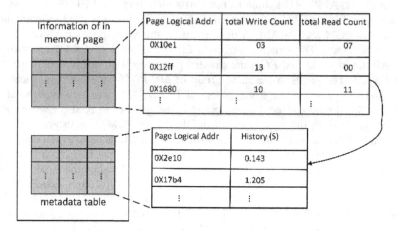

Fig. 3. Metadata for recording page access information

If a page is selected as a victim to be replaced, we process the recorded metadata using Equation (1).

$$S_{cur} = (1 - \alpha) \times R / W + \alpha \times S_{pre} = S_{pre} + \beta \times (R / W - S_{pre}),$$

$$(\beta = 1 - \alpha, \quad 0 \leq \alpha < 0.5) \tag{1}$$

In Equation (1), R and W are the total counts of read and write operations to the replaced page during its staying in the memory. S_{pre} is the ratio of page's read count to its write count in the past. Therefore, if the S_{pre} of a page exceeds a certain threshold, we regard this page as read-intensive. Otherwise, the page is marked as write-intensive. Since the influence of access histories on the prediction of read and write intensity is becoming weak with time, we introduce a degrading factor α to adjust the influence of access histories to the prediction. On the other hand, the current reads and writes have a big impact on the future access pattern, thus, it is necessary to introduce a factor to reflect the importance of R/W in the prediction, as denoted as β in (1). It is reasonable to set this factor larger than α because of the recency feature in data accesses. In our method, we let $\beta = 1 - \alpha$, and α is smaller than 0.5.

Each page's S_{pre} is stored in the metadata table, which is used to decide where to place if the page is accessed again in the future. The metadata table is stored in PCM, and can be found even after power failure accidents. We limit the memory space used for metadata table since the memory capacity is still small compared to disk. However, the concrete capacity of the metadata table is decided based on the actual environment. We also use LRU to manage the metadata table in order to remain relatively hot page access information in the metadata table. In order to alleviate wear out problem, we introduce a small SRAM to buffer metadata table, and the information stored in SRAM will be flush to PCM at set intervals. Since this method aims at logical pages, so we can get the access information from the OS level.

3.2   Page Replacement and Migration

In this section, we present the page replacement and migration procedure of APP-LRU. We maintain a LRU list and two sub-lists. These lists are used to select victims for replacement, as well as to perform page migrations.

When a page fault occurs, the space allocation for the faulted page is based on the access history information in the metadata table (if exists). The page allocation algorithm is shown in **Algorithm 1**. The function *get_free_page()* in Algorithm 1 return a free memory page. If this function is called with a parameter *dram* (or *pcm*), the function will allocate a DRAM (or PCM) page (if exist), but if there is no free DRAM (or PCM) page, the function will allocate a PCM (or DRAM) page (if exist), or allocate the selected victim page from LRU position of LRU list (Before the victim is evicted, we calculate its read/write ratio based on Equation (1), and store the value in metadata table). If the faulted page does not have access histories after looking through the metadata table (Line 1), we call the function without parameter which means faulted page has no specific medium type requirement (Line 17). Otherwise, if the read/write ratio of the faulted page exceeds a certain threshold $R\_W\_Threshold$, it means that the faulted page probably tends to be read and should be placed in PCM, so we call *get_free_page()* function with parameter *pcm* (Line 4). If the selected victim page is in DRAM, we move the page that is in the head group of List-PCM to the location occupied by the page to be replaced in DRAM (Line 6 ~ 8). Similarly, if the ratio is less than the threshold, it means that the faulted page possibly is write-intensive and should be stored in DRAM (Line 10 ~ 16). As a consequence, we get a free page for accommodating the faulted page.

Algorithm 1. *Page Allocation*

Input: faulted page addr p
Output: an empty memory page *q*

```
1:    history(p) = get access history of page p in metadata table;
2:    if (history(p) ≠ null) then      /* the page p has been accessed before*/
3:        if (history(p).Scur > R_W_Threshold) then
4:            q = get_free_page(pcm);
5:            if (q belongs to PCM) then return q;
6:            else    /*q belongs to DRAM*/
7:                select r from the head of List-PCM;
8:                move r to q and insert q to the tail of List-DRAM;
9:                return q=get_free_page(pcm); /*r is empty, r belongs to PCM*/
10:       else
11:           q = get_free_page(dram);
12:           if (q belongs to DRAM) then return q;
13:           else    /*q belongs to PCM*/
14:               select r from the head of List-DRAM;
15:               move r to q and insert q to the tail of List-PCM;
16:               return q=get_free_page(dram); /*r is empty, r belongs to DRAM*/
17:   return q = get_free_page();
```

Next, we explain the page replacement algorithm of APP-LRU, as shown in **Algorithm 2**. If a requested page is not found in memory, we allocate a new space for it using Algorithm 1. We also put the page to the MRU position in the LRU list (Line

1 ~ 5). If the page request is a read request and belongs to DRAM, we increment the read count of the page and adjust the page's position in *List_DRAM*. If the page request is a write request and belongs to PCM, we increment the write count of the page, set a dirty mark, and adjust the page's position in *List_PCM*. (Line 6 ~ 13).

The access pattern of normal data is not likely to change dramatically, so the page's read/write ratio can accurately reflect the access tendency after a long time accumulation based on the theory of statistics. Why we don't choose the read/write ratio as the assessment standard of the migration? It is because the read/write ratio of in memory pages is a short-term computed result, so have no statistical. Even more, the pages that have a similar read/write ratio value may reflect different access frequency, but the warmer page's ratio is much more accurate if the moment when they are read into main memory is close.

Algorithm 2. *Page Replacement*

Input : page *p* logical address, operation type *op*

1:   **if** (miss) **then** /* *page fault* */
2:       *q= Page_Allocation(p)*;
3:       insert *p* to *q* and adjust the position of *q* in LRU list;
4:   **else**
5:       adjust the position of *q* in LRU;
6:   **if** (*op* is read) **then**
7:       read_count(*p*)++;
8:       **if** (*p* is in DRAM) **then**
9:           adjust the position of *q* in the List-DRAM;
10: **else**
11:       dirty(*p*)=1; write_count(*p*)++;
12:       **if** (*p* is in PCM) **then**
13:           adjust the position of *q* in the List-PCM;

---

4   Experimental Results

In the experiments, we use the LRU policy [13] as the baseline method, and also compare two different state-of-the-art approaches including CLOCK-DWF [11] and Hybrid-LRU [10]. Both CLOCK-DWF and Hybrid-LRU are designed for DRAM/PCM-based hybrid memory systems.

4.1   Experimental Setup

We develop a hybrid memory system simulator to evaluate the performance of page replacement policies. The system adopts unified addressing mode, DRAM takes the low-end addresses and PCM takes the high-end addresses. The page size is set to 2 KB. The total size of memory space is constant, and we vary the size of PCM used in the hybrid memory system ranging from 50% to 86%, which corresponds to the ratio of PCM to DRAM from 1:1 to 1:6 to evaluate the performance.

We use both synthetic and real traces in the experiments, as shown in Table 1. Memory footprint in the table refers to the amount of different pages that the traces reference. There are six synthetic traces used with different localities and read/write ratios. For example, the trace T9182 means that the read/write ratio in this trace is 90% / 10%, i.e., 90% reads plus 10% writes, and the reference locality is 80% / 20%, indicating that 80% requests are focused on 20% pages. The real trace is a one-hour OLTP trace in a bank system and contains 470,677 reads and 136,713 writes to a 20GB CODASYL database (the page size is 2KB).

Table 1. Synthetic and real traces used in the experiments

Trace	Memory Footprint	Read/Write Ratio	Locality	Total Accesses
T9182	10,000	90% / 10%	80% / 20%	300,000
T9155	10,000	90% / 10%	50% / 50%	300,000
T1982	10,000	10% / 90%	80% / 20%	300,000
T1955	10,000	10% / 90%	50% / 50%	300,000
T5582	10,000	50% / 50%	80% / 20%	300,000
T5555	10,000	50% / 50%	50% / 50%	300,000
OLTP	51,880	77% / 23%	~	607,390

4.2   Results on the Synthetic Traces

We use Equation (1) to predict defaulted pages' access patterns. Before we conduct the comparison experiments, we have to first determine the appropriate value of β to minimize the total PCM writes. Fig. 4 shows the total PCM write counts under the T5555 trace when we vary β from 0.5 to 1. It shows an obvious decrease and increase trend of PCM writes when the value of β increases, and the write count is minimized when β is 0.7. Therefore, we set the value of β as 0.7 in the following experiments.

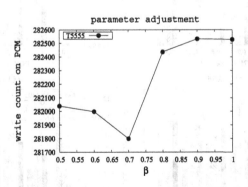

Fig. 4. PCM write counts when varying the parameter β

Figure 5 shows the number of total PCM writes induced by page faults, write operations of traces and migrations between PCM and DRAM. From the figures, we can see APP-LRU reduces maximum 11% total PCM writes with few migrate operations compared to LRU. This is because that APP-LRU can effectively distinguish write-intensive pages and store them in DRAM, making these pages' write operations take place on DRAM at the beginning. By doing so, it not only eliminates needless migrations but also reduce PCM writes. As APP-LRU has no history information to predict pages' read/write intensity when a page is first accessed, the improvement is limited, but we can get much more reduction as time goes by. The gap of PCM write counts between APP-LRU and LRU increases gradually as PCM/DRAM size ratio increases that means proposed policy perform much better when the PCM/DRAM ratio increases. However, APP-LRU incurs more PCM writes than CLOCK-DWF in most cases, that is because the PCM writes in CLOCK-DWF are only incurred by migration and

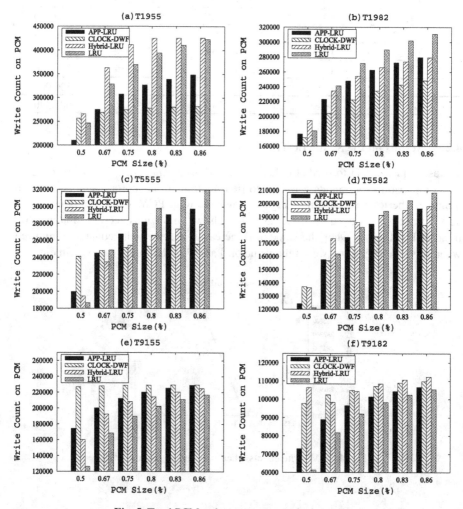

Fig. 5. Total PCM write counts on synthetic traces

page fault, and every write operation from workloads only happens on DRAM no matter where the page located in, which will induce a large number of migrations when the write operation is hit in PCM and have a significant effect on memory access latency.

Figure 6 shows the total migrations between PCM and DRAM of various replacement algorithms. Figure 5 shows CLOCK-DWF incurs minimum PCM writes compared to others, but Fig. 6 shows that it takes much more migrations in most cases which will introduce extra memory writes and reads. From this figure, both CLOCK-DWF and Hybrid-LRU incur much more migrations in most cases, but APP-LRU reduces nearly up to five times total migrations more than CLOCK-DWF. The migrations of our proposal on T9155 and T9182 are a bit larger than CLOCK-DWF. This is because that the migrations of CLOCK-DWF are only triggered by write operations, but in T9155 and T9182 there are only 10% write operations.

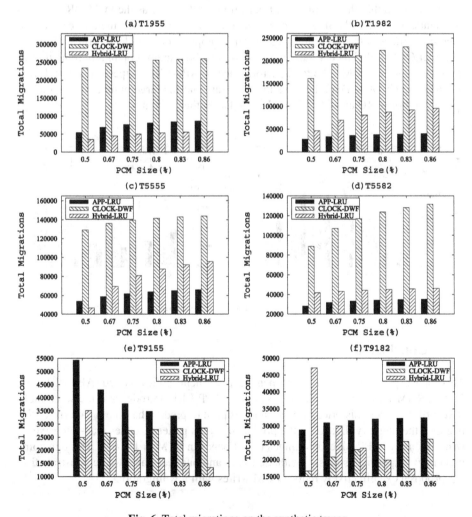

Fig. 6. Total migrations on the synthetic traces

4.3   Results on the Real OLTP Trace

Figure 7 shows the results on the real OLTP trace. The left part of Fig. 7 shows the total writes on PCM. The OLTP trace exhibits a read-incentive pattern and its read locality is much higher compared with write locality. These characteristics make APP-LRU cannot distinguish the write-intensive page since most pages are read-intensive with only few write operations. From the figure, we still can identify that APP-LRU reduce PCM's writes compared with LRU, which means APP-LRU policy is effective against reducing trace's write operations located on PCM. In conclusion, the APP-LRU algorithm has poor effect on reducing PCM write counts, but is better than both CLOCK-DWF and LRU. Furthermore, APP-LRU still can reduce the total PCM write counts as the size of PCM is larger than DRAM.

The right part of Fig. 7 shows total migrations for real OLTP trace. From the figure, we can see that the migrations of our proposal decrease as the PCM/DRAM ratio augments, and while the migrations of its competitors grow. Our method can reduce average 2 times total migrations against its competitors to reduce writes of PCM, while CLOCK-DWF incurs maximum migrations but cannot obtain any reduction of the total writes of PCM. The total performance of APP-LRU outperforms both Hybrid-LRU and CLOCK-DWF because the miss rate and the large number of migrations of both Hybrid-LRU and CLOCK-DWF are larger than others.

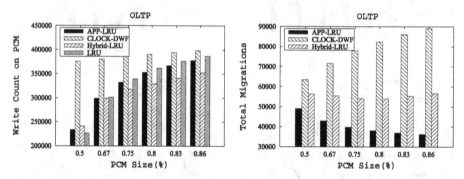

Fig. 7. PCM write counts and total migrations on the real OLTP trace

5   Conclusion

This paper proposes an efficient page replacement policy called APP-LRU for PCM/DRAM-based hybrid memory systems. APP-LRU introduces a metadata table to record the access histories of pages and propose to predict the access patterns of the pages in the memory. Based on the predicted access patterns, either read-intensive or write-intensive, APP-LRU determines to put pages in PCM or DRAM. Through comprehensive experiments on six synthetic traces and one real trace, we demonstrate that our proposal can effectively reduce PCM writes with few migrations.

Acknowledgement. This paper is supported by the National Science Foundation of China (No. 61073039, 61379037, and 61272317) and the OATF project funded by University of Science and Technology of China.

References

1. Lefurgy, C., Rajamani, K., Rawson, F., Felter, W., Kistler, M., Keller, T.W.: Energy management for commercial servers. IEEE Computer 36(12), 39–48 (2003)
2. Qureshi, M.K., Vijayalakshmi, S., Rivers, J.A.: Scalable high performance main memory system using phase-change memory technology. In: Proc. of ISCA, pp. 24–33. ACM, New York (2009)
3. Lee, B.C., Ipek, E., Mutlu, O., Burger, D.: Architecting phase change memory as a scalable DRAM alternative. In: Proc. of ISCA, pp. 2–13. ACM, New York (2009)
4. Chen, S., Gibbons, P.B., Nath, S.: Rethinking database algorithms for phase change memory. In: Proc. of CIDR, pp. 21–31 (2011)
5. Yang, B.-D., Lee, J.-E., Kim, J.-S., et al.: A Low Power Phase-Change Random Access Memory using a Data-Comparison Write Scheme. In: Proc. of ISCAS, New Orleans, USA, pp. 3014–3017 (2007)
6. Zhou, P., Zhao, B., Yang, J., Zhang, Y.: A durable and energy efficient main memory using phase change memory technology. In: Proc. of ISCA, pp. 14–23. ACM, New York (2009)
7. Cho, S., Lee, H.: Flip-N-Write: A simple Deterministic Technique to Improve PRAM Write Performance, Energy and Endurance. In: Proc. of MICRO, pp. 347–357. ACM, New York (2009)
8. Park, H., Yoo, S., Lee, S.: Power management of hybrid dram/pram-based main memory. In: Proc. of DAC, pp. 59–64. ACM, New York (2011)
9. Dong-Jae Shin, S.K., Park, S.M.: Kim and K. H. Park. Adaptive page grouping for energy efficiency in hybrid PRAM-DRAM main memory. In: Proc. of ACM RACS, pp. 395–402. ACM, New York (2012)
10. Seok, H., Park, Y., Park, K., Park, K.H.: Efficient Page Caching Algorithm with Prediction and Migration for a Hybrid Main Memory. ACM SIGAPP Applied Computing Review 11(4), 38–48 (2011)
11. Lee, S., Seoul Bahn, H., Noh, S.C.-D.: a write-history-aware page replacement algorithm for hybrid PCM and DRAM memory architectures. IEEE Transactions on Computers PP(99), 1 (2013)
12. Liu, S., Huang, X., et al.: Understanding Data Characteristics and Access Patterns in a Cloud Storage System. In: Proc. of CCGrid, pp. 327–334 (2013)
13. Coffman, E.G., Denning, P.J.: Operating Systems Theory, ch. 6, pp. 241–283. Prentice-Hall (1973)
14. Jin, P., Ou, Y., Haerder, T., Li, Z.: ADLRU: An Efficient Buffer Replacement Algorithm for Flash-based Databases. In: Data and Knowledge Engineering (DKE), vol. 72, pp. 83–102. Elsevier (2012)
15. Li, Z., Jin, P., Su, X., Cui, K., Yue, L.: CCF-LRU: A New Buffer Replacement Algorithm for Flash Memory. IEEE Trans. on Consumer Electronics 55(3), 1351–1359 (2009)
16. Yang, P., Jin, P., Yue, L.: Hybrid Storage with Disk Based Write Cache. In: Proc. of DASFAA Workshops 2011, pp. 264–275 (2011)
17. Yang, P., Jin, P., Wan, S., Yue, L.: HB-Storage: Optimizing SSDs with a HDD Write Buffer. In: Proc. of WAIM Workshops 2013, pp. 28–39 (2013)

Towards Relaxed Rollback-Recovery Consistency in SOA*

Jerzy Brzeziński, Mateusz Hołenko, Anna Kobusińska, Dariusz Wawrzyniak,
and Piotr Zierhoffer

Institute of Computing Science
Poznań University of Technology, Poland
{jbrzezinski,mholenko,akobusinska,dwawrzyniak,
pzierhoffer}@cs.put.poznan.pl

Abstract. Nowadays, one of the major paradigms of distributed processing is SOA. To improve the reliability of SOA-based systems, a RE-SERVE service that ensures recovery of consistent processing state, has been proposed. RESERVE introduces a high overhead during failure-free computing. Thus, in this paper we propose relaxed recovery consistency models that allow optimization of rollback-recovery in SOA. We propose their formal definitions, and discuss the conditions under which these models are provided by RESERVE.

Keywords: SOA, web services, fault tolerance, message logging, rollback-recovery, consistency.

1 Introduction

In the recent years, the rapid growth of development and deployment of service-oriented systems (SOA) has been observed [8]. Although SOA-based systems have many advantages, they are also highly error-prone. Failures of SOA components, lead to limitations in the availability of services, affecting the reliability of the whole system. Such a situation is highly undesirable from the viewpoint of SOA clients, who expect that provided services are reliable and available. To improve reliability of SOA-based systems and applications, different approaches may be applied. Among them are: replication, transaction-based forward recovery (which requires the user to explicitly declare compensation actions), and the rollback-recovery checkpoint-based approach [5].

In many existing SOA systems, in case of service failure, the compensation procedure is often applied to withdraw the effects of the performed request [2,9]. However, there are situations, when compensation procedure is either impossible, or it can be prohibitively expensive. In such situations, the rollback-recovery approach [6], known from the general distributed systems can be applied. Unfortunately, the rollback-recovery techniques for general distributed systems do

---

* This work was supported by the Polish National Science Center under Grant No. DEC-2011/03/D/ST6/01331

C.-H. Hsu et al. (Eds.): NPC 2014, LNCS 8707, pp. 96–107, 2014.

not into account specific properties of SOA systems, among which are: the autonomy of nodes, loose-coupling, heterogeneous nature of the environment, the dynamic nature and the longevity of interactions, and the inherent constant interaction with the outside world. As a consequence, web services should not be forced to take a checkpoint or to roll back in case of the fault-free execution. They can also refuse to inform other services on checkpoints they have taken. Therefore, there is a need for rollback-recovery mechanisms specially tailored for SOA architectures.

Responding to this need, we proposed RESERVE (Reliable Service Environment), which aims in increasing the SOA fault-tolerance [3,4]. RESERVE while preserving services autonomy, ensures at the same time that in the case of failure of one or more system components (i.e. web services or their clients), a coherent state of distributed processing is recovered. RESERVE focuses on seeking automated mechanisms that do not require the user intervention in the case of failures, and are *other* than transactions or replication. The proposed service can be used in any SOA environment, though it is particularly well-suited for the processing which does not have the transactional character, and for the applications that do not use the business process engines with internal fault-tolerance mechanisms (e.g. BPEL). It also respects the independence of the service providers, allowing them to implement their own fault-tolerant policies.

RESERVE guarantees that the recovered execution is perceived by all participants of the processing in a consistent manner. Since, according to our best knowledge, the notion of a consistent recovery state has not been clearly defined and formalized in the context of the SOA, during recovery we followed the intuitive approach, by which the recovered state is said to be consistent, if it reflects the observable behavior of the system before the failure. In this paper, we clearly define and formalize the notion of a strict SOA-based recovery consistency model, implemented in RESERVE until now. Because providing such a strict recovery consistency introduces a large overhead during the failure-free computing, we discuss under which conditions a strict recovery consistency can be relaxed. Consequently, we propose formal definitions of relaxed recovery consistency models that allow the recovered service state to differ from the one before the time of failure. We also determine which interactions (and in which order) have to be recovered by RESERVE service, to ensure the continuation of the processing consistent accordingly to the proposed relaxed recovery consistency models.

The rest of the paper is structured as follows: section 2 presents system model and basic definitions. Section 3 describes the general idea of RESERVE, which summarizes already presented service, and is included in order to make a paper self-contained. The main contribution of this paper is contained in Sections 4 and 5, where the formal definition of strict consistency model is presented, and relaxed recovery consistency models are proposed. Next, in Section 6 it is analyzed how the proposed recovery consistency models are realized within RESERVE service. Finally, Section 7 concludes the paper.

2   System Model and Basic Assumptions

Throughout this paper, SOA system model is considered. We focus on REST-ful web services [10], exposed as sets of resources, and identified by a uniform resource identifier (URI) mechanism. Resources can be characterized as a set of data items, which may be simple variables, files, objects of object-oriented programming language, etc. A client may interact with such services employing the HTTP protocol operations, with their customary interpretation. Services are published by service providers $S_k \in \mathcal{S}$ and accessed by service consumers (clients) $C_i \in \mathcal{C}$. The basic interaction between a client and a service consists of service invocation (an event at the client side), and its execution (an event at the server side). The code to be executed, i.e. the implementation of service functionality is termed a *method*. Invocations and executions correspond to communication events at the protocol level. Invocation starts with sending a request message from a client to a server, and matching receipt at the server side. Execution finishes with a reply message sent from the server to the client. The receipt of the reply completes the invocation. The sequence of interactions between clients and web services will be called a business process. Both clients and services are piece-wise deterministic. Services can concurrently process only such requests that do not require access to the same or interacting resources. Otherwise, the existence of a mechanism serializing access to resources, which uniquely determines the order of operations, is assumed.

According to the REST rules, communication in the considered system is stateless, which means that each request contains all the information necessary to understand the request, independently of any requests that may have preceded it. The considered communication channels are reliable (the reliability is ensured by retransmission of messages and appropriate filtering of duplicates), but they do not guarantee FIFO property. Additionally, the crash-recovery model of failures is assumed, i.e. system components may fail and recover after crashing a finite number of times [1]. Failures may happen at arbitrary moments, and we require any such failure to be eventually detected, for example by a Failure Detection Service [7]. Furthermore, we assume that each service provider may use different mechanisms to provide fault tolerance. By a recovery point we will denote an abstraction describing a consistent state of the service, which can be correctly recovered after a failure, but we do not make any assumptions on how and when such recovery points are made (to make a recovery point logs, checkpoints, replicas and other mechanisms may be used). Each service takes recovery points independently. Similarly, the client may also provide its own fault tolerance techniques to save its state.

3   ReServE — The General Idea

In this section, the design choices and concepts behind RESERVE service are presented. The detailed description of RESERVE has already been presented in [3,4], and is included here in order to make a paper self-contained. Due to the fact that interactions between clients and services result in possible resource state changes, they entail the client-service inter dependencies. Because in SOA the autonomy of services is assumed, the failure of one process should not influence the processing of other processes, and should not force them to rollback when they have not failed. Since service providers do not provide information on the internal implementation of services, it is not known which events introduce inter-process dependencies. Therefore, the recovery of a failed service should be isolated to avoid the cascading rollbacks of other processes.

The architecture of RESERVE is shown in Fig. 1. It has a modular construction, and includes Recovery Management Units (RMU), Client Intermediary Modules (CIM) and Service Intermediary Modules (SIM). The main task of RMUs is increasing the reliability of performed business processes. RMUs store all requests and responses exchanged by business process participants in their Stable Storage able to survive all failures. As a result, the RMU modules posses a complete history of communication, which is used during rollback and recovery of business processes. The remaining CIM and SIM units serve as proxies for clients and servers. They make RESERVE transparent to participants of the communication, and allow to fully control the flow of messages in the system by intercepting messages issued by clients and servers. Additionally, SIMs monitor the services status and react in the case of its failure by initiating and managing the service rollback-recovery procedure.

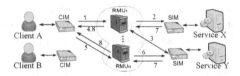

Fig. 1. RESERVE architecture

Each service is registered in one RMU (default or master RMU), but the single RMU can be used by many services. In turn, the client can be registered simultaneously in many RMUs, but always one of them stores information on other RMU's used by the client. The request issued by a client to a service is intercepted by client's CIM, and forwarded to its master RMU (1). If the required service is registered in RMU, the request is saved in RMU's Stable Storage, and forwarded to the service through its SIM (2). Otherwise, client's master RMU obtains the URI of requested service RMU from its SIM (3), and sends back this information to CIM (4), which reissues the request to a proper RMU (5, 6). The service processes request and sends the response back to RMU (7). The response is saved in the Stable Storage and forwarded to the client through CIM (8). If the RMU module obtains the client's request, to which the response has already been saved, then saved response is sent to the client, and there is no necessity to send the request once again to the service, which provides exactly-once execution of a client's request.

4   Strict Recovery Consistency Model

In RESERVE, the consistent recovery assumes the recovery of all events that have occurred before the failure in the same order as during the original execution. In effect, the recovered service reaches the state from before the failure. This approach lacks proper theoretical foundations — according to our best knowledge, neither the notion of a consistent recovery state has been clearly defined and formalized in the context of SOA, nor the requirements of the consistency have been specified. Finding the consistent state of SOA computation is important for analyzing, testing or verifying properties of these computations. Thus, the lack of formally specified and recognized consistency requirements for SOA-compliant processing gravely prohibits the construction of provably correct rollback-recovery protocols. Therefore, this paper aims at giving the necessary formal basis for any further in-depth research in this field.

In this section the ***strict recovery consistency model*** (***AllRequests***) that corresponds to RESERVE pessimistic approach is proposed. The failure occurrence in this case is fully masked, and the recovery is transparent from the viewpoint of clients and services. In the formal definition of this model, the notation presented below is used.

The set of all methods provided by a service is denoted by $\mathcal{M}$. They either *modify* (possibly also read) or *only read* the service state (they belong to sets $\mathcal{M}_M$ and $\mathcal{M}_R$ respectively). When a client C_i invokes a service S_j by sending the x-th request req that refers to a resource res an event denoted by $req_{C_i}^x(S_j, op, res)$ is produced. The parameter op of this event denotes the type of method ($op \in \mathcal{M}$) to be executed by the service in the result of obtaining the request. In turn, $recv\_rep_{C_i}^x(S_j, res)$ represents the event produced when a client C_i obtains from a service S_j the reply rep to its x-th request req; result of execution of req is return in res. The corresponding events at a service S_j, are: $recv\_req_{S_j}^x(C_i, op, res)$ and $rep_{S_j}^x(C_i, op, res)$. The former denotes the event produced when S_j receives the appropriate request from C_i. The latter represents the event produced when the service S_j has finished the execution of the request , and sends a reply to C_i. For the sake of the simplicity, if some element in the above notation is unimportant or obvious in the context, it can be omitted. The local history of a service S_j is denoted by $H_{S_j} = E_j^0 E_j^1 E_j^2 \dots E_j^n$.

Events that occur at service S_j are ordered by relation $\overset{S_j}{\longmapsto}$, called *service execution order*. In turn, the relation of events that occurs during service recovery is represented by $\overset{S_j}{\twoheadrightarrow}$, and is called *service recovery execution order*.

Each time when the failure of service S_j occurs, a crash event denoted by f^* is produced. In turn, in a moment of recovery a restart event $f^{\wedge}$ occurs. Thus, service state at the moment of event $f^{\wedge}$ occurrence is equivalent (in the result of the performed rollback) to the state saved in the latest recovery point RP_{S_j}. We denote the local history of a service S_j comprising events that occurred after the service recovery point RP_{S_j} was taken, but before the crash event f^* by $H_{S_j}^{\prec f^*}$. In turn, the local history of service S_j comprising events that occurred after the restart event is denoted by $H_{S_j}^{\succ f}$. Consequently, $reps_{S_j}(C_i, op, res) \in H_{S_j}^{\prec f^*}$ denotes the event of sending reply lost due to the failure by a service S_j to a client C_i, and $recv\_reqs_{S_j}(C_i, op, res) \in H_{S_j}^{\succ t}$ indicates that the event of receiving request by service S_j from client C_i was recovered after the restart event $\hat{f}$.

Informally, the recovered service state is said to be consistent according to strict recovery consistency model, if after recovery from a failure, the service state reflects the execution of all requests obtained from clients and other services, and performed by this service before its failure. Moreover, the order of recovered requests is the same as it was before the failure. Below, the formal definition of AllRequests recovery consistency model is presented:

Definition 1. *Let* $o1, o2 \in \mathcal{M}$ *be methods provided by a service* S_j. *The recovered service state is consistent according to* **strict recovery consistency model (AllRequests)**, *iff for all events* $recv\_reqs_{S_j}(C_i, o1)$, $recv\_reqs_{S_j}(C_k, o2)$ *that represent requests obtained by service* S_j, *and* $reps_{S_j}(C_i, o1)$, $reps_{S_j}(C_k, o2)$ *that are replies issued by* S_j *after performing methods* $o1$ *and* $o2$, *the following condition holds:*

$$reps_{S_j}(C_i, o1) \in H_{S_j}^{\prec f^*} \Rightarrow recv\_reqs_{S_j}(C_i, o1) \in H_{S_j}^{\succ f} \wedge$$

$$\forall reps_{S_j}(C_i, o1), reps_{S_j}(C_k, o2) \in H_{S_j}^{\prec f^*} :: reps_{S_j}(C_i, o1) \overset{S_j}{\rightarrowtail} reps_{S_j}(C_k, o2) \Rightarrow$$

$$recv\_reqs_{S_j}(C_i, o1)) \overset{S_j}{\twoheadrightarrow} recv\_reqs_{S_j}(C_k, o2)$$

The above definition says that if a method $o1$ was performed before the service failure (i.e. the event of sending a reply after performing $o1$ belongs to history $H_{S_j}^{\prec f^*}$ of events performed by S_j before the failure), then the method $o1$ is recovered. This implies that the event of receiving request that invokes $o1$ is applied again after the service restart, and belongs to history $H_{S_j}^{\succ f}$ of events performed by service S_j after its rollback. Moreover, if replies to $o1$ and $o2$ were issued before the failure in a specified service execution order, their execution order is the same during the recovery. A formal specification allows unambiguous determination of the set of requests that can not be missed during the recovery, because they are necessary to meet the recovery consistency model.

5   Relaxed Recovery Consistency Models

Service providers supply clients with a set of methods that allow them to benefit from the functionality offered by services. Depending on the characteristics of a service and the nature of its methods, the execution of these methods differently affects the service state. Some methods are past-operations-aware, i.e. they take into account the history of service processing in order to modify the service state, whereas the execution of other methods invalidates the previous service history, or part of it. Therefore, although some methods modify the service state, they are *irrelevant* to the overall service computation due to the method specificity.

To illustrate this, let us consider a counter service that provides the following methods: $inc(x)$ that increases a value of the counter resource by x, $dec(x)$ — decreasing a value of the counter by x, and $set(x)$, which sets the counter value for x. Further, let us assume that the following sequence of methods was performed: $inc(5)$, $dec(3)$, $set(7)$, $dec(1)$. After the failure occurrence only methods $set(7)$, and $dec(1)$ have to be recovered, because the result of execution of methods $inc(5)$, and $dec(3)$ was overridden by the execution of a method $set(7)$.

Re-execution of irrelevant methods can be omitted during the rollback-recovery, without changing the meaning of processing and its result. Consequently, such methods also need not to be logged. This implies that some services do not require a strict recovery consistency model to recover processing perceived as consistent. Below, we propose relaxed recovery consistency models that allow optimization of the rollback-recovery. In order to alleviate requirements regarding the consistent processing state, we assume that service provider delivers basic information on the character of methods it executes during service processing.

Every Modification Recovery Consistency Model. Lessons learned from the message-passing systems, in which read messages are neglected during the process rollback-recovery, enabled us to divide methods into lookup and modifying. Methods from the first group do not change the state of a service, so they can be considered irrelevant from the service point of view, and as such they can be omitted during the recovery of a service state. In turn, all modifying methods performed before the failure have to be recovered in the case of a service failure. Moreover, the order of their execution before the failure have to be maintained after the recovery. A recovery consistency model that ensures this assumption is called **every modification recovery consistency model (EveryMod)**.

Definition 2. *Let $o1, o2 \in \mathcal{M}_M$ be modifying methods provided by a service S_j. The recovered service state is consistent according to **every modification recovery consistency model (EveryMod)**, iff for all events $recv\_req_{S_j}(C_i, o1)$, $recv\_req_{S_j}(C_k, o2)$ that represent requests obtained by service S_j, and $rep_{S_j}(C_i, o1)$, $rep_{S_j}(C_k, o2)$ that are replies issued by S_j after performing $o1$ and $o2$, the following condition holds:*

$$rep_{S_j}(C_i, o1) \in H_{S_j}^{\prec f^*} \Rightarrow recv\_req_{S_j}(C_i, o1) \in H_{S_j}^{\succ f} \wedge$$
$$\forall rep_{S_j}(C_i, o1), rep_{S_j}(C_k, o2) \in H_{S_j}^{\prec f^*} :: rep_{S_j}(C_i, o1) \overset{S_j}{\rightarrowtail} rep_{S_j}(C_k, o2) \Rightarrow$$
$$recv\_req_{S_j}(C_i, o1)) \overset{S_j}{\rightarrowtail} recv\_req_{S_j}(C_k, o2)$$

EveryMod recovery consistency model loosens AllRequests model by taking into account only operations that modify service state ($o1, o2 \in \mathcal{M}_M$) instead of all operations performed before the failure. EveryMod can be applied to all e-commerce services. Let us consider an on-line store. Purchasing or returning products bought in this store changes the amount of available products and the store's budget. After a service failure, all performed purchases and returns have to be recovered. On the other hand, when a client just checks if the item is offered by on-line store or how much it costs, then the request corresponding to above method can be omitted during recovering a service state.

Important Modification Recovery Consistency Model. Let us consider that among modifying methods provided by a service, there is a set of methods that are significant for providing a service functionality. The execution of such methods does not take into account the history of other, previously performed methods. Therefore, during the rollback-recovery only significant methods have to be recovered.

A recovery consistency model that differentiates service modifying methods, and distinguishes a set of methods significant for supplying service functionality is called **important modifications recovery consistent model (ImpMod)**. The execution of significant methods does not take into account the history of previously performed methods, which are not significant. Informally ImpMod recovery consistency model implicates that all requests of significant methods have to be recovered. The execution order of recovered requests corresponds to their execution order before the failure occurrence. When significant methods have not been executed before the failure, then all modifying requests have to be recovered. Finally, requests modifying service state invoked after the execution of the last request of a significant method also have to be recovered.

Definition 3. *Let $o \in \mathcal{M}_M$ be modifying methods provided by a service S_j, and $o' \in \mathcal{M}_S$ be significant methods provided by S_j , where $\mathcal{M}_S$ denotes the set of significant methods $\mathcal{M}_S \subset \mathcal{M}_M$. Further let o1, o2 be methods of the same type $(o1, o2 \in \mathcal{M}_S$ or $o1, o2 \in \mathcal{M}_M)$. The recovered service state is consistent according to **ImpMod recovery consistency model**, iff for all events $recv\_reqs_{S_j}(C_i, o)$, that represent requests obtained by service S_j, and $reps_{S_j}(C_i, o)$ that are replies issued by S_j, the following condition holds:*

$$\left(\forall reps_{S_j}(C_i, o') :: reps_{S_j}(C_i, o') \in H_{S_j}^{\prec f^*} \right) \Rightarrow recv\_reqs_{S_j}(o') \in H_{S_j}^{\succ \hat{f}} \wedge$$

$$\forall reps_{S_j}(C_i, o) \in H_{S_j}^{\prec f^*} ::$$

$$\left[\left(\nexists reps_{S_j}(C_i, o') \in H_{S_j}^{\prec f^*} :: reps_{S_j}(C_i, o) \xrightarrow{S_j} reps_{S_j}(C_i, o') \right) \Rightarrow recv\_req_{C_i}(o) \in H_{S_j}^{\succ \hat{f}} \right] \wedge$$

$$\left(\forall recv\_reqs_{S_j}(C_i, o1), recv\_reqs_{S_j}(C_k, o2) \in H_{S_j}^{\prec f^*} :: reps_{S_j}(C_i, o1) \xrightarrow{S_j} reps_{S_j}(C_k, o2) \right)$$

$$\Rightarrow \left(recv\_reqs_{S_j}(C_i, o1) \xrightarrow{S_j} recv\_reqs_{S_j}(C_k, o2) \right)$$

Above definition states that every significant method performed before the failure is recovered, because when the reply issued after the execution of significant method o' belongs to history $H_{S_j}^{\prec f^*}$ of events performed by S_j before the failure, then the request of method $o1$ is re-invoked by S_j after its restart, and belongs to $H_{S_j}^{\succ \hat{f}}$ (first condition). Further, it is said that all modifying methods o executed before the failure (for which $reps_{S_j}(C_i, o) \in H_{S_j}^{\prec f^*}$) that were not followed by any significant method o'. In other words, if there exists no significant method o' invoked after the invocation of modifying methods o:

$$\left(\nexists reps_{S_j}(C_i, o') \in H_{S_j}^{\prec f^*} :: reps_{S_j}(C_i, o) \overset{S_j}{\rightarrowtail} reps_{S_j}(C_i, o') \right),$$ then the invocation of

modifying methods is recovered and belongs to the history $H_{S_j}^{\succ f}$ (second condition). Finally, the execution order during recovery procedure corresponds to the execution order before the failure.

To illustrate the application of ImpMod recovery consistency model let us assume that a service provides clients a virtual shopping basket, and supplies methods to operate on it (*add* and *remove*), as well as to finalize electronic shopping (*buy*). When a client adds or removes products from the basket, the amount of available products changes, what is reflected in the state of the on-line store. After the failure occurrence, when the on-line store restarts its work, the shopping basket of a client should comprise all products that have been added to it before the failure (the history of methods performed by a client consists of a sequence of *add* and *remove*). However, when the client finalizes its shopping the shopping basket is emptied. After recovery the history of performed actions contains only the information on finalizing shopping (there is just a buy *method*).

Latest Modification Recovery Consistency Model. Among modifying methods there can be distinguished those that override the service state, without taking into account the prior history of states. In such case, only the latest executed method is essential for the proper recovery of the service state, and as such it should be persistent. A recovery consistency model that ensures this assumption is called **latest modification recovery consistency model** (**LatestMod**).

Definition 4. *Let* $o1, o2 \in \mathcal{M}_L$ *be modifying methods that belong to the set* $\mathcal{M}_L$ *of methods that override a service state, where* $\mathcal{M}_L \subset \mathcal{M}_M$. *The recovered service state is consistent according to* **LatestMod recovery consistency model,** *iff for all events* $recv\_req_{S_j}(C_i, o1)$, $recv\_req_{S_j}(C_i, o2)$ *that represent requests obtained by service* S_j, *and* $reps_{S_j}(C_i, o1)$, $reps_{S_j}(C_i, o2)$, *that are replies issued by* S_j, *the following condition holds:*

$$\left(\forall reps_{S_j}(C_i, o1), reps_{S_j}(C_i, o2) \in H_{S_j}^{\prec f^*} :: reps_{S_j}(C_i, o1) \overset{S_j}{\rightarrowtail} reps_{S_j}(C_i, o2) \right) \Rightarrow$$

$$\left(recv\_req_{S_j}(C_i, o2) \in H_{S_j}^{\succ f} \right)$$

The key difference between ImpMod and LatestMod recovery consistency models consists in recovering only the single, latest request performed by the service before the failure in the case of the LatestMod mode. In contrast for the LatestMod recovery consistency model, in ImpMod a set of requests is recovered. Continuing the example of the on-line store, let us assume that a client of the on-line store manages its client's account profile. A client can change his/her personal details. Every modification of the client account is binding, so only the latest modification one is recovered.

No Modifications Recovery Consistency Model. In case of some services, the modifying methods can be unheralded from the viewpoint of such services. This is a case, of all services that mediate in the execution of methods requested by a client, and act as proxy services. Such services refer requests from clients to appropriate services providing functionality required by clients. A recovery consistency model that refers to intermediary services, that only mediate in the processing between clients and other services, is called **no modification recovery consistency model** (**NoMod**).

Definition 5. *Let* $o1, o2 \in \mathcal{M}_M$ *be modifying methods. The recovered service state is consistent according to* **NoMod recovery consistency model**, *iff for all events* $recv\_reqs_{S_j}(C_i, o1), recv\_reqs_{S_j}(C_i, o2)$ *that represent requests obtained by service* S_j, *and* $reps_{S_j}(C_i, o1), reps_{S_j}(C_i, o2)$, *that are replies issued by* S_j, *the following condition holds:*

$$\left(\forall reps_{S_j}(C_i, o1), reps_{S_j}(C_k, o2) \in H_{S_j}^{\prec f^*} \right) \Rightarrow H_{S_j}^{\succ t} = \varnothing$$

6 Discussion on the Consistent Recovery Problem

In this section we discuss the realization of the proposed recovery consistency models in the context of RESERVE. In order to recover a service state that is consistent according to a required recovery consistency model, a set of requests that should be re-executed after the service failure has to be designated. Also, the order in which the chosen requests are performed during the service recovery has to be determined. Therefore RESERVE service makes some necessary assumptions, and introduces internal mechanisms, to solve this problem. We discuss them briefly below.

In order to provide the correct recovery, the requests should be re-executed in the appropriate order. For this purpose, each reply sent by the service has a unique identifier, called *ResponseId*, which is assigned by a service. Relying on the provided formal specifications of the models presented in section 5, we determine which messages have to be kept by the RMU and resent to a service, during its recovery. Since AllRequests model is the most general recovery consistency model, we only describe the way it differs from other models. Moreover, actions performed by other modules (specifically SIM) are the same for all consistency models and are described in [3,4].

AllRequests recovery consistency model requires all requests to be saved. Only when a service informs about a new recovery point, RMU is allowed to remove older messages. Having received a request to start recovery process beginning with a certain message, denoted *lowestReqId*, RMU resends a set of messages determined by the following predicate:

$$toRecover = \{reqs_{S_j} : (rep_{reqs_{S_j}} \in SavedReplies \wedge$$
$$rep_{reqs_{S_j}}.ResponseId \geq lowestReqId) \vee (rep_{reqs_{S_j}} \notin SavedReplies)\}$$

The *toRecover* predicate chooses all messages directed to the given service, for which a reply has been saved with identifier greater or equal to the one requested

by the service. Also all requests without an answer kept by RMU are chosen to
be resent. EveryMod recovery consistency model differs from the strict one in
two aspects. Firstly, a receipt of reply allows RMU to forget the content of the
corresponding request. However, for the sake of a client recovery the reply must
be still kept by RESERVE. The request, on the other hand, will never be used
again, so it's content can be safely discarded. To preserve a possibility to recover
client states, the metadata of the requests has to be retained. After a failure, a
set of messages to be re-executed is described by:

$$toRecover = \{req_{s_j} : req_{s_j}\}.TheContent \neq \emptyset \wedge ((rep_{req_{s_j}} \in$$
$$SavedReplies \wedge rep_{req_{s_j}}.ReplyId \geq lowestReqId) \vee (rep_{req_{s_j}} \notin SavedReplies))$$

RMU chooses requests directed to the given service in a similar fashion to
AllRequests algorithm, but now it omits the requests without any content, as
they were deemed irrelevant to the recovery process. ImpMod recovery consistency model is a specific version of EveryMod model. Both models consider only
modifying requests, but ImpMod allows RMU to reduce the amount of repeated
messages even more. Upon receiving of a reply, RMU verifies if the corresponding
request was modifying. If not, it's content is discarded, as in EveryMod model.
If the request was modifying, it's importance, declared by the service, is verified.
Receipt of a reply to an important requests causes RMU to discard content of
previous unimportant requests directed to the same resource. A set of messages
to recover after a failure is calculated in the same way as in the EveryMod model.
Since the content of unimportant requests was removed, they won't become a
part of the recovery process. For even simpler services, supporting LatestMod
recovery consistency model, there is no concept of important modifications. Instead, after receiving a reply to a modifying request, RMU clears the content of
a previous request directed to the same resource. A response to a non-modifying
request, as in previous models, triggers clearing of this request's content. This
way there is at most one request saved for each resource.

7   Conclusions

Although some attempts to increase the fault-tolerance of SOA systems have
been undertaken, the proposed solutions, based on rollback-recovery mechanism,
require costly global recovery coordination, offering very strict consistency of the
recovered processing state. It is clear, based on the past experience, that many
SOA applications could benefit from less restrictive consistency models, allowing
the recovery of the processing state in a more efficient way. But, according to
best authors knowledge, neither the notion of a consistent recovery state has been
clearly defined and formalized in the context of SOA, nor the requirements of the
consistency have been specified. Therefore, this paper has dealt with a problem
of providing consistency models for rollback-recovery of SOA systems. In the
paper, the formal definitions of recovery consistency models were proposed, and
their features were discussed. A formal specifications allowed the unambiguous

determination of the set of requests that can not be missed during the recovery. The proposed recovery consistency models were applied in the context of ReServE service. Our future work encompasses carrying out the appropriate simulation experiments to quantitatively evaluate the overhead of the presented relaxed rollback-recovery protocols.

References

1. Avizienis, A., Laprie, J.-C., Randell, B., Landwehr, C.: Basic concepts and taxonomy of dependable and secure computing. IEEE Transactions on Dependable and Secure Computing 1(1), 11–33 (2004)
2. Cabrera, L.F., Copeland, G., Cox, B., Freund, T., Klein, J., Storey, T., Thatte, S.: Web services transactions specifications (2005)
3. Danilecki, A., Hołenko, M., Kobusińska, A., Szychowiak, M., Zierhoffer, P.: ReServE service: An approach to increase reliability in service oriented systems. In: Malyshkin, V. (ed.) PaCT 2011. LNCS, vol. 6873, pp. 244–256. Springer, Heidelberg (2011)
4. Danilecki, A., Hołenko, M., Kobusińska, A., Szychowiak, M., Zierhoffer, P.: Applying message logging to support fault-tolerance of SOA systems. Foundations of Computing and Decision Science 38(3), 145–158 (2013)
5. Dialani, V., Miles, S., Moreau, L., De Roure, D.C., Luck, M.: Transparent fault tolerance for web services based architectures. In: Monien, B., Feldmann, R.L. (eds.) Euro-Par 2002. LNCS, vol. 2400, pp. 889–898. Springer, Heidelberg (2002)
6. Elnozahy, N.E., Lorenzo, A., Wang, Y.-M., Johnson, D.B.: A survey of rollback-recovery protocols in message-passing systems. ACM Computing Surveys 34(3), 375–408 (2002)
7. Michal, K., Kobusińska, A., Kobusiski, J.: FAST failure detection service for large scale distributed systems. In: Proc. of the 17th Euromicro Int. Conf. on Parallel, Distributed and Network-Based Processing (PDP 2009), Weimar, Germany, pp. 229–236. IEEE Computer Society (February 2009)
8. Laskey, K., Estefan, J.A., McCabe, F.G., Thornton, D.: Reference Architecture Foundation for Service Oriented Architecture Version 1.0 Committee Draft 02. OASIS (2009)
9. Marinos, A., Razavi, A.R., Moschoyiannis, S., Krause, P.J.: RETRO: A consistent and recoverable RESTful transaction model. In: ICWS, pp. 181–188 (2009)
10. Richardson, L., Ruby, S.: RESTful Web Services. O'Reilly Media (2007)

A Novel Page Replacement Algorithm for the Hybrid Memory Architecture Involving PCM and DRAM

Kaimeng Chen[1], Peiquan Jin[1,2], and Lihua Yue[1,2]

[1] School of Computer Science and Technology,
University of Science and Technology of China, Hefei, China
[2] Key Laboratory of Electromagnetic Space Information, Chinese Academy of Sciences,
Hefei, China
jpq@ustc.edu.cn

Abstract. Recently, the development of phase change memory (PCM) motivates new hybrid memory architectures that consist of PCM and DRAM. An important issue in such hybrid memory architectures is how to manage the pages resisting in heterogeneous memories. For example, when a requested page is missing in the hybrid memory and the memory has no free spaces, what pages in which type of memory (PCM or DRAM) should be replaced? This problem is much different from traditional buffer replacement management, where they do not consider the special properties of different types of memories. In particular, differing from DRAM, PCM is non-volatile but it has lower access speeds than DRAM. Further, PCM has a limited write endurance which implies that it cannot be written endlessly. Therefore, we have to design a new page replacement algorithm that can not only maintain a high hit ratio as traditional algorithms do but also can avoid frequent writes to PCM. In this paper, aiming to provide a new solution to the page replacement problem in PCM/DRAM-based hybrid memories, we propose a new algorithm called MHR-LRU (Maintain-hit-ratio LRU). The objective of our algorithm is to reduce PCM writes while maintaining a high hit ratio. Specially, it keeps recently updated pages in DRAM and performs page migrations between PCM and DRAM. The migrations take into account both page access patterns and the influences of page faults. We conduct trace-driven experiments and compared our proposal with some existing algorithms including LRU, LRU-WPAM, and CLOCK-DWF. The results show that our proposal is able to efficiently reduce PCM writes without degrading the hit ratio. Thus, our study offers a better solution for the page replacement issue in PCM/DRAM-based hybrid memory systems than previous approaches.

Keywords: Page replacement, Phase change memory, Hybrid memory.

1   Introduction

Phase change memory (PCM) is one of the most promising non-volatile memories. PCM is byte-addressable and a type of random-access memories. Compared with DRAM, PCM has the advantages of durability, scalability, and low energy

C.-H. Hsu et al. (Eds.): NPC 2014, LNCS 8707, pp. 108–119, 2014.
© IFIP International Federation for Information Processing 2014

consumption. Thus, many researchers have proposed to incorporate PCM into the memory hierarchy of computer systems [1-3]. However, two problems of PCM make it difficult to totally replace DRAM in current computer systems. First, the write latency of PCM is about 6 to10 times slower than that of DRAM. Second, PCM has a worn-out problem because each PCM cell has limited write endurance. Thus, PCM is not suitable for update-intensive applications. As a summary, Table 1 shows a comparison between DRAM and PCM.

Table 1. Comparison between PCM and DRAM

Attributes	DRAM	PCM
Durability	Volatile	Non-volatile
Read Latency	50 ns	50 ns
Write latency	20 – 50 ns	350 – 1000 ns
Read Energy	~ 0.1 nJ/b	~ 0.1 nJ/b
Write Energy	~ 0.1 nJ/b	~ 0.5 nJ/b
Idle Power	~ 1.3 W/GB	~ 0.05 W
Density	Low	High (~ 4X DRAM)
Endurance	∞	10^8 for write

Therefore, a more practical way to utilize PCM in memory architectures is to use PCM and DRAM and thus to construct a hybrid memory architecture [4, 5]. Generally, there are two architectures to integrate PCM in DRAM-based main memory, namely *DRAM cache* architecture and *hybrid memory architecture*, as shown in Fig. 1. The *DRAM cache architecture* uses PCM as main memory and uses DRAM as the cache of PCM [4]. The DRAM cache is hidden to the operation system, like the L1 and L2 caches for CPU. The *hybrid memory architecture* puts PCM and DRAM at the same level in main memory [5]. The hybrid memory is regarded as the union of DRAM and PCM, and both of their storage capacities are used as main memory. In this situation, all the pages in DRAM and PCM are managed by the operation system.

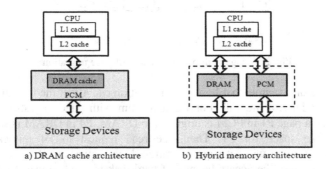

a) DRAM cache architecture   b) Hybrid memory architecture

Fig. 1. Memory architectures consists of PCM and DRAM

This paper focuses on the *hybrid memory architecture*. In particular, we concentrate on the page replacement problem for the hybrid memory architecture. Traditional page replacement algorithms are designed for DRAM-only main memory architecture. They are not suitable for the hybrid memory architecture because PCM and DRAM have different characteristics and the page replacement algorithms have to be aware of these differences. So far, a few page replacement algorithms for the hybrid memory architecture are proposed; some of them focus on PCM and DRAM [6, 7] while others are on flash memory and HDD [10, 11]. The similar idea of the existing algorithms is to keep write-intensive pages in DRAM and to let read-intensive pages in PCM so that DRAM can absorb most writes. For this purpose, specific page migration schemes are introduced in previous algorithms. The basic process of a page migration is as follows: when a page request comes to the memory, the page migration algorithm determines whether the requested page needs to be moved according to its access pattern. The read-intensive page in DRAM is moved to PCM and the write-intensive page in PCM is moved to DRAM.

However, there are two problems in the existing algorithms for hybrid memory systems. First, these algorithms always place pages read from disk in PCM and move read-intensive pages in DRAM to PCM. Because page placement and migration also incur writes to PCM, always caching read-intensive pages in PCM may lead to additional writes to PCM especially under read-intensive workloads. Second, moving a page between PCM and DRAM has to consider the problem that the memory is full. To accommodate the moved page in the target medium, the previous algorithms have to choose a victim page to release its space [6, 7]. This has an impact on the hit ratio of memory request. Thus, compared with conventional algorithms, the existing algorithms for hybrid memory usually introduce more page faults when processing memory requests.

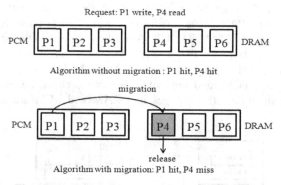

Fig. 2. A page fault occurs because of page migration

Fig. 2 shows an example that how page migration can affect the hit ratio. Initially, both PCM and DRAM are full. For the algorithm with page migration for hybrid memory, when a page P1 in PCM is migrated to DRAM, P4 in DRAM is selected as a victim to make space for P1. Then, the read request to P4 misses. For the conventional algorithm without page migration, both requests to P1 and to P4 hit in the memory. Because the access latency of hard disk is much slower than the write access latency of PCM, decreasing hit ratio to reduce write access count on PCM may lower the overall performance of hybrid memory.

In this paper, we present an efficient page replacement algorithm called MHR-LRU (Maintain-hit-ratio LRU) for PCM/DRAM-based hybrid memory. The algorithm aims to maintain a high hit ratio and to reduce PCM writes for the hybrid memory. Differing from previous algorithms, our algorithm does not move pages between PCM and DRAM when page requests arrive. Instead, we perform page migrations when page faults occur. Thus, the page migrations in our algorithm need not to release extra pages. This is helpful to maintain a high hit ratio, because releasing extra pages will lower the hit ratio. Besides, MHR-LRU places write-intensive pages in DRAM to reduce PCM writes. Under read-intensive workloads, DRAM is efficiently used to absorb most read requests and to limit the number of writes to PCM triggered by page placement and page migration.

We perform trace-driven experiments in a hybrid memory simulation environment to evaluate the performance of MHR-LRU. We use different types of workloads and conduct comparisons with other algorithms including LRU, LRU-WPAM [6], and CLOCK-DWF [7]. The results show that our algorithm is able to maintain a high hit ratio for different workloads and outperform the other three competitors considering PCM writes.

The remainder of this paper is organized as follows. In Section 2, we sketch the related work. In Section 3, we present the MHR-LRU page replacement algorithm for the hybrid memory architecture. Section 4 describes the details about the experiments and the performance evaluation results. Finally, Section 5 concludes the paper.

2   Related Work

Conventional page replacement algorithms have been designed for DRAM-based main memory with uniform access latency and unlimited write endurance. Hit ratio is the key metric to evaluate the performance.

LRU (Least Recently Used) is a conventional page replacement algorithm that has been widely used. LRU aligns all pages in memory in order of their most recent reference times. When a page fault occurs and the buffer pool is full, the least recently used page in memory is selected as a victim. LRU has also been widely used for buffer management over new types of storage media such as flash memory [12, 13].

Page replacement algorithms for hybrid main memory as shown in Fig. 1(b) should consider not only the hit ratio but also the number of PCM writes because PCM has the long write latency and limited endurance.

LRU-WPAM (LRU-With-Prediction-And-Migration) is an LRU-based page replacement algorithm for hybrid main memory [6]. The algorithm aligns all pages in hybrid main memory as a LRU queue, and use four monitoring queues: a DRAM read queue, a DRAM write queue, a PCM read queue and a PCM write queue. Each page is retained into both LRU list and one of the four queues according to its access pattern and located memory type. To measure the access pattern of a page in hybrid memory, the algorithm provides a weight value for each page. Each time a page hits in the memory, the page's weight is calculated again according to the type of this access request, if its weight value is above the threshold, the page will be migrated. If the memory need to choose a victim to release for receiving the migrated page, DRAM choose the least recently used page in DRAM read queue and PCM choose the least recently used page in PCM write queue.

CLOCK-DWF is a CLOCK-based page replacement algorithm for hybrid main memory [7]. When a page fault occurs, if the request is read, the page is put on PCM; otherwise the page is put on DRAM. When a page on PCM hits by write request, the page is migrated to DRAM. To get a free page frame while the memory is full, PCM use conventional CLOCK algorithm to select a victim page to release [8], but DRAM migrates a low write frequency page to PCM.

Both LRU-WPAM and CLOCK-DWF release pages in page migration, this would causes hit ratio degradation. Both of the two algorithms force read-bound pages to place on PCM, this may incurs higher PCM write count than conventional algorithms. For these problem, our study present a new method to reduce PCM write count without sacrificing hit ratio by merging page migration into page replacement process and just limiting write-bound pages to the DRAM. The details will be given in Section 3.

3   The MHR-LRU Algorithm

In this section, we present the details of the MHR-LRU algorithm for hybrid main memory. MHR-LRU aims to reduce the writes to PCM without degrading hit ratio so as to improve the overall performance of hybrid main memory. In order to accomplish this goal, we design the scheme that performs the page migration when page replacement occurs to make write-intensive pages on PCM.

3.1   The Main Idea

The main idea of MHR-LRU algorithm is described as follows:

(1) The algorithm use LRU list to manage pages together in hybrid main memory. All pages in hybrid memory are aligned in order of their most recent reference time. When a page fault occurs, the page in the LRU position will be selected as victim no matter where it locates.

(2) The algorithm uses a special data structure called DWL (DRAM Write-aware LRU list) to manage pages in DRAM. DWL aligns all pages in DRAM in order of their most recent write reference time.

(3) When a page fault occurs and the victim has been selected, MHR-LRU check the page access type and the victim's location, if the page's access request is write and the victim is located on PCM, MHR-LRU perform page migration: the victim on PCM is released and the page in the LRU position of DWL is migrated to PCM, then the requested page is put on DRAM. By doing so, MHR-LRU can get the following benefits: First, the page migration does not cause extra page release, so it does not affect the hit ratio; Second, since putting a page from disk on PCM and migrating a page in DRAM to PCM incur the same amount of write on PCM, compared with putting the requested page on PCM then performing write operation on it, migrating an in-DRAM page to PCM and putting the requested page on DRAM for write operation can immediately reduce the amount of write on PCM; Third, according to principle of temporal locality, page with the most recently write reference has a higher possibility to be write again than the page in the LRU position of DWL, this page migration can reduce the number of future write operation on PCM.

3.2   The Detailed Algorithm

Fig. 3 shows the detailed algorithm of MHR-LRU. If a requested page is found in DRAM, the page is also maintained in both the LRU list and DWL. Hence, we check the type of this page request. If it is a read request, we move the page to the MRU position of the LRU list. If it is a write request, we move the page to the MRU position of the LRU list and the MRU position of DWL (Line 1 ~ 7). If the requested page is in PCM, the page is maintained in LRU list, we move the page to the MRU position of the LRU list (Line 8 ~ 10).

Algorithm. *MHR-LRU*(request q)

Input: a page request q
Output: a reference to the requested page
Preliminary: (1) L is the LRU list of the memory, DWL is the DRAM write-aware list.
     (2) p is the requested page.

1:	**if** p is in DRAM **then**
2:	**if** q is a read request **then**
3:	move p to MRU position of L
4:	**else**
5:	move p to MRU position of L;
6:	move p to MRU position of DWL;
7:	**return** a reference to p;
8:	**else if** p is in PCM **then**
9:	move p to MRU position of L;
10:	**return** a reference to p;
	/*page fault occurs*/
11:	**else**
12:	**if** there is a free frame in hybrid main memory **then**
13:	put p into the free frame;
14:	**else**
15:	get *victim* from LRU position of L;
16:	**if** *victim* is in PCM and q is a write request **then**
17:	get page m from LRU position of DWL;
18:	release *victim* and migrate m to PCM;
19:	put p into the free frame of DRAM;
20:	**else**
21:	release *victim* and put p into the free frame;
22:	insert p into MRU position of L;
23:	**if** p is in DRAM **then**
24:	**if** q is a write request **then**
25:	insert p into MRU position of DWL;
26:	**else**
27:	insert p into LRU position of DWL;
28:	**return** a reference to p;

Fig. 3. The detailed algorithm of MHR-LRU

If a page is missing, we have to find a free frame to cache the requested page. If the memory has free spaces, we put the requested page into a randomly-selected free frame (Line 12 ~ 13). If the memory is full, we select the page in the LRU position of the LRU list as victim, if the victim is in PCM and the page's request is a write request, the victim is released. We do not put the requested page in PCM but move the page in the LRU position of DWL to PCM, and put the requested page into

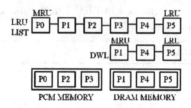

(a) Buffer initial situation for MHR-LRU algorithm

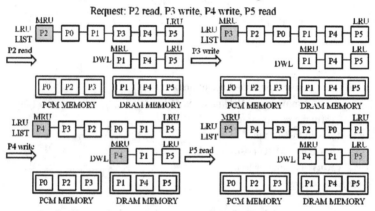

(b) The situation that pages in PCM and DRAM hit by read request and write request

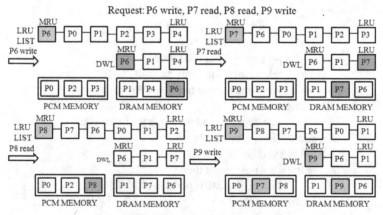

c) The situation that page replacement and page migration occur.

Fig. 4. An example of the MHR-LRU algorithm

DRAM. Otherwise, we just evict the victim for the requested page (Line 14 ~ 21). After putting the requested page into the hybrid memory, we insert the requested page to the MRU position of the LRU list. If the requested page is in DRAM, we insert it to the DWL according to its request type. If the page's request is a write request, it is inserted to the MRU position of DWL, else it is inserted to the LRU position of DWL (Line 22 ~ 28).

Fig. 4 gives an example of MHR-LRU. Fig. 4 (a) shows the initial state of the hybrid memory. The buffer contains P0, P1, P2, P3, P4, P5. P0, P2, P3 are in PCM, and P1, P4, and P5 are in DRAM. All pages are in LRU list and P1, P4, P5 are in DWL. Fig. 4 (b) shows the situation of page hits, and Fig. 4 (c) shows the situation of page faults.

Fig. 4 indicates that, when page faults occur, MHR-LRU selects and releases the least recently used page, which is similar to the LRU algorithm. This ensures that our algorithm can have the similar hit ratio as LRU. However, our algorithm does not release pages when page hits occurs, which is different from LRU-WPAM and CLOCK-DWF.

4   Performance Evaluation

In this section, we compare our algorithm with LRU, LRU-WPAM, and CLOCK-DWF. LRU is the reprehensive of traditional page replacement algorithms. LRU-WPAM and CLOCK-DWF are the recently proposed algorithms for the hybrid memory architecture.

4.1   Experimental Setup and Datasets

We use simulation experiments to evaluate our algorithm. We design the simulator for the hybrid memory architecture. In the experiments, the DRAM-to-PCM ratio is set to 1:4 because PCM density is expected to be four times higher than that of DRAM. Based on the simulator, the compared page replacement algorithms are implemented and trace-driven experiments are performed for performance evaluation. The parameters used in LRU-WPAM and CLOCK-DWF are the same as those in the original papers [6, 7].

We perform our simulation experiments with six types of synthetic traces. These traces are generated by DiskSim [9]. The characteristics of these traces are given in Table 2. The locality in Table 2, for example 80% / 20%, means that eighty percent of total references are focused on twenty percent of the pages.

4.2   Hit Ratios

Hit ratio is a key metric for the performance of page replacement algorithms. First, we compare the hit ratio of our algorithm with other three ones by varying the size of memory. We use the number of page faults to measure hit ratio. The results are shown in Fig. 5.

As Fig. 5 shows, when measures under the workloads with low localities (T9155, T5555, T1955), the hit ratios of LRU-WPAM and CLOCK-DWF are almost the same

Table 2. Six types of synthetic traces

Type	Total Reference	Different Pages Accessed	Read/Write Ratio	Locality
T9182	300,000	10,000	90% / 10%	80% / 20%
T9155	300,000	10,000	90% / 10%	50% / 50%
T5582	300,000	10,000	50% / 50%	80% / 20%
T5555	300,000	10,000	50% / 50%	50% / 50%
T1982	300,000	10,000	10% / 90%	80% / 20%
T1955	300,000	10,000	10% / 90%	50% / 50%

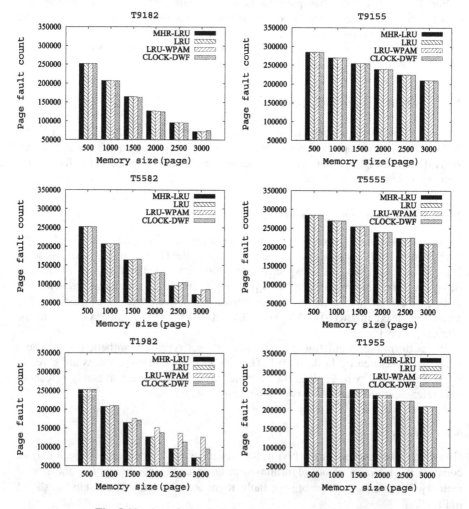

Fig. 5. Number of page faults under the six synthetic traces

as the hit ratio of LRU and MHR-LRU. Because all algorithms are based on temporal locality, a low locality access pattern leads to very similar hit ratios of four algorithms. When using the high-locality workloads (T9182, T5582, T1982), with the increase of the ratio of write operations in workloads, LRU-WPAM and CLOCK-DWF show higher number of page faults than LRU and MHR-LRU do.

LRU-WPAM and CLOCK-DWF usually release pages when they perform page migration. As shown in Fig. 2, this page release can introduce page fault. To show the relationship between page fault and page release, during the experiment, we collect page release count of LRU-WPAM and CLOCK-DWF under high-locality workloads that LRU-WPAM and CLOCK-DWF show higher number of page fault.   When page migration occurs and one page in the target medium has been released, the page release count increases. The result is shown in Fig. 6. As Fig. 6 shows, for LRU-WPAM and CLOCK-DWF, workloads with high ratio of write operations cause more pages to be released because of page migrations. This consequently leads to a higher number of page faults.

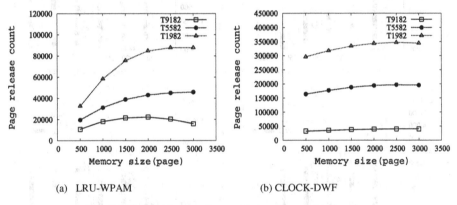

(a) LRU-WPAM   (b) CLOCK-DWF

Fig. 6. Number of page releases triggered by page migrations

4.3   Writes to PCM

The writes count to PCM is related to the overall write performance of the hybrid memory and the lifetime of PCM. In this section, we measure the number of write operations on PCM incurred by MHR-LRU in comparison with LRU, LRU-WPAM, and CLOCK-DWF.

Fig. 7 shows the number of PCM writes for LRU, LRU-WPAM, CLOCK-DWF, and MHR-LRU. MHR-LRU obtains less PCM writes than LRU-WPAM and CLOCK-DWF do in most cases. Compared with LRU, MHR-LRU reduces 17.45% of PCM writes on average, and reduces up to 34.1% of PCM writes. The write count reduction of LRU-WPAM is 1.01% on average, and the best result for write reduction is 8.69%. CLOCK-DWF is able to reduce averagely 9.82% more writes than LRU. Specially, MHR-LRU can still reduce 6.5% of PCM writes averagely in the worst case (under the workload T9155).

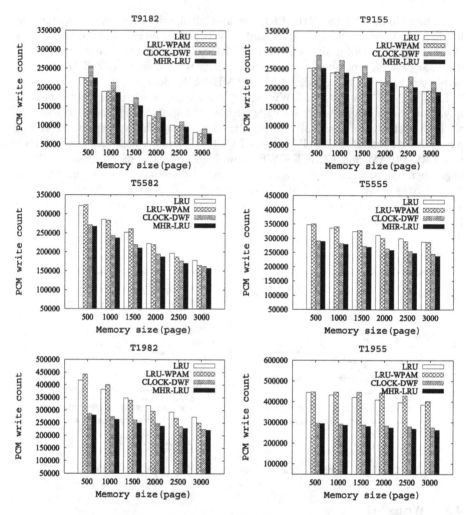

Fig. 7. PCM writes under the six synthetic traces

5   Conclusions

PCM has emerged as one of the most promising memories to be used in main memory hierarchy. A lot of studies propose to construct hybrid memory architectures involving PCM and DRAM to utilize the advantages of both media. In this paper, based on such hybrid memory architecture, we propose a new page replacement algorithm called MHR-LRU to handle the problems incurred by the hybrid memory architecture. MHR-LRU is able to maintain a high hit ratio and is able to reduce PCM writes effectively. We conduct trace-driven experiments in a simulation environment using six types of synthetic traces, and compare our algorithm with three competitors including LRU, LRU-WPAM, and CLOCK-DWF in terms of different metrics. The results show that our algorithm outperforms all the other algorithms.

Acknowledgement. This paper is supported by the National Science Foundation of China (No. 61073039, 61379037, and 61272317) and the OATF project funded by University of Science and Technology of China.

References

1. Burr, G.W., Kurdi, B.N., Campbell Scott, J., et al.: Overview of candidate device technologies for storage-class memory. IBM Journal of Research and Development 52(4-5), 449–464 (2008)
2. Freitas, R.F., Wilcke, W.W.: Storage-class memory: The next storage system technology. IBM Journal of Research and Development 52(4-5), 439–448 (2008)
3. Benjamin, C.: Lee, Engin Ipek, Onur Mutlu, et al., Architecting phase change memory as a scalable dram alternative. In: Proc. of ISCA, pp. 2–13 (2009)
4. Qureshi, M.K., Srinivasan, V., Rivers, J.A.: Scalable high performance main memory system using phase-change memory technology. In: Proc. of ISCA, pp. 24–33 (2009)
5. Dhiman, G., Ayoub, R.Z., Rosing, T.: PDRAM: a hybrid PRAM and DRAM main memory system. In: Proc. of DAC, pp. 664–669 (2009)
6. Seok, H., Park, Y., Park, K.W., et al.: Efficient page caching algorithm with prediction and migration for a hybrid main memory. ACM SIGAPP Applied Computing Review 11(4), 38–48 (2011)
7. Lee, S., Bahn, H., Noh, S.H.: Characterizing Memory Write References for Efficient Management of Hybrid PCM and DRAM Memory. In: Proc. of MASCOTS, pp. 168–175 (2011)
8. Corbato, F.J.: A Paging Experiment with the Multics System. In: Honor of P. M. Morse, pp. 217–228. MIT Press (1969)
9. Bucy, J.S., Schindler, J., Schlosser, S.W., et al.: The disksim simulation environment version 4.0 reference manual (cmu-pdl-08-101). Parallel Data Laboratory 26 (2008)
10. Yang, P., Jin, P., Yue, L.: Hybrid Storage with Disk Based Write Cache. In: Xu, J., Yu, G., Zhou, S., Unland, R. (eds.) DASFAA Workshops 2011. LNCS, vol. 6637, pp. 264–275. Springer, Heidelberg (2011)
11. Yang, P., Jin, P., Wan, S., Yue, L.: HB-Storage: Optimizing SSDs with a HDD Write Buffer. In: Gao, Y., Shim, K., Ding, Z., Jin, P., Ren, Z., Xiao, Y., Liu, A., Qiao, S. (eds.) WAIM 2013 Workshops 2013. LNCS, vol. 7901, pp. 28–39. Springer, Heidelberg (2013)
12. Jin, P., Ou, Y., Haerder, T., Li, Z.: ADLRU: An Efficient Buffer Replacement Algorithm for Flash-based Databases. Data and Knowledge Engineering (DKE) 72, 83–102 (2012)
13. Li, Z., Jin, P., Su, X., Cui, K., Yue, L.: CCF-LRU: A New Buffer Replacement Algorithm for Flash Memory. IEEE Trans. on Consumer Electronics 55(3), 1351–1359 (2009)

HiNetSim: A Parallel Simulator for Large-Scale Hierarchical Direct Networks[*]

Zhiguo Fan[1,2], Zheng Cao[1,**], Yong Su[1,2], Xiaoli Liu[1], Zhan Wang[1,2], Xiaobing Liu[1], Dawei Zang[1,2], and Xuejun An[1]

[1] Institute of Computing Technology,
Chinese Academy of Sciences, Beijing, China
[2] University of Chinese Academy of Sciences
{fanzhiguo,cz,suyong,liuxiaoli,wangzhan,liuxiaobing,
zangdawei,axj}@ncic.ac.cn

Abstract. As the scale of high performance computer keeps increasing, the hierarchical high dimension direct network, such as Cray Dragonfly and K computer 6D mesh, becomes commonly used. In such architecture, the variety of topologies in each hierarchy leads to the complexity of topology and routing algorithm. Facing to the high complexity and scalability, parallel network simulator is the suitable platform to design network architecture efficiently and study its performance. We design and implement a packet-level parallel network simulator HiNetSim which can achieve both high accuracy and efficiency. In addition, the simulator provides flexible interfaces and configuration files for establishing hierarchical topologies and implementing routing algorithms. As a demonstration of HiNetSim, studies on flattened butterfly, 4D Torus and a proposed hierarchical network are given. Evaluation shows that HiNetSim achieves linear parallel speedup and is capable of simulating the network with tens of thousands nodes.

1 Introduction

Today, the scale of interconnection network is keeping increasing and is expecting to hold hundreds of thousands of nodes [1]. To balance the scalability and performance, the hierarchical direct network architecture corresponding to the communication locality is widely used. In the hierarchical network, different hierarchies of the network often possesses different switching capacities, such as IBM BlueGene/Q 5D torus [2, 3] K tofu nested 6D torus [4] and Cray dragonfly [5]. Facing with different switching capacities, the network topology varies between different network hierarchies. In this case, the full system network architecture becomes more complicated and the fully adaptive routing algorithm is hard to design.

Network simulator is the most commonly used platform to perform the network evaluation. However, to study the complex hierarchical network efficiently, a network simulator must fulfill the following requirements.

---

[*] Supported by the National Natural Science Foundation of China under Grant No.61100014.
[**] Corresponding author.

C.-H. Hsu et al. (Eds.): NPC 2014, LNCS 8707, pp. 120–131, 2014.

1) *Scalability:* the network simulator must be capable of simulating large scale network. Only when the network scale is large enough, can many performance issues such as load balancing and network congestion show up.

2) *Accuracy:* the microarchitecture of network devices should also be simulated in detail, since they have great effect on the full system performance. For example, the number of virtual channels is a key factor for both the network performance and deadlock-free routing algorithm.

3) *Flexibility:* user interfaces should be friendly enough to quickly implement new architectures (topology and corresponding routing algorithm) for different hierarchies.

4) *Performance:* the simulation of the large scale network should be finished in a reasonable time.

However, most simulators are written with sequential codes and cannot meet the requirement of scalability and performance, such as BookSim [6], Xmulator [7], CINSim [8], MINSimulate [9] and INSEE [10]. Some parallel simulators, such as NSIM [11], simuRed [12] and topaz [13], are limited to a subset of network topologies and cannot meet the requirement of flexibility. BigNetSim [14] can perform efficient parallel simulation. However, it is designed with a new language Charm++ which introduces a long learning curve for users to develop new topologies and routing algorithms. The Network Simulator (ns) series [15] and DCNSim [16] are focus on internet system and lack of the micro-architecture details.

In this paper, we design and implement a parallel cycle-accurate network simulator HiNetSim to perform studies on the complex hierarchical network architecture. HiNetSim is written in C/C++ and uses a kernel-based framework. The simulation kernel SimK [17] is in charge of the functions needed by the PDES (parallel discrete event simulation) including the synchronization and communication mechanism, simulation task scheduling, and memory management. In this case, users can focus only on the simulation of network behavior which greatly reduces the developing time of new network models.

As the building block of hierarchical network, basic network architectures, such as fat-tree, all-to-all, *n*D torus, *n*D mesh, flattened butterfly and etc., have been implemented in HiNetSim. In addition, HiNetSim provides flexible user interfaces and configuration files to customize topologies and routing algorithms.

The reset of paper is organized as follows: Section 2 discusses key issues of designing HiNetSim; Section 3 describes the architecture and implementation of HiNetSim; Section 4 demonstrates the ability of HiNetSim by simulating some example networks. Section 5 shows performance result of HiNetSim. Section 6 gives the conclusion.

2   Key Issues and Design

2.1   Parallelism

In HiNetSim, each network component, such as NIC and switch, is defined as one *LE* (Logic Element). *LE* is the basic element for parallel simulation and scheduling.

Timing synchronization between *LEs* is the key issue regarding the correctness of simulation function. We adopted PDES (Parallel Discrete Event Simulation) mechanism [18] a parallel distributed synchronization mechanism to solve this.

There are two PDES mechanisms: conservative and optimistic. In the conservative model, events with later time stamp can only be processed after the earlier ones. In the optimistic one, events with later time stamp may be processed in advance. If an earlier time stamp arrives, a rollback mechanism is used to guarantee the correctness of simulation. However, the rollback needs large memory to store undetermined states and makes the debugging of network simulation much more difficult. To save the memory usage and shorten the developing time, we apply the conservative mechanism in HiNetSim.

2.2   Load Balancing

In the parallel simulation, if simulating workloads assigned to different threads/processes are not balance enough, the parallelism efficiency will be greatly decreased. To achieve the load balancing, we deploy both static and dynamic mechanisms.

At the initialization phase of the simulation, a static load balancing mechanism is used. According to different network topologies, HiNetSim provides an effective graph allocation strategy to put *LEs* into the same process based on their communication affinity. The problem statement of the *LE* allocation is: given a graph G with n weighted vertices and m weighted edges, how to divide the vertices into p sets so that every set has similar sum value of vertex weights and sum value of edge weights respectively. This problem is known to be NP complete, but there are some heuristic approximate solutions. We use Chaco (a graph partitioning package) to solve this problem which works well in partitioning hierarchical network topologies.

At the simulating phase, to achieve sub-millisecond granularity workload migration, a cooperated migration mechanism is proposed, which combines the merit of workload sharing and workload stealing. For each thread, our mechanism separates *run_list* and *mig_list* for normal execution and migration. Inside a thread, *LEs* are scheduled and stolen as follows:

1) All ready *LEs* are first put into the *run_list*. If the affinity flag of the *LE* indicates it has just been migrated, it is put to tail, otherwise to head.
2) Check the length of *run_list*, if it has beyond a threshold, excessive *LEs* are moved to the *mig_list*.
3) Check local *run_list*, if it is not empty, *LEs* in it are sent to execute, and LEs in local *mig_list* are moved to local *run_list*. Otherwise, it tries to steal *LEs* from remote *mig_lists*.

2.3   Cycle-Level Accuracy

To guarantee the cycle-level accurate, simulation in flit level may be the best solution. However, the flit-level simulation introduces plenty of simulation tasks and eventually leads to poor efficiency. To carry out the large-scale simulation with the same accuracy within a reasonable time, we use packet-level simulation in virtual cut through switching (VCT). In addition, VCT is the most commonly used switching technology. Our process of the packet-level simulation is:

1) When the first flit of a packet arrives at one switch, the switch accepts it only if there is enough space for the whole packet in its receiving queue.
2) The switch selects one packet from its receiving queues based on certain arbitration algorithm and calculates the flow control credit to check whether the receiving side has enough space to accept it.
3) If the flow control credit is enough, then the switch sends out the packet flit by flit until the last one is sent out.

In simulation, we assume that all switches in an interconnection network have the same bandwidth. If we define the length of flit as L, the bandwidth of switch as BW, T_R (w, k) and T_S (w, k) as the time stamps of switch w receiving and transmitting the kth flit respectively, T_C as the time of arbitration delay, routing delay, flow control and etc., then the T_S (w, k) can be described as:

$$\begin{cases} T_S(w,0) = T_R(w,0) + T_c & k = 0 \\ T_S(w,k) = T_S(w, k\text{-}1) + L/BW & 1 \le k \le n \end{cases} \qquad (1)$$

As shown in the equation (1), T_S (w, n) can be determined when T_R $(w, 0)$ and T_c is known. If we assume that all the ports of switches in an interconnection network have the same bandwidth, then T_S $(w, n) = T_R$ $(w, 0) + T_c + (n\text{-}1) \times L/BW$. Therefore, instead of simulating all the flits, the performance result can be obtained by simulating only the first flit and the last flit of each packet. Such simplification can accelerate the simulation without any loss of accuracy.

2.4   Flexibility

Network topology, routing algorithm, and flow control mechanism are tightly coupled with each other. In addition, many configurable parameters in network devices are only working with certain topologies and routing algorithms. Thus, achieving the flexibility of supporting various kinds of network architecture is rather difficult.

We implement a hierarchical structure to separate the simulation of microarchitecture of the network device and mechanisms for full simulated network (flow control and routing algorithm) from each other. Hierarchical structure is widely

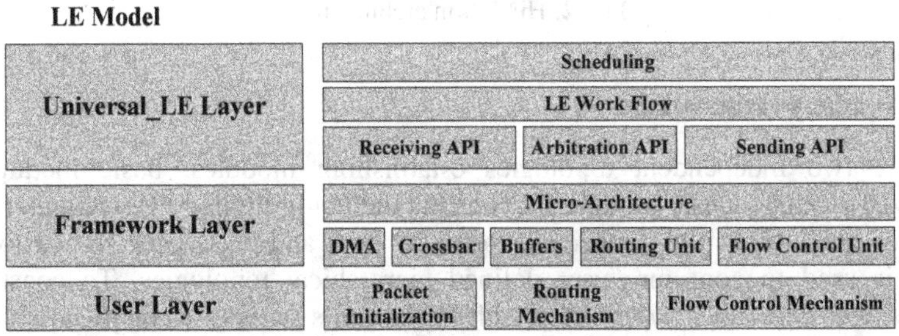

Fig. 1. LE hierarchical architecture

used in computer filed, such as operating systems, network, and etc. In HiNetSim, we borrow this idea and implement the *LE* with three layers. As shown in Figure 1:

- *Universal_LE Model*: takes charge of the scheduling of LE and defines the work flow of simulated network device including sending, receiving, arbitration and etc. The model does not implement any parameters or mechanisms of the target network.
- *Framework Model*: simulates the device micro-architecture including DMA, crossbar, buffers, routing unit and flow control unit and etc.. It also performs the function of performance statistics.
- *User Model*: implements the mechanisms of packet initialization, flow control and routing algorithm.

3   Implementation

3.1   HiNetSim Architecture

As is shown in Figure 2, in HiNetSim, *LE*s (can be switch or NIC) are connected with each other following the target network topology and SimK as the simulation kernel schedules *LE*s into execution and performs the synchronization and communication between *LE*s. Regarding a new network architecture, users can build the simulation from following four aspects: topology, routing algorithm, flow control mechanism, and switch/NIC micro-architecture. HiNetSim has implemented several well-known network architectures including fully connected, n-dimension torus, flattened butterfly, fat tree and etc. So, users can easily build their hierarchical networks by reusing codes of the implemented networks in proper network hierarchies.

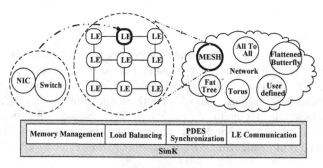

Fig. 2. HiNetSim architecture

3.2   Topology Generation

There are two independent topologies establishing modules: basic module and customized module. Basic module implements the configuration of our implemented topologies, including fully connected, torus, fat tree, and etc., while the customized module is used to configure user defined hierarchical topologies. To construct a topology, user can either write codes with HiNetSim's APIs (for complicated regular topologies) or describe the topology in configuration files (for irregular topologies).

3.3   Routing Mechanism

Since the routing algorithm is always tightly combined with topology, four routing mechanisms are supported to achieve the best flexibility:

1)   *Source address routing*: fill the destination port vector (record the destination port number in each hop) in the packet structure.
2)   *Table-based routing*: fill the address-to-port mapping table in each switch /router structure.
3)   *Dimension order routing*: especially for *n*-dimension mesh and torus topologies, fill the packet structure with the description of dimension ordering and fill the dimension-to-port mapping table in each switch/router structure;
4)   *Zone routing* [3]: an adaptive routing mechanism for direct networks, fill the zone identification, destination address and guidance bits of dimension ordering in the packet structure and fill the zone masks in each switch/router structure.

3.4   Flow Control Mechanism

HiNetSim implements the credit-based flow control mechanism as the default option. In PDES, two *LE*s are usually running at different timestamps, so we must buffer the flow control packet in a dedicated queue in the destination *LE* and pop it out when the destination *LE* has reached the timestamp of the flow control packet. To simplify the implementation without violating PDES synchronization policy, each flow control packet contains two different timestamps: one indicates the time to use the credit and the other one is the timestamp of the source *LE* for passing the flow control packet to the destination *LE*.

3.5   Simulation of Network Devices

HiNetSim simulates the detailed micro-architectures of NIC and switch. The router in HPC interconnection network is built from several NICs and a switch. As shown in Fig. 3, the NIC model contains seven modules: trace generator (generating artificial traffic patterns, such as uniform random, tornado, bit reversal and etc.), North Bridge (simulation of the I/O bus), DMA model (simulation of a RDMA engine), route generator (generating routing information to be carried with packets), receiver (receiving packets and putting them in the receiving buffers), transmitter (transmitting packet out) and flow control.

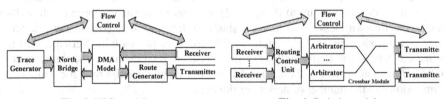

Fig. 3. NIC model   **Fig. 4.** Switch model

Fig. 4 shows an input-queuing switch model in HiNetSim. It contains five modules: receiver (receiving packets and putting them into corresponding virtual channels), transmitter (performing the output arbitration and transmitting packet out), crossbar (for each transmitter, selecting proper packets to send out), routing control (calculating destination port based on current routing mechanism), and flow control. Parameters such as the number and depth of virtual channels, receiving delay, arbitration strategy (round-robin, matrix arbiter or priority) and delay, internal bus bandwidth and etc. are configurable.

4   Simulation Examples

In this section, we perform simulations on both basic networks (flattened butterfly and 4D torus) and a proposed large-scale hierarchical network (4.5D Torus shown in Section IV.C) to demonstrate the simulation capability of HiNetSim.

4.1   Flattened Butterfly (FB): 1024 Nodes

Fig. 5 shows the topology of the two dimensions flattened butterfly [19]. In each row and column, switches are fully interconnected with each other. Table 1 shows 4 different kinds of configurations of 1024 nodes flattened butterfly, including 2 to 4 dimensions. First column in Table 1 shows the net name we called in our simulation. Configuration column shows the number of nodes per dimension, and the last column shows the number of nodes per switch directly connected with. We use VOQ (Virtual Output Queuing) microarchitecture and uniform random traffic [20-22].

Table 1. 1024 nodes fattened butterfly

Name	Configurations	# of nodes per switch
FB1	8×8	16
FB2	16×16	4
FB3	8×8×8	2
FB4	4×4×4×4	4

Fig. 6 shows the performance of flattened butterfly under different configurations. Network FB1 achieve much lower throughput (0.46) than others, because it is a flattened butterfly with oversubscription that connects 16 nodes per switch (standard fattened butterfly 8×8: 8 nodes per switch). On the contrary, network FB2 and FB3 can achieve throughputs up to (0.91~0.92) with very low latency, because these they are connecting with less nodes than the standard flattened butterfly (standard flattened butterfly 8×8×8: 8 nodes per switch, 16×16: 16 nodes per switch). Network FB4 is a standard flattened butterfly with high link occupation can achieve the throughput of 0.81. Users can perform these simulations by simply configuring the number of dimension and the number of nodes per dimension.

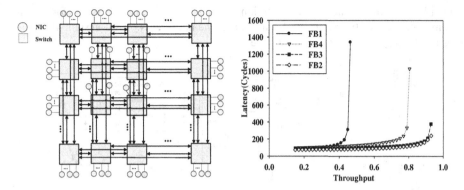

Fig. 5. Flattened butterfly topology   **Fig. 6.** Throughput vs. Latency: FB

4.2   4D Torus: 4096 Nodes

We simulate the 4D Torus network at the 4096 nodes scale (8 × 8 × 8 × 8: each dimension contains 8 nodes) and study the effect of virtual channels on network performance. One VC is used as the escape channel in these simulations. In addition, dimension order routing (DOR) and uniform random traffic is used.

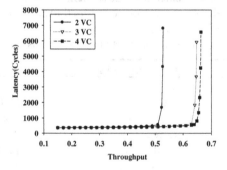

Fig. 7. Throughputs vs. Latency: 4D torus with different number of VCs

As shown in Fig. 7, with 2 VCs, the network throughput is 0.51. With 3 and 4 VCs, throughputs can increase to 0.63 and 0.65 respectively. The improvement is achieved by reducing the head-of-line (HOL) blocking. However, because of the limitation of using DOR algorithm, the throughput is difficult to reach 0.7.

4.3   D Torus Network: A Hierarchical Network

We proposed a 4.5D Torus network to show the simulation of hierarchical network. The 4.5D Torus topology aims to optimize local communication and build large-scale network with low radix routers. As is shown in Fig. 8 (a), the basic building block of network is the 8-port router (2 ports for the host, 1 port for I/O, and 5 for interconnection). As shown in Fig. 8 (b), 4 fully connected routers form a Superblock (8 nodes). The remaining 8 ports of the Superblock are used for external interconnection. Fig. 8 (c) shows the standard 4D torus topology built with

Superblocks. Since the interconnection inside Superblock is only for local communication, we treat it as 0.5D dimension. The network is of full-system 4D torus plus local 0.5D, so we name it 4.5D Torus.

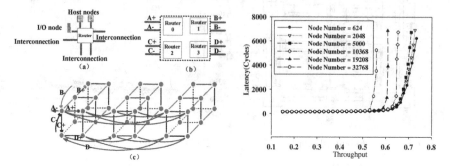

Fig. 8. Topology of 4.5D Torus   **Fig. 9.** Throughput vs. Latency: 4.5D torus

This simulation uses zone routing mechanism and 4 virtual channels (including 2 escape VCs). We set the virtual channel's buffer to 4096Byte and MTU (Maximum transmission Unit) to 1024Byte. We perform the simulation with a traffic that contains 70% intra-superblock communication, 20% neighbor-superblock communication within 3 hop counts, and 10% to the remaining superblocks.

Table 2. Configurations of 4.5D torus

A×B×C×D	# of Superblocks	# of Nodes
3×3×3×3	81	648
4×4×4×4	256	2,048
5×5×5×5	625	5,000
6×6×6×6	1,296	10,368
7×7×7×7	2,401	19,208
8×8×8×8	4,096	32,768

We simulate the 4.5D torus with different scales (648~32,768 nodes). As shown in Table 2, the first column shows the dimension length of A, B, C, and D. The other two columns show the number of superblocks and nodes (8 nodes per superblock).

As shown in Fig. 9, when network scale is small (e.g. 648 nodes), the throughput can reach to 0.75. As the network scale increases, the throughput keeps decreasing. When the number of nodes is 32,768, the throughput is only 0.56. The throughput decrement is mainly caused by the network load imbalance introduced by DOR routing algorithm. The ability of gathering network load imbalance information is very important for a simulator. To get heavily loaded devices or paths, HiNetSim provides detailed performance statistics for each network device and even each port. By comparing the throughput of each node, the bottleneck of network can be easily found out. We use HiNetSim to analyze the network load of 4.5D torus with 32,768 nodes. 3D graphic can compare only the loads of two dimensions, so we show the load balancing with three combinations of dimensions: A and B, B and C, C and D.

From Fig.10 (a) and (b), we can see that throughputs of B, C and D dimensions have very small variations. Fig.10 (c) shows that A dimension is load imbalanced as the throughput varies from 0.2 to 0.7. Some nodes are heavily loaded (exceed the saturation point of a router with 2VCs) in A dimension and become the bottleneck. Such imbalance is mainly caused by the DOR algorithm (A dimension first).

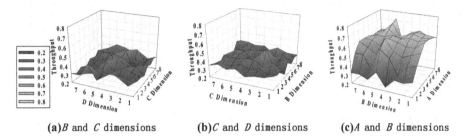

(a)B and C dimensions   (b)C and D dimensions   (c)A and B dimensions

Fig. 10. Load balancing condition of 4.5D torus network

5   Performance Evaluations on HiNetSim

This section evaluates the performance of HiNetSim on a 12-core Intel machine. The configuration of system is listed in Table 3.

Table 3. Experiment environment

CPU type	Xeon X5675
CPU number	2
Memory	96GB
OS	CentOS 6.3
Compiler	gcc 4.46
Library	Pthread

Table 4. Network types and configurations

Network Types	# of Switch numbers	# of Nodes
4.5D Torus	576 (3×3×4×4×4)	1152
Flattened Butterfly	64 (8×8)	1024
Fat Tree	320 (m=16,n=3)	1024
4D Torus	1296 (6×6×6×6)	1296

The performance of HiNetSim is evaluated with simulations of different types of networks. Table 4 shows the network type and configuration of each network. These networks are in the similar scale (1024~1296 node). All these simulations are using 1024Byte packets and 100% inject rate. The parallel speedup is calculated as: execution time on single core / execution time on multiple cores.

As shown in Fig. 11, HiNetSim can achieve linear speedup as the number of processor cores increases. Even super-linear speedup 15.6 is obtained when simulating 1,024 nodes flattened butterfly. The speedup is mainly related with the number of *LE*s: the fewer the *LE*s, the less communication and cache miss. So, 1024 nodes flattened butterfly with the fewest *LE*s can achieve super-linear speedup.

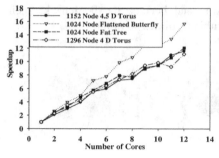
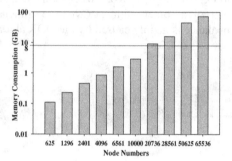

Fig. 11. Speedup of various networks   **Fig. 12.** Memory consumption of HiNetSim

Regarding the large scale network simulation, memory consumption is also an important issue. Fig. 12 shows the memory consumption of simulating 4D Torus which involves lots of *LE*s. When simulating no more than 10,000 nodes, less than 8GB memory is used. 8GB memory is easy to be fulfilled even in a personal laptop. When simulating 65,536 nodes, 72GB memory is used, which is also easy to get for a dual-processor blade server. So, with good parallel speedup and acceptable memory consumption, HiNetSim is capable of simulating large interconnection networks.

6   Conclusions and Future Work

HiNetSim is a parallel simulator that simulates large scale hierarchical interconnection networks with high efficiency, accuracy and flexibility. We use packet level simulation to guarantee the simulation efficiency, but still achieve the same accuracy as flit level. To shorten the development time of the simulation on new hierarchical network architectures, we provide flexible topology configuration, general purpose routing algorithm interfaces, and simulations of many commonly used networks. In this paper, we demonstrate the function of HiNetSim by simulating flattened butterfly, 4D Torus and a hierarchical network 4.5D Torus. Evaluation shows that HiNetSim can achieve linear parallel speedup. In addition, it can perform the simulation of 10,000 nodes network with less than 8GB memory and 65,536 nodes network with 72GB memory.

References

1. Top500 list, http://www.top500.org
2. Chen, D., Eisley, N.A., Heidelberger, P., Senger, R.M., Sugawara, Y., Kumar, S., Salapura, V., Satterfield, D.L., Steinmacher-Burow, B., Parker, J.J.: The IBM Blue Gene/Q interconnection fabric. IEEE Micro 32(1), 32–43 (2012)
3. Chen, D., Eisley, N.A., Heidelberger, P., Senger, R.M., Sugawara, Y., Kumar, S., Salapura, V., Satterfield, D.L., Steinmacher-Burow, B., Parker, J.J.: The IBM Blue Gene/Q interconnection network and message unit. In: Proc. SC Int. Conf. High Perform. Comput., Netw., Storage Anal., pp. 1–10 (2011)

4. Ajima, Y., Takagi, Y., Inoue, T., Hiramoto, S., Shimizu, T.: The Tofu Interconnect. IEEE Micro 32(1), 21–31 (2012)
5. Kim, J., Dally, W.J., Scott, S., Abts, D.: Cost-Efficient Dragonfly Topology for Large-Scale Systems. IEEE Micro 29(1) (January 2009)
6. BookSim 2.0, http://nocs.stanford.edu/booksim.html
7. Nayebi, A., Sarbazi-Azad, H., Shamaei, A., Meraji, S.: XMulator: An Object Oriented XML-Based Simulator. In: Proceedings of the First Asia International Conference on Modelling & Simulation, Phuket, Thailand, pp. 128–132 (2007)
8. Tutsch, D., Ludtke, D., Walter, A., Kuhm, M.: CINSim: A Component-based Interconnection net-work Simulator for Modeling Dynamic Reconfiguration. In: ESM 2005: European Conference on Modeling and Simulation, Riga, Latvia, pp. 32–39 (2005)
9. Tutsch, D., Brenner, M.: MINSimulate – A Mul-tistage Interconnection Network Simulator. In: ESM 2003: European Simulation Multiconference: Foundations for Successful Modeling & Simulation, Notingham, SCS, pp. 211–216 (2003)
10. Ridruejo Perez, F. J., Miguel-Alonso, J.: INSEE: An interconnection network simulation and evaluation environment. In: Cunha, J.C., Medeiros, P.D. (eds.) Euro-Par 2005. LNCS, vol. 3648, pp. 1014–1023. Springer, Heidelberg (2005)
11. Miwa, H., Susukita, R., Shibamura, H., et al.: NSIM: An Interconnection Network Simulator for Extreme-Scale Parallel Computers. IEICE Transactions on Information and Systems v E94-D(12), 2298–2308 (2011)
12. Pardo, F., Boluda, J.A.: SimuRed: A flit-level event-driven simulator for multicomputer network performance evaluation. Computers & Electrical Engineering 35(5), 803–814 (2009)
13. Abad, P., et al.: Topaz: An open-source interconnection network simulator for chip multiprocessors and supercomputers. In: Intl Symposium on Networks-on-Chip, NOCS (2012)
14. Bignetsim, http://charm.cs.illinois.edu/research/bignetsim
15. ns-3, http://www.nsnam.org/
16. Hu, N., Fu, B., Sui, X., Li, L., Li, T., Zhang, L.: DCNSim: a unified and cross-layer computer architecture simulation framework for data center network research. In: Proceedings of the ACM International Conference on Computing Frontiers (CF 2013), Article 19, 9 pages (2013)
17. Xu, J., Chen, M., Zheng, G., Cao, Z., Lv, H., Sun, N.: SimK: a parallel simulation engine towards shared-memory multiprocessor. Journal of Computer Science and Technology 24(6), 1048–1060 (2009)
18. Fujimoto, R.M.: Parallel discrete event simulation. Communications of the ACM 33(10), 30–53 (1990)
19. Kim, J., Dally, W.J., Abts, D.: Flattened butterfly: a cost-efficient topology for high-radix networks. ACM SIGARCH Computer Architecture News. 35(2) (2007)
20. Dally, W.J., Towles, B.: Principles and Practices of Interconnection Networks. Morgan Kaufmann, San Francisco (2004)
21. Dally, W.J.: Virtual-channel flow control. In: International Symposium on Computer Architecture, pp. 60–68 (1990)
22. Duato, J.: Deadlock-free adaptive routing algorithms for multicomputers: evaluation of a new algorithm. In: Proceedings of the Third IEEE Symposium on Parallel and Distributed Processing, pp. 840–847 (1991)

Wire Length of Midimew-Connected Mesh Network

Md Rabiul Awal[1,*], M. M. Hafizur Rahman[1], Rizal Mohd Nor[1],
Tengku Mohd Bin Tengku Sembok[2], Yasuyuki Miura[3], and Yasushi Inoguchi[4]

[1] Department of Computer Science, KICT, IIUM,
Jalan Gombak, Kuala Lumpur, 50728, Malaysia
[2] Cyber Security Center, National Defense University Malaysia,
Kuala Lumpur, 57000,Malaysia
[3] Graduate School of Technology, Shonan Institute of Technology,
1-1-25, Tsujido Nishikaigan, Fujisawa, Kanagawa, Japan
[4] Research Center for Advanced Computing Infrastructure, JAIST,
Nomi-Shi, Ishikawa 923-1292, Japan
{rabiulawal1,tmtsembok}@gmail.com, {hafizur,rizalmohdnor}@iium.edu.my,
miu@info.shonan-it.ac.jp, inoguchi@jaist.ac.jp

Abstract. Midimew connected Mesh Network (MMN) is a Minimal
DIstance MEsh with Wrap-around links (midimew) network. In this paper, we present the architecture of MMN and evaluate the total wire
length of MMN, TESH, mesh, and torus networks. It is shown that the
proposed MMN possesses simple structure and moderate wire length.
The total wire length of MMN is slightly higher than that of mesh network and lower than that of 2-D torus network. Overall performance
suggests that, MMN is an optimal network among these networks.

Keywords: Massively Parallel Computers, Interconnection Network,
MMN, and Total Wire Length.

1   Introduction

Current trend [1] suggests that, the demand for computation power is increasing rapidly and found as constant over the last half century. Massively parallel
computer (MPC) is introduced to meet this demand. Nevertheless, the scaling
of MPC is increasing as well. In nearby future, MPC will contain 10 to 100
millions of nodes [2] in a single system with computing capability at the tens of
petaflops or exaflops level. In MPC, interconnection network dominates the system performance [3, 4]. In relation, hierarchical interconnection network (HIN)
is a plausible alternative way to interconnect the future generation MPC [5] systems. Nevertheless, the performance of proposed HIN does not yield any obvious
choice of a network for MPC. Among a lot of HINs, several k-ary n-cube based
HIN have been proposed [6–9] for better performance.

---

* Corresponding author.

C.-H. Hsu et al. (Eds.): NPC 2014, LNCS 8707, pp. 132–143, 2014.
© IFIP International Federation for Information Processing 2014

The scaling of the processor is an arising concern with the attributes of high performance. Application driven technology trends pressing the geometry of silicon fabrication technology. This advancements make the transistor very small and allow greater transistor densities. Eventually, MPC with more than million nodes is feasible with current and future technology. Hence, the functionality becomes more complex of a MPC system with the shrinking geometry. As a matter of fact, interconnection network becomes the steering point, in the context of power dissipation and cost. In an MPC system, more than 50% of total power dissipated by the interconnection network. Also, the cost of MPC is related to the communication links of the network. In other words, interconnection network is composed of nodes and wires. Hence, the network is wire limited [10] on a VLSI surface. Wire length determines the communication delay [11–13] of the network. It also indicate the network size on a VLSI surface. Total wire length of network indicates the average locality of links of the network. It also explores the ease of Network-on-Chip implementation of the network. Therefore wire length is an influential factor for the network [14].

Midimew-connected Mesh Network (MMN) [15] was proposed to improve performance of fixed degree network while keeping the diameter short which is still desirable [7, 16]. Basic module of MMN is 2-D mesh and higher level network are midimew [17] network. Hence, MMN offers simple and hierarchical structure and this translate to the ease of VLSI implementation. The focus point of this paper is to explore the feasibility of VLSI implementation of MMN in terms of wire length. We compare the total wire length with several fixed degree network. For fair comparison we consider degree 4 networks only.

The remainder of the paper is organized as follows. In Section 2, we present the basic architecture of the MMN. Wire length evaluation is discussed in Section 3. Finally, in Section 4, we conclude this paper.

2   Architecture of the MMN

Midimew connected Mesh Network (MMN) is a hierarchical interconnection network. Multiple basic modules (BM) are hierarchically interconnected to form a higher level network of MMN. Architecturally the MMN consists of two major parts, the basic module (BM) and higher level networks. The BMs act as the basic building blocks of MMN whereas higher level networks determines the construction of MMN from BMs.

Basic Module is the basic building blocks of MMN. BM of MMN is a 2D-mesh network of size $(2^m \times 2^m)$. BM consists of 2^{2m} processing elements (PE). PEs are arranged in 2^m rows and 2^m columns, where m is a positive integer. Considering $m = 2$, a BM of size (4×4) is portrayed in Figure 1. Each BM has $2^{(m+2)}$ free ports at the contours for higher level interconnection. These free ports are used as communication links for higher levels and denoted by q. All Intra-BM links are done by free ports of the interior nodes. All free ports of the exterior nodes, either one or two, are used for inter-BM links to form higher level networks. In this paper, BM refers to a Level-1 network.

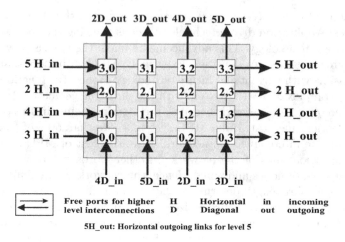

Fig. 1. Basic Module of MMN

Successive higher level networks are built by recursively interconnecting 2^{2m} immediate lower level subnetworks in a $(2^m \times 2^m)$ midimew network. In a midimew network, one direction (either horizontal or vertical) is symmetric tori connected and other direction is diagonally wrap-around connected. We have assigned the vertical free links of the BM for symmetric tori connection and horizontal free links are used for diagonal wrap-around links.

As portrayed in Figure 2, considering (m = 2) a Level-2 MMN can be formed by interconnecting $2^{(2\times2)} = 16$ BMs. Similarly, a Level-3 network can be formed by interconnecting 16 Level-2 sub-networks, and so on. Each BM is connected to its logically adjacent BMs. It is useful to note that for each higher level interconnection, a BM uses $4 \times (2^q) = 2^{q+2}$ of its free links, $2^{(2q)}$ free links for diagonal interconnections and $2^{(2q)}$ free links for horizontal interconnections. Here, $q \in \{0, 1, ..., m\}$,, is the inter-level connectivity. $q = 0$ leads to minimal interlevel connectivity, while $q = m$ leads to maximum interlevel connectivity.

A MMN(m, L, q) is constructed using $(2^m \times 2^m)$ BMs, has L levels of hierarchy with inter-level connectivity q. In principle, m could be any positive integer value. However, if $m = 1$, then the network degenerates to a hypercube network and if $m \geq 3$, the granularity of the family of networks is coarse. If $m = 2$, then it is considered the most interesting case, because it has better granularity than the large BMs. In the rest of this paper we consider m = 2, therefore, we focus on a class of MMN(2,L,q) networks.

The highest level network which can be built from a $(2^m \times 2^m)$ BM is $L_{max} = 2^{m-q} + 1$ with $q = 0$ and $m = 2$, $L_{max} = 5$, Level-5 is the highest possible level. The total number of nodes in a network having $(2^m \times 2^m))$ BMs is $N = 2^{2mL}$. If the maximum hierarchy is applied then number of total nodes which could be connected by MMN(m,L,q) is $N = 2^{2m(2^{m-q}+1)}$. For the case of (4×4) BM with $q = 0$, a MMN network consists of over 1 million nodes.

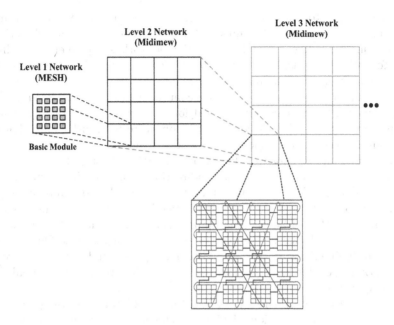

Fig. 2. Higher Level Networks of MMN

3   Wire Length Evaluation

Efficient use of wires is important to accomplish required performance from an interconnection network. Here we assume that all networks have a 2D-planar implementation and each node is implemented in one tile area. The width and height of a node depends upon its underlying CMOS technology. As the network consists of tiles (nodes), eventually the wire length depends on the size of tile. Let us consider, the tile height is x and tile width is y, hence tile area is xy. All the tiles are interconnected by wires to construct an interconnection network. For simplicity, we can consider total wires of the network are of two direction, Vertical and Horizontal direction. For Vertical and Horizontal direction, the wire length depends on the tile height and width respectively. Wire length between two particular nodes is the number of tiles needs to pass to interconnect the nodes. Consequently, total wire required to connect all the nodes of a network is the number of total tiles needs to be passed and can be expressed as,

$$Wire\ Length = Tile\ distance_X + Tile\ distance_Y$$

$$Tile\ distance = \#\ of\ tiles \times \#\ of\ groups$$

Here *# of groups* indicate the total number of same patterned communication links. For example, in a (4×4) 2D-mesh network, there are 4 columns and 4 rows with 16 nodes. So, in this network, *# of groups* for both vertical and horizontal directions is 4.

It is convenient to point out that, each node used in MMN have a router. These routers are used to interconnect all nodes, either directly or indirectly by the communication links. This interconnection network is implemented by direct wires. To evaluate the total wire length, we have calculated the length of the wires used to connect all the routers.

The communication links used to interconnect nodes are considered as bidirectional links. That is, each link is used for data in and data out by sharing the time. Therefore, each link contains just one wire to transfer data. For the intercommunication among nodes, unidirectional links can considered as well which contain multi wire for each link. Now, the point of using this type of links is, unidirectional links are faster than bidirectional links as they contain more channels for data passing. Thus, use of unidirectional links can improve the performance by saving time. Nevertheless, unidirectional links also require at least double wire than that of bidirectional links. As a result, unidirectional links increase the wire length, wiring complexity and cost of the network. On the other hand, use of bidirectional links save additional expenses and implement area of the network. Hence, for low cost, high performance network, bidirectional links are more appropriate.

We evaluated the total wire length of 2D-mesh, 2D-torus, TESH (2,2,0) and MMN (2,2,0). We have considered 45 nm technology to define the nodes size. According to 45nm technology [18], the tile height is 5.2 mm and tile width is 3.6 mm. Thus the tile size is 18.72 mm^2. So the node height, width and size are same as tiles. The wire length between two nodes suggests the number of tiles to be passed. So wire length between two nodes in horizontal direction is the product of number of tiles needs to be passed and tile width. Similarly for vertical direction, wire length is the product of number of tiles needs to be passed and tile height.

Hence, with the considered tile size, wire length between two neighbor nodes in horizontal direction is 3.6 mm and for vertical direction is 5.2 mm. For a 2D-mesh network, wire length depends on the grid size in vertical and horizontal direction. For example, in a $(N_x \times N_y)$ 2D-mesh network, wire length in one group in horizontal direction is $(N_x - 1) \times tilewidth$. Again for total N_x groups wire length is $N_x \times ((N_x - 1) \times tilewidth)$. Correspondingly, for total N_y groups $N_y \times ((N_y - 1) \times tileheight)$ is the wire length in vertical direction. Thus, for a (4×4) 2D-mesh network, wire length in vertical direction is 10.8 mm. With 4 groups and space for system interface, input/output (I/O), message class (MC), wire length in vertical direction is $(10.8 \times 4) + 4.9 = 48.1$ mm. Similarly for horizontal direction, wire length is 63 mm and total wire length is 111.1 mm. Figure 3(a) shows the wire length of a 4×4 mesh network. The wire length of a 16×16 (256 nodes) mesh is evaluated in same pattern and it is 211.75 cm.

In a 2D-torus network, with the mesh links, additionally there are wrap around torus links for both vertical and horizontal direction. Like mesh, 2D-torus is also dimension size dependent. For a $(N_X \times N_Y)$ 2D-torus network, two neighboring nodes in horizontal direction has the wire length of 3.6 mm, the width of a tile and in vertical direction wire length is 5.2 mm, the height of a tile. wire length of

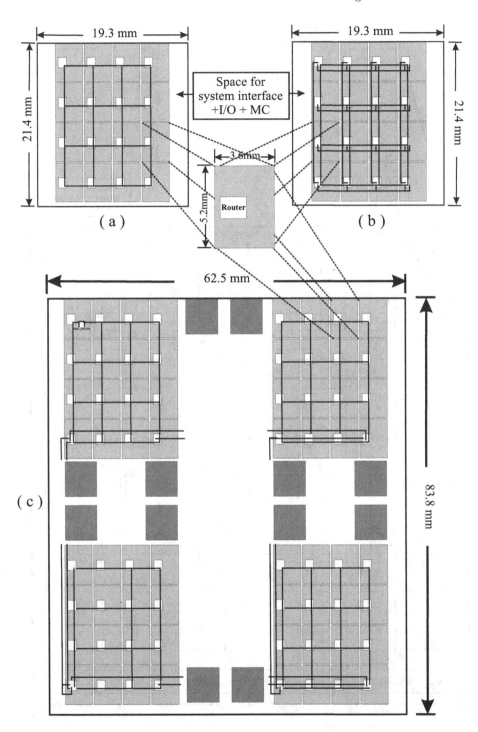

Fig. 3. Illustration of (a) 4×4 mesh, (b) 4×4 torus and (c) 256 nodes TESH Network

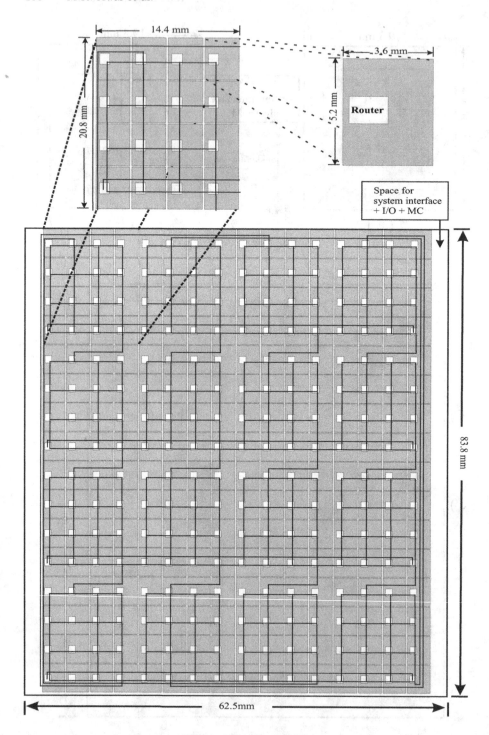

Fig. 4. 256 nodes MMN

the wrap around links in horizontal direction is N_{X-1}. Again in vertical direction, the wire length is N_{Y-1}. Number of groups are equal to N_X and N_Y. Figure 3(b) is showing a 4×4 2-D torus network. In horizontal direction wire length is 21.6 mm. # of groups is 4, therefore 86.4 mm is the wire length in horizontal direction. Similarly in vertical diction wire length of each group is 31.2 mm, for 4 groups, it is 124.8 mm. Finally with the reserved space for system interface, input/output (I/O), message class (MC) total wire length is 216.7 mm for a 4×4 2-D torus network. Wire length of a 16×16 (256 nodes) 2-D torus is calculated in a same manner and it is 422.95 cm in total. In Figure 3(b) a 4×4 2-D torus network is depicted.

TESH network is a hierarchical interconnection network with multiple basic modules. The basic module is a 2-D mesh network. Hence it is convenient to find out the wire length in basic modules, then calculate the connecting links for higher levels. The wire length of a 4×4 basic module is 105.6 mm which gives 1689.6 mm for 16 basic modules. In higher level links to horizontal direction wire length is 345.6 mm for 4 groups and 499.2 mm wire length for vertical direction. So in total the wire length of a 256 nodes TESH network is 253.99 cm. Figure 3(c) demonstrates the wire length of a 256 nodes TESH network.

Like TESH, Wire length of MMN evaluated by calculating the wires in BMs and in higher levels. Wire length in BMs of MMN is determined by the number of links in horizontal direction and in vertical direction and exactly equal to TESH, 1689.6 mm for 16 4×4 basic modules. Nevertheless, the links of higher levels is different from TESH. Higher level links of MMN are composed of wrap around and diagonal links. Each wraparound links has length of 54 mm which compute 216 mm wire length for 4 wrap around links. 4 diagonal links have length of 120 mm, 120 mm, 109.6 mm, and 109.6 mm. The rest inter BM links gives 480 mm. Hence 263.43 cm is the total wire length of a 256 nodes MMN. Figure 4 illustrates the wire length of a 256 nodes MMN.

The wire length dominates the initial system cost of networks. Networks with much wire eventually results a high installation cost and a large VLSI area which responsible for poor performance. In correlation, diameter indicates the worst case scenario of a network and has direct influence on the overall static network performance. Hence, the product of total wire length and diameter is a good criteria to get the static operating cost of the network. We can express the static operating cost as follows,

$$C_{static} = L \times D$$

Here, C_{static} represents the static operating cost, L for total wire length and D stands for diameter. It is already mentioned that, we have considered the links as bidirectional links. Hence, calculation of the links are the wire length. This calculation is valid for bidirectional links only.

Cost is one of the important parameter for evaluating an interconnection network. Though the actual cost of a system depends on the implemented hardware and the physical network in total but total wire length and diameter effect the performance metrics of the network including message traffic density, fault tolerance and average distance. Low diameter impose low cost, small space and better performance, while high diameter requires high cost, large space, and poor performance. Therefore, the static operating cost is a good criterion to indicate the relationship between cost and performance of a network. Hence, it can give a pre-idea about the network before installation. The evaluation of Total Wire Length and static operating cost of various networks are tabulated in Table 1,

Table 1. Comparison of Total Wire Length of Various Networks

Network	Wiring Complexity	Total Wire Length (cm)	Static Operating Cost
2D-Mesh	480	211.75	6652.5
2D-Torus	512	422.95	6767.2
TESH(2,2,0)	416	253.99	5333.79
MMN(2,2,0)	416	263.43	4478.31

From Table 1, it is clear that 2D-mesh network can be constructed with minimum amount of wires among the networks, 211.75 cm in total. On the other hand, 2D-torus network contains maximum 422.95 cm of wires to interconnect all nodes of it. Total wire length for TESH (2,2,0) is 253.99 cm and in case of MMN (2,2,0), it is slightly higher than that of TESH network, 263.43 cm. The static network performance of different networks are shown in Table 2[15]. For fair comparison we consider degree 4 networks only.

2D-mesh is a very simple network. It is very easy to construct and does not contain any wrap around links. So 2D-mesh results least amount of wire length in total, but the performance of mesh keeps the network under the table. The diameter of mesh network is 30. Hence, this large diameter results the network ending with relatively high static operating cost 6652.5. It is higher than TESH, MMN and less than 2-D torus network.

2-D torus network presents better performance than that of others. 2D-torus network consists of 2D-mesh and warp around torus links. The wrap around links are equal to the sum of column and row numbers. It has $N_x + N_y$ wrap around links where the network size is $N_x \times N_y$. These long wrap around links results a significant amount of wires. Therefore, 2-D torus network possess maximum wire length among the networks. Though the diameter of 2-D torus is better than other networks which is 16, there is no wonder that it includes the maximum static operating cost among the networks which is 6767.2.

TESH (2,2,0) is a hierarchical network. It has optimized architecture combined of 2-D mesh and 2-D torus network. Hence, the wiring complexity and total wire length both are optimized for this network. As a result, TESH network has smaller diameter than mesh network and slightly higher than MMN and 2-D torus network. But, TESH require less wire than 2-D torus network. Eventually, TESH has less static operating cost than mesh and 2-D torus network and higher than MMN and it is 5333.79.

Like TESH (2,2,0), MMN (2,2,0) is also a hierarchical network. MMN has the combination of mesh and midimew networks for the architecture. Now, mesh is

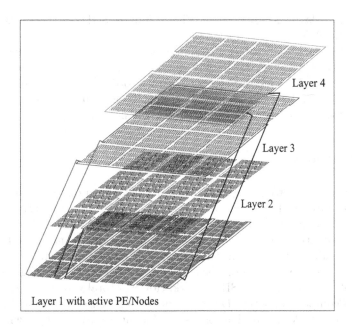

Fig. 5. Metal layers to implement MMN

the simplest network among all grid networks and midimew network has minimum diameter among all degree 4 networks. Hence, MMN is a perfect example of optimized network. So, naturally MMN has optimized diameter and total wire length. It possess less amount of communication links. Also the communication links increase with higher levels only not with the grid size. Therefore, MMN has better static operating cost than mesh, 2-D torus and TESH network and that is 4478.31.

Table 2. Comparison of Static Network Performance of Various Networks [15]

Network	Node Degree	Diameter	Average Distance	Ark Connectivity	Bisection Width
2D-Mesh	4	30	10.67	2	16
2D-Torus	4	16	8	4	32
TESH(2,2,0)	4	21	10.47	2	8
MMN(2,2,0)	4	17	9.07	2	8

The MMN can be implemented either on a 2-D or 3-D metal plane. For the case of 2-D plane, the network can be implemented on one metal layer only. In this case the implemented network will have a lot of jump crossing junction among the links. Jump crossing links cause serious affects. Therefore, multiple layers is a solution to avoid jump crossing of links. We have implemented the MMN on 4 layer 2-D plane [19]. Figure 5 depicts the metal layers used to implement the MMN.

Despite the fact that MMN consumes more wires to be constructed than mesh and TESH network, MMN has smaller diameter than mesh and TESH [15]. As a result, MMN possesses better static operating cost. Hence, among these networks, MMN is the optimal network in the context of static network performance and required wire to implement the network.

4 Conclusion

The architecture and wire length of the MMN have been discussed in detail. In addition the wire length evaluation of 2-D mesh, 2-D torus and TESH are also explored and compared with MMN as well. It is shown that the MMN possess a simple architecture, composed of 2-D mesh and midimew network. From the wire length evaluation, it is clear that, the MMN presents moderate wire length in total with fixed degree nodes. The total wire length of MMN is slightly higher than that of 2-D mesh and TESH network. However total wire length of MMN is far lower in comparison with 2-D torus. This paper focused on the architectural structure and wire length evaluation. Issues for future work include wire length evaluation of MMN in a 3-D environment.

Acknowledgments. This work is partly supported by FRGS13-065-0306, Ministry of Education, Government of Malaysia. The authors would like to thank the anonymous reviewers for their constructive comments and suggestions on the paper which have helped to improve the quality of the paper.

References

1. Koomey, J.G., Berard, S., Sanchez, M., Wong, H.: Assessing trends in the electrical efficiency of computation over time. In: IEEE Annals of the History of Computing (2009)
2. Beckman, P.: Looking toward exascale computing. In: 9th International Conference on Parallel and Distributed Computing, Applications and Technologies, p. 3 (2008)
3. Yang, Y., Funahashi, A., Jouraku, A., Nishi, H., Amano, H., Sueyoshi, T.: Recursive diagonal torus: an interconnection network for massively parallel computers. IEEE Transactions on Parallel and Distributed Systems 12, 701–715 (2001)
4. Rahman, M.M., Hafizur., J.X., Masud, M.A., Horiguchi, S.: Network performance of pruned hierarchical torus network. In: 6th IFIP International Conference on Network and Parallel Computing, pp. 9–15 (2009)
5. Abd-El-Barr, M., Al-Somani, T.F.: Topological properties of hierarchical interconnection networks: a review and comparison. J. Elec. and Comp. Engineering 1 (2011)
6. Lai, P.L., Hsu, H.C., Tsai, C.H., Stewart, I.A.: A class of hierarchical graphs as topologies for interconnection networks. J. Theoretical Computer Science 411, 2912–2924 (2010)

7. Liu, Y., Li, C., Han, J.: RTTM: a new hierarchical interconnection network for massively parallel computing. In: Zhang, W., Chen, Z., Douglas, C.C., Tong, W. (eds.) HPCA 2009. LNCS, vol. 5938, pp. 264–271. Springer, Heidelberg (2010)

8. Rahman, M.M.H., Horiguchi, S.: HTN: a new hierarchical interconnection network for massively parallel computers. IEICE Transactions on Information and Systems 86(9), 1479–1486 (2003)

9. Jain, V.K., Ghirmai, T., Horiguchi, S.: TESH: A new hierarchical interconnection network for massively parallel computing. IEICE Transactions on Information and Systems 80, 837–846 (1997)

10. Dally, W.J.: Performance Analysis of k-ary n-cube Interconnection Networks. IEEE Trans. on Computers 39(6), 775–785 (1990)

11. Chi-Hsiang, Y., Parhami, B., Emmanouel, A., Varvarigos, E.A., Hua Lee, H.: VLSI layout and packaging of butterfly networks. In: Proceedings of the Twelfth Annual ACM Symposium on Parallel Algorithms and Architectures, pp. 196–205 (2000)

12. Dally, W.J., Towles, B.: Route packets, not wires: On-chip interconnection networks. In: Proceedings of Design Automation Conference, pp. 684–689 (2001)

13. Parhami, B.: Introduction to parallel processing: algorithms and architectures, vol. 1. Springer (1999)

14. Parhami, B., Kwai, D.M.: Challenges in Interconnection Network Design In the Era of Multiprocessor and Massively Parallel Microchips. In: Proc. Int'l Conf. Communications in Computing, pp. 241–246 (2000)

15. Awal, M.R., Rahman, M.H., Akhand, M.A.H.: A New Hierarchical Interconnection Network for Future Generation Parallel Computer. In: Proceedings of 16th International Conference on Computers and Information Technology, pp. 314–319 (2013)

16. Camarero, C., Martinez, C., Beivide, R.: L-networks: A topological model for regular two-dimensional interconnection networks. IEEE Transactions on Computers 62, 1362–1375 (2012)

17. Puente, V., Izu, C., Gregorio, J.A., Beivide, R., Prellezo, J., Vallejo, F.: Improving parallel system performance by changing the arrangement of the network links. In: Proceedings of the 14th International Conference on Supercomputing, pp. 44–53 (2000)

18. Howard, J., Dighe, S., Vangal, S.R., Ruhl, G., Borkar, N., Jain, S., Erraguntla, V., Konow, M., Riepen, M., Gries, M., Droege, G., Larsen, T.L., Steibl, S., Borkar, S., De, V.K., Wijngaart, R.V.D.: A 48-core IA-32 processor in 45 nm CMOS using on-die message-passing and DVFS for performance and power scaling. IEEE Journal of Solid-State Circuits 46(1), 173–183 (2011)

19. Awal, M.R., Rahman, M.H.: Network-on-Chip Implementation of Midimew-Connected Mesh Network. In: Proceedings of 14th International Conference on Parallel and Distributed Computing, Applications and Technology, pp. 265–271 (2013)

Benchmarking the Memory Hierarchy of Modern GPUs

Xinxin Mei, Kaiyong Zhao, Chengjian Liu, and Xiaowen Chu

Department of Computer Science, Hong Kong Baptist University
{xxmei,kyzhao,cscjliu,chxw}@comp.hkbu.edu.hk

Abstract. Memory access efficiency is a key factor for fully exploiting the computational power of Graphics Processing Units (GPUs). However, many details of the GPU memory hierarchy are not released by the vendors. We propose a novel fine-grained benchmarking approach and apply it on two popular GPUs, namely Fermi and Kepler, to expose the previously unknown characteristics of their memory hierarchies. Specifically, we investigate the structures of different cache systems, such as data cache, texture cache, and the translation lookaside buffer (TLB). We also investigate the impact of bank conflict on shared memory access latency. Our benchmarking results offer a better understanding on the mysterious GPU memory hierarchy, which can help in the software optimization and the modelling of GPU architectures. Our source code and experimental results are publicly available.

1 Introduction

GPUs have become popular parallel computing accelerators; but their further performance enhancement is limited by the sophisticated memory system [1–6]. In order to reduce the default memory access consumption, developers usually utilize some specially designed memory spaces empirically [3–5]. It is necessary to have a clear and comprehensive documentation on the memory hierarchy. Despite the need, many details of memory access mechanism are not released by the manufacturers. To learn the undisclosed characteristics through third-party benchmarks becomes compelling.

Some researchers benchmarked the memory system of earlier GPU architectures [7–10]. They studied the memory latencies and revealed cache/translation lookaside buffer (TLB) structures. According to reports from vendor, recent generations of GPUs, such as Fermi, Kepler and Maxwell show significant improvement on memory access efficiency [11–16]. The memory hierarchies are different from those of earlier generations. To the best of our knowledge, a state-of-art work remains vacant.

In this paper, we explore the memory hierarchies of modern GPUs: Fermi and Kepler. We design a series of benchmarks to investigate their structures. Our experimental results confirm the superiority of recent architectures in memory access efficiency. Our contributions are summarized as follows:

C.-H. Hsu et al. (Eds.): NPC 2014, LNCS 8707, pp. 144–156, 2014.

Table 1. Comparison of NVIDIA Tesla, Fermi and Kepler GPUs

Generation	Tesla	Fermi	Kepler
Device	GeForce GTX 280	GeForce GTX 560 Ti	GeForce GTX 780
Compute Capacity	1.3	2.1	3.5
Shared Memory	size: 16 KB bank No: 16 bank width: 4 byte	size: 16/48 KB bank No: 32 bank width: 4 byte	size: 16/32/48 KB bank No: 32 bank width: 4/8 byte
Global Memory	non-cached . size: 1024 MB	cached in L1&L2 L1 cache size: 64 KB sub- tract shared memory size; L2 cache size: 512 KB size: 1024 MB	cached in L2 or read-only data cache L1 cache size: 64 KB sub- tract shared memory size; L2 cache size: 1536 KB size: 3071 MB
Texture Memory	per-TPC texture units	per-SM texture units	per-SM texture units

1. We develop a novel fine-grained P-chase benchmark to expose GPU cache and TLB features.

2. Based on the benchmark, we find a number of unconventional designs not disclosed by previous literatures, such as the special replacement policy of Fermi L1 data cache, 2D spacial locality optimized set-associative mapping of texture L1 cache and the unequal L2 TLB sets.

3. Our source code and experimental results are publicly available.[1]

The remainder of this paper is organized as follows. Section 2 introduces some background knowledge of GPU memory hierarchy. Section 3 presents our fine-grained benchmark design. Section 4 discusses the microarchitecture of various memory spaces of Fermi and Kepler. We conclude our work in Section 5.

2   Background: Modern GPU Memory Hierarchy

In the popular GPU programming model, CUDA (compute unified device architecture), there are six memory spaces, namely, register, shared memory, constant memory, texture memory, local memory and global memory. Their functions are described in [14–18]. In this paper, we limit our scope to the discussion of three common but still mysterious ones: shared memory, global memory and texture memory. Specifically, we aim at disclosing the impact of bank conflict on shared memory access latency, and the cache mechanism and latency of global/texture memory.

In Table 1, we compare the memory characteristics of the Tesla GPU discussed in [8, 9] and our two targeting GPU platforms. The *compute capacity* is used by NVIDIA to distinguish the generations. The Fermi devices are of compute capacity 2.x, and the Kepler devices are of 3.x. The two GPU cards we use, MSI N560GTX-Ti Hawk (repack of GeForce GTX 560 Ti) and GIGABYTE GeForce GTX 780 (repack of GeForce GTX 780), are of compute capacity 2.1 and 3.5 respectively. As we can find in Table 1, the most distinctive difference is the global memory. On Tesla devices, the global memory access is non-cached while on Fermi devices, it is cached in both L1 and L2 data cache. Kepler has

---

[1] http://www.comp.hkbu.edu.hk/~chxw/gpu_benchmark.html

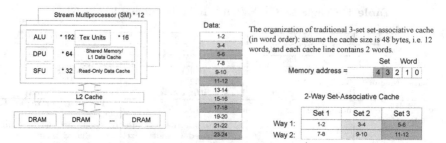

Fig. 1. Block Diagram of GeForce GTX 780

Fig. 2. Traditional Set-Associative Cache

L1 data cache; but it is designed for local memory accesses rather than global memory accesses. Besides L2 data cache, Kepler global memory accesses can be cached in read-only data cache for compute capacity 3.5 or above. It is also notable that modern GPUs have larger shared memory spaces and more shared memory banks. Tesla shared memory size is fixed as 16 KB. On Fermi and Kepler devices, shared memory and L1 data cache share a total of 64 KB memory space. The texture memory is cached in all generations. Tesla texture units are shared by three streaming multiprocessors (SMs), namely a thread processing cluster (TPC). However, Fermi and Kepler texture units are per-SM.

As shown in Fig. 1, the shared memory, L1 data cache and the read-only data cache are on-chip, i.e., they are within SMs. L2 cache and DRAMs are off-chip. The L2 cache is accessed by all the SMs, and a GPU board has several DRAM chips.

For ease of reference, we also review some fundamentals of cache systems. The cache backs up a piece of main memory on-chip to offer very instant memory accesses. Due to the performance-cost tradeoff, the cache sizes are limited. Fig. 2 shows the structure of a traditional set-associative cache. Data is loaded from main memory to cache at the granularity of a cache line. Memory addressing decides the location in the cache of a particular copy of main memory. For set-associative cache, each line in the main memory is mapped into a fixed cache set and can appear at any cache ways of the corresponding set. For example, in Fig. 2, word 1-2 can be in way 1 or way 2 of the first cache set. If the required data is stored in cache, there is a cache hit, otherwise a cache miss. When the cache is full and a cache miss occurs, some existing contents in the cache is replaced by the required data. One popular replacement policy is least-recently used (LRU), which replaces the least recently accessed cache line. Modern architectures usually have multi-level and multi-functional caches. In this paper, we discuss the data cache and TLB (cache for virtual-to-physical memory translation page tables). Previous cache studies all assume a cache model of equal cache sets, typical set-associative addressing and LRU replacement policy [7–10, 19, 20]. Based on our experimental results, such model is sometimes incorrect for GPU cache systems.

3 Methodology

3.1 Shared Memory Bank Conflict: Stride Memory Access

GPU shared memory is divided into banks. Successive words are allocated to successive banks. If some threads belonging to the same warp access memory spaces in the same bank, bank conflict occurs.

```
for ( i=0;i <= iterations; i++ ) {
    data=threadIdx.x*stride;
    if(i==1) sum = 0; //omit cold miss
    start_time = clock();
    repeat64( data=sdata[data];); //64 times of stride access
    end_time = clock();
    sum += (end_time − start_time);
}
```

Listing 1. Shared Memory Stride Access

To study the impact of bank conflict on shared memory access latency, we utilize the stride memory access introduced in [15]. We launch a warp of threads on GPU. Listing 1 is the kernel code of our shared memory benchmark. We multiply the thread id with an integer, called *stride*, to get a shared memory address. We do 64 times of such memory accesses and record the total time consumption. This consumption is actually the summation of 63 times of shared memory access and 64 times of *clock*() overhead. We then calculate the average memory latency of each memory access. If a bank conflict occurs, average memory latency is much longer.

3.2 Cache Structure: Fine-Grained Benchmark

The P-chase benchmark is the most classical method to explore cache memory hierarchy [7–10, 19, 20]. Its core idea is to traverse an array A by executing $j = A[j]$ with some stride. The array elements are initialized with the indices of the next memory access. We measure the time consumption of a great number of such memory accesses and calculate the average consumption of each access. Listing 2 and Listing 3 give the P-chase kernel and the array initialization respectively. The memory access pattern can be inferred from the average memory access latency. The smallest memory latency indicates cache hit and bigger latencies indicate cache misses.

For simplicity, we define the notations for cache and P-chase parameters in Table 2. Note that we access GPU memory k times but only N/s array elements are accessed ($k >> N/s$). Memory access pattern is decided by the combination of N and s [19].

Saavedra et al. varied both N and s in one experiment to study CPU memory hierarchy [19, 20]. Volkov et al. applied the same method on a G80 GPU [7]. Wong et al. developed the footprint experiment: fixing s and varying N, to study the multi-level caches one by one of a Tesla GPU [8, 9]. Recently, Meltzer et al. used both Saavedra's and Wong's footprint experiment to investigate Fermi L1 and L2 data cache structure [10]. They utilized Saavedra's method to get an overall idea and then analyzed each cache structure with footprint experiment. Experimental results based on the two methods coincided with each other perfectly in [10]. However, we got different results of cache line size of texture L1 cache when we applied the two methods. What happened?

The problem is caused by the usage of total or average time consumption. It indicates the existence of cache miss, but little information on the miss percentage or the causes of cache miss. In order to get all the information, we need to know the full memory access process. Motivated by the above, we design a fine-grained benchmark utilizing GPU shared memory to display the latency of every memory access.

```
start_time = clock();
for(it=0;it<iterations;it++){
    j=A[j];
}
end_time=clock();
    //average memory latency
tvalue=(end_time−start_time)/
    iteration;
```

Listing 2. P-chase Kernel

```
__global__ void KernelFunction(...){
    //declare shared memory space
    __shared__ unsigned int s_tvalue[];
    __shared__ unsigned int s_index[];

    for(it=0;it<iterations;it++) {
        start_time=clock();
        j=my_array[j];
            //store the element index
        s_index[it]=j;
        end_time=clock();
            //store the access latency
        s_tvalue[it]=end_time−start_time;
    }
}
```

Listing 4. Fine-grained P-chase Kernel

```
for(i=0;i<array_size;i++){
    A[i]=(i+stride)%array_size
    ;
}
```

Listing 3. Array Initialization

Listing 4 gives the kernel code of our fine-grained benchmark. We launch one thread on GPU devices each time. By repeatedly executing $j = my\_array[j]$, the thread visits the array elements whose indices are multiples of s. For ease of analysis, we also record the visited array indices. We time each procedure of reading the array element and storing the index into the shared memory. Because the CUDA compiler automatically omit meaningless data readings, we need to write the shared memory with the updated index, namely the index of the next element rather than of the current one [15]. In addition, for operations of calling *clock*() and writing shared memory are synchronous, to get convincible memory latency, we need to imbed writing shared memory in the timing. Although this brings extra measurement error, the error is relatively small compared with the memory latency and does not affect the disclosure of memory structures.

Specifically, we apply our benchmark with strategies below to get the cache characteristics. N and s are calculated on every word (i.e., the length of an unsigned integer) basis.

(1) Determine C: $s = 1$. We initialize N with a small value and increase it gradually until cache misses appear. C equals the maximum N where all memory accesses fit in the cache.

Table 2. Notations for Cache and P-chase Parameters

Notation	Description	Notation	Description
C	cache size	N	array size
b	cache line size	s	stride size
a	No. of cache sets	k	iterations

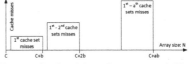

Fig. 3. Cache Miss Patterns of Various N

(2) Determine b: $s = 1$. We begin with $N = C + 1$ and increase N gradually again. When $N < C + b + 1$, only memory accesses to the first cache set are missed. If $N = C + b + 1$, memory accesses to the second cache set are also missed. Based on the increase of missed cache lines, we can find b.

(3) Determine a: $s = b$. We start with $N = C$ and increase N at the granularity of b. The cache miss patterns are decided by N, as shown in Fig. 3. Every increment of N causes cache misses of a new cache set. When $N > C + (a - 1)b$, all cache sets are missed. We can get a from cache miss patterns accordingly. The cache associativity, i.e., number of cache ways, equals $C/(ab)$.

(4) Determine cache replacement policy. In our fine-grained benchmark, we set $k > N/s$ so that we traverse the array multiple times. Because the array elements are accessed in order, if the cache replacement policy is LRU, then the memory access process should be periodic. For example, given a cache shown in Fig. 2, $N = 13$ and $s = 1$, the memory access pattern is repeated every 13 data loadings: whenever we visit the ith array element, it is fixed as a cache miss/hit. If the memory access process is aperiodic, then the replacement policy cannot be LRU. Under this circumstance, we set $N = C + b, s = b$, and follow the full memory access process with a considerable k. All cache misses belong to the first cache set. Because we also have information of accessed array indices, we can find which cache line is replaced of every cache miss. Based on this method, we get the particular Fermi L1 data cache replacement policy.

In addition, we design a special array initialization with non-uniform strides. We are motivated to exhibit as many memory latencies as possible within one experiment, similar with [19]. We apply this initialization on studying various global memory latencies. We manually fill the array elements with the indices rather than execute Listing 3.

To conclude, we propose a fine-grained benchmark that utilizes GPU shared memory to store all memory access latencies. This benchmark enables exhaustive study of GPU cache structures. We explore the global memory and texture memory hierarchy with our fine-grained benchmark. We also design a sophisticated array initialization to exhibit various memory latencies within one experiment.

Experimental Platform: the CPU is Intel Core^{TM} i7-3820 @3.60 GHz with PCI-e 3.0. Our operating system is a 64-bit CentOS release 6.4. CUDA runtime/driver version is 5.5. We use CUDA compiler driver NVCC, with options -arch=sm_21 and -arch=sm_35 to compile all our files on Fermi and Kepler devices respectively.

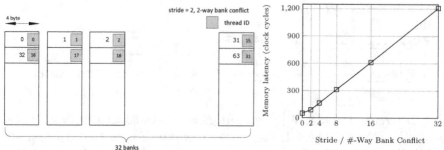

Fig. 4. Fermi Shared Memory Banks

Fig. 5. Latency of Fermi Bank Conflict

4   Experimental Results

4.1   Shared Memory

GPU shared memory is on-chip and non-cached. In many CUDA applications, researchers utilize shared memory to speed up memory accesses [3–5]. However, based on our experimental results, the shared memory access can be slower than global memory access if there are considerable bank conflicts. In this section, we investigate the impact of bank conflict on shared memory access latency.

Fig. 4 illustrates a 2-way bank conflict caused by stride memory access on Fermi architecture. The bank width is 4-byte. E.g., word 0 and word 32 are mapped into the same bank. If the stride is 2, thread 0 and thread 16 will visit word 0 and word 32 respectively, causing a bank conflict. The way of bank conflict equals the greatest common divisor of stride and 32. There is no bank conflict for odd strides.

In Fig. 5, we plot the average shared memory latency of Fermi. If stride is 0, i.e., the data is broadcasted [15], memory latency is about 50 cycles. Memory latency increases to 88 cycles for 2-way bank conflict, and 1210 cycles for 32-way bank conflict. The increment indicates that memory loads of different spaces in the same bank are executed sequentially. GPU kernel efficiency could be seriously degraded when there are considerable bank conflicts.

Kepler shared memory outperforms Fermi in terms of avoiding bank conflicts [18]. Kepler improves shared memory access efficiency by introducing the 8-byte wide bank. The bank width can be configured by calling *cudaDeviceSetShared-MemConfig()* [15]. Fig. 6 gives a comparison of memory mapping between the two modes: 4-byte and 8-byte. We use 32-bit data so that each bank row contains two words. In 8-byte mode, 64 successive integers are mapped into 32 successive banks. In 4-byte mode, 32 successive integers are mapped into 32 successive banks. Different from Fermi, bank conflict is only caused by two or more threads accessing different bank rows.

Fig. 7 shows the Kepler shared memory latency with even strides of both 4-byte and 8-byte modes. When stride is 2, there is no bank conflict for either 4-byte or 8-byte mode, whereas there is 2-way bank conflict on Fermi. When stride

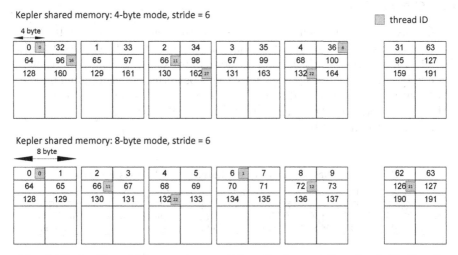

Fig. 6. Kepler Shared Memory Access: 4-Byte Bank v.s. 8-Byte Bank (Stride=6)

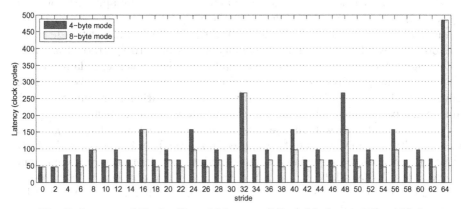

Fig. 7. Latency of Kepler Shared Memory: 4-Byte Mode v.s. 8-Byte Mode

is 4, there is 2-way bank conflict, half as Fermi. When stride is 6, there is 2-way bank conflict for 4-byte mode but no bank conflict for 8-byte mode. We illustrate this situation in Fig. 6. For 4-byte mode, half of the shared memory banks are visited. Thread i and thread $i + 16$ are accessing separate rows of the same bank ($i = 0, ..., 15$). For 8-byte mode, 32 threads visit 32 banks without conflict. Similarly, 8-byte mode is superior to 4-byte mode for other even strides whose number is not a power of two.

In summary, Kepler can provide higher shared memory access efficiency by the following two ways. First, compared with Fermi, 4-byte mode Kepler shared memory can halve the chance of bank conflict. Second, 8-byte mode further reduces bank conflict.

4.2 Global Memory

The CUDA term, global memory, includes physical memory spaces of DRAM, L1 and L2 cache. Previous studies show that there are two levels of TLB: L1 TLB and L2 TLB to support GPU virtual memory addressing [7–9]. In this section, we first exhibit memory latencies of various access patterns. We visit global memory spaces with non-uniform strides to collect as many access patterns as possible within one experiment. We then focus on the architectures of micro units, such as L1 data cache and TLB.

Table 3. Global Memory Access Latencies of Various Patterns

Pattern	1	2	3	4	5	6	Pattern	1	2	3	4	5	6
Kepler	230	236	289	371	734	1000	Data cache	hit	hit	hit	miss	miss	miss
Fermi: L1 enabled	116	404	488	655	1259	–	L1 TLB	hit	miss	miss	hit	miss	miss
Fermi: L1 disabled	371	398	482	639	1245	–	L2 TLB	–	hit	miss	–	miss	miss

Global Memory Latency. We collect global memory latencies of six access patterns in Table 3. Fermi global memory accesses are cached in both L1 and L2 data cache. The L1 data cache can be manually disabled by applying compiler option *-Xptxas -dlcm=cg*. We measure the memory latencies with Fermi L1 data cache both enabled and disabled, as listed in the last two rows of left side table.

Note that Kepler gets a unique memory access pattern (pattern 6 in Table 3) of page table context switching. We find that when a kernel is launched on Kepler, only memory page entries of 512 MB are activated. If the thread visits a page entry that is inactivated, the hardware needs a rather long time to switch among the page tables. This is so-called page table "miss" in [10].

View from Table 3, on Fermi devices, if the data is cached in L1, the L1 TLB miss penalty is 288 cycles. If data is cached in L2, the L1 TLB miss penalty is 27 cycles. Because the latter penalty is much smaller, we infer that physical memory places of L1 TLB and L2 data cache are close. Similarly, physical memory places of L1 TLB and L2 TLB are also close, which means that L1/L2 TLB and L2 data cache are off-chip shared by all SMs.

We can also find that unless the L1 data cache is hit, caching in L1 does not really save time. For four out of five patterns, enabling L1 data cache is about 6 or 15 clock cycles slower than disabling it.

Another interesting finding is that unless Fermi L1 data cache is hit, Kepler is about 1.5-2 times faster than Fermi although it does not utilize L1 data cache. Kepler has much smaller L2 data cache memory latency, L2 data cache miss penalty and L1/L2 TLB miss penalty. It confirms the superiority of Kepler in terms of memory access efficiency.

Fermi L1 Data Cache. We list the characteristics of Fermi L1 data cache and some other common caches in Table 4. Fermi cache can be either 16 KB or 48 KB, and we only report the 16 KB case in this paper due to limited space. According to [10], cache associativity is 6 if it is configured as 48 KB .

Table 4. Common GPU Cache Characteristics

Parameters	Fermi L1 data cache	Fermi/Kepler L1 TLB	Fermi/Kepler L2 TLB	Fermi/Kepler texture L1 cache
N	16 KB	32 MB	130 MB	12 KB
b	128 byte	2 MB	2 MB	32 byte
a	32	1	7	4
LRU	no	yes	yes	yes

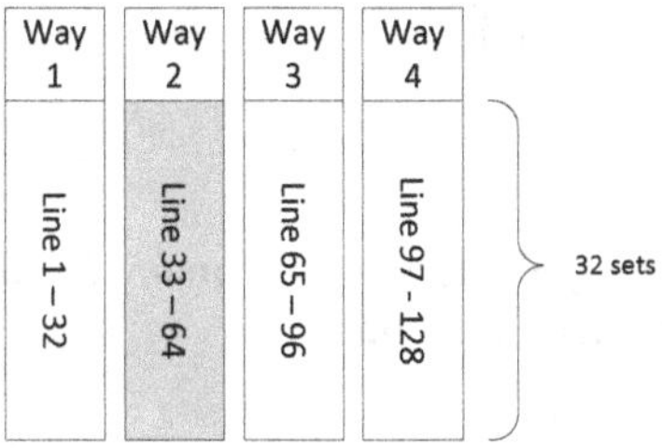

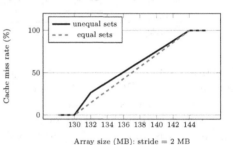

Fig. 8. Fermi L1 Cache Mapping

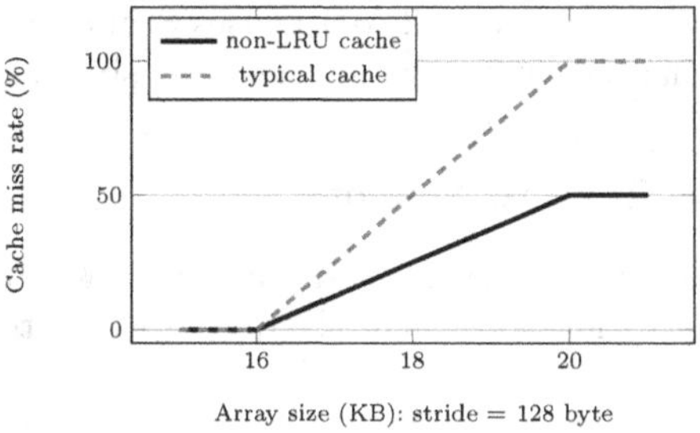

Fig. 9. Miss Rate of Non-LRU Cache

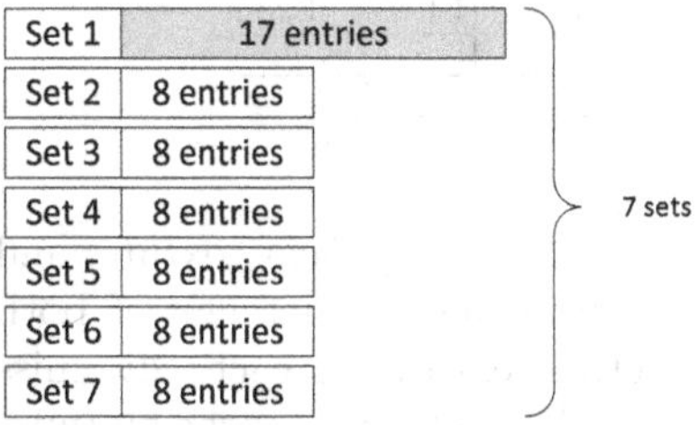

Fig. 10. Kepler/Fermi L2 TLB Structure

Fig. 11. Miss Rate of Unequal-Set Cache

One distinctive feature of Fermi L1 cache is that its replacement policy is not LRU, because the memory access process is aperiodic. We apply our fine-grained benchmark on arrays varying from 16 KB to 24 KB to study the replacement policy. Fig. 8 gives the L1 cache structure based on our experimental results. L1 cache has 128 cache lines mapped into way 1-4. Of all 32 sets, one cache way has triple the chance to be replaced than other three ways. It is updated every two cache misses. In our experiment, way 2 is replaced most frequently. The replacement probabilities of the four cache ways are $\frac{1}{6}, \frac{1}{2}, \frac{1}{6}, \frac{1}{6}$ respectively.

Fig. 9 shows the effect of the non-LRU replacement policy. The y-axis label, cache miss rate, is obtained from dividing the missed cache lines by the total cache lines. For the traditional cache, the maximum cache miss rate should be 100% [9, 19] yet the non-LRU Fermi cache has a maximum miss rate of 50% based on our experimental result.

Fermi/Kepler TLBs. Based on our experimental results, Fermi and Kepler have the same TLB structure: L1 TLB is 16-way fully-associative and L2 TLB is set-associative with 65 ways. The L2 TLB has unequal cache sets as shown in Fig. 10.

We plot the L2 TLB miss rate in Fig. 11. For the traditional cache, the miss rate increases linearly while the measured miss rate increases piecewise linearly: $N = 132$ MB causes 17 missed entries at once and varying N from 134 MB to 144 MB with $s = 2$ MB causes 8 more missed entries each time. Thus the big set has 17 entries, while the other six sets have 8 entries.

4.3   Texture Memory

Texture memory is read-only and cached. Fermi/Kepler texture memory also has two levels of cache. Here we discuss texture L1 cache only.

Table 5. Texture Memory Access Latency

Device	Texture cache		Global cache	
	L1 hit	L1 miss, L2 hit	L1 hit	L1 miss, L2 hit
Fermi	240	470	116	404
Kepler	110	220	–	230

Texture L1 Cache. We bind an unsigned integer array to linear texture, and fetch it with *tex1Dfetch()*. We measure the texture memory latency of both Fermi and Kepler as listed in Table 5. The Fermi texture L1 cache hit/miss consumption is about 240/470 clock cycles and Kepler texture L1 cache hit/miss consumption is about 110/220 clock cycles. The latter one is about two times faster.

In Table 5, we also find that Fermi texture L1 cache access is much slower than global L1 data cache access. In contrast, Kepler texture memory management is of low cost.

In addition, our experimental results suggest a special set-associative addressing as shown in Fig. 12. The 12 KB cache can store up to 384 cache lines. Each line contains 8 integers/words. 32 successive words/128 successive bytes are mapped into successive cache sets. The 7-8th bits of memory address define the cache set, while in traditional cache design, the 5-6th bits define the cache set. Each cache set contains 96 cache lines. The replacement policy is LRU. This mapping is optimized for 2D spatial locality [14]. Threads of the same warp should visit close memory addresses to achieve best performance, otherwise there would be more cache misses.

5   Conclusions

In this paper, we have explored many unexposed features of memory system of Fermi and Kepler GPUs. Our fine-grained benchmark on global memory and

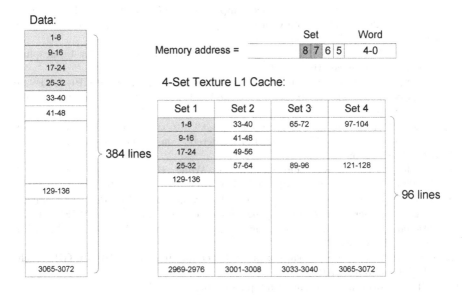

Fig. 12. Fermi & Kepler Texture L1 Cache Optimized Set-Associative Mapping

texture memory revealed some untraditional designs used to be ignored. We also explained the advantage of Kepler's shared memory over Fermi. We consider our work inspiring for both GPU application optimization and performance modeling. However, our work still has two limitations. First, we restrict ourselves to single thread or single warp memory access. The memory latency could be much different due to the multi-warp scheduling. Second, due to our preliminary experimental results on L2 cache investigation, the L2 cache design is even more complicated. Our fine-grained benchmark is incapable of L2 cache study due to the limited shared memory size. We leave these two aspects for our future study.

Acknowledgement. This research work is partially supported by Hong Kong GRF grant HKBU 210412 and FRG grant FRG2/13-14/052.

References

1. Li, Q., Zhong, C., Zhao, K., Mei, X., Chu, X.: Implementation and analysis of AES encryption on GPU. In: 2012 IEEE 14th International Conference on High Performance Computing and Communication 2012 IEEE 9th International Conference on Embedded Software and Systems (HPCC-ICESS), pp. 843–848 (2012)
2. Chu, X., Zhao, K., Wang, M.: Practical random linear network coding on GPUs. In: Fratta, L., Schulzrinne, H., Takahashi, Y., Spaniol, O. (eds.) NETWORKING 2009. LNCS, vol. 5550, pp. 573–585. Springer, Heidelberg (2009)
3. Li, Y., Zhao, K., Chu, X., Liu, J.: Speeding up K-Means algorithm by GPUs. Journal of Computer and System Sciences 79, 216–229 (2013)

4. Micikevicius, P.: 3D finite difference computation on GPUs using CUDA. In: Proceedings of 2nd Workshop on General Purpose Processing on Graphics Processing Units, pp. 79–84. ACM (2009)
5. Zhao, K., Chu, X.: G-BLASTN: accelerating nucleotide alignment by graphics processors. Bioinformatics (2014)
6. Mei, X., Yung, L.S., Zhao, K., Chu, X.: A measurement study of GPU DVFS on energy conservation. In: Proceedings of the Workshop on Power-Aware Computing and Systems, vol. (10). ACM (2013)
7. Volkov, V., Demmel, J.W.: Benchmarking GPUs to tune dense linear algebra. In: Proceedings of the 2008 ACM/IEEE Conference on Supercomputing, vol. (31). IEEE Press (2008)
8. Papadopoulou, M., Sadooghi-Alvandi, M., Wong, H.: Micro-benchmarking the GT200 GPU. Computer Group, ECE, University of Toronto, Tech. Rep. (2009)
9. Wong, H., Papadopoulou, M.M., Sadooghi-Alvandi, M., Moshovos, A.: Demystifying GPU microarchitecture through microbenchmarking. In: 2010 IEEE International Symposium on Performance Analysis of Systems & Software (ISPASS), pp. 235–246. IEEE (2010)
10. Meltzer, R., Zeng, C., Cecka, C.: Micro-benchmarking the C2070. In: GPU Technology Conference (2013)
11. NVIDIA Corporation: Fermi Whitepaper (2009)
12. NVIDIA Corporation: Kepler GK110 Whitepaper (2012)
13. NVIDIA Corporation: Tuning CUDA Applications for Kepler (2013)
14. NVIDIA Corporation: CUDA C Best Practices Guide - v6.0 (2014)
15. NVIDIA Corporation: CUDA C Programming Guide - v6.0 (2014)
16. NVIDIA Corporation: Tuning CUDA Applications for Maxwell (2014)
17. Micikevicius, P.: Local Memory and Register Spilling. NVIDIA Corporation (2011)
18. Micikevicius, P.: GPU performance analysis and optimization. In: GPU Technology Conference (2012)
19. Saavedra, R.H.: CPU Performance Evaluation and Execution Time Prediction Using Narrow Spectrum Benchmarking. PhD thesis, EECS Department, University of California, Berkeley (1992)
20. Saavedra, R.H., Smith, A.J.: Measuring cache and TLB performance and their effect on benchmark runtimes. IEEE Transactions on Computers 44, 1223–1235 (1995)

Parallel CYK Membership Test on GPUs

Kyoung-Hwan Kim[1], Sang-Min Choi[1], Hyein Lee[1], Ka Lok Man[2],
and Yo-Sub Han[1,*]

[1] Department of Computer Science, Yonsei University, Seoul, Republic of Korea
{kyounghwan,jerassi,hyein,emmous}@cs.yonsei.ac.kr
[2] Department of Computer Science and Software Engineering,
Xian Jiaotong-Liverpool University, Suzhou, China
ka.man@xjtlu.edu.cn

Abstract. Nowadays general-purpose computing on graphics processing units (GPGPUs) performs computations what were formerly handled by the CPU using hundreds of cores on GPUs. It often improves the performance of sequential computation when the running program is well-structured and formulated for massive threading. The CYK algorithm is a well-known algorithm for the context-free language membership test and has been used in many applications including grammar inferences, compilers and natural language processing. We revisit the CYK algorithm and its structural properties suitable for parallelization. Based on the discovered properties, we then parallelize the algorithm using different combinations of memory types and data allocation schemes using a GPU. We evaluate the algorithm based on real-world data and herein demonstrate the performance improvement compared with CPU-based computations.

Keywords: Parallel Computing, Context-Free Language Membership Test, CYK Algorithm, GPU Programming, CUDA.

1 Introduction

Graphics Processing Unit (GPU) computing involves the use of a GPU to improve general-purpose scientific applications, that were formerly handled by a CPU. A GPU consists of processors with different instruction set architectures (ISAs). GPUs designed with massively parallel single instruction multiple threads (SIMT) are many-core processors that provide an effective performance through low-latency and high-bandwidth. The limits of program scalability are often related to some combination of memory bandwidth saturation, memory contention, imbalanced data distribution or data structure/algorithm interactions. For a better performance, researchers and developers have therefore suggested particular data structures and formulated problems specifically for massive threading. They executed massive threads by leveraging shared memory resources including [7,23]. There are a few tools that support general purpose computing for GPUs such as the Compute Unified Device Architecture

---

* Corresponding author.

C.-H. Hsu et al. (Eds.): NPC 2014, LNCS 8707, pp. 157–168, 2014.
© IFIP International Federation for Information Processing 2014

(CUDA) [18] and Open Computing Language (OpenCL) [13]. We considered the Cocke-Younger-Kasami (CYK) algorithm [6,12,22], which is popular for several application domains such as RNA secondary structure prediction [4] and grammatical inference [17], and implement parallel CYK algorithms using GPUs. Note that the runtime of the CYK algorithm is $O(|G|n^3)$, where n is the length of an input string and $|G|$ is the size of the input context-free grammar (CFG) [1]. Namely, the runtime of the CYK algorithm is closely related to the size of the grammar and the length of the input string. We investigated the possible grammar mapping methods for hundreds of cores in a GPU, which may give rise to an overall performance improvement of the CYK algorithm. In particular, we considered three mapping methods: rule-based, left-variable sorting and right-variable sorting mappings. We applied each mapping to different architectural features of GPUs such as zero-copy host memory, page-locked memory, shared memory and texture memory. We then evaluated the algorithm for different combinations of mapping methods and features. We ran our experiments on NVIDIA GPUs (GTX560Ti) with 384 cores using the dataset from the Berkeley parser [16] and Penn Treebank [14].

In Section 2, we revisit previous research on the parallelization of the CYK algorithm. We then recall CFG and the CYK algorithm in Section 3. We describe three mapping methods and four memory structures in Section 4. We then present our experimental results and an analysis from applying the four memory structures to each mapping method in Section 5. Finally, some concluding remarks regarding this research are given in Section 6.

2   Related Work

The CYK algorithm allows us to determine whether an input string is in an input context-free language. The algorithm has been widely used in several domains such as parsing, grammatical inference and bioinformatics. The CYK algorithm is a classical dynamic programming algorithm and there have been many attempts to parallelize it depending on the applications used. Table 1 shows previous studies.

3   CFG Membership Test

We briefly recall the definition of context-free languages and the CYK algorithm. For more details on these topics, the reader is referred to Hopcroft and Ullman [10].

3.1   Context-Free Languages

A CFG G is specified by the tuple $G = (V, \Sigma, P, S)$, where V is a set of variables, Σ is a set of terminals, P is a set of production rules and S is the start symbol. Given a CFG $G = (V, \Sigma, P, S)$, let $\alpha A \beta$ be a string derived from S where $A \in V$

Table 1. Related work on the parallel CYK implementation

Authors	Year	Summary
Takashi et al. [19]	1997	They suggested an agenda-based parallel CYK parser on a distributed-memory parallel machine that consists of 256 nodes (single processors). This approach uses a specific parallel language and parallelizes the CYK algorithm by allocating each cell of the CYK matrix into a processor.
Bordim et al. [3]	2002	They studied the CYK algorithm on field programmable gate arrays (FPGAs) and developed a hardware generator that creates a Verilog HDL source performing CYK parsing for a given CFG. Their approach considers 2,048 production rules and 64 variables in an input CFG and shows a speedup factor of almost 750×.
Johnson [11]	2011	The author examined the CYK algorithm for a dense probabilistic context-free grammars (PCFG) and constructed a dense PCFG with 32 variables and 32,768 production rules with random probability. The author reported an 18.4× speedup obtained on NVIDIA Fermi s2050 GPUs, and suggested a reduction method in one block for calculating the probability.
Dunlop et al. [8]	2011	They presented a matrix encoding of CFGs using a multiplication method for a matrix low-latency parallelized CYK algorithm. They encoded the grammars of CFG in a matrix form in which the rows are the left-hand side variable of the production and the columns are the right-hand side variables (pairs in CNF).
Yi et al. [21]	2014	They proposed an efficient parallel CYK algorithm for natural language parsing of PCFG on GPUs. A PCFG is a CFG in which each production is augmented with the probability. Their algorithm assigns each production rule of an input PCFG to each core in a GPU and finds the valid parsing rules quickly.

and α and β are strings from $(V \cup \Sigma)^*$. When $A \rightarrow \gamma$, we say that A is rewritten to γ and denote this derivation step by $\Rightarrow$ symbol: namely, $\alpha A \beta \Rightarrow \alpha \gamma \beta$. When there are zero or more steps of derivation, we denote this step by $\overset{*}{\Rightarrow}$ symbol. The language $L(G)$ of G is then a set of terminal strings derived from the start symbol S; namely, $L(G) = \{w \in \Sigma^* \mid S \overset{*}{\Rightarrow} w\}$. We can say that a CFG $G = (V, \Sigma, P, S)$ is in Chomsky Normal Form (CNF) if every production rule in P is either of form $A \rightarrow BC$ or $A \rightarrow a$, where $A, B, C \in V$ and $a \in \Sigma$ [5]. It is well-known that every CFG can be transformed in to CNF [10]. From now on, we assume that an input CFG is in CNF.

Procedure 1. CYK Algorithm

```
1: procedure CYK ALGORITHM(G = (V, Σ, P, S), w)
2:     initialize table M[n][n + 1][|V|];                    ▷ |V| is size of variables
3:     n = length of input string w
4:     for i = 0 to n − 1
5:         if {A ∈ V | A → wᵢ ∈ P}
6:             M[i][i + 1][A] = T                            ▷ Initialize with terminal rules
7:     end for
8:     for len = 2 to n
9:         transitionRule(M, n, len, G);                    ▷ Procedure 2
10:    end for
11:    if M[0][n][S] = T
12:        return true
13:    else
14:        return false
15:    end if
16: end procedure
```

3.2   CYK Algorithm

Given an input string $w = w_1 w_2 \cdots w_n \in \Sigma^*$ and a CFG $G = (V, \Sigma, P, S)$, the CYK algorithm, which is based on the bottom-up dynamic programming, determines whether w is in $L(G)$. The algorithm constructs a triangular table M in which each cell $M[i-1][j][A]$, for $A \in V$, is T if $A \stackrel{*}{\Rightarrow} w_i w_{i+1} \cdots w_j$ in G. Once all of M is computed, the algorithm checks whether $M[0][n][S] = \text{T}$.

Procedure 2. transitionRule

```
1: procedure TRANSRULE(M, n, len, G = (V, Σ, P, S))
2:     for i = 0 to n − len do                              ▷ Start Index
3:         j = i + len;                                      ▷ End Index
4:         foreach production A → BC ∈ P
5:             for split = i + 1 to j − 1
6:                 if M[i][split][B] =T do
7:                     if M[split][j][C] =T do
8:                         M[i][j][A] =T;
9:         end foreach
10:    end for
11: end procedure
```

First, we initialize the bottom level of the table using the terminal rules (line 5 and 6). The algorithm then proceeds to repeatedly apply all binary rules and builds up for the table using Procedure 2. As illustrated in Procedure 1, the algorithm fills up M and checks whether $M[0][n][S]$ is T.

Fig. 1 illustrates the CYK table M for the string $w = cabac$ with respect to a CFG $G = \{\{S, A, B, C\}, \{a, b, c\}, P, S\}$, where $P = \{S \rightarrow AB \mid b, A \rightarrow CB \mid AA \mid a, B \rightarrow AS \mid b, C \rightarrow BS \mid c\}$.

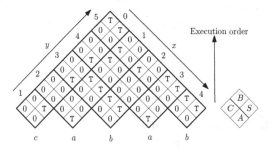

Fig. 1. An example of the CYK table for an input string, *cabab*

4   Our Approaches and Implementations

We next discuss the different implementations of Procedure 2 that account for the bulk of the overall execution time for the CYK algorithm. We consider three thread mappings, memory types for data access, and two data transfer methods.

4.1   Three Types of Thread Mappings

One of the important factors for designing parallel algorithms is how to map the input data to the threads for fast parallel processing. We consider the possible mappings of the grammar rules to the threads for the table cells or variables of the CYK algorithm. We select grammar rules for thread mapping instead of variables. Since the number of variables is usually fewer than the number of threads, it is possible to fail to provide enough parallelism to fully utilize the massive number of threads in GPUs. In addition, a load imbalance exists because of differences in the number of rules for each variables and it leads to different branches and degrades the performance. We can reduce the load imbalance by mapping the rules to the threads. There are three mapping methods used: rule-based, left-variable sorting ($\mathcal{LVS}$) and right-variable sorting ($\mathcal{RVS}$) mappings.

1. **Rule-Based Mapping:** We noticed that the **foreach** (line 4) loop in Procedure 2 is suitable for parallelization. We therefore simply map all rules in the input grammar to all available threads as described in Procedure 3.
2. $\mathcal{RVS}$ **Mapping:** The $\mathcal{RVS}$ mapping is to sort the production rules in a CFG, according to the first variable of the right-hand side (RHS) in the production rules. The left figure in Fig. 2 shows an example of $\mathcal{RVS}$. The main reason for introducing $\mathcal{RVS}$ mapping is to reduce the thread divergence. In Procedure 2, we first check whether the two variables on the RHS exist in each cell. If they exist, we store them in the current cell. Thread-divergence occurs since each rule has different first variables in the RHS. For example, when some threads that have the first RHS variable satisfying an if-condition to enter the if-statement, other threads must wait until the statement ends.

Procedure 3. RuleandRVSTR

```
 1: procedure RULEANDRVSTR(M, n, len, G = (V, Σ, P, S))
 2:     for i = 0 to n − len do in parallel                    ▷ Mapping to Thread Block
 3:         j = i + len;
 4:         __shared__ bool shVar[||V||];
 5:         foreach production A → BC ∈ P in parallel
 6:                                                              ▷ Mapping to Thread
 7:             for split = i + 1 to j − 1
 8:                 if M[i][split][B] = T do
 9:                     if M[split][j][C] = T do
10:                         shVar[||A||]= T;
11:         end foreach
12:         for A ∈ V in parallel
13:             M[i][j][A] =shVar[||A||];
14:     end for
15: end procedure
```

This situation degrades the performance since some threads must wait for the others. Thus, in the variable-based mapping of algorithm, we avoid this type of divergence by sorting the first-right variables in the production rules.

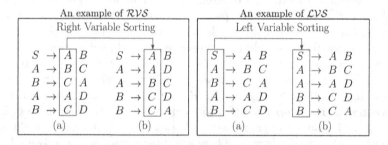

Fig. 2. An example of $\mathcal{RVS}$ and $\mathcal{LVS}$

3. **$\mathcal{LVS}$ Mapping:** The $\mathcal{LVS}$ mapping first sorts all production rules in a CFG, to the left-hand side (LHS) variable of the rules. The right figure in Fig. 2 shows examples of $\mathcal{LVS}$: (a) and (b) are the production rules before and after $\mathcal{LVS}$, respectively. We group the rules that have the same LHS variables. The purpose of $\mathcal{LVS}$ is to concurrently access variables with a set of rules that have the same LHS value. When we store the variables in Procedure 4, we aim to improve the performance by storing the sorted variables into single variable.

4. **Adding Dummy:** If we use dummy rules in $\mathcal{RVS}$ mapping, we could improve the overall performance since some threads may not need to wait on line 6 in Procedure 2. In $\mathcal{LVS}$ mapping, we use dummies because each warp has only one LHS value, which allows us to save a LHS value to one memory

---

Procedure 4. LVSTR

1: **procedure** LVSTR$(M, n, len, G = (V, \Sigma, P, S))$
2:     **for** $i = 0$ **to** $n - len$ **do in parallel**   ▷ Mapping to Thread Block
3:         $j = i + len$;
4:         __shared__ int shVar$[|W|]$;   ▷ $|W|$ is size of warps
5:         **foreach** production $A \rightarrow BC \in P$ **in parallel**
6:   ▷ Mapping to Thread
7:             **for** $split = i + 1$ **to** $j - 1$
8:                 **if** $M[i][split][B] = $ T **do**
9:                     **if** $M[split][j][C] = $ T **do**
10:                         shVar$[w] = $ T;   ▷ w is warp number
11:         **end foreach**
12:         **for** thread $t_w \in$ **each warp** w **in parallel**
13:             $M[i][j][shVar[|w|]] = $T;
14:     **end for**
15: **end procedure**

---

storage. By adding dummies, the memory access may be increased. However, we obtain performance improvement by reducing thread divergence and sharing one LHS value in each thread blocks. If the grammars are not ordered by LHS or RHS, the adding dummies is effective, since the performance improvement is greater than the overhead from the additional memory access. We describe this tendency and the results of adjusting this method to our implementation in the experimental results, in Section 5

4.2   Two Types of Memory for Data Access

In GPU programming, data are usually allocated and accessed in global memory. Since the access speed of global memory is slow, reducing access is important for high-performance. We therefore use texture memory and shared memory to reduce access.

- **Texture Memory:** Texture memory is read-only memory and is allocated by calling a binding API in CUDA. Unlike global memory, texture memory provides caching and reads all threads in a kernel. If the memory is frequently accessed, it becomes more efficient since it has a faster access speed than global memory. On the other hand, it has an overhead caused from binding the device data after the memory allocation is initiated from the host.
- **Shared Memory:** Shared memory is a memory block that can be accessed by all threads within a block. It is much faster than local and global memory. We use this memory in rule-based and $\mathcal{RVS}$ mapping by following two steps: First, we allocate the variables and their number to the shared memory and store them before saving them directly to the table. We then restore these variables to the global memory. These steps differ from those of Procedure 3. Since all threads in the same warp have the same LHS variable because of deploying dummy rules, we can save one variable instead of all variables in

the shared memory. Therefore, $\mathcal{LVS}$ mapping need smaller space than rule-based and $\mathcal{RVS}$ mapping. We add the following processes to Procedure 3 in order to implement $\mathcal{LVS}$ mapping; we allocate the shared memory based on the number of threads in a block and warp, and save the variables in the memory and restore them into the global memory.

4.3 Two Types of Data Transfer Methods

We transfer the input grammar from the host to the device before we start the membership test. After computation, we need to transfer the top cell of table, which is a set of variables deriving the input string, from device to host to verify the test. The data transfer between two devices often causes the degraded performance in GPU programming. It is crucial to reduce the data transfer time between the devices. We use the following two methods to improve the speed:

- **Page-locked Host Memory:** We generally allocate the data to the page-locked host memory. A page-locked buffer, also called pinned memory, save all data in physical memory. We can improve the speed of the data movement using page-locked host memory since this memory does not use paging.
- **Zero-copy Host Memory:** The zero-copy host memory enables GPUs to access host memory directly without transferring data to the device. In addition, GPUs can read and write data simultaneously in the host memory, which is not possible in a traditional PCI bus.

5   Experimental Results

We apply previous approaches to GPU. The details of the experimental platform are as follows: CPU is Core i3 3.10Ghz, RAM is 8GB, GPU is GTX 560 Ti and its memory is 1GB. The number of SM and SP are respectively 8 and 384. Shared Memory/SM is up to 48KB and L1 cache/SM is up to 512KB.

We use grammars by Petrov et al. [16] for our experiment. These grammars have been widely used for evaluating the performance of parsing with CFGs [2,9,20]. They suggested various methods such as splitting and merging variables for a high parsing performance. Because of splitting and merging rules, there are 1,043 variables and 1,725,570 binary rules for parsing in the resulting CFGs.

Since we only consider CFGs instead of PCFGs for the CYK algorithm, we ignore these splitting and merging variables in the experiment. We merge the same word class variables into a single variable. Therefore, we have 98 variables and 3,840 binary rules. We use Section 23 of the WSJ portion of the Penn Treebank [14] as our benchmark set.[1] The sequential version of the CYK algorithm was written in C. It requires $53,987$ ms per sentence. We compare the execution time of various implementations of the CYK algorithm in CUDA based on the thread mapping methods and different memory access patterns.

---

[1] In the benchmark set, an input string is a sentence, and the length of the input string is the number of words in the sentence.

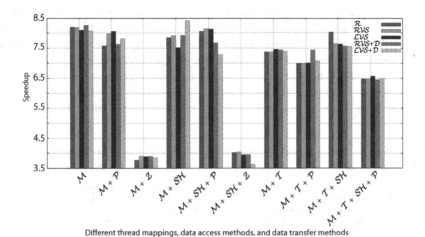

Fig. 3. Speedup of different implementations of a parallel CYK algorithm using different thread mapping methods, data access methods, and data transfer methods

Fig. 3 and Table 2 shows the speedup of the different parallel CYK algorithm implementations on a GTX 560 Ti.

- $\mathcal{M}$: Three thread mapping methods
- $\mathcal{R}$: Rule-based mapping
- $\mathcal{D}$: Deploying dummy rules to $\mathcal{RVS}$ and $\mathcal{LVS}$ mapping
- $\mathcal{P}$: Page-locked host memory
- $\mathcal{Z}$: Zero-copy host memory
- $\mathcal{SH}$: Storing data in shared memory
- $\mathcal{T}$: Placing grammar rules in texture memory

For each test, we randomly selected 1,000 sentences for the benchmark set and measure the runtime. We repeated this test 100 times and computed the average runtime for each case.

- **Five Mapping Methods:** We first implement rule-based, $\mathcal{LVS}$ and $\mathcal{RVS}$ mappings. We then add dummy rules to $\mathcal{LVS}$ and $\mathcal{RVS}$ mappings.
    1. $\mathcal{R}$: Rule-based mapping shows an 8.20× speedup.
    2. $\mathcal{RVS}$: The use of $\mathcal{RVS}$ shows an 8.18× speedup, which is similar to the result of rule-based mapping.
    3. $\mathcal{RVS} + \mathcal{D}$: Once we add dummies to $\mathcal{RVS}$, the size of the grammar increases by 46% to 5,632 compared with the original size of 3,840. Since the size of grammar increases, there might be a more frequent memory accesses in the kernel. However, we achieved a slightly improved performance of 8.26×, because of reducing thread divergence. Note that an advantage is achieved from all threads passing the first if-statement without any idle time.

4. $\mathcal{LVS}$: $\mathcal{LVS}$ shows a poorer performance than $\mathcal{R}$, with an 8.10× speedup. Since we sort the production rules according to the LHS variables, some rules that have different first RHS variables are processed in the same warp concurrently, which causes frequent thread divergences than $\mathcal{R}$.

5. $\mathcal{LVS} + \mathcal{D}$: When we add dummy rules, the grammar size increases by 21% to 4,630 compared with 3,840. The overhead becomes signification, so it shows only an 8.08× speedup, which is slower than $\mathcal{M}$.

Table 2. Speedups of different implementations of a parallel CYK algorithms by different thread mapping methods, data access methods, and data transfer methods

	$\mathcal{M}$	$\mathcal{M}+\mathcal{P}$	$\mathcal{M}+\mathcal{Z}$	$\mathcal{M}+\mathcal{SH}$	$\mathcal{M}+\mathcal{SH}+\mathcal{P}$	$\mathcal{M}+\mathcal{SH}+\mathcal{Z}$
$\mathcal{R}$	8.20	7.58	3.77	7.85	8.06	4.02
$\mathcal{RVS}$	8.19	7.98	3.90	7.92	8.16	4.05
$\mathcal{LVS}$	8.10	8.06	3.89	7.52	8.14	3.95
$\mathcal{RVS}+\mathcal{D}$	8.26	7.63	3.90	7.93	7.68	3.96
$\mathcal{LVS}+\mathcal{D}$	8.08	7.82	3.85	8.42	7.29	3.63

	$\mathcal{M}+\mathcal{S}$	$\mathcal{M}+\mathcal{T}+\mathcal{P}$	$\mathcal{M}+\mathcal{T}+\mathcal{SH}$	$\mathcal{M}+\mathcal{T}+\mathcal{SH}+\mathcal{P}$
$\mathcal{R}$	7.38	7.00	8.04	6.48
$\mathcal{RVS}$	7.38	7.00	7.65	6.48
$\mathcal{LVS}$	7.47	7.01	7.64	6.57
$\mathcal{RVS}+\mathcal{D}$	7.45	7.45	7.58	6.45
$\mathcal{LVS}+\mathcal{D}$	7.40	7.07	7.56	6.48

- **Page-Locked Host Memory:** Since our program uses a relatively small amount of memory, the page-locked host memory method shows a slower runtime compared with the memory allocation without a page-lock. This is because the paged-locked host memory has its own memory allocation function, which is slower than the traditional memory allocation function.
- **Zero-Copy Host Memory:** $\mathcal{M}+\mathcal{Z}$ and $\mathcal{M}+\mathcal{SH}+\mathcal{Z}$ show speedup of 4×, which is worse than $\mathcal{M}$, since the use of zero-copy host memory is very costly in our implementation as small amount of data are frequently moved.
- **Shared Memory:** In the case of shared memory, only $\mathcal{LVS}+\mathcal{D}+\mathcal{SH}$ shows a performance improvement. Since $\mathcal{LVS}+\mathcal{D}+\mathcal{SH}$ allocates shared memory according to the number of warps in each block, it can effectively utilize shared memory. This gives rise to a speedup of 8.42× at maximum. Note that the GTX 560 Ti has an L1 cache with a Fermi architecture [15]. We also observe that the other mappings have a shared memory table array in L1 cache and they also need more shared memory in proportion to the size of the variables and more access to the memory than those for $\mathcal{LVS}+\mathcal{D}$ mapping. The other mappings using shared memory therefore degrade the performance.
- **Texture Memory:** For texture memory, we observe a slower speed than the case without texture mapping for two reasons: First, the GPUs must fetch data from texture memory by calling a special fetch operation, which delays the process overall. Second, the texture memory is optimized for 2D data [18], whereas our data is a 1D string.

We also compared the implementation of a previous study by Yi et al [21]. Since their implementation is for parsing PCFG, it requires an additional operation to calculate the probability, atomic operation, and so on. We therefore cannot compare their implementation directly. The speedup of the fastest implementation of their work is 4.37×. This result is worse than our result 8.42×. This means that our result is more appropriate for a CFG membership test.

6   Conclusions

We explored a design for parallelizing the CYK algorithm. We analyzed different methods for thread mapping, data access using various types of memories and data transfer based on the memory design concepts. We then compared the different implementations of the CYK algorithm on a GTX560Ti. Our contributions can be summarized as follows:

– We evaluated various implementations of CYK on a GPU
– We utilized a memory access pattern in a warp using shared memory

The fastest implementation of the algorithm when using a GPUs is from $\mathcal{LVS} + \mathcal{D} + \mathcal{SH}$ mapping when the number of rules is relatively small (in our test case, it was almost 8k), i.e., left-variable sorting while deploying dummy rules with shared memory. This implementation is 8.42× faster than the sequential C version. However, the experimental results showed that except for $\mathcal{LVS} + \mathcal{D}$ mapping, using shared memory is slower than using global memory because the data are already in the L1 cache on the GTX560Ti using the $3,841$ production rules of the benchmark grammar. Using page-locked and zero-copy host memory results in more overhead, and compared to its benefit, it worsens the performance. We believe that these observations will be helpful for designing a fast parallel CYK algorithm for use on GPUs.

References

1. Aho, A.V., Ullman, J.D.: The theory of parsing, translation, and compiling (1972)
2. Bodenstab, N., Dunlop, A., Hall, K., Roark, B.: Beam-width prediction for efficient context-free parsing. In: Proceedings of the 49th Annual Meeting of the Association for Computational Linguistics: Human Language Technologies, pp. 440–449 (2011)
3. Bordim, J.L., Ito, Y., Nakano, K.: Accelerating the CKY parsing using fPGAs. In: Sahni, S.K., Prasanna, V.K., Shukla, U. (eds.) HiPC 2002. LNCS, vol. 2552, pp. 41–51. Springer, Heidelberg (2002)
4. Cai, L., Malmberg, R.L., Wu, Y.: Stochastic modeling of RNA pseudoknotted structures: a grammatical approach. Bioinformatics, 66–73 (2003)
5. Chomsky, N.: On certain formal properties of grammars. Information and Control, 137–167 (1959)
6. Cocke, J.: Programming languages and their compilers: Preliminary notes (1969)
7. D'Agostino, D., Clematis, A., Decherchi, S., Rocchia, W., Milanesi, L., Merelli, I.: Cuda accelerated molecular surface generation. Concurrency and Computation: Practice and Experience 26(10), 1819–1831 (2014)

8. Dunlop, A., Bodenstab, N., Roark, B.: Efficient matrix-encoded grammars and low latency parallelization strategies for CYK. In: Proceedings of the 12th International Conference on Parsing Technologies, pp. 163–174 (2011)
9. Foster, J.: "cba to check the spelling" investigating parser performance on discussion forum posts. In: Human Language Technologies: The 2010 Annual Conference of the North American Chapter of the Association for Computational Linguistics, pp. 381–384 (2010)
10. Hopcroft, J.E., Ullman, J.D.: Introduction to Automata Theory, Languages, and Computation (1979)
11. Johnson, M.: Parsing in parallel on multiple cores and GPUs. In: Proceedings of the Australasian Language Technology Association Workshop 2011, pp. 29–37 (2011)
12. Kasami, T.: An efficient recognition and syntax analysis algorithm for context-free languages. Technical report, Air Force Cambridge Research Laboratory (1965)
13. Khronos OpenCL Working Group. The OpenCL Specification, version 1.0.29 (2008), http://khronos.org/registry/cl/specs/opencl-1.0.29.pdf
14. Marcus, M.P., Santorini, B., Marcinkiewicz, M.A.: Building a large annotated corpus of english: The Penn Treebank. Computational Linguistics 19(2), 313–330 (1993)
15. Nvidia Corporation. NVIDIA's Next Generation CUDA Compute Architecture: Fermi. Technical report, Nvidia Corporation (2009)
16. Petrov, S., Barrett, L., Thibaux, R., Klein, D.: Learning accurate, compact, and interpretable tree annotation. In: Proceedings of the 21st International Conference on Computational Linguistics, pp. 433–440 (2006)
17. Sakakibara, Y.: Learning context-free grammars using tabular representations. Pattern Recognition 38(9), 1372–1383 (2005)
18. Sanders, J., Kandrot, E.: CUDA by Example: An Introduction to General-Purpose GPU Programming, 1st edn. Addison-Wesley Professional (2010)
19. Takashi, N., Kentaro, T., Taura, K., Tsujii, J.: A parallel CKY parsing algorithm on large-scale distributed-memory parallel machines. In: Proceedings of the 5th Pacific Association For Computational Lingustics, pp. 223–231 (1997)
20. Weese, J., Ganitkevitch, J., Callison-Burch, C., Post, M., Lopez, A.: Joshua 3.0: syntax-based machine translation with the thrax grammar extractor. In: Proceedings of the 6th Workshop on Statistical Machine Translation, pp. 478–484 (2011)
21. Yi, Y., Lai, C.-Y., Petrov, S.: Efficient parallel CKY parsing using GPUs. Journal of Logic and Computation 24(2), 375–393 (2014)
22. Younger, D.H.: Recognition and parsing of context-free languages in time n^3. Information and Control 10, 189–208 (1967)
23. Vu, V., Cats, G., Wolters, L.: Graphics processing unit optimizations for the dynamics of the HIRLAM weather forecast model. Concurrency and Computation: Practice and Experience 25(10), 1376–1393 (2013)

Designing Coalescing Network-on-Chip
for Efficient Memory Accesses of GPGPUs

Chien-Ting Chen[1], Yoshi Shih-Chieh Huang[1], Yuan-Ying Chang[1],
Chiao-Yun Tu[1], Chung-Ta King[1], Tai-Yuan Wang[1], Janche Sang[2],
and Ming-Hua Li[3]

[1] Department of Computer Science, National Tsing Hua University, Hsinchu, Taiwan
[2] Department of Computer and Information Science, Cleveland State University,
Cleveland, OH, USA
[3] Information and Communications Research Laboratories,
Industrial Technology Research Institute, Hsinchu, Taiwan

Abstract. The massive multithreading architecture of General Purpose
Graphic Processors Units (GPGPU) makes them ideal for data parallel
computing. However, designing efficient GPGPU chips poses many challenges. One major hurdle is the interface to the external DRAM, particularly the buffers in the memory controllers (MCs), which is stressed
heavily by the many concurrent memory accesses from the GPGPU.
Previous approaches considered scheduling the memory requests in the
memory buffers to reduce switching of memory rows. The problem is
that the window of requests that can be considered for scheduling is too
narrow and the memory controller is very complex, affecting the critical
path. In view of the massive multithreading architecture of GPGPUs
that can hide memory access latencies, we exploit in this paper the novel
idea of rearranging the memory requests in the network-on-chip (NoC),
called packet coalescing. To study the feasibility of this idea, we have
designed an expanded NoC router that supports packet coalescing and
evaluated its performance extensively. Evaluation results show that this
NoC-assisted design strategy can improve the row buffer hit rate in the
memory controllers. A comprehensive investigation of factors affecting
the performance of coalescing is also conducted and reported.

Keywords: Network-on-chip, general-purpose graphic processors unit,
memory controller, latency hiding, router design.

1 Introduction

Modern General Purpose Graphic Processors Units (GPGPUs) have over ten to
hundred times more computing power than general purpose processors [15,19].
GPGPUs are thus well suited for high performance computing [14,16,20]. A GPGPU
typically contains many *streaming multiprocessors* (SMs), sometimes referred to as
shader cores, each is composed of many small *streaming processors* (SPs).

A *warp*, consisting of multiple threads, is the basic unit of scheduling on a
SM. Multiple warps can be assigned to a SM and synchronized only within the

C.-H. Hsu et al. (Eds.): NPC 2014, LNCS 8707, pp. 169–180, 2014.

SM. When a warp is blocked due to memory access, other ready warps may be executed so that the SM is not idle. The amount of time when a warp is context-switched out until it is scheduled for execution again is known as the *slack time* [21]. If the slack time is longer than memory access time, the latency in memory accesses is effectively hidden.

The massive multithreading architecture of GPGPUs makes them ideal for data parallel computing. However, the many concurrently memory accesses out of data parallel computing also severely stress the memory, particularly the buffers in the memory controllers (MCs). The problem is made even worse due to the *many-to-few-to-many* traffic patterns [4] in GPGPUs, which is from *many* SMs to *few* MCs and then back to many SMs.

As DRAM cells are typically organized in a two-dimensional array and to access a cell, a whole row of cells need to be loaded into the *row buffer* first, previous approaches to improving memory performance in GPGPUs focus on scheduling memory requests in the request queue in MCs to increase the *row buffer hit rate* [11,18]. The problem is that the window of requests that can be considered for scheduling is too narrow and the memory controller becomes complicated, affecting the critical path [22].

In view of the latency-hiding capability of GPGPUs, we exploit in this paper the novel idea of rearranging the memory requests in the network-on-chip (NoC), called *packet coalescing*. The idea is to merge memory requests destined for the same row of the memory in the routers of the NoC. In this way, the *many* memory requests from the different SMs may be merged to a *few* large packets along the path. When they arrive at the MC, memory requests are already in proper order for continuous row buffer hits. Note that packets may be delayed in the NoC for coalescing opportunity. However, the gain in faster memory accesses may more than compensate the delays. To study the feasibility of this idea, we have designed an expanded NoC router that supports packet coalescing and evaluated its performance extensively.

The contributions of this paper are as follows:

- We propose the novel idea of coalescing and reordering memory requests in the NoC in a distributed manner to improve the row buffer hit rate of the memory controllers.
- We design an enhanced NoC that supports packet coalescing.
- We provide an in-depth evaluation of the proposed architecture, investigate possible sources of inefficiency, and study ways to mitigate the problems.

2   System Design

To study the feasibility of packet coalescing, we present in this section an expanded NoC router based on a typical five-stage pipeline, which consists of *Input Buffering* (IB), *Routing Computation* (RC), *Virtual-channel Allocation* (VA), *Switch Allocation* (SA), and *Link Traversal* (LT) [7,8]. To extend the router for packet coalescing, a number of components are added: *Coalescer*, *Scheduler*, *Detector* and *Grant Holder*. They are mainly implemented in the *IB* and *SA* stages.

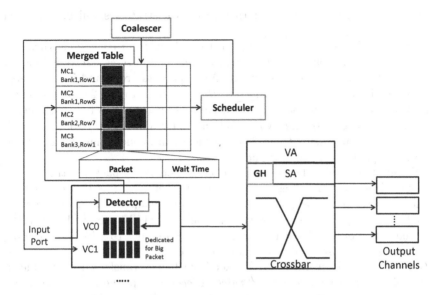

Fig. 1. The extended router microarchitecture for packet coalescing

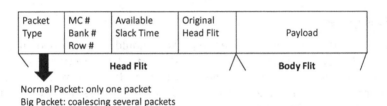

Normal Packet: only one packet
Big Packet: coalescing several packets

Fig. 2. Extended packet format for packet coalescing

2.1 Router Microarchitecture

Fig. 1 shows the proposed router microarchitecture. To match the extended router, the packet format should also be modified as shown in Fig. 2. The first field, *Packet Type*, indicates whether the packet is a normal packet or a coalesced, long packet. The second field contains information of the destination of the request to the row of a memory bank. This information is used to decide whether two packets can be merged together or not.

– *Detector*: When the router receives a head flit indicating it is a read request, Detector decides for how long the packet should wait for coalescing. The decision is affected by factors such as the router location, the routing algorithmth, available slack time of the packet, number of available warps, and GPGPU architecture. For example, if a router is closer to the memory controller, it will see more packets that could be coalesced, and thus it is nature to hold a packet longer there. Detailed strategies will be discussed later.

- *Coalescer*: If it is decided that a packet should wait for coalescing, then Coalescer stores this packet to the *Merged Table*. The *Merged Table* is indexed by the MC id, bank id, and row id. When packets are stored in the Merge Table, their packet type is changed to *Big Packet*, as Figure 2 shows. If a new packet arrives that can be merged with another packet already in the Merged Table, the headers of the two packets are merged with an updated packet size and available slack time. Their payloads are concatenated together to form the payload of the new packet.
- *Scheduler*: Scheduler checks in every cycle if there is any packet in the Merged Table whose held time has expired. Such packets contains the memory requests destined to the same row of the same bank in the same memory controller. They will be removed from the Merged Table and placed in the virtual channel to be sent to the next hop. Strategies to schedule these big packets will be discussed in the next section.
- *Grant Holder*: To avoid a Big Packet from being transferred apart due to the fairness mechanism of the *Switch Allocation* pipeline stage, the *Grant Holding* (GH) mechanism is added to let a Big Packet hold the grant until the entire packet is transferred.

2.2   Design Issues

One important design issue is where the packets should wait for opportunities of coalescing and for how long. The simplest idea is to delay every request packet for a fixed time in each router on the path to the MC. However, since all the packets are delayed for a fixed time interval in the routers, the overall traffic pattern will remain the same. A better strategy is to distribute the allowable delays of a packet wisely among the routers along its path to the destination MC. Since packets that can be merged are all destined to the same MC, the routers closer to the MC should have a higher probability of seeing packets that can be merged. Therefore, we can allocate more delays to the routers closer to the MC. This is called the *dynamic slack distribution policy*.

Specifically, we employ a design parameter, called *Fixed Delay per Hop* and multiply it with the number of hops in the path from the requesting SM to the destination MC. This gives the total delay that the packet will experience along the path. The amount of delay in each router on the path is then calculated as shown below. The idea is to allocate one portion of the total delays on the first router, two portions on the second router, and so on.

$$(\textit{Fixed Delay per Hop} \times \textit{Total Hop Count}) \times \frac{\textit{Traversed Hop Count}}{\sum_{i=1}^{\textit{Total Hop Count}} i} \quad (1)$$

Another issue is the head-of-line problem in the memory request queue that unavoidably arises when memory requests to the same rows are grouped together [10,12]. Modern DRAM chips are usually organized into banks, and memory requests to different banks can be serviced concurrently. These requests are queued in the memory request queue in the MC and served in a FCFS fashion. Any scheduling scheme, including packet coalescing, that attempts to increase row buffer hits will necessarily group the memory requests to the same DRAM row together in the request queue. However, this would inversely block requests to other banks, reducing the bank level parallelism. Therefore, advanced memory scheduling schemes are often complemented with mechanisms such as *banked FIFO*, in which each bank has its own request queue.

3   Evaluation

We use GPGPU-Sim [5], a cycle-accurate many-core simulator, to evaluate the proposed packet coalescing mechanism. The microarchitecture parameters used in the evaluations are shown in Table 1. Eleven benchmark programs are used in our evaluation, including three from GPGPU-Sim. The benchmark programs are shown in Table 2. The proposed packet coalescing mechanism is compared with two MC-side buffer scheduling methods: FIFO and FR-FCFS [11,18], where FIFO is used as the baseline. The design parameter, *Fixed Delay per Hop*, is set to 5 cycles. Note that, being a NoC-side solution, packet coalescing can be used together with FIFO or FR-FCFS.

3.1   Row Buffer Miss Rate

Packet coalescing aims to reduce the row buffer miss rate by rearranging memory requests in the NoC. A lower row buffer miss rate implies faster memory accesses. Fig. 3 shows the performance in terms of row buffer miss rate.

From the figure, we can see that packet coalescing, when used together with FR-FCFS (denoted FR+dynamic), can reduce the row buffer miss rate by 78.75% over that of pure FIFO. When compared with FIFO and FR-FCFS, packet coalescing can further improve row buffer miss rate by 8.7% and 2.87% respectively.

Table 1. Microarchitecture parameters of GPGPU-Sim

Parameter	Value
Number of Shader Cores	28
Warp Size	32
Number of Threads/Core	1024
Number of Registers/Core	16384
NoC Topology / Routing	Mesh / Dimension-Order
NoC Virtual Channel	1
NoC Virtual Channel Buffer	8
NoC Flit Size	32
Memory Controller	8
DRAM Request Queue	32
Memory Controller Scheduling Scheme	FR-FCFS / FIFO / Banked-FIFO
GDDR3 Memory Timing	tCL=9, tRP=13, tRC=34, tRAS=21, tRCD=12, tRRD=8

Table 2. Benchmark programs

Benchmark	Label	Suite
AES Encryption	AES	[5]
Graph Algorithm: Breadth-First Search	BFS	Rodinia[6]
Coulombic Potential	CP	Parboil[2]
3D Laplace Solver	LPS	[5]
LIBOR Monte Carlo	LIB	3rd Party[5]
MUMmerGPU	MUM	3rd Party[5]
Neural Network	NN	[5]
N-Queens Solver	NQU	[17]
Ray Tracing	RAY	3rd Party[5]
Weather Prediction	WP	3rd Party[5]
BlackScholes Simulation	BlackScholes	Nvidia [1]

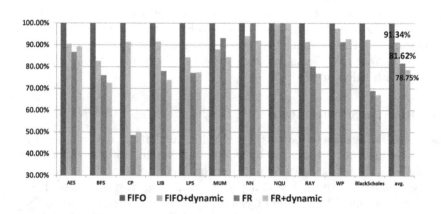

Fig. 3. Row buffer miss rate

The performance of individual benchmarks varies. The figure shows that benchmarks such as LIB, NN, and RAY can achieve a lower miss rate, because the injection patterns of these benchmarks are suitable for coalescing. However, WP does not perform well because the coalescing probability of WP is relatively low compared with other benchmarks. Benchmarks such as AES and NQU have a low packet injection rate to the NoC, and thus are hard to be improved.

The improvement in row buffer miss rate translates into improvement in DRAM accesses, as shown in Fig. 4. The figure shows a more than 25% reduction in the DRAM access time in average. This is because our design will delay packets in the NoC to rearrange their arrival sequence in the memory controllers. Thus, the average memory fetch time is higher than the baseline. However, if we deduct the average NoC traverse time from the average memory fetch time to get the average DRAM access time, our design does reduce the DRAM access time as shown in the figure.

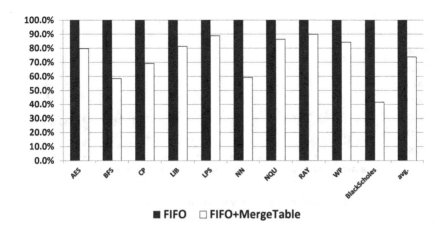

FIFO   □ **FIFO+MergeTable**

Fig. 4. Average DRAM access time

3.2   Instructions per Cycle

Next, we evaluate the overall performance of the system in terms of *instructions per cycle* (IPC) to see whether the improvement in DRAM accesses can translate into overall performance improvement. The results are shown in Fig. 5. Unfortunately, the IPC of the whole system does not improve much. Apparently, the performance gain in DRAM accesses is not enough to compensate the loss due to the delay in the NoC for packet coalescing. This can be verified in Fig. 5 with the configuration FIFO+extra5cycle, in which no packet coalescing is performed but every packet is delayed 5 cycles on each hop. In other words, this configuration will suffer from the delay in NoC but does not get any benefit from packet coalescing. From the figure, it can be seen that our approach did get some performance gain over FIFO+extra5cycle but not enough to compensate for the cost of delays in NoC.

3.3   Factors Affecting Performance

There are many factors affecting the overall performance of our design. These factors can be classified into two main categories. One category is related to application characteristics and the other is related to microarchitecture. These factors will be discussed below.

Application Characteristics. An important application characteristic is the number of *available warps* in the application. Packet coalescing is based on the assumption that applications have a sufficient amount of warps to hide the longer NoC latency due to coalescing. As shown in Fig. 6, most benchmarks only have 5 or few available warps in average. As the number of available warps is

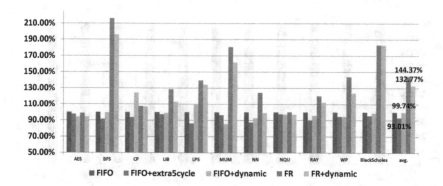

Fig. 5. Overall performance in terms of IPC

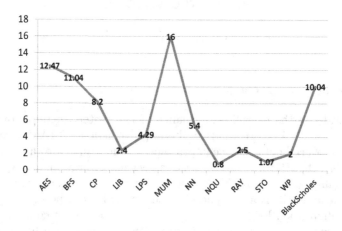

Fig. 6. Available warps of benchmark programs

proportional to the slack time [21], our design suffers from a lack of slack time to hide the overhead in the delay in NoC.

On the other hand, benchmarks such as *AES*, *BFS*, *MUM*, and *BlackScholes* have a relatively higher number of available warps. For these applications, we examine their *coalescing probability*, shown in Fig. 7. We can see that *MUM* only has a coalescing probability of 0.1 for a packet to merge with another. This probability is too low for effective packet coalescing. Furthermore, we found out that the benchmark programs doe not have enough number of memory requests to benefit from our design.

Router Microarchitecture. Modern DRAM chips are usually composed of many banks. *Bank level parallelism* thus plays an important role in DRAM accesses. Traditional memory controllers will queue the memory requests in the memory request queue and, if the requests are to access different memory banks, these requests can be serviced in parallel. As a result, the utilization of the banks

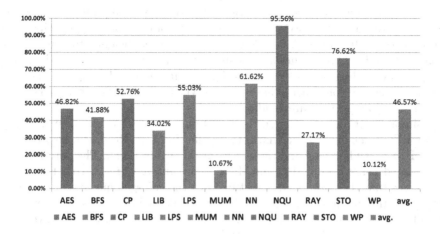

Fig. 7. Coalescing probability of benchmark programs

increases and the DRAM access latency is improved. Now, when we coalesce packets in the NoC, the memory requests going to the same memory bank will be grouped together, effectively serializing the accesses to the memory banks and resulting in the Head-of-Line problem.

A straightforward but effective solution is to distribute the memory request queue to each bank, or *banked FIFO*. Each bank has an independent request queue to buffer the memory requests to that bank. The overall performance of our design coupled with banked FIFO is shown Fig. 8. The figure shows that *BFS* and *BlackScholes* have better performance than the baseline architecture. *BFS* can improve the performance by about 2-3% and *BlackScholes* by 16-17%.

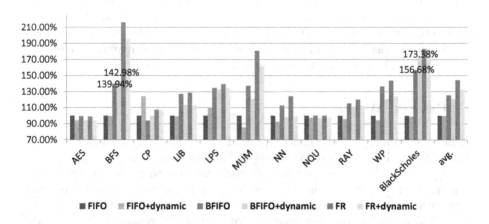

Fig. 8. Overall performance with banked FIFO

Even though banked FIFO can mitigate the Head-of-Line problem, the problem can still occur if the FIFO queue is too small. For example, suppose there are two packets heading to bank 2, followed by four packets heading to bank 0. Assume that the FIFO buffer in bank 0 can only hold two packets. Thus, the other two packets heading to bank 0 will be blocked in the interface queue between NoC and memory controller. These packets will further block other packets no matter which banks they are heading.

A simple solution is to enlarge the FIFO queue in each bank. As mentioned above, BFS is one of the benchmarks that suffer from the Head-of-Line problem. Thus, BFS is studied here and the results are shown in Fig. 9. The performance is evaluated using overall IPC and the metric *bank idle time*. From Fig. 9(a), we can see that the baseline architecture with the enlarged queues can improve the overall IPC by about 6%. Our design with enlarged queues can improve the overall IPC by about 9%. Obviously, there is an additional 3% improvement from eliminating the Head-of-Line problem.

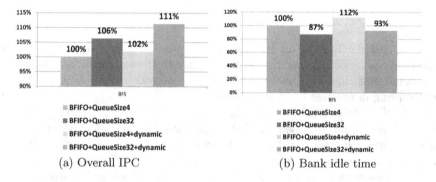

(a) Overall IPC   (b) Bank idle time

Fig. 9. Overall IPC and bank idle time with enlarged BFIFO queue

It is also interesting to note from Fig. 9(b) that the bank idle time drops 19% using our design with the banked FIFO, which is better than the baseline architecture with banked FIFO (13%). This further proves that the Head-of-Line problem does exist in configurations with small queues, and enlarging the queues of banked FIFO can eliminate the problem.

4   Related Works

To increase memory access efficiency, out-of-order scheduling such as FR-FCFS [12,13,18] has been studied extensively. Unfortunately, it requires a complex structure [3]. So far, there are very few works investigating memory scheduling in a massively parallel, many-core accelerators. Some works consider moving memory access scheduling out of the memory controller into the on-chip network and GPGPU shader core. For example, Yuan *et al.* [22] observed that memory requests sent from shader cores to DRAM will be disrupted by the NoC. Thus, they proposed a NoC arbitration scheme called *Hold Grant* to preserve the row buffer access locality of memory request streams. In [10], the idea of *superpackets* is proposed for the shader core to maintain row buffer locality for the memory requests out of the core. While these works focus on maintaining the row buffer locality from a single shader core, our work exploit the coalescing opportunity across the cores inside the NoC. Our design leverages the many-to-few-to-many traffic pattern [4] in GPGPU to merge packets from different shader cores.

In [5], Bakhoda *et al.* showed that non-graphics applications tend to be more sensitive to bisection bandwidth than latency, also known as *bandwidth-sensitive and latency-insensitive*. The slacks of memory accesses are also studied in [9,21]. In [9], memory latency hiding resulting from critical paths is investigated in the traditional SMP systems. The concept of GPGPU packet slack is presented in [21] to detour packets for energy saving. Our design differs in that packet slack time is used to merge packets destining to the same row in DRAM to improve memory access performance.

5   Conclusions

In this paper, we propose a novel NoC design that merges memory requests from different GPGPU cores destining to the same row in the DRAM. This in essence offloads the scheduling of memory requests from the memory controllers to the interconnection network. As a result, our design promotes in-network processing rather than in-memory processing. A rudimentary router with coalescing logic is presented, and the design is evaluated with GPGPU-Sim. The evaluation results show that our preliminary design performs similarly as FR-FCFS on row buffer hit rate. However, it suffers from the delays in the NoC waiting for coalescing. As a result, the overall IPC performance cannot be improved much. Possible sources of inefficiencies are analyzed and discussed. More research is needed to optimize the current the design to achieve the best performance.

Acknowledgements. This work was supported in part by the National Science Council, Taiwan, under Grant 102-2220-E-007-025 and by the Industrial Technology Research Institute, Taiwan.

References

1. Nvidia gpu computing sdk suite,
   https://developer.nvidia.com/gpu-computing-sdk
2. Parboil benchmark suite, http://impact.crhc.illinois.edu/parboil.php
3. Ausavarungnirun, R., Chang, K., Subramanian, L., Loh, G., Mutlu, O.: Staged memory scheduling: Achieving high performance and scalability in heterogeneous systems. In: Proceedings of the 39th International Symposium on Computer Architecture, pp. 416–427. IEEE Press (2012)
4. Bakhoda, A., Kim, J., Aamodt, T.: Throughput-effective on-chip networks for many-core accelerators. In: Proceedings of the 2010 43rd Annual IEEE/ACM International Symposium on Microarchitecture, pp. 421–432. IEEE Computer Society (2010)

5. Bakhoda, A., Yuan, G., Fung, W., Wong, H., Aamodt, T.: Analyzing cuda work-loads using a detailed gpu simulator. In: Proceedings of IEEE International Symposium on Performance Analysis of Systems and Software (ISPASS), pp. 163–174. IEEE (2009)

6. Che, S., Boyer, M., Meng, J., Tarjan, D., Sheaffer, J., Lee, S., Skadron, K.: Rodinia: A benchmark suite for heterogeneous computing. In: Proceedings of IEEE International Symposium on Workload Characterization (IISWC), pp. 44–54. IEEE (2009)

7. Dally, W.: Virtual-channel flow control. IEEE Transactions on Parallel and Distributed Systems 3(2), 194–205 (1992)

8. Dally, W., Towles, B.: Principles and practices of interconnection networks. Morgan Kaufmann (2004)

9. Das, R., Mutlu, O., Moscibroda, T., Das, C.: Aérgia: A network-on-chip exploiting packet latency slack. IEEE Micro 31(1), 29–41 (2011)

10. Kim, Y., Lee, H., Kim, J.: An alternative memory access scheduling in many-core accelerators. In: 2011 International Conference on Parallel Architectures and Compilation Techniques (PACT), pp. 195–196. IEEE (2011)

11. Mutlu, O., Moscibroda, T.: Stall-time fair memory access scheduling for chip multiprocessors. In: Proceedings of the 40th IEEE/ACM International Symposium on Microarchitecture, pp. 146–160. IEEE Computer Society (2007)

12. Mutlu, O., Moscibroda, T.: Parallelism-aware batch scheduling: Enhancing both performance and fairness of shared dram systems. In: ACM SIGARCH Computer Architecture News, vol. 36, pp. 63–74. IEEE Computer Society (2008)

13. Nesbit, K., Aggarwal, N., Laudon, J., Smith, J.: Fair queuing memory systems. In: Proceedings of the 39th IEEE/ACM International Symposium on Microarchitecture, pp. 208–222. IEEE (2006)

14. Nickolls, J., Dally, W.: The gpu computing era. IEEE Micro 30(2), 56–69 (2010)

15. NVIDIA: Nvidia's next generation cuda compute architecture: Fermi (2009)

16. Owens, J., Houston, M., Luebke, D., Green, S., Stone, J., Phillips, J.: Gpu computing. Proceedings of the IEEE 96(5), 879–899 (2008)

17. Pcchen: N-queens solver,
http://forums.nvidia.com/index.php?showtopic=76893

18. Rixner, S., Dally, W., Kapasi, U., Mattson, P., Owens, J.: Memory access scheduling. In: Proceedings of the 27th International Symposium on Computer Architecture, pp. 128–138. IEEE (2000)

19. Sanders, J., Kandrot, E.: CUDA by example: An introduction to general-purpose GPU programming. Addison-Wesley Professional (2010)

20. Stone, J., Gohara, D., Shi, G.: Opencl: A parallel programming standard for heterogeneous computing systems. Computing in Science and Engineering 12(3), 66 (2010)

21. Yin, J., Zhou, P., Holey, A., Sapatnekar, S., Zhai, A.: Energy-efficient non-minimal path on-chip interconnection network for heterogeneous systems. In: Proceedings of the 2012 ACM/IEEE International Symposium on Low Power Electronics and Design, pp. 57–62. ACM (2012)

22. Yuan, G., Bakhoda, A., Aamodt, T.: Complexity effective memory access scheduling for many-core accelerator architectures. In: Proceedings of the 42nd IEEE/ACM International Symposium on Microarchitecture, pp. 34–44. IEEE (2009)

Efficient Parallel Algorithms for Linear RankSVM on GPU

Jing Jin and Xiaola Lin

School of Information Science and Technology,
Sun Yat-sen University, Guangzhou, China
jinj5@mail2.sysu.edu.cn, linxl@mail.sysu.edu.cn

Abstract. Linear RankSVM is one of the widely used methods for learning to rank. Although using Order-Statistic Tree (OST) and Trust Region Newton Methods (TRON) are effective to train linear RankSVM on CPU, it becomes less effective when dealing with large-scale training data sets. Furthermore, linear RankSVM training with L2-loss contains quite amount of matrix manipulations in comparison with that with L1-loss, so it has great potential for achieving parallelism on GPU. In this paper, we design efficient parallel algorithms on GPU for the linear RankSVM training with L2-loss based on different queries. The experimental results show that, compared with the state-of-the-art algorithms for the linear RankSVM training with L2-loss on CPU, our proposed parallel algorithm not only can significantly enhance the training speed but also maintain the high prediction accuracy.

Keywords: Parallel Computing, GPU Computing, GPU sorting, Linear RankSVM, Learning to Rank.

1   Introduction

As a promising parallel device for general-propose computing, Graphics Processing Unit (GPU) not only provides tens of thousands of threads for applications with data-level or task-level parallelism, but also shows superb computational performance on floating point operations in comparison with the current multi-core CPUs [1]. Additionally, combining with Compute Unified Device Architecture (CUDA) programming model [2] released by NVIDA in 2007, quite a lot of existing applications can be conveniently programmed and ported to GPUs. Especially, the machines learning algorithms can be highly parallelizable on GPUs since they typically contain a large number of matrix manipulations [3].

According to the Chapelle et. al. [4], state of the art learning to rank models can be categorized into three types: *pointwise methods* such as [5], [6], *pairwise methods* such as [7], [8], [9], and *listwise methods* such as [10], [11]. Among these models, RankSVM, which can be consider as a special case of Support Vector Machine (SVM) [12], is a widely used pairwise approach for leaning to rank. There exists two types of RankSVMs: linear RankSVM [13], [14], [15], [16], [17] and nonlinear RankSVM [18], [19]. Although both of them have been extensively studied, the lengthy training remains a challenging issue.

C.-H. Hsu et al. (Eds.): NPC 2014, LNCS 8707, pp. 181–194, 2014.
© IFIP International Federation for Information Processing 2014

Given a set of training label-query-instance tuples $(y_i, q_i, \boldsymbol{x}_i)$, $y_i \in K \subset \mathbb{R}$, $q_i \in Q \subset \mathbb{Z}$, $\boldsymbol{x}_i \in \mathbb{R}^n$, $i = 1, \cdots, l$, where K is the set of possible relevance levels with $|K| = k$, Q is the set of queries with $|Q| = m$, l is the total number of training instances and n is the number of features for each training instance, as well as a defined set of *preference pairs*: $\mathcal{P} \equiv \{(i, j) \mid q_i = q_j, y_i > y_j\}$ with $p \equiv |\mathcal{P}|$, where (i, j) indicates $(\boldsymbol{x}_i, \boldsymbol{x}_j)$ for short, then the objective function $f(\boldsymbol{w})$ of linear RankSVM with L2-loss is presented by:

$$f(\boldsymbol{w}) = \min_{\boldsymbol{w} \in \mathbb{R}^n} \frac{1}{2} \boldsymbol{w}^T \boldsymbol{w} + C \sum_{(i,j) \in \mathcal{P}} \max(0, 1 - \boldsymbol{w}^T (\boldsymbol{x}_i - \boldsymbol{x}_j))^2 \qquad (1)$$

where $\boldsymbol{w} \in \mathbb{R}^n$ is a vector of parameters, $C > 0$ is a regularization parameter. The goal of RankSVM is to learn $\boldsymbol{w}$ such that $\boldsymbol{w}^T \boldsymbol{x}_i > \boldsymbol{w}^T \boldsymbol{x}_j$ if $(i, j) \in \mathcal{P}$.

Although there have been many serial algorithms for linear RankSVM, however, there is no empirical research exists on this issue for achieving linear RankSVM on some parallel systems. Moreover, on the one hand, although the linear RankSVM training using TRust regiON Newton methods (TRON) [20] instead of Cutting Plane Method (CPM) may obtain more quick convergence speed, it becomes less effective when dealing with the large-scale training data sets; on the other hand, the linear RankSVM with L2-loss contains more matrix-matrix or matrix-vector operations over that with L1-loss, so training linear RankSVM with L2-loss can be accelerated effectively on GPU. This motivates us to design efficient GPU algorithms to train linear RankSVM with L2-loss.

The main contributions of this paper can be summarized as follows: (1) We define a new rule of how to determine the preference pairs in terms of the different queries (Please see Definition 1); (2) Based on the new rule, we propose a parallel algorithm P-SWX for linear RankSVM training with L2-loss; (3) We propose an efficient GPU sorting algorithm, GPU-quicksorting, that can sort multiple sequences within a single GPU kernel. Meanwhile, we conduct extensive comparison experiments to prove the effectiveness of our proposed algorithms. To the best of our knowledge, this is the first work that achieves RankSVM training on GPU.

The rest of the paper is organized as follows: In Section 2, we briefly introduce the basic principle of linear RankSVM with L2-loss we are interest in solving, as well as its effective solution TRON. Section 3 is mainly devoted to designing parallel algorithms P-SWX and GPU-quicksorting on GPU to accelerate training speed of the linear RankSVM with L2-loss. Experiments, which indicate the performance of our proposed algorithms, are given and analysed in Section 4. Finally, Section 5 summarizes the conclusion of this project and points the future research work.

2   Linear RankSVM Training with L2-loss

This section briefly introduces the linear RankSVM training with L2-loss by using TRON.

2.1 Linear RankSVM Traing with L2-loss by Using Trust Region Newton Method

Typically, TRON can be viewed as an effective Newton method to solve the optimization problem $f(\boldsymbol{w})$, the primary goal of which, at the d-th iteration, is to find a $\boldsymbol{w}^{d+1}$ so that $f(\boldsymbol{w}^{d+1})$ is less than $f(\boldsymbol{w}^d)$. To update $\boldsymbol{w}^d$ by $\boldsymbol{w}^{d+1} = \boldsymbol{w}^d + \boldsymbol{v}$, TRON takes an improved Conjugate Gradient (CG) method to find an optimal direction $\boldsymbol{v} \in \mathbb{R}^n$ by iteratively minimizing $F_d(\boldsymbol{v})$ which is the second-order Taylor approximation of $f(\boldsymbol{w}^{d+1}) - f(\boldsymbol{w}^d)$.

$$F_d(\boldsymbol{v}) \equiv \nabla f(\boldsymbol{w}^d)^T \boldsymbol{v} + \frac{1}{2}\boldsymbol{v}^T \nabla^2 f(\boldsymbol{w}^d)\boldsymbol{v}$$

$$\min_{\boldsymbol{v}} \quad F_d(\boldsymbol{v}) \quad \text{subject to} \quad \|\boldsymbol{v}\| \leq \Delta_d \tag{2}$$

where Δ_d is the size of the trust region, and $\nabla f(\boldsymbol{w}^d)$ and $\nabla^2 f(\boldsymbol{w}^d)$ are indicated the first and second order differential function of $f(\boldsymbol{w})$, respectively. Apparently, TRON contains two levels iterations, inner iterations and outer iterations. The inner one is the CG iterations which are used to find an optimal $\boldsymbol{v}$ within the trust region iteratively for updating $\boldsymbol{w}$, while the outer one is Newton Method which is applied to generate a more optimal $\boldsymbol{w}$ for $f(\boldsymbol{w})$. The whole framework of TRON can be clearly presented by Algorithm 1. Our setting for updating Δ_d follows the work done by Lin et al. [21]. But for the stopping condition, we follow that of TRON in the package LIBLINEAR[1] [22] to check if the gradient is small enough compared with an initial gradient shown as follows.

$$\|\nabla f(\boldsymbol{w}^d)\|_2 \leq \epsilon_s \|\nabla f(\boldsymbol{w}^0)\|_2 \tag{3}$$

where $\boldsymbol{w}^0$ is the initial iteration and ϵ_s is the stopping tolerate given by users.

Algorithm 1. Trust Region Newton Method

Input $\boldsymbol{w}^0 \leftarrow \boldsymbol{0}$, maximum outer iterations N
Output $\boldsymbol{w}^d$
1: Initialize $\Delta_0 \leftarrow 0$ and $d \leftarrow 0$
2: **while** $d \leq N$ **do**
3:     //The *while*-loop indicates the whole outer iterations.
4:     **if** $\|\nabla f(\boldsymbol{w}^d)\|_2 \leq \epsilon_s \|\nabla f(\boldsymbol{w}^0)\|$ **then**
5:         **return** $\boldsymbol{w}^d$
6:     **else**
7:         Apply CG iterations (inner iterations) until subproblem (2) is solved or $\boldsymbol{v}$ reaches the trust-region boundary.
8:         Update $\boldsymbol{w}^d$ and Δ_d to $\boldsymbol{w}^{d+1}$ and Δ_{d+1} respectively.
9:         $d \leftarrow d + 1$
10:    **end if**
11: **end while**

---

[1] http://www.csie.ntu.edu.tw/~cjlin/liblinear/liblinear-1.94.tar.gz

Optimizing $f(w)$ by TRON refers to computing $\nabla f(w)$ and $\nabla^2 f(w)$. However, the $\nabla^2 f(w)$ doesn't exist because $\nabla f(w)$ is not differentiable. To derive a faster method to calculate $\nabla^2 f(w)v$, Lee et.al. [16] has explored the structure of $\nabla^2 f(w)v$ by defining some expressions as follows.

$$
\begin{aligned}
&\mathrm{SV}(w) \equiv \{(i,j) \mid (i,j) \in \mathcal{P}, 1 - w^T(x_i - x_j) > 0\} \\
&\mathrm{SV}_i^+ \equiv \{x_j \mid (j,i) \in \mathrm{SV}(w)\} \\
&\mathrm{SV}_i^- \equiv \{x_j \mid (i,j) \in \mathrm{SV}(w)\} \\
&p_w \equiv |\mathrm{SV}(w)|
\end{aligned}
\tag{4}
$$

$$
\begin{aligned}
\beta_i^+ \equiv |\mathrm{SV}_i^+|, \alpha_i^+ \equiv \sum_{x_j \in \mathrm{SV}_i^+} x_j^T v, \gamma_i^+ \equiv \sum_{x_j \in \mathrm{SV}_i^+} w^T x_j \\
\beta_i^- \equiv |\mathrm{SV}_i^-|, \alpha_i^- \equiv \sum_{x_j \in \mathrm{SV}_i^-} x_j^T v, \gamma_i^- \equiv \sum_{x_j \in \mathrm{SV}_i^-} w^T x_j
\end{aligned}
\tag{5}
$$

Following the above definitions, Lee et.al. [16] converted $f(w)$ and $\nabla f(w)$ and $\nabla^2 f(w)v$ into following expressions.

$$
\begin{aligned}
f(w) &= \frac{1}{2} w^T w + C(A_w X w - e_w)^T (A_w X w - e_w) \\
&= \frac{1}{2} w^T w + C(w^T X^T ((A_w^T A_w X w) - (2 A_w^T e_w)) + p_w)
\end{aligned}
\tag{6}
$$

$$
\nabla f(w) = w + 2C X^T ((A_w^T A_w X w) - (A_w^T e_w))
\tag{7}
$$

$$
\nabla^2 f(w)v = v + 2C X^T (A_w^T A_w X v)
\tag{8}
$$

where X indicates $[x_1, \cdots, x_l]^T$, $A_w \in \mathbb{R}^{p_w \times l}$ is a matrix indicated by:

$$
A_w \equiv \begin{array}{c} \cdots \quad i \quad \cdots \quad j \quad \cdots \\ \vdots \\ (i,j) \begin{bmatrix} 0 \cdots 0 +1\, 0 \cdots 0 -1\, 0 \cdots 0 \end{bmatrix} \\ \vdots \end{array}
$$

$e_w \in \mathbb{R}^{p_w \times l}$ is a vector of ones. Four of $X^T A_w^T A_w X v$, $A_w^T e_w$, p_w and $A_w^T A_w X w$, according to the derivation done by Lee et al. [16], can be computed by:

$$
X^T A_w^T A_w X v = X^T \begin{bmatrix} (\beta_1^+ + \beta_1^-) x_1^T v - (\alpha_1^+ + \alpha_1^-) \\ \vdots \\ (\beta_l^+ + \beta_l^-) x_l^T v - (\alpha_l^+ + \alpha_l^-) \end{bmatrix}
$$

$$
A_w^T e_w = \begin{bmatrix} \beta_1^- - \beta_1^+ \\ \vdots \\ \beta_l^- - \beta_l^+ \end{bmatrix}, \quad p_w = \sum_{i=1}^{l} \beta_i^+ = \sum_{i=1}^{l} \beta_i^-
$$

$$A_w^T A_w X w = \begin{bmatrix} (\beta_1^+ + \beta_1^-)w^T x_1 - (\gamma_1^+ + \gamma_1^-) \\ \vdots \\ (\beta_l^+ + \beta_l^-)w^T x_l - (\gamma_l^+ + \gamma_l^-) \end{bmatrix}$$

If all β_i^+, β_i^-, α_i^+, α_i^-, γ_i^+ and γ_i^- are already calculated, then computing $\nabla^2 f(w)v$ in terms of (8) would cost $O(ln + n)$, where $O(ln)$ is for computing $X^T A_w^T A_w X v$ and $O(n)$ is for vector addition. Similarly, the computations of $\nabla f(w)$ and $f(w)$ both cost $O(ln + n)$ if all β_i^+, β_i^-, γ_i^+ and γ_i^- are computed already. Furthermore, $\nabla^2 f(w)v$ can be viewed as the computational bottlenecks since it refers to not only the CG iteration but also the outer iteration of TRON. According to the definitions of SV_i^+ and SV_i^-, computing all parameter variables in (5) requires to determine whether $1 - w^T(x_i - x_j)$ or $1 - w^T(x_j - x_i)$ is greater than zero. So sorting all $w^T x_i$ before CG iterations of TRON must be a reasonable way to do a quick decision. If all $w^T x_i$ is sorted already, then computing the all parameter variables in (5) by DCM may cost $O(lk)$ [23]. If taking advantage of favourable searching performance of OST, then the $O(lk)$ term is would be reduced to $O(l\log(k))$ [15]. Therefore, by using TRON along with OST, the total computation complexity of linear RankSVM training with L2-loss is equal to $(O(l\log l) + O(ln + l\log(k) + n) \times$ average #CG iterations) $\times$ #outer iterations, where the $O(l\log l)$ term is the cost of sorting all $w^T x_i$.

3   Novel Parallel Algorithms for Linear RankSVM Training with L2-loss on Graphic Processing Units

In this section, we devote to designing efficient parallel algorithms for training linear RankSVM with L2-loss on GPU.

3.1   Efficient Parallel Algorithm for Computing Hessian-Vector Product on Graphic Processing Units

As shown in (5), each x_i has one-to-one relationship with the parameters β_i^+, β_i^-, α_i^+, α_i^-, γ_i^+ and γ_i^-. So we can assign a thread to calculate these variables that correspond to x_i. Although this rough parallel method can effectively achieve data-level parallelism on GPU, each assigned thread has to execute $O(l)$ steps, which is less effective over DCM ($O(lk)$) or OST ($O(l\log(k))$) if k is small.

However, according to definition of $\mathcal{P}$, x_i and x_j can combine into a preference pair if and only if $q_i = q_j$ holds true. Hence, all x_i (or all y_i) can be divided into m subsets because of existing m different queries in Q. We assume that for a query $Q(t) \in Q$, where $t = 1, \cdots, m$, $X_t = [x_{t1}, \cdots, x_{t|X_t|}]$ and $Y_t = [y_{t1}, \cdots, y_{t|Y_t|}]$ indicate the corresponding subsets of the training instances and labels respectively.

Theorem 1. *If all x_i (or all y_i) are divided into m subsets X_t (or Y_t) in terms of m different queries $Q(t), t = 1, \cdots, m$, then any two of X_t (or Y_t) are independent of each other.*

Proof. According to SV_i^+ and SV_i^-, computing the parameter variables corresponding to x_i (or y_i) only refers to all x_j (or all y_j) satisfying $q_j = q_i$. Therefore, it implies that any two of X_t (Y_t) are independent of each other.

According to Theorem 1, if $x_i \in X_t$ and $y_i \in Y_t$, then computing the parameters β_i^+, β_i^-, α_i^+, α_i^-, γ_i^+ and γ_i^- corresponding to x_i should go through only the subsets X_t and Y_t but not all x_i and all y_i, which can reduce the computation complexity significantly. Meanwhile, we should sort all subsets $w^T X_t = [w^T x_{t1}, \cdots, w^T x_{t|X_t|}]$ independently, instead of all $w^T x_i$. Moreover, if all X_t (or all Y_t) are obtained already, then computing $f(w)$, $\nabla f(w)$, and $\nabla^2 f(w)v$ based on $SV(w)$ is not suitable any more because it refers to all x_i and all y_i.

Definition 1. *For a query $Q(t)$, the rule of how to determine the preference pairs $(i,j), 1 \le i \le |X_t|, 1 \le j \le |X_t|, i \ne j$, is defined as $SV_t(w) \equiv \{(i,j) \mid 1 - w^T(x_{ti} - x_{tj}) > 0\}$ with $p_t \equiv |SV_t(w)|$.*

The $SV_t(w)$ is similar but essentially different from $SV(w)$ because it only involves the data information related to $Q(t)$. So if all X_t (or all Y_t) are obtained already, then the expressions of (4) and (5) should be transformed into (9) and (10) respectively.

$$SV_{ti}^+ = \{x_{tj} \mid y_{tj} > y_{ti}, 1 - w^T(x_{tj} - x_{ti}) > 0\}$$
$$SV_{ti}^- = \{x_{tj} \mid y_{tj} < y_{ti}, 1 - w^T(x_{ti} - x_{tj}) > 0\} \tag{9}$$

$$\beta_{ti}^+ = |SV_{ti}^+|, \alpha_{ti}^+ = \sum_{x_{tj} \in SV_{ti}^+} x_{tj}^T v, \gamma_{ti}^+ = \sum_{x_{tj} \in SV_{ti}^+} w^T x_{tj}$$
$$\beta_{ti}^- = |SV_{ti}^-|, \alpha_{ti}^- = \sum_{x_{tj} \in SV_{ti}^-} x_{tj}^T v, \gamma_{ti}^- = \sum_{x_{tj} \in SV_{ti}^-} w^T x_{tj} \tag{10}$$

Accordingly, $f(w)v$, $\nabla f(w)$ and $\nabla^2 f(w)$ have to be converted into:

$$f(w) = \frac{1}{2}w^T w + C(\tilde{A}_w \tilde{X}w - e_w)^T(\tilde{A}_w \tilde{X}w - e_w)$$
$$= \frac{1}{2}w^T w + C(w^T \tilde{X}^T((\tilde{A}_w^T \tilde{A}_w \tilde{X}w) - 2(\tilde{A}_w^T e_w)) + \sum_{t=1}^{m} p_t) \tag{11}$$

$$\nabla f(w) = w + 2C\tilde{X}^T((\tilde{A}_w^T \tilde{A}_w \tilde{X}w) - (\tilde{A}_w^T e_w)) \tag{12}$$

$$\nabla^2 f(w)v = v + 2C\tilde{X}^T(\tilde{A}_w^T \tilde{A}_w \tilde{X}v) \tag{13}$$

where $\tilde{X} = [X_1, \cdots, X_m]^T$, $\tilde{Y} = [Y_1, \cdots, Y_m]$, $\tilde{A}_w \in \mathbb{R}^{(\sum_{t=1}^{m} p_t) \times l}$ is as similar as A_w, $p_t = \sum_{i=1}^{|X_t|} \beta_{ti}^+ = \sum_{i=1}^{|X_t|} \beta_{ti}^-$. Of course, combined with (9) and (10), $\tilde{A}_w^T \tilde{A}_w \tilde{X}v$, $\tilde{A}_w^T \tilde{A}_w \tilde{X}w$ and $\tilde{A}_w^T e_w$ can be computed by:

$$\tilde{A}_w^T \tilde{A}_w \tilde{X} \boldsymbol{v} = \begin{bmatrix} (\beta_{11}^+ + \beta_{11}^-)\boldsymbol{x}_{11}^T \boldsymbol{v} - (\alpha_{11}^+ + \alpha_{11}^-) \\ \vdots \\ (\beta_{m|X_m|}^+ + \beta_{m|X_m|}^-)\boldsymbol{x}_{m|X_m|}^T \boldsymbol{v} - (\alpha_{m|X_m|}^+ + \alpha_{m|X_m|}^-) \end{bmatrix}$$

$$\tilde{A}_w^T \tilde{A}_w \tilde{X} \boldsymbol{w} = \begin{bmatrix} (\beta_{11}^+ + \beta_{11}^-)\boldsymbol{w}^T \boldsymbol{x}_{11} - (\gamma_{11}^+ + \gamma_{11}^-) \\ \vdots \\ (\beta_{m|X_m|}^+ + \beta_{m|X_m|}^-)\boldsymbol{w}^T \boldsymbol{x}_{m|X_m|} - (\gamma_{m|X_m|}^+ + \gamma_{m|X_m|}^-) \end{bmatrix}$$

$$\tilde{A}_w^T \boldsymbol{e}_w = \begin{bmatrix} \beta_{11}^- - \beta_{11}^+ \\ \vdots \\ \beta_{m|X_m|}^- - \beta_{m|X_m|}^+ \end{bmatrix}$$

According to Theorem 1, it needs to assign m thread blocks to compute all parameter variables shown in (10) in parallel on GPU. Moreover, each $\boldsymbol{x}_{ti}$ corresponds to β_{ti}^+, β_{ti}^-, α_{ti}^+, α_{ti}^-, γ_{ti}^+ and γ_{ti}^-, so do such computation can effectively achieve data-level parallelism on GPU in terms of the Definition 1. Assume that, for the t-th query $Q(t)$, $\boldsymbol{w}^T X_t'$ indicates the sorted $\boldsymbol{w}^T X_t$, i.e., $\boldsymbol{w}^T X_t' = [\boldsymbol{w}^T \boldsymbol{x}_{t\pi(1)}, \cdots, \boldsymbol{w}^T \boldsymbol{x}_{t\pi(|X_t|)}]$ satisfying $\boldsymbol{w}^T \boldsymbol{x}_{t\pi(1)} \leq, \cdots, \leq \boldsymbol{w}^T \boldsymbol{x}_{t\pi(|X_t|)}$, $X_t' \boldsymbol{v} = [\boldsymbol{x}_{t\pi(1)}^T \boldsymbol{v}, \cdots, \boldsymbol{x}_{t\pi(|X_t|)}^T \boldsymbol{v}]$ and $Y_t' = [y_{t\pi(1)}, \cdots, y_{t\pi(|X_t|)}]$. Then, we map three of $\boldsymbol{w}^T X_t'$, $X_t' \boldsymbol{v}$ and Y_t' into the t-th thread block of GPU jointly for parallel computing.

Based on the above discussions, we propose an efficient parallel algorithm, P-SWX, to compute parameter variables shown in (10) on GPU. The specific steps of P-SWX are clearly shown in Algorithm 2 in which the threads in the t-th thread block should execute at most $O(|X_t|)$ steps. Let $l_L \ll l$ indicates the largest $|X_t|$, then the threads on GPU should execute at most $O(l_L)$ steps.

However, to get more favourable training speed, the matrix operations, including matrix-matrix products, matrix-vector products and vector additions, should be calculated by respectively adopting *Segmm*, *Sgemv* and *Saxay* subroutines in CUBLAS [24]. So if all parameter variables shown in (10) are calculated already, then computing $\nabla^2 f(\boldsymbol{w})\boldsymbol{v}$, $\nabla f(\boldsymbol{w})$ and $f(\boldsymbol{w})$ on GPU by invoking CUBALS may be a more reasonable choice. Although P-SWX and CUBLAS may effectively improve the training speed of linear RankSVM with L2-loss, the sorting costs on CPU, $O(l \log l)$ term, is still high when addressing large-scale training data sets.

3.2   Efficient GPU Sorting for Linear RankSVM Training with L2-loss

As discussed in 3.1, we should assigning m thread blocks to sort all $\boldsymbol{w}^T X_t$ concurrently on GPU. As the subscript i of each $\boldsymbol{w}^T \boldsymbol{x}_{ti}$ needs to be applied in the next operations such as the operations in Algorithm 2, we should keep the subscript i of each $\boldsymbol{w}^T \boldsymbol{x}_{ti}$. Thus, we should convert each $\boldsymbol{w}^T \boldsymbol{x}_{ti}$ into a corresponding

---

Algorithm 2. P-SWX: m thread blocks should be assigned on GPU

Input $Y_t' \in \mathbb{R}^{|X_t|}$, $\boldsymbol{w}^T X_t' \in \mathbb{R}^{|X_t|}$, $X_t' \boldsymbol{v} \in \mathbb{R}^{|X_t|}$ and $t = 1, \cdots, m$
Output $\beta_{t\pi(i)}^+$, $\beta_{t\pi(i)}^-$, $\alpha_{t\pi(i)}^+$, $\alpha_{t\pi(i)}^-$, $\gamma_{t\pi(i)}^+$ and $\gamma_{t\pi(i)}^-$ ($t = 1, \cdots, m$ and $\pi(i) = 1, \cdots, |X_t|$).

1: Initialize:$\beta_{t\pi(i)}^+ \leftarrow 0$, $\beta_{t\pi(i)}^- \leftarrow 0$, $\alpha_{t\pi(i)}^+ \leftarrow 0$, $\alpha_{t\pi(i)}^- \leftarrow 0$, $\gamma_{t\pi(i)}^+ \leftarrow 0$ and $\gamma_{t\pi(i)}^- \leftarrow 0$,
   ($t = 1, \cdots, m$ and $\pi(i) = 1, \cdots, |X_t|$)
2:   $j \leftarrow 1$
3:   **while** $j \leq |X_t|$, $\boldsymbol{x}_{t\pi(j)} \in \mathrm{SV}_{t\pi(i)}^+$, $\pi(i) = 1, \cdots, |X_t|$ and $t = 1, \cdots, m$ **do**
4:        $\alpha_{t\pi(i)}^+ \leftarrow \alpha_{t\pi(i)}^+ + \boldsymbol{x}_{t\pi(j)}^T \boldsymbol{v}$
5:        $\beta_{t\pi(i)}^+ \leftarrow \beta_{t\pi(i)}^+ + 1$
6:        $\gamma_{t\pi(i)}^+ \leftarrow \gamma_{t\pi(i)}^+ + \boldsymbol{w}^T \boldsymbol{x}_{t\pi(j)}$
7:        $j \leftarrow j + 1$
8:   **end while**
9:   $j \leftarrow |X_t|$
10: **while** $j \geq 1$, $\boldsymbol{x}_{t\pi(j)} \in \mathrm{SV}_{t\pi(i)}^-$, $\pi(i) = 1, \cdots, |X_t|$ and $t = 1, \cdots, m$ **do**
11:       $\alpha_{t\pi(i)}^- \leftarrow \alpha_{t\pi(i)}^- + \boldsymbol{x}_{t\pi(j)}^T \boldsymbol{v}$
12:       $\beta_{t\pi(i)}^- \leftarrow \beta_{t\pi(i)}^- + 1$
13:       $\gamma_{t\pi(i)}^- \leftarrow \gamma_{t\pi(i)}^- + \boldsymbol{w}^T \boldsymbol{x}_{t\pi(j)}$
14:       $j \leftarrow j - 1$
15: **end while**

---

struct node that contains two elements *value* and *id*. Taking a $\boldsymbol{w}^T \boldsymbol{x}_{ti}$ for example, the *value* and *id* of its corresponding *struct* node store the value of $\boldsymbol{w}^T \boldsymbol{x}_{ti}$ and i, respectively.

In computer memory, $\boldsymbol{w}^T \tilde{X}^T$ is always stored instead of all $\boldsymbol{w}^T X_t$, thus $\boldsymbol{w}^T \tilde{X}^T$ should be converted into a *struct* sequence d^{pri}, and each $\boldsymbol{w}^T X_t$ corresponds to a subsequence d_t^{pri} of d^{pri}. Apparently, how to locate the boundaries of each d_t^{pri} in d^{pri} is crucial to achieve the sorting in parallel on GPU. Thus, we define a *struct* parameter *workset* with two elements *beg* and *end* to record the boundaries of each subsequence in d^{pri}, where *beg* and *end* store starting position and ending position of a subsequence respectively. Taking the t-th subsequence d_t^{pri} for example, both *beg* and *end* of *workset(t)* can be calculated by using following expression.

$$workset(t) = \begin{cases} beg = 1 + |X_1| + \cdots + |X_{t-1}| \\ end = |X_1| + |X_2| + \cdots + |X_t| \end{cases} \tag{14}$$

According to the above discussions and work done by D. Cederman et al. [25], we propose an efficient GPU sorting, GPU-quicksorting, by using an auxiliary buffer d^{aux} which is as large as d^{pri}. The basic principle of such a GPU sorting are primarily broken down into two steps. The first one is that if the $|X_t|$, in the t-th thread block, is larger than a user-defined *minsize*, then the d_t^{pri} would be partitioned into two sub-sequences by a randomly selected *pivot*; if not, the d_t^{pri} would be sorted directly by *bitornic sorting* [26]. The second one is that the each divided subsequence, generated in the first step, with the size $\leq minsize$

would be sorted by *bitornic sorting*, while those/that with the large size should be further divided by the first step until the size of each new divided subsequence has been $\leq minsize$. The specific steps of GPU-quicksorting are presented in Algorithm 3.

Theoretically, our proposed GPU-quicksorting would be an efficient GPU sorting algorithm since it can make full use of the unique properties of GPU to sort multiple sequences in parallel within a single *GPU Kernel*. Consequently, by using Algorithm 1, Algorithm 2, Algorithm 3 and CUBLAS, we can design an efficient GPU implementation P-SWXRankSVM to train linear RankSVM with L2-loss on GPU.

4   Performance Evaluation

In this section, we set two state-of-the-art applications OSTRankSVM[2] and DCMRankSVM as the comparison tools to evaluate P-SWXRankSVM in our experimental tests. The OSTRankSVM is an effective method that solves the linear RankSVM training with L2-loss by TRON along with OST, while DCM-RankSVM is another effective method that solves the linear RankSVM training with L2-loss by TRON along with DCM.

There are six real world training data sets, the size of each of which is clearly presented in Table 1, that are used in our experimental tests. We set C, ϵ_s and $minsize$ to be 1, 10^{-5} and 64 respectively. It is unclear yet if it is the best option, but certainly we would like to try custom setting first. The measurements are carried out in a single server with four Intel(R) Xeon(R) E5620 2.40GHz four-core CPUs and 32GB of RAM running Ubuntu 9.04(64 bit). The graphics processor used is a NVIDA Tesla C2050 card with 448 CUDA cores, and the frequency of each CUDA core is 1.15 GHz. The card has 3GB GDDR5 memory and a memory bandwidth of 144 GB/s. Besides, the CUDA driver and runtime versions used in our experiments are both 5.0, and only one Tesla C2050 card is used in all benchmark tests.

Table 1. Training Data Sets

Data Set	l	n	k	$|Q|$	p	l_L
MQ2007-list	743,790	46	1,268	1,017	285,943,893	1,268
MQ2008-list	540,679	46	1,831	471	323,151,792	1,831
MSLR-WEB10K	723,421	136	2	6,000	31,783,391	809
MSLR-WEB30K	2,270,296	136	5	18,919	101,312,036	1,251
MQ2007	42,158	46	2	1017	246,015	147
MQ2008	9,630	46	3	471	52,325	121

---

[2] http://www.csie.ntu.edu.tw/~cjlin/papers/ranksvm/ranksvml2_exp-1.3.tgz

---

Algorithm 3. GPU-quicksorting(GPU kernel)

Input $workset$, m, d^{pri} and d^{aux}
1: $bx \leftarrow xblockid$ //$xblockid$: the ID number of thread block
2: **if** $bx \leq m$ **then**
3:     $beg, end \leftarrow workset(bx).beg, workset(bx).end$
4:     **if** $end - beg < minsize$ **then**
5:         $d^{aux}(beg \rightarrow end) \leftarrow d^{pri}(beg \rightarrow end)$
6:         $bitonic(d^{aux}(beg \rightarrow end), d^{pri}(beg \rightarrow end))$ //Sort the data.
7:     **else**
8:         push both beg and end to $workstack$
9:         **while** $workstack \neq \emptyset$ **do**
10:             $d^{aux}(beg \rightarrow end) \leftarrow d^{pri}(beg \rightarrow end)$
11:             $pivot \leftarrow random(d^{aux}(beg \rightarrow end))$ //Select a $pivot$ randomly.
12:             $lt_{threadid}, gt_{threadid} \leftarrow 0, 0$ //$threadid$: the ID number of threads
13:             **for** $i \leftarrow beg + threadid, i \leq end, i \leftarrow i + threadcount$ **do**
14:                 **if** $d^{aux}(i).value \leq pivot.value$ and $pivot.id \neq d^{aux}(i).id$ **then**
15:                     $lt_{threadid} \leftarrow lt_{threadid} + 1$
16:                 **else**
17:                     $gt_{threadid} \leftarrow gt_{threadid} + 1$
18:                 **end if**
19:             **end for**
20:             $Cumulative\ Sum: lt_0, lt_1, lt_2, \cdots, lt_{sum} \leftarrow 0, lt_0, lt_0 + lt_1, \cdots, \sum_{i=0}^{threadcount} lt_i$
21:             $Cumulative\ Sum: gt_0, gt_1, gt_2, \cdots, gt_{sum} \leftarrow 0, gt_0, gt_0 + gt_1, \cdots, \sum_{i=0}^{threadcount} gt_i$
22:             $lp, gp \leftarrow beg + lt_{threadid}, end - gt_{threadid+1}$
23:             **for** $i \leftarrow beg + threadid, i \leq end, i \leftarrow i + threadcount$ **do**
24:                 **if** $d^{aux}(i).value \leq pivot.value$ and $pivot.id \neq d^{aux}(i).id$ **then**
25:                     $d^{pri}(lp) \leftarrow d^{aux}(i).value, lp \leftarrow lp + 1$ //Write the data to the left of $pivot$.
26:                 **else**
27:                     $d^{pri}(gp) \leftarrow d^{aux}(i).value, gp \leftarrow gp - 1$ //Write the data to the right of $pivot$.
28:                 **end if**
29:             **end for**
30:             **for** $i \leftarrow beg + lt_{sum} + threadid, i < end - gt_{sum}, i \leftarrow i + threadcount$ **do**
31:                 $d^{pri}(i) \leftarrow pivot$
32:             **end for**
33:             pop both beg and end from $workstack$
34:             **if** $|d^{pri}(beg \rightarrow (beg + lt_{sum}))| \leq minisize$ **then**
35:                 $d^{aux}(beg \rightarrow (beg + lt_{sum})) \leftarrow d^{pri}(beg \rightarrow (beg + lt_{sum}))$
36:                 $bitonic(d^{aux}(beg \rightarrow (beg + lt_{sum})), d^{pri}(beg \rightarrow (beg + lt_{sum})))$
37:             **else**
38:                 push both beg and $beg + lt_{sum}$ to $workstack$
39:                 $beg, end \leftarrow beg, (beg + lt_{sum})$
40:             **end if**
41:             **if** $|d^{pri}((end - gt_{sum}) \rightarrow end)| \leq minisize$ **then**
42:                 $d^{aux}((end - gt_{sum}) \rightarrow end) \leftarrow d^{pri}((end - gt_{sum}) \rightarrow end)$
43:                 $bitonic(d^{aux}((end - gt_{sum}) \rightarrow end), d^{pri}((end - gt_{sum}) \rightarrow end))$
44:             **else**
45:                 push both $(end - gt_{sum})$ and end to $workstack$
46:                 $beg, end \leftarrow (end - gt_{sum}), end$
47:             **end if**
48:         **end while**
49:     **end if**
50: **end if**

4.1 Performance Evaluation for P-SWXRankSVM

The specific performance comparisons among DCMRankSVM, OSTRankSVM and P-SWXRankSVM with respect to the different training data sets are presented in Table 2. As shown in the table, the OSTRankSVM performs better than OSTRankSVM, which mainly relies on the superior property of OST ($O(l\log(k))$) in reducing the computation complexity compared to DCM ($O(lk)$). As expected, the P-SWXRankSVM has greater speedup performance over both of DCMRankSVM and OSTRankSVM when addressing the large-scale training data sets. Apparently, such efficient speedup for P-SWXRankSVM mainly depends on that P-SWXRankSVM can make full use of the great computation power of GPU based on our designing.

Table 2. Performance Comparison among DCMRankSVM, OSTRankSVM, P-SWXRankSVM

Data Set	DCMRankSVM Training Time(s)	OSTRankSVM Training Time(s)	P-SWXRankSVM Training Time(s)	Speedup
MQ2007-list	380.51	203.02	22.46	16.94x/9.04x
MQ2008-list	493.12	276.46	37.17	11.81x/7.44x
MSLR-WEB10K	2791.22	2481.35	276.11	10.11x/8.99x
MSLR-WEB30K	19449.65	17019.16	939.38	20.70x/18.12x
MQ2007	12.67	10.18	5.90	2.18x/1.73x
MQ2008	0.67	0.48	1.37	0.49x/0.35x

Moreover, to analyse the convergence performance of DCMRankSVM, OSTRankSVM and P-SWXRankSVM in more detail, we investigate the relative difference η to the optimal function value shown as:

$$\eta = \left| \frac{f(\boldsymbol{w}) - f(\boldsymbol{w}^*)}{f(\boldsymbol{w}^*)} \right| \tag{15}$$

where the $\boldsymbol{w}^*$ is the optimum of (1), and the ϵ_s is also set to be 10^{-5}.

The measured results involving convergence speed with respect to the different training data sets are clearly illustrated in Figure 1. From the figure, we can observe that the OSTRankSVM converges faster than DCMRankSVM as training time goes, but the convergence speed of OSTRankSVM is not marked enough over that of DCMRankSVM as training time goes if the data sets have a small k. This may be because OST becomes more efficient over DCM if k is large enough. As expected, P-SWXRankSVM can converge much faster than both of DCMRankSVM and OSTRankSVM. However, it is special for "MQ2008". The reason for this case relies on that if the data sets with small size can't effectively utilize the great computation power of GPU, so invoking P-SWXRankSVM to train the small data set, such as "MQ2008", would cost too much time in launching GPU kernels and communicating between CPU and GPU, rather than in computing.

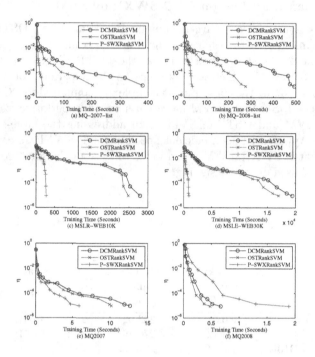

Fig. 1. A Convergence speed comparison among DCMRankSVM, OSTRankSVM, P-SWXRankSVM

4.2 Prediction Performance Evaluation for P-SWXRankSVM

If an optimum w^* of (1) is obtained, then we need to evaluate that such a w^* is whether good or not for doing prediction. In general, checking Pairwise Accuracy (PA) [27] is very suitable for measuring the prediction performance of pairwise approach such as RankSVM. Thus, we choose PA as the measurement in here.

$$\text{PA} \equiv \frac{|\,\{(i,j)\,|\in \mathcal{P}, w^{*T}x_i > w^{*T}x_j\}\,|}{p} \tag{16}$$

The specific measured results are presented in Table 3 clearly. As shown in the table, training linear RankSVM with L2-loss by using anyone of these implementations would result in almost same prediction performance, which effectively proves that P-SWXRankSVM not only can accelerate the linear RankSVM training with L2-loss significantly but also guarantee the prediction accuracy. However, please note that such a case can be explained as follows: In essence, four of DCM, OST, P-SWX and GPU-quicksorting are devoted to improving the training speed of the linear RankSVM with L2-loss, thus they, theoretically, couldn't influence the prediction accuracy.

Table 3. Measured Pairwise Accuracy of DCMRankSVM, OSTRankSVM, P-SWXRankSVM

Data Set	Pairwise Accuracy (PA)		
	DCMRankSVM(%)	OSTRankSVM(%)	P-SWXRankSVM(%)
MQ2007-list	81.11	81.11	81.11
MQ2008-list	82.11	82.11	80.72
MSLR-WEB10K	61.25	61.04	60.43
MSLR-WEB30K	60.96	60.79	60.45
MQ2007	70.59	70.59	70.60
MQ2008	80.24	80.24	80.24

5   Conclusion and Future Work

In this paper, we have proposed two efficient parallel algorithms P-SWX and GPU-quicksorting to accelerate the linear RankSVM training with L2-loss on GPU. To sum up, to design efficient parallel algorithms for the linear RankSVM training with L2-loss, we not only divide all training instances x_i and labels y_i into several independent subsets in terms of different queries, but also redefine a new rule of how to determine the preference pairs (i, j). Just because of this, our proposed parallel algorithms can achieve both task-level and data-level parallelism effectively on GPU. Since this is the initial work to design GPU implementations for training linear RankSVM with L2-loss on a single GPU, there are still many challenges that should to be addressed to further explore their multiple GPU implementations. So, the next extension of this work will use multiple GPU devices to solve even larger training problem in parallel fashion.

Acknowledgement. We would like to thank all anonymous referees for their valuable comments. This research is partially supported by the National Natural Science Foundation of China under Grants No. 60773199, U0735001 and 61073055.

References

1. Owens, J.D., Houston, M., Luebke, D., Green, S., Stone, J.E., Phillips, J.C.: Gpu computing. Proceedings of the IEEE 96(5), 879–899 (2008)
2. Nvidia, C.: Compute unified device architecture programming guide (2007)
3. Steinkraus, D., Buck, I., Simard, P.: Using gpus for machine learning algorithms. In: Proceedings of the Eighth International Conference on Document Analysis and Recognition, pp. 1115–1120. IEEE (2005)
4. Chapelle, O., Chang, Y.: Yahoo! learning to rank challenge overview. Journal of Machine Learning Research-Proceedings Track 14, 1–24 (2011)
5. Fuhr, N.: Optimum polynomial retrieval functions based on the probability ranking principle. ACM Transactions on Information Systems (TOIS) 7(3), 183–204 (1989)

6. Cooper, W.S., Gey, F.C., Dabney, D.P.: Probabilistic retrieval based on staged logistic regression. In: Proceedings of the 15th Annual International ACM SIGIR Conference on Research and Development in Information Retrieval, pp. 198–210. ACM (1992)

7. Freund, Y., Iyer, R., Schapire, R.E., Singer, Y.: An efficient boosting algorithm for combining preferences. The Journal of Machine Learning Research 4, 933–969 (2003)

8. Burges, C., Shaked, T., Renshaw, E., Lazier, A., Deeds, M., Hamilton, N., Hullender, G.: Learning to rank using gradient descent. In: Proceedings of the 22nd International Conference on Machine Learning, pp. 89–96. ACM (2005)

9. Quoc, C., Le, V.: Learning to rank with nonsmooth cost functions. Proceedings of the Advances in Neural Information Processing Systems 19, 193–200 (2007)

10. Wu, Q., Burges, C.J., Svore, K.M., Gao, J.: Ranking, boosting, and model adaptation. Tecnical Report, MSR-TR-2008-109 (2008)

11. Valizadegan, H., Jin, R., Zhang, R., Mao, J.: Learning to rank by optimizing ndcg measure. In: Advances in Neural Information Processing Systems, pp. 1883–1891 (2009)

12. Cortes, C., Vapnik, V.: Support-vector networks. Machine Learning 20(3), 273–297 (1995)

13. Joachims, T., Finley, T., Yu, C.N.J.: Cutting-plane training of structural svms. Machine Learning 77(1), 27–59 (2009)

14. Sculley, D.: Large scale learning to rank. In: NIPS Workshop on Advances in Ranking, pp. 1–6 (2009)

15. Airola, A., Pahikkala, T., Salakoski, T.: Training linear ranking svms in linearithmic time using red–black trees. Pattern Recognition Letters 32(9), 1328–1336 (2011)

16. Lee, C.P., Lin, C.J.: Large-scale linear ranksvm. Neural Computation, 1–37 (2014)

17. Chapelle, O., Keerthi, S.S.: Efficient algorithms for ranking with svms. Information Retrieval 13(3), 201–215 (2010)

18. Yu, H., Kim, Y., Hwang, S.: Rv-svm: An efficient method for learning ranking svm. In: Theeramunkong, T., Kijsirikul, B., Cercone, N., Ho, T.-B. (eds.) PAKDD 2009. LNCS, vol. 5476, pp. 426–438. Springer, Heidelberg (2009)

19. Kuo, T.M., Lee, C.P., Lin, C.J.: Large-scale kernel ranksvm.

20. Conn, A.R., Gould, N.I., Toint, P.L.: Trust region methods, vol. (1). Siam (2000)

21. Lin, C.J., Weng, R.C., Keerthi, S.S.: Trust region newton method for logistic regression. The Journal of Machine Learning Research 9, 627–650 (2008)

22. Fan, R.E., Chang, K.W., Hsieh, C.J., Wang, X.R., Lin, C.J.: Liblinear: A library for large linear classification. The Journal of Machine Learning Research 9, 1871–1874 (2008)

23. Joachims, T.: A support vector method for multivariate performance measures. In: Proceedings of the 22nd International Conference on Machine Learning, pp. 377–384. ACM (2005)

24. Nvidia, C.: Cublas library programming guide, 1st edn. NVIDIA Corporation (2007)

25. Cederman, D., Tsigas, P.: A practical quicksort algorithm for graphics processors. In: Halperin, D., Mehlhorn, K. (eds.) ESA 2008. LNCS, vol. 5193, pp. 246–258. Springer, Heidelberg (2008)

26. Batcher, K.E.: Sorting networks and their applications. In: Proceedings of the Spring Joint Computer Conference, April 30-May 2, pp. 307–314. ACM (1968)

27. Richardson, M., Prakash, A., Brill, E.: Beyond pagerank: machine learning for static ranking. In: Proceedings of the 15th International Conference on World Wide Web, pp. 707–715. ACM (2006)

A Real-Time Scheduling Framework
Based on Multi-core Dynamic Partitioning
in Virtualized Environment

Song Wu, Like Zhou, Danqing Fu, Hai Jin, and Xuanhua Shi

Services Computing Technology and System Lab
Cluster and Grid Computing Lab
School of Computer Science and Technology
Huazhong University of Science and Technology, Wuhan, 430074, China
{wusong,zhoulike,fdq1989,hjin,xhshi}@hust.edu.cn

Abstract. With the prevalence of virtualization and cloud computing,
many real-time applications are running in virtualized cloud environments. However, their performance cannot be guaranteed because current hypervisors' CPU schedulers aim to share CPU resources fairly and
improve system throughput. They do not consider real-time constraints
of these applications, which result in frequent deadline misses. In this
paper, we present a real-time scheduling framework in virtualized environment. In the framework, we propose a mechanism called *multi-core
dynamic partitioning* to divide *physical CPUs* (PCPUs) into two pools
dynamically according to the scheduling parameters of *real-time virtual
machines* (RT-VMs). We apply different schedulers to these pools to
schedule RT-VMs and non-RT-VMs respectively. Besides, we design a
global earliest deadline first (*vGEDF*) scheduler to schedule RT-VMs.
We implement a prototype in the Xen hypervisor and conduct experiments to verify its effectiveness.

Keywords: Virtualization, Real-time scheduling, Multi-core, Cloud
computing.

1 Introduction

Cloud computing is a rapidly emerging paradigm that cloud resources in data
centers are leased by users on demand. Cloud data centers, such as Amazon's
Elastic Compute Cloud (EC2) [1], use virtualization technology to provide such
on-demand infrastructure services. In cloud data centers, a *physical machine*
(PM) always hosts many *virtual machines* (VMs), and various kinds of applications are running in these VMs. Many of them have real-time constraints, such
as streaming server, VoIP server, and real-time stream computing platforms.

Although more and more real-time applications run in virtualized cloud environments, their performance is hardly guaranteed [11][13][18]. The main reason is that virtualization adds an additional layer, called hypervisor such as
Xen [8], between *guest operating systems* (guest OSes) and underlying hardware.

C.-H. Hsu et al. (Eds.): NPC 2014, LNCS 8707, pp. 195–207, 2014.
© IFIP International Federation for Information Processing 2014

CPU schedulers in hypervisors are not optimized for real-time applications, such as Xen's default Credit scheduler [9].

Previous studies [13][16][18] present some solutions to support real-time applications in virtualized environments. However, they are not good enough for these applications and cloud environments. RT-Xen [16] does not support VMs with multiple *virtual CPUs* (VCPUs). Schedulability analysis is important in real-time scheduling, but these studies [13][18] do not analyze their schedulability. More importantly, all these solutions favor the RT-VMs running real-time applications, which may affect the performance of non-real-time applications and violate the performance isolation guaranteed by cloud platforms.

Aiming at these problems, this paper presents a real-time scheduling framework based on *multi-core dynamic partitioning*. First, it divides PCPUs into two pools dynamically by taking *non-uniform memory access* (NUMA) architecture into account according to the scheduling parameters of RT-VMs. It allows RT-VMs to run on a pool and non-RT-VMs to run on the other pool, which brings good performance isolation. Second, we design a *global earliest deadline first* (*vGEDF*) scheduler to schedule RT-VMs. Moreover, we implement a working prototype of the real-time scheduling framework in the Xen hypervisor, named *Risa*, and evaluate its effectiveness through experiments.

In summary, the main contributions of this paper are as follows.

– We present a real-time scheduling framework to support real-time applications in virtualized environment. The framework provides good performance isolation through multi-core dynamic partitioning.
– Considering the domination of multi-core processors in server market, we present the vGEDF scheduler to schedule RT-VMs, which can support real-time applications well and take full advantage of multi-core processors.
– We implement a prototype in the Xen hypervisor, and conduct experiments to verify its effectiveness. The experimental results show that our framework can support real-time applications well, reduce operation expense caused by manual operations in VM management, and improve CPU utilization.

The rest of this paper is organized as follows. Section 2 presents the design of the real-time scheduling framework in detail. We explain the experimental environment and show the experimental results in Section 3. Section 4 briefly surveys the related work. Finally, Section 5 concludes this paper.

2   Design of Real-Time Scheduling Framework

In this section, we present the design of our real-time scheduling framework, which is shown in Fig. 1. In the framework, PCPUs are partitioned into two pools (i.e. *rt-pool* and *non-rt-pool*) automatically according to the scheduling parameters of RT-VMs. We apply our vGEDF scheduler to *rt-pool* to schedule RT-VMs and the Credit scheduler to *non-rt-pool* to schedule non-RT-VMs. In the following, we first describe how to partition PCPUs automatically. Then, we propose the design of the vGEDF scheduler.

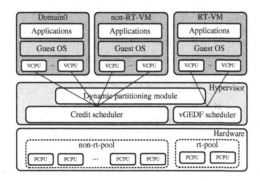

Fig. 1. The real-time scheduling framework

2.1 Multi-core Dynamic Partitioning Mechanism

In the multi-tenant cloud environment, a PM hosts many VMs that run various kinds of applications from different customers. However, a single CPU scheduler cannot support all the applications well. For example, although the Credit scheduler supports CPU-intensive and memory-intensive applications well, it is not suitable for real-time applications. Accordingly, the schedulers optimized for real-time applications [12][13][16][18] always favor these applications, which may affect the performance of non-real-time applications. Moreover, an important requirement of multi-tenant cloud environment is performance isolation. As a result, it is a challenge to support real-time applications while minimizing the impact on non-real-time applications running on the same PM. In this paper, we present the multi-core dynamic partitioning mechanism to meet this goal.

Currently, although administrators can divide PCPUs into multiple pools and apply different schedulers to these pools manually, this method is not fit for cloud environment. The reasons are as follows. On one hand, administrators need to estimate the requirements of RT-VMs, and statically allocate peak number of PCPUs to a pool, which probably results in resource over-provision and increases operation expense. On the other hand, when the requirements of RT-VMs change, administrators need to manually change the number of PCPUs allocated to the pool. Otherwise, the performance of real-time applications may not be guaranteed any more. Our multi-core dynamic partitioning mechanism addresses these drawbacks well.

If a PM has RT-VMs, the real-time scheduling framework partitions PCPUs into two pools automatically and applies different schedulers to these pools to schedule RT-VMs and non-RT-VMs respectively. So, first of all, we need to determine how many PCPUs should be allocated to *rt-pool*. Then, we allocate corresponding PCPUs to *rt-pool* by taking NUMA architecture into account.

How Many PCPUs Should Be Allocated to Rt-Pool. For the convenience of description, we define some variables as follows:

- C_i: the worst-case execution time of the ith task.
- T_i: the inter-arrival period of the ith task (assumed to be equal to the relative deadline).
- N_P: the number of PCPUs should be allocated to *rt-pool*.
- N_{RT}: the number of RT-VMs in a PM.
- NV_i: the number of VCPUs of the ith RT-VM.
- p_i: the *period* parameter of the ith RT-VM, which indicates the relative deadline.
- s_i: the *slice* parameter of the ith RT-VM, which represents the worst-case execution time.

According to the schedulability test of EDF scheduling [14], a set of real-time tasks is schedulable only if its total utilization does not exceed 100%.

$$\sum_{i=1}^{n} \frac{C_i}{T_i} \leq 1 \tag{1}$$

In virtualized environments, in order to guarantee the schedulability of RT-VMs in multi-core platforms, the scheduling parameters of RT-VMs and the number of PCPUs must satisfy the following equation:

$$\sum_{i=1}^{N_{RT}} \frac{s_i \times NV_i}{p_i} \leq N_P \tag{2}$$

Hence, derived from (2), N_P can be calculated by (3). Actually, N_P is the minimal number of PCPUs should be allocated to *rt-pool*. It has a strong relationship with the scheduler applied to *rt-pool*. Equation (3) defines how to calculate N_P for the vGEDF scheduler. Our real-time scheduling framework can be easily extended to support other real-time schedulers. The only thing needed to be done is to define how to calculate N_P.

$$N_P = \left\lceil \sum_{i=1}^{N_{RT}} \frac{s_i \times NV_i}{p_i} \right\rceil \tag{3}$$

How to Partition PCPUs. Cloud is a highly dynamic environment. Various operations are happened in a short time period, such as VM creation, VM destroy, and VM reconfiguration. As a result, N_P is changing as time goes on. Considering such dynamic characteristic, we design a multi-core dynamic partitioning algorithm to support cloud environment. All the operations that may change N_P trigger the algorithm to allocate adequate number of PCPUs to *rt-pool*. The pseudo-code of the algorithm is shown in Algorithm 1.

Algorithm 1. Multi-core Dynamic Partitioning Algorithm

---

1 $prev\_N_P \leftarrow num\_pcpus(rt\_pool)$;
2 **foreach** vm *in the list of RT-VMs* **do**
3 | $new\_num \leftarrow new\_num + (vm.nvcpus * vm.slice)/vm.period$;
4 **end**
5 $N_P \leftarrow ceil(new\_num)$;
6 delete $timer$;
7 **if** $N_P > prev\_N_P$ **then**
8 | $partition(non\_rt\_pool, rt\_pool, N_P - prev\_N_P)$;
9 **else if** $N_P < prev\_N_P$ **then**
10 | set $timer$ to call $partition(rt\_pool, non\_rt\_pool, prev\_N_P - N_P)$;
11 **end**

First, the algorithm reads the scheduling parameters of RT-VMs and calculates N_P (line 2~5). Then, it compares N_P with the previous one. If N_P is greater than the previous one, the algorithm allocates more PCPUs to *rt-pool* immediately. On the contrary, if it is less than the previous N_P, the algorithm shrinks *rt-pool*. However, the shrink operation is not executed instantly, because it may cause fluctuation. For example, administrators may destroy a RT-VM belonging to a customer and create the other RT-VM for the other customer immediately. If the algorithm shrinks *rt-pool* immediately, it needs to expand *rt-pool* after the shrink. In order to avoid such fluctuation, we adopt a delayed shrink manner, which uses a timer to delay the shrink operation (line 6~11).

Nowadays, an increasing number of new multi-core systems use the NUMA architecture. There are multiple memory nodes in modern NUMA systems, and the access latency of local nodes is shorter than that of remote nodes. Aimed at such characteristic, our multi-core dynamic partitioning algorithm takes the NUMA architecture into account when we partition PCPUs. It preferably allocates

---

Algorithm 2. NUMA-aware Partitioning Algorithm

---

1 $prev\_num \leftarrow num\_pcpus(rt\_pool)$;
2 **if** $prev\_num == 0$ *and* $dst\_pool == rt\_pool$ **then**
3 | select $pcpu$ on which a RT-VM currently running or previously run;
4 | remove $pcpu$ from src_pool;
5 | add $pcpu$ to dst_pool;
6 | $pcpu\_num \leftarrow pcpu\_num - 1$;
7 **end**
8 $local\_node \leftarrow$ the local node associated with dst_pool;
9 **while** $pcpu\_num! = 0$ **do**
10 | remove $pcpu$ from src_pool that belongs to $local\_node$ or other nodes if all PCPUs in $local\_node$ are allocated to dst_pool;
11 | add $pcpu$ to dst_pool;
12 | $pcpu\_num \leftarrow pcpu\_num - 1$;
13 **end**

PCPUs belonging to a NUMA node to *rt-pool* instead of randomly selected PC-PUs. The pseudo-code of the algorithm is shown in Algorithm 2, which shrinks *src_pool* and expands *dst_pool*. If *rt-pool* is empty, the algorithm selects the PCPU on which a RT-VM currently running or previously run, and allocates this PCPU to *rt-pool* (line 2∼7). Then, it gets the NUMA topology of the PM and finds the local node associated with *dst_pool* (line 8). Finally, the algorithm preferably allocates PCPUs belonging to this node to *dst_pool*. If all the PCPUs belonging to this node are allocated to *dst_pool*, the algorithm picks PCPUs from other nodes and allocates them to *dst_pool* (line 9∼13).

2.2   vGEDF Scheduler

Schedulability analysis is important in real-time scheduling. However, previous solutions [13][18] do not analyze their schedulability. In this paper, we design the vGEDF scheduler based on EDF scheduling algorithm, whose schedulability is analyzed by previous studies [7].

Nowadays, multi-core processors have dominated server markets. Schedulers must take full advantage of the multi-core processors. The *Simple Earliest Deadline First* (SEDF) scheduler [9] is not suitable for cloud environments because of the lack of load balance among multi-cores. On the contrary, our vGEDF scheduler supports real-time applications in multi-core platform well through global queues. Its architecture is shown in Fig. 2.

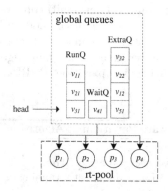

Fig. 2. Architecture of vGEDF

In the real-time scheduling framework, the vGEDF scheduler is applied to *rt-pool*. All the PCPUs in *rt-pool* share three global queues: runnable queue (*RunQ*), waiting queue (*WaitQ*), and extra queue (*ExtraQ*). Each VM also has following scheduling parameters: p_i, s_i, and x_i. The meaning of p_i and s_i is described in Section 2.1. x_i is a boolean value to indicate whether a VM can get extra CPU time (i.e. work-conserving mode). The scheduler inserts VCPUs into these queues according to their scheduling parameters. If a VCPU has remaining

CPU slice in current period, it is inserted into *RunQ*. Otherwise, it is inserted into *WaitQ* or *ExtraQ* according to the value of x_i of the VCPU. The priority of a VCPU is calculated according to their deadlines: the earlier the deadline, the higher the priority. VCPUs in *RunQ* are sorted by their priorities, and the VCPU in the head of *RunQ* has the highest priority. *ExtraQ* is used to support work-conserving mode.

Algorithm 3. vGEDF Scheduling Algorithm

---

1 handle the bookkeeping for *current* in *RunQ* or *ExtraQ*;
2 update_queues(*RunQ*, *WaitQ*);
3 snext ← CandidatePick(*RunQ*);
4 **if** *snext == NULL* **then**
5   snext ← CandidatePick(*ExtraQ*);
6   **if** *snext == NULL* **then**
7 | **return** *idle_vcpu[cpu]*;
8   **end**
9 **end**
10 ret.task ← snext.vcpu;
11 snext.picked ← 1;
12 **return** *ret.task*;

The pseudo-code of the vGEDF scheduling is shown in Algorithm 3. The scheduler first conducts bookkeeping for the current running VCPU and updates the parameters of VCPUs in *RunQ* and *WaitQ* (line 1~2). Then, it picks a VCPU from *RunQ* or *ExtraQ* to run (line 3~10). For the convenience of bookkeeping and updating queues, the picked VCPU is still in the queues. Therefore, when a VCPU is picked to run, we need to mark it as *picked* (line 11).

Because our vGEDF scheduler picks the VCPU from global queues to run, a VCPU may run on several PCPUs in a short time period, which may increase cache misses. We present some approaches to reduce cache misses. On one hand, the multi-core dynamic partitioning mechanism preferably allocates PCPUs belonging to a NUMA node to *rt-pool* and these PCPUs share the last-level cache. The vGEDF scheduler applied to *rt-pool* will not increase the last level cache misses if all the PCPUs in *rt-pool* belong to a NUMA node. On the other hand, in order to further mitigate the impact of cache misses, we present a cache-aware pick algorithm (shown in Algorithm 4), which takes cache affinity into account, to reduce L1 and L2 cache misses.

Besides, although the vGEDF scheduler uses global queues to manage VCPUs, the scalability is not a problem for the scheduler. This is because schedulers that use global queues can also scale to a certain number of PCPUs. Moreover, only a part of applications running in cloud environment is real-time applications. As a result, our framework allocates a small amount of PCPUs to *rt-pool* and only these PCPUs share the global queues. Even a PM has many PCPUs and all these PCPUs should be allocated to *rt-pool*, the scalability problem can also be addressed by our framework through partitioning multiple real-time pools.

Algorithm 4. CandidatePick Algorithm

```
 1  ret ← NULL;
 2  foreach vcpu in queue do
 3  │   if vcpu.cpu_mask&current_pcpu! = 0 then
 4  │   │   if vcpu.processor! = current_pcpu&&((vcpu.picked == 1&&vcpu! =
    │   │   current)||vcpu is cache hot) then
 5  │   │   │   continue;
 6  │   │   end
 7  │   │   ret ← vcpu;
 8  │   │   break;
 9  │   end
10  end
11  return ret;
```

---

3   Performance Evaluation

We implement a working prototype of the proposed real-time scheduling framework in Xen-4.2.1, called *Risa*. In this section, we evaluate the effectiveness of *Risa* through several experiments. We first describe the experimental environment, and then present the experimental results.

3.1   Experimental Environment and Methodology

Our evaluations are conducted on a server which has two quad-core 2.4GHz Intel Xeon CPUs, 24GB memory, 1TB SCSI disk, and 1Gbps Ethernet card. We use Xen-4.2.1 as the hypervisor and CentOS 5.5 distribution with the Linux-2.6.32.40 kernel as the OS. The network I/O of a VM is handled via a software bridge in Domain0. Unless otherwise specified, the configurations of VMs running on the server are as follows: 1VCPU, 1GB memory and 8GB virtual disk. Our experiments are targeted at understanding the effect of each component of *Risa*.

How to Evaluate the Effect of Multi-core Dynamic Partitioning Mechanism. As described in Section 2.1, a practical way to support different kinds of applications simultaneously and provide performance isolation in multi-tenant cloud environment is to partition PCPUs into multiple pools and to apply different schedulers to these pools. As a result, we conduct experiments under two multi-core partitioning mechanisms.

One is the multi-core dynamic partitioning mechanism of *Risa*, which can manage *rt-pool* automatically according to the scheduling parameters of RT-VMs. The other is the multi-core static partitioning mechanism. It uses *cpupools*, a new feature of Xen since Xen 4.2, to partition PCPUs into *rt-pool* and *non-rt-pool*, but in a static method. It allocates the peak number of PCPUs to *rt-pool* manually according to the estimation of the requirements of RT-VMs before the creation of them, and deletes *rt-pool* when all the RT-VMs are destroyed.

How to Evaluate the Effect of the vGEDF Scheduler. When we evaluate the vGEDF scheduler, we conduct experiments under four strategies to demonstrate the advantages of the vGEDF scheduler. We dedicate four PCPUs to Domain0 to handle communication and interrupts for other VMs, which isolates Domain0 to all other domains. Fourteen VMs (VM1~VM14) are running on the other PCPUs. VM1 hosts testing real-time applications and the others are interfering VMs which run lookbusy [4]. The details of these strategies are as follows.

baseline is the default configuration in cloud environment that only the Credit scheduler is adopted to schedule VMs.

Risa is our framework. In this strategy, seven VMs (VM1~VM7) are set as RT-VMs. The scheduling parameters of VM1 are set as (p_i=5ms, s_i=1ms). The others are set as (p_i=10ms, s_i=2ms). Therefore, *Risa* allocates two PCPUs to *rt-pool* according to (3) and applies the vGEDF scheduler to *rt-pool* automatically.

sp+SEDF uses the multi-core static partitioning mechanism to simulate an environment like *Risa*. It partitions PCPUs into two pools and allocates two PCPUs to *rt-pool* manually, and the SEDF scheduler is adopted to schedule RT-VMs in *rt-pool*. Because it does not support load balance among multiple PCPUs, the distribution of these RT-VMs is as follows: a PCPU hosts four RT-VMs (VM1~VM4) and the other hosts three RT-VMs (VM5~VM7).

sp+SEDF(overload) is similar with *sp+SEDF*, except that a PCPU is overloaded. Because the SEDF scheduler does not support load balancing among multiple PCPUs, it is possible that a PCPU is overloaded while the other has slight load. This strategy is used to simulate such situation that a PCPU hosts six RT-VMs (VM1~VM6) and only one RT-VM (VM7) runs on the other PCPU.

3.2 Effect of Multi-core Dynamic Partitioning Mechanism

In this test, we evaluate the effect of the multi-core dynamic partitioning mechanism. We launch two non-RT-VMs with 8 VCPUs on the server and each runs eight hungry loop applications as non-real-time applications, which can exhaust

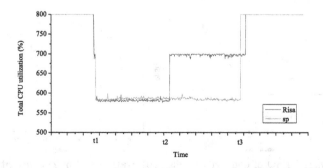

Fig. 3. Total CPU utilization of non-RT-VMs under different partitioning strategies. *Risa* uses dynamic partitioning, and *sp* means static partitioning.

the available CPU resources. We monitor the total CPU utilization of these VMs, which is the performance metric in this test. A shell script is running to create and destroy RT-VMs as time goes on, and the tasks of this script are as follows. 1) at time *t1*, it creates two RT-VMs and sets their scheduling parameters as $(p_i=10\text{ms}, s_i=6\text{ms})$; 2) at time *t2*, it changes s_i of a RT-VM to 2ms; 3) at time *t3*, it destroys these RT-VMs. In the multi-core static partitioning mechanism, the first thing needs to be done is to estimate the number of PCPUs which should be allocated to *rt-pool*. Then, two PCPUs are allocated to *rt-pool* before the creation of RT-VMs according to (3). Finally, *rt-pool* is destroyed at *t3* and the number of PCPUs of *non-rt-pool* is increased (it cannot be increased automatically when *rt-pool* is destroyed). Moreover, RT-VMs need to be assigned to *rt-pool* by administrators explicitly. In the multi-core dynamic partitioning, the only thing needs to be done is to run the shell script. The test results are shown in Fig. 3.

From the test results, we can observe that *Risa* automatically reduces the number of PCPUs of *rt-pool* at time *t2*. This is because the needed number of PCPUs of *rt-pool* turns to 1 according to (3) when the script adjusts the scheduling parameter of the RT-VM. Besides, because *Risa* adopts a delayed shrink manner, the increase of CPU utilization at *t3* under *Risa* is 15 seconds (implementation defined) later than *sp*. As a result, compared to the multi-core static partitioning mechanism, the multi-core dynamic partitioning mechanism of *Risa* can reduce operation expense and improve CPU utilization.

3.3   Effect of vGEDF Scheduler

In this test, we perform two experiments to evaluate the effectiveness of the vGEDF scheduler of *Risa*. They are conducted under different guest OSes. One is *general purpose operating system* (GPOS). The other is *real-time operating system* (RTOS), which is designed to serve real-time application requests.

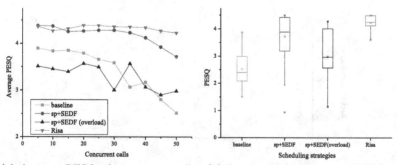

(a) Average PESQ of concurrent calls   (b) Statistics of 50 concurrent calls

Fig. 4. Call quality under different strategies

Experiments with VoIP Server Running in GPOS. *Voice over Internet Protocol* (VoIP) server is a typical soft real-time application. Asterisk [2] is a famous and open source telephone private branch exchange. In this test, we use Asterisk to conduct experiments to evaluate the vGEDF scheduler of *Risa*.

We use VM1 to host Asterisk, and run SIPp [6] on a machine in the same LAN as a VoIP client. We start up several concurrent calls that range from 5 to 50 to simulate the real world environment, and measure call quality with the ITU-T PESQ (*Perceptual Evaluation of Speech Quality*) metric [15], which ranges from 0 to 4.5. Typically, if the value is greater than 4, it means that the VoIP service has good quality. The test results are shown in Fig. 4.

Seen from Fig. 4(a), *Risa* is the best among these scheduling strategies, and the call quality is guaranteed under *Risa*. This is because *Risa* is designed for real-time applications and takes full advantage of underlying multi-core processors. The Credit scheduler is a proportional fair share scheduler and does not consider real-time constraints. Thus, it even cannot guarantee the call quality with small concurrent calls. With the increase of concurrent calls, the SEDF scheduler cannot support the VoIP server any more. This is because the SEDF scheduler cannot make full use of multi-core processors. Besides, the call quality under the strategy of *sp+SEDF(overload)* is very low, which also shows the importance of load balancing among multiple PCPUs. Compared with the Credit scheduler, *Risa* achieves 68.1% improvement in call quality according to the average PESQ when we start up 50 concurrent calls. Accordingly, compared with the SEDF scheduler, *Risa* enhances the call quality by 13.7%.

Moreover, Fig. 4(b) shows the statistics of the call qualities of 50 concurrent calls under different strategies. We find that call quality is very steady under *Risa*, which is crucial for the VoIP server to provide stable services.

Experiments with Cyclictest Running in RTOS. Cyclictest [3] is a widely used real-time testing tool, which can evaluate kernel latencies of real-time Linux kernel. In this test, we use cyclictest to conduct experiments under a RTOS to demonstrate whether *Risa* supports the RTOS and hardware-assisted VMs (HVMs).

Table 1. Cyclictest test results under different strategies

Strategy	Min Latencies (us)	Avg Latencies (us)	Max Latencies (us)
Credit	5	5862	181559
sp+SEDF	0	3224	58634
Risa	0	2342	55700

The guest RTOS is CentOS 5.5 with Linux-2.6.32.40 kernel plus PREEMPT-RT patch [5], which is installed in a HVM. We replace VM1 in the four strategies with the HVM, and use cyclictest to evaluate the kernel latency of the RTOS by collecting data for 500,000 times. However, we observe that the RTOS is not responded under the strategy of *sp+SEDF(overload)* because of the features of the HVM. As a result, the experimental results only include three strategies, which are shown in Table 1. From the test results, we can find that the kernel latency is the smallest under *Risa*. Compared with the Credit scheduler and the SEDF scheduler, the kernel latency is reduced by 60% and 27.4% according to the average latencies, respectively. However, the reduction on maximum latencies is small compared to the SEDF scheduler. This is because both SEDF and vGEDF are based on the EDF scheduling algorithm.

4   Related Work

Hu *et al.* [10] present an I/O scheduling model of VM based on multi-core dynamic partitioning. They divide PCPUs into three subsets, and apply an identical scheduler with different strategies to these subsets. However, real-time scheduling is much more complex than I/O scheduling. Designing different schedulers for various subsets is more suitable for supporting real-time applications.

Lee *et al.* [13] introduce a concept named *laxity* to denote the scheduling latency that a VM desires. The VCPU of a VM running soft real-time applications is inserted into the middle of run queue according to its *laxity* so that it can be scheduled within its desired deadline. Kim *et al.* [12] present an approach to reallocate credits for the VMs running client-side multimedia applications adaptively according to their qualities. Our previous work [17][18] proposes a parallel soft real-time scheduling algorithm, which addresses real-time constraints and synchronization problems simultaneously, to support parallel soft real-time applications in virtualized environment. Hwang *et al.* [11] design a soft real-time scheduling to support virtual desktop infrastructures. However, all these studies lack the schedulability analysis, which is important for real-time scheduling. RT-Xen [16] presents a hierarchical real-time scheduling framework for Xen, but it only supports single core VMs.

5   Conclusion

In this paper, we present a real-time scheduling framework based on multi-core dynamic partitioning in virtualized environment. If the system has RT-VMs, PCPUs are partitioned into two pools (*rt-pool* and *non-rt-pool*) automatically according to the scheduling parameters of RT-VMs. *rt-pool* uses the vGEDF scheduler, which takes full advantage of multi-core processors, to schedule RT-VMs. Non-RT-VMs are scheduled by the Credit scheduler in *non-rt-pool*. We implement a prototype in the Xen hypervisor and evaluate its effectiveness. The experiments results show that *Risa* supports real-time applications well, reduces operation expense, and improves CPU utilization.

Acknowledgments. The research is supported by National Science Foundation of China under grant No.61232008, National 863 Hi-Tech Research and Development Program under grant No.2013AA01A208, Doctoral Program of MOE under grant 20110142130005, EU FP7 MONICA Project under grant No.295222, and Chinese Universities Scientific Fund under grant No. 2013TS094.

References

1. Amazon's Elastic Compute Cloud (EC2), http://aws.amazon.com/ec2/
2. Asterisk, http://www.asterisk.org/
3. Cyclictest, https://rt.wiki.kernel.org/index.php/Cyclictest
4. Lookbusy - a synthetic load generator, http://www.devin.com/lookbusy/
5. Real-Time Linux Wiki, https://rt.wiki.kernel.org
6. SIPp, http://sipp.sourceforge.net/
7. Baker, T.P.: An analysis of edf schedulability on a multiprocessor. IEEE Trans. Parallel Distrib. Syst. 16(8), 760–768 (2005)
8. Barham, P., Dragovic, B., Fraser, K., Hand, S., Harris, T., Ho, A., Neugebauer, R., Pratt, I., Warfield, A.: Xen and the art of virtualization. In: Proc. SOSP 2003, pp. 164–177 (2003)
9. Cherkasova, L., Gupta, D., Vahdat, A.: Comparison of the three cpu schedulers in Xen. SIGMETRICS Perform. Eval. Rev. 35(2), 42 (2007)
10. Hu, Y., Long, X., Zhang, J., He, J., Xia, L.: I/O scheduling model of virtual machine based on multi-core dynamic partitioning. In: Proc. HPDC 2010, pp. 142–154 (2010)
11. Hwang, J., Wood, T.: Adaptive dynamic priority scheduling for virtual desktop infrastructures. In: Proc. IWQoS 2012 (2012)
12. Kim, H., Jeong, J., Hwang, J., Lee, J., Maeng, S.: Scheduler support for video-oriented multimedia on client-side virtualization. In: Proc. MMsys 2012, pp. 65–76 (2012)
13. Lee, M., Krishnakumar, A.S., Krishnan, P., Singh, N., Yajnik, S.: Supporting soft real-time tasks in the Xen hypervisor. In: Proc. VEE 2010, pp. 97–108 (2010)
14. Liu, C.L., Layland, J.W.: Scheduling algorithms for multiprogramming in a hard-real-time environment. Journal of the ACM (JACM) 20(1), 46–61 (1973)
15. Rix, A.W., Beerends, J.G., Hollier, M.P., Hekstra, A.P.: Perceptual evaluation of speech quality (pesq)-a new method for speech quality assessment of telephone networks and codecs. In: Proc. ICASSP 2001, vol. 2, pp. 749–752 (2001)
16. Xi, S., Wilson, J., Lu, C., Gill, C.: RT-Xen: Towards real-time hypervisor scheduling in Xen. In: Proc. EMSOFT 2011, pp. 39–48 (2011)
17. Zhou, L., Wu, S., Sun, H., Jin, H., Shi, X.: Supporting parallel soft real-time applications in virtualized environment. In: Proc. HPDC 2013, pp. 117–118 (2013)
18. Zhou, L., Wu, S., Sun, H., Jin, H., Shi, X.: Virtual machine scheduling for parallel soft real-time applications. In: Proc. MASCOTS 2013, pp. 525–534 (2013)

Automatic Data Layout Transformation for Heterogeneous Many-Core Systems

Ying-Yu Tseng, Yu-Hao Huang, Bo-Cheng Charles Lai, and Jiun-Liang Lin

Department of Electronics Engineering, National Chiao-Tung University
1001 Da-Hsueh Rd, Hsinchu, Taiwan
{yingyu.ee99,pcco001.ee99}@nctu.edu.tw,
bclai@mail.nctu.edu.tw, qazhphphphp3@gmail.com

Abstract. Applying appropriate data structures is critical to attain superior performance in heterogeneous many-core systems. A heterogeneous many-core system is comprised of a host for control flow management, and a device for massive parallel data processing. However, the host and device require different types of data structures. The host prefers Array-of-Structures (AoS) to ease the programming, while the device requires Structure-of-Arrays (SoA) for efficient data accesses. The conflicted preferences cost excessive effort for programmers to transform the data structures between two parts. The separately designed kernels with different coding styles also cause difficulty in maintaining programs. This paper addresses this issue by proposing a fully automated data layout transformation framework. Programmers can maintain the code in AoS style on the host, while the data layout is converted into SoA when being transferred to the device. The proposed framework streamlines the design flow and demonstrates up to 177% performance improvement.

Keywords: heterogeneous systems, data layout transformation, many-core, GPGPU.

1 Introduction

Heterogeneous many-core systems have demonstrated superior performance by leveraging the benefits from processing units with different characteristics. A heterogeneous system consists of a host and a device, where the host takes charge of sophisticated algorithm flow while the device performs massively parallel data processing [10]. Fig. 1 illustrates a widely adopted architecture of modern heterogeneous many-core systems. The system applies high-end CPUs as the host, and a GPGPU (General Purpose Graphic Processing Unit) as the device. CPUs perform control flow management and enable ease of programming, while GPGPUs support massive parallel execution to achieve high throughput data processing. Tasks of an application can then be dispatched to the best-suited processing resources to achieve efficient and high performance computing.

C.-H. Hsu et al. (Eds.): NPC 2014, LNCS 8707, pp. 208–219, 2014.

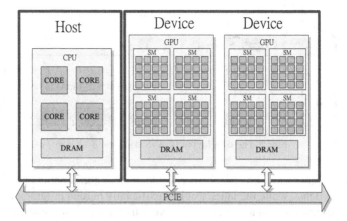

Fig. 1. The organization of a heterogeneous many-core system

The heterogeneity of the system has caused disparate design philosophy and resultant execution behavior between the host and device. A common design flow divides an application into two parts. The control of the execution flow is taken care of by the host processor, while the part with massive parallelism is transferred to the many-core engines on the device for high throughput computing. Since the massive parallel computation usually poses intensive data accesses, developing a proper data structure for the corresponding many-core device is a critical performance factor.

The preferred data structures of tasks are different on the two sides of the system. The programming paradigm of the host processor usually applies conventional object-oriented scheme, which tends to pack the associated elements of the same object into the same class. This scheme enhances both code readability and maintainability. However, the same data layout scheme does not provide efficient data accesses to the throughput processors on the device side.

Fig. 2 illustrates an example of multi-object operations on GPGPUs. This operation has been widely applied to various applications, such as image processing. As in Fig. 2, there are three types of data elements, R, G, and B. The application can simultaneously operate on the data belonging to the same type, and would process the data of different types in turns. An object can be represented by combining the associated data from different types. For example, a pixel in an image consists of color elements from red, green, and blue. To have better code readability, programmers tend to pack the elements for the same object into the same class. Such data layout is referred as the Array-of-Structure (AoS). However, AoS is not an efficient data layout for GPGPUs. The parallel tasks in a GPGPU are clustered into execution groups, called warps. Tasks in a warp perform the same operation on different data points. To enable efficient data accesses, the data elements of the same type are required to be arranged in a consecutive manner. This data layout scheme is referred as Structure-of-Arrays (SoA). Programmers need to transform the data layout from AoS to SoA before passing the execution to the device side. However, SoA is usually against the intuition of understanding an object, and makes the code hard to maintain. This issue has involved the tradeoff of programmers between the performance on devices and the readability

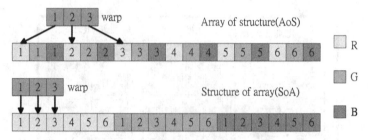

Fig. 2. The data layout of AoS style and SoA style

and maintainability of codes. The former would degrade the benefits of heterogeneous many-core systems, while the latter would significantly burden programmers.

This paper proposes an automatic data layout transformation framework to streamline the design flow as well as alleviate the overhead. The data is maintained as AoS structure on the host, and automatically transformed into the ASTA (Array-of-Structure-of-Tiled-Arrays) structure [1] during the data transfer from the host to device. ASTA arranges data into tiled arrays, which can be more effectively utilized by a GPGPU. The proposed framework involves the design of several novel hardware modules. The hardware Data Layout Transformer performs the data layout transformation to ASTA during the data transfer on the PCIe interface. In this way, the run-time overhead of data layout transformation can be hidden. When receiving the data on the device, a pipelined adapter is implemented to transpose the data efficiently. Specialized load and store units are also developed to translate the assigned data addresses to the target addresses. The proposed framework enables automatic data layout transformation between the host and device, and is transparent to programmers. The experimental results have demonstrated up to 177% performance improvement with the proposed framework.

The rest of the paper is organized as follows. Section 2 discusses the related work of data accesses of heterogeneous many-core systems. Section 3 introduces the hardware data layout transformation framework proposed in this paper. Section 4 shows the simulation results and analyzes the performance enhancement. Section 5 will concludes this paper.

2   Related Works

A heterogeneous system has applied disparate design philosophy and resultant execution behavior between the host and device. The corresponding data structure of an application also needs to be adapted to the characteristics and requirements of the system. GPGPUs on the device side have implemented memory coalescing, which combine consecutive data accesses into a single transaction. It has been demonstrated that to retain the benefit provided by memory coalescing, the data structure needs to be arranged as the SoA scheme [1][2][3][8].

The data layout transformation has been studied on both CPUs and GPGPUs. For CPUs, Karlsson [4] discussed an in-place transposition way and Gustavson and

Swirszcz [5] proposed an OpenMP-based approach. On GPGPUs, early researches gave the out-of-place transposition way and the performance was limited due to the ineffective usage of GPGPU DRAM [6]. The Dymaxion framework proposed by Che et al. [7] is a library-based software approach. It performs data transformation on the CPU side and overlaps with data transfers on PCI-e. Since the data transformation is performed by CPUs, the transformation speed is limited by the CPU memory band-width. Sung et al. [1] proposed another library-based approach that uses in-place algorithm transforming data layout from AoS to ASTA (Array-of-Structure-of-Tiled-Arrays) on GPGPUs. The ASTA arranges data into tiled arrays, which can be more effectively utilized by a throughput processor. An in-place marshaling algorithm was also developed for transforming the data layout, and has demonstrated to be fast-er than the optimized traditional out-of-place transformations while avoiding doubling the GPGPU DRAM usage. However, this software approach induces runtime over-head of transforming the data layout.

This paper proposes a hardware-based data layout transformation framework that is transparent to programmers. With the proposed hardware modules, the data layout transformation and address translation have been fully automated. The programmer can benefit from the low overhead transformation, and also be able to enhance the productivity by using the more intuitive SoA object-oriented code in both CPUs and GPGPU kernels.

3   Hardware Data Layout Transformation Framework

To achieve the best performance on a heterogeneous many-core system, programmers are required to take considerable effort to transform the data layout to enable data

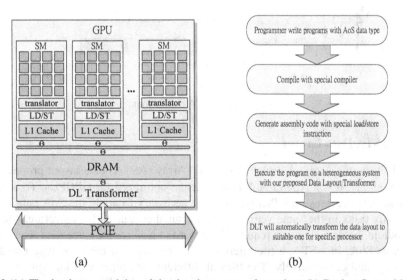

Fig. 3. (a) The hardware modules of the data layout transformation. (b) Design flow with the proposed data layout transformation framework.

accesses for the throughput processor on the device side. This paper proposes a fully automated data layout transformation framework to streamline the design flow as well as alleviate the overhead. This paper applies the proposed data transformation on a widely adopted heterogeneous system with CPU-GPGPU organization to demonstrate the fundamental functions and attained benefits.

3.1   Overview of System and Design Flow

The proposed data layout transformation consists of two hardware modules. As shown in Fig. 3(a), the first module is the Data Layout Transformer (DL Transformer) that is cascaded to the PCIe interface. The DL Transformer transforms the AoS data structure from the host to the ASTA structure, and stores the new data structure into the DRAM of the GPGPU. The second module is the specialized load/store (LD/ST) unit in GPGPUs. These LD/ST units are able to translate the data access addresses automatically for programmers. With the proposed hardware modules, the design flow of the heterogeneous program is illustrated in Fig. 3(b). Programmers maintain the more readable AoS codes for both GPGPU and CPU kernels. The AoS data structure can avoid discrete data layout with better code readability. Programmers only need to specify the AoS data structure that would be used by the parallel kernels on the device GPGPU. A simple function can be added to the current available compiler to recognize these data structures, and automatically send these data to the hardware DL Transformer. The appropriate PTX code for GPGPU will be generated to control the data receiving and address translation on the GPGPU side. By inserting the special flag into the PTX code, the load/store unit would access the data through a hardware address translator to get the transformed addresses.

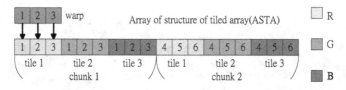

Fig. 4. The ASTA data layout

3.2   ASTA Data Layout

Fig. 4 illustrates Array of Structure of Tiled Array (ASTA) data layout proposed by Sung et al. [1]. It is a type of AoS data structure optimized for GPGPUs. To achieve efficient data accesses on GPGPUs, it is not necessary to apply the SoA data layout since only tasks in the same warp will be executed concurrently. Therefore, one can only adjoin the data elements required by a warp to achieve the same data access efficiency as SoA. In ASTA, a tile refers the data elements of the same type that have been allocated consecutively. The tiles of different data types will join together and form a mini AoS structure, named a chunk. The ASTA data layout is an array of these chunks. The hardware DL Transformer proposed in this paper also utilizes ASTA data layout on GPGPUs. With ASTA, the design of DL Transformer no longer needs to gather all the same elements together. This paper also proposes a pipeline design of DL Transformer that can achieve higher performance with low hardware complexity.

3.3   Data Layout Transformer

Fig. 5 illustrates the data layout transformation on the proposed DL Transformer module. The DL Transformer is designed to transform the AoS data layout to ASTA style while transferring data from CPUs to GPGPUs. Because the procedure between different chunks is independent, the following discussion will focus on one chunk. First, the buffer A in DL Transformer gathers a new chunk from PCIe. As it finishes receiving the entire chunk, it will send the chunk to the next stage of buffer B. The data layout of this chunk will be transformed from AoS to ASTA tile by tile. It is done by K iterations, where K is the number of data elements in a class. The first iteration is generating the first tile of this chunk. A set of multiplexers is controlled by K to determine which elements to form a new tile. In each cycle of this iteration, the first bit of these selected elements is sent to buffer C and the data in both buffer B and C are shifted by one bit simultaneously. Until all bits in buffer C are ready, the new tile will be sent to buffer D so that buffer C can do the next iteration of gathering the next tile. The buffer D is used to store the tile to the DRAM in a GPGPU.

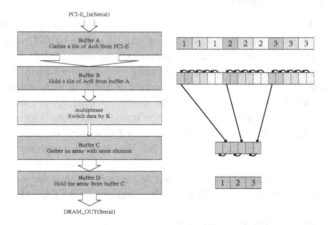

Fig. 5. Procedure of data layout transformation

Due to the limited bandwidth of PCIe and the concern of hardware cost, the iteration between buffer B and C should be separated by some proper number of cycles. The execution cycles of these stages of one chunk workload is shown in Table 1. The design of the pipeline structure is more efficient when the execution cycles of these stages are the same. That is, the multiplexer between buffer B and C should transfer $(bandwidth/W)$ bits in each cycle to balance the latency. The parameter W is the length for a tile. For example, the bandwidth is 128bit/transaction and W is 32, DL

Transformer should have 4 copies of multiplexer sets to transfer 4 bits, and the data in both buffer B and C are also shifted by 4 bits simultaneously.

Another transformation needed in our module is to transform the ASTA back to AoS when the data is transferred from a GPGPU to a CPU. The function can be achieved easily by reversing the flow of the previous transformation. The data will be sent from the GPGPU DRAM to Buffer D, and the multiplexer can be replaced by a decoder or de-multiplexer.

A possible design issue happens when the size of the whole array is not a multiple of W. It makes the last chunk of this array incomplete. To solve this issue, we choose to pad redundant bits to make the size of chunk as multiples of W. It will slightly increase the memory usage of the array. However, the number of objects of an array is usually much larger than W, and this overhead becomes negligible.

Table 1. Execution cycles in different stages

Stage	Cycles
PCIe to buffer A	$K \times W \times Size \times 8/bandwidth$
buffer B to C	$K \times Size \times 8/bit\_per\_cycle$

3.4   Specialized Load and Store Unit

The specialized load/store (LD/ST) unit is proposed to automatically translate the original data address to the target data address (ASTA). This LD/ST module relieves the programmers from reorganizing the complex transformed data accesses when programing GPGPU kernels. When performing the transformation from AoS to ASTA, the transformed addresses can be obtained by the following equations (**1**) and (**2**). Equation (**1**) derives the index of the datum (*Index*) from *Addr_origin* and *Addr_begin*. With *Index*, one can calculate the transformed data address (*Addr'*) by adding three offsets to the beginning of the array (*Addr_begin*). The offsets are respectively listed in equation (**2a**), (**2b**), and (**2c**). Equation (**2a**) represents the element index in its tile while equation (**2b**) gives the offset by the order of tile in the chunk. The chunk offset is represented by equation (**2c**) as well. With *Addr_begin* and these three offsets, one can translate an address to the transformed ASTA style data address.

$$Index = (Addr\_origin - Addr\_begin)/Size \tag{1}$$

$$Addr' = Addr\_begin + [$$
$$(Index/K)\%W + \tag{2a}$$
$$(Index\%K) \times W + \tag{2b}$$
$$(Index/K/W) \times K \times W \tag{2c}$$
$$] \times Size$$

4   Experiment Results

This section compares the performance of the proposed DLT framework. The experiment setup will be shown in section 4.1. Section 4.2 will illustrate the performance with no hardware delay time. Section 4.3 will explore the impact of different lengths of a tile, and section 4.4 will discuss the performance effect when adding hardware delays.

4.1   Experiment Setup

The performance of the proposed data layout transformation framework is verified with GPGPU-Sim, a cycle-accurate performance simulator for GPGPU [9]. The architecture parameters of GPGPU-Sim are configured to model NVIDIA GTX480, which consists of 15 streaming multiprocessors. Each warp contains 32 concurrent threads. The benchmarks used in this paper are listed in Table 2. The Black-Scholes benchmark is adopted from CUDA SDK [11] and the other two benchmarks are from Parboil Benchmark suite [12].

Table 2. Descriptions of test benchmark

Benchmarks	Description
Black-Scholes	This benchmark evaluates fair call and put prices for a given set of European options by Black-Scholes formula.
LBM	A fluid dynamics simulation of an enclosed, lid-driven cavity, using the Lattice-Boltzmann Method.
SPMV	Computes the product of a sparse matrix with a dense vector. The sparse matrix is read from file in coordinate format, converted to JDS format with configurable padding and alignment for different devices.

4.2   Performance Comparison with Different Data Layouts

Fig. 6 shows the normalized performance of designs with different data layout schemes. The CUDA_AoS and CUDA_ASTA apply only AoS and ASTA data structures respectively. The CUDA_AoS_DLT runs the CUDA_AoS on the platform with the proposed DLT framework. Note the performance is measured with no translator delay time. One can observe that CUDA_ASTA outperforms CUDA_AoS mainly because the GPGPU can access data efficiently with ASTA data structure. The benchmarks LBM and BlackScholes show more significant performance gain because these two applications pose regular data access behavior. In these applications, warps generate multiple accesses to the same cache line or adjacent memory locations, and therefore the performance benefits more from the ASTA structure. The SPMV benchmark, on the other hand, has irregular data access behavior. In this case, the ASTA data layout only provides minor performance gain.

Although having better performance, CUDA_ASTA applies the data structure that is not intuitive to programmers. Transforming the coding styles between AoS and

ASTA requires extra programming effort. The proposed DLT automatically transforms the data layout from AoS to ASTA without changing the coding style of kernel functions. An interesting observation is that the CUDA_AoS_DLT even outperforms CUDA_ASTA in all the benchmarks. This is because the coding of AoS structure has fewer instructions in the kernel function than the ASTA structure. The AoS data layout needs only one array pointer to manipulate the whole data while the ASTA data layout needs as many array pointers as the number of arrays. The code of ASTA style needs to pass more parameters into the kernel function and also requires more instructions to calculate the addresses of different structure elements. These overheads are not involved in the proposed DLT hardware since the code still retains the AoS data layout. Therefore the CUDA_AoS_DLT can return better performance than CUDA_ASTA.

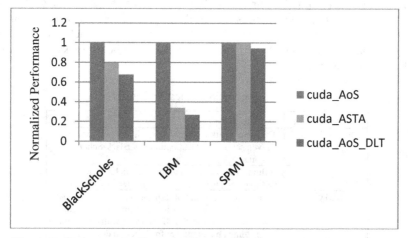

Fig. 6. The normalized performance of designs with different data layout schemes

4.3   Impact of Different Lengths of a Tile

Fig. 7 shows the normalized performance when the tile length is changing from 16, 32, to 64. The tile length is the parameter W discussed in section 3. This is an important factor since it affects not only the amount of transformer buffers and multiplexers but also the performance of the ASTA layout. The design with ASTA layout behaves like AoS layout when the parameter W is small. One can notice that the performance with $W = 16$ is worse than 32 and 64. However, increasing the W from 32 to 64 does not return more performance enhancement. This is because the performance does not gain further benefit from applying larger W, while the overhead of supporting larger W starts compromising the performance.

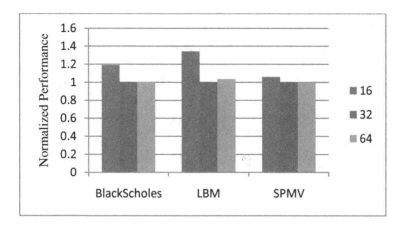

Fig. 7. The normalized performance of designs with different tile lengths (parameter *W*)

4.4   Performance Effect When Adding Hardware Delays

The proposed DLT framework uses hardware modules to perform the automatic data layout transformation. The experiments so far did not take hardware delays into account.   Fig. 8 shows organization of the arithmetic units for data layout transformation. This paper models these modules in the GPGPU-Sim. The address translator hardware is added into the streaming multiprocessor (SM) of the simulator. The address of GTX480 is 32bit and therefore the parameter *K* is 5bit. In this case, the translator needs a divider, a multiplier, and three 32-bit adders. The divider needs to support 32-bit divided by 5-bit, and the multiplier should support 32-bit multiplied by 5-bit. The delay of the hardware is estimated based on the integer ALU from the GTX480 configuration file. The latency of the DLT is modeled as 75 cycles in the simulator. Note that the PCIe module between CPUs and GPGPUs is not implemented in GPGPU-Sim. Fig. 9 shows the performance when the hardware delay is concerned. As shown in Fig. 9, the proposed design has achieved up to 177% performance improvement.

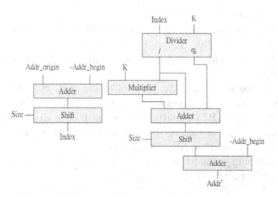

Fig. 8. Hardware architecture of address translator

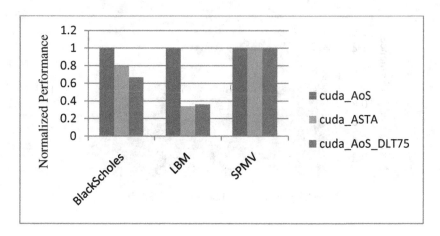

Fig. 9. The normalized performance of designs with hardware delays

5   Conclusion

This paper proposes a fully automated data layout transformation framework to help streamline the design flow as well as alleviate the overhead. Our programmer-friendly framework is composed of Data Layout Transformer and specialized Load/Store Unit. Our proposed framework is evaluated using three different applications with multiple input datasets. The results have demonstrated to achieve up to 177% performance improvement while retaining good program readability and maintainability.

References

1. Sung, I.-J., Stratton, J.A., Hwu, W.-M.W.: DL: A Data Layout Transformation System for Heterogeneous Computing. In: Proc. IEEE InPar, San Jose, pp. 513–522 (May 13, 2012)
2. Jang, B., Schaa, D., Mistry, P., Kaeli, D.: Exploiting Memory Access Patterns to Improve Memory Performance in Data-Parallel Architectures. Proc. IEEE Transactions on Parallel and Distributed Systems 22(1) (January 2011)
3. Che, S., Sheaffer, J.W., Skadron, K.: Dymaxion: optimizing memory access patterns for heterogeneous systems. In: Proc. SC, pp. 13–13 (2011)
4. Karlsson, L.: Blocked in-place transposition with application to storage format conversion. Technical report (2009)
5. Gustavson, F., Karlsson, L., Kagström, B.: Parallel and cache-efficient in-place matrix storage format conversion. ACM Transactions on Mathematical Software
6. Ruetsch, G., Micikevicius, P.: Optimizing matrix transpose in CUDA (January 2009)
7. Che, S., Sheaffer, J.W., Skadron, K.: Dymaxion: optimizing memory access patterns for heterogeneous systems. In: Proc. SC, p. 13 (2011)
8. CUDA C programming guide, http://docs.nvidia.com/cuda/cuda-c-programmingguide/index.html

9. Bakhoda, A., Yuan, G.L., Fung, W.W.L., Wong, H., Aamodt, T.M.: Analyzing CUDA Workloads Using a Detailed GPGPU Simulator. In: Ispass 2009: IEEE International Symposium on Performance Analysis of Systems and Software, pp. 163–174 (2009)
10. Garland, M., Grand, S.L., Nickolls, J.: Parallel Computing Experiences with Cuda. IEEE Computer Society (2008)
11. GPU Computing SDK,
    https://developer.nvidia.com/gpu-computing-sdk
12. Parboil Benchmarks,
    http://impact.crhc.illinois.edu/Parboil/parboil.aspx

mpCache: Accelerating MapReduce with Hybrid Storage System on Many-Core Clusters

Bo Wang[1], Jinlei Jiang[1,2], and Guangwen Yang[1]

[1] Department of Computer Science and Technology
Tsinghua National Laboratory for Information Science and Technology (TNLIST)
Tsinghua University, Beijing 100084, China
bo-wang11@mails.tsinghua.edu.cn, {jjlei,ygw}@tsinghua.edu.cn
[2] Technology Innovation Center at Yinzhou
Yangtze Delta Region Institute of Tsinghua University
Zhejiang 314006, China

Abstract. As a widely used programming model and implementation for processing large data sets, MapReduce does not scale well on many-core clusters, which, unfortunately, are common in current data centers. To deal with the problem, this paper: 1) analyzes the causes of poor scalability of MapReduce on many-core clusters and identifies the key one as the underlying low-speed storage (hard disk) can not meet the requirements of frequent IO operations, and 2) proposes mpCache, a SSD based hybrid storage system that caches both Input Data and Localized Data, and dynamically tunes the cache space allocation between them to make full use of the space. mpCache has been incorporated into Hadoop and evaluated on a 7-node cluster by 13 benchmarks. The experimental results show that mpCache gains an average speedup of 2.09 when compared with the original Hadoop, and achieves an average speedup of 1.79 when compared with PACMan, the latest in-memory optimization of MapReduce.

1 Introduction

The human society has stepped into the big data era where applications that process terabytes or petabytes of data are common in science, industry and commerce. Usually, such applications are termed IO-intensive applications, for they spend most time on IO operations. Workloads from Facebook and Microsoft Bing data centers show that IO-intensive phase constitutes 79% of a job's duration and consumes 69% of the resources [2].

MapReduce [5] is a programming model and an associated implementation for large data sets processing on clusters with hundreds or thousands of nodes. Due to its scalability and ease of programming, MapReduce has been adopted by many companies, including Google [5], Yahoo, Microsoft [9], and Facebook [20].

Although MapReduce scales well with the increase of server number, its performance, however, improves less or even remains unchanged with the increase

C.-H. Hsu et al. (Eds.): NPC 2014, LNCS 8707, pp. 220–233, 2014.

of CPU-cores per server. Figure 1 shows the execution time of *self-join* with varied CPU-cores per server on a 7-node cluster, in which the line with pluses denotes the time taken by Hadoop and the line with squares denotes the time in an ideal world. As the number of CPU-cores increases, the gap between the plus-line and square-line gets wider and wider. The fundamental reason behind this is that the underlying low-speed storage (hard disk) can not meet the requirements of MapReduce frequent IO operations: in the Map phase, the model reads in raw input data to generate set of intermediate key-value pairs, which are then written back; Shuffle phase, the model reads the intermediate data out from the disk once again and sends to corresponding nodes which Reduce tasks are scheduled on. In addition, during the whole execution of jobs, temporary data is also written to local storage when memory buffer is full. Although more tasks are concurrently running as more CPU-cores equipped, the IO speed of the storage system which backs MapReduce remains unchanged and can not meet the IO demand of high-concurrency tasks, resulting in the unchanged performance of MapReduce. Unfortunately, it is common that servers in data centers are often equipped with a large quantity of CPU-cores (referred to as **many-core**).

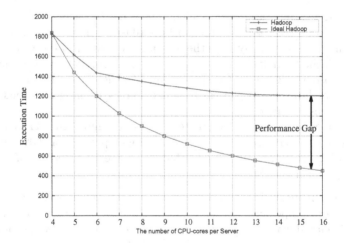

Fig. 1. Execution time of *self-join* running with varied number of CPU-cores per server using settings in Section 3 with 60GB Input Data

To overcome the bottleneck of low speed storage, caching data in memory is an effective way to improve IO-intensive applications. Indeed many studies have been done on in-memory cache [6] [13]. With the volume of memories scales with hardware technology, it seems more feasible to cache data in memory to provide high IO speed. However, caching data in memory inevitably occupies additional memories and drops down the task parallelism degree (that is the number of concurrent running tasks). What's more, some machine-learning algorithms such as *k-means* and *term-vector* are memory-intensive that consume very large volume of memories. For these applications, task parallelism degree drops significantly due to insufficient memories, leaving some CPU-cores idle. Although adding more memories could alleviate the situation, the volume of data scales even faster. Taking cost into consideration, it is not cost-effective to provide high IO speed by in-memory caching.

Flash memory based Solid State Drive (SSD), emerges as an ideal storage medium for building high performance storage systems. However the cost of building a storage system completely with SSDs is often above the acceptable threshold in most commercial data centers. Even considering the price-drop trend, the average cost per GB of SSDs is still unlikely to reach the level of hard disks in the near future [8]. Thus, we believe that in most systems, SSDs should not be simply viewed as a replacement for the existing HDD-based storage, but instead SSDs should be a means to enhance it.

Taking all the concerns discussed above into consideration, we proposed mp-Cache, SSD based hybrid storage system, to support MapReduce scalable on many-core clusters, which not only provides high IO for IO-intensive applications but also maintains task parallelism degree of memory-intensive jobs. The contributions of our paper are as follows.

- We propose a new approach, called mpCache, to cache both Input Data and Localized Data to speedup the IO-intensive phases. We also devise an algorithm to dynamically tune the allocations between Input Cache and Localized Cache to make full use of the cache and provide better performance.
- We propose an algorithm to replace Input Cache efficiently, taking replacement cost, data set size, access frequency, all-or-nothing into consideration for better performance.
- Extensive experiments are conducted to evaluate mpCache. The experiment results shows that mpCache gets an average speedup of 2.09 when compared with original Hadoop and achieves an average speedup of 1.79 when compared with PACMan.

The rest of this paper is organized as follows. Section 2 describes the key ideas and algorithms of mpCache. Section 3 shows the experimental results. Section 4 reviews the related work and the paper ends in Section 5 with some conclusions.

2   mpCache Design

As shown in Figure 2, mpCache adopts a master-slave architecture with one mpCache Master and several mpCache Slaves. mpCache Master acts as a co-ordinator to globally manage mpCache slaves to ensure that a job's input data blocks, which are cached on different mpCache slaves, present in an all-or-nothing manner, for some prior research work [2] found that a job is sped up only when inputs of all tasks are cached. mpCache Slave tunes the cache space allocation between Input Cache and Localized Cache, and serves cached blocks.

mpCache Master consists of two components–*Dynamic Space Manager* and *Replace Arbitrator*. *Dynamic Space Manager* is responsible for collecting the

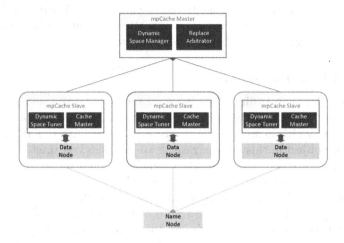

Fig. 2. mpCache architecture

information of allocation of dynamic space from each mpCache Slave and record into history data with job type and input data set size. *Replace Arbitrator* leverages the cache replacement scheme.

mpCache Slave seats on each data node and consists of two components–*Dynamic Space Tuner* and *Cache Master*. *Dynamic Space Tuner* is corresponding to tuning the space allocation between Input Cache and Localized Cache. *Cache Master*'s role is to serve cached blocks and cache new blocks. *Cache Master* on each data node intercepts the data reading requests from Map task, checking whether the requested data block cached. If does, *Cache Master* servers the data request from cache and request to *Replace Arbitrator* of mpCache Master for the block's hit. If the requested block is not cached and cache space does not have sufficient space to hold it, *Cache Master* will send replace request to *Replace Arbitrator* and evicts cached blocks to make room for new cache according to the return information from *Replace Arbitrator*.

2.1   Optimal Allocation Determination

Dynamic Space Tuner divides the whole cache space into three parts, i.e., Input Cache, Dynamic pool, and Localized Cache. Since the distributed file systems (e.g., GFS [7] and HDFS [17]), which back MapReduce applications up, store data as blocks, we divide Dynamic pool into blocks. When caching input data, free Dynamic pool blocks are allocated to Input Cache when Input Cache is full. As the execution of job going, *Dynamic Space Tuner* constantly monitors the used Localized Cache size. When Localized Data size exceeds Localized Cache size, *Dynamic Space Tuner* checks if there are free blocks in Dynamic pool, if not *Dynamic Space Tuner* excludes cached input data from Dynamic pool using the same scheme described in Section 2.2, then allocates blocks of Dynamic pool to

Localized Cache one by one. All the Dynamic pool blocks allocated to Localized Cache are withdrawn back when Localized Cache used ratio is below the *guard value* (in our implementation, *guard value* is set to 0.5).

2.2   Input Data Cache Model

Admission Control Policy. We use an admission control policy to decide whether or not it is worthwhile caching an object in the first place. We use an auxiliary cache which maintains the *identities* of input data sets from different jobs. For each object in this auxiliary cache we also maintain time-stamps of the last access, measured both in terms of the number of data set accesses and time.

Using the admission control policy, we would like to ensure that at the ith iteration the potential incoming input data jd_i is popular enough to offset the loss of the input data it displaces. So we process as follows: If there is enough free space for jd_i, we simply put jd_i into the main cache. Otherwise, we check if jd_i occurs in the auxiliary cache. If it does not, jd_i is not put into the main cache. However, we put jd_i into the auxiliary cache in accordance with LRU rules. On the other hand, if jd_i does occur in the auxiliary cache, then we determine if the decision which the replacement policy heuristic makes would be profitable. That is we compare the value $1/Size(jd_i)\Delta_{jd_i i}$ ($\Delta_{jd_i i}$ is at the ith iteration the number of accesses since the last time jd_i was accessed) with the sum $\sum_j 1/(Size(jd_j)\Delta_{jd_j i})$ of the set of candidate outgoing data blocks. We admit jd_i only if it is profitable to do so.

Main Cache Replacement Scheme. We now describe the data replacement scheme of the main cache. With the data set in the main cache we associate a *frequency* $Fr(jd)$ counting how many times jd was accessed since the last time it entered the main cache. We also maintain a priority queue for the data sets in the main cache. When a data set of a job is inserted into the queue, it is given priority $Pr(jd)$ computed in the following way:

$$Fr(jd) = Blocks\_Access(jd)/Size(jd) \tag{1}$$

$$Pr(jd) = Full + Clock + Fr(jd)/Size(jd) \tag{2}$$

where *Blocks_Access(jd)* is the number of accesses of all blocks of data set jd; $Fr(jd)$ is the frequency count of data set jd; *Full* is a *bonus* value for the data set which have all the blocks cached in the main cache (due to the *all-or-nothing* characteristic of MapReduce cache [2]); *Clock* is a running queue "clock" that starts at 0 and is updated, for each evicted data set $jd_{evicted}$, to its priority in the queue, $Pr(jd_{evicted})$; and $Size(jd)$ is the number of blocks of data set jd. When mpCache Master receives update message from mpCache Slave, we use Algorithm 1 described below to update $Pr(jd)$ of the data set to which the update message corresponding. *To_Del* is a list of tuples such as $< data\_node, blocks_{evicted} >$.

Algorithm 1. Main Cache Replacement Scheme

1: **if** the request for the block bk a hit update **then**
2:    get the data set jd, to which bk belongs.
3:    $Clock$ do not change.
4:    $Blocks\_Access(jd)$ increased by one.
5:    $Pr(jd)$ is update using Equation 1~2 and jd is moved according in the queue.
6: **else**
7:    **if** the request does not need replace **then**
8:       bk is cached.
9:    **else**
10:       identify $mpSlave$ where the request comes from.
11:       identify $data\_node$ where $mpSlave$ seated on.
12:       **if** To_Del list contains $data\_node$ **then**
13:          return $blocks_{evicted}$ to $mpSlave$, $mpSlave$ evicts $blocks_{evicted}$ and cache bk.
14:       **else**
15:          identify the data set $jd_{evicted}$ to evict, which has the lowest priority
16:          $Clock$ is set to $Pr(jd_{evicted})$.
17:          set $blocks_{evicted}$ to all the blocks of $jd_{evicted}$.
18:          return $blocks_{evicted}$ to $mpSlave$, which evicts $blocks_{evicted}$ and cache bk.
19:          identify all the data nodes $allnodes$ which store $blocks_{evicted}$.
20:          **for** $dn \in allnodes$ **do**
21:             add $< dn, blocks_{evicted} >$ to To_Del.
22:          **end for**
23:       **end if**
24:    **end if**
25:    $Blocks\_Access(jd)$ increased by one.
26:    **if** all the blocks of jd are cached **then**
27:       $Full = BONUS\_VALUE$.
28:    **else**
29:       $Full = 0$.
30:    **end if**
31:    $Pr(jd)$ is computed using Equation 2 and jd is enqueued accordingly.
32: **end if**

---

3   Evaluation

We implement mpCache by modifying Hadoop distributed file system HDFS
(version 2.2.0) and use YARN (version 2.2.0) to execute the benchmarks.

3.1   Platform

The cluster used for experiments consists of 7 nodes. Each node has two eight-
core Xeon E5-2640 v2 CPUs running at 2.0GHz, 20MB Intel Smart Cache, 32GB
DDR3 RAM, one 2TB SATA hard disk and two 160GB SATA Intel SSDs configured as RAID0. All the nodes run Ubuntu 12.04, have a Gigabit Ethernet
card and connect to a Gigabit Ethernet switch. Since our SSD cache space is
160*2=320GB on each node, which is large enough to hold most of the input

data set, and in real data centers, the input data of jobs is TB or even PB magnitudes, we only use 80GB cache in our experiment.

3.2 Benchmarks

We use 13 benchmarks released on PUMA [1], covering shuffle-light, shuffle-medium, and shuffle-heavy categories. We vary the input data size of each benchmark to 20 classes. As the input data size has Zipf-like frequency distributions [11], we set a chosen probability to each data size using Equation 3.

$$f(k; s, N) = \frac{1/k^s}{\sum_{i=1}^{N} 1/i^s} \tag{3}$$

Table 1 summarizes the characteristics of the benchmarks in terms of input data size (data of the right three column is when $k=10$), data source, the number of Map/Reduce tasks, shuffle size, and execution time on Hadoop.

Shuffle-light cases have very little data transfer in shuffle phase, including *grep*, *histogram-ratings*, *histogram-movies*, and *classification*. Shuffle-heavy cases, the shuffle data size of which is very large (as shown in Table 1, almost the same volume as the input data size), include *k-means*, *self-join*, *adjacency-list*, *ranked-inverted-count*, and *tera-sort*. The shuffle data size of shuffle-medium cases is between shuffle-light and shuffle-heavy, including *word-count*, *inverted-index*, *term-vector*, and *sequence-count*.

Table 1. Input data size of benchmarks. (k=1,2,...,20) and characteristics

Benchmark	Input size(GB)	Data source	#Maps & #Reduces	Shuffle size(GB)	Map&Reduce time on Hadoop(s)
grep	k*4.3	wikipedia	688 & 40	$6.9*10^{-6}$	222&2
histogram-ratings	k*3	netflix data	480 & 40	$6.3*10^{-5}$	241&5
histogram-movies	k*3	netflix data	480 & 40	$6.8*10^{-5}$	261&5
classification	k*3	netflix data	480 & 40	$7.9*10^{-3}$	286&5
word-count	k*4.3	wikipedia	688 & 40	0.318	743&22
inverted-index	k*4.3	wikipedia	688 & 40	0.363	901&6
term-vector	k*4.3	wikipedia	688 & 40	0.384	1114&81
sequence-count	k*4.3	wikipedia	688 & 40	0.737	1135&27
k-means	k*3	netflix data	480 & 4	26.28	450&2660
self-join	k*3	puma-I	480 & 40	26.89	286&220
adjacency-list	k*3	puma-II	480 & 40	29.38	1168&1321
ranked-inverted-count	k*4.2	puma-III	672 & 40	42.45	391&857
tera-sort	k*3	puma-IV	480 & 40	31.96	307&481

When submitting job to the cluster, we randomly select a job from the 13 benchmarks, and we choose input data size according to the attached probability.

3.3 Experimental Results

Comparison with Hadoop and PACMan. We compare the execution time of benchmarks on mpCache with that on both Hadoop and PACMan. We run the benchmarks on mpCache, Hadoop, and PACMan separately and get the average value.

PACMan uses memory to cache input data, the bigger the cache size is, the more data is cached in memory, causing the faster Map phase. However, in YARN, the concurrent running tasks number is relative to the available CPU-cores and free memory. Using too much memory for cache will decrease the parallelism degree of the tasks. We set the memory cache size to 12GB as recommended in PACMan [2].

Figure 3 shows the normalized execution time of Map/Reduce phase. For shuffle-light jobs *grep*, *histogram-movies*, *histogram-ratings*, and *classification*, the execution time is short (about 241s, 253s, 279s, and 304s of Hadoop when $k=10$), most of the time is spending on data IO, caching the input data of Map accelerates the execution of Map phase significantly (gets a speedup of 2.42 times of Map phase averagely). The Reduce phase time of mpCache is almost the same as that of Hadoop for three reasons: i) The Reduce phase of shuffle-light jobs is vert short (about 2s, 4s, 4s, and 5s when $k=10$); ii) Shuffle-light jobs have very little shuffle data (less than 10 MB); iii) The localized data size is very small (less than 1 MB), thus, caching localized data has little acceleration. The job execution time of shuffle-light jobs on mpCache gets a speedup of 2.23 times, averagely. When running on PACMan, each task runs well with 1GB memory, thus PACMan and mpCache gets the same parallelism degree of the tasks. Although PACMan's memory cache provides a fast IO than SSD cache of mpCache, mpCache size is much bigger than PACMan's memory cache size, mpCache's auxiliary cache scheme also prevents too frequent replacement, causing **a higher hit ratio** than PACMan does. Therefore, PACMan gets an average speedup of 2.17 times, which is slightly lower than mpCache.

For shuffle-medium jobs *word-count*, *inverted-index*, *term-vector*, and *sequence-count*, the execution time is longer than shuffle-light jobs(about 779s, 932s, 1209s, and 1174s), the acceleration of caching Map input data is also smaller (gets a speed of 1.25 times of Map phase averagely). The shuffle data size of these jobs is about 318~737MB, and the localized data size is 1~3GB, thus, caching localized data has bigger acceleration of Reduce phase than that of shuffle-light jobs, getting a average speed up of 1.60 times of Reduce phase. The job execution time of shuffle-medium jobs on mpCache gets a speed up of 1.25 times, averagely. When running on PACMan, *word-count* and *inverted-index* run well with 1GB memory, thus the speedup is roughly the same as mpCache. *term-vector* task needs at least 3GB memory, thus the parallelism degree is 10 on Hadoop and mpCache, while 6 on PACMan, causing the performance of PACMan drops to 0.762 of Hadoop. *sequence-count* needs at least 2GB memory, thus the parallelism degree is 16 on Hadoop and 10 on PACMan, causing the performance of PACMan drops to 0.868 of Hadoop.

For shuffle-heavy jobs *k-means*, *self-join*, *adjacency-list*, *ranked-inverted-index*, and *tera-sort*, the shuffle data size and localized data size is very big, thus caching Map input data and localized data both reduce the Map&Reduce phase time significantly. The Map time of *k-means*, *self-join*, *ranked-inverted-index*, and *tera-sort* is shorter than that of *adjacency-list*, thus the front three jobs get a speedup of 1.82~2.69, while, the *adjacency-list* Map time is longer (1168s), thus, getting

a speedup of only 1.04 times. Since the localized data size of shuffle-heavy jobs
is the biggest of the three types, caching localized data accelerates the Reduce
phase most, getting a speedup of 3.87 times of Reduce phase. The job execution
time of shuffle-heavy jobs on mpCache gets a speed up of 2.65 times, averagely.
When running on PACMan, *self-join*, *adjacency-list*, *ranked-inverted-index*, and
tera-sort need 2 GB memory for each task, thus the parallelism degree is 10 on
PACMan, and get an average performance of 0.981 of Hadoop. *k-means* benchmark clusters input data into 4 clusters, thus Reduce tasks number is set to 4.
The Reduce phase of *k-means* is a heavy part (2660s of 3087s), and needs at
least 8GB memory for each task. Therefore, the Map phase time is 2.46 times
of Hadoop, and Reduce time is the same as Hadoop, causing a performance of
0.808 of Hadoop.

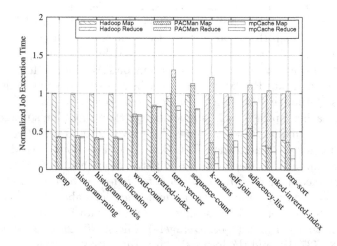

Fig. 3. Job execution time comparison with Hadoop and PACMan

PACMan used 12GB memory for data cache and got considerable performance using MapReduce v1 of Hadoop, the task parallelism degree of which was
configured by "slots" number. And slots number was set as constant value in
configuration files, both Hadoop and PACMan used the same configuration, thus
the same task parallelism degree. However, in MapReduce v2–YARN, the concurrent running task number is determined by free CPU-cores and free memory,
allocating memory for data cache inevitably reduce the task parallelism degree of
some jobs. In our cluster, each node contains 16 CPU-cores and 32GB memory,
PACMan used 12GB for memory cache, thus the memory left for computing is
20GB. When running "1GB jobs" (which consume 1GB memory for each task,
such as *grep*, *histogram-rating*, *histogram-movies*, *classification*, *word-count*, and
inverted-index) on PACMan, the task parallelism degree is 16, which is the same
as that of Hadoop and mpCache. Therefore, PACMan gets a better performance
than Hadoop and almost the same as mpCache. For other jobs, each task needs

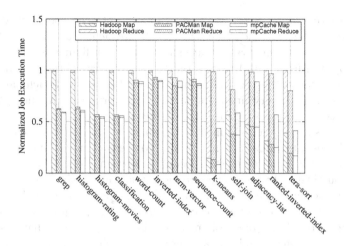

Fig. 4. Job execution time comparison with Hadoop and PACMan on 8 CPU-cores

at least 2GB memory (3GB for *term-vector*, and 6GB for *k-means*), which results in the task parallelism degree of PACMan drop to 10 (6 of *term-vector*, and 3 of *k-means*). Although PACMan's memory cache could significantly speedup Map phase IO, the drop of task parallelism degree slows down the job worse, thus as illustrated in Figure 3, PACMan even performs worse than Hadoop of these "at least 2 GB" jobs.

For all these benchmarks, mpCache gains an average speedup of 2.09 when compared with the original Hadoop, and achieves an average speedup of 1.79 when compared with PACMan.

In order to trade off the influence of memory cache of PACMan, we also do an experiment using only 8 CPU-cores of each node for Hadoop, PACMan, and mpCache. As shown in Figure 4, when using only 8 CPU-cores, most of the benchmarks run with the same task parallelism degree on Hadoop, mpCache, and PACMan(except *term-vector* and *k-means*). For shuffle-light jobs, mpCache and PACMan run with the same task parallelism degree, speedups over Hadoop are 1.74 and 1.67, separately. For shuffle-medium jobs, *word-count* and *inverted-index* is 1GB-task job, getting speedups over Hadoop of 1.12 and 1.08. *term-vector* is 3GB-task job, when running on Hadoop and mpCache, task parallelism degree is 8, while, running on PACMan is 6, causing a high Map phase time than Hadoop. Thus, the whole performance of PACMan is still worse than Hadoop. For shuffle-heavy jobs, the localized data size is also very big, mpCache caches both input data and localized data, resulting in an average speedup of 1.63 times of Map phase, while PACMan gets an average speedup of 1.35 times of Map phase. mpCache's caching localized data also gets an average speedup of 2.09 times of Reduce phase, while PACMan does not affect the Reduce phase. For all the benchmarks, mpCache gets an average speedup of 1.62 times, while, PACMan gets an average speedup of 1.25 times.

Sensitivity to Cache Size. We now evaluate mpCache's sensitivity to cache size by varying the available cache size of each mpCache Slave between 5GB and 160GB. The experimental results are shown in 3 sub-figures, i.e., Figure 5(a), Figure 5(b), and Figure 5(c), corresponding to the 3 categories of benchmarks.

Figure 5(a) shows the effect of cache size on *Shuffle-light* benchmarks. These benchmarks all have very little shuffle date and very short Reduce phase (the Reduce phase is no longer than 2.1% of the whole time), thus, the Localized Cache occupies little space and most of the space is allocated to Input Space, the speedup of these benchmarks is mostly due to the caching of Input Data. When the cache size is 5GB per node, the speedup is very small due to insufficient space to hold Input Data. As the cache size increases, the speedup rises significantly and getting the maximum point when the cache size is about 90GB.

Figure 5(b) shows the effect of cache size on *Shuffle-medium* benchmarks. These benchmarks have some volume of shuffle data (no more than 1GB), both Map and Reduce phase could be accelerated by caching Localized Data. When the cache size per node is 5GB, all the Localized Data is cached, thus Reduce phase gets an average speedup of 59.99%. However, the Reduce phase only occupies 3.43% of the whole time, resulting in the speedup of the whole job of only 1.40%. As the cache size increases, the speedup increases due to the reduction of Map phase time and getting the maximum speedup when the cache size is about 100GB.

Figure 5(c) shows the effect of cache size on *Shuffle-heavy* benchmarks. These benchmarks have very large volume of shuffle data, resulting in the Localized Data space occupies as large as 32GB when running *tera-sort* with 30GB Input Data. Thus ,when the cache size is below 40GB, most of the cache is allocated to Localized Cache, and the speedup is due to caching Localized Data.

4   Related Work

MapReduce Optimization on Multi-core Server. With the emerging of multi-core systems, MapReduce frameworks were also proposed and optimized on multi-core server [15][19][18]. All of these frameworks are designed for a single server, of which [18] mainly focused on graphics processors and [15][19] were implemented on symmetric-multiple-processor server. Obviously, these single-node frameworks could only process gigabytes of data at most and are stretched so thin to handle terabytes or petabytes of data.

MapReduce Optimization via In-Memory Cache. PACMan [2] and HaLoop [3] cached input data in memory to reduce IO cost of hard disks and optimize performance. Since the task parallelism degree of new generation of MapReduce (e.g., YARN) is more concerns about free memory. Caching data in memory consumes additional memory and cuts down the task parallelism, thus leading to low performance for some memory-intensive jobs. Due to limitation of memories and the large volume of Localized Data, PACMan only cached Input Data, thus only Map phase was improved. However, many MapReduce

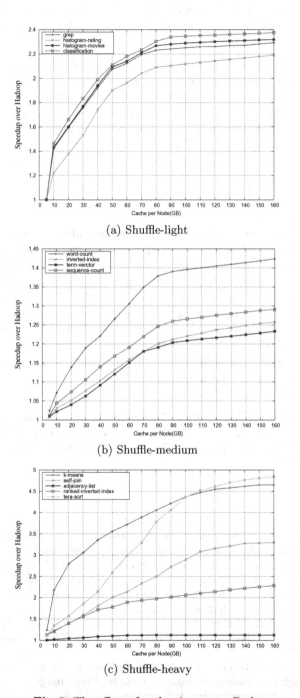

(a) Shuffle-light

(b) Shuffle-medium

(c) Shuffle-heavy

Fig. 5. The effect of cache size on mpCache

applications consist of heavy Reduce phase (e.g., *k-means* and *tera-sort*), our caching Localized Data also significantly improves Reduce phase and gets better acceleration of the whole job.

IO Optimization via SSD Cache. Yongseok et al. [12] proposed balancing data in cache and update cost for optimal performance of SSD. Hystor [4], Proximal IO [16], SieveStore [14], and HybridStore [10] used SSD as the cache of hard disks. However, these works only cache small files (e.g., size below 200KB), and only work for a single node. mpCache works in unison of all the nodes and makes use of relatively complex and efficient eviction scheme to make better support for MapReduce.

5 Conclusion

As a widely used programming model and implementation for processing large data sets, MapReduce does not scale well on many-core clusters due to the IO restriction of storage. Emerging of SSD provides a good trade off between cost and performance and caching data in SSD also prevents the problem of in-memory's degradation of computing parallelism degree. In this paper, we proposed mpCache, an SSD-based universal caching system for MapReduce, which caches both Input Data and Localized Data to speed up all the IO-consuming phases–**Read**, **Spill**, and **Merge**. We implemented mpCache in Hadoop and evaluated it on a 7-node cluster. The results show that mpCache can get a speedup of 2.09 times over Hadoop, and 1.79 times over PACMan.

Acknowledgment. This Work is co-supported by National Basic Research (973) Program of China (2011CB302505), Natural Science Foundation of China (61170210), and National High-Tech R&D (863) Program of China (2011AA01A203).

References

1. Ahmad, F., Lee, S., Thottethodi, M., Vijaykumar, T.: Puma: Purdue mapreduce benchmarks suite (2012), http://web.ics.purdue.edu/~fahmad/benchmarks.htm
2. Ananthanarayanan, G., Ghodsi, A., Wang, A., Borthakur, D., Kandula, S., Shenker, S., Stoica, I.: Pacman: Coordinated memory caching for parallel jobs. In: Proceedings of the 9th USENIX conference on Networked Systems Design and Implementation, NSDI 2012, p. 20. USENIX (2012)
3. Bu, Y., Howe, B., Balazinska, M., Ernst, M.D.: Haloop: Efficient iterative data processing on large clusters. Proceedings of the VLDB Endowment 3(1-2), 285–296 (2010)
4. Chen, F., Koufaty, D.A., Zhang, X.: Hystor: making the best use of solid state drives in high performance storage systems. In: Proceedings of the International Conference on Supercomputing, ICS 2011, pp. 22–32. ACM (2011)
5. Dean, J., Ghemawat, S.: Mapreduce: simplified data processing on large clusters. Communications of the ACM 51(1), 107–113 (2008)

6. Feeley, M.J., Morgan, W.E., Pighin, E., Karlin, A.R., Levy, H.M., Thekkath, C.A.: Implementing global memory management in a workstation cluster. ACM (1995)

7. Ghemawat, S., Gobioff, H., Leung, S.-T.: The google file system. ACM SIGOPS Operating Systems Review 37, 29–43 (2003)

8. Handy, J.: Flash memory vs. hard disk drives - which will win?, http://www.storagesearch.com/semico-art1.html

9. Isard, M., Budiu, M., Yu, Y., Birrell, A., Fetterly, D.: Dryad: distributed data-parallel programs from sequential building blocks. ACM SIGOPS Operating Systems Review 41(3), 59–72 (2007)

10. Kim, Y., Gupta, A., Urgaonkar, B., Berman, P., Sivasubramaniam, A.: Hybridstore: A cost-efficient, high-performance storage system combining ssds and hdds. In: 2011 IEEE 19th International Symposium on Modeling, Analysis & Simulation of Computer and Telecommunication Systems, MASCOTS 2011, pp. 227–236. IEEE (2011)

11. Knuth, D.E.: The art of computer programming, vol. 3. Addison-Wesley, Reading Mass. Pearson Education (2005)

12. Oh, Y., Choi, J., Lee, D., Noh, S.H.: Caching less for better performance: Balancing cache size and update cost of flash memory cache in hybrid storage systems. In: Proceedings of the 10th USENIX Conference on File and Storage Technologies, FAST 2012, p. 25. USENIX (2012)

13. Ousterhout, J., Agrawal, P., Erickson, D., Kozyrakis, C., Leverich, J., Mazières, D., Mitra, S., Narayanan, A., Parulkar, G., Rosenblum, M., et al.: The case for ramclouds: scalable high-performance storage entirely in dram. ACM SIGOPS Operating Systems Review 43(4), 92–105 (2010)

14. Pritchett, T., Thottethodi, M.: Sievestore: a highly-selective, ensemble-level disk cache for cost-performance. In: Proceedings of the 37th Annual International Symposium on Computer Architecture, ISCA 2010, pp. 163–174. ACM (2010)

15. Ranger, C., Raghuraman, R., Penmetsa, A., Bradski, G., Kozyrakis, C.: Evaluating mapreduce for multi-core and multiprocessor systems. In: IEEE 13th International Symposium on High Performance Computer Architecture, HPCA 2007, pp. 13–24. IEEE (2007)

16. Schindler, J., Shete, S., Smith, K.A.: Improving throughput for small disk requests with proximal i/o. In: Proceedings of the 9th USENIX Conference on File and Storage Technologies, FAST 2011, pp. 133–147. USENIX (2011)

17. Shvachko, K., Kuang, H., Radia, S., Chansler, R.: The hadoop distributed file system. In: 2010 IEEE 26th Symposium on Mass Storage Systems and Technologies, MSST 2010, pp. 1–10. IEEE (2010)

18. Stuart, J.A., Owens, J.D.: Multi-gpu mapreduce on gpu clusters. In: 2011 IEEE International Parallel & Distributed Processing Symposium, IPDPS 2011, pp. 1068–1079. IEEE (2011)

19. Talbot, J., Yoo, R.M., Kozyrakis, C.: Phoenix++: modular mapreduce for shared-memory systems. In: Proceedings of the Second International Workshop on MapReduce and Its Applications, pp. 9–16. ACM (2011)

20. Thusoo, A., Sarma, J.S., Jain, N., Shao, Z., Chakka, P., Anthony, S., Liu, H., Wyckoff, P., Murthy, R.: Hive: a warehousing solution over a map-reduce framework. Proceedings of the VLDB Endowment 2(2), 1626–1629 (2009)

Online Mechanism Design for VMs Allocation in Private Cloud

Xiaohong Wu[1], Yonggen Gu[1], Guoqiang Li[2,*], Jie Tao[1], Jingyu Chen[3], and Xiaolong Ma[4]

[1] School of Information and Engineering, Huzhou University, Zhejiang, 313000, China
[2] School of Software, Shanghai Jiao Tong University, Shanghai, 200240, China
[3] Institute of Computer Application Technology, Hangzhou Dianzi University, Zhejiang, China
[4] School of Information Management and Engineering, Shanghai University of Finance and Economics, Shanghai, China

Abstract. Resource allocation mechanism plays a critical role towards the success of cloud computing. Existing allocation mechanisms in public cloud is unsuitable for private IaaS cloud because they either cannot maximize the sum of users' value, or provide no service guarantee. This paper proposes a novel online, model-free mechanism that makes different allocations for flexible jobs and inflexible jobs. Users presenting job are incentivized to be truthful not only about their valuations for VM units, but also about their arrival, departure and the character of jobs (flexible or inflexible). We simulate the proposed online mechanism using data from RICC, showing that, compared with the mechanism which adopts same allocation method for all jobs, using our mechanism leads to high social welfare and percentage of served users.

Keywords: mechanism design, incentive compatible, resource reservation, greedy allocation.

1 Introduction

With the development of cloud computing technology, *Infrastructure-as-a-Service (IaaS)* has gained popularity in recent years due to the flexibility, scalability and reliability. For a private IaaS cloud, the objective of resource allocation is to maximize the efficiency of resources. That is, the IaaS private cloud provider needs to find an optimum resource allocation for all users in order to maximize the social welfare which is the sum of users value.

Existing allocation mechanisms in public IaaS cloud are pay-as-you-go and bid-based allocation. Pay-as-you-go is a first-come first-serve allocation mechanism which does not concern about the value of an allocation. In fact, the efficiency of an allocation can be improved if the cloud allocates VMs to users with higher valuation by knowing user-centric valuation. Amazon [1] has used bid-based mechanism in spot instance market to make up for this shortcoming, where users periodically

---

* Corresponding author.

C.-H. Hsu et al. (Eds.): NPC 2014, LNCS 8707, pp. 234–246, 2014.
© IFIP International Federation for Information Processing 2014

submit bids to the provider, who in turn posts a series of spot prices. Users gain resource access, until the spot price rises above their bids. Thus, due to the dynamic changing of the spot price, it provides no service guarantee to those jobs which should be completed by VMs during multiple time unit periods.

To overcome above shortcomings in existing mechanisms, we are motivated to design a new auction mechanism for VM allocation in private IaaS cloud which is presented as an *online greedy allocation with reservation*(OGAWR) mechanism. The OGAWR mechanism has three characteristics compared with the auction in spot instance. First, the auction in our online mechanism is carried out in each time unit as long as user comes, while the auction in spot instance is carried out in each period that includes multiple time units. Second, OGAWR mechanism will provide service guarantee, that is, each job which should be processed during multiple time units will not be terminated before it is completed. Third, especially, we use different allocation methods of VMs for the flexible jobs and inflexible jobs. *Flexible jobs* refer to those jobs that the users only care about whether they could be completed before their deadline, and the process details are ignored. For example, a finance firm has to process the daily stock exchange data for guaranteeing the trading in next day. Obviously, the finance firm only cares about whether the job can be finished before the next trading day, and does not care about how the job is processed. Contrarily, *inflexible jobs* refer to those jobs that must be processed continuously when they start to be processed.

The rest of paper is organized as follows. In section 2 we discuss related work. After formalizing the problem model in Section 3, in section 4 we design an online greedy allocation with reservation(OGAWR) mechanism, and analyze the properties of OGAWR mechanism in section 5. The experiment evaluation are showed in section 6. Finally, conclusions appear in section 7. Due to the lack of space, we omit proofs of lemmas and theorems; these can be found in the extended version [16].

2   Related Work

The resources allocation in cloud computing is an important topic because it is closely related to the revenue of both cloud users and providers. Many literatures have conducted the studies focusing on this topic, and there are two main lines of research for this problem. One of these investigates the VMs allocation by solving an optimization problem. These works focus on the optimization of object functions, but generally without considering any strategic behaviours among users (e.g., the VM allocation approach for spot markets in paper [9]). The other is game theory based approach to analyze and design a reasonable mechanism. For instance, a cloud resource allocation approach based on game theory [7] is proposed, and assumes that the allocation would start after all users submit their request. Combinatorial auctions are supposed to apply in VMs allocation in some literatures [8] [10] [11], and all these work only consider resource allocations in one time unit and restrict their discussions in a single offline auction period. However, in cloud computing, the cloud users arrive and leave randomly, so the statistic analysis and design based on game theory are not suitable for it.

Online mechanism is an important expansion of mechanism theory in the multi-agent and economics literature, generally applied in dynamic environment, which is consistent with the environment characters in cloud computing. According to the research on online mechanism, there are two frameworks of research in this field. One of these is model-based approach which aims for developing online variants of Vickrey-Clarke-Groves (VCG) mechanisms [3] [4]. These works rely on a model of future availability, as well as future supply (e.g., Parkes and Singh [3] use an MDP-type framework for predicting future arrivals). The other is model-free approach which requires fewer assumptions, and makes computing allocations more tractable than the first one (e.g., the online mechanism in electric vehicle charging in [5]).

The online mechanisms have been used in cloud computing [12] [13] [14]. [14] only introduces an online mechanism framework for cloud resources allocation without detail allocation algorithm. The online mechanism in [12] is a resource allocation approach for batch jobs, and the value functions for users are continuous. Zaman et al [13] design a truthful mechanism that allocates the VMs to users by greedy allocation, and allows those allocated users continuously use those VMs for the entire period requested.

Based on those works in [12] [13] [14], we also aim to design an online truthful mechanism for VMs allocation. Further, we pay attention to the following points:

1. In our model, a user requests one VM for multiple time units to finish the job during the arrival-departure interval. According to the demand in process time, all jobs are classified into two classes: flexible jobs and inflexible jobs.
2. We choose different allocation methods for the two classes of jobs, and especially design a discontinuous resource allocation based on reservation-ratio for the flexible jobs, by which the distribution of workload of users can be adjusted at their arrival-departure interval and the total workloads processed in cloud will be improved.
3. We focus on all the users with single-valued preference. That is, each user could get a non-zero constant value brought by the job only if it could be finished completely.

3   Modeling and Notations

We consider a private cloud provider who provides only one type of VM instances, and the total number of VM instances is denoted by C. Consider discrete time periods $T = 1, 2, ...$, indexed by t and possible infinite.

An agent presents a user i who submits its job to the cloud randomly, which can be characterized by the 'type' $\theta_i = (a_i, d_i, l_i, e_i, V_i) \in \Theta_i$, where Θ_i is its type space. Here, a_i and d_i present the arrival and departure time of agent i, and l_i is its total computation workload, i.e, the job size. Assume that each agent requires at most one VM in one time unit. The workload l_i is the number of time units for which agent i requires one VM. The last component of θ_i is V_i, the value agent i obtains if its job is completed, and $V_i \geq 0$.

As described in section 1, the jobs are classified into flexible jobs and inflexible jobs. In order to distinguish the job classes, a character parameter e_i is used to point out the agent is flexible $(e_i = 1)$ or inflexible $(e_i = 0)$.

We define $\pi_i = (\pi_i^{a_i}, \pi_i^{a_i+1}, ..., \pi_i^{d_i})$ as the allocation for agent i. $\pi_i^t = 1$ if agent i is allocated one VM at time $t \in [a_i, d_i]$, otherwise $\pi_i^t = 0$. The allocation result for agent i is denoted by A_i.

$$A_i(\pi_i) = \begin{cases} 1 & if \quad \Sigma_{t \in [a_i, d_i]} \pi_i^t \geq l_i \ and \ \pi_i^t \leq 1 \\ 0 & otherwise \end{cases} \tag{1}$$

Each agent i is characterized by a valuation function v_i defined as follows:

$$v_i = \begin{cases} V_i & if \quad A_i = 1 \\ 0 & otherwise \end{cases} \tag{2}$$

The challenge of the cloud provider is to make allocation decisions π^t dynamically while trying to maximize the sum of agents value. The problem is described as follows:

$$\max \Sigma v_i$$
$$s.t \quad \pi_i^t \leq 1 \tag{3}$$
$$\Sigma_{i=1}^n \pi_i^t \leq C, t \in T$$

4   The Online Greedy Allocation with Reservation

4.1   Description of Mechanism

In this section we design a model-free online mechanism for the above setting.

The number of idle VMs at time t is denoted by $s(t)$. The definition of greedy allocation is as follows.

Definition 1. *(Greedy allocation) At each step t allocate the $s(t)$ VMs to the active agents with the highest valuations.*

If all agents request one VM only for one time unit, greedy allocation with appropriate payment could constitute a truthful mechanism [2]. However, in the case of multiple time units demands, according to equation (2), whether agent i could get the value V_i is decided by all of its allocation in period $[a_i, d_i]$. That is, the value brought by one VM at some time unit cannot be decided at first, so greedy allocation for each time unit can not be performed. In order to maintain incentive compatibility, we extend the greedy allocation policy by allowing the system to reserve VMs for agents. By such allocation approach, the agent is not only allocated one VM at current time t but also reserved one VM for multiple time units in future period. We define unit valuation as the valuation of one VM per unit time, and it is expressed as V_i/l_i to each agent i.

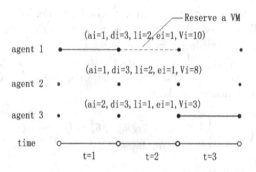

Fig. 1. An example for multi-time unit demand($C = 1$)

Definition 2. *(Online greedy allocation with reservation(OGAWR)) At each step t allocate the s(t) VMs to the active agents with the highest unit valuations, at the same time, make the VM reservation for allocated agent i during period $[t + 1, d_i]$ if $l_i > 1$.*

Consider an example with 3 time units and 3 agents in Fig. 1, where $\theta_1 = (1, 3, 2, 1, 10), \theta_2 = (1, 3, 2, 1, 8), \theta_3 = (2, 3, 1, 1, 3)$ showing the agents arrival, departure, job size, job class and valuation. Suppose furthermore that $C = 1$, and we sort the agents by their unit valuation V_i/l_i. Because agent 1 has the highest unit valuation at time 1, OGAWR method would allocate the VM to agent 1, and reserve one VM for it. Since it is a flexible job ($e_1 = 1$), there are two choices for reserving: reserving at time 2 or at time 3. In Fig. 1, the VM in time unit 2 is chosen to reserve for agent 1, so there is no idle VM to be allocated at time 2. At time 3, although agent 2 has higher unit valuation than agent 3, the VM is still allocated to agent 3, because agent 2 has no sufficient time to finish the job at that time.

It is worth to note that OGAWR might not be performed in some cases. That is, an agent with highest unit valuation cannot be allocated although there is sufficient time from departure for process. In the above example, suppose that the VM in time unit 3 is reserved for agent 1 at time 1. In that case, at time 2, although agent 2 has higher unit valuation than agent 3 and there is sufficient time to process, agent 2 still cannot be allocated. The reason for this result is that the supply in future is less than that in current time. Therefore, the OGAWR can be realized only if it makes 'non-increasing reserving'.

Definition 3. *(non-increasing reserving) Non-increasing reserving refers to a class of reserving schemes which always satisfies $s(t) \leq s(t + 1) \leq s(t + 2) \leq \dots$ after allocation at each time t.*

In OGAWR mechanism, the agent participating the allocation at time t satisfies three conditions:(1)It arrives before time t. (2)Its departure time is longer than $t + l_i - 1$. (3)It is still unallocated. The OGAWR mechanism consists of allocation rule and payment rule described as follows.

- **Allocation Rule.** At each time t, it makes allocation as follows.
  Stage 1 *Greedy allocation*: Allocate the $s(t)$ VMs using greedy allocation, breaking ties at random.
  Stage 2 *Non-increasing reservation*: Make non-increasing reservation for agents who are allocated in stage 1 if necessary. If one VM is reserved for agent i at time k, $\pi_i^k = 1$.
  Let $\theta^t = (\theta_1, \theta_2, ..., \theta_n)$ denote the set of agent types participating the allocation at time t, and π^t denotes the decision policy at time t. The mechanism makes a sequence of allocation decisions $(\pi^1, \pi^2, ...)$, and π^t includes all those agents allocated at time t.
- **Payment Rule.** We design a critical payment which is equal to the critical value for allocated agents, and the definition of critical value is as follows. Given type $\theta_i = (a_i, d_i, l_i, e_i, V_i)$, the critical value for agent i is defined as

$$V_{(a_i,d_i,l_i,e_i)}^c(\theta_{-i}) = \begin{cases} \min V_i' & s.t. \ A_i(\theta_i', \theta_{-i}) = 1, \\ & for \ \ \theta_i' = (a_i, d_i, V_i') \\ \infty & no \ such \ V_i' \ exists \end{cases} \quad (4)$$

where $\theta_{-i} = (\theta_1, \theta_2, ..., \theta_{i-1}, \theta_{i+1}, ...)$.
We define payment policy $p_i(\theta)$ as

$$p_i(\theta) = \begin{cases} V_{(a_i,d_i,l_i,e_i)}^c(\theta_{-i}) & if \ A_i = 1 \\ 0 & otherwise \end{cases} \quad (5)$$

4.2   The Algorithm Design of OGAWR Mechanism

In this section, the algorithm based on the proposed rules for allocation and payment is designed. First, we introduce two reserving methods for inflexible agents and flexible agents respectively.

Continuous reserving: Continuous reserving is suitable for inflexible agents, which is similar to the allocation in MOVMPA mechanism proposed in paper [13]. If agent i wins the auction at time t, one VM will be reserved continuously for it in next $l_i - 1$ units. That is, $\pi_i^k = 1, k = t+1, ..., t+l_i-1$, if $\pi_i^t = 1$.

Discontinuous reserving based on reservation-ratio(Discontinuous reserving): This reserving method reserves one VM for agent i in next $l_i - 1$ time units with lowest reservation-ratio, and reserve the VM in earliest time unit if there are multiple time units with same reservation-ratio.

Reservation ratio denoted by $r(k)$ is the ratio of the number of reserved VMs to total capacity C at future time k expressed as $r(k) = s(k)/C$. Obviously, $r(k)$ is changed with time.

For inflexible agents, continuous reserving and discontinuous reserving both could be used. Since discontinuous reserving can adjust the distribution of users' workload, so in our mechanism we choose discontinuous reserving for inflexible agents. The steps of the allocation algorithm at time t are as follows:

Step 1. Sort all agents which participate the allocation at time t in non-increasing order of V_i/l_i.

Table 1. Allocation algorithm: *Allocate*

Input: θ^t, S^t, t
Output: S^t, π^t, A
1: if $s(t) = 0$, goto end
2: sort all $\theta^t \subseteq \Theta$ in non-increasing order of V_i/l_i
3: $(\pi^t, A) = greedyallocate(\theta^t, S^t)$
4: sort all $i \in \pi^t$ in non-decreasing order of d_i
5: for each $i \in \pi^t$
6:    if $e_i = 1$
7:       $(\pi_i, S^t) = DiscontinuousReserve(l_i - 1)$
8:    else
9:       $(\pi_i, S^t) = ContinuousReserve(l_i - 1)$
10:   end if
11: end for
12: $S^{t+1} \leftarrow S^t \setminus \{s(t)\}$
13: end

Step 2. Allocate $s(t)$ idle VMs to $s(t)$ agents with highest valuation, breaking ties at random.

Step 3. Choose a suitable reserving method for each agent allocated at step 2. Continuous reserving is chosen if $e_i = 0$, and discontinuous reserving is chosen if $e_i = 1$.

Define a status vector $S^t = (s(t), s(t+1), s(t+2), ..s(t+m-1))$ as the VM supplies in period $[t, t+m-1]$ before allocation at time t, where $s(t+k)$ is denoted as the supply at future time $(t+k) \in T$, and m satisfies $s(t+m-1) < C$ and $s(t+m) = C$. For computing critical value, we define $v_{-i,t}^{(m)}$ to be the mth highest of unit valuations V_j/l_j from all agents j in θ^t, $j \neq i$. Then $v_{-i,t}^{s(t)}$, for supply $s(t)$, is the lowest value that is still allocated a unit, if agent i were not present not only at current t but also before t. Henceforth, we refer to $v_{-i,t}^{(s(t))}$ as the marginal clearing value of the idle VM for agent i at time t.

OGAWR Mechanism runs in each time unit t, and the algorithm is described as follows:

Step 1. According to the allocation rule of OGAWR, the allocation is performed based on S^t, θ^t, which generates an allocation set π^t and a new status set S^{t+1}, and updates allocation result A.

Step 2. For each agent i who got its first unit at step 1, the critical value for agent i at time t is computed using equation $v_{i,t}^c = v_{-i,t}^{s(t)}$. Then, we execute a suppositional allocation in which i is not present, and get suppositional results π_{-i}^t and S_{-i}^{t+1}.

Step 3. For each i who got the allocation before time t and $t \leq d_i - l_i + 1$, according to the suppositional result S_{-i}^t which suppose that i had been not present before t, we compute the critical value for agent i as $v_{i,t}^c = v_{-i,t}^{s_{-i}(t)}$. We also execute a suppositional allocation in which i is not present based on the suppositional status S_{-i}^t, and get suppositional results π_{-i}^t and S_{-i}^{t+1}.

Table 2. Mechanism algorithm: OGAWR

Input: t, $\theta^t = \{\theta_1, \theta_2, ..., \theta_n\}$, S^t
Output: S^{t+1}, π^t, p_i, A
1:   $\pi^t = \varnothing$
2:   if $s(t) = 0$, goto end
3:   $(S^{t+1}, \pi^t, A) = Allocate(\theta^t, S^t, t)$
4:   for each $\pi_i \in \pi^t$ do
5:      $v_{i,t}^c = v_{-i,t}^{s(t)}$
6:      $(S_{-i}^{t+1}, \pi_{-i}^t, A_{-i}) = Allocate(\theta_{-i}^t, S^t, t)$
7:   end for
8:   for each $i \notin \pi^t$ and $A_i = 1$ and $t \le d_i - l_i$ do
9:      $v_{i,t}^c = v_{-i,t}^{s_{-i}(t)}$
10:    $(S_{-i}^{t+1}, \pi_{-i}^t, A_{-i}) = Allocate(\theta_{-i}^t, S_{-i}^{t-1}, t)$
11: end for
12: for each i: $t = d_i - l_i + 1$
13:     if $A_i = 0$, $p_i = 0$
14:     else $p_i = \displaystyle\min_{t \in [a_i, d_i - l_i + 1]} v_{i,t}^c \cdot l_i$
15: end for
16: end

Step 4. For each i who satisfies $t = d_i - l_i$, the payment p_i is computed. If $A_i = 0$, the payment p_i is zero, otherwise the payment can be computed as

$$p_i = (\min_{t \in [a_i, d_i - l_i + 1]} v_{i,t}^c) \cdot l_i$$

Lemma 1. *The payment in above algorithm is a critical payment. That is,* $(\displaystyle\min_{t \in (a_i, d_i - l_i + 1)} v_{i,t}^c) \cdot l_i = V_{(a_i, d_i, V_i, l_i, e_i)}^c(\theta_{-i})$ *for each allocated agent* i.

5   Analysis of OGAWR Mechanism

We assume no early-arrival no late-departure misreports with $a_i \le a_i' \le d_i' \le d_i$, because generally agent i don't know its type until a_i and the value of agent will be zero if it is finished after d_i. We also assume no less job size misreports with $l_i' \ge l_i$ because the agent i will have no sufficient time to process if $l_i' < l_i$.

Definition 4. *(Monotonic with resource demand) An allocation policy is monotonic with resource demand l_i if for any arrival-departure interval $[a_i, d_i]$, any valuation V_i and any job size report $l_i' \ge l_i$, we have $A_i(a_i, d_i, V_i, l_i') = 1 \Rightarrow A_i(a_i, d_i, V_i, l_i) = 1$.*

Definition 5. *(Monotonic with arrival-departure interval) An allocation policy is monotonic with arrival-departure time if for any job size l_i, any valuation V_i and any arrival-departure time report $a_i' \ge a_i$ and $d_i' \le d_i$, we have $A_i(a_i', d_i', V_i, l_i) = 1 \Rightarrow A_i(a_i, d_i, V_i, l_i) = 1$.*

Lemma 2. *The allocation policy in OGAWR mechanism is monotonic with re-source demand and arrival-departure interval.*

Next, we discuss about whether an agent would get more utility by misreport e_i. First, an inflexible agent would not misreport $e_i = 1$ because discontinuous allocation for this class job will cause zero value. Second, we find there is no difference in allocation and payment to flexible agent between reporting $e_i = 1$ and reporting $e_i = 0$. For allocation, due to the greedy allocation and non-increasing reserving, whether an agent can be allocated is only decided by the order of its valuation and not related to e_i. For payment, according to the critical value equation(4), the critical value of agent i would not changes when e_i changes, and the payment of the agent is equal to the critical value which is also not related to e_i. We assume that each agent is rational, that is, the agent will choose to report true type when misreport cannot improve its utility.

Theorem 1. *The OGAWR mechanism is incentive compatible with no-early arrival, no-late departure misreports and no less job size misreports.*

We define the competitive ratio on social welfare as follows. An auction mechanism M is $c - competitive$ with respect to the social welfare if for every bidding sequence θ , $E_M(\theta) \geq E_{opt}(\theta)/c$. Accordingly, c is the competitive ratio of M. Where, E_M is the sum of agents value in mechanism M, and E_{opt} denotes the sum of agents value by the optimal algorithm.

Assume that VM to all agents has a same maximal unit valuation v_{max} and same minimal unit valuation v_{min}, i.e, $v_i \in [v_{min}, v_{max}]$. Define $N = \frac{v_{max}}{v_{min}}$. At the same time, we assume the maximal job size is L and $L \geq 2$.

Theorem 2. *OGAWR mechanism has a competitive ratio on social welfare* $\frac{C \cdot N \cdot (L+1)}{2}$.

6   Evaluation and Simulation

As analysed above, the competitive ratio c of OGAWR mechanism might be very large because it is decided by L and N. That is, it may lead to very low social welfare at the worst case. In this section, we will present the simulation results and compare the OGAWR mechanism with two allocation methods. one is an offline optimal approach designed under the assumption that we know all the agents valuation beforehand and completely ignore the allocation time constraint in $[a_i, d_i]$. Although it is not reasonable that OGAWR mechanism is compared with the offline allocation without time constraint, we can understand the actual level of proposed mechanism on social welfare and percentage of served agents by comparing the curves. The other method compared is a good online mechanism (MOVMPA) designed in paper [13]. The main difference between MOVMPA mechanism and OGAWR mechanism is that MOVMPA uses continuous allocation for each agent.

Same as [13], the input data of the experiments are collected from the Parallel Workload Archive [15], which collect many workload logs from large scale parallel systems in various places around the world. We select 10 thousands continuous records from log RICC-2010-2. In the log, the minimal time unit recorded is second. In our experiment, we choose 10 minutes as one time unit, and all records selected are distributed randomly from time 0 to time 8000. Each record corresponds to one task, and the information of a task includes arrival time , wait time, runtime, number of allocated processors, etc. Each task is processed by at most 8 thousands processors. According to the number of allocated processors k, a task can be divided into k subtasks each of which must be processed serially in one processor. That is, one subtask requests at most one VM in each time unit which is consistent with the assumption in our model. Let each agent present one subtask(also is one job). After the step of task decomposition, there are about 285 thousands agents in these records.

Next, we discuss how the type of agent $\theta = (a_i, d_i, l_i, e_i, V_i)$ can be got. First, a_i and l_i can be got from the log, where the real arrival time of the record is a_i and the runtime can be converted to the size l_i. As described above, if k agents are generated from one same record, they will have same arrival time and job size. Second, we produce the other information d_i and V_i. Assume that the deadline and the valuation are exponential distribution. Deadline d_i and valuation V_i/l_i are computed as $d_i = a_i + l_i + l_i \cdot exp(d_{avg})$ and $V_i/l_i = exp(v_{avg})$. Finally, the parameter e_i is generated randomly. The table II shows the simulation parameters.

Table 3. Simulation Parameters

Type	Notaion	Value	Parameter
Arrival time	a_i	form workload archive	
departure time	d_i	$a_i + l_i + l_i \cdot exp(d_{avg})$	$d_{avg} = 2$
job size	l_i	from workload archive	
valuation	V_i	$V_i/l_i = exp(v_{avg})$	$v_{avg} = 50$
job character (flexible)	e_i	1 or 0, generate randomly	

Fig. 2 and 3 shows the distribution of all those records we selected. Fig. 2 shows the number of arrival subtasks at each time unit, while Fig. 3 is the size distribution of all agents.

Before running of the mechanism, we initialize the supply, the total number of VMs, which is closely related to the allocation results. we define an initial supply C_0 is equal to average requirement for each time unit, i.e., $C_0 = \Sigma_{i=1}^n l_i/|T|$, where $|T| = 8000$ is total time units we select.

Fig. 4 shows the social welfare, the sum of agents value with different C, and C changes continuously from $C = 0.5 \cdot C_0$ to $C = 1.5 \cdot C_0$. First, we note that the trends for the two scenarios in OGAWR mechanism are different C when supply is low and close to $C = 0.5 \cdot C_0$, the OGAWR mechanism results only in a small overall improvement in social welfare, However, when it grow to more than C_0, there is a very obvious improvement. Especially, when $C = 1.5 \cdot C_0$, the social welfare in OGAWR mechanism is very close to it in the condition of offline allocation, while it still keep a low level in MOVMPA mechanism.

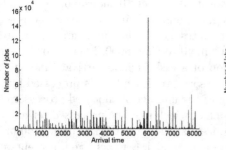

Fig. 2. Distribution of arrival time   **Fig. 3.** Distribution of job size

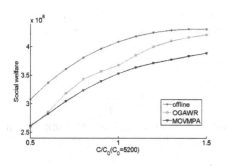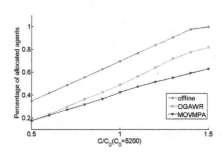

Fig. 4. The number of competed jobs under three mechanisms   **Fig. 5.** The sum of agents value under three mechanisms

With respect to the number of completed jobs of individual agents, the results are shown as Fig. 5. The percentage of completed jobs increases with the increase of supply in all allocation approaches, and in OGAWR, it is obviously higher than that in MOVMPA when they are in the same supply capacity.

7   Conclusion

In this paper, we propose an online VM allocation mechanism for private IaaS cloud resources, whose goal is to improve the social welfare. We construct a online resource allocation model in which jobs are divided into two classes: inflexible jobs and flexible jobs. Then, an online greedy allocation with reservation(OGAWR) mechanism under the dynamic cloud environment is designed and proved truthfully. We also performed extensive experiments to observe the results of the mechanism. The results show that, from the aspects of improving social welfare and the number of completed jobs, OGAWR is better than the mechanism which allocates the inflexible agents as well as flexible agents.

For future work we plan to consider several issues. First, in this paper we assumed all agents need only one VM per time unit, but in the future we plan to extend the allocation model to deal with multiple VMs demands per time unit.

Second, it would be interesting to design model-based mechanism and compare the performance with the model-free online mechanism proposed in this paper. Finally, we also plan to study online mechanism design for public IaaS cloud in future work, where the goal of mechanism is to maximal the revenue of cloud provider.

Acknowledgments. The workload log from the RICC cluster was graciously provided by Motoyoshi Kurokawa. This Work was supported by the National Natural Science Foundation of China (61170029, 61100052, 61373032, 91318301), Zhejiang Provincial Natural Science Foundation of China under Grant No. Y1111000, and Zhejiang Provincial Science and Technology Plan of China under Grant No. 2013C31097.

References

1. Amazon. Amazon EC2 spot instances,
   http://aws.amazon.com/ec2/spot-instances/
2. Nisan, N. (ed.): Algorithmic game theory. Cambridge University Press (2007)
3. Parkes, D.C., Singh, S.: An MDP-Based approach to Online Mechanism Design. In: Proc. of NIPS 2003 (2003)
4. Gershkov, A., Moldovanu, B.: Efficient sequential assignment with incomplete information. Games and Economic Behavior 68(1), 144–154 (2010)
5. Gerding, E.H., Robu, V., Stein, S., et al.: Online mechanism design for electric vehicle charging. In: Proceeding of the 10th International Conference on Autonomous Agents and Multiagent Systems (AAMAS 2011), pp. 811–818 (2011)
6. Nahir, A., Orda, A., Raz, D.: Workload Factoring with the Cloud: A Game-Theoretic Perspective. In: Proceedings of the 31st Annual Joint Conference of the IEEE Computer and Communications Societies. Networking (INFOCOM 2012), pp. 2566–2570. IEEE Society (2012)
7. Wei, G., Vasilakos, A.V., Zheng, Y., et al.: A game-theoretic method of fair resource allocation for cloud computing services. The Journal of Supercomputing 54(2), 252–269 (2010)
8. Zaman, S., Grosu Combinatorial, D.: auction-based allocation of virtual machine instances in clouds. Journal of Parallel and Distributed Computing 73(4), 495–508 (2013)
9. Zhang, Q., Gurses, E., Boutaba, R.: Dynamic resource allocation for spot markets in cloud computing environments. In: 2011 Fourth IEEE International Conference on Utility and Cloud Computing (UCC), pp. 178–185. IEEE (2011)
10. Danak, A., Mannor, S.: Resource allocation with supply adjustment in distributed computing systems. In: Proceeding of the 30th International Conference on Distributed Computing Systems (ICDCS), pp. 498–506. IEEE (2010)
11. Wang, Q., Ren, K., Meng, X.: When cloud meets eBay: Towards effective pricing for cloud computing. In: Proceedings of the 31st Annual Joint Conference of the IEEE Computer and Communications Societies. Networking (INFOCOM 2012), pp. 936–944. IEEE Society (2012)

12. Jain, N., Menache, I., Naor, J(S.), Yaniv, J.: A truthful mechanism for value-based scheduling in cloud computing. In: Persiano, G., et al. (eds.) SAGT 2011. LNCS, vol. 6982, pp. 178–189. Springer, Heidelberg (2011)
13. Zaman, S., Grosu, D.: An Online Mechanism for Dynamic VM Provisioning and Allocation in Clouds. In: Proceeding of the 5th International Conference on Cloud Computing (CLOUD), pp. 253–260. IEEE (2012)
14. Zhang, H., Li, B., Jiang, H., et al.: A framework for truthful online auctions in cloud computing with heterogeneous user demands. In: Proceedings of the 32st Annual Joint Conference of the IEEE Computer and Communications Societies. Networking (INFOCOM 2012), pp. 1510–1518. IEEE Society (2012)
15. Feitelson, D.G.: Parallel Workloads Archives: Logs, http://www.cs.huji.ac.il/labs/parallel/workload/logs.html
16. Wu, X., Gu, Y., Li, G., et al.: Online Mechanism Design for VMs allocation in Private Cloud, http://basics.sjtu.edu.cn/~liguoqiang/paper/Onlinefull.pdf

Threshold Based Auto Scaling of Virtual Machines in Cloud Environment

M.K. Mohan Murthy, H.A. Sanjay, and Jumnal Anand

Nitte Meenakshi Institute of Technology, Bangalore
{maakem,sanju.smg,anandsbj1989}@gmail.com

Abstract. Cost effectiveness is one of the reasons behind the popularity of Cloud. By effective resource utilization cost can be further reduced and resource wastage can be minimized. The application requirement may vary over time depending on many factors (for instance load on the application); user may run different types of application (a simple MS word to complex HPC application) in a VM. In such cases if the VM instance capacity is fixed there is a high possibility of mismatch between the VM capacity and application resource requirement. If the VM capacity is more than the application resource requirement then resource will be wasted; if the VM capacity is less than the application resource requirement then the application performance will degrade. To address these issues we are proposing threshold based auto scaling of virtual machines in which VMs will be dynamically scaled based on the application resource utilization (CPU and Memory). Using our approach effective resource utilization can be achieved.

Keywords: Cloud Computing, Auto Scaling, Virtual Machines.

1 Introduction

In cloud paradigm software, infrastructure, and platform are given as services. In this work we are considering infrastructure (Virtual Machine). IaaS providers provide Virtual Machine (VM) to end user. User will use VM instance to host/run his applications and he will pay some amount as per the SLA (Service Level Agreement). Many organizations moving towards private cloud; effective resource utilization, cost reduction, and easy maintenance are some of the reasons behind this. Employees in the organization will get the VM instances. They have to login to these instances to use them. Whether it is commercial cloud or private cloud following two scenarios are possible

1.1 Scenario 1: User Hosts Different Application on the VM

User may use VM to host different applications from a simple MS word to complex accounting software. If the VM instance is static (normally this will be the case) user has to select VM instance in such a way to match the application which has the maximum resource requirement. In this case for instance if the user uses the VM to

C.-H. Hsu et al. (Eds.): NPC 2014, LNCS 8707, pp. 247–256, 2014.

run his application which has the maximum requirement only for 2 hours in a day then in remaining 22 hours resource will be wasted. If the application resource requirement is more than the VM then it leads to application performance degradation.

1.2   Scenario 2: Application Requirement Vary over Time

Consider a database application which needs more resource when the transactions are happening. If the transactions are not there it doesn't need high resources. In case of the static VM instance this will lead to resource wastage.

Migration of application from one VM to another address' above mentioned issues but it is having many disadvantages. It is time consuming, tedious, not cost effective, and error prone. If VM is dynamically scaled according to the application requirement resource wastage can be minimized.

To address the above mentioned issues we have developed and tested threshold based auto scaling of VM mechanism, in which the VM is auto configured according to the application requirement. In threshold based auto scaling the resource utilization of the VM is monitored. If they exceed the predefined threshold values then VM capacity will be increased or decreased dynamically without shutting them down according to the need, which minimizes resource wastage.

1.3   Up-Scaling

In this work we have considered RAM and CPU utilization of the VM. As the resource requirement of the application increases, the RAM and CPU utilization of the VM increases. At some point the application resource requirement will become more when compare to VMs capacity as a result performance of the application degrades and ultimately it will hang. To avoid this problem when the CPU and Memory utilization of the VM crosses the predefined maximum threshold value we will increase the RAM and CPU capacity of the VM.

1.4   Down-Scaling

As the resource requirement of the application decreases, the RAM and CPU utilization of the VM decreases. This will lead to resource wastage since the VM capacity is not fully utilized. To avoid resource wastage when the CPU and Memory utilization of the VM crosses the predefined minimum threshold value we will decrease the RAM and CPU capacity of the VM. Monitoring and scaling of RAM and CPU of the VM are two independent tasks.

Rest of the paper is organized as follows section 2 gives brief description about the related work; section 3 explains the threshold based auto scaling of VM; section 4 describes the algorithms used to upscale/downscale the VM; section 5 talks about the experimental setup and results, followed by conclusion.

2   Related Work

There are couple of efforts related to dynamic resource provisioning in cloud environment. In [1] auto-scaling of the VM instances with respect to the load, where load is defined as number of jobs submitted and the deadline and budget to complete the submitted jobs are considered. In the proposed system the VM must be rebooted after scaling it. So there will be time delay and performance degradation. In some scenarios rebooting of VM is not acceptable.

In [2] a novel architecture is presented for the dynamic scaling of web applications based on thresholds in a virtualized cloud computing environment. This work illustrates the scaling approach with a front-end load balancer for routing and balancing user requests. Web applications are deployed on web servers installed in virtual machine instances. In [3] a cloud computing architecture is constructed with a front-end load balancer, a virtual cluster monitor system and an auto-provisioning system. The front-end load balancer is utilized to route and balance user requests to cloud services deployed in a virtual cluster. The virtual cluster monitor system is used to collect the statistics of the usage of physical resources in each virtual machine in the virtual cluster. The auto-provisioning system is used to dynamically provision the virtual machines based on the number of the active sessions or the use of the resources in the virtual cluster.

In the works [2] [3] front end load balancer is used for load balancing on virtual machines. In these works a new instance of VM is added to the VM cluster if the resource utilization crosses the upper threshold. If the utilization is below the lower threshold then VM instances are removed from the cluster. In these works scaling of the VM based on the hosted application requirement is not addressed. In [4] a model-driven engineering approach is presented to optimize the configuration, energy consumption, and operating cost of cloud auto-scaling infrastructure to create greener computing. This work concentrates on energy consumption and budget constraints. In this work pre-configured static VM instances are used. This will lead to resource wastage as well as application performance degradation.

In all of these works cloud is scaled by adding new VMs. They are not considering auto scaling of a single VM which is required in the scenario where user will be using a VM to run his applications in private or public cloud. Our work is about to auto scale a VM based on the threshold values.

3   Threshold Based Auto Scaling of VM

Application requirement may change over time and also user may host different applications (which have different resource requirement) on the VM. In these cases fixed VM capacity may lead to resource wastage or application performance degradation. This can be addressed by dynamically scaling the VM according to the hosted application requirement. In threshold based auto scaling the resource utilization of the VM is monitored. If they exceed the predefined threshold values then VM capacity will be increased or decreased dynamically according to the need without shutting down the VMs, which minimizes resource wastage. High level system overview is shown in figure 1.

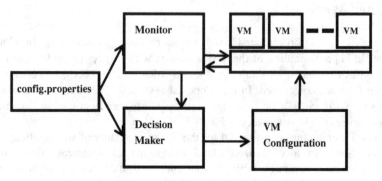

Fig. 1. Auto Scaling system overview

Auto-scaling system has the following components

3.1   Monitor

The monitor component monitors the VMs; it reads the CPU and Memory utilization and passes this data to Decision Maker component. It uses Xen APIs to get the CPU and Memory utilization of the VMs. It sends request for the CPU and Memory utilization of VMs to the XCP using Xen APIs. By default it monitors all the active VMs or we can make it to monitor only specific VMs by configuring the corresponding values in config.properties. The time interval to send the request to XCP to get the VMs statistics can be configured in config.properties.

When the Monitor module starts it will read all the configuration properties from the config.properties and monitors the VMs as per the values set to different property parameters in config.properties file.

3.2   Decision Maker

Decision maker module gets the VM statistics from Monitor module and it also read the threshold values from the config.properties file, compares against the VM statistics and decides whether to up/down scale the VM and conveys this decision to VM configuration module. The information passed to the VM configuration module includes the VM ID which should be scaled, whether scaling should happen to RAM or CPU and how much scaling should happen. All the threshold values and scaling values (helps in to take the decision of how much scaling should happen) are configurable which are stored in the config.properties file.

There is a possibility that VM's CPU and RAM utilization may exceed the threshold value for few seconds and again come back to the normal values. If the monitor module gets these values it will trigger up/downscaling of the RAM/CPU of the VM. In the next iteration monitor module gets the normal values again this triggers down/up-scaling of the RAM/CPU of the VM which results in unnecessary up/down scaling of VMs. To avoid this problem we have introduced configurable properties called cpuiteration (min and max) and memoryiteration (min and max).

Any positive integer value from 0 to n can be set to the cpuiteration and memoryiteration. Both are independent of each other, min memoryiteration and min cpuiteration are used in case of down-scaling, max memoryiteration and max cpuiteration are used in case of up-scaling. The Decision Maker initiates up/downscaling only if the RAM and CPU utilization of the VM exceeds the threshold values in the successive number of iterations specified in the cpuiteration (min and max) and memoryiteration (min and max) .

4   Scaling Algorithms

We have written two separate algorithms for memory scaling and CPU scaling. The working principle of both the algorithms is same.

In case of the memory scaling algorithm each VM's memory utilization (Mx) is read and compared with max memory threshold value (Mmx). If Mx is greater than or equal to Mmx then the max memory utilization counter (MTx) is increased and min memory utilization counter (MTm) is reset.

4.1   Memory Scaling

Step 1: for each VMx Read Memory utilization Mx
Step 2: if the Mx>=Mmx
   - Increment the MTx for the VMx
   - Reset MTm for the VMx
else if Mx<=Mmn
   - Increment the MTm for the VMx
   - Reset MTx for the VMx

Step 3: if MTx>TTMt and if free memory available
   - initiate the VM up-scaling for memory
   - go to step 5
else if MTm >TTMt
   - initiate the VM down-scaling for memory
   - go to step 5
Step 4: Go to Step 1
Step 5: Reset the MTx and MTm
Step 6: Go to Step 1

4.2   CPU Scaling

Step 1: for each VM_x Read CPU utilization C_x
Step 2: if the $C_x>=C_{mx}$
   - Increment the CT_x for the VM_x
   - Reset CT_m for the VM_x
   else if $C_x<=C_{mn}$

$\quad$ - *Increment the CT_m for the VM_x*
$\quad$ - *Reset CT_x for the VM_x*
Step 3: if $CT_x > TTC_t$ and if computing resources available
$\quad$ - *initiate the VM up-scaling for CPU*
$\quad$ - *go to step 5*
$\quad$ *else if $CT_m > TTC_t$*
$\quad\quad$ - *initiate the VM down-scaling for CPU*
$\quad\quad$ - *go to step 5*
Step 4: Go to Step 1
Step 5: Reset the CT_x and CT_m
Step 6: Go to Step 1

VMx - Virtual Machine identifier
Mmx - Memory maximum threshold defined
Mmn - Memory minimum threshold defined
Cmx - CPU maximum threshold defined
Cmn - CPU minimum threshold defined
T – Time interval defined to read the Memory, CPU utilization of VMs
TTMt - Time threshold counter defined for Memory.
TTCt - Time threshold counter defined for CPU.
CTx - Max CPU iteration count.
MTx - Max memory iteration count.
CTm - Min CPU iteration count.
MTm - Min memory iteration count.
Cx - CPU utilization of VMx
Mx - Memory utilization of VMx

5   Experimental Setup and Results

A Cloud Environment is set up using Xen Cloud Platform (XCP) [5]. XCP includes Xen Hypervisor, Xen API tool-stack, vSwitch etc. XCP is an open source enterprise-ready server virtualization and cloud computing platform. Many of the existing IaaS providers are using the customized XEN to create the virtualization infrastructure. XCP delivers the Xen hypervisor with support for a range of guest operating systems including Windows and Linux network and storage support, management tools in a single, tested installable image, which is also called XCP appliance. It also supports the dynamic scaling of virtual machine. XCP APIs are used to get the memory and CPU utilization statistics of the VMs and to up-scale and down-scale the VMs.

5.1   Memory Scaling

XCP supports two types of memories: static and dynamic. Each will have minimum and maximum range. The static memory maximum defines the maximum amount of physical memory that the guest operating system can address from the time the guest boots up until the time the guest shuts down again. It is not possible to change static memory when the VM is running. In case of the dynamic memory it is possible to increase/decrease the range when the VM is running. XCP provides a feature called dynamic memory controller. Using the following API's provided by the XCP we increase/decrease the dynamic memory within the valid range whenever required.

xe vm-param-set uuid=<*uuid*> memory-dynamic-{min, max};

uuid is the identifier which uniquely identifies a VM.

5.2   CPU Scaling

CPU scaling can be done by either modifying the CPU cap or CPU weight. The CPU cap optionally fixes the maximum amount of CPU a domain will be able to consume. The cap is expressed in percentage of one physical CPU: 100 is 1 physical CPU, 50 is half a CPU, 400 is 4 CPUs, etc... The default, 0, means there is no upper cap [5]. CPU weight of a VM decides how much CPU is allocated to that VM. A domain with a weight of 512 will get twice as much CPU as a domain with a weight of 256 on a contended host. Legal weights range from 1 to 65535 and the default is 256 [5]. In our work we have used the CPU cap to scale the CPU allocated to VM. The following API provided by the XCP is used.

xe vm-param-set uuid<*uuid*> VCPUs-params:cap=<*value*>

The Cloud Server is setup on a 4 Core Machine with Intel Xeon W3250 processor with 2.67 GHz, 12 GB of DDR3 RAM, 1 TB Hard disk with 7200 RPM. The desktop machine which is used to monitor the VMs for memory and CPU utilization of the application has the Intel Core2 Duo processor with 2.66 GHz clock speed, 1 GB of RAM, 500 GB hard disk, connected over an Ethernet LAN. CentOS 5.7 Operating System is used.

To generate load on VMs we have used both computing intensive programs and memory intensive programs. Once the programs are started the CPU and memory utilization of the VMs will increase. We have set the scaling factor for memory as 1.25 and for CPU it is 2. The utilization count is set to 3 minutes i.e. if the resource usage exceeds the upper threshold value for 3 minutes continuously, then the corresponding VMs will be allocated more resources as specified in the scaling factor (up-scaling). If the resource usage is below the lower threshold value for 3 minutes continuously, then the resource will be de-allocated from the VM as per the scaling factor (down-scaling).

We have setup the threshold values as follows

Upper threshold – 80%, Lower threshold – 25%

Figure 2 and 3 shows memory up-scaling and downscaling respectively. Figure 4 and 5 shows CPU up-scaling and downscaling respectively. Since we have set the utilization count to 3 minutes, we can observe the scaling at 4th minute in all the cases.

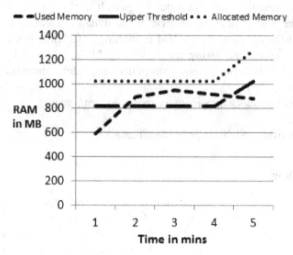

Fig. 2. Memory up-scaling

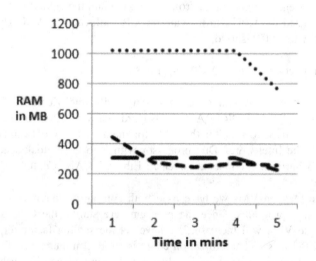

Fig. 3. Memory down-scaling

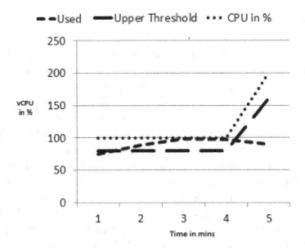

Fig. 4. CPU up-scaling

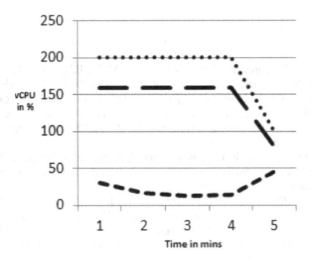

Fig. 5. CPU down-scaling

Following is our observations

- Downscaling minimizes the resource wastage.
- Up-scaling make sure that the application performance is not compromised.
- Choosing the right threshold values is very important for the success of our approach.

A lower threshold value result in fluctuation of the VM capacity and a higher threshold value makes our algorithms less responsive to the change in resource utilization of the VM.

6   Conclusion

By adopting effective resource utilization techniques resource wastage can be minimized. Our threshold based auto-scaling is one such technique in which VM is dynamically scaled as per the application resource requirement, thereby minimizing the resource.

Selecting proper threshold values is very important factor in the success of our approach. A lower threshold value leads to frequent change in VM configuration and a higher value reduces the responsiveness of VM to adapt to the new resource requirement. We can use several techniques to find out optimum threshold values such as history based, mathematical model etc. In future we are planning to build a feedback based system to dynamically scale the VM according to the application requirement. At present our dynamic scaling system is threshold based where threshold values are static and predefined. In feedback based system we will monitor the application's resource utilization and it will be used as feedback to define the threshold values.

References

1. Mao, M., Li, J., Humphrey, M.: In: Schwarz, T.S.J., Miller, E.L.: Cloud Auto-scaling with Deadline and Budget Constraints. Department of Computer Science University of Virginia Charlottesville, VA, USA 22904 {ming, jl3yh, humphrey}@cs.virginia.edu (2011)
2. Chieu, T.C., Mohindra, A., Karve, A.A., Segal, A.: Dynamic Scaling of Web Applications in a Virtualized Cloud Computing Environment. In: 2009 IEEE International Conference on e-Business Engineering (2009)
3. Hung, C.-L., Hu, Y.-C., Li, K.-C.: Auto-Scaling Model for Cloud Computing System. Dept of Computer Science & Information Engineering, Providence University {clhung, ychu, kuancli}@pu.edu.tw
4. Doughertya, B., Whiteb, J., Schmidta, D.C.: Model-driven Auto-scaling of Green Cloud Computing. Institute for Software Integrated Systems, Vanderbilt University, Campus Box 1829 Station B, Nashville, TN 37235, Email:{briand,schmidt}@dre.vanderbilt.edu bECE, 302 Whitemore Hall, Virgnia Tech, Blacksburg, VA 24060, Email:julesw@vt.edu
5. http://wiki.xen.org/XCP_Design_and_Architecture

A Novel Resource Provisioning Model for DHT-Based Cloud Storage Systems

Jingya Zhou[1,2] and Wen He[2]

[1] School of Computer Science and Technology, Soochow University,
215006 Suzhou, P.R. China
jyz@seu.edu.cn
[2] School of Computer Science and Engineering, Southeast University,
211189 Nanjing, P.R. China
wenhe@seu.edu.cn

Abstract. Cloud storage providers build a distributed storage system by utilizing cloud resources located in data centers. The interactions among servers in a DHT (Distributed Hash Table)-based cloud storage system depend on the routing process, and its execution logic is more complicated. Hence, how to allocate resources to not only guarantee service performance (*e.g.*, data availability, response delay), but also help service providers to reduce cost became a challenge. To address this challenge, this paper presents a novel resource provisioning model for cloud storage systems. The model utilizes queuing network for analysis of both service performance level and cost calculation. Then the problem is defined as a cost optimization with performance constrains, and a novel algorithm is proposed. Furthermore, we implemented a DHT-based storage system on top of an infrastructure platform built with OpenStack. Based on real-world traces collected from our system, we show that our model could effectively guarantee the target data availability and response delay with lower cost.

1 Introduction

Cloud storage utilizes cloud technologies to build storage systems based on IT resources located in datacenters, and provides customers with data storage, data sharing, data access and management, and so on. Recently cloud storage services have attracted more and more attention from both academia and industry [1][2]. One of the most attractive features of cloud storage is the ability to provide customers with convenient data access services without worrying about data loss. When customers use services they are mainly concern about data availability and response delay. The former represents the probability that customers can successfully access the target data, and the latter refers to the time required for the system to respond to requests. Both of them directly affect the service level that customers experienced, and become the preferred performance metrics discussed in this paper.

High amount of concurrent access requests is another feature of cloud storage, which makes storage providers choose to build distributed storage systems

C.-H. Hsu et al. (Eds.): NPC 2014, LNCS 8707, pp. 257–268, 2014.

based on P2P structure (*e.g.*, Dynamo [1], Cassandra [2]). It is a type of shared nothing architecture (SNA) [3], in which each server has its own disk for storage. DHT mechanism is responsible for both storing data to all servers and requests routing. It can provide an "always-on" experience as the continuous growth of system scale. Due to the distributed nature of systems, customers' requests need to be matched and forwarded among many servers after they arrive at systems. There are many interactions among servers during requests being processed. Different from multi-tier web applications, servers interact sequentially layer by layer according to the hierarchy, while the interactions occurred in cloud storage systems depend on the routing process and are more complicated. Hence how to model the relationship between service performance and resource provisioning becomes a challenge. In addition, cloud storage systems are based on the infrastructure services offered by IaaS providers, for example, Dropbox chooses IT resources that come from Amazon as its servers to store data and deal with requests [4]. Storage providers only pay for resources that are needed according to the current amount of access requests, which will reduce cost.

We explore the problem from the cloud storage provider's point of view. The overall cost paid by a storage provider mainly includes server cost, storage cost and traffic cost. As mentioned above, this paper mainly concerns access performance, so we make assumptions that all data have been stored in the system, and then the storage cost has been fixed. Most traffic is generated by both retrieving data from datacenter and geo-replication across multi-datacenter. Traffic cost caused by retrieving data can be reduced by data compression techniques, while traffic cost caused by geo-replication depends on the specific replication scheme. Both of them are outside the scope of this paper. Therefore, the cost discussed here mainly refers to server cost, and the final objective of resource provisioning is to generate the server level resource demands to minimize cost while satisfying performance requirements. In this paper we propose a novel model to achieve server level resource provisioning with optimal cost-performance trade-off. Our proposed model strives to rent just enough resources for systems to minimize resource waste, while avoiding performance degradation.

2   Related Work

Jing *et al.* [5] proposes a novel resource auto-scaling scheme that try to find the optimal number of VMs by modeling system as a M/M/m queue so as to achieve cost-latency trade off. However, It assume a simple scenario that VMs run independently, and the interactions among VMs are not considered completely. Ferretti *et al.* [6] designs a middleware architecture for resource management that aims to satisfying quality of service (QoS) requirements as well as optimizing resource utilization. It only provides a common framework for analysis, and does not optimize for addressing a specific execution logic.

For multi-tier applications, Jing *et al.* [7] focuses on how to minimize cost while satisfying response delay constraint. It employs a flexible hybrid queuing model that consists of one M/M/c queue and multiple M/M/1 queues to determine the number of VMs at each tier. Different from layer-by-layer research ideas, Lama *et al.* [8] suggests employing fuzzy theory to guide server provisioning and designs a model-independent fuzzy controller, so as to minimize VMs while guarantee end-to-end response delay. The works in [7][8] are based on the assumption that VMs are identical, but usually IaaS providers provide various types of VMs. Furthermore, the assumption of single VM type results in coarse-grained resource provisioning and limited cost optimization.

Zhu *et al.* [9] creates a resource provisioning model by employing M/G/1 queuing system, and develop meta-heuristic solutions based on the mixed tabu-search optimization algorithm to solve the provisioning problem. It only take response delay into consideration, and focus on the maximization of IaaS provider's profit which is different from the goal of this paper. By considering budget constraint as well as response delay, Zhu *et al.* [10] presents a feedback control based dynamic resource provisioning algorithm for maximizing application QoS.

For cloud storage services, customers' requests usually should be matched and forwarded among many servers after they arrive at systems. The interactions among servers depend on the routing process, and do not be executed in accordance with the fixed order. Hence the interactions occurred in cloud storage systems are complicated and lack of an effective resource provisioning model for characterization. Zhang *et al.* [11] presents a resource management algorithm for cloud storage systems. The proposed algorithm aims to achieve load balancing by using two types of operation, i.e., merge operation and split operation. However, such an algorithm does not consider server interactions during the execution of services, and only consider load balancing as performance metrics. This paper explores the resource provisioning model based on the execution logic of cloud storage services. We consider two performance metrics in the model, *i.e.*, data availability and response delay, and strive to optimize cost as well as guarantee performance.

3 Resource Provisioning Model

3.1 System Model

Cloud storage systems run on the infrastructure of datacenter, and the system overview is described by Figure 1. Cloud storage providers rent servers from IaaS providers and build the system by organizing servers into a distributed network, so that the system can store massive data in a distributed manner. When customers' requests arrive at the system, they are dispatched to servers and will be processed according to DHT mechanism. It is assumed that the data have been stored in the system, and then the primary performance metrics concerned by customers should be data availability, denoted by P_{suc} which represents the probability that customers can successfully access the target data, and response delay, denoted by R which represents the time required for the system to respond to requests. This paper strives to research on resource provisioning from the cloud storage provider's point of view. Our problem is how to generate a resource provisioning demand according to the current customers' requests, so that

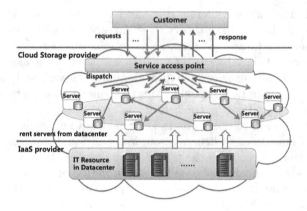

Fig. 1. Cloud storage system overview

it can meet performance metrics while optimize economic metrics. The resource provisioning demand consists of three parameters, *i.e.*, the number of servers, the processing capacity of each server, and cost.

3.2 Resource Provisioning Problem

To tackle the above problem, we need to establish a resource provisioning model. As we know, cloud storage system is distributed, when it receives requests it will dispatch them to servers randomly. The server matches the received requests with the data stored upon it. If match success, server will return results directly, otherwise server will forward requests to the next one according to DHT rules till finding the target data. Servers interact with each other through forwarding requests. For better describing this kind of interactions, we propose a resource provisioning model based on queuing network. As shown in Figure 2, the system consists of N servers, and each one is modeled as an M/G/1/k queue with independent general execution time distribution. The request arrivals are poisson with rate λ_1. Servers are classified and charged by processing capacity, *e.g.*, the processing capacity of server i is represented by μ_i ($\mu_{min} \le \mu_i \le \mu_{max}$), where μ_{max}, μ_{min} are the upper bound and lower bound respectively. The cost of server is represented by the function of processing capacity $f(\mu_i)$. Due to the limit of processing capacity, server cannot simultaneously receive and process an unlimited number of requests. As requests increase, the length of queue becomes larger, which results in a higher response delay. To avoid high response delay, we set up a size limit k for each queue. When the length of queue reaches k, the workload of server will be saturated, and then the new arrived requests will be denied. Once a request is denied, the customer's access will fail, and as a consequence the data availability will decrease. The formal definition of resource provisioning problem is described as follows:

Given that the thresholds of performance metrics (*i.e.*, data availability and response delay) are P^*_{suc} and R^*, and the threshold of server rejection rate is

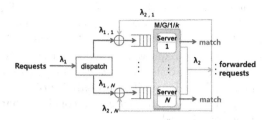

Fig. 2. Queuing network model for resource provisioning

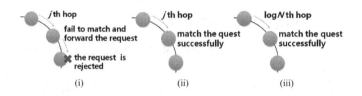

Fig. 3. An example of request forwarding

P_{rej}^*. The server cost is $f(\mu_i)$ that is a non-decreasing function of μ_i, and the request arrival rate is λ_1. We need to generate the optimal resource provisioning demand $(N, \mu, \text{Cost}(\mu))$ that meets performance metrics while optimize server cost. In the demand, N represents the number of servers, μ represents the vector of server's processing capacities, and $\text{Cost}(\mu)$ is the sum of server cost. *i.e.*,

$$
\begin{aligned}
\text{Min} \quad & \text{Cost}(\mu) = \sum_{i=1}^{N} f(\mu_i) \\
\text{s.t.} \quad & (1)\ P_{suc} \geq P_{suc}^* \\
& (2)\ R \leq R^* \\
& (3)\ P_{rej} \leq P_{rej}^* \\
& (4)\ \mu_{\min} \leq \mu_i \leq \mu_{\max}
\end{aligned}
\tag{1}
$$

In cloud storage systems, customers' requests can be satisfied within $O(\log N)$ hops forwarding according to DHT rules, so that the mean match rate at each hop is at least $1/(\log N + 1)$. Assume that the mean rejection rate of server is P_{rej}, then

$$
P_{suc} = \sum_{j=0}^{\log N} A(j)B(j)\frac{j+1}{\log N + 1}
\tag{2}
$$

where $A(j) = (1 - P_{rej})^{j+1}$ represents the probability that the request arrives at the $j + 1$th server after it finish j hops forwarding without being denied, while $B(j) = \prod_{m=0}^{j} (1 - \frac{m}{\log N + 1})$ represents the probability that the request has not been matched at previous j servers. The probability of being matched successfully at the $j + 1$th server is $\frac{j+1}{\log N + 1}$. Assume that the request stops at the

$j + 1$th server, and then there exists three cases, as shown in Figure 3: (i) The request is not matched at the $j + 1$th server. Then the request is forwarded to the $j + 2$th server, and is denied by the server. The probability of such case should be $B(j + 1)P_{rej}$. (ii) The request is matched successfully at the $j + 1$th server. The probability of such case should be $B(j)\frac{j+1}{\log N+1}$. (iii) The request has arrived at the last hop, i.e., $j = \log N$. The probability of such case should be $A(\log N)B(\log N)$. Combining the above cases, we conclude that the mean hop counts of request can be represented by

$$H = \sum_{j=0}^{\log N-1} \left(A(j) \cdot B(j)((1 - \tfrac{j+1}{\log N+1})P_{rej} + \tfrac{j+1}{\log N+1})j\right) \\ + A(\log N)\mathrm{B}(\log N) \cdot \log N \tag{3}$$

We can deduce the mean number of forwarded messages in the same way:

$$M = \sum_{j=0}^{\log N-1} \left(A(j) \cdot B(j)\left((1 - \tfrac{j+1}{\log N+1})P_{rej} \cdot (j+1) + \tfrac{j+1}{\log N+1} \cdot j\right)\right) \\ + A(\log N)\mathrm{B}(\log N) \cdot \log N \tag{4}$$

As described by Figure 2, the arrival rate of servers consists of both the requests λ_1 issued from customers and the forwarded requests λ_2, and $\lambda_2 = \lambda_1 M$. So the mean arrival rate can be calculated by λ_1/N. It is noted that the probability of receiving requests depends on the access frequency of data stored on server. $Q_i(0 < Q_i < 1)$ is used to represent the access frequency of server i, and then the arrival rate of forwarded requests at server i should be $\lambda_{2,i} = Q_i\lambda_2$. For server i, the arrival rate can be represented by

$$\lambda(i) = \lambda_{1,i} + \lambda_{2,i} \tag{5}$$

Response delay consists of two parts, i.e., the mean time required to forward the request, denoted by T, and the mean sojourn time at a server, denoted by W. Thus the mean response delay should be

$$R = T \cdot H + W \cdot (H + 1) \tag{6}$$

We should deduce the sojourn time by analyzing M/G/1/k queuing system. This paper chooses to use two-moment approximation approach [13] that is based on diffusion theory [14]. The key idea of approach is concluded that the discrete queuing process is approximated to a continuous diffusion process. The rejection rate of server i equals the probability of having k requests in the queue, i.e.,

$$P_{k,i} = \frac{\rho_i^{(\Phi_i+2k)/(2+\Phi_i)}(\rho_i-1)}{\rho_i^{2(\Phi_i+k+1)/(2+\Phi_i)}-1} \\ \text{where } \Phi_i = \sqrt{\rho_i e^{-s_i^2} s_i^2} - \sqrt{\rho_i e^{-s_i^2}} \tag{7}$$

$\rho_i = \lambda(i)/\mu_i$ represents the service intensity of server i, and s_i represents the co-efficient of variation of the service process. The mean rejection rate is calculated by

$$P_{rej} = \frac{1}{N} \sum_{i=1}^{N} P_{k,i} \tag{8}$$

Because server may deny the incoming requests, the effective arrival rate at server i should be less than $\lambda(i)$, and can be represented by $\lambda_e(i) = \lambda(i)(1 - P_{k,i})$. Thus the probability of empty workload at server i is given by

$$P_{0,i} = 1 - \frac{\lambda_e(i)}{\mu_i} = \frac{(\rho_i - 1)}{\rho_i^{2(\Phi_i + k + 1)/(2 + \Phi_i)} - 1} \tag{9}$$

The probability that there are j requests waiting in the queue of server i is $\rho_i^j P_{0,i}$, and then the mean number of requests waiting in the queue of server i should be

$$L_i = \sum_{j=0}^{k-1} j \rho_i^j P_{0,i} + k P_{k,i} \tag{10}$$

Based on Little's Formula [12], the sojourn time at server i is represented by $W_i = L_i/\lambda_e(i)$. Therefore, the mean sojourn time is given by

$$W = \frac{1}{N} \sum_{i=1}^{N} W_i \tag{11}$$

3.3   Solution

Recall that the cloud storage provider's greatest concern is to maximize profit (*e.g.*, by minimizing cost) while providing high quality service (*e.g.*, by guaranteeing data availability and response delay). The resource provisioning is defined as a non-linear cost optimization problem with performance constraints from the cloud storage provider's point of view. By solving the problem, we can achieve the optimal resource demands for system resource provisioning. The previous works only focus on the optimization of number of servers. However, in practice the minimal number of servers does not reflect the lowest cost. In our solution, we are not only trying to answer how many servers need to rent, but also answer what the capacities vector of these servers is. μ is used to represent the vector of server capacities, while N is the number of rented servers, and is also the dimension of capacities vector. We should determine the feasible range of N at the first step.

Substitute P_{suc}^* and P_{rej}^* in constraints (1) and (3) into equation (2), then we can obtain the value of N that satisfies constraints (1) and (3), denoted by N'. In the same way we can obtain the value of N, denoted by N'' that satisfies constraints (2) and (3) by substituting R^* and P_{rej}^* in constraints (2) and (3) into equation (6). It is noted that the server rejection rate $P_{k,i}$ is the non-increasing function of μ_i, then substitute $\mu_{\max}(\mu_{\min})$ in constraint (4) and $P_{k,i} = P_{rej}^*$ into equation (7), we can deduce the maximal (minimal) arrival rate $\lambda_{\max}(\lambda_{\min})$. Combine equations (4) and (5) together, we find that $\lambda(i)$ is related to total customers' requests arrival rate λ_1, rejection rate P_{rej} and the number of servers N. By substituting λ_1, P_{rej}^* and $\lambda_{max}(\lambda_{min})$ into equation (5), we can achieve the feasible range of N, denoted by $[N_1, N_2]$ that satisfies the threshold of rejection rate. In order to satisfy all constraints, the feasible range should be trimmed by N' and N''. Proposition 1 shows us the proof of feasible range of N.

Algorithm Resource_provisioning

Input

λ_1: the total customers' requests arrival rate

μ_{max}: the upper bound of processing capacity

μ_{min}: the lower bound of processing capacity

Q_i: the access frequency of server i

T: the mean time required to forward the request

Output

Opt_solution$(N, \mu, Cost(\mu))$: the optimal resource demands

1. Calculate N' by subjecting P_{suc}^* and P_{rej}^* to equation (2);
2. Calculate N'' by subjecting R^* and P_{rej}^* to equation (6);
3. Calculate $\lambda_{max}(\lambda_{min})$ by subjecting $\mu_{max}(\mu_{min})$ and $P_{k,i} = P_{rej}^*$ to equation (7)
4. Calculate N_1 (N_2) by subjecting $\mu_{max}(\mu_{min})$, P_{rej}^* and λ_1 to equation (5)
5. $N_{min} = \max(N', N_1, N'')$, $N_{max} = \max(N', N_2)$;
6. Opt_solution $(N, \mu, Cost(\mu)) = $ **NLP_OPT** (N_{min});
7. **if** $N_{min} \neq N_{max}$
8.   **for** $N = N_{min} + 1 \text{to} N_{max}$
9.   solution $(N, \mu, Cost(\mu)) = $ **NLP_OPT** (N);
10.   **if** solution$(N, \mu, Cost(\mu))$ is better than Opt_solution$(N, \mu, Cost(\mu))$
11.   Opt_solution $(N, \mu, Cost(\mu)) = $ solution $(N, \mu, Cost(\mu))$;
12.   **end if**
13.   **end for**
14. **end if**
15. **return** Opt_solution $(N, \mu, Cost(\mu))$;

Proportion 1. *In the server provisioning problem, the feasible range of number of servers that satisfies all constraints is* $[\max(N', N_1, N''), \max(N', N_2)]$.

Proof: P_{rej} is a non-increasing function of N by analyzing equations (7) and (8). If $N' \leq N_1$, the lower bound of N, denoted by N_{min}, takes the value of N_1 for satisfying constraint (3). Otherwise, N_{min} takes the value of N' for satisfying constraint (1). In addition, R is a non-increasing function of N by analyzing equation (6) (T is much smaller when compared with W). In order to satisfying constraints (2), N_{min} takes the value of N'', *i.e.*, $N_{min} = \max(N', N_1, N'')$. Assume the optimal value $N^* < N_{min}$, and then it will result in that one constraint or all of constraints cannot be satisfied. Therefore, N_1 should take the value of $\max(N', N_1, N'')$.

In the same way, if $N' \leq N_2$, the upper bound of N, denoted by N_{max}, takes the value of N_2 for satisfying constraint (3). Otherwise, N_{max} takes the value of N' for satisfying constraint (1), *i.e.*, $N_{max} = \max(N', N_2)$. Assume the optimal value $N^* > N_{\max}$, and the corresponding optimal cost is $Cost^* = \sum_{i=1}^{N^*} f(\mu_i), (\mu_{\min} \le \mu_i \le \mu_{\max})$. Then all constraints can be satisfied, and N_2 is located in the feasible range. The corresponding cost $Cost\_N_2 = N_2 f(\mu_{\min})$, but $Cost\_N_2 < Cost^*$, which conflicts with the assumption. Therefore, $N_{\max}$ should take the value of $\max(N', N_2)$.

To solve the optimization problem, an novel algorithm is proposed, called **Resource_provisioning**. In the algorithm, lines 1-5 are used to compute the feasible range of N, and then for each N in the feasible range, lines 6-15 use **NLP_OPT**(N) to solve the sub-optimization problem with the fixed value of N.

There are non-linear functions in constraints, so that the sub-optimization problem is a non-linear programming problem which can be formalized as follows:

$$
\begin{aligned}
\text{Min} \quad & Cost(\mu) = \sum_{i=1}^{N} f(\mu_i) \\
\text{s.t.} \quad & (1)\ g_1(\mu) = P^*_{suc} - P_{suc} \le 0 \\
& (2)\ g_2(\mu) = R - R^* \le 0 \\
& (3)\ g_3(\mu) = P_{rej} - P^*_{rej} \le 0 \\
& (4)\ g_4(\mu) = \mu_{\min} - \mu_i \le 0 \\
& (5)\ g_5(\mu) = \mu_i - \mu_{\max} \le 0
\end{aligned}
\tag{12}
$$

In this paper we use augmented lagrangian approach to solve the problem. By introducing slack variable z_j, the inequality constraints become equality constraints, i.e., $g_j(\mu) - z_j^2 = 0$, $j = 1, 2, 3, 4, 5$. We design the augmented lagrangian function, as follows:

$$
F(\mu, \gamma, c) = Cost(\mu) + \frac{1}{2c} \sum_{j=1}^{5} \left\{ [\max\{0, \gamma_j + cg_j(\mu)\}]^2 - \gamma_j^2 \right\}
\tag{13}
$$

where γ is multiplier vector, c is penalty factor, and $z_j^2 = \frac{1}{c} \max\{0, \gamma_j + cg_j(\mu)\}$. Thus the problem is transformed into a simple unconstrained optimization problem, i.e., Min $F(\mu, \gamma, c)$. The solution of non-linear programming can be obtained by iteratively solving unconstrained optimization problem.

4 Experimental Evaluation

4.1 Experiment Setup

We implemented a DHT-based cloud storage system on top of project Voldemort which is an open source implementation of Dynamo. The infrastructure platform is constructed on top of a cluster of 14 IBM HS22 blade servers which are connected in a 1Gbps LAN. These underlying resources are managed by an infrastructure platform built with OpenStack. Servers in our system can be classified as control servers and storage servers. The former is in charge of dispatching requests to storage servers, recording run-time log, and performance statistics. The latter is in charge of processing the incoming requests.

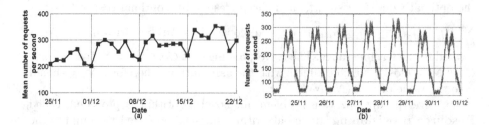

Fig. 4. Distribution of service performance levels

4.2   Trace-Driven Evaluation

We collected real-world traces from November 25, 2013 to December 22, 2013. Figure 4(a) reports the requests received by the system during the period. The mean number of requests per second became larger as the growth of customers scale from 337 to 512. It reflects a weekly pattern that the amount of concurrent visits is lower on weekends. A daily pattern is reflected by Figure 4(b). There are two peaks appeared in the morning and afternoon separately, and the trough appears at noon and midnight. Note that request for files larger than 4MB will be split into several requests, so the actual arrival rate of requests will be higher.

The amount of concurrent visits was too low to evaluate our provisioning scheme. We reprocessed the traces by adding the last three weeks dataset to the first week. Then we used LoadRunner [15] to test our system. The most common resource provisioning approach is based on Utilization-oriented Principle (UoP) [16]. The UoP approach tries to reduce cost by improving resource utilization (*i.e.*, equals ρ) to a predetermined range. We choose UoP approach to compare with our scheme, and the ranges are set as [60%, 70%] and [80%, 90%]. The thresholds of P_{suc}^*, R^* and P_{rej}^* are set as 99%, 200ms and 0.3%. The processing capacity depends on the type of VM. We measured the capacities through deploying each type of VM in our system, and the values are 224, 535 and 1372.

Figure 5 shows separately the CDF of P_{suc}/P_{suc}^*, R/R^* and P_{rej}/P_{rej}^*. It is concluded from equations (7) and (8) that the rejection rate has a positive correlation with utilization rate. For UoP [60%, 70%] approach concerned, the mean utilization rate are restricted in a low level without large variations, which results in a low level of rejection rate without large variations. When the rejection rate is low, the data availability is so high that we can neglect the influence of other factors on data availability. For UoP [80%, 90%] approach concerned, if the arrival rate is low, system could maintain a high level of both utilization rate and rejection rate. As the arrival rate increases, in order to satisfy performance constraints, both utilization rate and rejection intend to decrease. Note that compared with the threshold, our scheme can achieve much closer data availability and response delay.

Figure 6 describes the comparison of hourly server cost by using different provisioning approaches. UoP approach is sensitive to ρ^*. It appears to be relatively conservative when ρ^* is in the interval [60%, 70%]. Then excessive provisioning of resources results in a much higher performance level than the threshold level. Furthermore, UoP approach pays 72.9% higher cost than our scheme, *i.e.*, the higher cost in exchange of the higher performance level. When ρ^* is in the interval [80%, 90%], it pays 31.8% higher cost than our scheme. Hence the cost can be reduced by increasing ρ^*, however, excessive increase in ρ^* will greatly increase rejection rate. As a consequence, the data availability decreases and becomes lower than the threshold.

The fixed number of types of VMs indicates the number of processing capacities available for selection is small. Therefore, the practical efficiency of our algorithm became high, and the mean execution time was 2.37 seconds.

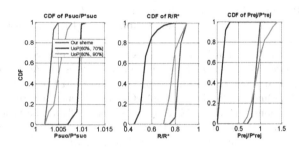

Fig. 5. Comparison of distribution of service performance levels

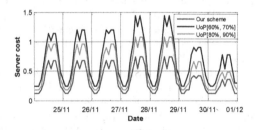

Fig. 6. Comparison of server cost

5   Conclusions

In this paper, we explore the resource provisioning from cloud storage provider's point of view, and propose a novel resource provisioning model. The model considers the complex interactions among servers during system running by using queuing network, and captures the relationship between performance metrics and the allocated resources. Then based on the model, the resource provisioning problem is defined as a cost optimization with performance constraints. We put forward solution algorithms for solving the optimization problem. We have built a DHT-based storage system in our campus network. Based on real-world traces collected from system, the experimental results demonstrate that the proposed scheme can reduce cost while guaranteeing both data availability and response delay.

References

1. DeCandia, G., Hastorun, D., Jampani, M., Kakulapati, G., Lakshman, A., Pilchin, A., et al.: Dynamo: Amazon's Highly Available Key-value Store. In: ACM Symp. Operating Systems Principles (SOSP 2007), pp. 205–220. ACM Press (2007)
2. Lakshman, A., Malik, P.: Cassandra: a decentralized structured storage system. ACM SIGOPS Operating Systems Review 44, 35–40 (2010)
3. Stonebraker, M.: The Case for Shared Nothing. IEEE Database Engineering Bulletin 9, 4–9 (1986)
4. Idilio, D., Marco, M., Maurizio, M.-M., Anna, S., Ramin, S., Aiko, P.: Inside Dropbox: Understanding Personal Cloud Storage Services. In: ACM Conf. Internet Measurement Conference (IMC 2012), pp. 481–494. ACM Press (2012)
5. Jing, J., Jie, L., Quan, Z.-G., Dong, L.-G.: Optimal Cloud Resource Auto-Scaling for Web Applications. In: IEEE/ACM Symp. Cluster, Cloud and Grid Computing (CCGrid 2013), pp. 58–65. IEEE CS Press (2013)
6. Ferretti, S., Ghini, V., Panzieri, F., Pellegrini, M., Turrini, E.: QoS-Aware Clouds. In: IEEE Conf. Cloud Computing (CLOUD 2010), pp. 321–328. IEEE CS Press (2010)
7. Jing, B., Liang, Z.-R., Xiong, T.-R., Bo, W.-Q.: Dynamic Provisioning Modeling for Virtualized Multi-tier Applications in Cloud Data Center. In: IEEE Conf. Cloud Computing (CLOUD 2010), pp. 370–377. IEEE CS Press (2010)
8. Lama, P., Xiao, B.-Z.: Efficient Server Provisioning with Control for End-to-End Response Time Guarantee on Multitier Clusters. IEEE Trans. Parallel and Distributed Systems 23, 78–86 (2012)
9. Zhu, Z., Bi, J., Yuan, H., Chen, Y.: SLA Based Dynamic Virtualized Resources Provisioning for Shared Cloud Data Centers. In: IEEE Conf. Cloud Computing (CLOUD 2011), pp. 630–637. IEEE CS Press (2011)
10. Zhu, Q., Agrawal, G.: Resource Provisioning with Budget Constraints for Adaptive Applications in Cloud Environments. In: ACM Symp. High Performance Distributed Computing (HPDC 2010), pp. 304–307. ACM Press (2010)
11. Zhang, C., Chen, H.-P., Gao, S.-T.: ALARM: Autonomic Load-Aware Resource Management for P2P Key-Value Stores in Cloud. In: IEEE Conf. Dependable, Autonomic and Secure Computing, pp. 404–410. IEEE CS Press (2011)
12. Gross, D., Shortle, J.-F., Thompson, J.-M., Harris, C.-M.: Fundamentals of queueing theory, 4th edn. John Wiley & Sons (2008)
13. MacGregor, S.-J.: Properties and performance modelling of finite buffer M/G/1/K networks. Computers & Operations Research 38, 740–754 (2011)
14. Tijms, H.: Heuristics for finite-buffer queues. Probability in the Engineering and Informational Sciences 6, 277–285 (1992)
15. HP LoadRunner Tutorial (2010)
16. AWS Elastic Beanstalk, http://aws.amazon.com/elasticbeanstalk/

BIDS: Bridgehead-Employed Image Distribution System for Cloud Data Centers

Zhongzhao Wang[1], Yuebin Bai[1,*], Kun Cheng[1], Jihong Ma[2], Duo Lv[3],
Yuanfeng Peng[4], and Yao Ma[1]

[1] School of Computer Science, Beihang University, Beijing 100191, China
[2] Handan Polytechnic College, Handan 056000, China
[3] Department of Computer Science, Arizona State University,
Tempe, AZ 85281, USA
[4] Department of Computer Science, Pennsylvania University, Philadelphia,
PA 19104, USA

Abstract. To provide elastic cloud services with QoS guarantee, it is essential for data centers to provision Virtual Machine(VM) instances rapidly. Due to bandwidth bottleneck of centralized model, the P2P-like distribution schemes are recently adopted. However, most of them just focus on the transmission speed, but ignore the impact on network bandwidth, especially for cloud data centers which are connected by Wide Area Network(WAN). In this paper, we propose a bridgehead-employed VM image distribution system(BIDS), which aims to minimize the repetitive data flows of WAN while speeding up the image distribution. In BIDS, we also design a version based image sharing mechanism, which tries to make a balance between efficiency and management complexity. Besides, we implement a Remote Management Console(RMC). The final evaluation shows that BIDS is of high efficient and low overhead.

Keywords: virtual machine(VM), image distribution, bridgehead, cloud data centers.

1 Introduction

Generally speaking, cloud data centers keep plenty of VM images. For good system elasticity and scalability, it is critical for the cloud data centers to provision VM images fast, even in the case of massive concurrent requests. In order to eliminate the bottleneck of conventional centralized model, researchers recently proposed BitTorrent-like distribution model[1,2]. This model relieves the burden on storage servers, but it just allows VM instances that start from the same image files to share chunks. Prior studies[3,4] have shown that different VM images could still have lots of common chunks. Then Peng et al.[5] proposed a cross-image distribution model, called VDN. VDN is a complete sharing model. It means that image chunks can be shared among any VM instances regardless

---

* Corresponding author.

C.-H. Hsu et al. (Eds.): NPC 2014, LNCS 8707, pp. 269–280, 2014.

of image types. But we must be aware of the fact that VDN had made the system indexing unit, eg., *lookup*, *publish*, etc, changed from images to chunks. So VDN has a complex index structure and expensive computing cost. In addition, all current known distribution models mainly focus on distribution speed, but ignore the impact on network bandwidth. We all know that cloud data centers usually consist of multi data centers which are deployed in different regions and connected by WAN. Because WAN often refers to low bandwidth and long delay, it's inexpedient to treat WAN and Local Area Network(LAN) equally in the image distribution system.

In this paper, we propose a bridgehead-employed VM image distribution system(BIDS), which aims to minimize the repetitive data flows of WAN while speeding up the image file distribution. Different from VDN and other similar paradigms, BIDS has several novel features. First, we introduce bridgehead mechanism in the distribution model. Here we assume that the cloud data centers consist of multi Independent Data Centers(IDCs) and all these IDCs are connected via WAN. In each IDC, we specify some Designated Bridgehead(DB) hosts to decrease the bandwidth consumption of inter-IDCs. Second, we propose version-based image sharing scheme, which tries to make a balance between efficiency and management complexity. And *Delta files* are used to speed up distribution and optimize storage of each physical host. Third, we implement a Remote Management Console to facilitate the management of image resources in cloud data centers.

The rest of the paper is organized as follows. Sect. 2 describes the design principle of BIDS and Sect. 3 presents the detailed implementation. Sect.4 evaluates our proposed model. We discuss the related work in Sect. 5, followed by conclusions in Sect. 6.

2   Design Principle of BIDS

In designing the BIDS distribution framework, our primary objective is to maximize the amount of VM image data that is available within one IDC or on nearby IDCs when the image is needed.

2.1   Execution Mechanism of Bridgehead Mode

We all know that WAN has a characteristic of low bandwidth and long delay. So when one IDC own a image file, it's improper to allow the hosts in other IDCs to "download" the image data arbitrarily. We should find a way which can speed up image file distribution while minimizing WAN bandwidth consumption. In this paper, we introduce the concept of bridgehead. In each IDC, we specify some particular hosts, called DBs. Here the DB is just a normal host except for the ability of sharing image data with other IDCs. In BIDS, the ordinary hosts are forbidden to exchange image data with other IDCs' hosts directly. When a ordinary host must have to obtain image data from other IDCs, it will send request to DB(s) firstly. Here the DBs form the upper-level distribution network. All the inter-IDC image data transmission is accomplished via this network. Thus, the inter-IDC image data exchange can be completely restricted within DBs. The waste of WAN bandwidth caused by plenty of repetitive data flows can be avoided.

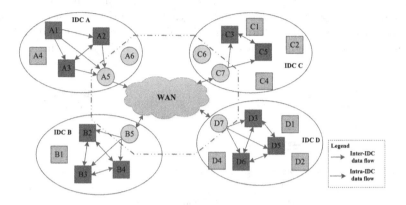

Fig. 1. The brief diagram of bridgehead_employed distribution mode

Now, we briefly illustrate the bridgehead mechanism by an example. Figure 1 shows a skeleton diagram of BIDS distribution process. The host A5, A6, B5, C6, C7, D7 are DB nodes and they form a upper-level network. Now suppose that host A1 own a image file X, host A2, A3, B2, B3, B4, C3, C5, D3, D5, D6 need to get image X. For A2, A3, they belong to the same IDC with A1, so they can get image data from A1 directly. Meanwhile, A2, A3 can share the image data they have already obtained. In such scenario, host A5, A6 are just normal hosts. They make no sense for image distribution. For B2, B3, B4, they can't get image data from A1 directly. In this case, the DB node B5 has to communicate with A5 for image data. Then host B2, B3, B4 get image data from B5. Of course, they can also share the obtained data with each other. Note that the data transmission between DBs, between DB and hosts can proceed in parallel. Analogously, IDC C, IDC D have similar processing. Here, host C7, D7 may be able to obtain image file X from multi DBs simultaneously.

As you can see from Fig. 1, A6 and C6 are DB hosts, but they don't participate in the distribution of image X. They can be viewed as normal hosts in this scenario, but they perhaps play a role of DB in other image distribution. In BIDS, the distribution of one image usually corresponds to a special hierarchical network view. In this view, part of DBs form upper-level network. A DB host may play a role of DB in one view, but act as a normal host in another view. The role of DB depends on the host_list constructed by GIS(General Index Server, detail in Sect. 2.2). This dynamic, non-immobilized scheme can improve distribution efficiency, and at the same time, avoid performance bottleneck problem caused by static scheme.

2.2   Efficient Collaborative Sharing

In cloud data centers, metadata management is one key factor of affecting the performance and efficiency. Here, the metadata consists of the list of hosts who have certain images. In BIDS, in order to manage massive metadata, we set up a particular server, called GIS. In GIS, it stores information about hosts, images, and the relationships between hosts and images, between IDCs and hosts. Besides these, GIS also needs to keep the information about *Delta files*, more details can be found in Sect.2.3. Figure 2 illustrates the work flow of *Publish* and *Lookup*.

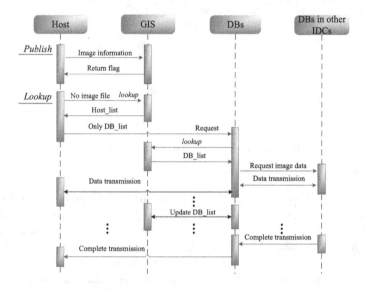

Fig. 2. The sequence char of *Publish* and *Lookup*

In BIDS, when a host, including DB, has obtained a new image, or upgraded an old image, it will execute the *publish* process. Then GIS will do some update operation. For another case, when a host, including DB, needs to get a image, it will execute the *lookup* process. In Fig. 2, we can see that the *lookup* result just contains DB hosts. This informs the requester that the request image is stored in other IDC(s). So the requester send request(s) to the specified DB(s). After that, the data transmission between DBs, between DB(s) and host begin. During the transmission, the DB(s) may communicate with GIS periodically to get the latest host information. Note that centralized structure may turns into the bottleneck of reliability. But it can be resolved easily by mature duplex backup technology.

Distribution Security. For the hosts within one IDC, because they are deployed in LAN, the malicious nodes outside the network are unable to interact with these hosts. In addition, the host themselves can also reject the local requests because of authorization failed, invalid request, or just in order to guarantee the user service. For inter-IDC distribution, because all the DB nodes are designated by administrators with unique DB IDs, it's impossible for malicious nodes to pose as DBs to grab image files.

2.3 Image Version Management

Crossing-image sharing already become an indispensable part of improving performance. But allowing data sharing among any images, like VDN[5] does, often brings up high system overhead. In another aspect, Satyanarayanan et al.[6] show that if a set of images is based on the same major version of operating system, the similarity is high(more than 50%). Peng.c et al.[5] have concluded that the most popular images can contribute to more than 85% of all instances. So it's quiet common that users' VM requests may mainly focus on several types of images. Here each type of image may contain many versions.

Consequently, we propose a version-based image sharing scheme. In this scheme, VM instances that belong to different versions can share their data. Here, we use *Delta file* to record the difference between images that derived from the same base images, but belong to different versions. In this way, a VM instance can quickly upgrade to newer version with just one *Delta file*. And the host can quickly build a new image with just one *Delta file* if it already owns some version of the base image. Of course, it is also feasible for a host to run multi VM instances with just one image file and a series of delta files. In BIDS, *Delta file* information, relationships between *Delta files* and image versions are stored in GIS. Thus, when a host needs to upgrade its image to certain version, it can quickly find which *Delta file* is needed and where to find the *Delta file*.

Image Storage. In BIDS, we employ a distributed storage mechanism. We set up a local storage server in each IDC. These servers act as image "providers". Note that the DB and storage server play a similar role to some extent. The DB can totally act as a storage server and we have done in this way for system testing. However, if the DB is not employed for storage, its useless, outdated, or duplicate image files can be removed by administrators via RMC.

2.4 Remote Management Console

In order to facilitate the management of all the image files, we design a management console. Note that RMC is mainly used for image file management, not a sophisticated resource management platform, like RHEV[7]. To be specific, RMC mainly achieve the following functions.

– Network Information Statistics: In order to facilitate the administrator to know running status of cloud data centers, RMC communicates with GIS periodically to maintain some global statistic information. Alternatively, RMC display these information by the graph way.

- Distribution Control: RMC could control hosts remotely, like limiting "upload", "download" speed, switching sharing status. Besides, RMC could also be used to designate or change IDCs' DBs, designate some hosts to *publish* images, or manipulate hosts to "download" certain image files automatically.
- Image Management: In BIDS, we adopt flexible storage mechanism. Images may be stored in ordinary hosts and DBs. After long-time running, the hosts may store some old, or useless images. RMC can be used to remove images according to certain policies, like oldest, rerely used, or just randomly.

3   Components Implementation of BIDS

In this section, we present the details of components implementation of BIDS.

3.1   Architecture of GIS

GIS is one of key component of BIDS. It holds the running information of the whole system and makes corresponding responses for each arrived request. Figure 3 shows the main function modules of GIS.

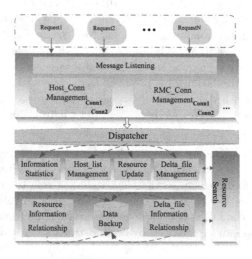

Fig. 3. Architecture of GIS

Host Conn and RMC Conn Modules are mainly used for handling interactions with other components. These two modules need to maintain the information of each received connection. Normally, these two modules may deal with plenty of connection requests concurrently. Resource Search Module is responsible for locating resource position rapidly. Here, we propose an improved hash function which bases on the implementation of Python Dictionary. In Host_list Management Module, we design lots of filter policies which apply to pick out the optimal host list. With the host list, the requester can obtain image data with a minimum cost. Information Statistics Module mainly in response to the RMC's remote commands. The other modules are responsible for managing images, hosts, *Delta files* and image versions information.

3.2 Architecture of Host Service Part

This component is the core of BIDS, all the real image data distribution is accomplished via this part. At runtime, this component needs to communicate with GIS, RMC and other hosts. Figure 4 shows the major modules of this part.

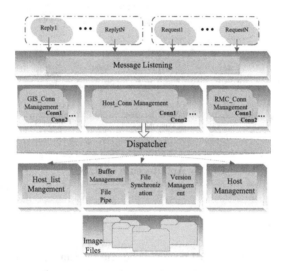

Fig. 4. Architecture of Host Service Part

Similar to SIN, we implement three Conn Modules. Besides, we implement Node Management Module in response to operation instructions sent by RMC. Host_list Management Module can identify the locally stored image information, and *publish* the image information to the GIS if necessary. It also can manage the host list received from GIS and guide the host where to obtain the required image data. File Synchronization Module mainly achieve:(i)build delta file; (ii) merge for the target file. For Version Management Module, it is mainly used to control procedure of version operation. Buffer Management and File Pipe Modules accomplish memory mapping mechanism: the file data is mapped into the memory pages directly. This method can make user process access file data directly and avoid inefficient data copy between user space and kernel space like the conventional file read mode does.

3.3   Architecture of RMC

In BIDS, RMC is implemented based on WEB using MVC design pattern. Its framework can be broadly divided into five layers: View Layer, Model Layer, Service Layer and Persistence Layer. Figure 5 shows the hierarchy architecture of RMC. Using such hierarchy, on the one hand, can decrease interdependence among modules and bring convenience to developers. On the other hand, it can achieve code reuse.

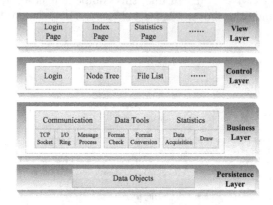

Fig. 5. Architecture of RMC

4   Evaluation

In this section, we compare BIDS with the model that does not perform the "bridgehead" mechanism. But in other aspects, it has similar collaborative sharings as BIDS does. We call it *Baseline*. We use provision time and WAN bandwidth consumption as performance metrics. Meanwhile, the influence of delay variation on BIDS's performance is also evaluated.

In order to better exhibit the BIDS's performance, we construct a simplified cloud data center network with a small amount of physical hosts. Within each IDC, we assign 200Mbps for intra-IDC links. All the physical hosts are connected via switches. For Inter-IDC, we construct diverse WAN environment by adjusting bandwidth size and delay time. The testing VM image can vary from 450MB to 4GB. Considering that the testing network size is small, it's improper to assign WAN bandwidth in the order of Gbps as real cloud data center does. Thus, we limit the bandwidth value to a small range.

4.1   Provision Time

In this part, we set up four IDCs act as "provider". About eight hosts in another IDC request image data in a random order. The WAN delay is set to 15ms.

For WAN bandwidth, some typical WAN types, like CAT-3 cable, CAT-4 cable, E-3 Europe and others, are emulated in the test. We repeated test, while varying the size of VM images:450MB, 1.6GB and 4GB. We record time each host takes, the final average results are shown in Fig. 6.

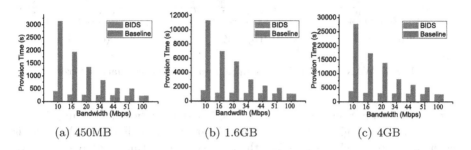

(a) 450MB   (b) 1.6GB   (c) 4GB

Fig. 6. Provision time for VM images over time using *Baseline*

Here, we make the following observations. First, the provision times both decrease as the WAN bandwidth increases. But the rate of decline in BIDS is lower. The reason is that *Baseline*'s bandwidth variation will affect all the requesters. But in BIDS, it only affects largely on DB nodes and has little influences on the requesters. Second, when the bandwidth is low, the performance gain of BIDS is significant, as much as 7x speedup. That's because BIDS fully utilizes the advantage of locality and high-speed LAN makes the image data quickly distributed to each host. But in *Baseline*, requesters have to put up with the low efficient of WAN. Third, when the bandwidth increases to certain degree, the decline rate in BIDS become quietly low. The reasonable explanation is that as bandwidth increases, the key factor of affecting performance in BIDS has changed from bandwidth to DB's distribution efficiency. But we have to say that BIDS is still quiet efficient, especially when the available bandwidth is low. Note that we can improve BIDS's performance manyfold by employing additional DBs.

4.2   Bandwidth Consumption

An efficient distribution model should keep low bandwidth consumption while improving distribution performance. In BIDS, we achieve it by decreasing the repetitive data flows of cross-IDCs. In this subsection, we analysis the bandwidth consumption of the two distribution models. Considering that each image file is divided into fixed-length chunks for distribution, we evaluate the bandwidth consumption through the statistical number of image chunks which are transferred via WAN. In this part, we employ the same test environment as Sect. 4.1 does. We conduct multiple tests, Fig. 7 shows the final statistical results.

It's obvious that BIDS has a fixed bandwidth consumption which comes from DB. Because just single DB node is employed for image distribution in our

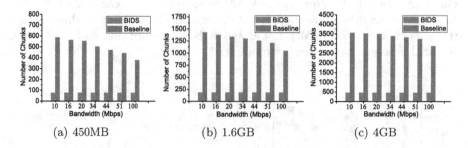

Fig. 7. WAN bandwidth consumption under different image file size

tests, the consumption value is changeless, but the bandwidth consumption for *Baseline* is quiet high. Considering that the image data sharing within IDC is faster than inter-IDC transmission, the request hosts within same IDC will own the same image data after some time running. Then they must have to require the chunks from other IDCs via WAN, which leads to high bandwidth consumption. In another aspect, we can see that the WAN bandwidth consumption reduces gradually as the bandwidth increases. The reason is that higher bandwidth makes it more possible for hosts to obtain chunks from the hosts within the same IDC.

4.3   Delay

In this subsection, we evaluate the influences of system performance when different delay time is assigned to WAN. Similar to Sect. 4.1, the provision time is employed as evaluation metric. Three typical delay times are adopted in our test:10ms, 30ms, 50ms. The testing results are shown in Fig. 8.

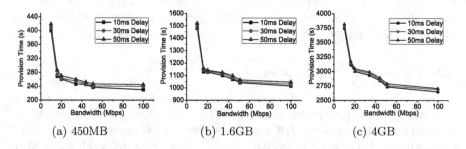

Fig. 8. Influence of delay variation on BIDS's provision time

As you can see from Fig. 8, delay variation doesn't bring about remarkable changes on provision time. The reason is as follows. In BIDS, chunk data is transferred in a pipelined manner. The receiver does not have to return acknowledge messages until a complete chunk is received. Then MD5 checksums of chunks are used to ensure the correctness of transmission. We know that delay acts on distribution only when plenty of message exchange happen among hosts. But in BIDS, message exchange occurs only when the host needs to request new chunks, or retransmit error received chunks, or send checksums. But these only make up a small part of total distribution. Therefore, delay has limited influence on system performance.

5   Related Work

Nowadays, improving distribution efficiency of VM instances has great influence on the overall system performance. Therefore, many efforts have been made on this topic and lots of novel solutions are proposed.Among these researches, Schmidt et al.[8] discussed several distribution methods, including unicast, multicast, BitTorrent-like distribution. Wartel et al.[9] also proposed BitTorrent-like distribution model. In their model, they treat an entire VM image file as a Bit-Torrent seed file. Then Chowdhury et al.[10] revised the BitTorrent protocol and presented an architecture called Orchestra that controls both inflow and outflow data transmission to optimize performance. BJorkqvist et al[11] proposed a tow-tier network topology ignoring different network connections among edge nodes and this solution can reduce the retrieval latency for data centers. Different from the above distribution mechanisms, Peng et al.[5] proposed a more efficient sharing mechanism via utilizing common chunks in different VM images. Zhu et al[12] designed a new distribution mechanism called Twinkle. Twinkle reduces provisioning time by speeding up the initialization of VM instances using demand predication and partial page lunch. Epstein et al[13] focused on data placement on centralized storage servers. They tried to minimize the provision time via the optimization of staging schedules.

6   Conclusions

In cloud data centers, the low bandwidth and long delay of WAN is an important factor of affecting distribution. In this paper, we propose bridgehead mode to minimize the repetitive data flows of WAN while speeding up the image file distribution. Meanwhile, we design the version based collaborative sharing mechanism to speed up the image distribution and RMC make the administrators easy to manage all the image files. Final tests show that our system is efficient.

Acknowledgements. This work is supported by the National Science Foundation of China under Grant No.61340031,61073076,and 61202425, Ph.D. Programs Foundation of Ministry of Education of China under Grant No.20121102110018, and Key Technology R&D Program of Hebei Province, China under Grant No. 13200326D.

References

1. Chen, Z., Zhao, Y., Miao, X., Chen, Y.: Rapid provisioning of cloud infrastructure leveraging peer-to-peer networks. In: Proceeding of 29th IEEE International Conference on Distributed Computing Systems Workshops (ICDCS), Washington, DC, pp. 22–26 (2009)
2. Chowdhury, M., Zaharia, M., Ma, J., Jordan, M.I.: Managing data transfers in computer clusters with orchestra. In: Proceeding of the ACM SIGCOMM 2011 Conference (SIGCOMM 2011), New York, pp. 98–109 (2011)
3. Reimer, D., Thomas, A., Ammons, G., Mummert, T.: Open black boxes: using semantic information to combat virtual machine image sprawl. In: Proceeding of the 4th ACM SIGPLAN/SIGOPS International Conference on Virtual Execution Environments (VEE), New York, pp. 111–120 (2008)
4. Jin, K., Miller, E.L.: The effectiveness of deduplication on virtual machine disk images. In: Proceeding of the Israeli Experimental Systems Conference (SYSTOR), New York, vol. (7) (2009)
5. Peng, C., Kim, M., Zhang, Z., Lei, H.: VDN: Virtual Machine Image Distribution Network for Cloud Data Centers. In: Proceeding of IEEE INFOCOM (INFOCOM 2012), Orlando, pp. 181–189 (2012)
6. Satyanarayanan, M., Richter, W., Ammons, G., Harkes, J.: The case for content search of vm clouds. In: IEEE 34th Computer Software and Applications Conference Workshops (COMPSACW), Seoul, pp. 382–387 (2010)
7. RHEV: Red Hat Enterprise Virtualization,
   http://www.redhat.com/products/cloud-computing/virtualization
8. Schmidt, M., Fallenbeck, N., Smith, M., Freisleben, B.: Efficient distribution of virtual machines for cloud computing. In: 18th Euromicro International Conference on Parallel, Distributed and Network-Based Processing (PDP), Pisa, pp. 567–574 (2010)
9. Wartel, R., Cass, T., Moreira, B., Roche, E.: Image distribution mechanisms in large scale cloud providers. In: 2th IEEE International Conference on Cloud Computing Technology and Science (CloudCom), Indianapolis, pp. 112–117 (2010)
10. Chowdhury, M., Zaharia, M., Ma, J., Jordan, M.I.: Managing data transfers in computer clusters with orchestra. In: Proceedings of the ACM SIGCOMM 2011 Conference (SIGCOMM 2011), New York, pp. 98–109 (2011)
11. Bjorkqvist, M., Chen, L.Y., Zhang, X.: Minimizing retrieval latency for content cloud. In: Proceedings of the IEEE INFOCOM (INFOCOM 2011), Shanghai, pp. 1080–1088 (2011)
12. Zhu, J., Jiang, Z., Xiao, Z.: Twinkle: A fast resource provisioning mechanism for internet services. In: Proceedings of the IEEE INFOCOM (INFOCOM 2011), Shanghai, pp. 802–810 (2011)
13. Epstein, A., Lorenz, D.H., Silvera, E., Shapira, I.: Virtual appliance content distribution for a global infrastructure cloud service. In: Proceedings of IEEE INFOCOM(INFOCOM 2010), San Diego, pp. 1–9 (2010)

A Broker-Based Self-organizing Mechanism for Cloud-Market

Jie Xu and Jian Cao[*]

School of Electronic Information and Electrical Engineering
Shanghai Jiao Tong University, Shanghai, 200240, China
{xujieasd,cao-jian}@sjtu.edu.cn

Abstract. Cloud computing becomes an increasingly popular computing paradigm which leads to an increasingly sophisticated and growing influence of the social business model for cloud computing. A robust and orderly operating mechanism is the foundation of the maturity and stability of cloud commerce market. Since the cloud commerce negotiation is a dynamic and adaptive process, an approach of self-organizing based on multi-agent systems is proposed to achieve the required macroscopic properties of locally interacting agents in cloud market. The novel establishes a three-layered self-organizing multi-agents mechanism to support cloud commerce parallel negotiation activities. Purpose of our work is simulating the mechanism to follow the trend of development in line with economic market rules between cloud consumer and cloud provider. The experimental results indicate that the multi-agents system is successful in handling the commerce negotiation and completing expected requirements.

Keywords: cloud computing, multi-agent systems, self-organizing.

1 Introduction

Cloud computing [1][2] is the development of distributed computing, parallel computing and grid computing. It can be defined as [3] "a large-scale distributed computing paradigm that is driven by economies of scale, in which a pool of abstracted, virtualized, dynamically-scalable, managed computing power, storage, platforms, and services are delivered on demand to external customers over the internet." Similar with the utility service as water, gas, and electricity in daily life, cloud consumer pay service providers for their usage of cloud utility services [4]. The business model of cloud computing bears a strong resemblance to the social commercial model. Cloud consumer select from cloud provider market to find a most satisfied provider and cloud provider wish its service to be mostly accepted to obtain the maximum profit.

However, most of cloud consumers are not experienced enough to obtain the best selection from cloud market. They simply trust the quality information published by cloud provider. Another issue is that it's inconvenient for an individual to compare

---

[*] Corresponding author.

C.-H. Hsu et al. (Eds.): NPC 2014, LNCS 8707, pp. 281–293, 2014.

around from the numerous providers. Therefore, it is necessary to propose a scheduling and resource allocation mechanism for cloud services market to achieve a stable market adaptation [5].

Holland and Miller [7] suggest studying economic systems as complex adaptive systems which containing adaptive agents, networked. Similarly, to maintain the stability of cloud market, we propose a broker-based self-organizing mechanism based on multi-agents to simulate the operating mechanism of cloud market in this novel. The mechanism enables a set of broker agents as third party services to handling the negotiation between cloud consumers and cloud providers.

Mechanism we proposed borrows the ideology of "invisible hand [6]", posed by Adam Smith, which reveals that individuals only consider their own interests in economic life. Driven by "invisible hand", producers seek to maximize profits and consumers pursuit to maximize utility. The broker agent is designed to obtain the instinctive behavior of both consumers and providers. This broker-based mechanism will keep the system changing its internal structure without explicit external command as it is dynamically changeable. As system executing conducts, cloud market forms differentiation and the entire system keeps in general equilibrium.

Hence, the intention of this mechanism we designed mainly involves three aspects: 1) Establish and implement a negotiation tunnel between cloud consumer and cloud provider via broker agent. 2) Maximum to meet customer and provider needs and devise a protocol to keep the cloud market self-organized under a healthy competition. 3) Gradually refining cloud market segmentation so that each cloud provider could make its market positioning precisely.

The broker-based self-organizing framework and communicating stratagem will be introduced in section 3. The detail self-organizing mechanism will be elaborated in section 4. The research simulation and the respective results are described in section 5. Section 6 concludes the paper.

2   Related Work

The research of cloud commerce model and mechanism for cloud computing have been widely studied in recent years. In [8] authors proposed computational economy as a metaphor for effective management of resources and application scheduling. They suggested that market-oriented resource management is necessary to regulate the supply and demand of cloud resources at market equilibrium, and discussed some representative economy-based systems. In [5], authors presented a vision of 21th century computing and described an architecture of market-oriented clouds which contains cloud consumer, cloud provider and cloud allocator to manage cloud resource. But both of the authors did not mention an explicit, appropriate and usable mechanism or algorithm for cloud resource allocation.

Not many cloud commerce mechanisms have been used as a solution for scalable cloud resource management. Existing cloud market based negotiation model such as "auctions model" [9][10] and "recommendation model" [11], all focus on the cooperation quality between cloud service markets and individual cloud consumer. Author in [12][13][14] proposes a cloud commerce negotiation model based on multi-agent systems. The negotiation model consists of provider agents and consumer agents acting on behalf of resource providers and consumers, and a set of broker agents coordinating the negotiation between consumer agents and provider agents.

3   Broker-Based Self-organizing on Cloud Commerce

3.1   Broker-Based Self-organizing Framework

Agents play a major role of negotiating, communicating and decision making between providers and consumers in loud computing model [12][13]. Cloud users can access cloud market through multi-agent system to find a sensible and optimal decision.

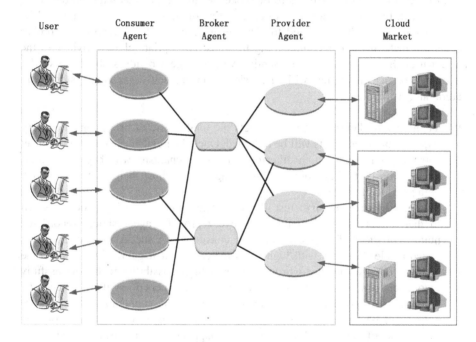

Fig. 1. Broker-based negotiation Framework of cloud computing

Fig 1 demonstrates the architecture of Broker-based cloud computing. The multi-agent system consists of three portions: consumers, providers and brokers. Consumer agents and provider agents are acting to be responsible for cloud users and cloud providers from cloud market. Each cloud provider has a set of properties such as "service using price", "virtual machine CPU" to evaluate its service quality. We define $S_i(p_1, p_2, p_3 ... p_n)$ to describe a service with its properties with each value of p_i refers to the objective assessment of the corresponding property. Cloud requesters also have a set of properties to describe the demanding of cloud users, which are defined as $U_i(p_1, p_2, p_3 ... p_n)$. Broker agents play roles like intermediaries between consumer agent and provider agent. Their fundamental responsibility is matching the properties of consumers and providers and achieves maximum benefits for both sides.

Two types of many-to-many negotiation activities are handled: consumer agents negotiate with broker agents for satisfying cloud user requests and provider agents negotiate with broker agents for cloud market management and differentiation.

3.2   Broker Agent Properties and Characteristics

Broker agent, can be regarded as a set of service agents, which is the integrated services body of cloud services managing, takes care of coordination, mediation and communication. Broker agent is based on the conception of BDI agent [21], with beliefs, desires and intentions. Desires are goals or expectations and judgments on the state of the environment. The desire of broker agent corresponds with the desire of cloud market. Intentions refer both to an agent's commitments to its desires and its commitment to the plans selected to achieve those goals. The intentions of broker agents are matching and recommending the most appropriate cloud provider to the current user. Beliefs are facts representing what an agent believes about the world. Several properties and beliefs will be considered in that self-organizing system, both natural and artificial.

- **Transaction:** Transaction [15] reflects the total traffic of broker agents. Every request from user agents will be recorded. Once the number of such request meet some certain condition, a filtering service mechanism will begin to work. Transaction is the key point for broker agents to adjust their internal topology with provider agents.
- **Sale and Failure History:** Just like merchants count how many goods they sell to their clients in modern business, every provider agent should record the number of successful cooperation with consumers. A successful cooperation is called a sale. Provider with high sales indicates that it gains a warm welcome from its clients. In other words, it owns a high possibility to be successfully recommended to consumers. On the contrary, consumers don't always accept the recommended providers. There exists unsuccessful cooperation. The failure record can be learned by broker agent with learning mechanism to avoid the same type of unsuccessful cooperation happening again. Both success and failure record history are important indicators for agent filter and mining.
- **Satisfaction:** Consumer will score for service provider as feedback when it successfully cooperates with a provider. The satisfaction of a cloud provider is the average value of scores from consumers which is defined as:

$$\mathrm{Sat}_j = \frac{\sum_{i=0}^{n} s_{ij}}{n}$$

The satisfaction of a service provider reflects its popularity and quality to some extent. It also plays an important role on cloud market differentiation.

3.3   Multi-agent Communication Mechanism

The task of multi-agent computing process can be regarded as a process to match consumer's request with resources of cloud providers. Consumer agent, broker agent and provider agent handles different problem respectively, and the detailed mechanism will be discussed in Section 4.

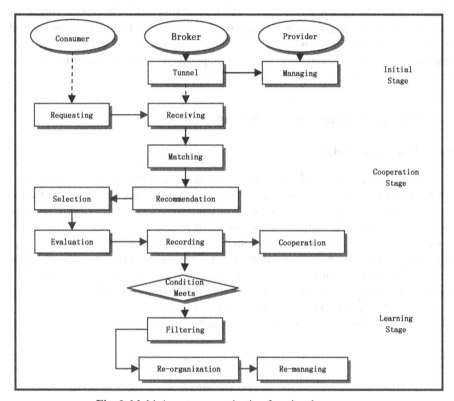

Fig. 2. Multi-Agent communication functional processes

- Consumer agent: represents for cloud consumer, its function mainly involves: 1) Representing cloud user's requirement into formalization. 2) Contacting some broker agents and selecting the most satisfied provider. 3) Combing a single service with corresponding broker agent's outputs and returning evolution value.
- Broker agent: a coordinator between consumer agent and provider agent, its work includes: 1) Establishing communication tunnels for both consumer agent and provider agent. 2) Matching consumer requests with managed providers and recommending the most appropriate one 3) learning and filtering from cooperation records between consumer agents and provider agents to enhance the success rate and evolution value of discovering cloud resources.
- Provider agent: administrator of a set of cloud resources. It manages the interface of cloud resources. It accepts the requests from broker agents and transforms the corresponding output to the corresponding cloud services.

Fig 2 illustrates the communication function process of multi-agent system with three stages. First of all, initial stage performs an original state of agent registration. As communication tunnel constructed, the connections between broker agents and provider agents are randomly established. Cooperation stage shows the complete procedure of how broker agents negotiate with both consumer agents and provider agents to accomplish successful collaborations between buyers and sellers. And learning stage carries out when the broker transaction reaches a certain condition. This stage is designed to classify the quality of collaboration between consumers and providers. With classification and filtering, broker agents will gain the preference of consumer groups and adjust their internal compositions for an improvement of user satisfaction and higher rate of successful cooperation.

4   Self-organizing Model and Algorithm

4.1   Consumer Model

"Consumer First", from Marshall Field, as a marketing concept, should be traced back to the late 19's Marshall Field's department store. The concept tells us that the consumer is the principal part of commercial trading. It is very important to make an accurate definition for consumer model closer to consumer's request.

Behaviors and requirements vary from consumer to consumer. Yet there always exists a group of consumers, their interests and demands are similar to each other. For example some cloud consumers prefer "cheap" service while others are inclined to high performance. Hence the same type of consumer owns identical user preference and each type of the consumer should have a preference function to show its satisfaction of a cloud provider which we defined as *preference(s):*

$$\text{Perference(s)} = \sum property_i \cdot pv_i$$
$$where \sum pv_i = 1$$

Here pv_i is the weight coefficient for each property vector. The value of pv_i depends on the realistic user type. When consumer receives the recommended cloud providers from broker, it will refer to its preference and choose the most satisfactory service for cooperation.

In traditional commerce, consumer always tends to cooperate with the provider once it used, but it would also like to try other provider it seldom used. We define a choose function for the probabilistic of a broker service chosen by consumer.

$$Pro_i = \frac{1 + B\_serive_i}{N + service_{all}}$$

Here B_serive_i denotes the number of cooperation between consumer agent and broker agent i. N is the number of broker agent in the multi-agent system.

And service$_{all}$ is the total number of cooperation between consumer and all brokers. On the basis of the regulations we've discussed above, we proposed our consumer model running mechanism using the algorithm below:

Algorithm 1. Consumer Model Running Mechanism

Sending
1.   Get user property $U_i(p_1, p_2, p_3 \dots p_n)$
2.   For each Broker i
3.   Calculate the chosen probability Pro_i
4.   End for
5.   Chosen_Broker[] ← three Broker with maximum Pro_i value
6.   For each chosen broker i
7.   Send_request(Chosen_Broker[i], request_content)
8.   End for

Receiving
1.   When receive recommendation from broker agent A
2.   Calculate Perference(s)
3.   If all three recommendation recieved
4.   Chosen_Provider ← top rate Perference(s) provider
5.   Cooperate(Chosen_Provider, evolution)
6.   Feedback(Corresponding_Broker, evolution)
7.   End if

User requirements are always changing, but the overall demand follows with certain rules for a certain type of consumer. Hence, user property in our user model is a set of uncertain vectors based on user preference.

4.2   Service Selection and Response Model

When customer selecting merchandise in shops, many factors are taken into consideration to find the most satisfied goods: whether the goods match his needs, whether it sells well, or what are the comments from other customers. Service selection and response model simulates the consumer psychology of customer. The function $R_{recommond}$ is defined to represents a provider's recommended probability which mainly involve three factors: matching indicator, sales indicator and satisfaction. The probability formula is defined as follows:

$$\begin{cases} R_{recommond_i} = \alpha \cdot R_{match_i} + \beta \cdot R_{sale_i} + \gamma \cdot Sat_i \\ R_{match_i} = \dfrac{\sum S_{p_{kj}} \times U_{p_{ij}}}{\sqrt{\sum S_{p_{kj}}^{2}} \times \sqrt{\sum U_{p_{ij}}^{2}}} \\ R_{sale_i} = 1 - \dfrac{rank_i}{N_{provider}} \end{cases}$$

R_{match} denotes the cosine similarity [16] of properties between recommended provider and target user. R_{sale} indicates the rank and popularity of a provider where $N_{provider}$ denotes the total number of providers agent managed by broker agent. Hence, the function $R_{recommond}$ signifies the combination of the three indicators where α, β, γ are corresponding weight coefficients.

After broker agent receives the request from consumer agent, it firstly calculates the recommended probability of each provider agents in its managing list. Secondly it chooses the provider with the highest value and recommend to consumer and then wait for consumer's feedback. A decision threshold is very necessary to distinguish feedbacks from positive and negative examples with the response evaluation value.

4.3   Learning Model

A notable feature of free market is that buyers and sellers do not coerce each other, in the sense that they obtain each other's property rights without physical force. Correspondingly, our multi-agent system is designed to maintain in accordance with the market discipline. Hence, the intention for the filtering and learning mechanism mainly involve two aspects:

- Excluding service provider of poorer quality: a poor quality service provider means provider has few successful cooperation records or even seldom be made inquiries from consumers. This kind of provider does not meet the needs of cloud market. They shall be eliminated in the competition of other providers
- Establishing market position: with the increasing number of access requests from consumers, broker agent will learn to know the customer type it mainly orients and the provider service of favorable managing. That is, broker agent gains knowledge of the consumer's selection pattern. As learning mechanism conduction, a market differentiation gradually appears. It mainly performs that a certain broker majors in a particular type of providers. And the total cloud market is partitioned by broker agents according to consumer preferences.

The learning mechanism contains three steps as follows:

- **Step 1, Eliminating**: broker agents first re-group the managed provider agents in a descending order according to Sail and then delete the provider services from manage-list which fall behind others by a certain percentage.
- **Step 2, Modeling**: screening all success and failure cooperation from the record and constructing a training set based on a certain machine learning method which we will talk about later.
- **Step 3, Selecting:** selecting unsaturated provider agents from cloud service market based on the training model constructed in step 2. Broker will continue searching the qualified provider until it reaches its managing limitation.

We choose ID3 decision tree [17][18] for consumer preference filtering and classification. We choose the attribute of user property as the decision tree's attribute. The information gain is defined to measure the quantitative of the worth of an attribute for a most useful choice of classifying examples. And the entropy is defined to characterize the purity of an arbitrary collection of examples. The detail definition [20] shows blow:

$$
\begin{cases}
Entropy(S) \equiv \sum_{i=1}^{n} -p_i log_2 p_i \\
Gain(S, A) \equiv Entropy(S) - \sum_{v \in Values(A)} \frac{|S_v|}{|S|} Entropy(S_v)
\end{cases}
$$

5   Experimental Evaluation

The simulation environment of our experiment is established based on java agent Development Framework (JADE) [20]. As many performance indicators of cloud service will influence cloud consumers' choices, we considerate five indicators to represent the capability of a cloud service: {service cost, service CPU, service storage, bandwidth, service response time}. Each of them is valued based on its performance level ranging from 1 to 10. Contemporary, the service property represents the interest of a group of particular person, also known as the preference of the consumer.

To evaluate the performance of our self-organizing mechanism, the expecting result of the experimental includes three fields: 1) a cloud market differentiation takes shape. 2) With the conduction of learning mechanism, success rate between consumer and provider performs a remarkable improvement. 3) As the adjustment time grows, the satisfaction feedback from consumer agent also has been significantly improved.

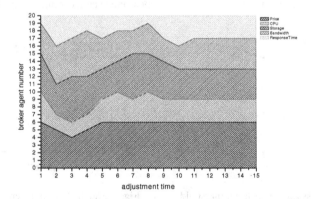

Fig. 3. Cloud market differentiation revolution

Fig 3 illustrates the cloud market differentiation evolution from one set of experiment, where 20 broker agents collaborate to connect and negotiate with consumers and providers. The work division of broker agents was ambiguous at first. After about 10 adjustment steps, a clear division of labor gradually appears. That phenomenon verifies the first expectation we've talked about above.

Fig 4 and Fig 5 shows the comparison empirical result of three different strategies: self-organizing mechanism contains complete three modules (CMLM), strategy without learning mechanism (CM), no consumer and learning mechanism (NM). From the comparison, we see that both success rate and satisfaction performs a significant improvement under our mechanism with adjustment time grows, which is in full compliance with the second and the third experiment expectation. When we remove the consumer mechanism and learning mechanism, the cloud market is keeping chaos as performance of success rate and satisfaction doesn't change at all.

Note that when we only eliminate the learning mechanism, there is still an improvement for both success rate and satisfaction. In fact, consumers can find their most satisfied provider through numerous times of attempts, but the process is slowly. Hence, we can conclude that the learning mechanism improve the efficiency of cloud market differentiation and stability.

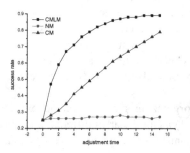
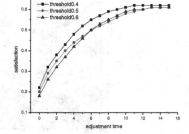

Fig. 4. Success rate with/without consumer mechanism and learning mechanism

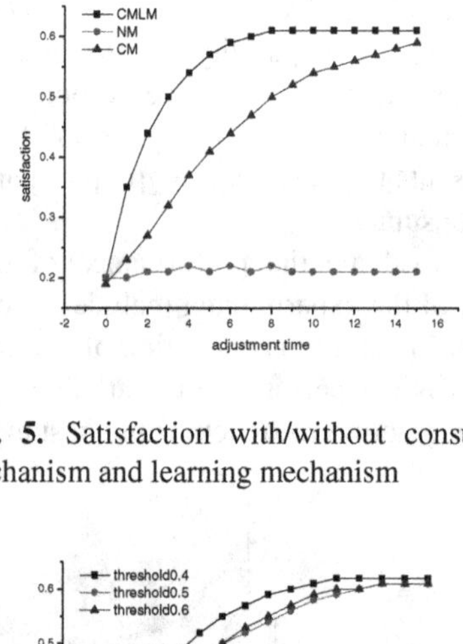

Fig. 5. Satisfaction with/without consumer mechanism and learning mechanism

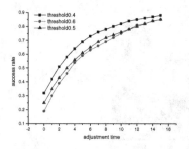

Fig. 6. Success rate in different threshold

Fig. 7. Satisfaction in different threshold

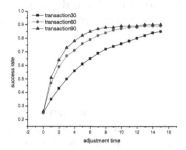

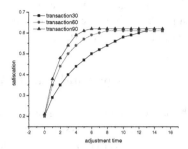

Fig. 8. Success rate in different transaction   **Fig. 9.** Satisfaction in different transaction

Fig 6 to Fig 9 shows the empirical result of our self-organizing mechanism in different measurements. We set up two sets of variables {decision threshold and broker transaction} which we think may have influence in Algorithm performance.

Broker agents adjust their management constructions based on their average transaction number. The experimental truth is the higher of the transaction number, the more rapid increase of the success rate and satisfaction's improvement. Because a higher transaction number indicates that consumer agents access broker agent for more times. But it doesn't mean we should choose a high value for transaction number. We always wish that the market system can achieve a stable and orderly state in a short time. Yet the high value transaction number implies more time is waste before learning and classification mechanism.

Decision threshold is a parameter to classify positive and negative examples. Apparently, the cooperation record could be easily classified into positive example set when we set up a lower decision threshold. Fig 6 and Fig 7 illustrates this point: threshold with 0.4 performances slightly better in both satisfaction and success rate. But the performance of threshold with 0.5 and 0.6 are not very different. That because there exists a satisfaction critical value. Practically, the satisfaction value always reaches a critical value in all of our experiments.

The reason for the phenomenon is caused by the criteria inconsistent between consumer accepting and broker recommending. Consumer agents choose provider agents for cooperation of most preference values. But Broker agents recommend providers mainly based on property matching as they do not know the preference of an individual agent. Note that the preference formula and the matching formula are not corresponding. We show the ideal mathematical expectation of satisfaction below:

$$E_{satisfaction} = \frac{\sum_{s \in Positive(E)} preference(s)}{|Positive(E)|} = \sum_{s \in Positive(E)} E_{S\_property_i} \cdot S\_pv_i$$

Here Positive(E) means the set of positive example and $E_{S\_property_i}$ is the mathematical expectation of consumer property$_i$. In ideal state, consumer agents accept all recommendation from broker agents, which indicates that satisfaction is the average value of all preference values feedback from successful cooperation. And also in ideal situation, the provider recommended from broker agent exactly matches the consumer agent's request. Therefore, the feedback preference directly related to the value of consumer properties.

6   Conclusions and Future Work

With the tremendous growing number of web cloud service and the sharp increasing demands from cloud users, establishing an integrated, scalable and fully distributed framework and strategy of the cloud market becomes an important issue. The significance of our work is that: 1) we borrow the idea of free commercial market in modern cloud computing systems. 2) We proposed a broker-based self-organizing mechanism to simulate the progress of cloud market conduction. And the simulation experiment performs a highly stable and auto-adapt market system that both cloud consumer and cloud provider achieve a win-win development.

As a satisfaction critical value exists in our model, we will focus on the improvement of service selecting and response mechanism in our strategy in the future. To avoid the criteria inconsistent of consumer accepting mechanism and broker recommending mechanism, a more reasonable matching strategy should be taken into consideration in our future work.

Acknowledgements. This work is partially supported by China National Science Foundation (Granted Number 61272438), Research Funds of Science and Technology Commission of Shanghai Municipality (Granted Number 14511107702, 12511502704).

References

1. Armbrust, M., et al.: A view of cloud computing. Communications of the ACM 53(4), 50–58 (2010)
2. Weiss, A.: Computing in the Clouds. netWorker 11(4), 16–25 (2007)
3. Twenty Experts Define Cloud Computing, http://cloudcomputing.syscon.com/
4. Foster, I., et al.: Cloud Computing and Grid Computing 360-Degree Compared. In: Grid Computing Environments Workshop, pp. 1–10 (2008)
5. Buyya, R., Yeo, C.S., Venugopal, S.: Market-oriented cloud computing: Vision, hype, and reality for delivering it services as computingutilities. In: High Performance Computing and Communications, pp. 5–13 (2008)
6. Invisible Hand Theory, http://www.ecocommerce101.com/invisible-hand-theory.htm
7. Holland, J.H., Miller, J.H.: Artificial adaptive agents in economic theory. American Economic Review 81(2), 365–370 (1991)
8. Buyya, R., Abramson, D., Venugopal, S.: The Grid Economy. Proceedings of the IEEE 93(3), 698–714 (2005)
9. Song, B., Hassan, M.M.: EN Huh A novel Cloud market infrastructure for trading service. Computational Science and Its Applications, pp. 44–50 (2009)

10. Grosu, D., Das, A.: Auction-based resource allocation protocols in grids. In: The 16th IASTED International Conference on Parallel and Distributed Computing and Systems, pp. 20–27 (2004)

11. Han, S.-M., Mehedi Hassan, M., Yoon, C.-W., Lee, H.-W., Huh, E.-N.: Efficient service recommendation system for cloud computing market. In: Ślęzak, D., Kim, T.-h., Yau, S.S., Gervasi, O., Kang, B.-H. (eds.) GDC 2009. CCIS, vol. 63, pp. 117–124. Springer, Heidelberg (2009)

12. Sim, K.M.: Agent-Based Cloud Commerce. Industrial Engineering and Engineering Management, 717–721 (2009)

13. Sim, K.M.: A market-driven model for designing negotiation agents. Comput. Intell. 18(4), 618–637 (2002)

14. Sim, K.M.: Towards Complex Negotiation for Cloud Economy. Advances in Grid and Pervasive Computing, 395–406 (2010)

15. Klos, T.B., Nooteboom, B.: Agent-based computational transaction cost economics. Journal of Economic Dynamics and Control, 503–526 (2001)

16. Tan, P.-N., Steinbach, M., Kumar, V.: Introduction to Data Mining, pp. 499–501. Addison-Wesley (2005)

17. Quinlan, J.R.: induction of decision trees. Machine Learning 1(1), 81–106 (1986)

18. Quinlan, J.R.: Decision trees and multi-valued attributes. In: Hayes, Michie, & Richards, Mechine intelligence, vol. 11, pp. 305–318. Oxford University Press, Oxford (1988)

19. Mitchell, T.M.: Machine Learning, pp. 38–56. McGraw-Hill (1997)

20. JADE document, http://jade.tilab.com/

21. Georgeff, M., Pell, B., Pollack, M., et al.: The Belief- Desire-Intent ion Model of Agency. In: Proc of the 5th Workshop on Agent Theories, Architectures, and Language, pp. 1–10 (1999)

Group Participation Game Strategy for Resource Allocation in Cloud Computing

Weifeng Sun[1], Danchuang Zhang[2], Ning Zhang[1], Qingqing Zhang[1], and Tie Qiu[1,*]

[1] School of Software, Dalian University of Technology
116621 Dalian Liaoning, China
{wfsun,qiutie}@dlut.edu.cn, zhang_ning@mail.dlut.edu.cn,
zhang901140@163.com
[2] Meteorological Administration of Dalian
116621 Dalian Liaoning, China
zhangdanchuang@163.com

Abstract. Based on the characteristics of cloud—resources belonging to the same institution and independent resource pool, we proposed a model for the complex task-resource and task-task interactions in cloud by game theory, and proved the existence of Nash equilibrium in the game. In this game model, every task selects resources by itself, rather than the resources are allocated by cloud system. We propose two cloud resource allocation game models—CT-RAG and CS-RAG. A new cloud resource allocation strategy—Group Participation Game Strategy (GPGS) is proposed based on these two game models. We also find out and analyze the equilibrium state of the game with GPGS. The theory analysis shows that GPGS can reduce the total cost of the system in the condition that all tasks/subtasks are rational. Simulation compares Nash, GPGS, Opt and "Round-Robin". The results of evaluation show that the GPGS is better.

Keywords: Cloud computing, resource allocation, game theory, Nash equilibrium.

1 Introduction

Recently, the cloud computing[1] has brought another innovation in IT industry. Cloud computing is a model for enabling ubiquitous, convenient, on-demand network access to a shared pool of configurable computing resources that can be rapidly provisioned and released with minimal management effort or service provider interaction[2]. Cloud computing can now be delivered as services over the internet. For example, CloudCast[3] provides the short-term weather forecasts depending on cloud computing services. The superiority of cloud computing compared to other parallel computing is the concept of resource pool. The resource pool is a virtual set of resources with discretionary combination and allocation, which can be expanded, allocated and recycled dynamically. The resources of cloud are diverse, like compute,

---

* Corresponding author.

C.-H. Hsu et al. (Eds.): NPC 2014, LNCS 8707, pp. 294–305, 2014.

storage, bandwidth, and so on. The cloud providers rent the resources to users and charge by the time or other metrics. For example, for Google App Engine [4], the Stored Data is charged by per gigabytes monthly.

However, the present pricing mechanisms and resource allocation strategies are far from optimal. When cloud system is in a high load state, the existing algorithms (e.g. FIFO, Round-Robin etc.) can't achieve good performance. This problem will become more and more prominent with the increase of cloud users. Moreover, the cloud users aim to reduce the turnaround time and payment of the tasks, and the cloud providers aim to improve the performance of the whole system. Hence, resource allocation in cloud is a very important issue for not only the whole system but also every task.

It is generally accepted that game theory is effective to solve many issues in computer science, such as in grid resource allocation [5], node stimulation in wireless networks and P2P networks[6] [7].The basic elements of a game include: player, action, payoff, information, strategy, outcome and equilibrium. In practice, a game is defined to model the issue to be solved with the basic elements, and the purpose is to find the Nash Equilibrium by game analysis. Nash equilibrium is a stable state with strategy set of all players. John F. Nash has proved that every game has Nash equilibrium [8]. Consequently, game theory can be applied to solve many issues in computer science. In cloud, the system manages and schedules different sources with the form of resource pool by virtualization, and the tasks of different users compete for these resources. So it is reasonable to define a game for cloud resource allocation. By setting a series of reasonable allocation strategies, we can adjust the Nash equilibrium state of this game. And these may improve the performance and load balancing of system.

In this paper, we combine the cloud resource allocation with game theory, and propose a new resource allocation strategy in cloud. It can minimize the total cost by change the payoff of each player, analyze the process and the result of the equilibrium state, and prove the allocation strategy we proposed can reduce the total cost of the system.

The main contributions of this paper are:

- We propose a new cloud resource allocation game model and a new resource allocation strategy GPGS based on the overall interests assuming that all tasks are rational;
- We proved the existence of Nash equilibrium and GPGS equilibrium in GPGS;
- Analysis demonstrates that the GPGS equilibrium state achieved from GPGS has smaller total cost of the whole system.

2   Related Work

With the development of cloud, traditional resource allocation strategy is no longer suitable in cloud computing environment, [9] compare the difference of resource allocation between cloud computing and traditional environments. That is:

- Divide the independent resource pool, allocate and release different physical and virtual resources according to the need of tasks dynamically;
- Provide and release the resources flexibly and fast;
- Cloud system need to optimize the use of resource automatically.

Cloud computing and grid computing are similar. Game theory has been widely used in the research of grid resource allocation problems [10] [11].Combined with the characteristics of cloud computing resource allocation, game theory can also be applied to solve the problem of resource allocation in cloud computing. [12] proposed a cloud resource allocation strategy in continuous double auction framework based on Nash equilibrium which can allocation the resources in the cloud environment effectively. [13] proposed a cloud resource allocation strategy based on the evolutionary game, achieving a minimum cost by change the resource selection strategy individually. [14] proposed a market-based resource allocation strategy, experiments results show that this strategy could achieve the Nash equilibrium and a balance between supply and demand effectively.

There are few papers which considered the conflict between the rationality of each task and the total cost of the system. Usually, the allocation strategies of tasks in cloud environments aim at the overall optimal system cost in the process of resource selection. If a task is always considering itself to obtain a better payoff, then we call it rational task. Rational tasks can change their strategies to enhance their own payoffs, however raising the overall system costs at the same time. In this paper, on condition that all tasks/subtasks are rational, we present a new cloud resource allocation game model and proposed a new strategy based on the overall interests. The system can achieve the minimum total cost while all tasks select resources base on this strategy. And all tasks can obtain maximum payoff in the game.

3   Resource Allocation Game Model and Nash Equilibrium

In this section, a Cloud Task-Resource Allocation Games (CT-RAG) is proposed and defined. CT-RAG models the resource allocation in cloud computing and captures the task-resource and task-task interactions. Next, it shows the existence of Nash equilibrium and the defect in an instance of CT-RAG because of the task rationality. This paper considers the tasks which clients submit during some time as a batch. Therefore, the resource allocation strategy of CT-RAG is considered as a static scenario. We leave the real-time situation to future work.

3.1   Resource Allocation Game Modeling

In our model, the tasks act the player of a CT-RAG. The resource allocation determines the strategy of the tasks (players). In other words, task obtains the payoff by means of selecting different resources. In this paper, there are several assumptions about CT-RAG as follow:

1. Subtask is defined as the smallest execution unit in a cloud. Every task can be separated by several same or similar subtasks. And all the subtasks of different tasks have the same requirement of resource and execution time on a determinate resource. The subtasks of one task are independent. One task finished implies that all the subtasks of this task are finished.
2. There is only one kind of resource (e.g. CPU) in this model. The tasks or subtasks are charged base on execution time. It means that tasks or subtasks have to pay to

cloud provider based on the expense function. The execution time will increase with the increase of task number on one resource.

3. All tasks or subtasks are rational. It means that the only thing tasks considered is how to increase their own payoff, rather than how to increase the system's payoff.

4. The cost of one task is composition of execution time and the expense of price charged by resource. The execution time of a task is the sum of all subtasks' execution time. In this work, the cost of one task is a sum with the weight of execution time and expense. And we defined the ratio is 1:1.

$$cost = completion\ time + expense\ . \tag{1}$$

Suppose there are m tasks $S = (S_1, S_2, ..., S_m)$ and n resources $R = (R_1, R_2, ..., R_n)$ in the cloud. All the tasks and subtasks simultaneously use the resources of cloud. There is no limit to the amount of subtasks executed on one resource. For each subtask, the execution time would enhance with the increase in amount of subtasks executed on the same resource.

Each task $S_i \in S$ can be divided into x_i subtasks, therefore the task-resource interactions can be considered as task-task interactions. Each subtask can only execute on one resource. Assume that the amount of all subtasks is M, which is $\sum_{i=1}^{m} x_i = M$. Each resource $R_j \in R$ is associated with an expense function $f_j(\cdot)$ ($f_j \in IR_+$) and single execution time t_j of each subtask. $f_j(y)$ is the expense of every subtask when there are y subtasks executed on resource R_j. This paper assumes that f_j is a monotonic increasing function and $y \cdot f_j$ is also a monotonic increasing function. The vector $f = (f_1, f_2, ..., f_n)$ shows the expense functions of all the resources in the cloud. By changing the expense function of each resource, various resources can be distinguished in the cloud. Such as the increase of f_j' can result in the decrease of y_j, and y_j is the amount of subtask executed on resource R_j at Nash equilibrium. Obviously, $\sum_{i=1}^{m} x_i = \sum_{j=1}^{n} y_j = M$ is obtainable. The costs (completion time and expense) of each subtask executed on the same resource are consistent. The vector $t = (t_1, t_2, ..., t_n)$ denotes the execution time of all the resources in the case of one resource only executes one subtask. The completion time of each subtask on resource R_j equals the product of the execution time t_j and y_j of this resource, which is $T_j = y_j \times t_j$.

The expense function of each resource represents an abstraction of expense when the task or subtask is executing on the resource, and is proportional to the ability of the resource. All tasks must pay the money for the execution on the selected resources, this is where expense occurs. On the condition that the cloud defines the expense function of each resource according to its ability, the priority of each task can be distinguished by given them different amount of money. But in our paper, there is no limit of the amount of money for each task. We leave the discussion of it to future work.

In this paper, the allocation interaction between tasks and resources is represented as a global resource allocation matrix A. Matrix A is composed of m rows, one for each task, and n columns, one for each resource (Fig. 1(a)). $a_{ij} = q$ indicates that q subtasks of task S_i are allocated to resource R_j, and $a_{ij} = 0$ indicates there are not any subtasks allocated to resource R_j. Global resource allocation matrix A is also regarded as a m-dimensional vector $(a_1, a_2, ..., a_m)^T$. a_i is the strategy adopted by task S_i in CT-RAG and is given by the vector $(a_{i1}, a_{i2}, ..., a_{in})$. The feasibility of the global resource allocation matrix A depends on the following conditions:(1) $\sum_{j=1}^{n} a_{ij} = x_i$ and

(2) $a_{ij} \geq 0$ $\forall i,j$. Similarly, there is a subtask-resource allocation matrix B. It can reflect the allocation interaction between subtasks and resources (Fig. 1 (b)). In CT-RAG, each subtask can only execute on one resource, so b_{ij} can only be two values $b_{ij}=0$ or $b_{ij}=1$ and there is only one "1" in each row (strategy of each subtask).

The 3-tuple (S, A, P) represents a Cloud Task-Resource Allocation Game (CT-RAG). In CT-RAG, the player is task, and the strategy of S_i is the i-th row of matrix A— $(a_{i1}, a_{i2}, ..., a_{in})$. The vector $P = (P_1, P_2, ..., P_m)$ is the payoff of all players (tasks), and P_i is the reciprocal of the cost C_i of task S_i. P_i and C_i is shown as Formula (2). And the performance of the whole system is reflected by the total cost C which is the sum of the cost of all tasks according to Formula (2).

$$A = \begin{pmatrix} a_{11} & a_{12} & \cdots & a_{1n} \\ a_{21} & a_{22} & \cdots & a_{2n} \\ \vdots & \vdots & \ddots & \vdots \\ a_{m1} & a_{m2} & \cdots & a_{mn} \end{pmatrix} \begin{matrix} x_1 \\ x_2 \\ \vdots \\ x_m \end{matrix} \qquad B = \begin{pmatrix} b_{11} & b_{12} & \cdots & b_{1n} \\ b_{21} & b_{22} & \cdots & b_{2n} \\ \vdots & \vdots & \ddots & \vdots \\ b_{M1} & b_{M2} & \cdots & b_{Mn} \end{pmatrix} \begin{matrix} 1 \\ 1 \\ \vdots \\ 1 \end{matrix}$$
$$\begin{matrix} y_1 & y_2 & \cdots & y_n \quad M \end{matrix} \qquad\qquad \begin{matrix} y_1 & y_2 & \cdots & y_n \quad M \end{matrix}$$

(a)   (b)

Fig. 1. Allocation matrixes of tasks-resources and subtasks-resources: (a) tasks-resources matrix A ;(b)subtasks-resources matrix B

$$C_i = \sum\nolimits_{j=1}^{n} a_{ij} \times (T_j \times y_j + f_j(y_j))$$
$$P_i = 1/C_i = 1/\sum\nolimits_{j=1}^{n} a_{ij} \times (T_j \times y_j + f_j(y_j)) \qquad (2)$$
$$C = \sum\nolimits_{i=1}^{m} \sum\nolimits_{j=1}^{n} a_{ij} \times (T_j \times y_j + f_j(y_j))$$

The cloud system aims to minimize the total cost C, and every task also tries to decrease its own cost C_i by altering the strategy.

3.2   Nash Equilibrium in CT-RAG

CT-RAG has a Nash equilibrium certainly like other games. In CT-RAG, each task always tries to reduce its own cost by altering strategy continually according to the strategies of others. This dynamic process with continuous changing can't be stop until the system is in a stable state. In other words, all tasks can't reduce its cost by changing its strategy. This state is the Nash equilibrium of CT-RAG.

Theorem 1: If all the expense functions of CT-RAG are linear, the Nash equilibrium of CT-RAG is not unique. And there is the same z_j, $z_j = \sum_{i=1}^{m} a_{ij}$, in all Nash equilibriums.

Proof: In Nash equilibrium of CT-RAG, no task has motivation to change the stable state. It means the cost of subtask executed on each resource is the same. If a new subtask need to execute, its cost is the same whichever resource it selected. Assume that the amount of subtask executed on each resource is $(z_1, z_2, ..., z_n)$. This can be express as follow for each resource:

$$\begin{cases} t_1(z_1+1)+f_1(z_1+1) = \cdots = t_n(z_n+1)+f_n(z_n+1) \\ \sum_{j=1}^{n} z_j = M \end{cases} \tag{3}$$

Since t_i, f_i, M is given, the homogeneous linear system consisting of n equations in n unknowns can be solved. There is the same z_j, $z_j=\sum_{i=1}^{m} a_{ij}$, in all Nash equilibriums. Therefore, a resource allocation matrix A is Nash equilibrium if it satisfies the following properties: (1) $\sum_{j=1}^{n} a_{ij}=x_i$, (2) $\sum_{i=1}^{m} a_{ij}=z_j$ and (3) $a_{ij}\geq0$ $\forall i,j$. So the Nash equilibrium of CT-RAG is not unique.

Theorem2. If CT-RAG has linear expense function then the total cost of any Nash equilibrium is at most 4/3 times as much as the total cost of theory optimal [15].

The proof of theorem 2 is shown in [16]. The gap of the two total cost is caused by the rationality of tasks. In most instances, the strategy change of one task can result in the cost increase of other tasks and the total cost C.

4   The Group Participation Game Strategy

To reduce the influence mentioned in section 3, we proposed a new resource allocation Group Participation Game Strategy (GPGS). Every task/subtask selects its strategy according to GPGS by itself. It ensures the cost of the whole system at Nash equilibrium is close to the global optimum. In this section, we assume the expense function is linear. Other cases of expense function exceed the scope of this paper, and linear expense function is feasible for cloud to adjust the Nash equilibrium. In this section, a Cloud Subtask-Resource Allocation Games (CS-RAGs) is proposed and defined firstly. The players of CS-RAGs are subtasks, rather than tasks. The analysis of total cost belongs to CT-RAGs is similar as that of CS-RAGs, so we can calculate the amount of subtasks executed on each resource $(Y_1, Y_2, ..., Y_n)$. Then all tasks select the resources in order according to this vector.

4.1   CS-RAGs and Nash Equilibrium

The 3-tuple (s, B, p) represents a Cloud Subtask-Resource Allocation Game (CS-RAG). CS-RAG is a sequential game, and every subtask selects its strategy one by one. In CS-RAG, the player is subtask. s_i represents the i-th subtask, and the strategy of s_i is the i-th row of matrix B— $(b_{i1}, b_{i2}, ..., b_{in})$. Every subtask can only be allocated to one resource, so the strategy of s_i is also represented as w_i, $w_i \in Z$ and $1\leq w_i \leq n$, it means the subtask has been allocated to resource R_{w_i}. The vector $p= (p_1, p_2, ..., p_M)$ is the payoff of all players (subtasks), and p is the reciprocal of the cost c_i of subtask s_i. c_i and the total cost C is shown as follow:

$$c_i = T_{w_i} \times y_{w_i} + f_{w_i}(y_{w_i})$$
$$C = \sum_{i=1}^{M} c_i = \sum_{i=1}^{M} \left[T_{w_i} \times y_{w_i} + f_{w_i}(y_{w_i}) \right] \tag{4}$$

And the payoff of every subtask is defined as follow:

$$p_i = 1/c_i = 1/T_{w_i} \times y_{w_i} + f_{w_i}(y_{w_i}) \tag{5}$$

As the analysis above, CS-RAG also has Nash equilibrium, and it is not unique. We can get the number of subtask on every resource in Nash equilibrium of the game with M subtasks and n resources according to formula (3), (4), (5).

$$Y_j' = (M - \sum_{h=1}^{n}((b_j - b_h)/(t_h + a_h)))/((t_j + a_j)\sum_{h=1}^{n}(1/t_h + a_h)) \tag{6}$$

4.2   Spillover Effect or Externality

Consider the situation that m tasks compete for two resources R_1 and R_2. Assuming that number of all subtasks is M. Each subtask has only two choices—R_1 or R_2. Strategy of subtask s_i depends on the strategy of other M-1 subtasks; and strategy of each subtask will have an impact on other subtasks, which is called spillover effect. Supposing there are y subtasks which choose R_1, the cost of each subtask is $c_1(y)$, and M-y subtasks which choose R_2, the cost of each subtask is $c_2(y)$, then the total cost of the system is as Formula (7)

$$C(y) = yc_1(y) + (M - y)c_2(y) \tag{7}$$

If subtask s_i choose R_2 at beginning, and change the strategy to choose resource R_1, then the number of subtasks which choose R_1 rise to $y+1$. The cost of s_i change from $c_2(y)$ to $c_1(y+1)$, and the total cost of the system is as Formula (8).

$$C(y+1) = (y+1)c_1(y+1) + (M - y - 1)c_2(M - y - 1) \tag{8}$$

The difference between $C(y)$ and $C(y+1)$ is the increment of total payoff.

$$C(y+1)-C(y)=(c_1(y+1)-c_2(M-y))+y(c_1(y+1)-c_1(y))+(M-y-1)(c_2(M-y-1)-c_2(M-y)) \tag{9}$$

The first item $c_1(y+1)-c_2(M-y)$ in Formula (9) is the payoff alteration of strategy changer, called the marginal private gain. When the change of one subtask affects other subtasks, the payoff alteration of other subtasks is called marginal spillover effect, which is the second and third item of Formula (9). The spillover effect leads to the payoff conflict between tasks and the whole system.

4.3   The Group Participation Game Strategy (GPGS)

Because of the subtask rationality, Nash equilibrium of CS-RAG can't minimize the total cost. Thus this paper proposes a group participation game strategy (GPGS) to adjust CS-RAG, and all players in this game must observe this strategy. There are three regulations of resource allocation strategy GPGS:

Regulation 1: x_i is subtask number of task S_i. Task S_1, S_2, ..., S_m are sequenced according to x_i. Assuming that S_1, S_2, ... , S_m is a sequential vector and S_1 is the task with least subtasks. The regulation of resource selecting for all tasks is: S_1 selects x_1 resources firstly. The next is S_2, and S_m is the last one. All the subtasks will be executed synchronously when all tasks have already selected resources.

Regulation 2: c_1, c_2, ... , c_n are the cost of subtask on each resource. Every task selects resource according to the vector c_1, c_2, ..., c_n, and it can be calculated by this:

$$c_j = Y_j \times t_j + f_j(Y_j) \qquad (10)$$

In this paper, $f_j(\cdot)$ is linear, so c_j can also be expressed as follow:

$$c_j = Y_j \times t_j + (a_j \times Y_j + b_j) \qquad (11)$$

Regulation 3: The payoff of every subtask is defined as follow:

$$p_i = 1/(c_i + \lambda c_\Delta) \qquad (12)$$

When some subtask is selecting resource, λ is the number of subtask which has already selected this resource, and c_Δ is the increment of every subtask on this resource.

In practice, tasks select resources according to these three regulations, and it can be seen as a CT-RAG with GPGS. The game with GPGS will converge to equilibrium state. And we call it GPGS equilibrium in this paper. We attempt to ensure the total cost of the GPGS equilibrium is close to optimal.

4.4   The Theory Analysis of GPGS

The aim of cloud computing resource allocation is achieving the least overall cost. So the cloud computing resource allocation game can be regard as group game, and it is appropriate that analyze the whole interest of cloud resource allocation by group game theory. In group game, the strategy every player selected is not necessarily known. The group game analysis focus on the player number of each strategy. We can judge the performance of an allocation strategy by comparing the gap between the Nash equilibrium and the GPGS equilibrium.

In CT-RAG, task S_i can be divided into x_i subtasks, so it has $C_{x,n}$ strategies. It is complicated to analyze the overall interest by the unit of task. In this paper, the overall interest of all tasks is the same as the overall interest of all the subtasks, and every subtask only has n strategies. Therefore, the overall interest of collective action can be discussed by the unit of subtask. Then the analysis of CT-RAG turns into the analysis of CS-RAG. First, spillover effect or externality will be described in CS-RAG. Next, an example of m tasks and two resources will be given in order to show the convergence process of Nash equilibrium. At last, the gap of the total cost between the Nash equilibrium and the GPGS equilibrium will be deduced with liner expense function by a general example. In this section, the increasing of overall interest is replaced by the decreasing the total cost.

We have already analyzed the Nash equilibrium of CS-RAG in section 4.1. The primary difference between CS-RAG and CS-RAG with GPGS is the definition of payoff. In CS-RAG with GPGS, the payoff is defined as the reciprocal of $c_i + \lambda c_\Delta$.

If some subtask intends to enhance its own payoff, it is necessary to reduce not only its cost, but also the impact of its strategy on other subtasks. Therefore, the rationality is combined with the interest of whole system.

The convergence process of GPGS equilibrium is almost the same as Nash equilibrium. Every subtask chooses the strategy which can maximize its own payoff. At the same time, it can minimize the whole cost. We can get it from the definition of payoff easily.

In the example of m tasks composed of M subtasks and two resources we mentioned in section 4.1, the equilibrium state will change with the increase of GPGS strategy in the game. The total cost can be represented by this:

$$C = y \times c_1(y) + (M - y) \times c_2(y)$$
$$= (t_1 + a_1) \times y^2 + b_1 \times y + (t_2 + a_2) \times (M - y)^2 + b_2 \times (M - y) \tag{13}$$

The GPGS equilibrium is the state with minimum total cost. So we can get the value of y:

$$y = (M(t_2 + a_2) + 0.5(b_2 - b_1)) / (t_1 + t_2 + a_1 + a_2) \tag{14}$$

We can calculate the total cost in the two states and the difference between them:

$$C_{Nash} = M^2(t_2 + a_2) + Mb_2 - (M^2(t_2 + a_2)^2 + M(t_2 + a_2)(b_2 - b_1)) / (t_1 + t_2 + a_1 + a_2)$$
$$C_{GPGS} = M^2(t_2 + a_2) + Mb_2 - (M^2(t_2 + a_2)^2 + M(t_2 + a_2)(b_2 - b_1) + (b_2 - b_1)^2) / 4(t_1 + t_2 + a_1 + a_2) \tag{15}$$
$$C_{Nash} - C_{GPGS} = (b_2 - b_1)^2 / 4(t_1 + t_2 + a_1 + a_2)$$

Consider the general situation. Assuming there are m tasks composed of M subtasks and n resources. GPGS equilibrium is the state which can minimize the whole cost. And it can be shown as follow:

$$min\ C = \sum_{j=1}^{n} (Y_j'' \times t_j + a_j \times Y_j'' + b_j) \quad \sum_{j=1}^{n} Y_j'' = M \quad 0 \le y_j \le M, 1 \le j \le n \tag{16}$$

Where Y_j'' is the number of subtasks on resource R_j in GPGS equilibrium.

It can be solved by Lagrange Multipliers method. The process of the solution is shown as follow:

Introduce a function: If C is the minimum, it means. And we get a system of linear equations of n unknowns:

$$\begin{cases} 2(t_1 + a_1)Y_1'' + b_1 + \lambda = 0 \\ \vdots \\ 2(t_n + a_n)Y_n'' + b_n + \lambda = 0 \\ Y_1'' + Y_2'' + \cdots + Y_n'' = M \end{cases} \tag{17}$$

Therefore, we can get the solution of the GPGS equilibrium:

$$Y_j'' = (M - \sum_{h=1}^{n} ((b_j - b_h) / 2(t_h + a_h))) / ((t_j + a_j) \sum_{h=1}^{n} 1 / (t_h + a_h)) \tag{18}$$

By the above analysis, there is a less total cost of the system in CS-RAG with GPGS, although all players aim to enhance their own payoff. In practice, the resource allocation scheme is every player select resource by itself according to GPGS, rather than the resource provider allocate integrally.

5   Experimental Evaluation

In this paper, we implement the evaluation test to verify the feasibility and performance of our resource allocation strategy. In cloud environment, resource usually consists of virtual resource pools and physical resources. These resources can be selected by each user dynamically as required. Physical host is the most common cloud computing node resource. In GPGS, resources are selected by each task based on group game to reduce the total system cost and improve the efficiency.

The aim of a resource allocation is obtain the best performance of the whole system. The total cost is an important index of the performance of the system. We compare the total cost of the Nash, Optimal, "Round-Robin" and GPGS by the model we proposed in section 3.1. "Round-Robin" has already been used well in system like Hadoop. In the "Round-Robin" method, all resources are numbered from 1 to n. when a task wants to execute with k resources, it is scheduled on the next k resources, as a Round-Robin manner.

In practice, there are sorts of resources in cloud. And we can distinguish these resources by different expense function in our model. We used two different examples to analyze different strategies:

- The capacities of all resources are similar. It means the expense function of them is similar too, and the functions are all linear.
- The gap between the capacities of different resources is large. They have obvious different linear expense function.

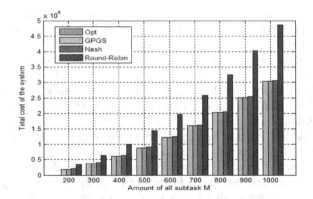

Fig. 2. The Comparison of total cost with homogeneous resources in different strategies

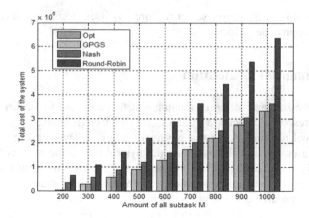

Fig. 3. The Comparison of total cost with heterogeneous resources in different strategies

For comparing the performance of different resource allocation strategies, we used five host resources with heterogeneous expense function. We recorded the total cost of each resource allocation strategies when the number of subtask is from 200 to 1000.Fig. 2 compares the performance of the various strategies with homogeneous resources, and Fig. 3 compares the performance of the various strategies with heterogeneous resources. In both two cases, the total cost of GPGS is less the "Round-Robin" obviously. When the expenses of different resources are quite different, the total cost of GPGS is less than Nash's, and it is quite close to Opt's.

6   Conclusion and Future Work

In this paper, we proposed a new resource allocation game model in cloud. Further, we demonstrated the existence of Nash equilibrium in the game and found that Nash equilibrium can't reduce the total cost. For reduce the total cost, we proposed a new cloud resource allocation strategy—group participation game strategy (GPGS), and compared the difference between Nash equilibrium state and GPGS equilibrium state in the game. By the analysis of the difference between the two states, we concluded that rational tasks lead to the increase of total cost. The gap between Nash equilibrium and GPGS equilibrium was shown by means of a special example. Simulations compared the total and load balance between Nash, Optimal, "Round-Robin" and GPGS. The result showed GPGS can reduce the total cost effectively.

However, limited to the page limit, we don't analyze the load balance and the task fairness deviation which represents the fairness of tasks. In addition, the game in this paper is static, and different subtasks are relative in many cases of cloud resource allocation. We do not take these into consideration in this paper. In future work, we will talk about the analysis the load balance and the task fairness deviation, and we will take the dynamic resource allocation strategy into consideration.

Acknowledgments. This work is supported in part by Natural Science Foundation of China under grant No. 61103233, 61202442, 61202443.

References

1. Jadeja, Y., Modi, K.: Cloud computing - concepts, architecture and challenges. In: International Conference on Computing, Electronics and Electrical Technologies, pp. 877–880 (2012)
2. Mell, P., Grance, T.: The NIST Definition of Cloud Computing. National Institute of Standards and Technology (2011)
3. Krishnappa, D.K., Irwin, D., Lyons, E., Zink, M.: CloudCast: Cloud computing for short-term mobile weather forecasts. In: IEEE International, Performance Computing and Communications Conference, pp. 61–70 (2012)
4. Google app engine, http://appengine.google.com/
5. Yaghoobi, M., Fanian, A., Khajemohammadi, H., Gulliver, T.A.: A non-cooperative game theory approach to optimize workflow scheduling in grid computing. In: Pacific Rim Conference on Communications, Computers and Signal Processing, Victoria BC, pp. 108–113 (2013)
6. Michiardi, P., Molva, R.: A collaborative reputation mechanism to enforce node cooperation in mobile ad-hoc networks. In: Proceedings of the IFIP TC6/TC11 6th Joint Working Conference on Communications and Multimedia Security, Deventer, The Netherlands, pp. 1072–1121 (2002)
7. Wang, T.-M., Lee, W.-T., Wu, T.-Y., Wei, H.-W., Lin, Y.-S.: New P2P Sharing Incentive Mechanism Based on Social Network and Game Theory. In: International Conference on Advanced Information Networking and Applications Workshops, Fukuoka, pp. 915–919 (2012)
8. Nash, J.: Non-cooperative Games. Annals of Mathematics 54, 289–295 (1951)
9. Foster, I., Zhao, Y., Raicu, I., Lu, S.Y.: Cloud Computing and Grid Computing 360-degree compared. In: Grid Computing Environments Workshop, Austin TX, pp. 1–10 (2008)
10. Li, Z.J., Cheng, C.T.: An Evolutionary Game Algorithm for Grid Resource Allocation under Bounded Rationality. Concurrency and Computation: Practice and Experience 9, 1205–1223 (2009)
11. Caramia, M., Giordani, S.: Resource allocation in grid computing:An economic model. WSEAS Transactions on Computer Research 3, 19–27 (2008)
12. Guiran, C., Chuan, W., Yu, X.: Efficient Nash Equilibrium Based Cloud Resource Allocation by Using a Continuous Double Auction. In: International Conferenceon Computer Design and Applications, Shenyang China, pp. 94–99 (2010)
13. Wei, G., Vasilakos, A.V., Zheng, Y., Xiong, N.: A game-theoretic method of fair resource allocation for cloud computing services. The Journal of Supercomputing 54, 252–269 (2010)
14. You, X.D., Wan, J.: ARAS-M: Automatic Resource Allocation Strategy based on Market Mechanism in Cloud Computing. Journal of Computers 6, 1287–1296 (2011)
15. Jalaparti, V., Nguyen, G.D., Gupta, I., Caesar, M.: Cloud Resource Allocation Games. Technical Report, University of Illinois (2010), http://hdl.handle.net/2142/17427
16. Roughgarden, T., Tardos, E.: How bad is selfish routing. Journal of the ACM 49, 236–259 (2002)

Towards Optimal Collaboration of Policies in the Two-Phase Scheduling of Cloud Tasks

Cong Xu[1,2], Jiahai Yang[1,2], Di Fu[1,2], and Hui Zhang[1,2]

[1] Institute for Network Sciences and Cyberspace, Tsinghua University,
Beijing 100084, China
[2] Tsinghua National Laboratory for Information Science and Technology (TNList),
Tsinghua University, Beijing 100084, China
xucong10@mails.tsinghua.edu.cn, {yang,hzhang}@cernet.edu.cn,
fudi@bupt.edu.cn

Abstract. The use of virtualization technology makes software applications more scalable and cost effective when they are deployed over cloud computing platforms, but virtualization technology also brings challenges to task scheduling over cloud. The commonly used list scheduling schemes split the scheduling process into two phases: ordering and dispatching. However, majorities of recent researches about scheduling of cloud tasks concentrate on optimizing the schedulers' performance in one phase, but seldom consider the collaborations of scheduling policies used in different phases. This paper summarizes some representative ordering and dispatching policies used in list schedulers, models the execution processes of these ordering and dispatching policies using Stochastic Petri Nets (SPN), and simulates the list scheduling process of cloud tasks. Based on the modeling and experimental results, we further evaluate which composition of ordering and dispatching policies provides optimal performance in the two-phase scheduling process of cloud tasks.

Keywords: list scheduling, ordering policy, dispatching policy, Stochastic Petri Net, queuing theory.

1 Introduction

Cloud computing service providers are interested in improving the task scheduling mechanisms to provide better Quality of Service (QoS) to their users. However, with the increasing scale of cloud computing platform, a single cloud may host and provide more and more diverse services, which brings new challenges to the scheduling of cloud tasks. The dynamicity of virtual environment [1], diversity of software applications [2] and elasticity of cloud services [3] exacerbate the dynamicity and complexity of the scheduling mechanisms: a cloud task's processing rate tends to have significant variations since the virtual resources allocated to the same task may be different. Hence, how to optimally dispatch the task requests to the proper virtual resources for processing is an important issue. Moreover, there will also be times

C.-H. Hsu et al. (Eds.): NPC 2014, LNCS 8707, pp. 306–320, 2014.

when a task's arrival rate is greater than its maximum possible processing rate, then how to determine an optimal task execution order to reduce the peak load of a cloud computing platform is another significant issue.

List schedulers [4] are widely used in the dynamic scheduling of cloud tasks. As shown in Fig. 1, a list scheduler splits the scheduling process into two phases: one is the ordering phase, where tasks are sorted according to a specific ordering policy; the other is the dispatching phase, where tasks are dispatched to the allocated virtual resources (VMs) for processing according to a specific dispatching policy. The existing studies on task scheduling over cloud mostly concentrate on improving the schedulers' performance in one phase, such as optimizing the task processing sequence in the first phase to minimize the overall response time [4-11]; or optimizing the assignment of the task requests to the VMs to improve the utilization of cloud resources [12-18] and to ensure the fairness of each task [19-21]. However, only few researches have further studied the optimal collaboration of ordering and dispatching policies in different phases [22].

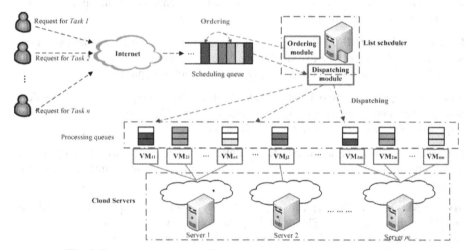

Fig. 1. Two-phase task scheduling process in a cloud computing platform

This paper summarizes some representative ordering and dispatching policies which are widely used in both industry and academic communities. Using Stochastic Petri Nets (SPN), we theoretically and consistently model the execution processes of these ordering and dispatching policies for the first time, and analyze the performance of a list scheduler under different compositions of policies. Based on the modeling and experimental results, we further evaluate which composition of ordering and dispatching policies provide optimal performance in the two-phase scheduling process of cloud tasks.

The rest of this paper is organized as follows. Section 2 summarizes representative ordering and dispatching policies. Section 3 proposes a Stochastic Petri Net model to describe the scheduling process, studies some features of different ordering and dispatching policies and analyzes the performance of a list scheduler under different ordering and dispatching policies. Section 4 evaluates the performance of the list scheduler under different collaborations of ordering and dispatching policies. Section 5 concludes the paper.

2   Scheduling Policies in the Two Phases

This section summarizes some representative ordering and dispatching policies used in the list scheduler of cloud computing platforms. These policies are commonly used in both industry and academic communities.

2.1   Ordering Policies in the First Phase

When the average task arrival rate exceeds the platform's processing rate, the unhandled tasks will be stalled in the scheduling queue, and the platform tends to be overloaded. At this time, an appropriate ordering policy is needed to determine an optimal task processing sequence to slow down the growth rate of the scheduling queue. The commonly used ordering policies are listed below:

Random Ordering Policy: This policy randomly chooses one type of the cloud tasks for processing. All the tasks have equal chances to be scheduled in this policy, which achieves better fairness of tasks.

First in First Out (FIFO) Policy: This is a simple and widely used ordering policy, which makes the tasks to be executed in the order they arrived. This policy ensures all the tasks suffer almost the same waiting delay in the ordering phase.

Shortest Remaining Time First (SRTF) Policy: This policy ensures the smallest task in the scheduling queue to be scheduled first [5], aiming to improve the responsiveness of the scheduler when the load is heavy.

Longest Remaining Time First (LRTF) Policy: This policy ensures the largest task in the scheduling queue to be scheduled first, aiming to improve the throughput of the scheduler.

Myopic MaxWeight Policy: This policy can be viewed as an improvement of SRTF or LRTF policy. Neither SRTF nor LRTF policy is a starvation-free ordering since the large sized tasks under SRTF or the small sized tasks under LRTF are likely to wait forever when the load is heavy [22]. To solve this problem, a weight is assigned to each task in the scheduling queue in this policy, and the value of a task's weight is the task's size (for LRTF) or task's execution rate (for SRTF) multiplies its waiting time. This policy schedules the task with the maximum weight first, which ensures the tasks suffering long waiting time have chances to be processed.

2.2   Dispatching Policies in the Second Phase

The dispatching policies assign tasks to virtual resources for processing. An appropriate dispatching policy optimizes the resource utilization of a cloud platform and further improves the performance of the scheduler. The commonly used dispatching policies are listed below:

Random Routing Policy (RR): This policy randomly dispatches a task to one of the VMs for processing, which ensures each allocated VM has an equal chance to process a task.

Shortest Queue Routing Policy (SQR): This policy dispatches a task to the VM with the shortest processing queue, which achieves better fairness by balancing the load on each VM [19, 20].

Shortest Expected Delay Routing Policy (SEDR): This policy dispatches a task to the VM with the shortest processing delay, which can be viewed as a generalization of the SQR policy for homogeneous servers [12].

Overall Shortest Expected Delay Routing Policy (OSEDR): This policy dispatches a task to the appropriate VM to keep the overall processing delay of a server minimum [21], it optimizes the sum of the execution delays of all the tasks on each server.

3   Modeling and Analysis of Scheduling Policies

In this section, we describe the list scheduling process using the SPN model. By modeling different ordering and dispatching policies, we formulate some performance metrics (e.g. average resource utilization of a service). Furthermore, we evaluate the performance of a list scheduler according to our modeling results.

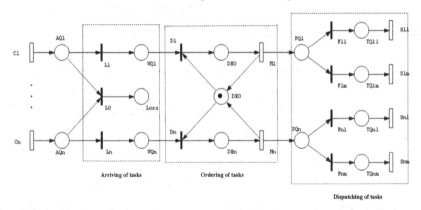

Fig. 2. SPN model of the two-phase task scheduling process

3.1   Description of Scheduling Process Using SPN Model

Fig. 2 shows the SPN model of the two-phase list scheduling process shown in Fig. 1. It describes a scenario that a cloud computing platform comprises m servers, and processes n types of different tasks. Some important notations and definitions used in the SPN model and subsequent derivations are illustrated in Table 1. The scenario considered here is dynamic or online scheduling of small sized tasks onto a fixed non-preemptive cloud system.

Table 1. Summary of Key Notations and Definitions

Notations	Definitions
$C_i.$	Timed transition, indicates the arrvial of task i
λ_i	Poisson arrival rate of the task i
$L_i.$	Free choice conflict transition, decides if task i can be buffered in the global scheduling queue
WQ_i	Place, indicate a logical sub scheduling queue of task i
$WQ_i(t)$	Length of logical sub scheduling queue WQ_i at time t
D_i	Free choice conflict transition, decides if task i can be processed under a specific ordering policy
$P_i[D(t)]$	Probability that a request of task i passes D_i at time t
M_i	Transportation of task i from global scheduling queue to a specific VM for processing
F_{ij}	Free choice conflict transition, decides if task i can be dispatched to the allocated VM located on server j
$P_{ij}[F(t)]$	Probability that requests of task i pass transition F_{ij} at time t
TQ_{ij}	Processing queue of task i on server j
$TQ_{ij}(t)$	Length of processing queue TQ_{ij} at time t
l_{max}	Maximum length of each processing queue
λ_{ij}	Arrival rate of task i to its processing queue on server j
S_{ij}	Timed transition, indicates the processing of task i on server j
μ_{ij}	Processing rate of task i on its allocated VM located on server j
ρ_{ij}	Utilization of the VM allocated to task i on server j
T_{avg}	Average completion time of a task
$\rho_{avg}(i)$	Average resource utilization of task i
$\rho_{worst}(i)$	Worst case resource utilization of task i

For analytic tractability, we assume the arrival of task i satisfies Poisson distribution with mean rate λ_i. After arriving, a token representing task i in the SPN will come to place AQ_i and decide if it can pass through transition L_i to be buffered in the global scheduling queue. For analytic tractability, we assume that the size of the global scheduling queue is properly set to avoid task losses.

An ordering policy determines the value of $P_i[D(t)]$, which is the probability that a request of task i in the scheduling queue can be handled at time t. To accurately describe the ordering policies, we assume that there exists a sub logical scheduling queue WQ_i which buffers the arrived requests for task i. Suppose the arrival rate of task i changes to $\overline{\lambda_i}$ after the token passes through transition L_i, then $\overline{\lambda_i}=\lambda_i P_i[D(t)]$.

A dispatching policy determines the enabling function of each transition F_{ij}, which further determines the value of $P_{ij}[F(t)]$. $P_{ij}[F(t)]$ is the probability that a request of task i is dispatched to a VM located on server j for processing. Finally, the arrival rate of task i to its processing queue TQ_{ij} on server j is: $\lambda_{ij}=\overline{\lambda_i} P_{ij}[F(t)] =\lambda_i P_i[D(t)] P_{ij}[F(t)]$.

Then the tasks in the processing queue will be serially processed by the program running on the corresponding VM, which is similar to the scenario described in $M/G/1$ model. For analytic tractability, we assume the processing rate of each task i on server j is exponentially distributed with mean value μ_{ij}, and the tasks' sizes are sorted in ascending order from task 1 to task n. Suppose the VMs on the same server have the same configuration, then the execution rates of the tasks dispatched to the same server satisfy: $\mu_{1j} \geq \mu_{2j} \geq ... \geq \mu_{nj}$ $(1 \leq j \leq m)$.

Since the utilization metrics and responsiveness metrics are the most frequently used metrics to evaluate the performance of a scheduling policy, we derive the expressions of average resource utilization and average completion time of task i based on existing modeling results introduced in queue theory [24]:

$$\rho_{avg}(i) = \sum_{j=1}^{m} \frac{\rho_{ij}}{m} = \sum_{j=1}^{m} \frac{\lambda_i \cdot \lim_{t \to \infty} P_i[D(t)]P_{ij}[F(t)]}{\mu_{ij} m} \tag{1}$$

$$T_{avg} = \sum_{i=1}^{n}\sum_{j=1}^{m} \frac{E[TQ_{ij}(t)]}{\lambda_{ij}(1 - \dfrac{1-\rho_{ij}^{l_{max}+1}}{1-\rho_{ij}})mn} = \frac{1}{mn}\sum_{i=1}^{n}\sum_{j=1}^{m} \lim_{t \to \infty} \frac{\rho_{ij}(1-\rho_{ij}^{l_{max}+1}) - (l_{max}+1)\rho_{ij}^{l_{max}+1}(1-\rho_{ij})}{\lambda_i P_i[D(t)]P_{ij}[F(t)](1-\rho_{ij}^{l_{max}+1}) + \rho_{ij} - 1} \tag{2}$$

$$\forall i, j, \quad \sum_{i=1}^{n} P_i[D(t)] = 1 \quad \sum_{j=1}^{m} P_{ij}[F(t)] = 1$$

The value of $\rho_{avg}(i)$ and T_{avg} are determined by the value of $P_i[D(t)]$ and $P_{ij}[F(t)]$. Hence, we need to derive the expressions of $P_i[D(t)]$ and $P_{ij}[F(t)]$ under different ordering and dispatching policies.

3.2   Modeling of Ordering Policies

First, we derive the expressions of $P_i[D(t)]$ in the steady-state under different ordering policies.

Random Ordering Policy. Since this policy randomly chooses one type of the cloud tasks for processing, the probability is time-independent, so the expression of $P_i[D(t)]$ in the steady-state is:

$$P_i[D(t)] = \lim_{t \to \infty} P_i[D(t)] = 1/n$$

FIFO Policy. Using FIFO policy, the value of $P_i[D(t)]$ in the steady-state is positively correlated to the arrival rate of task i [24]. Thus:

$$\lim_{t \to \infty} P_i[D(t)] = \lambda_i / \sum_{j=1}^{n} \lambda_j$$

SRTF Policy. This policy ensures the smallest task in the queue to be scheduled first. Using this policy, if task i is to be processed, then the logical scheduling queue of task 1 to task i-1 should be empty, hence the expression of $P_i[D(t)]$ is:

$$P_i[D(t)] = \prod_{j=1}^{i-1} P[WQ_j(t) = 0] \cdot P[WQ_i(t) > 0]$$

Consider the steady-state, if the logical scheduling queue of task j is not empty, then at least one of this task's processing queue is full. Therefore, we get:

$$\lim_{t \to \infty} P[WQ_j(t) = 0] = \prod_{s=1}^{m} P[\lim_{t \to \infty} TQ_{js}(t) < l_{max}], \quad \lim_{t \to \infty} P[WQ_j(t) > 0] = 1 - \prod_{s=1}^{m} P[\lim_{t \to \infty} TQ_{js}(t) < l_{max}]$$

Based on the modeling results of $M/G/1$ model, we derive the expression of $P_i[D(t)]$ in the steady-state:

$$\lim_{t \to \infty} P_i[D(t)] = \lim_{t \to \infty} \prod_{j=1}^{i-1} P[WQ_j(t) = 0] \cdot P[WQ_i(t) > 0]$$

$$= \prod_{s=1}^{m} \prod_{j=1}^{i-1} \frac{(1 - \rho_{js}) \rho_{js}^{l_{max}}}{1 - \rho_{js}^{l_{max}+1}} \cdot [1 - \prod_{s=1}^{m} (\frac{(1 - \rho_{is}) \rho_{is}^{l_{max}}}{1 - \rho_{is}^{l_{max}+1}})]$$

LRTF Policy. This policy ensures the largest task in the scheduling queue to be scheduled first. Similar to the derivation in SRTF policy, we get the expression of $P_i[D(t)]$ in the steady-state:

$$\lim_{t \to \infty} P_i[D(t)] = \lim_{t \to \infty} \prod_{j=i+1}^{n} P[WQ_j(t) = 0] \cdot P[WQ_i(t) > 0]$$

$$= \prod_{s=1}^{m} \prod_{j=i+1}^{n} \frac{(1 - \rho_{js}) \rho_{js}^{l_{max}}}{1 - \rho_{js}^{l_{max}+1}} \cdot [1 - \prod_{s=1}^{m} \frac{(1 - \rho_{is}) \rho_{is}^{l_{max}}}{1 - \rho_{is}^{l_{max}+1}}]$$

Myopic MaxWeight Policy. This policy determines the weight of a task based on a task's size and waiting time. To approximately model a task's waiting time, we assume that the waiting time of task i is positively correlated to $WQ_i(t)$, (If the first task in WQ_i cannot be handled, all the followed tasks will be blocked. So the queue length reflects the waiting time of the first task). Based on SRTF policy, the expression of $P_i[D(t)]$ under Myopic MaxWeight policy should be modified as:

$$P_i[D(t)] = (\prod_{j=1}^{i-1} P[WQ_j(t) = 0] \cdot P[WQ_i(t) > 0]) \cdot WQ_i(t) / \sum_{k=1}^{n} WQ_k(t)$$

Then the expression of $P_i[D(t)]$ in the steady-state can be derived as follows:

$$\lim_{t \to \infty} P_i[D(t)] = \lim_{t \to \infty} \prod_{j=1}^{i-1} P[WQ_j(t) = 0] \cdot P[WQ_i(t) > 0] \cdot WQ_i(t) / \sum_{k=1}^{n} WQ_k(t)$$

$$= \prod_{s=1}^{m} \prod_{j=1}^{i-1} \frac{(1 - \rho_{js}) \rho_{js}^{l_{max}}}{1 - \rho_{js}^{l_{max}+1}} \cdot [1 - \prod_{s=1}^{m} \frac{(1 - \rho_{is}) \rho_{is}^{l_{max}}}{1 - \rho_{is}^{l_{max}+1}}]$$

$$\cdot \frac{\sum_{s=1}^{m} \rho_{is} / (m - \sum_{s=1}^{m} \rho_{is}) - \sum_{s=1}^{m} [\frac{\rho_{is}}{1 - \rho_{is}} - \frac{(l_{max} + 1)\rho_{is}^{l_{max}+1}}{1 - \rho_{is}^{l_{max}+1}}]}{\sum_{k=1}^{n} \{\sum_{s=1}^{m} \rho_{ks} / (m - \sum_{s=1}^{m} \rho_{ks}) - \sum_{s=1}^{m} [\frac{\rho_{ks}}{1 - \rho_{ks}} - \frac{(l_{max} + 1)\rho_{ks}^{l_{max}+1}}{1 - \rho_{ks}^{l_{max}+1}}]\}}$$

Based on the above derivations, we get the specific expressions of $P_i[D(t)]$ under different ordering policies, which is the foundation of further evaluations.

3.3   Modeling of Ordering Policies

In the second phase, we need to formulate $P_{ij}[F(t)]$ in the steady-state under different dispatching policies.

Random Routing Policy (RR). This policy randomly dispatches a task to one of the m allocated VMs for processing, so the probability is time-independent:

$$P_{ij}[F(t)] = \lim_{t \to \infty} P_{ij}[F(t)] = 1/m$$

Shortest Queue Routing Policy (SQR). This policy dispatches a task to the VM with the shortest processing queue. The probability $P_{ij}[F(t)]$ can be formulated as:

$$P_{ij}[F(t)] = \begin{cases} \dfrac{1}{\|SQR(F)\|}, & if \quad j \in SQR(F) \\ 0 \quad, & if \quad j \notin SQR(F) \end{cases}$$

$$SQR(F) = \{j \mid TQ_{ij}(t) = Min(TQ_{i1}(t), ..., TQ_{im}(t))\}$$

Consider the steady-state, the probability that task i is dispatched to VM located on server j is positively correlated to its expected processing rate on server j. Therefore, the expression of $P_{ij}[F(t)]$ in the steady-state is:

$$\lim_{t \to \infty} P_{ij}[F(t)] = \mu_{ij} / \sum_{s=1}^{m} \mu_{is}$$

Shortest Expected Delay Routing Policy (SEDR). This policy dispatches a task to the VM with the shortest processing delay. $P_{ij}[F(t)]$ can be formulated as:

$$P_{ij}[F(t)] = \begin{cases} \dfrac{1}{\|SEDR(F)\|}, & if \quad j \in SEDR(F) \\ 0 \quad, & if \quad j \notin SEDR(F) \end{cases}$$

$$SEDR(F) = \{j \mid TQ_{ij}(t)/\mu_{ij} = Min(TQ_{i1}(t)/\mu_{i1}, ..., TQ_{im}(t)/\mu_{im})\}$$

Consider the steady-state, the probability that task i is dispatched to VM located on server j is positively correlated to the square of its processing rate on server j. Therefore, the expression of $P_{ij}[F(t)]$ in the steady-state is:

$$\lim_{t \to \infty} P_{ij}[F(t)] = \mu_{ij}^2 / \sum_{s=1}^{m} \mu_{is}^2$$

Overall Shortest Expected Delay Routing Policy (OSEDR). This policy dispatches a task to the appropriate VM to keep the overall processing delay of a server minimum. The probability $P_{ij}[F(t)]$ can be formulated as:

$$P_{ij}[F(t)] = \begin{cases} \dfrac{1}{\|OSEDR(F)\|}, & if \quad j \in OSEDR(F) \\ 0 \quad, & if \quad j \notin OSEDR(F) \end{cases}$$

$$OSEDR(F) = \{j \mid \sum_{i=1}^{n} TQ_{ij}(t)/\mu_{ij} = Min(\sum_{i=1}^{n} TQ_{i1}(t)/\mu_{i1}, ..., \sum_{i=1}^{n} TQ_{im}(t)/\mu_{im})\}$$

This policy minimizes the sum of all the tasks' processing delays on a server, aiming to improve the overall execution time of a server. However, in the scenario described in Fig. 1, the VMs located on the same server will process different tasks simultaneously; hence the optimization goal should be the processing delay of the slowest task, but not the sum of processing delays. This policy may be not applicable in the scheduling of cloud tasks, hence will not be modeled in the following context.

3.4   Performance Analysis of Scheduling Policies

Substitute the expressions of $P_i[D(t)]$ and $P_{ij}[F(t)]$ into formula (1), we can calculate the value of $\rho_{avg}(i)$, which can be further used to evaluate the performance of different collaborations of ordering and dispatching policies. Some useful conclusions are illustrated below:

Based on the modeling results, we prove that SEDR and SQR optimize the utilization of each task in average and worst cases respectively, no matter what ordering policy they are collaborated with.

Optimizing the average resource utilization of task i is to minimize the value of $\rho_{avg}(i)$. Substitute the expression of $P_{ij}[F(t)]$ into (1), we get the expressions of $\rho_{avg}(i)$ under different dispatching policies:

SQR:
$$\rho_{avg}(i) = \frac{\overline{\lambda_i}}{m} \cdot \sum_{j=1}^{m} \frac{\mu_{ij}^2}{\mu_{ij}\sum_{j=1}^{m}\mu_{ij}^2} = \frac{\overline{\lambda_i}}{m} \cdot \sum_{j=1}^{m}\mu_{ij} / \sum_{j=1}^{m}\mu_{ij}^2$$

(3)

SEDR:
$$\rho_{avg}(i) = \frac{\overline{\lambda_i}}{m} \cdot \sum_{j=1}^{m}[\mu_{ij} / (\mu_{ij}\sum_{j=1}^{m}\mu_{ij})] = \overline{\lambda_i} / \sum_{j=1}^{m}\mu_{ij}$$

(4)

Calculate the value of (4)-(3):

$$\Delta\rho_{avg}(i) = \overline{\lambda_i} \cdot \frac{1}{\sum_{j=1}^{m}\mu_{ij}} - \frac{\overline{\lambda_i}}{m} \cdot \frac{\sum_{j=1}^{m}\mu_{ij}}{\sum_{j=1}^{m}\mu_{ij}^2} = \overline{\lambda_i} \cdot \frac{m\sum_{j=1}^{m}\mu_{ij}^2 - (\sum_{j=1}^{m}\mu_{ij})^2}{m\sum_{j=1}^{m}\mu_{ij}^2\sum_{j=1}^{m}\mu_{ij}} = \overline{\lambda_i} \cdot \frac{\sum_{i=1}^{m-1}\sum_{k=i+1}^{m}(\mu_{ij}-\mu_{ik})^2}{m\sum_{j=1}^{m}\mu_{ij}^2\sum_{j=1}^{m}\mu_{ij}} \geq 0$$

Thus, SEDR policy provides better resource utilization of a task than SQR policy in average case. Similarly, we can prove that SEDR policy provides better resource utilization of a task than the other dispatching policies shown in this paper. Due to the space limitation, we omit the proof details here.

On the other hand, in the worst case, a request of task i is likely to be blocked in the scheduling queue when task i's processing queue with the heaviest load is full. Hence the worst case resource utilization of task i is determined by the utilization of task i's VM on the heaviest load:

$$\rho_{worst}(i) = Max\{\frac{\overline{\lambda_i}\lim_{t\to\infty}P_{i1}[F(t)]}{\mu_{i1}}, ..., \frac{\overline{\lambda_i}\lim_{t\to\infty}P_{im}[F(t)]}{\mu_{im}}\}$$

An optimal scheduling policy should minimize the value of $\rho_{worst}(i)$. We know $\rho_{worst}(i)$ gets the minimum value when:

$$\lim_{t\to\infty} P_{i1}[F(t)]/\mu_{i1} = \lim_{t\to\infty} P_{i2}[F(t)]/\mu_{i2} = ... = \lim_{t\to\infty} P_{im}[F(t)]/\mu_{im} \qquad (5)$$

To satisfy (5), the expression of $P_{ij}[F(t)]$ should be:

$$\lim_{t\to\infty} P_{ij}[F(t)] = \mu_{ij}\,/\sum_{s=1}^{m}\mu_{is}$$

(6)

We find that (6) is the same as the expression of $P_{ij}[F(t)]$ under SQR policy. Hence SQR dispatching policy provides optimal utilization of tasks in the worst case.

Next, we prove that, when the requests of different tasks are arriving uniformly, SRTF is the optimal ordering policy to collaborate with SEDR in the average case, while LRTF is the worst ordering policy to collaborate with SEDR.

Average resource utilization of all the tasks can be expressed as follows:

$$\rho_{total} = \frac{1}{n}\sum_{i=1}^{n}\rho_{avg}(i) = \sum_{i=1}^{n}\sum_{j=1}^{m}\frac{\lambda_i \cdot \lim_{t\to\infty} P_i[D(t)]P_{ij}[F(t)]}{\mu_{ij}mn} \qquad (7)$$

Since the dispatching policy SEDR is chosen, the value of $P_{ij}[F(t)]$ is determined. The requests of different tasks are uniformly arrived, so the value of λ_i is basically identical. And we have assumed $\mu_{1j}\ge\mu_{2j}\ge ...\ge\mu_{nj}$, hence we get:

$$\lambda_1\sum_{j=1}^{m}\frac{1}{\mu_{ij}} \le \lambda_2\sum_{j=1}^{m}\frac{1}{\mu_{2j}} \le ... \le \lambda_n\sum_{j=1}^{m}\frac{1}{\mu_{nj}}$$

And the value range of ρ_{total} should be:

$$\lambda_1\sum_{j=1}^{m}\frac{1}{\mu_{1j}}\cdot\sum_{j=1}^{m}\frac{\lim_{t\to\infty} P_{ij}[F(t)]}{mn} \le \rho_{total} \le \lambda_n\sum_{j=1}^{m}\frac{1}{\mu_{nj}}\cdot\sum_{j=1}^{m}\frac{\lim_{t\to\infty} P_{ij}[F(t)]}{mn}$$

At this time, the value of ρ_{total} is minimum when:

$$\lim_{t\to\infty} P_1[D(t)] \to 1, \quad \lim_{t\to\infty} P_i[D(t)] \to 0, \quad \forall 2\le i\le n$$

And the value of ρ_{total} is maximum when:

$$\lim_{t\to\infty} P_n[D(t)] \to 1, \quad \lim_{t\to\infty} P_i[D(t)] \to 0, \quad \forall 1\le i\le n-1$$

In the average case, the processing queue is not full, hence:

$$1-\rho_{ij} >> 0 \quad \forall 1\le i\le n, \quad \forall 1\le j\le m$$

By calculating the value of $P_i[D(t)]$ under different ordering policies, we get the following conclusions:

- The value of $P_1[D(t)]$ in the steady-state is closest to 1 under the SRTF ordering policy, which indicates that SRTF is the optimal ordering policy to cooperate with SEDR
- The value of $P_n[D(t)]$ in the steady-state is closest to 1 under the LRTF ordering policy, which indicates that LRTF is not an appropriate ordering policy to achieve optimal resource utilization.

- The value of $P_i[D(t)]$ is fixed under the FIFO ordering policy, which indicates that FIFO is a moderate ordering policy.

- $P_1[D(t)]$ also gets the maximum value under the Myopic MaxWeight ordering policy, but the value is not so close to 1 compared with the value of $P_1[D(t)]$ under the SRTF policy. Thus, using Myopic MaxWeight policy, we can also achieve relatively good resource utilization in the average case, but it is not the best choice.

If the requests of different tasks are not uniformly arrived, similarly we can prove that the optimal ordering policy to collaborate with SEDR should satisfy:

$$\lim_{t \to \infty} P_i[D(t)] \to 1 \quad \forall \lambda_i \sum_{j=1}^{m} \frac{1}{\mu_{ij}} = Min\{\lambda_1 \sum_{j=1}^{m} \frac{1}{\mu_{1j}}, \lambda_2 \sum_{j=1}^{m} \frac{1}{\mu_{2j}}, ... \lambda_n \sum_{j=1}^{m} \frac{1}{\mu_{nj}}\}$$

However, in the worst case, the processing queue is nearly full, and when a request of task i is blocked in the scheduling queue, it will not be processed. So, there is a probability that:

$$\lambda_1 \sum_{j=1}^{m} \frac{1}{\mu_{1j}} \to \infty$$

At this time, SRTF is not the optimal ordering policy since:

$$\sum_{i=1}^{n} \{\lambda_i \cdot \lim_{t \to \infty} P_i[D(t)] \sum_{j=1}^{m} \frac{1}{\mu_{ij}}\} \to \infty, \quad if \quad \lim_{t \to \infty} P_1[D(t)] \to 1$$

And Myopic MaxWeigtht is an optimal ordering policy to cooperate with SQR, since it reduces the value of $P_1[D(t)]$, but also keep it maximum. The collaboration of Myopic MaxWeight ordering and SQR dispatching has been proved to be throughput optimal elsewhere [22, 25].

Using our model, we can also evaluate the average responsiveness of the tasks under different collaborations of ordering and dispatching policies, by substituting the expressions of $P_i[D(t)]$ and $P_{ij}[F(t)]$ into (2) and comparing the value of T_{avg}. Due to the space limitation, we omit the evaluation of other performance metrics here.

4   Experiments and Evaluations

In this section, we realize different collaborations of ordering and dispatching policies in the scheduling process of cloud tasks. Based on the experimental results, we evaluate the performance of the list schedulers and validate our modeling results.

We simulate the scenario where a cloud computing platform comprises N servers, and processes tasks with 5 different sizes (i.e. 5 types of tasks). The tasks simulated here are the simple character counting tasks, thus we can approximately predict the processing time of a task according to the task's size. The task scheduling process simulated in our experiment is the same as shown in Fig. 1. The arrival rate of task i satisfies Poisson distribution with mean rate λ_i, and the requests of different tasks are uniformly arrived, thus $\lambda_1 = \lambda_2 =...= \lambda_5$. The tasks' sizes are sequenced in ascending order, hence the processing rate of each task on the platform satisfies: $\mu_{1j} \geqslant \mu_{2j} \geqslant ... \geqslant \mu_{5j}$ ($1 \leq j \leq N$). The simulation time is set long enough (1000 time units) to make the scheduling process reach its steady-state.

Since the utilization metrics reflect the throughput of a system, we record the percentage of processed tasks at each time point to evaluate the throughput of the platform. To make our simulation more convincible, we simulate dynamic scheduling of tasks onto a large scale cloud system with 500 servers (N=500). Twenty-five list schedulers work together to order the arrived tasks and dispatch them to 2500 VMs located on the 500 cloud servers.

Fig. 3 shows the throughput of the cloud computing platform at each time point under different collaborations of ordering and dispatching policies. We simulated the collaborations of all the dispatching policies introduced in this paper and ordering policies FIFO (shown in Fig. 3A), SRTF (shown in Fig. 3B), LRTF (shown in Fig. 3C) and Myopic MaxWeight (shown in Fig. 3D).

We can see from Fig. 3A-3D that, no matter what ordering policy is used, SQR and SEDR dispatching policies achieve better throughput to the cloud platform among the four dispatching policies. This phenomenon validates our modeling results in Section 3 that SEDR and SQR achieve better resource utilization of a task in the scheduling process.

We also notice that the scheduling results using OSEDR is not effective: sometimes, the scheduling results of OSEDR are even no better than Random policy. The reason of this phenomenon is that optimizing the sum of execution delays on a server is not reasonable in cloud computing platforms just as previously discussed in Section 3, since the VMs co-located on the same cloud server can process different tasks simultaneously, the applicable dispatching policy is to optimize the execution delay of the slowest task on a server.

Although the platform achieves better throughput using SEDR and SQR policies, there are still some differences in the scheduling results. Using SEDR policy, the throughput is the best in the initial and middle periods of the scheduling (typically from time unit 1-600), but the throughput will then drop down below SQR policy; on the other hand, using SQR policy, the throughput of the platform rises to the best in the final period of the scheduling. This fact can be explained using the conclusions presented in Section 3: SEDR is the optimal dispatching policy to collaborate with in the average case, hence it provides best throughput in the initial and middle periods when the task loads are not heavy enough. However, when it comes to the final periods of the scheduling, the accumulated unhandled tasks will affect the scheduling results, and the scenario will be changed from the average case scheduling to the worst case scheduling. According to our conclusions in Section 3, SQR is the utilization optimal dispatching policy in the worst case; it explains the phenomenon that using SQR, the platform gets the best throughput in the final period of the scheduling.

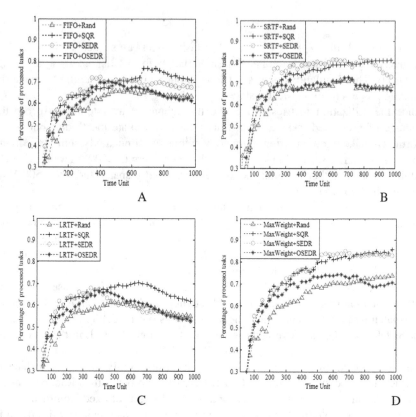

Fig. 2. Throughput of the cloud platform under different collaborations of ordering and dispatching policies

Comparing the results shown in Fig. 3A-3C, we find that the collaboration of SRTF ordering and SEDR dispatching achieves best throughput in the initial and middle scheduling periods; the collaboration of FIFO and SEDR performs moderately; and the collaboration of LRTF and SEDR performs worst. This fact confirms to our modeling results that SRTF is the optimal ordering policy to cooperate with SEDR in the average case when the task requests are uniformly distributed, while LRTF is the worst policy to collaborate with.

We notice from Fig. 3B and 3C that, using SRTF and LRTF policy, the throughput will suffer attenuation at a specific time point (around time unit 400-500 for LRTF, 700-800 for SRTF). This is because SRTF and LRTF are not starvation-free orderings: some tasks have already been stalled in the scheduling queue even if their processing queues are not full; to make things worse, if the shortest (for SRTF) or longest (for LRTF) remaining time tasks are blocked, all the arrived tasks at this time point will not be processed, which will dramatically attenuate the system's throughput close to zero at this time point. However, we can see in Fig. 3D that Myopic MaxWeight policy solves the throughput attenuation problem by improving the SRTF policy. The collaboration of Myopic MaxWeight and SQR provides best throughput in the final period of scheduling (after time unit 700), which theoretically and experimentally validate the conclusion that the collaboration of Myopic MaxWeight ordering and SQR dispatching is the utilization optimal list scheduling policy in the worst case.

5   Conclusion

We briefly summarize some representative ordering and dispatching policies which are commonly used in both industry and academic communities, model the execution processes of these ordering and dispatching policies using the SPN model, and apply different collaborated scheduling policies to schedule cloud tasks in simulation environment. Based on the modeling and experimental results, we have evaluated that SEDR and SQR are utilization optimal dispatching policies to collaborate with in the average case and worst case scheduling respectively; the collaboration of SRTF ordering and SEDR dispatching achieves optimal throughput in the average case, while the collaboration of Myopic MaxWeight ordering and SQR dispatching achieves optimal throughput in the worst case.

References

1. Marty, M., Hill, M.: Virtual Hierarchies to Support Server Consolidation. In: Proceedings of the 34th Annual International Symposium on Computer Architecture, pp. 46–56 (2007)
2. Speitkamp, B., Bichler, M.: A mathematical programming approach for server consolidation problems in virtualized data centers. IEEE Transactions on Services Computing, 266–278 (2010)
3. Beloglazov, A., Buyya, R.: Energy efficient allocation of virtual machines in cloud data centers. In: 2010 10th IEEE/ACM International Conference on Cluster, Cloud and Grid Computing, pp. 577–578 (2010)
4. Burkimsher, A., Bate, I., Indrusiak, L.S.: A survey of scheduling metrics and an improved ordering policy for list schedulers operating on workloads with dependencies and a wide variation in execution times. In: Future Generation Computer Systems (2012, 2013)
5. Topcuoglu, H., Hariri, S., Wu, M.Y.: Performance-effective and low-complexity task scheduling for heterogeneous computing. IEEE Transactions on Parallel and Distributed Systems, 260–274 (2002)
6. Lu, X., Sitters, R.A., Stougie, L.: A class of on-line scheduling algorithms to minimize total completion time. Operations Research Letters 31(3), 232–236 (2003)
7. Laili, Y., et al.: A Ranking Chaos Algorithm for dual scheduling of cloud service and computing resource in private cloud. Computers in Industry, 448–463 (2013)
8. Oracle: N1 grid engine 6 administration guide—configuring the share-based policy (2010), http://docs.oracle.com/cd/E19080-01/n1.grid.eng6/817-5677/i999588/index.html
9. Östberg, P.O., Danie, E., Erik, E.: Decentralized scalable fairshare scheduling. Future Generation Computer Systems, 130–143 (2013)
10. Chang, H., Kodialam, M., Kompella, R.R., et al.: Scheduling in mapreduce-like systems for fast completion time. In: Proceedings of IEEE INFOCOM Conference, pp. 3074–3082 (2011)

11. Chen, F., Kodialam, M., Lakshman, T.V.: Joint Scheduling of Processing and Shuffle Phases in MapReduce Systems. In: Proceedings of IEEE INFOCOM Conference (2012)
12. Lui, J.C.S., Richard, R.M., Don, T.: Bounding the mean response time of the minimum expected delay routing policy: an algorithmic approach. IEEE Transactions on Computers 44(12), 1371–1382 (1995)
13. Albers, S.: Better bounds for online scheduling. In: Proceedings of the 29th Annual ACM Symposium on Theory of Computing (STOC 1997), New York, USA, pp. 130–139 (1997)
14. Bender, M.A., Chakrabarti, S., Muthukrishnan, S.: Flow and stretch metrics for scheduling continuous job streams. In: Proceedings of the 9th Annual ACM–SIAM Symposium on Discrete Algorithms, SODA 1998, Philadelphia, PA, USA, pp. 270–279 (1998)
15. Kong, X., Lin, C., Jiang, Y., Yan, W., Chu, X.: Efficient dynamic task scheduling in virtualized data centers with fuzzy prediction. Journal of Network and Computer Applications 34(4), 1068–1077 (2011)
16. Calheiros, R.N., Ranjan, R., Buyya, R.: Virtual machine provisioning based on analytical performance and qos in cloud computing environments. In: IEEE ICPP (2011)
17. Yuan, Y., Wang, H., Wang, D.: On Interference-aware Provisioning for Cloud-based Big Data Processing. In: IEEE 20th International Workshop on Quality of Service 2013 (IWQoS 2013) (June 2013)
18. Jung, G., Hiltunen, M.A., Joshi, K.R., Schlichting, R.D., Pu, C.: Mistral: Dynamically Managing Power, Performance, and Adaptation Cost in Cloud Infrastructures. In: IEEE ICDCS 2010 (June 2010)
19. Mitzenmacher, M.: The power of two choices in randomized load balancing. Ph.D. dissertation, University of California at Berkeley (1996)
20. He, Y.T., Down, D.G.: Limited choice and locality considerations for load balancing. Performance Evaluation 65(9) (2008)
21. Lin, C., Shan, Z., Yang, Y.: Integrated schemes of request dispatching and selecting in Web server clusters. In: Proceedings of Conference on Software: Theory and Practice, 16 th World Computer Congress 2000 (WCC 2000), Beijing, China (August 2000)
22. Maguluri, S.T., Srikant, R., Ying, L.: Stochastic models of load balancing and scheduling in cloud computing clusters. In: Proceedings of IEEE INFOCOMM Conference (2012)
23. Khan, A.A., McCreary, C.L., Jones, M.S.: A comparison of multiprocessor scheduling heuristics. In: IEEE International Conference on Parallel Processing (ICPP) (1994)
24. Kleinrock, L.: Queueing Systems. Theory, vol. I, p. 187. John Wiley & Sons, New York (1975)
25. Maguluri, S.T., Srikant, R.: Scheduling Jobs with Unknown Duration in Clouds. In: IEEE INFOCOM Conference (2013)

Gossip Membership Management with Social Graphs for Byzantine Fault Tolerance in Clouds*

JongBeom Lim[1], Joon-Min Gil[2], Kwang-Sik Chung[3], Jihun Kang[1],
Daewon Lee[4], and Heonchang Yu[1],**

[1] Department of Computer Science Education, Korea University, Seoul, Korea
{jblim,k2j23h,yuhc}@korea.ac.kr
[2] School of Computer & Information Communications Engineering,
Catholic University of Daegu, Daegu, Korea
jmgil@cu.ac.kr
[3] Department of Computer Science, Korea National Open University, Seoul, Korea
kchung0825@knou.ac.kr
[4] Department of General Education, SeoKyeong University, Seoul, Korea
daelee@skuniv.ac.kr

Abstract. As computer systems have become more complex and dynamic, unstructured and decentralized techniques serve as basic building blocks in large-scale systems such as cloud computing systems. In particular, we consider a gossip-based algorithm, one of the unstructured overlay construction techniques. In this paper, we propose a membership management mechanism using the gossip-based algorithm with social graphs for the Byzantine fault tolerance problem. Experimental results show that our membership management mechanism copes with Byzantine nodes effectively in a scalable way without a bottleneck in dynamic computing environments, requiring only $n \geq 2f + 1$ nodes.

1 Introduction

In recent years, the epidemic or gossip-based communication model has been employed in many applications in large-scale distributed systems and cloud computing systems. These applications include information dissemination [1], [2], clock synchronization [3], mutual exclusion [4], deadlock detection [5], termination detection [6], video streaming service [7], and BitTorrent (Tribler) [8]. In cloud computing environments, nodes can join or leave the system at will by virtue of virtualization technology [9]. Because of the characteristics of typical cloud computing environments, that is, the overlay network is often not fully connected and is constantly changing, the existing communication models are not able to suitably address reliability and scalability problems [10]. Therefore,

---

* This work was supported by the National Research Foundation of Korea (NRF) grant funded by the Korea goverment (MEST) (No. NRF-2012R1A2A2A02046684).
** Corresponding author.

C.-H. Hsu et al. (Eds.): NPC 2014, LNCS 8707, pp. 321–332, 2014.
© IFIP International Federation for Information Processing 2014

as cloud computing matures, the gossip-based communication model has received significant attention because of its inherent ability to handle the dynamic behavior of nodes or resources [11].

Because modern gossip-based protocols use *local view*, which is a membership table that contains a small number of neighbor nodes, rather than maintaining full membership information of the system, the uniformity of peer sampling has become an important basic factor for evaluating the protocol. In this regard, several membership management mechanisms of the gossip-based protocols have been devised [12], [13], [14] to maintain the uniformity of peer sampling. Although biased peer sampling may not influence the correctness of the gossip protocol, it leads to performance degradation for applications. Furthermore, malicious or Byzantine nodes may subvert the system even though the number of Byzantine nodes is sufficiently small, and therefore, existing membership management mechanisms are not suitable for preserving the uniformity of random sampling.

In this paper, we propose a membership management solution over social graphs in the presence of Byzantine nodes. Although previous solutions focus on the uniform sampling of nodes, including Byzantine nodes, we endeavor to sample nodes within the set of correct nodes disregarding Byzantine nodes from local views. In brief, when a correct node encounters a suspicious (Byzantine) node, the correct node does not accepting the membership information of the suspicious node and leverages the pre-existing social graph for membership management.

The rest of this paper is organized as follows. We describe the gossip protocol, social graph, and Byzantine fault tolerance problem with related work in Section 2. In Section 3, we provide our system model and algorithms for membership management using social graphs. We present the results of performance evaluation in Section 4. Then, we conclude the paper in Section 5.

2   Related Work

An epidemic or gossip protocol is a method to communicate among uniquely identifiable nodes in a cycle-based fashion, inspired by the spread of disease. Diseases such as airborne diseases, contagious diseases, or HIV can be spread when individuals encounter others through networking connections. Another analogy of a gossip protocol can be found in the social behavior of persons. For example, if person P has just been updated for some data, P is willing to spread that information to other persons. Subsequently, P will contact some neighbors and try to push the data. In contrast, if person P has not yet obtained new data, P wants to be updated and P will try to obtain the data by pulling other neighbors. A gossip protocol guarantees message delivery with a high probability even if failures occur because of its inherent properties [15]. Refer to [16] and [17] for a correctness proof of the gossip protocol. The simplest form of the gossip protocol comes in two states: susceptible and infected. This form of the gossip protocol is called the SI model [18]. In the gossip protocol, each node maintains little membership information, which is called *local view*, instead of full membership information in the system. Hence, the overlay network can be greatly simplified. At each cycle, a node selects o(fanout) gossip targets from its local view and then communicates with the gossip targets using one of the following methods: (1) push mode, (2) pull mode, and (3) push-pull mode.

As for membership management of the gossip protocol, several schemes have been proposed. In [12], the authors proposed the *view-shuffling* operation, where pairs of nodes regularly and continuously swap portions of their local views. Unfortunately, the naive version of the view-shuffling operation has some drawbacks in that the overlay network may be partitioned in some cases. Hence, an enhanced version of view shuffling has been proposed [13]. The difference between naive view shuffling and enhanced view shuffling is that in the enhanced version, when swapping local views, the initiator includes the *id* of the gossip target in the *sent view*, which will be included to the local view of the gossip target, and then replaces the *id* of the gossip target with its own *id* before transmission. This modification results in the uniformity of random sampling even when starting from a non-uniform distribution of nodes in the local views [19].

In Newscast [14], each node performs a view-swapping operation periodically, keeping only the most up-to-date local view entries of the union of the two local views. This idea is based on the assumption that nodes exhibit dynamic behavior, and therefore, the probability of existing in the local views of two nodes is high for newly joined nodes. In Brahms [20], the authors proposed a Byzantine-resilient and uniform peer sampling algorithm based on view shuffling, requiring multiple samplers and validators, where a unique hash function is used in each. Because of this, to obtain a uniform sample for a sampler, a sufficiently long sequence of shuffle operations is required. Moreover, the uniformity is valid only for one instance. In other words, another sequence of shuffling operations needs to be performed for another instance.

On the other hand, the membership management proposed in this paper does not require multiple samplers at each node, and the additional overhead for uniformity is minimized. Furthermore, the uniformity of local views is *always* evolving as the number of gossip cycles increases, retaining the previous uniformity regardless of different instances of membership management operations. In addition, as discussed, we endeavor to sample nodes within the set of correct nodes disregarding Byzantine nodes from local views, unlike the previous solutions, which focus on the uniform sampling of nodes including Byzantine nodes.

We consider social graphs to enhance the uniformity of peer sampling, disregarding Byzantine nodes. An informal definition of a social graph is a graph representation of an overlay network, of which every two nodes with a social relationship are connected through an overlay. In a typical gossip protocol, the overlay network is constructed only by local views of nodes. In addition to this, if Node A has relationships with Node G and Node H, Node A has an outdegree of seven (if the gossip protocol uses push mode).

Assume that Node A has data informative to its neighbors (i.e., nodes in a social view), but the data are sensitive and private. In such a case, Node A does not want to expose the data to nodes (although the data are beneficial to the nodes) other than its neighbors. Similarly, if Node A has sent sensitive and private data to its neighbor (Node G), Node A requires that Node G not send the data because the social relationships are not transitive. We note that the social relationships are symmetric. That is, if Node A trusts Node G, Node G also trusts Node A. We note that even though Node A and G have a trust relationship, they may not have contact information between them. For instance, if Node A contacts Node G, which does not have Node A in its own contact list, Node G will recognize Node A, and vice versa.

We use these properties of social graphs to solve the Byzantine fault tolerance problem. As far as confidentiality and privacy are concerned, explicit mechanisms should be employed when using social graphs. Because we focus on the Byzantine fault tolerance problem, these confidentiality and privacy mechanisms are beyond the scope of this paper. Several studies have been devoted to these mechanisms [21], [22].

3   Proposed Membership Management

In this study, we propose an enhanced version of gossip membership management with social graphs. The basic idea of our proposed solution is to utilize an existing social relationship in order to increase the expectations of the correct nodes in local views. More precisely, when a node encounters a suspicious node, the node utilizes its social neighbors to replace the suspicious node with a trustworthy node. As gossip cycles progress, a correct node may contact a Byzantine node, which outputs an incorrect decision value. In this case, we let the correct node perform a membership management algorithm that we provide. The pseudocode of the algorithm is provided in Section 3.2. In brief, in our membership management, the correct node contacts its social neighbor and then retrieves the social view of one of the social neighbors. Afterwards, the correct node replaces the Byzantine node information in the local view with the retrieved information.

One of the simplest forms that solve the Byzantine consensus problem is based on broadcast primitives. In this approach, the leader periodically sends a broadcast message to every node in the system, and then the leader waits until it receives all of the acknowledgements. Next, the leader performs the consensus algorithm to decide whether consensus is reached. If consensus is not reached (because some distributed computations are not finished), the leader sends another broadcast message. The drawbacks of this approach are: (1) the leader should remain stable during the whole epoch (single point of failure), (2) the message complexity of the algorithm is $O(n^2)$ (scalability problem), (3) it is not good at handling the dynamism of the system (not churn-resilient), and (4) no node (except for the leader) knows the system-wide information (not globally optimized).

To solve the global optimization problem, one can use gossip algorithms based on a broadcast primitive. In such a case, at each cycle, every node sends its local information to every other node in the system. Although the broadcast-based algorithms require fewer gossip cycles to reach consensus, the message complexity of the algorithms is $O(n^2)$ *at each cycle.* Unlike the previous approaches, our solution is not based on the broadcast primitive or the leader and is able to properly address the scalability problem in terms of the number of nodes even in the presence of Byzantine nodes. Furthermore, as gossip cycles progress, the system-wide information is distributed across the nodes in the system. To the best of our knowledge, several previous studies have dealt with the Byzantine fault tolerance problem in a dynamic system. The implicit assumptions of some previous studies are: no Byzantine nodes exist in the system, and the system is static (i.e., nodes are not allowed to join or leave).

3.1   System Model

There is a set of nodes or processes and all the nodes are functionally equivalent to each other. Henceforth, we use the terms "node" and "process" interchangeably. There is no notion of global memory. Therefore, message passing is the only way to communicate in the system. Communication channels are reliable but are not restricted to FIFO. In terms of failures, we assume that any node can be subject to Byzantine failures (i.e., they arbitrarily deviate from the specification of the algorithm intentionally or inadvertently, outputting an incorrect decision value by definition). In the worst case, a malicious Byzantine node performs covert activities in collusion with other Byzantine nodes to hinder or delay the objectives of other correct nodes. To prevent identification forgery, we use a digital signature scheme that uses public and private keys to sign and verify a message. That is, a node signs a message with a private key before transmission to a gossip target, and a receiver verifies a message using a public key of a sender. This guarantees the identity and the reputability of the signatory.

For Byzantine consensus, we consider the *interactive consistency* problem [23], where $n \geq 2f + 1$. In the problem in the presence of Byzantine nodes, each node sends and receives its DecisionVector by gossiping and checks DecisionVector in order to reach the consensus. If over half of the DecisionVector has non-empty elements, and their values are identical, the nodes can conclude the consensus value. We assume that Byzantine nodes exhibit malicious behavior. To be more precise, they send an empty DecisionVector except for their own elements. This behavior is the best effort of malicious Byzantine nodes, if we use a cryptographic scheme for DecisionVector.

3.2   Detailed Algorithms

To realize our proposed scheme, an additional data structure is required (i.e., social view). In our scenario, however, the additional overhead resulting from the data structure is marginal because the size of the social view is small compared to that of the local view. Recall that the size of the local view is significantly

---

Algorithm 1. Management of social view for P_i

```
 1  begin at each cycle
 2  |   if P_i makes a new social neighbor P_j then
 3  |   |   if socialView P_i is full then
 4  |   |   |   if there is P_k that has less friendship than P_j then
 5  |   |   |   |   socialView P_i ← socialView P_i − P_k;
 6  |   |   |   |   socialView P_i ← socialView P_i ∪ P_j;
 7  |   |   else
 8  |   |   |   socialView P_i ← socialView P_i ∪ P_j;
 9  |   if P_i breaks up with P_j then
10  |   |   socialView P_i ← socialView P_i − P_j;
```

---

less than that of the membership information of the system. We note that we consider the size of the social view a global system parameter with the same value for all nodes. In the following algorithms, a subscript indicates the owner of the data structure. We assume that P_i is a correct node in the algorithms.

Algorithm 1 shows the pseudocode for social view management. At each cycle, P_i manages its social view (`socialView`) based on relationships with other nodes. If P_i has a new social neighbor P_j, it tries to add P_j to `socialView` (line 2-8). During this phase, P_i checks the empty slot for P_j. If no empty slot is available in `socialView` (line 3), it tries to find P_k that has less friendship than that of P_j (line 4). If there is P_k that meets the condition, it replaces P_k with P_j (line 5-6). If an empty slot is available in `socialView`, it adds P_j to `socialView` (line 8). When P_i breaks up with P_j, it removes P_j from `socialView` (line 10).

We assume that no correct node deviates from the specification of the protocol. The gossip-based protocol consists of two threads: an active thread that initiates communication at each cycle and a passive thread that waits for incoming messages. The proposed membership management mechanism uses the Byzantine consensus algorithm running in the system. By inspecting the result of the decision value of the encountered node, individual nodes differentiate correct nodes and Byzantine nodes. When a correct node encounters a suspicious node, the correct node does not accept the membership information of the suspicious node and performs the membership management algorithm proposed in this paper. Furthermore, we assume that correct nodes do not violate trust relationships with others. In other words, no correct node will intentionally disclose membership information and create friendships with Byzantine nodes.

A full analysis of criteria determining friendships is out of the scope of this paper, because it depends on the specific characteristics of the applications using the gossip protocols. In fact, we can use an application-specific criterion that works best for the application. For example, Gossple [24] uses a *set item cosine similarity* metric to measure the friendships between nodes. If we apply the set item cosine similarity to measure the friendships, a node that has the larger metric value can replace the existing node. In addition, the application may have a threshold value to determine the friendships for nodes. In this case, a node can remove (break up) one of the friends in `socialView` when a metric value between the two nodes is below the threshold value.

For the active thread of the gossip protocol, each time P_i selects a gossip target P_j it checks the decision value of P_j. We note that the `verify()` function returns *true* when two input parameters are identical; otherwise, it returns *false*. If `verify()` returns true, it assigns true to the `activate` variable. If the protocol is in push mode, P_i includes its own *id* in the `sendingView` and then sends this view to P_j. If the protocol is in pull mode, it tries to receive the `sendingView` from P_j and then updates its local view with the received view.

When the `verify` function returns false, P_i neither sends its view information to P_j nor receives the view information from P_j because `sendingView` from P_j may contain harmful information that pollutes the local view of P_i with Byzantine nodes. At this stage, P_i sets the `activate` variable to false and then selects one of the social neighbors from its `socialView`. After selecting the social neighbor, P_i tries to receive the `socialView` of the social neighbor. Then, P_i selects P_k, that is, one of the nodes from the `socialView` of the social neighbor. Afterwards, P_i replaces P_j with P_k in its `localView`. If P_i has no social neighbor, or `rand` function returns null, P_k cannot be inserted into `localView`. For brevity, this checking procedure is omitted. Lastly, P_i performs the `ByzantineConsensusAlgorithm()` function or not, based on the `activate` value.

For the passive thread of the gossip protocol, whenever P_i is selected from another node P_j it first checks `requestType`. If `requestType` is for a local view, P_i compares the `decisionValue` of P_j with its own value. If the two values are coherent, it accepts the `sendingView` of P_j and updates its local view with the received view in push mode. If the protocol is in pull mode, P_i includes its own *id* in `sendingView` and sends the view to P_j. If `requestType` is for the social view, and P_j is a friend, P_i sends its `socialView` to P_j.

4   Evaluation

In this section, we provide performance results of our membership management mechanism using social graphs. We do not include Shuffling [12] and Newscast [14] because those methods cannot tolerate Byzantine nodes even if the number of the Byzantine nodes is negligible. In our observation, Shuffling places less than 30% of the correct nodes in decision vectors on average when performing the Byzantine consensus algorithm if the Byzantine probability is 0.1, and the shuffle ratio is 50%. Newscast can be considered as view shuffling with a shuffle ratio of 100%. In other words, Newscast is more vulnerable to Byzantine nodes compared to Shuffling.

4.1   Experimental Settings

Table 1 shows the parameters and their values used in the evaluations. We note that the numbers in parentheses are the default values unless specified otherwise.

Table 1. Evaluation parameters and their values (numbers in parentheses are the default values unless specified otherwise)

Parameter	Value
Number of nodes	10^4
Gossip mode	Push-pull
Size of local view	20
Size of social view	8
Fanout	1
Gossip cycles per instance	20
Byzantine probability	0.1, 0.2, 0.3, (0.4)

Because we need at least $f + 1$ correct nodes, the Byzantine probability is not configured to be higher than 0.5. Note also that because the probability is a measure of the expectation that an event will occur, the actual number of Byzantine nodes will be different from the number calculated with the Byzantine probability parameter.

Starting with the initial overlay network and local views in the presence of Byzantine nodes, we show how our membership management based on social graphs improves the uniformity of peer sampling. Then, we detail the effects on the local view to show how our proposed solution can improve the occurrence of correct nodes in local views. We note that we only show the results for correct nodes in the system because the results for Byzantine nodes are meaningless. Lastly, to show the scalability of the proposed approach, we present performance results by increasing the number of nodes exponentially. There were three objects for comparison: the default Byzantine consensus algorithm without membership management (NoMgmt), membership management performing random node sampling when a node encounters Byzantine nodes (Previous); and our membership management with social graphs when the social view size is 8 (Social(8)).

4.2   Performance Results

One of the design goals of our membership management is to reduce the possibility that a correct node contacts Byzantine nodes. Thus, we measured the number of Byzantine nodes in the local view to see how effectively our proposed membership management copes with Byzantine nodes. We assume that local views of individual nodes contain gossip partners selected at random from the system. Therefore, Byzantine nodes are in the local views of the correct nodes. Figures 1, 2, and 3 show the normalized percentages of Byzantine nodes in local views.

Figure 1 shows the results of the first instance. Because NoMgmt has no facility to perform membership management, the number of Byzantine nodes in local views is the same during the whole execution of the Byzantine consensus algorithm. Compared with Previous and Social(8), the percentage of Byzantine

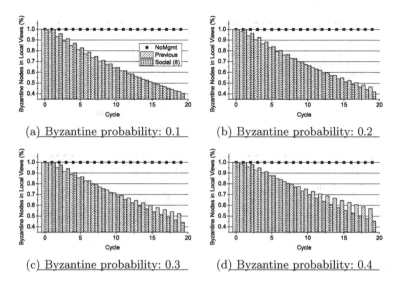

Fig. 1. Normalized percentage of Byzantine nodes in local views (first instance)

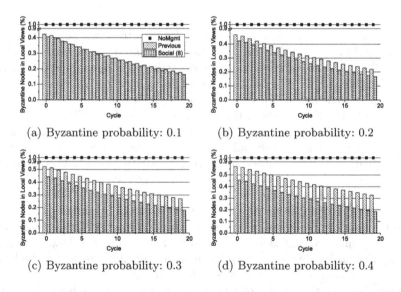

Fig. 2. Normalized percentage of Byzantine nodes in local views (second instance)

nodes in local views decreases as the gossip cycle proceeds in both methods, whereas Social(8) results in a greater reduction in the number of Byzantine nodes in local views than Previous in late cycles. It is interesting to note that in early cycles, Social(8) has a higher percentage of Byzantine nodes in local views than Previous. The reason for this phenomenon is that some nodes have

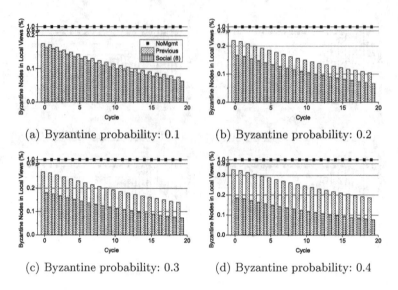

(a) Byzantine probability: 0.1   (b) Byzantine probability: 0.2

(c) Byzantine probability: 0.3   (d) Byzantine probability: 0.4

Fig. 3. Normalized percentage of Byzantine nodes in local views (third instance)

no social neighbors. In other words, when P_i tries to select `socialNeighbor`, this cannot be accomplished because the node has no social neighbors. Similarly, if P_i, who has some social neighbors, tries to receive `socialView` from `socialNeighbor`, it is possible that `socialNeighbor` has no social neighbors except P_i. In this case, no local view exchange is executed.

Figure 2 shows the results of the second instance. As in Figure 1, NoMgmt shows no change in the Byzantine nodes in local views. As the gossip cycle proceeds, and the Byzantine probability increases, Social(8) has a lower percentage than Previous and always outperforms Previous. By the specification of the algorithms, the nodes have a greater chance to exchange their local views when they encounter Byzantine nodes frequently. In this regard, there is a trade-off between the number of Byzantine nodes and the probability of exchanging local views. When the number of Byzantine nodes is small, the probability of performing membership management is low. Conversely, if the number of Byzantine nodes is large, the probability of performing membership management is high, and there are a number of local view slots to be changed.

Figure 3 shows the results of the second instance. As in Figures 1 and 2, Social(8) outnumbers Previous in the total reduction of Byzantine nodes, and the performance gap is greater with a larger Byzantine probability. At cycle 20, the percentages of Byzantine nodes in local views for Previous (resp. Social(8)) are approximately 7.49% (resp. 6.31%), 10.47% (resp. 6.69%), 14.02% (resp. 7.32%), and 18.64% (resp. 7.69%) when the Byzantine probability is 0.1, 0.2, 0.3, and 0.4, respectively. This means that our proposed membership management has 1.19, 1.56, 1.92, and 2.42 times fewer Byzantine nodes in local views then Previous when the Byzantine probability is 0.1, 0.2, 0.3, and 0.4, respectively.

5 Conclusion

In this paper, we have presented a membership management mechanism based on social relationships on the gossip overlay for the Byzantine fault tolerance problem. Rather than utilizing a traditional control method, where the centralized medium monitors the system and performs corrective functions, we let each node perform membership management with social graphs in a self-organizing way. Our self-organized construction of membership management using social graphs provides scalability, reliability, and resiliency in the presence of Byzantine nodes. The experimental results show that our membership management mechanism for Byzantine fault tolerance is globally optimized as the gossip cycle proceeds. Furthermore, our proposed membership management surpasses existing methods and effectively eliminates Byzantine nodes in the view of other nodes.

References

1. Lim, J., Lee, J., Chin, S., Yu, H.: Group-based gossip multicast protocol for efficient and fault tolerant message dissemination in clouds. In: Riekki, J., Ylianttila, M., Guo, M. (eds.) GPC 2011. LNCS, vol. 6646, pp. 13–22. Springer, Heidelberg (2011)
2. Antulov-Fantulin, N., Lancic, A., Stefancic, H., Sikic, M.: Fastsir algorithm: A fast algorithm for the simulation of the epidemic spread in large networks by using the susceptible–infected–recovered compartment model. Information Sciences 239, 226–240 (2013)
3. Iwanicki, K., van Steen, M., Voulgaris, S.: Gossip-based clock synchronization for large decentralized systems. In: Keller, A., Martin-Flatin, J.-P. (eds.) SelfMan 2006. LNCS, vol. 3996, pp. 28–42. Springer, Heidelberg (2006)
4. Lim, J., Chung, K.-S., Chin, S.-H., Yu, H.-C.: A gossip-based mutual exclusion algorithm for cloud environments. In: Li, R., Cao, J., Bourgeois, J. (eds.) GPC 2012. LNCS, vol. 7296, pp. 31–45. Springer, Heidelberg (2012)
5. Lim, J., Suh, T., Yu, H.: A deadlock detection algorithm using gossip in cloud computing environments. In: Han, Y.H., Park, D.S., Jia, W., Yeo, S.S. (eds.) Ubiquitous Information Technologies and Applications. Lecture Notes in Electrical Engineering, vol. 214, pp. 781–789. Springer, Netherlands (2013)
6. Lim, J., Chung, K.S., Gil, J.M., Suh, T., Yu, H.: An unstructured termination detection algorithm using gossip in cloud computing environments. In: Kubátová, H., Hochberger, C., Daněk, M., Sick, B. (eds.) ARCS 2013. LNCS, vol. 7767, pp. 1–12. Springer, Heidelberg (2013)
7. Chu, Y.H., Ganjam, A., Ng, T.S.E., Rao, S.G., Sripanidkulchai, K., Zhan, J., Zhang, H.: Early experience with an internet broadcast system based on overlay multicast. In: Proceedings of the Annual Conference on USENIX Annual Technical Conference, ATEC 2004, p. 12. USENIX Association, Berkeley (2004)
8. Zeilemaker, N., Capotă, M., Bakker, A., Pouwelse, J.: Tribler: P2p media search and sharing. In: Proceedings of the 19th ACM International Conference on Multimedia, MM 2011, pp. 739–742. ACM, New York (2011)
9. Mahajan, K., Makroo, A., Dahiya, D.: Round robin with server affinity: A vm load balancing algorithm for cloud based infrastructure. Journal of Information Processing Systems 9(3), 379–394 (2013)

10. Matos, M., Sousa, A., Pereira, J., Oliveira, R., Deliot, E., Murray, P.: Clon: Overlay networks and gossip protocols for cloud environments. In: Meersman, R., Dillon, T., Herrero, P. (eds.) OTM 2009, Part I. LNCS, vol. 5870, pp. 549–566. Springer, Heidelberg (2009)

11. Wuhib, F., Stadler, R., Spreitzer, M.: A gossip protocol for dynamic resource management in large cloud environments. IEEE Transactions on Network and Service Management 9(2), 213–225 (2012)

12. Stavrou, A., Rubenstein, D., Sahu, S.: A lightweight, robust p2p system to handle flash crowds. IEEE Journal on Selected Areas in Communications 22(1), 6–17 (2004)

13. Voulgaris, S., Gavidia, D., Steen, M.: Cyclon: Inexpensive membership management for unstructured p2p overlays. Journal of Network and Systems Management 13(2), 197–217 (2005)

14. Tölgyesi, N., Jelasity, M.: Adaptive peer sampling with newscast. In: Sips, H., Epema, D., Lin, H.-X. (eds.) Euro-Par 2009. LNCS, vol. 5704, pp. 523–534. Springer, Heidelberg (2009)

15. Ganesh, A., Kermarrec, A.M., Massoulie, L.: Peer-to-peer membership management for gossip-based protocols. IEEE Transactions on Computers 52(2), 139–149 (2003)

16. Allavena, A., Demers, A., Hopcroft, J.E.: Correctness of a gossip based membership protocol. In: Proceedings of the Twenty-Fourth Annual ACM Symposium on Principles of Distributed Computing, PODC 2005, pp. 292–301. ACM, New York (2005)

17. Gurevich, M., Keidar, I.: Correctness of gossip-based membership under message loss. In: Proceedings of the 28th ACM Symposium on Principles of Distributed Computing, PODC 2009, pp. 151–160. ACM, New York (2009)

18. Newman, M.: Networks: An Introduction. Oxford University Press, Inc., New York (2010)

19. Busnel, Y., Beraldi, R., Baldoni, R.: On the uniformity of peer sampling based on view shuffling. Journal of Parallel and Distributed Computing 71(8), 1165–1176 (2011)

20. Bortnikov, E., Gurevich, M., Keidar, I., Kliot, G., Shraer, A.: Brahms: Byzantine resilient random membership sampling. Comput. Netw. 53(13), 2340–2359 (2009)

21. Schiavoni, V., Riviére, E., Felber, P.: Whisper: Middleware for confidential communication in large-scale networks. In: 2011 31st International Conference on Distributed Computing Systems (ICDCS), pp. 456–466 (2011)

22. Singh, A., Urdaneta, G., van Steen, M., Vitenberg, R.: Robust overlays for privacy-preserving data dissemination over a social graph. In: 2012 IEEE 32nd International Conference on Distributed Computing Systems (ICDCS), pp. 234–244 (2012)

23. Pease, M., Shostak, R., Lamport, L.: Reaching agreement in the presence of faults. J. ACM 27(2), 228–234 (1980)

24. Bertier, M., Frey, D., Guerraoui, R., Kermarrec, A.-M., Leroy, V.: The gossple anonymous social network. In: Gupta, I., Mascolo, C. (eds.) Middleware 2010. LNCS, vol. 6452, pp. 191–211. Springer, Heidelberg (2010)

An Ensemble Multivariate Model for Resource Performance Prediction in the Cloud

Jean Steve Hirwa⋆ and Jian Cao

Shanghai Jiao Tong University
Department of Computer Engineering
800 Dongchuan Road, Minhang District, Shanghai 200240,
P.R. China
hirwasteve@hotmail.com, cao-jian@sjtu.edu.cn

Abstract. In cloud environment, multiple resources performance prediction is the task of predicting different resources by considering the differences from multiple task inferences based on the historical values to make effective and certainty judgmental decisions for the future values. One resource performance prediction can conclude the performance of another, which implies dependency (i.e., multi-resources) or independency (i.e., one resource), but that cannot be directly confirmed accurately. We use time series algorithms to investigate possible approaches, which can greatly assist us to analyze and predict the future values based on previously observed values. The goal of this paper is to review the theory of the common several models of multivariate time series, and to emphasize the practical steps to take in order to fit those models to real data and evaluate the outcome. Moreover, ensemble-learning algorithms are applied to the best-fit models to improve performance. Finally, we will discuss the results.

Keywords: Time series, Statistics, Ensemble learning.

1   Introduction

In cloud computing [2], since applications complete for resources with unknown workloads from other users, resources contention causes host load and availability to vary over time [3], and makes the load prediction problem even more harder. The host can be viewed as a collection of resources i.e., CPU, memory usage and I/O. If one of the components in cloud computing will not work or at least will execute below par, cloud computing will never work. Certain support measures, for example [6], have to be implemented to prevent any form of downtime.

⋆ The authors thank the reviewers for their valuable comments and effort to improve this paper. This work is partially supported by China National Science Foundation (Granted Number 61073021, 61272438), Research Funds of Science and Technology Commission of Shanghai Municipality (Granted Number 11511500102, 12511502704).

C.-H. Hsu et al. (Eds.): NPC 2014, LNCS 8707, pp. 333–346, 2014.

The behavior of cloud computing is highly dynamic [3], wherein the only way the process would be possible is through proper interaction of the application and hardware. Historical data can provide an adequate amount of information for modeling and predicting components in cloud computing behaviors [14]. In [15], [16], [1] the accuracy of prediction is subject to the choice of model chosen, which in turn may be limited by characteristics of the time series observations and the availability of labeled training data.

The available literature on Forecasting consider time series predictions of the status of distributed systems resources both CPU and available memory [1], [2], [4], [9], and their predictions are based on historical information provided by monitoring systems. In [7], and [13], they have evaluated and compared univariate and multivariate normality, and performance by applying graphical and statistical procedures. Obviously, it makes sense to put all available resources into consideration, which would provide more information rather than investigating each resource independently. Ensemble learning methods would be applied to the best fit models, in order to improve performance [11].

2   Related Work

Previously, research into resource prediction has focused on determing appropiate predictive models for a single or multiple resources [1], [8] for host behavior. Therefore, this work is mainly focused on multivariate model approach.

For example in [5], they proposed a new means of characterizing correlated workload patterns across Virtual Machines (VMs) resulted from the dependencies of applications running on them. Their applied multiple time series approach, and the workload was analyzed at the group level rather than at the individual VM level.

In [1], they proposed a multi-resource prediction model (MModel) that uses both the autocorrelation (a single resource) and the cross correlation (between two resources such as CPU and Memory usage). And their adaptation approaches were able to adapt to changing characteristics of the resources, especially for highly dynamic resources and long time predictions.

In [9], the approach focuses on the usage prediction for a specific node between CPU and Memory. They have found out that using both resources data can improve the forecasting performance. Moreover, a number of other techniques have been taken into account, from many and different factors of a cloud environment [3], [6], and [14].

In this investigation, regardless unstable behaviors may exist among resources [9] and interdependence, all resources available are taken into consideration as they can provide more information than any other autonomous resources. The idea of ensemble learning approaches is not new [11] [24], [27], but we intended to improve the outcome from the best fit models.

3   Prediction Theory and Techinques

In this work, we choose few models, which work better with univariate and multivariate time series similitaniously. In general, random variables may be uncorrelated but highly dependent [19]. But if a random vector has a multivariate normal distribution then any two or more of its components that are uncorrelated are independent. This implies that any two or more of its components that are pairwise independent are independent. But it is not true that two random variables that are separately, normally distributed and uncorrelated are independent.

Formally, dependence refers to any situation in which random variables do not satisfy a mathematical condition of probabilistic independence. Correlation can be considered as any departure of two or more random variables from independence, but technically it refers to any of several more specialized types of relationship between mean values.

3.1   Prediction Theory

In many situations, it is desirable or necessary to transform a time series data set before using the sophisticated methods [21], [22]. Since we have nonstationary data, an approriate preliminary transformation of the data to get stationarity might succed in stabilizing the variance and then we might use one of the familiar time series models.

Even if some models can be applied directly to nonstationary time series without requiring a preliminary transformation of the data [17], in this case study, univariate functions can be applied point-wise to multivariate data to modify their marginal distributions. It is also possible to modify some attributes of a multivariate distribution using an appropriately constructed transformation [21]. Details for techniques to transform and analyze stationality are introduced in [22].

In the prediction of time series, based on the correlations over time and among the variables, we can estimate the future behavior of time series by using various information extracted from current and past observations [22]. In this study we are looking for an approach which would provide us more accurate information in term of correlation from the previous and current observations comparatively.

3.2   Prediction Techniques

In our research process, we proposed two commonly used algorithms for our study and investigation:

Stable Vector Autoregressive Model. The vector autoregression (VAR) model is one of the most successful, flexible, and easy to use models for the analysis of multivariate time series. [18], [20]. Forecasts from VAR models are quite flexible because they can be made conditional on the potential future paths of specified variables in the model, see [20], [18]. In its basic form, a VAR consists of a set of d endogenous variables $Y_t = (Y_{1t}, \ldots, Y_{kt}, \ldots, Y_{dt})$ for $k = 1, \ldots, d$. A VAR model of order p (Stable Vector Autoregressive Model VAR(p)) is a special case represented by:

$$Y_t = v + \phi_1 Y_{t-1} + \cdots + \phi_p Y_{t-p} + W_t, \tag{1}$$

with A_i are $(d \times d)$ coefficient matrices for $i = 1, \ldots, p$, and where W_t is a *Gaussian* white noise and d-dimensional process with $E(W_t) = 0$. The VAR(p) process is stationary, which means, Y_t generates stationary time series with time invariant mean, variance and covariance structure given sufficient starting values.

$$det(I_d - A_1 z - \cdots - A_p z^p) \neq 0 \quad for \quad |z| \leq 1. \tag{2}$$

If the solution of the above equation has a root for $z = 1$, then either some or all variables in the VAR(p) process are integrated of order 1, i.e., $I(1)$. It might be the case, that cointegration between the variables does exist [28].

The stability of emprical VAR(p) process can be analyzed by considering the companion and calculating the eigenvalues of the coefficient matrix, and can be represented by:

$$\xi_t = A\xi_{t-1} + v_t, \tag{3}$$

Once a VAR(p) model has been estimated [18], the next step is to go for further analysis. Causal inference and forecasting are based upon Wold moving average decomposition for stable VAR(p) processes, which is given below as:

$$Y_t = \phi_0 W_t + \phi_1 W_{t-1} + \phi_2 W_{t-2} + \ldots, \tag{4}$$

with $\phi_0 = I_d$ and ϕ_s can be computed recursively according to;

$$\phi_s = \sum_{j=1} s\phi_{s-j} A_j \quad for \quad s = 1, 2, \ldots, \tag{5}$$

where $A_j = 0$ for $j > p$.

Therefore, forecasts for horizons $h \geq 1$ of an emprical VAR(p) process can be generated recursively according to;

$$Y_{T+h|T} = A_1 Y_{T+h-1|T} + \cdots + A_p Y_{T+h-p|T}, \tag{6}$$

where $Y_{T+j|T} = Y_{T+j}$ for $j \leq 0$.

Dynamic Linear Models. Dynamic Linear Models (DLM) are represented as a special case of general state space models, being linear and Gaussian e.g., [23], [25]. State-space models can be used for modeling univariate or multivariate time series, also in presence of non-stationarity, structural changes, irregular patterns.

Estimation and forecasting can be obtained recursively by the well know Kalman filter [25], and the first important class of state space models is given by Dynamic Linear Models (DLM), which are represented by the following two equations:

$$Y_t = F_t\theta_t + v_t, \quad v_t \sim N_m(0, V_t)$$
$$\theta_t = G_t\theta_{t-1} + w_t, \quad w_t \sim N_p(0, W_t), \tag{7}$$

where G_t and F_t are matrices and (v_t) and (w_t) are two independent white noise sequences, with mean zero and covariance matrices V_t and W_t respectively. Y_t equation is named *observation equation* and θ_t equation is named *state equation*. Moreover, it is assumed that θ_0 has a Gaussian distribution.

$$\theta_0 \sim M_p(m_0, C_0), \tag{8}$$

for some non-random vector m_0 and matrix C_0, and it is independent on (v_t) and (w_t). In contrast to (7), the general state space model can be provided in the form:

$$Y_t = F_t(\theta_t, v_t)$$
$$\theta_t = G_t(\theta_{t-1}, w_t), \tag{9}$$

with arbitrary functions F_t and G_t, it is therefore more flexible. Linear state space models specify f_t and g_t as linear functions, and Gaussian linear models add the assumptions of Gaussian distributions. Model details summary; filtering, smoothing and forecasting [23], [25].

4   Ensemble Learning Approach

Ensemble learning is a machine learning paradigm where multiple learners are trained to solve the same problem [26], [27], and it performs better than single learning model and discovers regularities in dynamic. Generally, it is primarily used to improve the (classification, prediction, function approximation, etc.) performance of a model, or reduce the likelihood of an unfortunate selection of a poor one.

The bagging approach is being taken into consideration for this study. It is a device intended for reducing the prediction error of learning algorithms. And following, a brief process of a bagging algorithm:

- Bagging method:
  - Create many data sets by bootstrapping or cross validation.
  - Create one decision tree for each data set.
  - Combine decision trees by averaging or voting final decisions.
  - Primarily reduces model variance rather than bias.
- Results:
  - On average, better than any individual tree.

Therefore, given a data set $S = (x_1, y_1), \ldots, (x_N, y_N)$ of size N, where $x_n \in X$, $y_n \in Y = \{0, 1\}$, M base models h_m, bagging constructs M classifiers with bootstrap replicas Sm of S, where Sm is obtained by drawing examples from original the data set S with replacement, usually having the same number of examples as S. The diversity among the classifiers is introduced by independently constructing different subsets of the original data set [10], [12]. After constructing ensembles, the prediction of the class of a new example is given by majority voting.

Algorithm 1. Ensemble learning algorithm

Input: S, M
1: **for** $m = 1, 2, \ldots, M$ **do**
2: S_m = Sample with replacement (S, N)
3: Train a base learner $h_m \rightarrow Y$ using S_m
4: **end for**
Output: $H(x) = argmax_{y \in Y} \sum_{m=1}^{M} I(h_m(x) = y)$

Moreover, it has been proved by [24] that the perfomance of bagging has goodness and badness. It does not simply reduce variance in its averaging process. But instead, it takes multiple random samples (with replacement) from training data set, and uses each of those samples to construct a separate model and separate predictions for test set, which in the end, those predictions are then averaged to create a more accurate and final predictive value. As result, it may underperform its ensemble members. In such situation, reweighting on training set is applicable to some of the learning algorithms.

Algorithm 2. Improved Ensemble learning algorithm

1: Initialize base models h_m for all $m \in 1, 2, \ldots, M$
2: **for all** training examples **do**
3:     **for** $m = 1, 2, \ldots, M$ **do**
4:     Set w = poisson (1) // a random variable w has poison distribution
5:     Update h_m with the current examples with weight w
6: **Anytime output:**
7: **return:** $H(x) = argmax_{y \in Y} \sum_{m=1}^{M} I(h_m(x) = y)$

Finally, we evaluate the outcome and investigate if an Ensemble Learning *Alg.* 1 underperformed its previous ensemble members. Furthermore, in order to reduce prediction errors, an Improved Ensemble Learning *Alg.* 2 should be applied afterward. The results and discussion are given in *Section*6.

Table 1. An overview of ensemble learning algorithm

$Y \to model_1 \searrow$	
$Y \to \quad \ldots \quad \to \sum \to Y_{ens}(t)$	
$Y \to model_m \nearrow$	

5 Evaluation Techniques

The datasets are localized from different datasets collected from different time sets. To conduct the numerical analysis, the dataset are selected from 2 different clusters and 3 variables are chosen from each cluster with the same time set and host: CPU, Memory usage and I/O. Furthermore, 1000 observations were randomly taken for each study separately. We analyze and investigate our data dependently and independently to reach our goal.

The models used for our study have many parameters, and they may be difficult to interpret due to complex interactions and feedback between variables in the model. As a result, we tried to find common various types of structural analysis, but putting more emphasize into correlation relationships Moreover, our samples are transformed stationary and normally distributed, i.e., $Y \sim N(0, \sigma^2)$; each variable Y is independent and identically distributed with mean zero, standard deviation σ^2, normal variate, in order to maintain the same condition for a good investigation.

The Root Mean Square Error (RMSE) is moslty applied to measure the difference between values predicted by a model and the values actually observed from the environment that is being modelled, and those differences are *residuals*. The RMSE of a model prediction with respect to the estimated variable Y_model is defined as the square root of the mean squared error:

$$RMSE = \sqrt{\frac{\sum_{i=1}^{n}(Y_{obs,i} - Y_{model,i})^2}{n}} = \sqrt{\frac{\sum_{i=1}^{n}(residuals)^2}{n}} \tag{10}$$

A granger causality analysis has been also carried out in order to assess whether there is any potential predictability power of one indicator for the other. A granger causality requires that the series has to be covariance stationary [18], [28], so an Augmented Dickey-Fuller test has been calculated. For all of the series the null hypothesis H_0 of non stationarity can be rejected at a 5% confidence level. A granger causality is normally tested in the context of linear regression models [29].

Finally, an Ensemble learning algorithm has been introduced, see *Table 1*, it involves combining multiple predictions derived by different techniques in order to create a stronger overall prediction. In [27] an ensemble with two techniques that are very similar in nature will perform more poorly than a more diverse model set. In this situation, we select the best performed model from each group and combine it with best from a different group.

Table 2. Ensemble learning outcome for multivariate data (Initially = Initial state, Ensemb. = Ensemble learning approach, and Impr. Ens. = Improved Ensemble learning approach)

Time	Ensemble: CPU and Memory			Ensemble: CPU and I/O		
	Initially	Ensemb.	Impr. Ens.	Initially	Ensemb.	Impr. Ens.
*Cl.*1						
60 sec	1.0850	1.0456	0.9171	1.0968	1.0719	0.9640
10 min	1.0410	1.0211	0.9694	1.0467	1.0223	0.9290
60 min	1.0403	1.0251	0.9492	1.1083	1.0776	0.9742
*Cl.*2						
60 sec	1.1431	1.1295	0.9855	1.0697	1.0661	0.9980
10 min	1.0758	1.0412	0.9346	1.0692	1.0579	0.9872
60 min	1.0516	1.0167	0.9281	1.0698	1.0592	0.9563

6 Discussion

We have selected our dataset from 2 different clusters and each cluster we only study one host. We have chosen 3 variables from each cluster with the same time set and host: cpu, memory usage and I/O.

The first step is to analyze the accuracy; by looking onto *RMSE*, it shows that mostly, a multivariate model always has to provide promising results over its univariate counterparts. Surprisingly, few cases of univariate series performed better, as shown in *Tables 5-12*, (all numbers in bold). For VAR(p); once we increase the value of *p*-lags, more we have a better outcome from multivariate model and it distiguishes itself from its equivalent univariate, as provided in *Tables 5-8*. This might be different from a DLM Model, where the results stay constant *Tables 9-12*. Once we set an initial *p*-lag value "1" to both selected multivariate algorithms (VAR(p) and DLM); VAR(p) performed poorly than its coequal univariate, but while increasing the *p*-lag value, a multivariate model outperformed its univariate model.

Compare both used models, we came to the conclusion that it depends on the condition of the initial values of the parameters. At the time *p*-lag was set to "1", DLM model *Fig. 1-(a)* performed well than VAR(p) model *Fig. 1-(b)*, but once VAR(p) increased its *p*-lag values *Fig. 2-(a) and 2-(b)*, it performed much better. Therefore, we cannot conclude directly that this model is better than another without looking into its initial state. Generally speaking, VAR(p) would be a promising model once a *p*-lag is much higher in our situation *Fig. 2-(b)*.

We had a look at Granger causality whether there is any potential predictability of one indicator for the other. It is hard to judge, but in general more chances will be given to CPU. *Tables 3 and 4*, show that the granger causality value have changed in disorder, which does not make any sense at all. And we conclude that, it is always beneficial if we may apply Granger Causality for each initial Models' conditions independently to find out a variable has a potential predictability, without making a general and fixed conclusion.

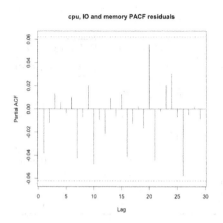

(a) DLM model overall Residuals (CPU, Memory, IO)

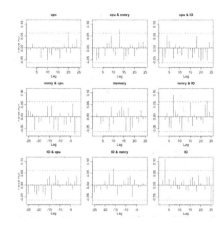

(b) VAR(p) model Residuals: p-lag "1" (CPU, Memory, and IO)

Fig. 1. DML and VAR(p) models for multivariate data

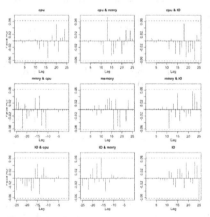

(a) VAR(p) model Residuals: p-lag "10" (CPU, Memory, and IO)

(b) VAR(p) model Residuals: p-lag "20" (CPU, Memory, and IO)

Fig. 2. VAR(p) models for multivariate data

Finally, as seen above multivariate models are promising approaches. If we want to make effective use of information extracted from them, it may always be beneficial to combine the best performed models from each group to obain the best overall and highest performance accuracy *Table 2*.

Table 3. Cluster-1: Granger Causality

Time	Granger: CPU and Memory		Granger: CPU and I/O	
	|cpu-memory|	memory-cpu	||cpu - I/O|I/O	- cpu
$p = 1$				
60 sec	0.0825	0.3053	0.2835	1.0385
10 min	0.5562	1.0261	0.1984	1.4754
60 min	0.8310	1.0622	0.5492	1.0950
$p = 10$				
60 sec	1.6182	2.1973	0.0765	0.0514
10 min	1.4778	0.6243	0.9124	0.5372
60 min	1.0580	0.6848	1.3795	0.8603
$p = 20$				
60 sec	0.3008	0.0601	0.2541	2.6377
10 min	0.9812	0.6081	1.5446	1.4462
60 min	1.1616	0.7966	1.3042	1.2351

Table 4. Cluster-2: Granger Causality

Time	Granger: CPU and Memory		Granger: CPU and I/O	
	|cpu-memory|	memory-cpu	||cpu - I/O|I/O	- cpu
$p = 1$				
60 sec	0.2696	0.7267	0.2333	0.4009
10 min	1.0079	2.3926	0.4070	1.1025
60 min	0.8015	1.3143	0.7693	0.9387
$p = 10$				
60 sec	0.7965	0.0346	0.2333	1.4252
10 min	0.6610	0.8483	0.5458	1.0681
60 min	0.8015	1.0465	0.7770	0.8215
$p = 20$				
60 sec	0.0653	2.5657	0.2036	1.8821
10 min	0.9035	1.5681	0.6837	1.1332
60 min	0.8310	1.0750	0.6173	1.0845

7   Conclusion

In this work we provide a more comprehensive look at the issue of investigating performance by using more appropriate statistical tests of comparative predictive ability. Moreover, we compare univariate versus multivariate models to provide evidence based real data experiments. We conclude that, in general multivariate outperform univariate counterparts. However, we cannot just conclude the best multivariate model because as seen from the results, it all depends on the initial condition of each model.

This was not enough, we have applied a granger causality to find out if there is any potential predictability of one indicator for the other, and we conclude that CPU has many chances than other resources, but it cannot always be a definitive conculsion according to the unstable results have been evaluated. Therefore, as multivariate contains more information, it might be reasonable to take advantage of ensemble learning approach and apply it to the best fit models to improve the performance from different groups.

References

1. Liang, J., Nahrstedt, K., Zhou, Y.: Adaptive Multi-Resource Prediction in Distributed Resource Sharing Environment. In: IEEE International Symposium on Cluster Computing and the Grid, pp. 293–300 (2004)
2. Armbrust, M., Fox, A., Griffith, R., Joseph, A.D., Katz, R., Konwinski, A., Lee, G., Patterson, D., Rabkin, A., Stoica, I., Zaharia, M.: A View of Cloud Computing. Communications of the ACM 53(4) (April 2010)
3. Yang, R., Van Der Mei, R.D., Roubos, D., Seinstra, F.J., Bal, H.E.: Resource optimization in distributed real-time multimedia applications. Multimedia Tools and Applications 59(3) (August 2003)
4. Hu, R.D., Jiang, J.F., Liu, G.M., Wang, L.X.: Efficient Resources Provisioning Based on Load Forecasting in Cloud. In: The 10th International Conference on Services Computing (July 2013)
5. Khan, A., Yan, X.F., Tao, S., Anerousis, N.: Workload Characterization and Prediction in the Cloud: A Multiple Time Series Approach. In: Network Operations and Management Symposium (NOMS), pp. 1287–1294 (April 2012)
6. Antonescu, A.F., Braun, T.: Improving Management of Distributed Services Using Correlations and Predictions in SLA-Driven Cloud Computing Systems. In: Conference Proceeding, 14th IEEE/IFIP Network Operations and Management Symposium (NOMS), Krakow, Poland (May 2014)
7. Burdenski, T.: Evaluating Univerariate, Bivariate, and Multivariate Normality Using Graphical and Statistical Procedures. ERIC, 61 (April 2000)
8. Dinda, P.A.: Design, Implementation, and Performance of an Extensible Toolkit for Resource Prediction in Distributed Systems. IEEE Transactions on Parallel and Distributed Systems 17(2) (February 2006)
9. Tan, J., Dube, P., Meng, X.Q., Zhang, L.: Exploiting Resource Usage Patterns for Better Utilization Prediction. In: 31st International Conference on Distributed Computing Systems Workshops, pp. 20–24 (June 2011)
10. Xiao, D.Z., Cao, S., Wong, F.: Optimization of bagging classifiers based on SBCB algorithm. Machine Learning and Cybernetics (ICMLC) 1, 262–267 (2010)
11. Chitra, A., Uma, S.: An Ensemble Model of Multiple Classifiers for Time Series Prediction. International Journal of Computer Theory and Engineering 2(3) (June 2010)
12. He, Q., Zhuang, F.Z., Zhao, X.R., Shi, Z.Z.: Enhanced Algorithm Performance for Classification Based on Hyper Surface using Bagging and Adaboost. Machine Learning and Cybernetics 6, 3624–3629 (2007)
13. Williges, R.C., Willinges, B.H.: Univariate and Multivariate Evaluation of Computer-Based Data Entry. In: Proceedings of the Human Factors and Ergonomics Society Annual Meeting, vol. 25(1), pp. 741–745 (October 1981)
14. Guim, F., Goyeneche, A., Corbalan, J., Labarta, J., Terstyansky, G.: Grid computing performance prediction based in historical information. In: Proceedings of the 7th IEEE/ACM International Conference on Grid Computing (2006)
15. McGovern, A., Rosendahl, D.H., Brown, R.A., Droegemeier, K.K.: Identifying Predictive Multi-dimensional Time Series Motifs: An Application to severe weather prediction. Data Mining and Knowledge Discovery 22(1-2), 232–258 (2011)
16. De Gooijer, J.G., Hyndman, R.J.: 25 Years of Time Series Forecasting. International Journal of Forecasting 22(44:1), 443–473 (2006)
17. Kugiumtzis, D., Bora-Senta, E.: Simulation of Multivariate Non-Gaussian Autoregressive Time Series with Given Autocovariance and Marginals. Similation and Modelling Practice and Theory, Elsevier (March 2014)

18. Lutkepohl, H.: New Introduction to Multiple Time Series Analysis, New York, pp. 13–26, 31-39, 41, 90-100, 102-106. Springer (2006)
19. Ebrahini, N., Hamedani, G., Soofi, E.S., Volkmer, H.: A Class of Models for Uncorrelated Random Variables. Journal of Multivariate Analysis 101(8) (September 2010)
20. Hamilton, J.: Time Series Analysis. Princeton University Press, Princeton (1994)
21. Rehfeld, K., Marwan, N., Heitzig, J., Kurths, J.: Comparison of Correlation Analysis Techniques for Irregularly Sampled Time Series. Nonlinear Processes in Geophusics 18, 389–404 (2011)
22. Kitagawa, G.: Introduction to Time Series Modeling, pp. 8–29. CRC Press, Boca Raton (2010)
23. West, M., Harrison, J.: Bayesian Forecasting and Dynamic Models, 2nd edn. Springer, New York (1997)
24. Grandvalet, Y.: Bagging equalizes influence. Journal of Machine Learning 55(3) (June 2004)
25. Durbin, J., Koopman, S.J.: Time Series Analysis by State Space Methods, vol. 24. Oxford University Press (June 2001)
26. Dietterich, T.G.: Approximation Statistical Tests for Comparing Supervised Classification Learning Algorithms. Neural Computation 10(7), 1895–1923 (2006)
27. Dietterich, T.G.: Ensemble Methods in Machine Learning. In: Kittler, J., Roli, F. (eds.) MCS 2000. LNCS, vol. 1857, pp. 1–15. Springer, Heidelberg (2000)
28. Engle, R.F., Granger, C.W.J.: Cointegration and Error Correction: Representation, Estimation, and Testing. Economica 55(2), 251–276 (1987)
29. Zhidong, B., Wong, W.K., Zhang, B.: Multivariate linear and nonlinear causality tests. Mathematics and Computers in Simulation 81(1), 5–17 (2010)

8 Appendix

Table 5. Cluster-1: VAR(p) model "CPU and Memory usage"

Time	Multivariate		Univariate			
	RMSE	Cov	RMSE		Cov	
	cpu-memory	cpu-memory	cpu	memory	cpu	memory
$p = 1$						
60 sec	**0.9743**	**0.0105**	**0.9631**	**0.9833**	**0.9304**	**0.9718**
10 min	0.9857	-0.3560	0.9756	0.9976	0.9527	0.9983
60 min	**0.9811**	**-0.0169**	**0.9657**	**0.9862**	**0.9441**	**0.9908**
$p = 10$						
60 sec	0.9652	0.0105	0.9631	0.9833	0.9304	0.9718
10 min	0.9767	-0.3560	0.9756	0.9976	0.9527	0.9983
60 min	0.9696	-0.0169	0.9657	0.9862	0.9441	0.9908
$p = 20$						
60 sec	0.9600	0.0105	0.9631	0.9833	0.9304	0.9718
10 min	0.9665	-0.3560	0.9756	0.9976	0.9527	0.9983
60 min	0.9610	-0.0169	0.9657	0.9862	0.9441	0.9908

Table 6. Cluster-2: VAR(p) model "CPU and Memory usage"

Time	Multivariate		Univariate			
	RMSE	Cov		RMSE		Cov
	cpu-memory	cpu-memory	cpu	memory	cpu	memory
$p = 1$						
60 sec	**0.9789**	**0.0167**	**0.9645**	**0.9904**	**0.9426**	**0.9820**
10 min	**0.9924**	**-0.0012**	**0.9601**	**1.0211**	**0.8524**	**0.5819**
60 min	0.9660	0.0530	0.9866	0.9841	0.9743	0.9719
$p = 10$						
60 sec	0.9681	0.0167	0.9645	0.9904	0.9426	0.9820
10 min	0.9857	-0.0012	0.9601	1.0211	0.8524	0.5819
60 min	0.9728	0.0530	0.9866	0.9841	0.9743	0.9719
$p = 20$						
60 sec	0.9561	0.0167	0.9645	0.9904	0.9426	0.9820
10 min	0.9737	-0.0012	0.9601	1.0211	0.8524	0.5819
60 min	0.9660	0.0530	0.9866	0.9841	0.9743	0.9719

Table 7. Cluster-1: VAR(p) model "CPU and I/O"

Time	Multivariate		Univariate			
	RMSE	Cov		RMSE		Cov
	cpu-I/O	cpu-I/O	cpu	I/O	cpu	I/O
$p = 1$						
60 sec	**1.0078**	**0.0032**	**0.9818**	**1.0177**	**0.9649**	**1.0687**
10 min	**1.0147**	**-0.0198**	**0.9955**	**1.0321**	**0.9920**	**1.0680**
60 min	**0.9810**	**-0.0094**	**0.9845**	**0.9770**	**0.9702**	**0.9554**
$p = 10$						
60 sec	0.9951	0.0032	0.9818	1.0177	0.9649	1.0687
10 min	1.0030	-0.0198	0.9955	1.0321	0.9920	1.0680
60 min	0.9690	-0.0094	0.9845	0.9770	0.9702	0.9554
$p = 20$						
60 sec	0.9829	0.0032	0.9818	1.0177	0.9649	1.0687
10 min	0.9897	-0.0198	0.9955	1.0321	0.9920	1.0680
60 min	0.9592	-0.0094	0.9845	0.9770	0.9702	0.9554

Table 8. Cluster-2: VAR(p) model "CPU and I/O"

Time	Multivariate		Univariate			
	RMSE	Cov		RMSE		Cov
	cpu-I/O	cpu-I/O	cpu	I/O	cpu	I/O
$p = 1$						
60 sec	**1.0040**	**-0.0619**	**1.0421**	**0.9597**	**1.0871**	**0.9347**
10 min	**1.0095**	**-0.0365**	**1.0252**	**0.9850**	**1.0521**	**0.9896**
60 min	0.9851	-0.0125	1.0271	0.9456	1.0560	0.8957
$p = 10$						
60 sec	0.9959	-0.0619	1.0421	0.9597	1.0871	0.9347
10 min	1.0040	-0.0365	1.0252	0.9850	1.0521	0.9896
60 min	0.9811	-0.0125	1.0271	0.9456	1.0560	0.8957
$p = 20$						
60 sec	0.9837	-0.0619	1.0421	0.9597	1.0871	0.9347
10 min	0.9878	-0.0365	1.0252	0.9850	1.0521	0.9896
60 min	0.9734	-0.0125	1.0271	0.9456	1.0560	0.8957

Table 9. Cluster-1: DML model "CPU and Memory usage"

Time	Multivariate			Univariate			
	RMSE|	Cov		RMSE		Cov	
	cpu-memory	cpu-memory		cpu	memory	cpu	memory
$p=1$							
60 sec	**1.0432**	**0.0026**		**1.0429**	**0.7815**	**1.0871**	**0.9623**
10 min	0.9931	0.0161		0.9911	0.9965	0.9855	0.9924
60 min	**1.0024**	**0.0273**		**1.0026**	**0.9307**	**1.0046**	**0.8657**

Table 10. Cluster-2: DML model "CPU and Memory usage"

Time	Multivariate			Univariate			
	RMSE|	Cov		RMSE		Cov	
	cpu-memory	cpu-memory		cpu	memory	cpu	memory
$p=1$							
60 sec	0.9780	0.0209		0.9769	1.0066	0.9560	1.0143
10 min	0.9383	0.0357		0.9390	0.9820	0.8809	0.9634
60 min	**1.0126**	-0.0015		**1.0120**	**0.9966**	**1.0243**	**0.9925**

Table 11. Cluster-1: DML model "CPU and I/O"

Time	Multivariate			Univariate			
	RMSE|	Cov		RMSE		Cov	
	cpu-I/O	cpu-I/O		cpu	I/O	cpu	I/O
$p=1$							
60 sec	**1.0412**	**-0.0619**		**1.0429**	**0.9673**	**1.0871**	**0.9347**
10 min	1.0020	-0.0051		1.0018	1.0113	1.0030	1.0220
60 min	0.9770	0.0322		0.9768	1.0290	0.9545	1.0579

Table 12. Cluster-2: DML model "CPU and I/O"

Time	Multivariate			Univariate			
	RMSE|	Cov		RMSE		Cov	
	cpu-I/O	cpu-I/O		cpu	I/O	cpu	I/O
$p=1$							
60 sec	**1.0070**	**0.0299**		**1.0036**	**1.0085**	**1.0139**	**1.0165**
10 min	1.0172	-0.0171		1.0172	1.0266	1.0339	1.0554
60 min	0.9513	0.0076		0.9509	0.9409	1.9042	0.8852

Prediction-Based Optimization
of Live Virtual Machine Migration

Changyuan Chen and Jian Cao[*]

Department of Computer Science and Engineering, Shanghai Jiao Tong University, China
changych@sjtu.edu.cn, cao-jian@cs.sjtu.edu.cn

Abstract. Virtual Machine (VM) migration is an important technology to support Infrastructure as a Service (IaaS). Traditional pre-copy and post-copy strategies could function well in LAN but will need considerable time to migrate between remote hosts in WAN. In this paper, we propose a prediction-based strategy to optimize cloud VM migration process over WAN. In this strategy, information about size increments of snapshots is used to determine appropriate time points for migration in order to reduce the downtime during migration. Specifically, we utilize Markov Chain Model to predict the future increasing speed of snapshots. The experiments on KVM showed our approach could achieve satisfying results.

1   Introduction

Cloud computing helps enterprises take advantage of resources provided by large cloud service vendors. Typically, enterprises need to expand their IT capabilities during workload peaks; meanwhile migrating a VM to a cloud is a cost-efficient choice. As a result, attention is being attracted to live VM migration.

The entire process of VM migration can be divided into three stages: the pre-copy, the down time and the synchronization stage [1]. During the pre-copy stage, a VM keeps running while the modified data is transferred [2]. After that, the VM shuts down and synchronizes the latest data [3]. In post migration, the VM resumes on the destination host before all the modified data is transferred [4]. So data on both sides should be synchronized. The durations of these three periods are important metrics and most of the migration strategies are designed for optimizing these metrics.

There are three classic basic algorithms for VM migration, namely pure stop-copy, pre-copy and post-copy algorithm. Pure stop-copy algorithm is designed to shut down the VM and copy all its state to the destination host [5, 6, 7]. Although pure stop-copy algorithm can minimize the total migration time, it creates long down time. In order to reduce the down time, pre-copy algorithm is widely used. For example, Khaled Z. presents a pre-copy based algorithm on-line (OL) to provide minimal downtime [2]. Post-copy algorithm is another way to reduce the down time during VM migration. Michael designs a post-copy based strategy using adaptive pre-paging across a

---

[*] Corresponding author.

C.-H. Hsu et al. (Eds.): NPC 2014, LNCS 8707, pp. 347–356, 2014.

Gigabit LAN [8]. Pre-copy algorithm and post-copy algorithm could reduce down time, but they both require a high bandwidth environment like LAN.

From the strategies above, we learn that the strategy to reduce the down time during VM migration is a critical issue. Lots of strategies work well in LAN, where the need of high bandwidth is meet. But they could hardly perform well in WAN. In this paper, we propose a prediction-based migration strategy, aiming to minimize the down time during VM migration. The prediction-based strategy could initiatively learn the VM's state and select the optimal points to complete the migration. While a VM running on a host, snapshots are taken and transferred to the destination host iteratively. Every time one snapshot is transferred, we predict an increasing curve of snapshot sizes using Markov Chain. Based on the prediction, we can capture the growth platform, which is the optimal time to finish the whole migration.

The rest of this paper is organized as follows. In the following section, we describe some related work about our problem. Then, we analyze the characteristics of snapshots on KVM platform in Section 3. Section 4 discusses the actual design and implementation of our migration strategy. Section 5 describes the experiments and their results. Finally, we draw some conclusions and describe the future work.

2   Related Work

VM migration technology enables most of the cloud services to work for a surge of customers. Lots of achievements about VM migration have been gained in recent years. XenMotion [9] is the migration module in Xen which adopts a pre-copy algorithm to address the issue, and VMotion [10] developed by VMware also allows a running VM to be moved from one host to another. They both aim at the LAN environment [11]. Especially, Xen implements live migration but it requires shared storage between hosts [12]. But migration in LAN can no longer meet the demand, so in this paper we propose a VM migration strategy which is adapted for WAN.

Liu proposed a novel approach to provide fast, transparent VM migration for both LAN and WAN environments, which is called CR/TR-Motion[11]. Liu's experiments demonstrated that CR/TR-Motion works well in LAN environment, but its performance in WAN is unsatisfactory. Timothy presented architecture, namely CloudNet, as a cloud framework with a VPN based network infrastructure to provide VM migration in WAN [13]. He optimizes the cost for transferring storage and VM memory in WAN environment, but CloudNet he implemented is built on the base of VPN. As is known, most VM migrations work in the general Internet environment, and we can hardly transfer data through VPN. On contrary, the VM migration strategy we propose is suitable for the general Internet environment. In our strategy, we make use of the incremental characteristic of snapshots and use pre-copy mechanism to reduce the down time during migration. In order to get the minimum snapshot increment during migration, we propose a prediction-based strategy using Markov chain as a theoretical basis. VM snapshot is a collection of all the states of the VM, including storage data, memory pages and CPU states. So we propose a prediction strategy to forecast the growth trends of VM snapshots, which will help to optimize the down time during migration.

3   Prediction-Based Model

In this section we describe our prediction-based model, which will smooth the way to our migration strategy. Two core aspects will be presented in the following sub-sections: snapshot size growth and the prediction model.

3.1   The Growth of the Size of a Snapshot

VM snapshots are files containing storage data, memory pages and CPU states at some time. A traditional snapshot at time t is defined as $SN_t = U\,M\,U$, where   represents the storage data, M represents the memory pages and   represents the CPU state. An incremental snapshot means the differences between the current and the former ones. So an incremental snapshot created at time t_i is defined as $sn_{t_i} = SN_{t_i} - SN_{t_{i-1}}$, and all the states of a VM at time t_i is $SN_{t_n} = U_{t_0}^{t_n} sn_{t_i}$.

3.2   The Prediction Model for Snapshot Size Growth

The growth of the size of a snapshot can be modeled as a time series and we try to find a prediction model to predict its future trend. We adopt Markov Chain as the prediction model.

Markov Chain and Transition Matrix. A Markov Chain is a mathematical system that undergoes transitions from one state to another on a state space [15]. It is a random process that the next state depends on the current one. The growth curve of snapshot size is a time series with some regular characteristic (Fig. 1 to Fig. 4).

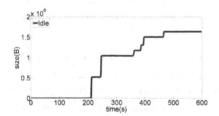

Fig. 1. No extra program on VM

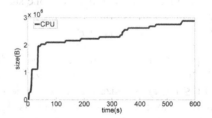

Fig. 2. CPU intensive program on VM

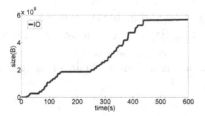

Fig. 3. IO intensive program on VM

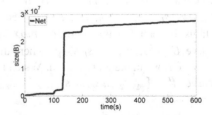

Fig. 4. Network intensive program on VM

In order to analyze and forecast the increasing curve, we set an *n-sized* window to capture the continuous discrete states of *n* as a status (Fig. 5). Each state in an *n-sized* window represents a size of an incremental snapshot in a time slot, and the *n* states compose a status, which is the base unit in our model. Optimal value of *n* depends on the learning data and the migration platform. The optimal value we set in experiments will be detailed in the evaluation section.

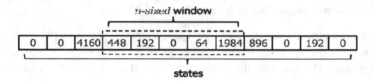

Fig. 5. N-sized window

Step 1. We extract patterns using *n-sized* window and build transition matrix using Markov Chain. Patterns are some typical snapshots growth sub-sequences, each of which represents a cluster of original growth curves. We extract the patterns from the historical data using a pattern fusion model which is based on Euclidean distance [14]. Then we make up the pattern set, $\square = \{P_1, P_2, \ldots \ldots, P_N\}$, where N is the number of patterns. We define pattern $P_i = \{s_1, s_2, \ldots \ldots, s_n\}$, in which s_i is a single state representing the size of an incremental snapshot. The length of pattern P_i is determined by the size of the window. The transition matrix is defined as

$M = \begin{pmatrix} p_{11} & \cdots & p_{1N} \\ \vdots & \ddots & \vdots \\ p_{N1} & \cdots & p_{NN} \end{pmatrix}$, which stores all the transition probabilities. In the matrix, the

rows $R = \{R_1, R_2, \ldots \ldots, R_N\}$ represent the current statuses while the columns $C = \{C_1, C_2, \ldots \ldots, C_N\}$ represent the following one. So each value in the transition matrix means a probability from one status to the successor. For instance, the i_{th} row in the transition matrix is $R_i = \{p_{i1}, p_{i2}, p_{i3}, \ldots \ldots, p_{iN}\}$, where $p_{ij} = Probability: P_i \rightarrow P_j$.

Step 2. In this step we formalize the prediction process based on the transition matrix M. The growth of the snapshot size can be represented as $L = \{s_1, s_2, \ldots \ldots, s_l\}$, each $s_i (1 \leq i \leq l)$ is a size increment while the curve L represents the snapshot growing from t_1 to t_l. The latest status is $S_i = \{s_{l-n+1}, s_{l-n+2}, \ldots \ldots, s_{l-1}, s_l\}$. The best matched pattern P_{best} will be found according to S_i, where P_{best} is a pattern P_j that meets such condition $min_{1 \leq j \leq N}\{Dist(S_i, P_j)\}$. Here, we use Euclidean distance to calculate $Dist(S_i, P_j)$. Then we will forecast the next status $S_{i+1} = \{s_{l-n+2}, s_{l-n+3}, \ldots \ldots, s_l, s_{l+1}\}$ according to P_{best} (Fig. 6). The status S_{i+1} is a status that satisfies the condition $max_{1 \leq j \leq N}\{M[P_{best}][S_j]\}$. After that we get the new curve $L' = \{s_1, s_2, \ldots \ldots s_l, s_{l+1}\}$, where the state s_{l+1} is what we predict.

So far, we make a prediction. We can repeat the predictions to obtain a long future curve $L'' = \{s_1, s_2, \ldots \ldots, s_l, s_{l+1}, \ldots \ldots, s_m, s_{m+1} \ldots \ldots\}$.

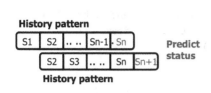

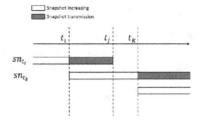

Fig. 6. Iterative prediction process   Fig. 7. Part of migration process

We find the curve sometimes go steep and sometimes go slow, so we could perform the last transmission during slow segment. Therefore, we need to identify these segments, which we call them growth platforms. We define $d_{ij} = \sum_i^j s_k \ (i \le k \le j)$, meaning the whole size increment from time i to j. Given a length of period m and a curve L'' with length n, a segment L_{ij} that meets the condition $min\{d_{ij}, (j - i = m, 1 \le i, j \le n)\}$ is the growth platform L^* of L''.

4   Prediction-Based Migration Strategy

During migration the efficiency depends on the snapshots' sizes with a given bandwidth. We define an increasing curve of a snapshot as $L = \{s_{t_0}, s_{t_1}, \dots \dots, s_{t_n}\}$, which represents the growing size of a snapshot. The element s_{t_i} in L is the size of sn_{t_i}: an incremental snapshot at t_i. Part of the migration is as follows (Fig. 7).

We consider the process starts at time t_i with sn_{t_i} and a given stable bandwidth . Snapshot sn_{t_i} is created at t_i. Let $\Delta t = \frac{s_{t_i}}{}$ and $t_j = t_i + \Delta t$, snapshot sn_{t_i} starts being transmitted at t_i and completes at t_j. At the same time, the VM keeps running. Thus, at time t_k $(j \le k)$, the next snapshot sn_{t_k} will be transmitted. And so forth, snapshots are transmitted to the destination host until the VM shuts down.

4.1   Feedback-Based Migration Strategy

Based on the prediction model described above, we propose a VM migration strategy: feedback based migration (FM) strategy. It is mainly composed of four steps. First, to transmit the base image and forecast a snapshot increasing curve using the prediction model. Second, to capture the time when the incremental snapshot is the smallest. Third, to adjust the predicted curve according to real-time feedback. Finally, to shut down the VM and synchronize the status when it reaches the time we predicted.

Predicting snapshot increasing curve is described in section 3, this section would describe the snapshots transmission process. Given a snapshot size growth curve and a bandwidth, a period that the smallest incremental snapshot is generated could be captured using depth-first search and greedy algorithm, which is described here.

Algorithm 1. Feedback-based migration algorithm

```
Input : a snapshot size growth curve p_list and a base_size
Output : finish_t, the proper point to shut down the VM
FindFinishTime (p_list, base_size)
begin
  min_size = MAX   finish_t = 0
  DFFind(p_list, base_size, 0)
  return finish_t
end

  DFFind (p_list, base_size, start_t)
begin
  if(base_size == 0)
    min_size = 0   tf = start_t
    return
  current_size = base_size
  while current_size not reach finish time
    update next_t and next_size
    DFFind(p_list, sub_size, start_t + next_t)
    if(min_size > next_size)
      min_size = next_size   finish_t = start_t + next_t
end
```

The algorithm FindFinishTime (FFT) would find the finish time of the migration with $O(n^2)$ time. Every time an incremental snapshot is transmitted, a predicted curve and a real-time would be compared. If the two curves match, the migration will work as predicted. Otherwise, a new predicted curve would be made and another finish time would be calculated. FM strategy works efficiently if the prediction is accurate. But when the predicted curve deviates from the actual curve, the finish time should be calculated every time a snapshot is transmitted. Thus, the efficiency would be lower. And an enhanced strategy is proposed below.

4.2   Adjustment-Based Migration Strategy

We enhance the former strategy by adding the adjustment factors during prediction and propose another strategy: adjustment based prediction (AM) strategy.

Every time we make prediction, the times of continuously repeated patterns is recorded. Once the time exceeds the threshold (one single pattern repeats for more than m times, which will be detailed in evaluation), we get the second popular status as the next status instead of the most popular one. The complexity of the algorithm is $O(n^2)$, and the length of the increasing curve is n. The algorithm improves the prediction efficiency, and the transmission is the same as FM strategy.

Algorithm 2. Adjustment-based migration algorithm

```
Input : markov_matrix, a base_size
Output : p_list, the predicted curve
Predict(markov_matrix, base_size)
begin
  current_size = base_size  p_list = null  pattern_time = 0
  build history_list from current
  while not reach finish time
    pattern = getPattern(history_list)
    if pattern_time > threshold
      pattern = getFollowPattern(history_list)
    next_status = predictNextStatus(markov_matrix)
    update p_list and history_list
    if pattern equals next_pattern
      pattern_time ++
    pattern = next_pattern
  return p_list
end
```

5   Experiments

In this section, we present an evaluation of our prediction-based migration. The experimental platform we used is built between SJTU, China and UFL, USA. We use KVM as the virtualization layer and lib-virt as the control layer.

We extract a pattern set through learning from history data. In Section 3, we know that the length of a pattern will affect the migration. In Fig. 8, we choose different lengths of patterns to compare the prediction accuracy and the efficiency. Finally, we select 50 as the pattern length according to our experiment.

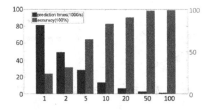

Fig. 8. Pattern length experiment

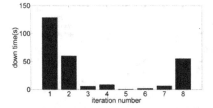

Fig. 9. Down time on iteration number

Considering migration over WAN, the strategy pure stop-copy (PSC) and the strategy fixed number iterations (FNI) are suitable. We find that the PSC strategy can minimize the whole migration time while its down time is long. The FNI strategy can reduce the down time, but it depends on the iteration numbers (Fig. 9).

The FNI strategy cannot detect the size of snapshot automatically. Fig. 9 reveals that snapshots become smallest during the 5th iteration. The FNI strategy cannot minimize the down time, since the iterations number is fixed. Compared with PSC and FNI strategies, FM and AM strategies can minimize the down time. We evaluate the performance of FM and AM strategies, compared with PSC and FNI strategies. In Fig. 10 to Fig. 13, we analyze the performance with different types of snapshots.

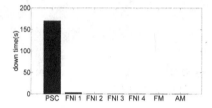

Fig. 10. Result on CPU intensive program

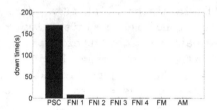

Fig. 11. Result on memory intensive program

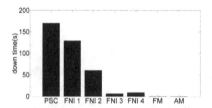

Fig. 12. Result on network intensive program

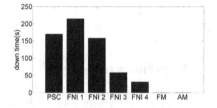

Fig. 13. Result on IO intensive program

From the figures above, we know that the network and IO intensive snapshots reflect the real performance about our strategy. What's more, we consider the size of the base image as a factor in our evaluation. In Fig. 14 and Fig. 15, we give a performance comparison using FM and AM strategies with PSC and FNI strategies.

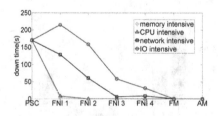

Fig. 14. Down time with 500M base image

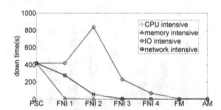

Fig. 15. Down time with 1G base image

VMs in evaluation run different programs, including CPU intensive, memory intensive, network intensive and IO intensive programs. In addition, two sizes of base image are considered. In evaluation, four migration strategies are taken, and the migration iterations from 1 to 4 are selected in FNI strategy. PSC strategy always produces a constant down time and the down time varies for FNI strategy. We can see that FM and AM work well and stably in all cases with almost zero down time.

As mentioned above, FM strategy is less efficient than AM strategy whenever the predicted curve deviates from the actual curve. AM strategy could adjust the predicted result so that the predicted curve matches the actual curve better. Here, we set m=5 as the threshold to avoid patterns repetition considering the snapshots size and bandwidth in our evaluation platform. The prediction times of AM strategy is fewer, and the effective prediction ratio is higher. Effective Prediction Ratio is defined as EPR = $N_{correct}/N_{total}$, where $N_{correct}$ is the times of correct prediction and N_{total} is the times of total prediction. In fig.16, it is indicated that the EPR of AM strategy is higher in different types of VMs and it is 21.1% higher than FM strategy overall.

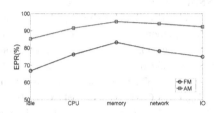

Fig. 16. EPR comparison between FM and AM strategies

6   Conclusion and Future Work

In this paper, for optimizing VM migration over WAN, we propose a prediction-based strategy which can forecast the increasing curve of snapshots about VMs. Our main contribution is to predict the increments of VM snapshot and select the proper segment to shut down the VM which minimizes the VM down time. Compared with two migration strategies, the evaluation shows that our PB strategy works well and stably during migration, which minimizes the down time among all the strategies.

In the future, there are two parts of work we can focus on. First, more migration metrics can be considered like the whole migration time and the bandwidth limitation. Second, we could split the snapshot finer, such as dirty page in memory and storage.

Acknowledgement. This work is partially supported by China National Science Foundation (Granted Number 61073021, 61272438), Research Funds of Science and Technology Commission of Shanghai Municipality (Granted Number 14511107702, 12511502704).

References

1. Clark, C., Fraser, K., Hand, S., Hansen, J.G., Jul, E., Limpach, C., Pratt, I., Warfield, A.: Live Migration of Virtual Machines. In: NSDI 2005 (2005)
2. Ibrahim, K.Z., Hofmeyr, S.A., Iancu, C., Roman, E.: Optimized pre-copy live migration for memory intensive applications. In: SC 2011, p. 40 (2011)

3. Ma, F., Liu, F., Liu, Z.: Live virtual machine migration based on improved pre-copy approach. In: ICSESS 2010, pp. 230–233 (2010)
4. Hines, M.R., Deshpande, U., Gopalan, K.: Post-copy live migration of virtual machines. Operating Systems Review 43(3), 14–26 (2009)
5. Kozuch, M., Satyanarayanan, M.: Internet suspend/resume. In: Proc. IEEE Workshop on Mobile Computing Systems and Applications, Washington, DC, USA, pp. 40–46 (2002)
6. Sapuntzakis, C.P., Chandra, R., Pfaff, B., Chow, J., Lam, M.S.: Optimizing the migration of virtual computers. ACM SIGOPS OSDI 2002, 377–390 (2002)
7. Whitaker, A., Cox, R.S., Shaw, M., Gribble, S.D.: Constructing Services with Interposable Virtual Hardware. In: NSDI 2004, pp. 169–182 (2004)
8. Hines, M.R., Gopalan, K.: Post-copy based live virtual machine migration using adaptive pre-paging and dynamic self-ballooning. In: VEE 2009, pp. 51–60 (2009)
9. Nelson, M., Lim, B.H., Hutchins, G.: Fast Transparent Migration for Virtual Machines. In: Proc. USENIX Ann. Technical Conf., pp. 391–394 (April 2005)
10. Nelson, M., Lim, B.H., Hutchins, G.: Fast Transparent Migration for Virtual Machines. In: Proc. USENIX Ann. Technical Conf., pp. 391–394 (April 2005)
11. Liu, H., Jin, H., Liao, X.: Live Virtual Machine Migration via Asynchronous Replication and State Synchronization. IEEE Trans. Parallel Distrib. Syst. 22(12), 1986–1999 (2011)
12. Williams, D., Jamjoom, H., Weatherspoon, H.: The Xen-Blanket: virtualize once, run everywhere. In: EuroSys 2012, pp. 113–126 (2012)
13. Wood, T., Ramakrishnan, Prashant, K.K., Shenoy, J.: CloudNet: dynamic pooling of cloud resources by live WAN migration of virtual machines. In: VEE 2011, pp. 121–132 (2011)
14. Yang, D., Cao, J., Fu, J.: A pattern fusion model for multi-step-ahead CPU load prediction. Journal of Systems and Software 86(5), 1257–1266 (2013)
15. Geyer, C.J.: Practical markov chain monte carlo. Statistical Science, 473–483 (1992)

Control Protocol and Self-adaptive Mechanism for Live Virtual Machine Migration over XIA*

Dalu Zhang**, Xiang Jin, Dejiang Zhou, Jianpeng Wang, and Jiaqi Zhu

Department of Computer Science and Technology, Tongji University,
Shanghai, China
daluz@acm.org,
{jinxiang8910,dejiang_zhou,wangjianpeng4321,garyzjq}@163.com

Abstract. FIA (Future Internet Architecture) is supported by US NSF
for future Internet designing. XIA is one of the projects which comply
with clean slate concept thoroughly. Meanwhile, virtual machine migration technique is crucial in cloud computing. As a network application,
VM migration should also be supported in XIA. This paper is an experimental study aims at verifying the feasibility of VM migration over XIA.
We primarily present intra-AD (Administrative Domain) and inter-AD
VM migration with KVM instances. The procedure is achieved by a migration control protocol which is suitable for the characters of XIA architecture. Moreover, an elementary self-adaptive mechanism is introduced
to maintain VM connectivity and connection states. It is also beneficial
for VM migration in TCP/IP network. Evaluation results show that our
solution well supports live VM migration in XIA and all the communications leading to VM can be kept uninterrupted after migration.

1 Introduction

For decades, Internet has become one of the most useful tools in our daily life.
It achieved great flourish because of large quantity of applications and various
kinds of media. However, TCP/IP network at present is suffering from serious
issues such as difficulties on scalability, mobility and security problems. This
leads to the emergence and development of future network.

XIA is one of the FIA projects supported by US NSF in 2010. It is also one
of the FIA-NP (Next Phase) projects announced in May 2014. XIA [1] aims
at getting rid of TCP/IP concepts. Network, host, service and content can be
abstracted as *principals*. New principal types can be defined for special use, even
if they have not been natively supported [2]. Network address is replaced by
DAG (Directed Acyclic Graph), which is flexible for addressing. In addition,
fallback allows communicating entities to choose an alternative action if intent
node is unreachable. Addresses are managed by name service, which provides a
mapping converting human-readable names to DAGs.

---

* Supported by the NSF of China (No. 61073154).
** Corresponding author.

C.-H. Hsu et al. (Eds.): NPC 2014, LNCS 8707, pp. 357–368, 2014.
© IFIP International Federation for Information Processing 2014

Virtualization is necessarily a key technology in cloud computing, which allows to run multiple operating systems on a single platform, utilizing host's expensive resources independently, such as CPU cycles and memory space. Data centers can achieve load balancing, host maintenance, energy management or disaster recovery [3] by VM migration.

Extensive research has been carried out on VMs with shared-storage [4], but shared-storage VMs cannot be applied in all scenarios [5]. For example, a user may not necessarily have access to a particular data center permanently. If a shared virtual disk is allocated through network, abnormal latency would occur. Thus, we prefer full VM migration, during which virtual disk is transferred as well as memory and CPU information. We choose KVM since block (storage) migration is intrinsically supported. KVM is a full virtualization solution frequently used in research area. KVM module is integrated in the kernel of common Linux distributions. However, direct kernel modules access is not permitted for users. This issue can be solved by QEMU which is also a piece of open-source virtualization software and is adopted as a management tool in user space.

In this paper, we first design VM migration platform in two different situations, in a single AD and between ADs. Since VM migration in XIA network is quite different to that in TCP/IP network, we adopt VM migration control protocol to manage migration procedure. Moreover, a current-network based self-adaptive mechanism is introduced to keep up all the connections leading to VM. We can achieve VM migration over XIA with the control protocol and self-adaptive mechanism. The experimental results demonstrate that VMs can get migrated with downtime no longer than 2s for full migration over XIA network.

Virtualization is necessary to maintain unified management for various cloud computing platforms, even in future data centers. It is also beneficial to keep user diversity and application isolation. Therefore, virtual machine will be in existence for a long period of time in the future. As a typical application in future networks, it should also be well supported in XIA. Base on the research about VM migration over traditional TCP/IP network, we try to study VM migration techniques in future Internet. On the one hand, it can test whether VM migration is supported in XIA. On the other hand, in comparison with the technologies used for VM migration in TCP/IP network, it is beneficial to perfect the design of future networks.

The rest of this paper is organized as follows: In Sect. 2 we discuss related work. In Sect. 3, we introduce the VM migration system design and migration modules processing migration. After that, we demonstrate the control protocol and self-adaptive mechanism to achieve VM migration in Sect. 4. Sect. 5 further discusses the experimental results. Some special issues and future works are discussed in Sect. 6 and Sect. 7 concludes this paper.

2   Related Work

Most of recent researches on VM migration are dedicated in studying the mechanisms of VM migration and factors that trigger it. In general, VM migration method can be mainly classified as pre-copy [6], post-copy [7]. There are also some optimizations based on pre-copy algorithms, such as transferring bitmaps[8] or log file [9] of dirty pages, or delivering "hot pages" in final round [10] to minimize the number of pages being transferred.

In TCP/IP network, an important issue is to get the migrated VM noticed by all the network elements after migration. It can be achieved by generating an unsolicited ARP reply on destination host, advertising location change of VM. But the fact is that this method may not be effective in all scenarios. If source host and destination host are in different subnets, some hosts or routers would not receive the ARP messages broadcasted by the migrated VM because of network isolation.

In order to solve the problem, lots of researches has been carried out, which can be classified into two categories. One is based on the concept of mobile IP. Article [11] presented to build a tunnel between original address and the new address so as to keep all the communications that have been set up before. In addition, dynamic DNS is utilized to record address update, so clients can connect to VM by obtaining the new address after VM migration. Network agents [12] are presented to be set in both source and destination subnet with ARP agents maintained on. The ARP agent in source subnet will broadcast ARP messages to advertise the information of VM's new location. But the limitation is that clients should locate in source subnet, otherwise, they cannot receive the ARP messages. Mobile IPv6 is introduced in [13], one of the benefits is that hosts supporting Mobile IPv6 can bypass the tunnel and connect to the VM through route optimization mode.

The other method depends on overlay network. In [14], source and destination network of VM migration procedure are repartitioned into the same VPN. ARP message can be forwarded at VPN level to update Ethernet switch mappings at both sites. This will help to redirect network traffic to VM's new location. In ViNe [15], hosts can be addressed by virtual network addresses first. Overlay network methods require to build virtual network before migration occurs, while in fact VM migration is triggered by some particular factors, virtual networks should be reorganized for migration each time since the source and destination network may not be constant.

We seldom find research about VM migration technologies over future Internet architectures. Therefore, it is contributory for us to conduct virtual machine migration research on XIA. It is contributive for the design of future networks.

3   System Design

3.1   Testbed Design

Our research goal can be summarized as four rules which we name as *"four any"*, that is, VMs can be deployed on any physical host and be migrated to any one, name service can run on any host in the network and any of the applications should not be interrupted during VM migration.

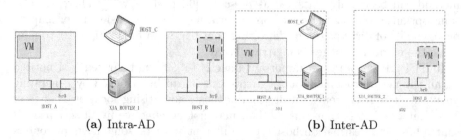

(a) Intra-AD   (b) Inter-AD

Fig. 1. VM migration testbed design in XIA network, (a) is the testbed in single AD and (b) is a typical testbed for VM migration between different ADs

The XIA prototype is developed base on software router click[16]. Common routers in TCP/IP network can't be recognized in XIA because of the differences in protocol formats. As a solution, XIA routers are realized by physical machines with two or more NICs. Name service is necessary for host address query in XIA. Any host can run as name server and provide global name resolution service. When the addresses of hosts or services are changed, they should be registered to name server.

AD is introduced in XIA to partition the network. It is convenient for network management. A VM in different AD will obtain different addresses as the AD number is changed. Therefore, inter-AD VM migration is more complex than that in a single AD. We propose two VM migration testbeds, in single AD and between ADs, concerning the issue of whether DAG has to be changed. Fig. 1a shows the testbed of VM migration in single AD. HOST_A, HOST_B and HOST_C represent the source host, destination host and client host respectively. HOST_VM depicted in dashed box denotes the virtual machine to be migrated. Name service runs on HOST_A because it can be put on any hosts. ROUTER_1 indicates a XIA router, routing and forwarding packets. In Fig. 1b, the topological structure is partitioned into two independent ADs and each XIA router manages its AD respectively. Name service still runs on HOST_A. All the hosts or services can register their DAG-style addresses to name service.

3.2 Migration Control Modules

We attempt to conduct VM migration in XIA network with now available virtualization product KVM and take the advantages of CHUNK provided in XIA for data delivery. The whole structure of VM migration consists of three modules and their relationship are shown in Fig. 2.

Migration Data Sending and Receiving. There are four migration modes in KVM. Among them, *tcp* mode is primarily used for VM migration in TCP/IP network by default. In *exec* mode, migration data are read and sent to standard I/O by the sender, while on the receiver side KVM hypervisor obtains data from

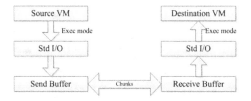

Fig. 2. Data flow between different modules for exec mode VM migration

standard I/O and then reload VM, no matter how data are transferred. *Tcp* mode cannot be adopted here since TCP connection is not supported in XIA. We choose to get KVM migration run in *exec* mode.

Migration Data Transfer. Three data transmission methods are provided in XIA, namely STREAM, DGRAM and CHUNK. STREAM is connection oriented and provides reliable transmission, just as TCP in TCP/IP protocol stack. Correspondingly, DGRAM is connectionless like UDP. Concept of CHUNK is widely used in content-centric future Internet architectures, especially XIA and NDN. All the data should be divided into chunks when transmitting in CHUNK mode. CID of a chunk is obtained by hash of the whole content block, so it can get self-verified. Network traffic is well controlled because each transaction is originated by the receiver and the sender just need to put the data that are required into content cache.

CHUNK mode is quite reliable because of its error control and intrinsic traffic control mechanisms though it is connectionless. We employ it as a transmission method for VM migration in XIA. When migration data are sent to standard I/O, migration sending process acquires and delivers them to the destination host. Meanwhile, receiving process accepts the chunks and writes them into standard I/O. The details of chunk mode data transmission procedure and the control protocol for its management will be introduced in Sect. 4.1.

Migration Test and Verify. In order to test whether VM migration procedure is live or not, we propose to run some applications in VM. Since traditional applications cannot work efficiently in XIA network environment, a calculation application (expressed as Cal in the context) is introduced, which is developed with APIs provided in XIA. A calculation server daemon runs in VM, calculating and verifying *Goldbach conjecture* (every even number can be expressed as a sum of two prime numbers). A client process runs on client host (HOST_C in Fig. 1), acquiring answers from server and printing them onto screen.

We propose to use *Xping* provided in XIA prototype as a way for downtime evaluation. For example, if time interval of Xping packets is set as Δt and n packets are dropped during downtime, we can get informed that downtime measured is $(n \pm 1) * \Delta t$, that means the downtime is $n * \Delta t$ with deviation of Δt. This is quite accurate if value Δt is small enough.

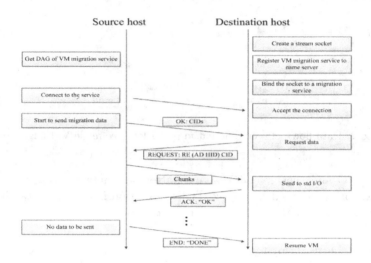

Fig. 3. Detailed working process of VM migration control protocol

4   Control Protocol and Self-adaptive Mechanism

We present a migration control protocol to manage the VM migration procedure in XIA. Since keeping the migrated VM accessible is significant, we introduce the self-adaptive mechanism for network work recovery after VM migration.

4.1   VM Migration Control Protocol

Fig. 3 shows the process of data transmission. Control messages are delivered by STREAM because it is simple and reliable. The destination site starts a stream socket first and binds it to a migration service. The socket is in listening state, waiting for connection of migration data sender host. After connection is set up, the source host (sender) will notify the destination host (receiver) of CIDs of the chunks that needed to be delivered. The destination host will construct messages to request for these chunks. The receiver then acknowledges for this round of transmission if the data are check to be correct and the sender continues its data transmission procedure till nothing to be delivered. If the data sender is sure of the end of migration, a "DONE" message will be sent out to announce the termination of VM migration.

4.2   Self-adaptive Mechanism

In implementation of VM migration in WAN of TCP/IP network, VM will get unreachable after being migrated to destination subnet. There are mainly three challenges. Firstly, the IP address obtained before migration belongs to the source subnet and it can't be recognized in new subnet, even the destination

Fig. 4. An simple example of XIA address expressed in the DAG form (*src* indicates a virtual source of DAG. *AD* is a 160-bits number identifying an AD. Similarly, *HID* and *SID* are 160-bits identifiers presenting a host or a service).

host which the VM lies on is not aware of the existence of VM. Secondly, if a new address is acquired, e.g. by DHCP, it is also difficult to get the new address information propagated to the whole Internet. Thirdly, all the communications related to the migrated VM should be recovered and the communications set up afterward must be routed to the right location.

Therefore, we present self-adaptive mechanism after VM is resumed on destination host. In order to solve the above-mentioned problems, self-adaptive procedure mainly focuses on three aspects, namely VM mobility perception, new location notification and traffic redirection.

Migration Perception. One basic precondition for VM migration accomplishment and traffic recovery is that migration of VM should be detected as soon as possible. A general solution is to intercept and capture signals from the hypervisor when particular event occurs. In XIA network, this goal can be achieved conveniently. XIA gateway router inside an AD broadcast beacons periodically which contain identifiers of the AD and router. Any host that receive the broadcast packets can easily determine which AD they belong to at present.

New Location Notification. Addresses in XIA are expressed by DAG and a simple form is depicted in Fig. 4. This structure is constructed with all kinds of IDs that are necessary, so it is convenient for re-construction. AD should be changed when a VM is migrated to a new AD, and a new DAG form address should be re-registered to name service as soon as VM migration is detected. Additionally, since a router is to manage the AD it locates in, the VM should also make itself noticed by the gateway router in the destination AD and the router will append its routing table with an entry directing to the VM.

Traffic Redirection. Network traffic related to VM should be resumed after it is migrated to destination host. Most of the researches that studying live VM migration in WAN adopt agents on source host and tunnels between agent and VM. Neither is needed when it comes to XIA because of its particular characteristics. Information contained in either source or destination address field of XIP layer header is not yet IP, but DAG instead. *Lastnode* field stores an identifier that indicates the node which is last processed by router. When a router receives a packet, it first checks *Lastnode* field and then processes the nodes afterward. Thus, a packet is routed and forwarded based on the information of a particular node in DAG, not DAG as a whole.

According to the analysis, we can take some modifications to the routing tables of routers on the migration path. In this way, packets forwarding to VM are still able to be delivered correctly according to "HID" routing entries, even though "AD" information is changed. We just have to change the *next-hop* field of VM's HID entry to make the path directing to the new location. If a router in source AD receives a packet with VM's obsolete DAG as destination address, it will direct the packet to next hop router which is nearer to destination host. For example, if ROUTER_1 in Fig. 1 receives a packet with VM's original DAG, this packet should be routed to ROUTER_2 according to the routing table that has been modified and finally it will arrive at VM because ROUTER_2 knows the location of VM exactly.

The rules of routing table in XIA also bring some troubles. When a VM is running on source host, a HID entry is added into it with the host's HID as destination and next hop address. Similarly, there is also an entry pointing to VM's HID in source host's routing table. This will lead to trouble as both of these entries can't get modified automatically and packets will be routed incorrectly when VM is migrated. Therefore, these two entries should be deleted in order to keep connectivity between source host and VM.

5   Implementation and Evaluation

We carry out VM migration over XIA network with the testbeds depicted in Section 3. With the evaluation results, we can easily get to know the deficiencies of our design and get improvement in next phase. We do not focus on iteration phases during migration or factors that trigger migration. Therefore, we don't need to take any modifications to QEMU-KVM. This is beneficial to make the current virtualization products flourish in the future when future networks such as XIA takes the place of TCP/IP. VM is configured with 4GB virtual disk and 640MB physical memory for full migration. The size is necessary for installation of XIA software. Hosts are configured with Intel core I3 processor and 8GB RAM. Computers with multiple network interface cards are used as XIA routers. All the physical hosts and VM are running Ubuntu 12.04 with kernel 3.5.0. Source code of XIA prototype v1.1 is obtained from Github.

5.1   Comparison of Migration Modes

First of all, it is necessary to compare migration performance in *tcp* and *exec* modes so as to get the differences between them. We implement *exec* mode data transmission by using SOCK_STREAM sockets in TCP/IP network, comparing to the default *tcp* method. Two kinds of workload along with calculation application we developed are introduced, which are widely used in network research areas.

Dbench: an open source benchmark tool to generate I/O workloads, simulating a variety of real file servers. We choose it as an I/O intensive application.

Netperf: a benchmark that can be used to measure the performance of many different types of networks. Here we run it as a workload inside VM and it does not communicate with clients because of limitations of protocol stack.

Fig. 5 shows the total migration time and downtime of VM migration in two modes with different VM workload. We can get concluded from comparison that total migration time and downtime will increase obviously if we use *exec* mode for migration with same workload, especially downtime. As a self-defined transmission method, the throughput of *exec* mode transmission is slightly lower than that of *tcp*. Thus, migration method selection affects the performance and we will complete *exec* mode VM migration over XIA for a comparison to that over TCP/IP network.

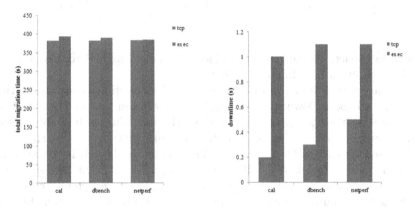

Fig. 5. Total migration time and downtime of two migration mode (*tcp* and *exec*)

5.2 Connectivity Test

We test VM migration in exec mode over both TCP/IP and XIA networks. Processing programs is required for data sending and receiving with sockets provided in TCP/IP and XIA networks respectively. A calculation service always runs in the VM for connectivity test. We just take one application as an example because VM will be unreachable in WAN as a matter of experience, no matter which kind of workload it takes along.

First of all, the service runs in VM never get interrupted during the migration procedure. Xping drops several packets during downtime but recovers soon after VM's resuming on destination host. Both connection-oriented and connection-less services will not be interrupted during VM migration, even without agents or tunnels used for network recovery in WAN of TCP/IP network.

Total migration time and downtime of above experiments are demonstrated in Table 1. We can conclude that full VM migration in LAN of TCP/IP network takes the least total migration time and downtime. When it comes to WAN, the VM and its services are all inaccessible after it has been migrated to the

Table 1. Performance of VM migration in different networks

	Intra-AD		Inter-AD	
	total time	downtime	total time	downtime
TCP/IP	6.5 min	1 s	-	-
XIA	14 min	1.2 s	15 min	1.2 s

Table 2. Migration performance in XIA network with different workload

	Intra-AD		Inter-AD	
	total time	downtime	total time	downtime
Calculation	14 min	1.2 s	15 min	1.2 s
Dbench	12 min	1.0 s	13 min	1.5 s
Netperf	12 min	1.7 s	14 min	1.7 s

destination subnet. The migrated VM has kept the original IP address and this can't be recognized in a different subnet.

In XIA network, VM migration can be achieved successfully though the performance isn't so good. Downtime is about 0.2s longer than that in TCP/IP while total migration time is about twice longer. The long time is probably caused by chunk cache mechanism in XIA routers. Chunks that are passing through a router would be cached for future use. The router will search its cache when a chunk request comes and it will deliver this chunk to client if found, or it will continues to forward this request. Thus the time cost for chunk search will sharply increase chunk transmission time. It can also reduce network throughput to some extent. Lots of effort has to be made for performance optimization in XIA. We have made some modifications to the cache algorithms, that is, to release the first chunk in the cache when extra space is required, which reduces total migration time and downtime sharply.

5.3   Workload Test

We evaluate VM migration performance in XIA with different workloads, representing typical server applications in today's data centers. Experimental results are shown in Table 2.

Calculation is CPU-intensive and network-intensive because it calculates results and delivers the data rapidly. Both *netperf* and *dbench* can be regarded as I/O intensive. We can see in Fig. 6 that total migration time varies little between the migrations in intra-AD and inter-AD. In contrast, migration of VM with *dbench* has the largest downtime variation. Among the applications listed, VM running *netperf* and *dbench* suffers longer downtime while the calculation application has longer total time. We can draw a conclusion that network intensive services will suffer longer total migration time, while downtime is longer for I/O intensive services.

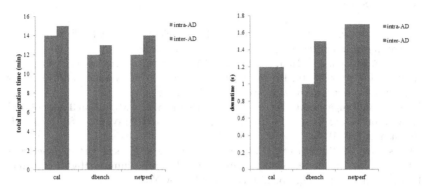

Fig. 6. Total migration time and downtime of VM migration in XIA network with different workload test

6 Future Works

This paper takes the first step towards the research of VM migration over XIA and our future studies will base on the testbeds designed. There are still many open issues that need to be further explored.

First of all, though we have achieved VM migration over XIA, the performance isn't so ideal. Performance optimization is an urgent matter. We hope to reduce total migration time and downtime in XIA to be as short as in TCP/IP. Another research point is migration strategies such as load balancing. Besides, we can study VM migration in more future Internet architectures in order to find one that is most suitable for future demand.

7 Conclusion

This paper designs experimental testbeds in future Internet prototypes comparing against VM migration in LAN and WAN of TCP/IP network. We propose KVM virtual machines to be migrated with independent sending and receiving programs. Data are transmitted in chunks and this procedure is managed by a migration control protocol. We then introduce a self-adaptive mechanism in order to solve the application interruption problem after VM is migrated, especially among ADs. All the traffics directed to VM can be recovered even if they are still using original VM addresses. Evaluation results show that VMs can be migrated in XIA networks successfully with downtime in the acceptable range. Performance improvement can leave for future research.

Acknowledgments. The authors are sincerely grateful for the technical support from Prof. Peter Steenkiste and Mr. Dan Barrett in Carnegie Mellon University and financial support from Shanghai INGEEK Information Technology Co. Ltd.

References

1. Han, D., Anand, A., Dogar, F., et al.: XIA: Efficient Support for Evolvable Inter-networking. In: 9th NSDI. USENIX Association, Berkeley (2012)
2. Anand, A., Dogar, F., Han, D., et al.: XIA: An architecture for an evolvable and trustworthy Internet. In: Proceedings of the 10th ACM Workshop on Hot Topics in Networks, Article No. 2. ACM, New York (2011)
3. Kang, T.S.: Tsugawa. M., Fortes, J., et al.: Reducing the Migration Times of Multiple VMs on WANs Using a Feedback Controller. In: IPDPSW, pp. 1480–1489. IEEE, Piscataway (2013)
4. Al-Kiswany, S., Subhraveti, D., Sarkar, P., et al.: VMFlock: virtual machine co-migration for the cloud. In: 20th International Symposium on High Performance Distributed Computing, pp. 159–170. ACM, New York (2011)
5. Comer, D.: A future Internet architecture that supports Cloud Computing. In: 6th International Conference on Future Internet Technologies, pp. 79–83. ACM, New York (2011)
6. Ibrahim, K.Z., Hofmeyr, S., Iancu, C., et al.: Optimized pre-copy live migration for memory intensive applications. In: International Conference for High Performance Computing, Networking, Storage and Analysis, pp. 1–11. ACM, New York (2011)
7. Michael, R.H., Umesh, D., Kartik, G.: Post-copy live migration of virtual machines. ACM SIGOPS Operating Systems Review 43(3), 14–26 (2009)
8. Luo, Y.W., Zhang, B.B., Wang, X.L., et al.: Live and incremental whole-system migration of virtual machines using block-bitmap. In: IEEE International Conference on Cluster Computing, pp. 99–106. IEEE, Piscataway (2008)
9. Liu, H.K., Jin, H., Liao, X.F., et al.: Live migration of virtual machine based on full system trace and replay. In: High Performance Distributed Computing, pp. 101–110. ACM, New York (2009)
10. Fei, M., Feng, L., Zhen, L.: Live virtual machine migration based on improved pre-copy approach. In: Software Engineering and Service Sciences (ICSESS), pp. 230–233. IEEE, Piscataway (2011)
11. Bradford, R., Kotsovinos, E., Feldmann, A., et al.: Live Wide-Area Migration of Virtual Machines Including Local Persistent State. In: 3rd International Conference on Virtual Execution Environments, pp. 169–179. ACM, New York (2007)
12. Silvera, E., Sharaby, G., Lorenz, D., et al.: IP Mobility to Support Live Migration of Virtual Machines across Subnets. In: SYSTOR 2009, Article No. 13 (2009)
13. Harney, E., Goasguen, S., Martin, J., et al.: The Efficacy of Live Virtual Machine Migrations over the Internet. In: 2nd International Workshop on Virtualization Technology in Distributed Computing, pp. 8–14. ACM, New York (2007)
14. Wood, T., Ramakrishnan, K.K., Shenoy, P., et al.: CloudNet: Dynamic Pooling of Cloud Resources by Live WAN Migration of Virtual Machines. In: 7th VEE, pp. 121–132. ACM, New York (2011)
15. Tsugawa, M., Riteau, P., Matsunaga, A.: User-level Virtual Networking Mechanisms to Support Virtual Machine Migration over Multiple Clouds. In: GLOBE-COM Workshops, pp. 568–572. IEEE, Piscataway (2010)
16. Kohler, E., Morris, R., Chen, B., et al.: The Click modular router. ACM Transactions on Computer Systems 18(3), 263–297 (2000)

Efficient Live Migration of Virtual Machines with a Novel Data Filter

Yonghui Ruan, Zhongsheng Cao, and Yuanzhen Wang

School of Computer Science and Technology
Huazhong University of Science and Technology, Wuhan, 430074, China
caozhongsheng@126.com

Abstract. Live migration of virtual machines (VM) is useful for resource management of data centers and cloud platforms. The pre-copy algorithm is widely used for memory migration. It is very efficient to deal with the memory migration of read-intensive workloads. But for write-intensive workloads, the pre-copy's straightforward iteration strategy will become inefficient. In this paper, we propose a novel data filter to improve the pre-copy algorithm in this inefficient situation. In each round of iteration, the data filter forecasts the pages which will be subsequently dirtied, and then filters them from the send list. This prevents the pages from being repeatedly transmitted, thus reducing migration time and bandwidth resource consumption. Meanwhile, the data filter also checks if the previously filtered pages should be re-added to the send list. This ensures that the downtime will not be increased. Experimental results show that the improved algorithm effectively reduces the amount of migrated data, while keeping the downtime at the same level.

1 Introduction

Live migration of virtual machines (VM) is a powerful tool which allows for the relocation of VM between different physical hosts [1, 3–6, 9, 15, 20]. The whole software stack can be consistently transferred, while the continuous execution of the workload is guaranteed. Live VM migration provides considerable flexibility for many tasks of data centers and cloud platforms, including load balancing, online maintenance and fault management of the system [12, 14], and physical server integration [13], etc.

Live VM migration involves migrating the VM's memory data, network connection and virtual devices. In practice, the VM image file is usually stored in a network-attached storage (NAS) device. Therefore the disk storage does not need to be migrated. In this paper, we focus on the memory migration issues.

The pre-copy algorithm is a widely used memory migration approach which consists of two phases: an iteration phase and a stop-and-copy phase. In the iteration phase, the memory pages are copied to the destination in an iterative way, while the VM is still running at the source. This phase continues until either a maximum iteration count is reached, or a sufficient number of pages are synchronized, whichever comes first. Then, in the stop-and-copy phase, the VM is suspended and the remaining pages are copied to the destination.

C.-H. Hsu et al. (Eds.): NPC 2014, LNCS 8707, pp. 369–382, 2014.
© IFIP International Federation for Information Processing 2014

In each round of the iteration phase, the pre-copy's iteration strategy tries to transmit all the pages which have not yet been synchronized. If a transmitted page is subsequently dirtied, it is re-sent in the next round. When encountered with write-intensive workloads, this strategy will cause a lot of repeated transmissions, which waste bandwidth resources and can not improve the downtime.

In this paper, we propose a novel data filter to improve the pre-copy algorithm in this inefficient situation. In each round, the data filter forecasts the pages which will be subsequently dirtied, and then filters them from the send list. This prevents the pages from being repeatedly transmitted, thus reducing the migration time and bandwidth resource consumption. Meanwhile, previously filtered pages will be reconsidered, to see if they can be added to the send list. Therefore, our migration algorithm can still transmit as many pages as possible in the iteration phase. This ensures that the downtime will not be increased.

The core of the data filter is a forecasting algorithm, which is used to forecast dirty pages in the iteration phase. To reduce the cost of analyzing the high rate input data stream of memory write, we propose a *state transition model of memory write* based on the analysis of the principle of locality. Furthermore, we propose the concept of the *local writable working set* (LWWS) to facilitate the analysis of the memory write behavior in a local time period. Based on these conceptions, we designed an applicable forecasting algorithm with sufficient forecasting accuracy.

We implement our algorithm based on Xen virtualization software and run experiments on a variety of workloads. Experimental results show that our algorithm effectively reduces bandwidth resource consumption, while achieving the same level of downtime.

The main contributions of this paper are as follows:

- We propose a state transition model to analyze memory write pattern, and propose the concept of the local writable working set to facilitate the analysis of memory write behavior in a short time period.
- We propose a novel data filter based on the state transition model and the local writable working set to improve the pre-copy's iteration strategy.
- We present the improved pre-copy algorithm, show detailed analysis of the algorithm, and provide a thorough evaluation using a variety of workloads.

The rest of the paper is organized as follows. Section 2 provides a survey of related literature, section 3 describes the data filter, section 4 describes the live migration process with our algorithm, section 5 evaluates our algorithm with a variety of workloads, and section 6 concludes this paper.

2 Related Work

Nicolae et al. [10] propose an approach of live virtual disk migration. For a disk I/O intensive workload, the local storage is required. Therefore, the migration of massive data in the virtual disk is involved in the live VM migration. While different from their study, we consider the general case of a shared storage structure, in which the VM accesses the virtual disk data through a NAS.

The pre-copy algorithm is widely used for memory migration. In the study of Clark et al. [1], the concept of the *writable working set* (WWS) is proposed. They track dirty pages under various workloads during normal operational phase of VM, and use this information to adjust the network rate for optimization. The WWS in their research is extended to the LWWS to facilitate the analysis of the memory write behavior in a short time period.

Liu et al. [6] propose a live migration algorithm called CR/TR-Motion that is based on checkpointing/recovery and trace/replay technology. Their algorithm sends the logs of execution trace instead of memory pages to achieve good migration efficiency for both LAN and WAN environments. The idea of forecasting and filtering in our algorithm can not be applied in combination with their method, since the trace/replay technology processes VM operations but not the memory pages.

Jo et al. [20] propose a technique to reduce the migration time while keeping the downtime to a minimum. They track the I/O operations between the VM and the NAS to maintain a map of the pages that reside on the storage device. For these pages, the memory-to-disk map is transmitted instead of the data itself. So these pages can be directly obtained from the NAS after the map is transmitted. As less pages are transmitted, the migration time is saved. On the other side, our algorithm largely improves bandwidth resource consumption and maintains the downtime at the original level.

There are many other approaches which optimize memory migration process, such as memory compression [4], migration throttling [1, 2, 9], and DSB(Dynamic Self-Ballooning) [3]. These studies try to optimize migration without changing the pre-copy algorithm itself. As a result, the data filter can be used in combination with these approaches to get better performance.

3   Data Filter

In this section we present the design of the data filter. As shown in figure 1, The data filter filters the original send list of each round to make a new send list. The source then sends pages to the destination according to the new list. Meanwhile, the pages that are filtered and updated in current round form the send list of the next round.

The core of the data filter is a forecasting algorithm, which forecasts dirty pages in the iteration phase. Below we introduce the state transition model of memory write, the framework of our forecasting algorithm.

3.1   State Transition Model of Memory Write

Given an observation period, let the frame number of dirty pages be the input. To forecast which pages are going to be dirtied in a given time interval, a forecasting model based on the analysis of the input data is needed.

Assume a workload with 1GB/sec rate of memory access, where the proportion of memory write is 10%. With a 4KB page size, 25.6K pages are dirtied

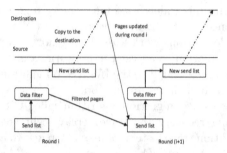

Fig. 1. Data filter

per second. That is, the input data stream has a rate of over 26,000 data points per second. In fact, some workloads may have even faster rates of memory write. The live migration task cannot afford the cost of analyzing such a high rate data stream.

In order to cope with this difficulty, we note that most of the repeated transmissions are actually caused by the frequently modified pages. This suggests that a forecasting model can be built by analyzing these frequent pages, which usually account for a small part of the VM memory.

A straightforward way to do this is to count how many times each memory page is modified during a normal operational phase of the VM, and identify the frequent pages among all the memory pages. However, the frequent pages which are analyzed in this way are the global frequent pages and almost useless. Because once they are filtered, there is no way to re-add them to the send list. If all of them are filtered, the downtime may be increased. But if only part of them are filtered, there may be many repeated transmissions which cause waste of bandwidth resources.

To avoid these disadvantages, a dynamic forecasting model based on the analysis of the frequent pages in a local time period is needed. To build such a model, the best knowledge we have is the principle of locality. The temporary locality principle states that if a page is currently being accessed, it is likely to be accessed again in the near future. The spatial locality principle states that the pages that will soon be accessed are close to the page that is currently being accessed. Based on these two principles, we infer that *within a short time duration, the pages which are frequently accessed are more likely to concentrate in some local regions of memory space.*

If we only consider memory write, the frequently modified pages will still gather in the same regions. Furthermore, if the observation period lasts for a long time, we'll find different groups of "hot spot" regions appearing in different short time durations. These groups of hot spot regions can be seen as states of memory write.

Assume that the VM's memory space is divided into a certain number of continuous linear regions of equal length. Within a given short time duration, we use a group of hot spot regions to describe a memory write state. When the time duration of a state has passed, it may stay or convert to a different state. If the state transition rules are also defined, the state transition model of memory writes is determined.

The state transition model is useful in that it helps to simplify the problem of the dirty page forecasting to the memory write state forecasting. Considering the example in the beginning of this section. For a 50ms time duration of each state, the input data stream will have a rate of only 20 states per second. Meanwhile, this rate is independent of the load characteristics.

3.2   Local Writable Working Set

The state transition model is used to predict hot spot regions of memory write. However, each hot spot region may also contain rarely modified pages, which should not be filtered. Therefore, the model needs to be further refined.

In the pre-copy algorithm implemented by Xen [1], Clark et al. proposed the concept of the writable working set. It is the set of the global frequently modified pages of the iteration phase. In order to avoid repeated transmission and achieve a better migration performance, these pages should be transferred via the stop-and-copy phase. To refine the state transition model, we extend the writable working set to the local writable working set.

Definition 1. Local Writable Working Set (LWWS). In the state transition model, each state corresponds to a group of hot spot regions. The frequently modified pages within these regions constitute a local writable working set.

Compared to the WWS, a LWWS is a set of frequently modified pages in a local time period. The LWWS has two useful properties.

Property 1. If a LWWS is associated with a frequent state, then it is a subset of the WWS.

If a state frequently occurs in the iteration phase, the pages of the corresponding LWWS will be the global frequent pages. In other words, these pages also belong to the WWS. Therefore, the LWWS is actually a subset of the WWS.

Property 2. If a LWWS is associated with a infrequent state, then the pages of it are infrequent pages.

Although a LWWS contains frequent pages under a corresponding state, the "frequent" pages related to the infrequent state will still be rarely modified. According to properties 1 and 2, the set of the LWWSs covers both frequent and infrequent pages of memory write.

3.3   Markov Model

In the above discussion, we present the framework of the forecasting model. In this section we discuss the implement of it.

We start from determining how to describe the transition rules between the memory write states. There are many factors that may affect the transition rules, including but not limited to system architecture, load characteristics, resource usage, etc. It involves extensive analytical work to learn how these factors affect the transition rules, and this is beyond the scope of this paper.

We use an alternative probabilistic method that is easier to implement and understand. The state transition process is considered as a stochastic process, where the state depends on previous states in a non-deterministic way.

In order to reduce the algorithm cost, we further simplify the model into two aspects. Firstly, we assume that the state transition process has the Markov property. So the state transition model becomes a Markov model. Secondly, when a group of hot spot regions is observed, only the hottest region is used to describe the corresponding state. Meanwhile, other hot spot regions are still recorded and associated to the state. In this way, we do not need to worry about the state explosion problem in practice.

Build the Markov Model: At the normal operational stage of the VM, we use the shadow page table to track dirty pages. Within a given duration, we identify a group of hot spot regions of memory writes, record all the dirty pages, and use the hottest region to describe a memory write state. We also record all the state transitions in a state transition matrix. When the modeling time is over, we calculate the LWWS of each state by identify the frequent pages among all the recorded dirty pages. Finally, the set of the calculated LWWSs alone with the state transition matrix are outputted and used for forecasting dirty pages in the migration process.

Figure 2 shows the 4 different state distribution of the experimental workloads. Xen was running on a machine with a two quad-core 2.13GHz Inter Xeon CPU. We start each workload in one virtual machine with 1GB RAM and 2 VCPU. The dirty bitmap is read every 50ms to identify a state. The size of the state space is 256, and the size of each region is 4MB. During the whole observation period, a total of 12,000 states are identified. More detailed information about the workloads can be found in section 5.1.

From this data we observe that the state distribution varies between the different workloads. For each workload, there is a group of states which have high frequency of occurrence. These frequent states represent the memory write pattern of each workload. When we treat each state as a local feature of memory write and learn transition rules between different states, we are able to make a fine grained prediction.

A key challenge of applying the Markov model is keeping the time-effectiveness of it, since the workload behavior may change with time. If the workload behavior changes during the migration process, there is no time to rebuild the Markov model. In this case, the data filter is disabled, and the original pre-copy algorithm is performed. In the following discussion, we assume that the memory write pattern does not change during the migration process.

Maintain the Markov Model: After we build the Markov model, we calculate the probability distribution of states and state transitions. Then, we perform a periodically sampling to test whether the current memory write pattern complies with the established Markov model. More specifically, we check the sampling data

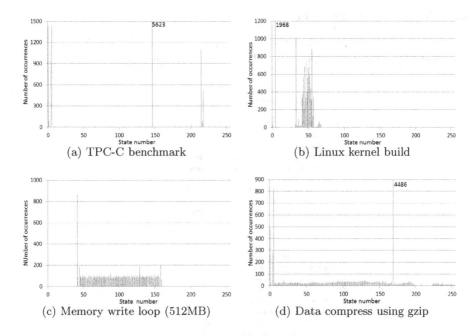

Fig. 2. Distribution of memory write states

to see if it obeys the probability distribution of states and state transitions that are calculated before. If these examinations fail, the Markov model is considered to be out of date and is rebuilt.

4   Live Migration with Improved Pre-copy Algorithm

4.1   Performance Metrics

We use the downtime, the migration time and the amount of migrated data to evaluate the performance characteristics of the VM migration algorithm.

Downtime: Overall suspend time of the VM during the migration process.

The migration downtime measures the availability of the VM during the migration process. An ideal optimization method should not cause the downtime to be increased.

Migration Time: Overall time of the VM migration.

The migration time is the interval between the time migration is initiated and the time the VM is consistently migrated to the destination.

Amount of Migrated Data: Total number of memory pages transferred during the migration process.

We use this metric to measure bandwidth resource consumption of the VM migration. It should be as low as possible on the premise of the unchanged downtime.

4.2   Migration Algorithm

This section presents the improved pre-copy algorithm. Figure 3 shows the pseudo-code of the algorithm (line 2-12) and the data filter (line 13-23).

```
1. let N := memory size of VM

2. MigrationAlgorithm(iterclue, itercount, duration)
3.     let iter := 1
4.     let unsyn := N
5.     let dirtylist := set of all VM pages; filterlist := empty set
6.     while iter < itercount and unsyn > iterclue do
7.         let sendlist := dirtylist + filterlist
8.         set (sendlist, filterlist) := DataFilter(sendlist, duration)
9.         set dirtylist := SendData(sendlist)
10.        set unsyn := length(filterlist) + length(dirtylist)
11.        iter++
12.    Stop-and-copy()

13. DataFilter(sendlist, duration)
14.    let LWWS := empty set
15.    let filterlist := empty set
16.    let sendtime := length(sendlist) / netrate()
17.    let curr := current identified state
18.    while sendtime >= duration
19.        set (curr, LWWS) := Forecast(curr)
20.        set filterlist := filterlist + LWWS
21.        set sendtime:= sendtime − duration
22.    set sendlist := sendlist − filterlist
23.    return(sendlist, filterlist)
```

Fig. 3. Improved pre-copy algorithm

In line 2, the parameter 'iterclue' is the threshold of the number of the remaining pages which have not yet been synchronized. When the stop-and-copy phase starts, this number is directly proportional to the downtime. The parameter 'itercount' is the maximum iteration count. The parameter 'duration' is the time duration for each memory write state.

In the migration algorithm, the pages that are dirtied and filtered in each round are recorded in the 'dirtylist' and 'filterlist'. In line 7, we use these two sets to calculate the 'sendlist'. It contains the pages which have not yet been synchronized in the beginning of each round. In line 9, the function SendData() transmits all the pages in the sendlist and returns dirty page set during the transmission process.

The data filter forecasts and filters dirty pages during the transmission time of the given 'sendlist'. In line 16, the function netrate() calculates network rate (number of pages transmitted per second). The variable 'sendtime' is the transmission time of the pages in the 'sendlist'. In line 17, the variable 'curr' is set to an identified state. In line 19, based on the identified state, the future states are forecasted using the state transition matrix. Each forecasted state is assigned to the 'curr' and used for forecasting in the next loop. Then, the pages of the corresponding LWWS is added to the 'filterlist' in line 20. As previously discussed, the state transition matrix and all the LWWSs are outputted after the Markov model is built.

5   Experiment

5.1   Test Setup

Our experimental platform consists of 3 identical physical servers, each with a two quad-core 2.13GHz Inter Xeon E5606 CPU, 4GB DDR RAM and Intel 82576 Gigabit Network Connection. The migrated VM is configured to use 2 VCPU and 1024MB of RAM. Xen-3.3.0 is used as the virtual machine monitor. The guest kernel is Linux 2.6.18, and the host kernel is a modified version of Linux 2.6.18 for both the source and the destination. Storage is accessed via iSCSI protocol from the third physical server configured as a NAS.

We implement the improved algorithm based on Xen virtualization software. The experiments use the following workloads:

TCP-C Benchmark: Mysql database and the open source test tool DBT2 [16] are used for the experiment. DBT2 is an implementation of the TPC's TPC-C Benchmark specification. We use a 60 warehouses dataset and 40 client connections. The Mysql database version is 5.1.7, with default settings.

Linux Kernel Build: The second experiment runs a system call intensive load — kernel compilation of Linux 2.6.18.

Memory Write Loop: We write a simple C program that writes constantly to a 256MB region and a 512MB region of memory.

Data Compression with gzip and bzip2: The test data is approximately 7GB of the XML text dump of the English version of Wikipedia [21] on June 4th, 2013, history 4 (approximately 7GB after decompressing with bzip2). We use the command 'gzip' and 'bzip2' to compress the data with the best compression ratio.

Unixbench: It's a fundamental high-level Linux benchmark suite that integrates CPU, file I/O, process spawning and other workloads. The following tails are performed: Load system with concurrent shell scripts, compiler throughput, recursion, dhrystone2 using register variables, arithmetic, pipe throughput, pipe-based context switching, process creation, and execl throughput.

To reduce the effect on other ongoing network services hosted on the source host, we limit the network bandwidth to 500Mbit/sec for the migration daemon. In all cases, the existing parameters of the pre-copy algorithm are set as default. For the improved algorithm, the observation interval is set to 50ms. For each workload, the VM migration of the two algorithms is started at the same time point.

5.2   Overhead of Data Filter

Table 1 shows the time cost for building the Markov model and applying the data filter. For the Markov model, the sampling interval of each state is 50ms, and the computation time is about 10ms. It takes about 60ms in all to identify and record a state. In each round of iteration, the data filter has to spend 50ms in waiting for the sampling results of the dirty page bitmap. After that, it takes a short time to forecast and filter dirty pages. From the third column of table 1 we can see that the time cost of the data filter is between 1.6 to 2 seconds. Noted that the maximum iteration count is 30 by default in Xen, it takes a total of 1.5 seconds to wait for the sampling results.

Let N be the memory size of the VM, let S be the size of the state space. After some simple optimizations, the space cost to record the state transition matrix, the LWWSs and some intermediate results is $O(N+S^2)$ (2.79MB memory space is used in our implementation). In the migration process, the space cost of the data filter is also $O(N + S^2)$ (1.63MB memory space is used in our implementation).

Table 1. Time cost of the Markov model and the data filter

Workloads	Time cost for modeling (millisecond per state)	Time cost of the data filter (millisecond)
TPC-C benchmark	59.735	1673
kernel-build	59.642	1636
gzip	58.232	1640
bzip2	59.982	1667
MW(512MB)	59.973	2000
MW(256MB)	59.987	1972
Unixbench	59.721	1662

5.3   Migration Performance for Different Size of State Space

We first evaluate the migration performance of the improved algorithm with different size of the state space. The experiment uses the TPC-C benchmark.

Figure 4 (a), 5 (a), 6 (a) show the downtime, the migration time and the amount of transferred pages of the original pre-copy algorithm and the improved algorithm with 64, 128, 256, 512 and 1024 states. From this figure we observe that when the size of the state space is set to 256 (the region size is 4MB), we obtain the best migration performance.

When a smaller size is used, the performance is worse because the corresponding regions are getting larger. The more a region covers memory pages, the more difficult the corresponding state transfers to other states in memory write process. This makes it hard to reconsider transmitting the previously filtered pages to maintain a low downtime. At one extreme, the whole memory space contains only one region and our forecasting algorithm becomes a static method. In this case, there is no way to re-add the filtered pages to the send list of each round.

On the other side, the size of the state space should not be set too large. If the memory region covers few pages, more than one region may be full with dirty pages during the time duration of each state. At the other extreme, each region contains only one memory page. It is difficult for the forecasting algorithm to identify the real memory write state in this situation. Therefore, the forecasting accuracy will be reduced and the performance will be worse.

The following experiments are focused on comparison between the pre-copy algorithm and the improved algorithm with 256 states.

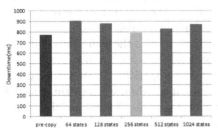 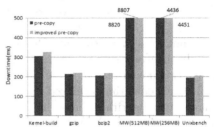

(a) Pre-copy and improved algorithm with different size of state space

(b) Pre-copy and improved algorithm with 256 states

Fig. 4. Comparison of downtime

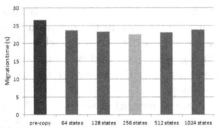 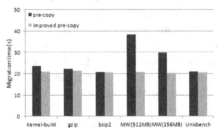

(a) Pre-copy and improved algorithm with different size of state space

(b) Pre-copy and improved algorithm with 256 states

Fig. 5. Comparison of migration time

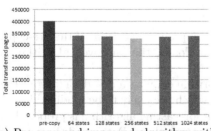 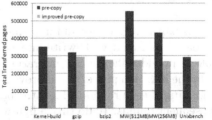

(a) Pre-copy and improved algorithm with different size of state space

(b) Pre-copy and improved algorithm with 256 states

Fig. 6. Comparison of total transferred pages

5.4   Downtime

Figure 4 (b) shows the migration downtime for the six remaining workloads, where "MW" refers to the memory write loop workload. First we notice that in the memory write loop workloads, the downtime of the two algorithms is nearly the same. Compared to approximately 8 seconds and 4 seconds downtime, a difference of dozens of milliseconds can be ignored.

Among the other four workloads, the improved algorithm has more downtime than the original pre-copy algorithm. More precisely, the downtime of the improved algorithm increases by 5.5% on average with respect to the pre-copy algorithm. This shows the data filter efficiently maintains the same level of downtime. In the worst case (the kernel-build workload), the improved algorithm has more 21ms downtime than the original pre-copy algorithm. Compared to the total 305ms downtime achieved by the pre-copy algorithm, we can still consider that the two algorithms have the same level of downtime. Therefore, the downtime is not significantly increased because of the data filter.

5.5   Migration Time and Amount of Migrated Data

Figure 5 (b) and 6 (b) show the migration time and the total transferred pages for the six workloads run. For the memory write loop workloads, we see excellent performance of the improved algorithm: both the duration and the bandwidth resources are significantly reduced with nearly no increase in the downtime. In fact, the artificial workloads have regular memory write patterns, which are easy to be captured by the data filter. Although their constant and high dirty rates cause the poor performance of the pre-copy algorithm, they are the ideal workloads for the data filter to show its efficiency.

For the rest of the four workloads, the improved algorithm achieves 73.5MB to 236.1MB reduction in the amount of migrated data compared to the pre-copy algorithm. When it comes to the migration time, the improvement is 0.2 to 1.6 seconds. This is because the data filter spends time in forecasting and filtering dirty pages, as shown in table 1.

6   Conclusion

In this paper we propose and implement an improved algorithm of the pre-copy. When encountered with write-intensive workloads, the improved algorithm is able to provide efficient live migration of VM.

In the iteration phase, the improved algorithm employs a new data filter at the beginning of each round to filter the pages which are likely to be modified in the subsequent rounds. To do this, a lightweight forecasting algorithm is proposed to forecast dirty pages generated during the iteration phase. We extend the concept of the writable working set to the local writable working set, and propose a state transition model. This model largely reduces the algorithm cost, while ensuring the forecasting accuracy. With the data filter, the original send list of each round is filtered. After that, the pages of the new send list are sent to the destination. Unlike any other optimization methods, the improved algorithm still tries to send as many pages as possible in the iteration phase, instead of simply postponing to send them in the stop-and-copy phase.

In the future, we plan to find a way to efficiently shorten the migration time of the live VM migration. On the other side, we also plan to find a more sophisticated model than the Markov model. Based on the complex model, the same level of the migration time and the bandwidth resource consumption as the stop-and-copy algorithm, and the same level of the downtime as the pre-copy algorithm can be achieved.

References

1. Clark, C., Fraser, K., Hand, S., Hansen, J.G., Jul, E., Limpach, C., Pratt, I., Warfield, A.: Live migration of virtual machines. In: NSDI, pp. 273–286 (May 2005)
2. Elmore, A.J., Das, S., Agrawal, D., El Abbadi, A.: Zephyr: live migration in shared nothing databases for elastic cloud platforms. In: SIGMOD, pp. 301–312 (June 2011)
3. Hines, M.R., Deshpande, U., Gopalan, K.: Post-copy live migration of virtual machines. SIGOPS Oper. Syst. Rev. 43(3), 14–26 (2009)
4. Jin, H., Deng, L., Wu, S., Shi, X., Pan, X.: Live virtual machine migration with adaptive memory compression. In: Cluster, pp. 1–10 (August-September 2009)
5. Song, X., Shi, J., Liu, R., Yang, J., Chen, H.: Parallelizing live migration of virtual machines. In: VEE, pp. 85–96 (May 2013)
6. Liu, H., Jin, H., Liao, X., Hu, L.: Live migration of virtual machine based on full system trace and replay. In: HPDC, pp. 101–110 (June 2009)
7. Deshpande, U., Wang, X., Gopalan, K.: Live gang migration of virtual machines. In: HPDC, pp. 135–146 (June 2011)
8. Ma, Y., Wang, H., Dong, J., Li, Y., Cheng, S.: Efficient Live Migration of Virtual Machine with Memory Exploration and Encoding. In: CLUSTER, pp. 610–613 (September 2012)
9. Liu, Z., Qu, W., Liu, W., Li, K.: Xen live migration with slowdown scheduling algorithm. In: PDCAT, pp. 104–107 (December 2010)
10. Nicolae, B., Cappello, F.: A Hybrid Local Storage Transfer Scheme for Live Migration of I/O Intensive Workloads. In: HPDC, pp. 85–96 (June 2012)
11. Shetty, J., Anala, M.R., Shobana, G.: A Survey on Techniques of Secure Live Migration of Virtual Machine. International Journal of Computer Applications 39(12), 34–39 (2012)
12. Nagarajan, A.B., Mueller, F., Engelmann, C., Scott, S.L.: Proactive Fault Tolerance for HPC with Xen Virtualization. In: ICS, pp. 23–32 (June 2007)
13. Nathuji, R., Schwan, K.: VirtualPower: Coordinated Power Management in Virtualized Enterprise Systems. SIGOPS Oper. Syst. Rev. 41(6), 265–278 (2007)
14. Jhawar, R., Piuri, V., Santambrogio, M.: Fault Tolerance Management in Cloud Computing: A System-Level Perspective. IEEE Syst. J. 7(2), 288–297 (2013)
15. Nelson, M., Lim, B.H., Hutchins, G.: Fast Transparent Migration for Virtual Machines. In: USENIX ATC, pp. 391–394 (April 2005)
16. Database Test Suite, http://sourceforge.net/apps/mediawik-i/osdldbt/

17. Kumar, S., Schwan, K.: Netchannel: A VMM-level Mechanism for Continuous, Transparent Device Access During VM Migration. In: VEE, pp. 31–40 (March 2008)
18. Shea, R., Liu, J.: Performance of Virtual Machines Under Networked Denial of Service Attacks: Experiments and Analysis. IEEE Syst. J. 7(2), 335–345 (2013)
19. de Gooijer, J.G., Hyndman, R.J.: 25 years of time series forecasting. Int. J. Forecast. 22(3), 443–473 (2006)
20. Jo, C., Gustafsson, E., Son, J., Egger, B.: Efficient Live Migration of Virtual Machines Using Shared Storage. In: VEE, pp. 41–50 (May 2013)
21. Enwiki Dump Progress, http://dumps.wikimedia.org/enwi-ki/

Energy-Efficient and Adaptive Algorithms for Constructing Multipath Routing in Wireless Sensor Networks

Shaohua Wan

School of Information and Safety Engineering,
Zhongnan University of Economics and Law, 430073 Wuhan, China
shwanhust@gmail.com

Abstract. In this paper, we design and implement a k-multipath routing algorithm that allows a given source node send samples of data to a given sink node in a large scale sensor networks. Construction and dynamic selection of alternative routing structures, for the purpose of extending the networks lifetime, while providing a balance between QoS(Quality of Service) requirements and the minimization of the variance of the energy. The proposed multipath routing algorithm tries to keep multipath as node disjoint routes. Our view is that balancing load distribution while meeting acceptable delays for applications can lead to significant power savings. The simulation results demonstrate that our multipath routing algorithm can not only achieve load balancing, but also can be help to prolong the life-span of network, compared with the shortest path routing(single path routing SPR).

1   Introduction

Wireless Sensor networks are composed of hundreds, or possibly thousands of tiny low-cost nodes which, once deployed in a particular physical environment, can measure various values of interest, perform some limited computation and communicate with other in order to achieve a desired task in a cooperative manner. Sensor networks can be deployed in large geographic areas to actively monitor a variety of operations ranging from long-term ones (e.g., security alerts) to short-term ones with high degree of dynamics (disaster management). A major research problem, critical to the real world operation of sensor networks, is to design networks that are efficiently and dynamically adaptable to the energy and QoS requirements. The main goal of the proposed research will be to develop energy- efficient and adaptive algorithms for constructing routing trees.

An important aspect of energy-efficiency is performing in-network aggregation while routing data from source sensors through intermediate nodes in the network. Servicing an aggregate query, say Q_i, involves disseminating the query from a given sink s_i, that requested it to all the target sensing nodes relevant for its processing; and sending the results from each of the target nodes back to the sink. An effective way of disseminating the queries and gathering the query answer is using a tree structure

C.-H. Hsu et al. (Eds.): NPC 2014, LNCS 8707, pp. 383–394, 2014.

rooted at the sink. Once the tree is constructed, each of its nodes has a dual role: forward the answer-sets measured by the children towards the sink; and perform some local aggregation of the data, in order to reduce the communication overhead.

The rest of the paper is organized as follows. In section 2, we provide related work into the area of multipath routing for wireless sensor networks. We model the query component and formulate the general construction point-to-point routes problem in section 3. Section 4 discusses route establishment, data transmission and route maintenance of the k-multipath routing. Based on simulation results, section 5 presents a detailed analysis of load distribution, energy consumption, lifetime for both multipath and the shortest path routing mechanisms. Section 6 concludes the paper.

2   Related Work

There has been recent research on distributed algorithms for construction of low-weight connected sub graphs and spanners in the context of wireless sensor networks(motivated by energy-efficient routing and fault- tolerant deployment) [1,2,3,4,5,9,10,11]. There has been little work on localized and distributed construction of routing trees for data aggregation in wireless sensor networks. Li et al. give a local algorithm to construct a low-weight sub graph (called as k-Local MST) that has many desirable properties: connectivity, sparseness, spanner, bounded degree, and planarity; but it is not a tree. A structure is low weight if its total edge length is within a small constant factor of the total edge length of the minimum spanning tree. Since the structure is not a tree, it is not suitable for query applications where an aggregation tree is needed. However, low weight structures and spanners, in particular, are useful in reducing the complexity of the underlying graph. The tree construction algorithms can be run on "top" of such spanner structures. MST cannot be constructed in a purely localized manner, i.e., each node cannot determine which edge is in the defined structure by using only the information of the nodes within some constant hops.

Data aggregation has been studied extensively [6, 7, 8]. The main motivation is to minimize the transmission of packets containing individual measurements whenever the semantics of the application needs a summarized picture of the environment, e.g., a weighted sum of the signals, and allows for functional decomposition when calculating the statistical values. When the data based on the actual measurements is categorical, even pattern identification techniques can be used for aggregation. Important parameters that impact data aggregations in wireless sensor networks has been addressed from the perspective of database-like query processing and, recently, the energy efficiency of node clustering with data aggregation trees has been studied.

The focus is on efficient processing of a mix of aggregate queries and not on constructing the routing trees themselves in an energy-efficient fashion. In contrast, the objective of our research is to construct such trees considering the evolution of the network as a sequence of generated queries with different semantics and adapting the routing structures both in the sense of constructing a new one and modifying the existing ones.

3   Query Model and Problem Formulation

3.1   Query Model

Users need to be able to interact with the sensor network, typically by connecting to a (sink) node and submitting queries of interest for which the network must provide accurate answers in a timely manner. While the most common, standard query specification language is SQL, which is typically used in database systems, it has also been adopted in wireless sensor network application based on the abstraction that the network represents, in fact, a largely distributed database system. However, specific aspects that distinguish a typical database from a sensor network infrastructure brought modifications to SQL and the most recognized SQL-specification for wireless sensor network is TinySQL. Regardless of the query specification language, a wireless sensor network needs to provide mechanisms for query processing that are both energy and bandwidth conscious. For example, as we have shown in the following, it is imperative, for resource usage efficiency, that a sensor network to implement a triggering (or similar) mechanism in order to better implement monitoring queries (continuous queries). The typical SQL style is as follows: a network user connects to one of the sink nodes, formulates and submits a query of the following form:

Q: SELECT   ALL/MIN/MAX/AVG (measurement)
    FROM   Region $(R_1(x_1, y_1, ... , x_n, y_n))$
    WHERE   Condition (measurement)
    FOR   Lifetime
    SAMPLE EVERY Sampling Interval

R_1 represents the geographical bounds of the region in which the samples for the query are to be collected from. If R_1 is not explicitly specified, it defaults to the entire sensor network deployment area. Sampling interval indicates the frequency each node must acquire the measurements and ship the data towards the sink. The sensor must stop sensing and sending the data towards the sink node after the lifetime period expires. We only consider the sink node is outside of region R_1.

Figure 1 gives an illustration of this case that we will exclusively consider. Therefore, we will have to construct point-to-point routes from the aggregation root node, which is situated inside the sampling region, to the ultimate destination, the sink node. The aggregation results should be shipped along with these paths.

3.2   Problem Formulation

Sensor nodes that are outside the sampling region are also important as they might be used in data-relay duties, making the connection between the producer, in the sampling region, and its consumer, the sink node. For each source-destination pair, a single (shortest) path is always discovered and used for data transmission, as seen in Figure 1, the aggregated information will be sent to the sink through the bold intermediate nodes. Obviously, in wireless sensor network, with a high density of nodes the shortest paths connecting any pair of nodes tend to be very close to the line segment connecting those two nodes. Hence, that area close to the line segment will be very likely to develop hot-spots, which is the situation we are trying to avoid in the first place. The fact that these nodes are overused is one of the major causes for hot spots. This paper provides a new multipath protocol for mitigating the sensor network hot- spot problem, considering load balancing as well as quality of data.

4   K-Multipath Routing Algorithm

4.1   Route Establishment

We assume that each node knows its location and the location of its neighbors. This simulator provides us with the heartbeat algorithm, which is already implemented and executed in the first hour of the simulation, and finds the neighbors for us.

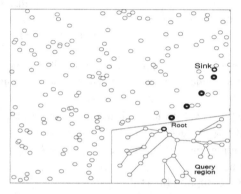

Fig. 1. Sink node is physically located outside the sampling region

The algorithm for constructing the routing structure should be as follows. For a given source-sink pair of nodes, the sink will unicast on a shortest path routing (along a straight imaginary line) the query request to the source node. Subsequently, based on the query specification, referring to Figure 2, we will draw a segment orthogonal to source-sink line segment. We will split the segment in k places, which will correspond to k intermediate destination points (breakpoints) of the paths between the sink and the source. The distance between two consecutive paths on the line which is orthogonal to the source-sink segment will be equal. For each line segment, we forward the data packet using nodes closest to the line segment. Since we have k breakpoints for a given source-sink pair, we will establish k multipath to offer more opportunities for regulating the traffic over the network.

Multipath routing protocol can try to find node disjoint, link disjoint, or non-disjoint routes. Node disjoint routes, also known as totally disjoint routes, have no nodes or links in common. Link disjoint routes have no links in common, but may have nodes in common. Non-disjoint routes can have nodes and links in common. Since we assume the whole topology is known, finding node-disjoint multiple paths is not a difficult task. Figure 2 shows an example of how to construct k-multipath which are node-disjoint routes given a source-sink pair of nodes. As can be seen in this Fig., that k-multipath from source to sink does not interfere with each other except that they share the resources at source and sink. To the best of my knowledge, even if the multiple paths are node-disjoint, transmissions along the routes may interfere if some nodes among the routes are in the same collision domain. When we establish multiple paths, it is important to establish paths that are as independent as possible to ensure the least interference between the paths.

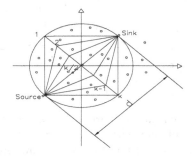

Fig. 2. K-multipath routing protocol model

The theoretical principle is adopted in our approach relies on the concept of Bezier curves, developed by Paul de Casteljau (1959) and independently by Pierre Bezier (1962). In its general form, a Bezier curve of a given set of n+1 points: Pi ($i=0, 1, 2\ldots\ldots n$), and a parameter $t \in [0, 1]$, is defined as:

$$p(t) = \sum_{i=0}^{n} P_i B_{i,n}(t) \tag{1}$$

Where $B_{i,n}(t)$ Bernstein polynomials, defined as:

$$B_{i,n}(t) = \frac{n!}{i!(n-i)!} t^i (1-t)^{n-i} \tag{2}$$

Sum to one for any t in [0, 1],

$$\sum_{i=0..n} B_i^n(t) = 1 \tag{3}$$

For 3 control points, n = 2,

$$p(t) = (1-t)^2 p_0 + 2t(1-t)p_1 + t^2 p_2 \tag{4}$$

For 4 control points, n = 3,

$$p(t) = (1-t)^3 p_0 + 3t(1-t)^2 p_1 + 3t^2(1-t)p_2 + t^3 p_3 \tag{5}$$

$$p(t) = (-t^3 + 3t^2 - 3t + 1)p_0 + (3t^3 - 6t^2 + 3t)p_1 + (-3t^3 + 3t^2)p_2 + (t^3)p_3 \tag{6}$$

$$p(t) = (-p_0 + 3p_1 - 3p_2 + p_3)t^3 + (3p_0 - 6p_1 + 3p_2)t^2 + (-3p_0 + 3p_1)t + (p_0)t \tag{7}$$

If we regroup the equation by terms of exponents of t, we get it in the standard cubic form. This form is very good for fast evaluation, as all of the constant terms (a, b, c, d) can be recomputed. The cubic equation form obscures the input geometry, but there is a one-to-one mapping between the two and so the geometry can always be extracted out of the cubic coefficients.

$$p(t) = a\,t^3 + b\,t^2 + c\,t + d$$

$$
\begin{aligned}
a &= \left(-\,p_0 + 3p_1 - 3p_2 + p_3\right)\\
b &= \left(3p_0 - 6p_1 + 3p_2\right)\\
c &= \left(-\,3p_0 + 3p_1\right)\\
d &= \left(p_0\right)
\end{aligned}
\tag{8}
$$

$$
p(t) = \begin{bmatrix} t^3 & t^2 & t & 1 \end{bmatrix} \cdot \begin{bmatrix} a \\ b \\ c \\ d \end{bmatrix}
\qquad
\begin{bmatrix} a \\ b \\ c \\ d \end{bmatrix} = \begin{bmatrix} -1 & 3 & -3 & 1 \\ 3 & -6 & 3 & 0 \\ -3 & 3 & 0 & 0 \\ 1 & 0 & 0 & 0 \end{bmatrix} \cdot \begin{bmatrix} p_0 \\ p_1 \\ p_2 \\ p_3 \end{bmatrix}
\tag{9}
$$

We can rewrite the equations in matrix form. This gives us a compact notation and shows how different forms of cubic curves can be related. It also is a very efficient form as it can take advantage of existing 4x4 matrix hardware support. For example, given three points P0, P1, and P2, a quadratic Bezier curve is the path traced by the equation (4) as shows in Figure 3.

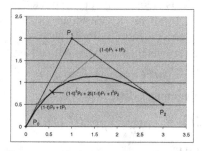

Fig. 3. Construct a Bezier curve from given three points

The curve passes through the first, P0 and last vertex points, P_n. The tangent vector at the starting point P0 must be given by $P_1 - P_0$ and the tangent P_n given by $P_n - P_{n-1}$. The properties of the Bernstein polynomials ensure that all Bezier curves lie in the convex hull of their control points. Hence, even though we do not interpolate all the data, we cannot be too far away. Figure 4 describes convex polygon formed by connecting the control points

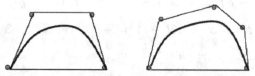

Fig. 4. Curve resides completely inside its convex hull

We have relied on the flexibility of the Bezier curves in order to overcome some of the cause of premature lifetime termination: lack of appropriate workload balancing in the most critical of the network-around the sink and source nodes. By using the Bezier curve as the trajectory model, we are able to control the coverage of the sink/source nearby nodes implicated in the routing and attain, in a practical setting, a near 100% utilization of them. Figure 2 shows that the routing coverage, for workload balancing, by means of trajectory-based alternating routes, in comparison with the ones which provide routes that approximate, to some degree, the shortest path routing.

The route's information, which is represented through a Bezier curve, must be transmitted from node for the routing purposes. A node, however, needs only to communicate the coordinates of the control points in order to be able to generate an entire Bezier curve, no matter its shaped and length. This property will save both time and energy, a clear advantage of using parametric curves such as Bezier. Moreover, not only on curve can be computed from a set of control points, but an entire family of curves can be also generated, based on the affine property of Bezier curves, which will prove benefit when managing multiple routes between two source-sink points. Bezier curves add flexibility to the routes. If we consider two fixed endpoints, the shape of the curve can be adjusted by using the remaining control points. Figure 5 shows the type of shapes Bezier trajectories can take by simply relocating these control points given the source-sink endpoints p_0 and p_1.

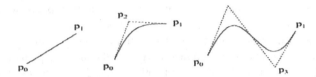

Fig. 5. Linear, quadratic and cubic

4.2 The Analysis of Finding Multiple Node- Disjoint Paths

Due to the independence of the paths, disjoint paths have been received considerable attention in the recent literature. The main reason is that disjoint paths offer certain advantages over non-disjoint paths. When using non-disjoint routes, a single link or node failure can result in multiple routes to fail while in node or link disjoint routes, a link failure will only cause a single route to fail. What is more, both the nodes and the wireless links are error-prone, which leads to multiple paths that share those nodes and links to fail in non-disjoint paths. Hence, node-disjoint paths can provide the highest degree fault-tolerance.

Many algorithms to find node-disjoint paths make use of request/reply cycles. Typically, a source node initiates a route discovery procedure by broadcasting a Route Request packet, and then this ROUTE REQUEST message is flooded to the entire network. Contrary to the above general algorithm, our k-multipath algorithm to build node-disjoint routes does not generate too much RREQ/RREP packets and then increases the routing overheads. Instead, we fully make use of geometrical knowledge to discover routes. According to the Fig. 2, all the coordinates of k breakpoints can be more easily calculated, in a segment orthogonal to source-sink line segment. In each of k-1 surrounded regions, we only construct one route from the source node to the sink node. Those intermediate nodes in one route are selected in a way that they should be closest to source-sink line segment. This is easily explained by the fact that it takes more time to deliver packets along the path farther away from the source-sink line segment. Multiple paths may present differences in the end-to-end delay of each path. Such scenarios require that data coming from different flows needs to be buffered till the flow from the path with the highest delay arrives for reordering the data correctly. This solution poses another problem, as high speed memory is extremely expensive, and therefore we should minimize the differential delay. In our simulation, we don't need to consider packet reordering.

5   Performance Evaluation

Our simulation setting is as follows. We create 500 nodes uniformly deployed in a 2×2km2 area, which use 802.11 protocol at the MAC layer, and the heartbeat node discovery protocol in order to determine the neighbors. We randomly pick up one pair of nodes as source-sink nodes from the physical terrain, and we don't consider the characteristic of the mobility of the nodes. Although how the number of the paths affects the performance remains unknown, there are 5 paths to be used in the simulation. We choose a path randomly from the multiple paths with the same probability. Moreover, we try to keep the number of paths odd.

We study two different ways to use the multiple paths. In one method, called multipath routing 1, we choose a path randomly from the multiple paths with the same probability. The other method, called multipath routing 2, is to choose a path with a probability inversely proportional to the length of the path. We vary the sampling rate in order to observe the effects of packet loss in the nodes due to the interferences among the multipath. We will compare the performance of the shortest path routing and multipath routing in different aspects. We evaluate the performance according to the following metrics:

•The load distribution: This metric provides the average relayed traffic in packets as function of the distance to the network center, in accordance with the Pham and Perreau's analytical model [3]. We use load distribution as a metric to evaluate the load balancing.

•Average energy consumption: The energy consumption is averaged over all nodes in the network.

•The lifetime extension: The metric studied is the number of hours of communication achieves when 1 percent, 25 percent, 50 percent, and 100 percent of the nodes die using multipath routing and the shortest path routing.

•Query Turn-Around Time: A measure of the initial responsiveness of the query; the time lapsed from the moment the query is submitted to the network by the user until the very first data-packet is received at the user. This will measure and penalize the multipath-construction algorithm with a high set-up time.

These measures are intended to provide insight into the ability of the protocols to route packets to their intended destination, and the energy efficiency of the protocols in accomplishing that task. The routing overhead is defined as the ratio of the number of routing messages generated by a routing protocol to the number of received data packets at the destinations. This metric is a measure of how many routing messages are needed to receive one data packet. It captures the efficiency of the routing protocol. Since the routing overhead is similar and much lower between multipath and the shortest path routing in our simulation, we don't present the results of routing overhead in this paper.

Figure 6 portrays the load distribution of the two protocols as function of the distance from the network center. In our simulation, the center is the midpoint of the segment between a pair of source-sink nodes. With the increase of the distance to the center, there is a much more slight decrease of the load for the multipath routing while the load is greatly reduced for the shortest path routing. This simulation shows that our multipath routing can achieve better load balancing. This result can be explained by the fact that the traffic of the network is evenly regulated to the different paths while the single path always chooses the geographic-based shortest path, which will unfairly distribute more loads to the nodes along this optimal route than their neighboring nodes. According to this Figure, we conclude that the shortest path is likely to be overloaded because this route is across or very close to the center. In addition, due to the fact that we adopt load balancing policy, theoretically, all the nodes should experience approximately the same loads in the multipath routing 1, however, there exists a smooth decrease of the loads as the distance increases. The possible reason is that those packets that travel through longer routes are dropped due to more latency.

Still, we notice that as the distance from the network center increases, the number of average load for multipath routing 2 drops faster than multipath routing 1. This can be explained that multipath routing 2 is to choose a path with a probability inversely proportional to the length of the path. In other words, the further the distance to the center, the lower the probability that the nodes are used to relay the packets. Moreover, since our load balancing policy is not optimal, those nodes close to the optimal route have to be assigned more traffic in comparison with ones at the rear. Nevertheless, it is important to stress the fact that our multipath routing outperforms the shortest path routing in terms of load balancing.

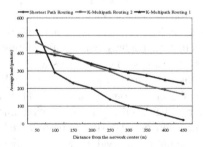

Fig. 6. The average load distribution as function of distance from the network center

Figure 7 portrays the average energy consumption of the three protocols as function of the number of the hours of communication. Clearly, both two multipath routing have smaller energy consumption than that of the shortest path routing. This demonstrates that both multipath routing can distribute the traffic load more fairly than the shortest path routing. This result can be explained by the fact that the traffic of the network is evenly regulated to the different paths while the single path always chooses the geographic-based shortest path, which will unfairly distribute more loads to the nodes along this optimal route than their neighboring nodes. According to this Figure, we conclude that the nodes along this shortest path are likely to be overused because this route is only one. Therefore, the energy of those nodes on this route will drop faster than the other nodes. Moreover, we also notice that there exists a slightly improvement of energy consumption between multipath routing 1 and multipath routing 2, even compared to the shortest path routing. This is because the nodes, even with no routing tasks, have to passively listen to neighboring nodes' radio transmission, which inevitably consumes battery energy. Even though our multipath routing is not optimal, it is important to stress the fact that our multipath routing outperforms the shortest path routing in terms of energy consumption.

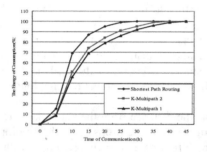

Fig. 7. The average energy consumption as function of the number of hours of communication

Figure 8 illustrates the lifetime extension as function of the percentage of node death. We study the number of hours of communication when 1 percent, 25 percent, 50 percent, and 100 percent of the nodes die using k-multipath routing and the shortest path routing. As can be seen in Figure 10, both of the two multipath routing can yield improvements over the shortest path routing in all cases while the lifetime extension of the multipath routing 1 is trivial compared to the multipath routing 2. To the best of our knowledge, the battery energy of a network node is mainly consumed on forwarding control and data packets. Multipath routing usually increases the energy consumption on the transmission of data messages because some data packets traverse sub-optimal paths. On the other hand, it will decrease the energy consumption on the transmission of control messages. This reveals that k-multipath routing 1 can achieve the best balanced energy dissipation among the sensor nodes to have full use of the complete sensor network. In Figure 9 we have plotted query turn-around time as function of sampling interval. One can see that there is less responsive time in the shortest path. But for the long term and continuous query, since the nodes close the shortest path routing, which are called "hot spots", will quickly deplete the sensor nodes' energy, the impact brought by link failure will greatly increase query response time. This confirms the more significance that we have explored K-Multipath Routing Scheme for Energy Efficient Wireless Sensor Networks.

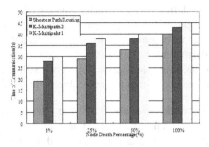

Fig. 8. The lifetime of the network as function of the percentage of node death

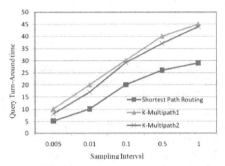

Fig. 9. Query turn-around time as function of sampling interval

6   Conclusions and Future Work

We present a novel load-balancing mechanism for wireless sensor networks. The new scheme is simple but very effective to achieve load balancing and congestion alleviation. We have explored an experimental comparison between k-multipath routing and the shortest path routing. Our performance study shows that the network traffic can be distributed more evenly onto multipath routing. Load balancing is important to fairly distribute the routing task among the nodes of the network. It can also protect a node from failure considering that a node with heavy duty is likely to deplete its energy quickly.

Although it takes much more time for the packet delivery along those multiple paths than the shortest path, the packet delivery fraction of our technique has been improved obviously and the network resource can be utilized efficiently. Also, we use the k-multipath routing to balance the energy dissipation to maximize the lifetime of the nodes in a sensor network. However, minimizing energy in isolation has drawbacks because energy efficiency often brings additional latency. Clearly, several practical applications set limits on acceptable latency, as specified by QoS requirements. For example, the data transmission delay per packet may have a bound. Beyond this bound, this packet may be dropped. Therefore, our motivation of this paper is to investigate the trade-off that arises between the end-to-end delay of the data transmission and the lifetime extension of the individual nodes and the network as a whole. We have explored an experimental comparison between k-multipath routing and the shortest path routing. So through distributing the energy load among the nodes, we can increase the lifetime and quality of data in a sensor network. However, multipath routing techniques are not without pitfalls. It is worthwhile to mention them clearly, even though they are not captured in our simulation. The primary disadvantages of multipath routing protocols compared to single path protocol are complexity and overhead. We have to consider the overheads that we maintain multiple routes to a destination, which leads to large routing tables at intermediate nodes. Also, we need to take into consideration how to allocate the packets to the multiple routes. Hence, we still need to expand our design to provide the solution to the above-mentioned problems in the future.

Acknowledgments. We would like to thank the anonymous reviewers for their insight and suggestions which have substantially improved the content and presentation of this paper. This work was supported by the Fundamental Research Funds for the Central Universities of China under Grant No. 31541311303 and the Research Project Funds (32514113005).

References

1. Chen, X., Chamania, M., Jukan, A., Drummond, A.C., da Fonseca, N.L.S.: QoS-Constrained Multi-path Routing for High-End Network Applications. In: IEEE INFOCOM2009 High-Speed Networks Workshop, Rio de Janeiro, Brazil (April 2009)
2. Ganjali, Y., Keshavarzian, A.: Load balancing in ad hoc networks: single-path routing vs. multipath routing. In: Twenty-Third Annual Joint Conference of the IEEE Computer and Communications Societies (INFOCOM 2004) (March 2004)
3. Pham, P.P., Perrau, S.: Performance Analysis of Reactive Shortest Path and Multipath Routing Mechanism with Load Balance. In: Proc. IEEE INFOCOM Conf., pp. 251–259 (April 2003)
4. Kwon, S., Shroff, N.B.: Analysis of Shortest Path Routing for Large Multi-Hop Wireless Networks. IEEE/ACM Transactions on Networking 17(3), 857–869 (2009)
5. Wan, S., He, Y.: Performance analysis of single-tree and split-tree approach in wireless sensor networks. In: CyberC 2009: International Conference on Cyber-Enabled Distributed Computing and Knowledge Discovery, pp. 132–135 (October 2009)
6. Fan, K.-W., Liu, S., Sinha, P.: Structure- free Data Aggregation in Sensor Networks. IEEE Transactions on Mobile Computing (TMC) 6(8), 929–942 (2007); an earlier version also appeared in INFOCOM 2006
7. Skraba, P., Fang, Q., Nguyen, A., Guibas, L.: Sweeps over wireless sensor networks. In: 5th Int'l Conference on Information Processing in Sensor Networks (IPSN), pp. 143–151 (2006)
8. Shrivastava, N., Buragohain, C., Agrawa, D., et al.: Medians and beyond: new aggregation techniques for sensor networks. In: Proc. of the Second International Conference on Embedded Networked Sensor Systems (SenSys 2004), pp. 239–249. ACM Press, New York (2004)
9. Chanak, P., Samanta, T., Banerjee, I.: Fault-tolerant multipath routing scheme for energy efficient wireless sensor networks. International Journal of Wireless & Mobile Networks (IJWMN) 5(2) (April 2013)
10. Vasudevan, S., Adler, M., Goeckel, D., Towsley, D.: Efficient Algorithms for Neighbor Discovery in Wireless Networks. IEEE/ACM Trans. Networking 21(1), 69–83 (2013)
11. Patel, P., Bansal, D., Yuan, L., Murthy, A., Greenberg, A.G., Maltz, D.A., Kern, R., Kumar, H., Zikos, M., Wu, H., Kim, C., Karri, N.: Ananta: cloud scale load balancing. In: SIGCOMM 2013, pp. 207–218 (2013)

An Adaptive Channel Sensing Approach Based on Sequential Order in Distributed Cognitive Radio Networks

Guangsheng Feng[1], Huiqiang Wang[1], Qian Zhao[2], and Hongwu Lv[1]

[1] College of Computer Science and Technology, Harbin Engineering University,
Harbin, China
{fengguangsheng,wanghuiqiang,lvhongwu}@hrbeu.edu.cn
[2] School of Computer and Information Engineering, Harbin University of Commerce,
Harbin, China
zhaoqian@hrbcu.edu.cn

Abstract. We design an efficient sensing order selection strategy for distributed Cognitive Radio Networks (CRNs), where multiple CRs sense the channels sequentially for spectrum opportunities according to a channel Latin Square. We are particularly interested in the case that CRs' quantity is more than the available channels', where traditional approaches will have high probabilities of collision. We first introduce a system model and an adaptive sensing threshold for available channels which is estimated according to the sensing probability of the specific sequential order. Then, we propose a channel sensing and access strategy that can adjust its sensing and access probabilities based on the crowded degree of sequential order. Last, we conduct extensive simulations to compare the performance of our approach with other typical ones. Simulation results show that the proposed scheme achieves an outstanding performance on channel utilization in the case of heavy channel workload.

1 Introduction

The rapid growth of new wireless communication services is now facing the difficulty of no enough available spectrum resource due to the fact that the fixed spectrums have been granted to some licensed entities exclusively. According to tremendous statistics[1-4], a great deal of allocated spectrums are severely underutilized. According to this fact, a new technology, namely Cognitive Radio (CR), is contrived, which enable wireless services to operate over those licensed but temporally or geographically unused spectrums through secondary opportunistic access. Cognitive Radio Networks, abbreviated as CRNs, are built on the platform of Cognitive Radio, where primary users (PUs), i.e., the licensed users, have arbitrary rights to transmit over those licensed channels whenever necessary. However, the secondary users (SUs) or CR nodes must perform spectrum sensing to attain transmission opportunities under the premise of protecting PUs' communications. Due to the hardware advancement, most of the wireless terminals are able to sense more than one channel within a same transmission slot, which is also our concern in this paper.

C.-H. Hsu et al. (Eds.): NPC 2014, LNCS 8707, pp. 395–408, 2014.

For the arbitrary PUs' rights to use licensed channels, a proper sensing mechanism should be designed to ensure a lower rate of transmission collisions among CRs. This mechanism can also evacuate the occupied channels immediately once some PU reclaims them, even if there are some SUs' communications over them. Provided a centralized coordinator and a common control channel (CCC), every CR may achieve a high efficiency of channel sensing and allocation. Otherwise, each of them has to sense the spectrum opportunity independently and then accesses an idle channel depending on the sensed results. In this case, each CR hunts for the opportunities of access channel by periodic or sequential channel sensing. In the first approach, each CR senses a specific channel first and then transmits over it if available. Otherwise, the CR has to wait until the next transmission slot and repeat this process periodically. In the second one, in order to find some available channels, each CR has to sense the channels sequentially according to an elaborated order designed in advance. After spectrum sensing, each CR makes its own decision on whether to sense the next channel continually or to start transmission based on the sensed results. Contrast to the periodically sensing strategies, the sequential approach allows a CR to identify an idle channel quickly by sensing more than one channel successively. If the sensed channel is occupied by other entities currently, there is little time delay before sensing the successive channels. Due to the above justifications, sequential channel sensing is of our concern in this paper.

Traditional researches have mainly focused on improving the throughput of CRNs. However the majority of them have a common assumption or implied assumption that the temporal idle channels could accommodate the majority of CRs, and only in this case some scheduling approaches could achieve a better performance. For example, Khan's work[1] has an excellent performance under the condition that the channel's quantity is not less than the CRs', which has been demonstrated in our experiment in Section 5, but Khan's contribution inspires our work greatly. On the basis of Latin Square utilized in [1], we are interested in the sequential channel sensing strategy without a centralized coordinator under the case of heavy channel workload, i.e., more CRs but fewer available channels.

In this paper, we propose a distributed and sequential sensing approach in a decentralized CRN on the basis of Khan's approach and random access. The contributions of our work are summarized as follows. First, a dynamic sensing threshold for available channels is proposed, which can reflect the crowded degree of a specific sequential channel order. In consideration of the CRs' computation capabilities, the threshold adjustment should be simple, dynamic and low complicated. Once the quantity of sensed available channels reaches the threshold, the related CR will randomly make a decision on whether to choose one channel or to observer continuously. If lots of CRs are crowded on a common sequential order, our approach prefers observation to transmission. Otherwise, there will be a mass of collisions among those CRs, resulted in all the frames invalid as well as a whole transmission slot wasted. Furthermore, if a CR gets a spectrum opportunity and transmits successfully, its access probability to the sequential channel order will be increased; otherwise it will be decreased correspondingly at the next transmission slot. Meanwhile, the sensing threshold of available channel is updated based on the transmission result, i.e., success or failure on this sequential channel order.

The remainder of the paper is organized as follows. In Section 2, we introduce the related work of interest. In Section 3, we design a distributed system model, including the system process mechanism, the stop condition of sensing, the threshold of available channels required to sense, and the collision avoidance approach. In Section 4, we evaluate our proposed design at different channel workload through numerical experimental results. Finally, Section 5 concludes the paper.

2   Related Work

To solve the open problem of spectrum sensing and channel access in distributed CRNs, lots of researches have been conducted and some typical frameworks have been proposed, such as the work in [2-4], where the issue of Opportunistic Spectrum Access, abbreviated as OSA, is still a hot issue.

In order to attain more spectrum opportunities, each CR has to perform periodic sensing or sequential sensing under the premise of protecting PUs' transmission. Centralized and decentralized approaches are two typical branches in dealing with such problems. In centralized ones, a coordinator is required to schedule all CRs' sensing and transmission activities, such as in [5, 6]. The work in [5] takes the statistical features of channel availabilities into consideration, and attains an optimal sensing sequential order with the assistance of coordinator, but this scheme is only suitable for two CRs existed. If lots of CRs are desired to communicate simultaneously, a heavy workload on channels will definitely deteriorate the network performance due to massive collisions. The work in [6] is established on an assumption that CRs and PUs cooperate with each other, where each CR reports its channel sensing result to a centralized Dynamic Spectrum Access (DSA) base station. Therefore, the overall throughput will be maximized through scheduling each CR's transmission opportunity by the DSA. In consideration of DSA unknowing all the operation parameters of PUs, this work proposed a sequential channel sensing order based on estimated traffic. However, all CR devices may not be managed by the same service provider in actual scenarios, and hence it is impossible to attain an optimal scheduling strategy with several different coordinators.

Sensing channel in CRNs with a distributed manner is another branch. Traditional researches are mainly focused on studying periodical sensing strategies, which are easy to implement especially only one authorized channel existed[7]. Moreover, these approaches are easily extended to multi-channel scenarios. In other words, in a given slot, a CR selects a channel to sense in a random way or according to its prior knowledge, and then it accesses this channel to transmit if available. Otherwise, this CR should stay quiet in the whole transmission slot. In this point, a distributed learning and allocation approach is investigated in the work [8, 9], where an adaptive random selection strategy on orthogonal channels is employed. The implementation of this approach is simple but high collision probability.

Using sequential channel order to sense spectrum opportunity has become a hot issue[10], in which a CR probes multiple channels one by one with an elaborated order in a given time slot. Generally, high throughput and low collision are two main objectives of system optimization [11-17]. In the work[11, 12], a low-load approach jointing transmission optimization is proposed to sense channels sequentially. The priori knowledge of authorized channels is not necessary in this approach but requires perfect bandwidth and data rate. The work [13] proposes a simple channel sensing order in multi-channel CRNs without the prior knowledge of PUs' activities, where all CRs sense the channels according to the descending order of their achievable rates. However, this approach is only suitable for OFDM surroundings, and also requires all channel gains in advance.

In the work[14], the statistics characteristics of Signal-to-Noise Ratio for each channel are explored using pilot signals and PU's activities. Based on the fluctuating nature of heterogeneous channels as well as the QoS requirements of various applications, two approaches for channel sensing order are proposed, which are suitable for real-time and best-effort applications respectively. Nevertheless, a Cognitive Pilot Channel, abbreviated as CPC, is required to exchange control information between CRs and the base station. The work[15] is focused on identifying the sensing order and sensing-access strategy such that it can achieve the maximum of energy efficiency. This problem is formulated as a stochastic sequential decision-making process and solved by means of dynamic programming. In addition, the long-term statistical features and short-term diversity features[16], as well as the fast channel sharing[17] are taken into account.

Recently, an efficient strategy for sensing order selection in distributed CRNs surroundings is proposed in Khan's work[1], where two or more autonomous CRs sense the channels sequentially (in some sensing order) for spectrum opportunities. The key contribution of this work is the adaptive persistent sensing order selection strategy in the case that CRs with false alarms autonomously select the sensing orders. This approach may achieve a better performance only when the quantity of CRs is not more than the quantity of available channels.

Different with existing work, we propose a novel sequential order strategy for sensing multiple channels in distributed CRNs jointing Khan's work and random access, but the two works have essential differences. Given that the sensing duration for a single channel is much shorter than the transmission duration, it is worth to attain a much lower collision probability at the cost of part transmission time, which is the foundation of this work.

3   An Adaptive Model for Multiple Channels Sensing

3.1   System Model

In a distributed CRN, M CRs and N authorized channels are coexisted, which are denoted as $\mathbf{CR} = \{CR_1, CR_2, \cdots, CR_M\}$ and $\mathbf{C} = \{C_1, C_2, \cdots, C_N\}$ respectively. If some channels are idle and sensed simultaneously by some CRs, they could transmit over those channels. In this case, if a PU reclaims one of the channels occupied by some CR, it will be evacuated by the related CR at once, which is consistent with the basic principle of Cognitive Radio. Given that all PUs and CRs employ the same time slot system as figure 1 shown, a CR maybe have experienced i sensing sub-slots when k idle channels are found, where k is the sensing threshold of available channels, i.e., a CR is required to find k idle channels and then makes a decision on whether to transmit or sense continually. The maximum of sensing duration is an allowable sensing interval, and the sensing process will be stopped and stay quiet if there is no any idle channel found until this upper bound. A PU's communication activity starts only in the beginning of a time slot and last to its end.

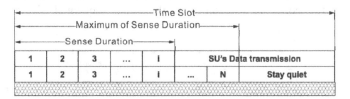

Fig. 1. Multiple channels access with the same time slot system

Similar to Khan's approach, all channels are organized as a form of Latin Square such as in(1):

$$\mathbf{CS} = \begin{bmatrix} C_1, C_2, C_3, \cdots, C_{N-1},\ C_N \\ C_2, C_3, C_4, \cdots, C_N\ ,\ C_1 \\ C_3, C_4, C_5, \cdots, C_1\ ,\ C_2 \\ \vdots\ \ \vdots\ \ \vdots\ \ \ddots\ \ \vdots\ \ \ \vdots \\ C_N, C_1, C_2, \cdots, C_{N-2}, C_{N-1} \end{bmatrix} \tag{1}$$

where there are $N*N$ elements and each row $CS_i\,(i=1,2,...,N)$ stands for a sequential channel order whose elements are consisted of $CS_{ij}\,(j=1,2,...,N)$. Every CR maintains a sensing probability for each CS_i, i.e., $P^{(CS)} = \{p_i^{(CS)}, i=1,2,...,N\}$, which the CR senses sequential channel order CS_i according to. At the beginning, each CR will select some CS_i according to the probability $p_i^{(CS)} - 1/N_{CS} = 1/N$. With the process going, the $p_i^{(CS)}$ will be updated according to its transmission and collision states, the objective of which is lowering the sensing probability to crowded channel orders. Note that the specific adaptive updating approach for $p_i^{(CS)}$ will be elaborated in next section. Due to the limitation of hardware devices, sensing and transmission could not be conducted simultaneously.

This model is established on the analysis of contending spectrum resource and one CR will make a decision on communicating over an idle channel only when k available channels are found. If two or more CRs are crowded at the same sequential channel order, it is required to sensing more available channels before making a transmission decision. Otherwise, a smaller number of available channels can help make a transmission decision. As shown in figure 2, C_1, C_2, C_3 and C_4 four channels are existed in a CRN, whose front part is a Latin Square based on channels, and its columns stand for sensing sub-slots, such as Sense 1 to Sense 4. In a transmission slot, a CR should find some idle channels first and then transmit in the remaining time of this slot. Suppose that CR_1 and CR_2 are crowded at the same CS_1 to perform sequential channel sensing simultaneously. In this case, if both CRs transmit immediately once they find one idle channel, a collision event between them is destined to occur. On the contrary, if they start their transmission when more than one idle channel is found, such as C_1 and C_2 available, they maybe avoid this collision event for CR_1 choosing one idle channel but CR_2 choosing the another idle one. Instinctively, the collision probability at the same sequential channel order is decreased.

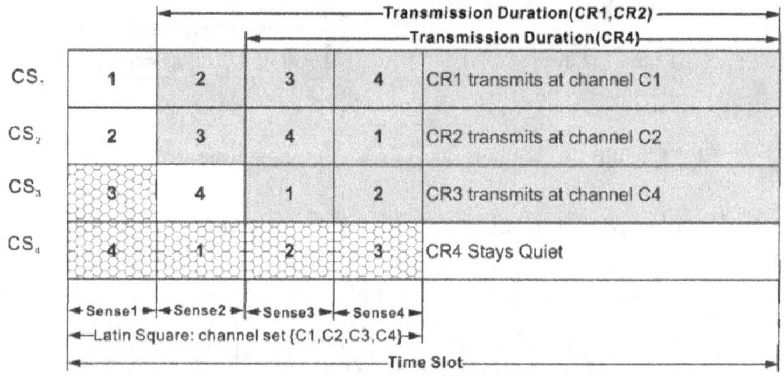

				Transmission Duration(CR1,CR2)	
				Transmission Duration(CR4)	
CS_1	1	2	3	4	CR1 transmits at channel C1
CS_2	2	3	4	1	CR2 transmits at channel C2
CS_3	3	4	1	2	CR3 transmits at channel C4
CS_4	4	1	2	3	CR4 Stays Quiet
	◄ Sense1 ►◄ Sense2 ►◄ Sense3 ►◄ Sense4 ►				
	◄ Latin Square: channel set {C1,C2,C3,C4} ►				
	◄ Time Slot ►				

Fig. 2. Schematic diagram of channel sensing

3.2   Stop Condition and Sensing Threshold for Available Channels

In this paper, we mainly concern the distributed approach for sequential channel sensing and there is no possibility of cooperative communications among CRs as well as PUs. Given that the sensing threshold for available channel is k, each CR will sense the sequential channel order CS_i successively, i.e., $\{CS_{i1}, CS_{i2},...,CS_{im}\}$, based on its sensing probability $p_i^{(CS)}$ until k available channels are found. Afterwards, the CR makes a decision on whether to transmit or to sense continuously. In contrast to existing work, we do not consider the traditional stop condition that once an idle channel is found, the process will be transferred to transmission from channel sensing. In the case of heavy channel load, i.e., more CRs but fewer available channels, two or more CRs are crowded at the same sequential channel order which leads to a high rate of collision correspondingly. If we continue to sense until k available channels (at least one) found, each CR on this channel order will have an opportunity to choose a different channel C_j to transmit according to its access probability $p_{CH}(CS_i, C_j)$.

Therefore, the value of k is sensitive to the collision probability. If it is too small, more collision will be caused, but on the contrary, the overall sensing time will be increased and the transmission time is shortened correspondingly.

As discussed above, $p_i^{(CS)}$ is the foregoing sensing probability that a CR attends at sequential channel order CS_i, which is estimated according to its transmission success or not on CS_i. A smaller of $p_i^{(CS)}$ stands for a higher collision probability on CS_i. On this basis, the threshold k of available channels could be estimated as (2):

$$k = \min\left\{ \lfloor 1/p_i^{(CS)} \rfloor, C_a \right\} \tag{2}$$

where C_a is the total quantity of available channels. Therefore, k's value stands for the crowded degree of the current channel order. If k equals to 1, our approach is simplified to Khan's. In conclusion, the stop condition of sensing channel is that k available channels have been found by the current CR.

3.3   Mechanism of Collision Avoidance

In a distributed CRN, collision events will occur frequently due to different CRs contending spectrum opportunities as well as lacking coordinated mechanism among CRs. If two or more CRs are crowded at the same sequential channel order, each CR may attain a similar sensing result and they surely collide with each other even the idle channels being found. In this case, all the transmission frames will be corrupted. To solve those problems, we propose a dynamic collision avoidance mechanism in this paper.

Suppose that a CR senses on sequential channel order CS_i, and do not take transmission activity until k available channels are found, where k is estimated according to section 3.2. If the specific quantity channels are found, the CR will randomly make a choice to transmit or to sense continuously. If continuous sensing is selected, the similar decision will be made in next sensing round. In other words, once k available channels are found, the CR faces two choices:

■   Select channel C_j to transmit based on $p_{CH}(CS_i, C_j)$ that denotes the probability of selecting channel C_j:

$$p_{CH}(CS_i, C_j) = \frac{2 \times r_j}{(1+k) \times k} \tag{3}$$

where k is the sensing threshold of available channels and r_j is the index number of channel C_j in current available channel set. As shown in(3), the last available channel in sensing result set has the highest access probability. Let r $(r=1,2,\ldots,k)$ denotes the index number in available set, and I_r is the subscript of some channel, i.e., $C_{I_r} \in C$. Therefore, C_{I_k} is the last element and $p_{CH}(CS_i, C_{I_k})$ is

$$p_{CH}(CS_i, C_{I_k}) = \frac{2 \times k}{(1+k) \times k} = \frac{2}{(1+k)} \tag{4}$$

To sum up, the access probability of each element in the available set is sensitive to its index number in this set as well as the total quantity k.

■   Continue to sense at the current sequential channel order CS_i.

If the first choice is selected, i.e., transmit over channel C_j, the following two cases maybe happen.

Case 1: If there is no collision over channel C_j during the transmission interval, this time of transmission is successful, which can be inferred from whether the related ACK is correctly received or not. In this case, the sensing probability CS_j, whose first item is C_j, is increased correspondingly:

$$\begin{cases} p_j^{(CS)} = p_j^{(CS)\,\prime} + \sigma_j \\ p_{k\neq j}^{(CS)} = \dfrac{1 - p_j^{(CS)}}{\sum\limits_{q\neq j} p_{q\neq j}^{(CS)\,\prime}} \times p_{k\neq j}^{(CS)} \end{cases} ,\ \text{if}\ p_j^{(CS)\,\prime} + \sigma_j < 1 \tag{5}$$

where $p_j^{(CS)\,\prime}$ is the sensing probability of CS_j at the last transmission slot and $\sigma_j \geq 0$ denotes the augmentation of sensing probability to CS_j at this transmission slot. The value of σ_j should meet the requirement $\lceil 1/p_j \rceil - \lceil 1/p_j{}' \rceil \geq K^{(CS_j)}$, which means that the sensing threshold of available channels should be increased by $K^{(CS_j)}$ such that the hit rate of channel C_j will be increased correspondingly. In this updating process, if $p_j^{(CS)\,\prime} + \sigma_j \geq 1$ holds true, the sensing probability to CS_j will be set to 1 and other one be set to 0, i.e., $p_{k\neq j}^{(CS)} = 0$.

Case 2: If the ACK is not received correctly, it is deemed that a collision occurs on channel C_j. In this case, the sensing probability to sequential channel order CS_j will be decreased, but others will be increased as shown in(6):

$$\begin{cases} p_j^{(CS)} = p_j^{(CS)\,\prime} - \sigma_j \\ p_{k\neq j}^{(CS)} = \dfrac{1 - p_j^{(CS)}}{\sum\limits_{q\neq j} p_{q\neq j}^{(CS)\,\prime}} \cdot p_{k\neq j}^{(CS)} \end{cases} ,\ \text{s.t.,}\ p_j^{(CS)\,\prime} - \sigma_j \geq 0 \tag{6}$$

Similarly,   the   value   of $\sigma_j \geq 0$ should   meet   the   requirement $\lceil 1/p_j{}' \rceil - \lceil 1/p_j \rceil \geq K^{(CS_j)}$ such that the hit rate of CS_j and C_j will be decreased. If there is a contradictory between the two inequalities $p_j^{(CS)\,\prime} - \sigma_j \geq 0$ and $\lceil 1/p_j{}' \rceil - \lceil 1/p_j \rceil \geq K^{(CS_j)}$, the former one should be assured first.

In case 1, it is possible that a CR continues to sense at the current sequential channel order CS_i. In this case, this CR starts to sense from the first element in CS_i in next sensing round, but those channels that have been found busy in the first sensing round will be omitted. Similarly, the process will transfer to transmission or selection decision when k available channels are found. When the whole time of sensing rounds reaches to the upper bound, i.e., the maximum of sensing duration, the sensing process will be stopped at once. As an example shown in figure 3, in the first sensing round (Round 1), CR_1, CR_2, CR_3 and CR_4 employ the same order $CS_1 < C_1, C_2, C_3, C_4, C_5 >$ to sense k (k=3) available channels. As a result, C_2 is busy and C_1, C_3 and C_4 are idle. In this case, if CR_1 selects channel C_1 to transmit but others decide to sense continuously, C_3, C_4 and C_5 are found available and C_1 is observed in this round. In this case, if CR_2 and CR_3 make a decision on transmission over C_3, a collision happens. Therefore, in the next transmission slot, CR_2 and CR_3 will decrease the sensing probabilities to $CS_3 < C_3, C_4, C_5, C_1, C_2, >$, and meanwhile increase the others. Instinctively, what we do can lower the collision probability in contrast to immediately transmission while one available channel is found.

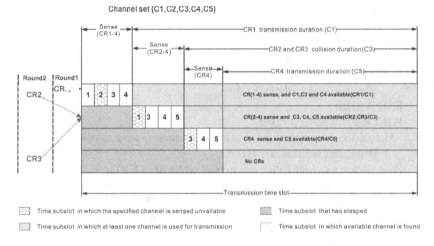

Fig. 3. Illustration of sense, collision and transmission in a transmission slot

Our proposed adaptive multiple channels sensing strategy can be summarized as the following pseudo-code algorithm CRN_MCST, which is executed in each CR independently and there is no any information exchanging among them.

Each CR will execute algorithm CRN_MCST one time in every single transmission slot. In initialization stage, the sensing probabilities to all sequential channel order are identical. With the iterating of transmission, each CR independently make a judgment on whether the current sequential channel order is crowded or not, and then adjust its sensing probability accordingly. In line 2-3, the threshold k of available channels sensing is calculated based on the sensing probability, and meanwhile a sequential channel order is selected from the channel Latin Square, i.e., CS_i. In line 4-8, the CR senses the sequential channel order successively, in which all the available channels are stored into the pre-allocated buffer. This process will be executed repeatedly until k available channels found or all the items in CS_i have been checked. Thus, the complexity of line 4-8 is proportional to the total channel quantity, i.e., $O(n)$. In the process of line 9-20, the CR makes a decision on which channel should be selected for transmission, and the sensing probability and access probability are also updated according to the transmission result. The time complexity is proportional to buffer size, thus it is $O(k)$ and $k <= n$. In line 21-22, it is the case that no available channels are found and the CR will stay quietly in the whole transmission slot. To sum up, the time complexity in a transmission slot is O(n).

Algorithm. CRN_MCST

   Initialization: The sensing probability vector P$^{(CS)}$, and each $p_i^{(CS)} = 1/n, i = 1, 2, ..., n$

   The channel matrix CS with Latin Square form;
   buffer_free is empty;// used for store the available channels sensed
   transmit_flag=false;

1.   **BEGIN**
2. CS_i is selected from CS based on $p_i^{(CS)}$
3.   Calculate k based on E.q.(2)
4.   **WHILE** ! endof(CS_i) && sizeof(buffer_free)<k //k is the threshold of free channels sensed by the current CR
5.   **IF** CS_{ij} is busy **THEN** j++;
6.   **ELSE**
7.   Store the CS_{ij} into the buffer_free;
8.   **END WHILE**
9.   **WHILE** sizeof(buffer_free)>0
10.   Make a decision on whether to transmit or continue to sense randomly;
11.   **IF** deciding transmission **THEN**
12.   Select C_j from buffer_free to transmit based on E.q.(3)
13.   Set transmit_flag=true and Transmit at the remaining transmission slots
14.   **IF** transmission is successful at C_j in CS_i **THEN**
15.   Increase the probability CS_i based on sensing probability E.q.(5) ;
16.   **ELSE** decrease the probability CS_i based on sensing probability E.q.(6);
17.   Evacuate the buffer_free; // CR will transmit at the remaining period
18.   **ELSE** //continue to sense the free channel in buffer_free
19.   Goto step 2;
20.   **END WHILE**
21.   **IF** transmit_flag=flase **THEN**
22.   Stay quiet until next transmission slot
23.   **END**

Fig. 4. Algorithm CRN_MCST: multiple channel sense and transmission

4   Experiments and Analysis

In order to verify the performance and compare with other typical approaches, some numerical experiments has been conducted in this section, where the mainly parameters in our experiment are similar to Khan's approach. The channel busy probability Pu is set 0.0, 0.1, 0.3 and 0.5, such that we can check the performance of different approaches at different channel workloads. The total channel quantity is 10 and the quantity of CRs are various from 2 to 20. The performance of channel utilization can be inferred from the wasted ratio of transmission slot, including collision interval and idle interval. Moreover, we set 50 transmission slots in each time experiment and total 10 experiments are conducted. Thus, we have attained 100 times experimental data. Meanwhile, we set 11 sub-slots as a transmission slot, i.e., if a CR has sensed the last item in current sequential order, there is only one sub-slot for transmission. The experimental results are shown in figure 5 - figure 8.

Figure 5 and figure 6 are the comparisons between our approach and Khan's. Khan's approach has an excellent performance under the case that there is a light load with a fewer number of CRs on the channels, where the wasted ration of transmission is no more than 20%. While the CR quantity is more than 10, the wasted ratio is soaring. Even all the channel are not occupied by PUs, i.e., $Pu=0.0$, the wasted ratio reaches 60% with 20 CRs. But in the case of $Pu=0.5$, the wasted ratio is about 33% in Khan's approach. Figure 6 shows the experimental result of our approach. It is obvious that the proposed approach has a better overall performance compared with Khan's, and the wasted ratio is constrained about 10% at different probabilities of Pus. Only when the CR quantity is 2 or 3, the performance is not superior to Khan's.

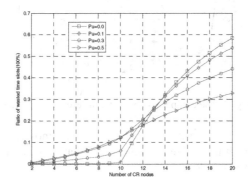

Fig. 5. Khan's method at different busy probabilities of channels with various CR quantities

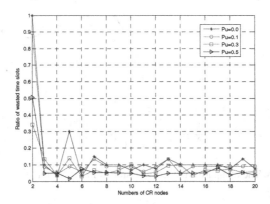

Fig. 6. The proposed method at different Pus with various CR quantities

Figure 7 shows the comparison at the channel busy probability $Pu=0.1$. Only when the CR quantity is less than channel quantity, Khan's method has a better performance. After that point, this approach has an intolerable increasing on channel wasted ratio. On the contrary, our approach remains a comparative stable wasted ration about 10%, only when the CR quantity is 2 or 3, the performance is poor. In the case of heavy channel workload, our proposed approach will be a quite effective complement to Khan's approach. In those three approaches, the Random LS strategy[13] has the least performance and the channel wasted ratio is reached 70% when there are 20 CRs in the network.

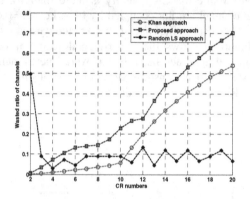

Fig. 7. The comparison between different approaches

When there are 10 CRs, each CR could attain an almost equitable transmission chance about 10% in all those three approaches, and all of them have achieved a well fairness, as shown in Figure 8.

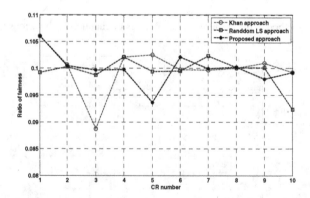

Fig. 8. The comparison in transmission ratio of different CR nodes

5   Conclusion

In this paper, we have investigated the distributed channel sensing strategy in a CRN environment with heavy load channels and obtained some important observations. In the system model, a sensing threshold for available channels is estimated based on the crowded degree of the current sequential channel order. On this base, each CR can adjust its sensing probability to sequential order and access probability to a channel according to whether this transmission success or not. Moreover, we presented an algorithm with low computational complexity, in which the process of each CR sensing the sequential channel order and deciding channel to transmit is elaborated in detail. Simulation results demonstrate the effectiveness of our proposed approach.

Acknowledgments. This work was supported in part by the Research Fund for the Doctoral Program of Higher Education of China under Grant 20122304130002, the Natural Science Foundation in China under Grant 61370212, the Natural Science Foundation of Heilongjiang Province under Grant ZD 201102 and F201037, the Fundamental Research Fund for the Central Universities under Grant HEUCFZ1213 and HEUCF100601, and Postdoctoral Science Foundation of Heilongjiang Province under Grant LBH-210204.

References

1. Khan, Z., Lehtomaki, J.J., DaSilva, L.A., Latva-aho, M.: Autonomous sensing order selection strategies exploiting channel access information. IEEE Transactions on Mobile Computing 12(2), 274–288 (2013)
2. Akyildiz, I.F., Lee, W.-Y., Vuran, M.C., Mohanty, S.: A survey on spectrum management in cognitive radio networks. IEEE Communications Magazine 46(4), 40–48 (2008)
3. Khozeimeh, F., Haykin, S.: Brain-inspired dynamic spectrum management for cognitive radio ad hoc networks. IEEE Transactions on Wireless Communications 11(10), 3509–3517 (2012)
4. Salami, G., Durowoju, O., Attar, A., Holland, O., Tafazolli, R., Aghvami, H.: A comparison between the centralized and distributed approaches for spectrum management. IEEE Communications Surveys & Tutorials 13(2), 274–290 (2011)
5. Fan, R., Jiang, H.: Channel sensing-order setting in cognitive radio networks: A two-user case. IEEE Transactions on Vehicular Technology 58(9), 4997–5008 (2009)
6. Liu, C.-H., Tran, J.A., Pawelczak, P., Cabric, D.: Traffic-aware channel sensing order in dynamic spectrum access networks. IEEE Journal on Selected Areas in Communications 31(11), 2312–2323 (2013)
7. Liang, Y.-C., Zeng, Y., Peh, E.C., Hoang, A.T.: Sensing-throughput tradeoff for cognitive radio networks. IEEE Transactions on Wireless Communications 7(4), 1326–1337 (2008)
8. Anandkumar, A., Michael, N., Tang, A.: Opportunistic spectrum access with multiple users: learning under competition. In: The 29th IEEE Conference on Computer Communications (INFOCOM 2010), San Diego, USA, pp. 1–9. IEEE Communications Society (2010)
9. Anandkumar, A., Michael, N., Tang, A.K., Swami, A.: Distributed algorithms for learning and cognitive medium access with logarithmic regret. IEEE Journal on Selected Areas in Communications 29(4), 731–745 (2011)
10. Theis, N.C., Thomas, R.W., DaSilva, L.A.: Rendezvous for cognitive radios. IEEE Transactions on Mobile Computing 10(2), 216–227 (2011)
11. Jiang, H., Lai, L., Fan, R., Poor, H.V.: Optimal selection of channel sensing order in cognitive radio. IEEE Transactions on Wireless Communications 8(1), 297–307 (2009)

12. Chang, N.B., Liu, M.: Competitive analysis of opportunistic spectrum access strategies. In: The 27th IEEE Conference on Computer Communications (INFOCOM 2008), Phoenix, AZ, USA, pp. 2207–2215. IEEE Computer Society Press (2008)
13. Cheng, H.T., Zhuang, W.: Simple channel sensing order in cognitive radio networks. IEEE Journal on Selected Areas in Communications 29(4), 676–688 (2011)
14. Huang, J., Zhou, H., Chen, Y., Chen, B., Zhu, X., Kong, R.: Optimal channel sensing order for various applications in cognitive radio networks. Wireless personal communications 71(3), 1721–1740 (2013)
15. Pei, Y., Liang, Y.-C., Teh, K.C., Li, K.H.: Energy-efficient design of sequential channel sensing in cognitive radio networks: optimal sensing strategy, power allocation, and sensing order. IEEE Journal on Selected Areas in Communications 29(8), 1648–1659 (2011)
16. Li, B., Yang, P., Wang, J., Wu, Q., Tang, S., Li, X., Liu, Y.: Almost optimal dynamically-ordered channel sensing and accessing for cognitive networks. IEEE Transactions on Mobile Computing, 1–14 (2013)
17. Lai, J., Dutkiewicz, E., Liu, R., Vesilo, R.: Opportunistic Spectrum Access with Two Channel Sensing in Cognitive Radio Networks. IEEE Transactions on Mobile Computing, 1–14 (2013)

A Location Privacy Preserving Method
Based on Sensitive Diversity for LBS

Changli Zhou[1,*], Chunguang Ma[1,*], Songtao Yang[1,2], Peng Wu[1], and Linlin Liu[3]

[1] Harbin Engineering University, Harbin City 150001, China
[2] Jia Mu Si University, Jiamusi City 154007, China
[3] Harbin Crystal Commercial Photography Co. Ltd, Harbin City 150001, China
zhouchangli888@gmail.com, machunguang@hrbeu.edu.cn

Abstract. A user's staying points in her trajectory have semantic association with privacy, such as she stays at a hospital. Staying at a sensitive place, a user may have privacy exposure risks when she gets location based service (LBS). Constructing cloaking regions and using fake locations are common methods. But if regions and fake positions are still in the sensitive area, it is vulnerable to lead location privacy exposure. We propose an anchor generating method based on sensitive places diversity. According to the visiting number and peak time of users, sensitive places are chosen to form a diversity zone, its centroid is taken as the anchor location which increases a user's location diversity. Based on the anchor, a query algorithm for places of interest (POIs) is proposed, and precise results can be deduced with the anchor instead of sending users' actual location to LBS server. The experiments show that our method achieves a tradeoff between QoS and privacy preserving, and it has a good working performance.

1 Introduction

Location Based Service (LBS) brings convenience to people's lives, at the same time, it also poses a risk of location privacy leakage. Location based query is a widely used LBS, a user sends a query request with her current location to LBS provider (LSP) to get places of interest (POIs). Such as "find the K nearest neighbor restaurants around me" or "find all the restaurants in the range of R kilometers", the former one is called KNN query and latter one is range query. Due to the spatial and temporal relevance, an exposure of location privacy may lead deeply privacy leakage, such as a user's home address, hobbies, health condition and so on. Location privacy is significantly important to us and should be protected carefully.

Places on a user's trajectory can be divided into two kinds: passing-by places and staying-at places. A mobile user issues LBS query with her current location at any time in a trajectory. A passing-by place has no relationship with a user, it only means a user has passed by a location without any semantic association. But a staying-at place, especially a sensitive place, has semantic association with a user staying at it, such as a user is staying at an infectious hospital.

---

* Corresponding author.

C.-H. Hsu et al. (Eds.): NPC 2014, LNCS 8707, pp. 409–422, 2014.

Location obfuscation is a general protecting method for location privacy preserving. Such as constructing cloaking region to achieve *k*-anonymity[1,2,3], as shown in Fig 1, user C sends her actual location to an anonymous server (AS), then AS expands her actual location to a rectangle R_2 including 2 other users, and R_2 will be sent to LSP for POIs instead of her actual location. But there is a problem, if the cloaking region is in a sensitive area, such as dash line rectangle in Fig.2. A query is sent with R_2 means the user is in a hospital. And when a user stays or moves a short distance in a sensitive area, all her cloaking regions may be included in it. Location diversity is a solution that requires users in a cloaking region to appear in diverse places, but that may lead a large cloaking region, such as R_3.

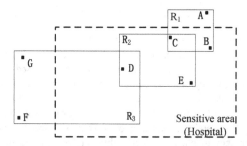

Fig. 1. Cloaking regions

Another protecting method is using fake locations[6,7], that is sending an actual location accompanied with some fake locations, and all the locations will be used in query operations, that brings too much burden to LSP. Then query methods with significant object[8] or anchor[9] are proposed, they have more improvements and more precise query results. Especially, SpaceTwist[9] is an effective method to get *K*NN POIs without providing a user's actual location to LSP. But these methods have the same drawback, which is if the fake locations or anchors are still picked in a sensitive area, location privacy of a user will be leaked anyway.

Staying at a sensitive place causes a semantic association with a user, continuous sensitive places lead to deep-going leakages[10,11]. We focus on the privacy preserving when a user is staying at or moving short distance around a sensitive place. The contents and contributions of this paper are as follows:

1).We propose a location privacy preserving method based on sensitive places diversity when a user is staying at a sensitive place. A center server (CS) generates a diversity anchor for a user. The diversity anchor is used to replace a user's actual location. CS sends a query with the anchor. The diversity anchor is in the overlap area of several sensitive places, which increases uncertainty of a user's actual location.

2).We propose a query algorithm with the diversity anchor. In a query request, a diversity anchor is sent to LSP instead of a user's actual location. LSP takes the anchor as a centroid and returns a candidate POIs set to CS, and CS can deduce precise result of *K*NN POIs for a user. Without providing any user's actual location, our algorithm achieves location privacy preserving and gets precise *K*NN POIs for a user.

2   Related Works

In order to achieve location privacy preserving, a user obscures her actual location before getting LBS. Gruteser et al[1] brought in k-anonymous idea from database for LBS privacy preserving. Mokbel et al[12] proposed an architecture with center server(CS), CS is between users and LSP, most of the CSs are credible. CS cloaks a user's actual location and returns refined results. Chow and Mokbel[13,14] proposed a P2P architecture without CS, it removes bottleneck when CS faces lots of users.

Anonymity is achieved by these methods, but if users crowd together in a place, cloaking regions may still in a small area, in extreme case they are at the same spot. To solve this problem, Bamba et al[4] introduced l-diversity idea from data publication into location anonymity, they proposed a cloaking method which satisfies location diversity. Xue et al[17] proposed a location diversity method to ensure each query can be associated with at least l different semantic places. Xu et al[5] proposed an anonymous cell with diversity roads. Yang et al[18] proposed cloaking cycle and forest which include diversity roads to ensure that a user locates at diversity roads equally in a cloaking cycle. Meng et al[11] proposed sensitive trajectory location protection method in data publication. Liu[19] gives query l-diversity in location privacy preserving for the first time.

Using fake locations is another way to achieve protection. A general method is sending several fake locations in order to obscure a user's actual location [6-9]. A user sends a fake location in SpaceTwist [9], which is called "anchor", to LSP and the user deduces POIs result according to the returned candidate set. The main procedure is as follows:

As shown in Fig. 2, a solid "•" denotes a user's actual location, "×" denotes an anchor. A user sends a query with the anchor to LSP, LSP performs INN (incremental nearest neighbor) query to get POIs candidate set and then sends it to the user gradually. Firstly, LSP takes the anchor as the centriod of supply space to search POIs. When a POI is found in Fig.2(b), the supply space expends and the demand space centred with user's location shrinks. As POIs are found gradually, SpaceTwist terminates when the supply space covers the demand space. Meng[15] and Gong[16] have proposed improvement to make SpaceTwist achieve k-anonymity respectively.

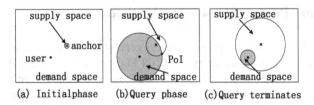

(a) Initialphase   (b)Query phase   (c)Query terminates

Fig. 2. SpaceTwist processing procedure

Both cloaking region and anchor will cause privacy leakage when they are still in a sensitive place. In this paper, we use an anchor referring to SpaceTwist, and ensure a user at sensitive place to pick the anchor with location diversity. Based on the anchor, we propose a query algorithm to get precise KNN POIs result for a user.

3   System Architecture

We pick the architecture with a CS, CS is between users and LSP, as shown in Fig. 3. A user with a GPS sensor of her intelligent terminal sends her location and query to CS. CS computes an anchor and sends anonymous query with the anchor to LSP. LSP performs INN search in its database according to the anchor location and returns POIs candidate set to CS. CS deduces precise results to the user.

Definition 1. There are 3 entity sets $< U, CS, LSP >$, $u_k \in U$ represents an energy constrained mobile user. $CS_i \in CS$ is a central server, deployed at crowded location, it has stronger abilities. LSP is an LBS provider, which is powerful in energy and processing, it stores all POIs in its database. CS is credible, users and LSP may be not.

Definition 2. A user's query $< u_k, loc_{uk}, l, C, R >$, u_k is her identity, loc_{uk} is an actual location, l is sensitive diversity degree, C and R are her query request content and personal requirement in the query respectively.

Definition 3. CS sends a piece of query $< CS_i, loc_{anchor}, C, \beta >$, CS_i is identity of a CS and loc_{anchor} is the anchor location which is computed and satisfied with location diversity, β is the number of POIs returned from LSP each time.

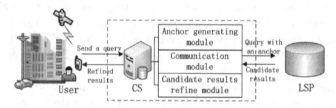

Fig. 3. System architecture

Definition 4. POIs are denoted as $\mathcal{P} = \{\mathcal{P}_1, \mathcal{P}_2, \ldots, \mathcal{P}_n\}$, $\mathcal{P}_i \in \mathcal{P}$ is a POI or a sensitive place. POIs also have semantic association with users, so we usually consider some POIs as sensitive places.

4   Location Privacy Preserving Method

Our method includes two main phases: the CS generates a diverse anchor for the user who is at a sensitive place, and query for *KNN* POIs with the anchor. The first phase contains sensitive location definition method based on users visiting frequency characteristics, and the anchor generating method is based on sensitive locaiton diversity. The second phase presents the query algorithm with a diversity anchor.

4.1   Diversity Anchor Generating Phase

We assign different sensitive weights based on users visiting number and visiting time period firstly. The sensitive weights are used to generate a diversity anchor then.

4.1.1   Sensitive Location Definition

Visiting number and peak visiting time period of a place reflect a sociality of a kind of people. When the users are staying at the place, the semantic associations will lead a privacy leakage of these users. For example, the visiting users to a place becomes more in every weekday morning, it may be a company rather than a bar, a user stays at this place may expose her working place. A place is often visited at night, it may be a bar rather than a hospital. Nearly all sensitive places have bigger visiting numbers and regular peak visiting time. These may lead a correlation with a category of places, so we take visiting number and peak visiting time as main factors.

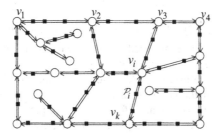

Fig. 4. Road networks with POIs

As the sensitive places are distributed in road networks, a user always finds a path to reach a sensitive place. So when we discuss users visiting number, we consider sensitive places (or POIs) are on the edge of the road graph. We define a directed graph of road networks as $G = (\mathbf{V}, \mathbf{E})$, $\mathbf{V}$ is a set of vertexes, each $v_i \in \mathbf{V}$ has a visiting weight $\mathcal{R}(v_i) = \lambda_i$. $\mathbf{E}$ is a set of edges, $e_{ik} \in \mathbf{E}$ is a directed edge between v_i and v_k. If there is no other vertex $v_x \in \mathbf{V}/\{v_i, v_k\}$ between v_i and v_k, a road directly connects v_i and v_k. Users arrive from v_i to v_k follows Poisson process with arrival rate $\lambda_{ik} > 0$, and $e_{ik} = \lambda_{ik}$, or else $e_{ik} = 0$. So we define visiting weight of a vertex v_i:

$$\mathcal{R}(v_i) = \lambda_i = \lambda_i' + \sum_{v_j \in \mathbf{V}, k \neq i} e_{ki} = \lambda_i' + \sum_{v_j \in \mathbf{V}, k \neq i} \lambda_{ki} \tag{1}$$

λ_i' is a accumulation of user arrival rate who doesn't start from a vertex. Suppose a user chooses each outgoing edge of a vertex with equal probability, each outgoing edge has a visiting weight $\mathcal{R}(v_i) / \deg_{out}(v_i)$, $\deg_{out}(v_i)$ is the outgoing degree. A road segment with two vertexes v_i and v_k has a weight $\mathcal{M}$ in the Formula (2). As shown in Fig.4, black square points are denoted as sensitive places. As we known, a user doesn't stays at each places in a road segment $v_i v_k$, she may only stay at one place according to her destination.

$$\mathcal{M} = [\mathcal{R}(v_i) / \deg_{out}(v_i)] + [\mathcal{R}(v_k) / \deg_{out}(v_k)] \tag{2}$$

Suppose a place P_i on $v_i v_k$ has n users passed by in a certain time period of a day and the probability of staying-at users is p, so the users staying at a place P_i on $v_i v_k$ follows Poisson process with an arrival rate $\mu_i = np$. The probability of staying-at number X of users when X is greater than a threshold X_T is:

$$P(X > X_T) = 1 - P(X \leq X_T) = 1 - \frac{e^{-\mu}}{0!} - \frac{\mu e^{-\mu}}{1!} - \cdots - \frac{\mu^{X_T} e^{-\mu}}{X_T!} \tag{3}$$

So each place can be assigned with the weight as:

$$\mathcal{R} = \mathcal{M} \cdot P(X > X_T) \tag{4}$$

We choose typical time periods of a day, such as rush hour, leisure time and so on, to get a sensitive weights sequence of a place $\mathcal{R}(P_i) = (\mathcal{R}_1, \mathcal{R}_2, \mathcal{R}_3, \ldots, \mathcal{R}_n)$, we can get its peak visiting time periods of a day. The average value $\overline{\mathcal{R}(P_i)}$ in Formula (5) reflects average visiting number of a place.

$$\overline{\mathcal{R}(P_i)} = \sum_{i=1}^{n} \mathcal{R}_i \Big/ n \tag{5}$$

If a place satisfies $\overline{\mathcal{R}(P_i)} > R_T$, we call it a sensitive place, R_T is a sensitive threshold. The sensitive weights are used to generate diversity anchor in next section.

Anchor generating based on sensitive location diversity

In this section, we pick a user's neighbor sensitive places to form a diversity zone, the anchor is generated at the centroid of the zone, a user querying with the anchor improves the probability of staying at different sensitive places.

When CS chooses neighbor sensitive places for a user, we divide neighbor sensitive places into 3 categories:

A. Disparate places, this kind of places have disparate peak visiting time period, a user choose this place may lead severely uneven distributing probability of each sensitive places for a user, such as a hospital and a bar, so CS excludes these places.

B. High correlation places, this kind of places do not only have similar peak visiting time period but also shows a linear correlation with the sensitive place which the user is staying at. These places may be the same kind neighbor places, such as two neighbor bars. For achieving diversity, CS excludes these places.

C. Similar places, this kind of places have similar peak visiting time period but they are not the same places, choosing this kind of places ensures sensitive diversity.

There are other measures to pick diversity places, we focus on user visiting number and its variation tendency according to the sensitive weight sequence of a place $\mathcal{R}(P_i) = (\mathcal{R}_1, \mathcal{R}_2, \mathcal{R}_3, \ldots, \mathcal{R}_n)$, which we have discussed below Formula (4).

CS has the sensitive weight sequences of all the POIs in its coverage area, one of the sequences of a place P_i is denoted as $\mathcal{R}(P_i) = (\mathcal{R}_1^i, \mathcal{R}_2^i, \mathcal{R}_3^i, \ldots, \mathcal{R}_n^i)$, each $\mathcal{R}_i^i \in \mathcal{R}(P_i)$ at different time periods is computed by Formula (4). Suppose a user is staying at P_i , and P_k is one of its neighbor sensitive places. CS compares the sequence $\mathcal{R}(P_i)$ to all the neighbor sensitive places $\mathcal{R}(P_k)$ and excludes the ones belonging to category A. We use cosine similarity to achieve this goal, in Formula (6), since cosine similarity can reflect the tendency similarity of two data sequences, $sim(P_i, P_k) \in [0,1]$, low similarity means a disparate place.

$$sim(P_i, P_k) = \frac{\mathcal{R}(P_i) \cdot \mathcal{R}(P_k)}{\|\mathcal{R}(P_i)\| \cdot \|\mathcal{R}(P_k)\|} = \frac{\sum_{j=1}^{n} \mathcal{R}_j^i \times \mathcal{R}_j^k}{\sqrt{\sum_{j=1}^{n} (\mathcal{R}_j^i)^2} \times \sqrt{\sum_{j=1}^{n} (\mathcal{R}_j^k)^2}} \tag{6}$$

Formula (6) only filters the disparate places. If two sequences of $\mathcal{P}_i$ and $\mathcal{P}_k$ show similar tendency, such as 2 simple examples (2000, 400, 100) and (1000, 200, 50), they have similar variation tendency, and shows linear similarity, these may belong to category B. We exclude these places to guarantee sensitive diversity. We use Pearson correlation coefficient to achieve this goal, which represents the linearly dependent of two data sequences.

$$r(\mathcal{P}_i, \mathcal{P}_k) = \frac{1}{n-1} \sum_{j=1}^{n} \left(\frac{\mathcal{R}_j^i - \overline{\mathcal{R}_i}}{s_{\mathcal{R}_i}} \right) \left(\frac{\mathcal{R}_j^k - \overline{\mathcal{R}_k}}{s_{\mathcal{R}_k}} \right) \tag{7}$$

As shown in Formula (7), $\overline{\mathcal{R}_i}$ 和 $S_{\mathcal{R}i}$ are mean value and standard deviation respectively. The more $|r|$ approaches 1, the higher linearly dependent is. We exclude places of category B with high $|r|$. There is no negative correlation ($r<0$) after the filter of Formula (6).

$$Dist(\mathcal{P}_i, \mathcal{P}_k) = \sqrt{\sum_{j=1}^{n} (\mathcal{R}_j^i - \mathcal{R}_j^k)} \tag{8}$$

CS filters disparate places and high correlation places by Formula (6) and (7), the remaining places satisfy sensitive diversity and refrains from inferring attack according to peak visiting time period difference. We rank the remaining candidate places according to similar degree, as defined in Formula (8), CS chooses better places to form a diversity zone according to diversity degree. We use Euclidean distance to estimate the similar degree in the candidate set. The greater Euclidean distance is, the higher diversity degree of a neighbor sensitive place is.

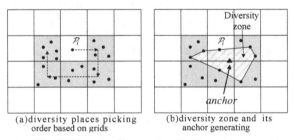

(a) diversity places picking order based on grids   (b) diversity zone and its anchor generating

Fig. 5. Diversity zone and anchor generating

As the area is divided into grids by default, when CS receives a query from a user staying at $\mathcal{P}_i < u_k, loc_{u_k}, l, C, R >$, it picks a neighbor grid randomly, as shown in Fig.5 (a), and clockwise get all the sensitive places in its neighbor grids, all the grids are in an angle range of $180°$ from the first grid, there is an angle limit because if the other sensitive places surround $\mathcal{P}_i$, $\mathcal{P}_i$ will be the sensitive place where the user is staying at. CS compares each sensitive place with $\mathcal{P}_i$ using Formula (6) and (7), filters disparate places and high correlation places, and ranks the remaining places according to Formula (8). Finally, CS chooses l sensitive places to form a diversity zone and takes its centroid as the anchor location, l is sensitive diversity degree defined by the user in query request. The Algorithm is as follows:

Algorithm 1. Diversity zone and anchor generating

1. **Procedure :** CS receives a query request $<u_k, loc_{uk}, l, C, R>$ from a user at P_i
2. generate a max heap W
3. randomly pick a neighbor grid, denote the vector from P_i to the grid as v_i
4. **while** $\theta(v_1, v_i) \leq 180°$ // v_i is the vector which u_k points to the ith neighbor grid
5.   clockwise get all neighbor grids
6. $S \leftarrow$ all the sensitive places in these grids
7. **for** each $P_k \in S$ **do**
8.   compute $sim(P_i, P_k)$
9.   **while** $sim(P_i, P_k) > \xi_s$ **do**   // ξ_s is a threshold
10.   compute $r(P_i, P_k)$
11.   **if** $r(P_i, P_k) < \xi_r$ **then**   // ξ_r is a threshold
12.   compute $Dist(P_i, P_k)$
13. $W \leftarrow P_k, Dist(P_i, P_k)$
14. **while** $|W| \geq l$ // satisfy sensitive l-diversity
15. connect the top l $P_k \in W$ to form a $Zone_{div}$
16. *centroid* $\leftarrow$ compute the centroid of $Zone_{div}$ // take the centroid as an anchor for the user
17. **return** *centroid*
18. **End Procedure.**

   In this section, we propose the picking method of sensitive diversity places according to user visiting number and its variation tendency. Then we use diversity places to form a diversity zone, the anchor is the centroid of the zone. CS uses this anchor to replace the user's actual location and issues users' query with the anchor. We can find that the anchor can be reused by other users in the sensitive places which form a diversity zone, the reuse decreases the overhead of CS.

4.2   Query Phase

In this phase, CS sends user's query request $<CS_i, loc_{anchor}, C, \beta>$ with a diversity anchor. When LSP receives a query request, it takes the anchor as a dimcenter and executes INN search. LSP returns the POIs candidate set gradually to CS. CS performs Algorithm 2 to deduce precise *KNN* PoIs for a user.

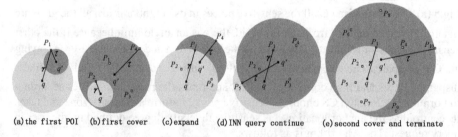

(a) the first POI   (b) first cover   (c) expand   (d) INN query continue   (e) second cover and terminate

Fig. 6. K nearest neighbor PoIs query for a user

As show in Fig.6(a), a user locates at q and q' is the diversity anchor, when the first POI is found, supply space (the dark grey cycle) expands and demand space (light grey cycle) shrinks. As POIs are found gradually, supply space covers demand space for the first time in Fig.6(b), K POIs are found around the anchor. Then demand space updates, containing K POIs in its cycle and keeps its radius unchanged after the expand, as shown in Fig.6(c) $K=3$. In Fig.6(d-e), query procedure continues until supply space covers demand space for the second time, K POIs are found around user. The algorithm running at CS end and referring to SpaceTwist is as follows:

Algorithm 2. CS performs the algorithm for KNN PoIs around a user at q

1. **Procedure :** K is defined by u_k, $q \leftarrow loc_{u_k}$, $q' \leftarrow loc_{anchor}$, β is the package capacity of PoIs returned from LSP
2. CS generates a max heap W_K
3. insert K pairs of $<NULL, \infty>$ into W_K
4. $\gamma \leftarrow$ the top distance in W_K // initialize demand space
5. $\tau \leftarrow 0$ // initialize supply space
6. send INN query to LSP with diversity anchor q'
7. **while** $\gamma + dist(q,q') > \tau$ **do**
8. $S \leftarrow$ get next package of PoIs from LSP
9. $\tau \leftarrow$ get the maximum $dist(q', \mathcal{P}_x)$ in S // update supply space
10.   **for** each $\mathcal{P}_w \in S$ **do**
11.   **if** $dist(q, \mathcal{P}_w) < \gamma$ **then**
12. $W_K \leftarrow <\mathcal{P}_w, dist(q, \mathcal{P}_w)>$
13. $\gamma \leftarrow dist(q, \mathcal{P}_w)$
14. $\gamma \leftarrow$ get $dist(q, \mathcal{P}_K)$ in W_K // update demand space
15. **while** $\gamma + dist(q,q') > \tau$ **do**
16. $S \leftarrow$ get next package of PoIs from LSP
17. $\tau \leftarrow$ get the maximum $dist(q', \mathcal{P}_u)$ in S // expand supply space gradually
18.   **if** $dist(q, \mathcal{P}_u) < \gamma$ **then**
19. $W_K \leftarrow <\mathcal{P}_h, dist(q, \mathcal{P}_u)>$
20. terminate INN query
21. **return** bottom K PoIs in W_K
22. **End Procedure.**

In our algorithm, demand space expands and covers at least K PoIs, which is the key point guarantees the user to get K PoIs around him nearly in 100% success rate. The query process will not terminate until supply space covers demand space again. As shown in Fig.6(e), LSP returns 10 PoIs in total. Alogrithm 2 picks $K=3$ PoIs $\{\mathcal{P}_2, \mathcal{P}_5, \mathcal{P}_7\}$ of them, the 3 POIs are around the user q, our algorithm is better than SpaceTwist. When we consider a user stay in a sensitive place, that means all the users are static or moves short distance, Algorithm 2 is snapshot query rather than continuous query, a user in a query procedure always uses one diversity anchor. As we known, a continuous query is composed of several snapshot queries, so Algorithm 2 is applicable for continuous query if continuous anchor sequence is generated. We will consider it in future work.

4.3   Performance Analysis

In this section, we will discuss security in the procedure of diversity anchor generating and querying with the anchor, then we analysis the algorithm complexity.

   (1) Security analysis

   An anchor is chosen in the overlap region of several sensitive places, it increases the probability of a user appearing in different sensitive places, the user's location semantic privacy is preserved. The diversity sensitive places are filtered by Formula (6), the disparate places are discarded to ensure the user is staying at each places with fequal opportunity. Formula (7) filters the sensitive places which may be the same to the one a user is staying at, such as a user is staying at a hospital, CS choose neighbor other hospital for her, which reduces the diversity. At last, CS picks l sensitive places in the remaining places to form a diversity zone, since the sensitive places is chosen from a randomly direction firstly and different users at the same sensitive place have different l-diversity degrees, so CS generates different anchors for users from the same place, that avoids inferring attacks which all the users using the same anchor are from the same sensitive place.

   When CS generates an anchor according to l sensitive places around him, she is staying at each place with equal probability $p(x_i) = 1/l$, so the information entropy of querying with this anchor one time is:

$$H(q) = \sum_{i=1}^{l} p(x_i) \log \frac{1}{p(x_i)} = \sum_{i=1}^{l} \frac{1}{l} \log l = \log l \qquad (9)$$

   That is the maximum information entropy for a single time, an adversary is hard to correlate any anchor with a user at sensitive place.

   (2) Complexity analysis of query algorithm

   Algorithm 2 is running at CS end, it compares the returned POIs from LSP, and decides when to terminate the query process, as demand space expanded in Algorithm2 Line14, the query terminated time has set already, so the algorithm will not last long or loop over and over again. The time complexity depends on amount of POIs returned in two phases in Algorithm 2 Line 8 and 16, it is $O(|\mathcal{P}_i|+|\mathcal{P}_h|)$. When $K=3$, LSP has to return 10 POIs to get precise KNN around a user, it is a little more, but the searching time complexity is not large. In the other hand, it is a tradeoff between ensuring privacy preserving and query efficiency.

5   Experiments

In this section, we discuss 3 main indicators: anonymity success rate, data traffic and average response time. We do experiments on two different data sets to manifest the good performance of our method.

5.1   Parameter Configuration

Simulation experiments are running on Windows 7, CPU is 3.5GHz Intel Core i7 processor and RAM is 16GB. We write the algorithms with Java, and we use two data sets, one is a real data set from Board on Geographical Names[1,] denoted as GDS, it includes 358957 PoIs. The other one is simulated data set[2], denoted as TDS, this data set is generated by widely used Thomas Brinkhoff Generator which is based on road networks of Oldenburg in Germany, it generates a city area about 24km×27km. The bandwidth between CS and users is 3Mbps. At LSP end, each data set of POIs is indexed by a 2K bytes R-tree structure. The parameter configurations are shown in the following Table 1:

Table 1. Parameters configuration

Parameters	Value range	Defaults
Number of users U	$100000 \leq U \leq 400000$	300000
Threshold of users at a sensitive place X_T	$100 \leq X_T \leq 1000$	200
Sensitive places similarity threshold ξ_s	$0 \leq \xi_s \leq 1$	0.4
Package capacity of PoIs β	$1 \leq \beta \leq 11$	6
PoIs query number K	$1 \leq K \leq 15$	8
Distance between user and anchor $dist(q,q')$	$200 \leq dist(q,q') \leq 1600$	1000

5.2 Success Rate of Anchor Generating

We run the experiments on both data set GDS and TDS, we discuss the success rate of anchor generating when thresholds X_T and ξ_s vary in Formula (4) and Algorithm 2.

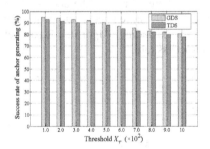
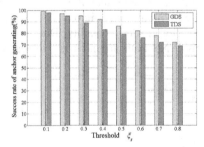

Fig. 7. Threshold X_T varys   **Fig. 8.** Threshold ξ_s varys

In Fig.7, when X_T increases, success rate of anchor generating is coming down and keeps stable around 80%, that is due to some places with smaller visiting number are not considered sensitive any more, in a valid region, CS is hard to find enough sensitive places around the user. To the same in Fig. 8, when similarity threshold is increasing, the sensitive places around a user must be similar enough to visiting number and visiting time, it means some places will be filtered. So the anchor generating is affected by these factors.

---

[1] http://geonames.usgs.gov/index.html
[2] http://iapg.jade-hs.de/personen/brinkhoff/generator/

5.3   Compare with SpaceTwist

We compares our Algorithm 2 to SpaceTwist on data set GDS and TDS, and mainly discuss the communication cost when K and $dist(q,q')$ are changing.

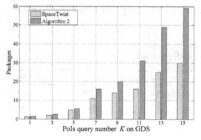 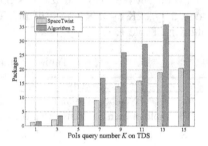

Fig. 9. K varies on GSD   **Fig. 10.** K varies on TDS

As shown in Fig.9-10, when K is increasing, packages are going up on both data set, and Algorithm 2 is higher than SpaceTwist, especially K varies from 11-15, packages are nearly twice than SpaceTwist. That is due to our algorithm expands demand space and continue query until supply space covers it again. LSP has to continue returning POIs until precise KNN POIs are obtained by CS, therefore the communication is increasing, and when K becomes larger, LSP needs to search more area to get enough POIs, packages are even more. Although Algorithm 2 has higher communication, it is much more precise than SpaceTwist, because the POIs found in our algorithm are around a user rather than the anchor, but SpaceTwist's are all around the anchor q', as shown in Fig.6(b) and Fig.6 (e), our algorithm pays a little more in communication but earns a lot in service quality. Due to demand space expanding, Algorithm 2 can get precise KNN POIs around a user in nearly 100% success rate.

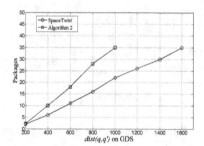 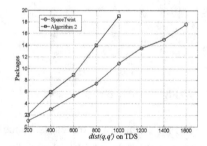

Fig. 11. $dist(q,q')$ varies on GSD   **Fig. 12.** $dist(q,q')$ varies on TDS

As shown in Fig.11-12, when an anchor is further from the user, LSP has to search a large area to get enough POIs, so its communication increases on both data set, as we discuss the anchor generating in our algorithm is not far away from a user based on grids, that ensures the communication cost of Algorithm 2 is in a reasonable range, in our experiments, we suppose there is no more than 1000 meters between neighbor grids. Communication of Algorithm 2 is higher than SpaceTwist, because it searches a larger area as demand space expands.

6   Conclusions

For location privacy preserving when a user is in a sensitive area, we propose an anchor generating method using a user's neighbor sensitive places to achieve l-diversity. By filtering places unsatisfied, CS generates an anchor and uses it to replaces a user's actual location in a query. As the anchor locates at an overlap area of several sensitive places, it increases the probability of appearing at different sensitive places for a user, it avoids the leakage of location privacy when a user and her anchor are both in the same sensitive area. In the query phase, CS needn't submit any user's actual location instead of the generated anchor. According to the POIs set returned by LSP, CS can deduce precise KNN POIs around a user, which is much more precise than SpaceTwist. Experiments and performance analysis show that our method is better in security and quality aspects, and its complexity and communication are in a reasonable range.

At the same time we also have some defects such as the factors to define sensitive place are single, we only consider user visiting number and its variation tendency. There is also a defect that the deployment of CS is not discussed, since when a CS is confronting lots of users, the response time may be a bottleneck for the CS. We will focus on these problems in our future works.

Acknowledgements. This research is supported by a grant from National Natural Science Foundation of China (No. 61170241, 61073042), The Fundamental Research Funds for the Central Universities (HEUCFZ1105), Specialized Research Fund for the Doctoral Program of Higher Education (No. 20132304110017), Excellent Youth Foundation of Heilongjiang Province in China (No. JC 201117), Science and Technology Research Project of Heilongjiang Education Department (No. 12513049, NO. 12541788), and this paper is also funded by the International Exchange Program of Harbin Engineering University for Innovation-oriented Talents Cultivation.

References

1. Gruteser, M., Grunwald, D.: Anonymous usage of location-based services through spatial and temporal cloaking. In: Proceedings of the 1st International Conference on Mobile Systems, Applications and Services, pp. 31–42. ACM (2003)
2. Gedik, B., Liu, L.: Location privacy in mobile systems: A personalized anonymization model. In: Proceedings of the 25th IEEE International Conference on Distributed Computing Systems, ICDCS 2005, pp. 620–629. IEEE (2005)
3. Chow, C.Y., Mokbel, M.F.: Trajectory privacy in location-based services and data publication. ACM SIGKDD Explorations Newsletter 13(1), 19–29 (2011)
4. Bamba, B., Liu, L., Pesti, P., et al.: Supporting anonymous location queries in mobile environments with privacygrid. In: Proceedings of the 17th International Conference on World Wide Web, pp. 237–246. ACM (2008)
5. Xu, J., Xu, M., Lin, X., et al.: Location privacy protection through anonymous cells in road network. Journal of Zhejiang University (Engineering Science) 3, 006 (2011)

6. Kido, H., Yanagisawa, Y., Satoh, T.: An anonymous communication technique using dummies for location-based services. In: Proceedings of the International Conference on Pervasive Services, ICPS 2005, pp. 88–97. IEEE (2005)

7. Lu, H., Jensen, C.S., Yiu, M.L.: Pad: Privacy-area aware, dummy-based location privacy in mobile services. In: Proceedings of the Seventh ACM International Workshop on Data Engineering for Wireless and Mobile Access, pp. 16–23. ACM (2008)

8. Hong, J.I., Landay, J.A.: An architecture for privacy-sensitive ubiquitous computing. In: Proceedings of the 2nd International Conference on Mobile Systems, Applications, and Services, pp. 177–189. ACM (2004)

9. Yiu, M.L., Jensen, C.S., Huang, X., et al.: Spacetwist: Managing the trade-offs among location privacy, query performance, and query accuracy in mobile services. In: IEEE 24th International Conference on Data Engineering, ICDE 2008, pp. 366–375. IEEE (2008)

10. Pellegrini, S., Ess, A., Schindler, K., et al.: You'll never walk alone: Modeling social behavior for multi-target tracking. In: 2009 IEEE 12th International Conference on Computer Vision, pp. 261–268. IEEE (2009)

11. Huo, Z., Meng, X., Hu, H., Huang, Y.: you *can* walk *a*lone: Trajectory privacy-preserving through significant stays protection. In: Lee, S.-g., Peng, Z., Zhou, X., Moon, Y.-S., Unland, R., Yoo, J. (eds.) DASFAA 2012, Part I. LNCS, vol. 7238, pp. 351–366. Springer, Heidelberg (2012)

12. Mokbel, M.F.: Towards privacy-aware location-based database servers. In: Proceedings of the 22nd International Conference on Data Engineering Workshops, pp. 93–93. IEEE (2006)

13. Chow, C.Y., Mokbel, M.F., Liu, X.: A peer-to-peer spatial cloaking algorithm for anonymous location-based service. In: Proceedings of the 14th Annual ACM International Symposium on Advances in Geographic Information Systems, pp. 171–178. ACM (2006)

14. Chow, C.Y., Mokbel, M.F., Liu, X.: Spatial cloaking for anonymous location-based services in mobile peer-to-peer environments. GeoInformatica 15(2), 351–380 (2011)

15. Huang, Y., Huo, Z., Meng, X.F.: Coprivacy: A collaborative location privacy-preserving method without cloaking region. Jisuanji Xuebao(Chinese Journal of Computers) 34(10), 1976–1985(2011)

16. Gong, Z., Sun, G.Z., Xie, X.: Protecting privacy in location-based services using k-anonymity without cloaked region. In: Mobile 2010 Eleventh International Conference on Data Management (MDM), pp. 366–371. IEEE (2010)

17. Xue, M., Kalnis, P., Pung, H.K.: Location diversity: Enhanced privacy protection in location based services. In: Choudhury, T., Quigley, A., Strang, T., Suginuma, K. (eds.) LoCA 2009. LNCS, vol. 5561, pp. 70–87. Springer, Heidelberg (2009)

18. Xue, J., Liu, X.Y., Yang, X.C., et al.: A location privacy preserving approach on road network. Jisuanji Xuebao(Chinese Journal of Computers) 34(5), 865–878 (2011)

19. Liu, F., Hua, K.A., Cai, Y.: Query l-diversity in location-based services. In: Tenth International Conference on Mobile Data Management: Systems, Services and Middleware, MDM 2009, pp. 436–442. IEEE (2009)

Message Passing Algorithm for the Generalized Assignment Problem

Mindi Yuan, Chong Jiang, Shen Li, Wei Shen, Yannis Pavlidis, and Jun Li

Walmart Labs and University of Illinois at Urbana-Champaign
{myuan,wshen,yannis,jli1}@walmartlabs.com, {jiang17,shenli3}@illinois.edu

Abstract. The generalized assignment problem (GAP) is NP-hard. It is even APX-hard to approximate it. The best known approximation algorithm is the LP-rounding algorithm in [1] with a $(1 - \frac{1}{e})$ approximation ratio. We investigate the max-product belief propagation algorithm for the GAP, which is suitable for distributed implementation. The basic algorithm passes an exponential number of real-valued messages in each iteration. We show that the algorithm can be simplified so that only a linear number of real-valued messages are passed in each iteration. In particular, the computation of the messages from machines to jobs decomposes into two knapsack problems, which are also present in each iteration of the LP-rounding algorithm. The messages can be computed in parallel at each iteration. We observe that for small instances of GAP where the optimal solution can be computed, the message passing algorithm converges to the optimal solution when it is unique. We then show how to add small deterministic perturbations to ensure the uniqueness of the optimum. Finally, we prove GAP remains strongly NP-hard even if the optimum is unique.

1 Introduction

GAP in its most general form is as follows [2]: There are multiple agents and tasks. Any agent can be assigned to perform any task with some cost or profit depending on the agent-task assignment. Each agent has a budget, and we wish to find an assignment in which no agent exceeds their budget, and the total cost of the assignment is minimized. Many practical problems can be modeled as GAP, for example finding the best locations to build distribution centers for a retail company, or assigning jobs to machines for the minimum cost in a data center. In this paper, we consider the following version of GAP:

- **Problem:** there are J jobs and M machines. Each machine has a capacity c_j. The processing cost is w_{ij} if job i is assigned to machine j.
- **Objective**: find a way to assign jobs to machines so that every job is assigned, the capacity constraints are satisfied, and the total cost is minimized.

Various algorithms have been developed for GAP. Shmoys and Tardos [3] implicitly proposed the first known algorithm, an LP-rounding 2-approximation

C.-H. Hsu et al. (Eds.): NPC 2014, LNCS 8707, pp. 423–434, 2014.
© IFIP International Federation for Information Processing 2014

algorithm. Subsequently, Chekuri and Khanna [4] explicitly presented that algorithm and developed a polynomial time approximation scheme for the multiple knapsack problem, which is a special case of GAP when each item has the same size and the same profit for every bin. They also proved the APX-hardness for two special cases of GAP. Recently, Fleischer *et. al.* [1] proposed two algorithms. One is a polynomial-time LP-rounding based $((1 - 1/e)\beta)$-approximation algorithm, which is the best known approximation for GAP so far. The other is a simple polynomial-time local search $(\beta/(\beta + 1) - \epsilon)$-approximation algorithm. Cohen *et. al* [5] developed an efficient approximation algorithm, which has the same $(\beta/(\beta+1) - \epsilon)$-approximation as Fleischer's second algorithm, but is much faster.

All of the above methods are approximate. In fact, [1] showed that the results cannot be approximated within a factor better than $1 - 1/e$ unless $NP \in DTIME(n^{O(\log \log n)})$. However, few researchers have investigated whether better algorithms can be designed under the additional condition that the optimum is unique.

Among the message passing algorithms (MPA), belief propagation (BP) and max-product algorithms are developed corresponding to the two main problems in probabilistic inference on graphical models (GM) [6]: evaluating the marginal and maximum *a posteriori* (MAP) estimation. For loopy graphs, the correctness and convergence of BP are still open problems for arbitrary GM's. However, even for GM's with cycles, the message passing algorithms are observed to perform surprisingly well in many cases, some of which are also with rigorous proof of optimality and convergence. For example, in [7] and [8], Yuan *et. al.* proposed message passing algorithms for the minimax weight matching and the constrained assignment problem respectively. Both algorithms were proved to be correct, given uniqueness of the optimum. For the maximum weighted matching (MWM) problem, as another example, Bayati *et. al.* [9] formulated a max-product algorithm by calculating the MAP probability on a well defined GM, which encodes the data and constraints of the optimization problem. For the proof of convergence and correctness of the algorithm, they constructed an alternating path on a computation tree to show each node would choose the correct edge in a MWM after enough iterations. However, this technique does not work in our problem, where half of the nodes have a capacity constraint. In [10], Bayati *et. al.* also provided the first proof of convergence and correctness of an asynchronous BP algorithm for a combinatorial optimization. They showed that when the LP relaxation has no fractional solutions, the BP algorithm converges to the correct solution. In [11], Sanghavi showed the equivalence of LP relaxation and max-product for the weighted matching in general graphs. He provided an exact, data-dependent characterization of max-product performance, and a precise connection to LP relaxation: if the LP relaxation is tight, max-product always converges to the correct answer, and inversely, if the LP relaxation is loose, max-product does not converge.

In this paper, we propose a message passing algorithm for GAP, which computes the optimal assignment on a tree graph. The basic algorithm passes an exponential number of real-valued messages per iteration, but a more refined version of this requires only a linear number of real-valued messages per iteration. In particular, the computation of the messages from machines to jobs decomposes into two knapsack problems, which are also present in each iteration of the LP-rounding algorithm. We observe that the algorithm can solve the GAP exactly in less than 10 iterations for small problems, when the best assignment is unique. We choose to test small problems, because their optima can be computed in reasonable amount of time. For large problems, it is hard to verify the correctness.

The rest of the paper is organized as follows. Section 2 presents the basic message passing algorithm. Section 3 derives a simplified version of the algorithm that uses fewer messages. Section 4 compares our algorithms with other algorithms. Section 5 discusses the extension of the algorithm when the optimum is not unique. Section 6 proves GAP is strongly NP-hard, even if there is a unique solution. Conclusion and future works are in Section 7.

2   Message Passing Algorithm

Consider the problem on an undirected weighted complete bipartite graph $\mathcal{G} = (\mathcal{J}, \mathcal{M}, \mathcal{E})$, where $\mathcal{J} = \{J_1, J_2, ..., J_n\}$ denotes the n jobs and $\mathcal{M} = \{M_1, M_2, ..., M_m\}$ denotes the m machines. Machine j $(1 \leq j \leq m)$ has a capacity c_j. Label each edge as $(J_i, M_j) \in \mathcal{E}$, with associated cost w_{ij}. The load of a machine is the sum of the weights of its adjacent edges. Assume all jobs can and need to be assigned, otherwise leaving all jobs unassigned will have the minimum cost. Although one machine can have multiple jobs, each job can only be assigned to one machine. Define an assignment matrix X, where an entry $x_{ij} = 1$ means job i is assigned to machine j and $x_{ij} = 0$ means it is not assigned to machine j. Thus the problem can be mathematically written as the following integer program:

$$\min_X \sum_{i,j} w_{ij} x_{ij}$$

$$s.t. \sum_j x_{ij} = 1, \forall i$$

$$\sum_i w_{ij} x_{ij} \leq c_j, \forall j$$

$$x_{ij} \in \{0, 1\}$$

Call the solution of the above problem X^*, the minimum cost assignment (MCA).

We first consider this problem on a graphical model, $\mathcal{G}$, of finding the minimum marginal distribution where the joint probability distribution can be completely specified between two nodes using the product of their functions. With abuse of notation, we will use J_i as the random variable in node J_i and M_j as the random variable for node M_j. J_i can then take on any single value l_i from $\mathcal{M}$ because each job can only be assigned to one machine. Meanwhile, M_j can take on any *subset* $\mathcal{S}_j$ of $\mathcal{J}$, resulting in 2^n different possible values. Denote the joint probability distribution $p(J_1 = l_1, J_2 = l_2, ...J_n = l_n, M_1 = \mathcal{S}_1, M_2 = \mathcal{S}_2, ...M_m = \mathcal{S}_m)$ as

$$p(J, M) = C \prod_{i,j} \phi_{J_i, M_j}(l_i, \mathcal{S}_j) \prod_i \alpha_i(l_i) \prod_j \beta_j(\mathcal{S}_j)$$

where

$$\phi_{J_i, M_j}(l_i, \mathcal{S}_j) = \begin{cases} 1, & \text{if } l_i = j, \ J_i \in \mathcal{S}_j \\ 1, & \text{if } l_i \neq j, \ J_i \notin \mathcal{S}_j \\ +\infty, & \text{otherwise} \end{cases} \tag{1}$$

$$\alpha_i(l_i) = e^{w_{il_i}}$$

$$\beta_j(\mathcal{S}_j) = \begin{cases} e^{\sum_{q \in \mathcal{S}_j} w_{qj}}, \text{if } \sum_{q \in \mathcal{S}_j} w_{qj} \leq c_j \\ +\infty, \text{otherwise} \end{cases} \tag{2}$$

and C is a constant for normalization. According to the definition of the compatibility function (1), a necessary condition for $p(J, M)$ to be finite is that the assignment must be compatible, i.e. M_j must accept J_i if J_i chooses M_j, and M_j must not accept J_i if J_i does not choose M_j. According to (2), the other necessary condition is that the assignment must be feasible, i.e. the capacity constraint for each machine must be satisfied. These two conditions together are also sufficient for $p(J, M)$ to be finite, and in particular, $p(J, M) = Ce^{2 \sum_i w_{il_i}}$. Note that when $p(J, M)$ is finite, it is a monotone function due to the positive edge weights. Let $p(J^*, M^*) = \arg\min p(J, M)$. By definition, $\{J_1 = l_1^*, J_2 = l_2^*, ...J_n = l_n^*\}$ will then be the MCA.

Define a message vector from J_i to M_j at iteration k: $M_{J_i \to M_j}^k = [m_{J_i \to M_j}^k(1), m_{J_i \to M_j}^k(2), ..., m_{J_i \to M_j}^k(2^n)]$. Likewise, define the message vector from M_j to J_i: $M_{M_j \to J_i}^k = [m_{M_j \to J_i}^k(1), m_{M_j \to J_i}^k(2), ..., m_{M_j \to J_i}^k(m)]$. Let $b_{J_i}^k$ be the belief vector for job J_i at the end of iteration k and let $a_{J_i}^k$ be job J_i's choice at that iteration, where $a_{J_i}^k = j$ means job J_i chooses machine M_j. Consequently, the standard message passing algorithm is as follows.

---

(1) Initialization:
$$M_{J_i \to M_j}^0 = M_{M_j \to J_i}^0 = 0$$

(2) At kth iteration:

$$m_{J_i \to M_j}^k(\mathcal{S}) = \min_{l \in \mathcal{M}} \phi_{J_i, M_j}(l, \mathcal{S}) \Big[\sum_{p \neq j} m_{M_p \to J_i}^{k-1}(l) + w_{il} \Big]$$

$$m_{M_j \to J_i}^k(l) = \min_{\mathcal{S} \subseteq \mathcal{F}_l} \phi_{J_i, M_j}(l, \mathcal{S}) \Big[\sum_{p \neq i} m_{J_p \to M_j}^{k-1}(\mathcal{S}) + \sum_{q \in \mathcal{S}} w_{ql} \Big]$$

where $\mathcal{F}_l$ is the set of all the feasible subset assignments to machine M_l.

(3) Beliefs at kth iteration:

$$b^k_{J_i}(l) = w_{il} + \sum_{p \in \mathcal{M}} m^k_{M_p \to J_i}(l)$$

(4) Assignment at the end of kth iteration:

$$a^k_{J_i} = \arg \min_{l \in \mathcal{M}} \{b^k_{J_i}(l)\}$$

In each iteration, every job/machine node sends and receives one message from every machine/job node. In computing its message, a node gathers the incoming messages at the last iteration from all neighboring nodes except the destination. Note the dimension of the vector $M^k_{J_i \to M_j}$ is 2^n. Similarly, in computing each entry for the vector $M^k_{M_j \to J_i}$, we potentially need to compare all 2^n subsets of $\mathcal{J}$, when the particular machine has enough capacity for the entire job set. As a result, the algorithm has exponential running time.

Most of the BP algorithms are formulated on trees, which are known as computation trees. In this paper, we use the same definition of computation trees as in [9]. Define the feasible tree assignment:

Definition 1. *A feasible tree assignment is an assignment on the computation tree, where 1) the capacity constraint of each machine is satisfied and 2) all the jobs, except the leaves, are assigned.*

Define $t^k_{J_i}(l)$, the total cost on the computation tree of node J_i after k iterations with the root choosing edge (J_i, M_l), i.e. J_i is believed to be assigned to machine M_l.

Lemma 1. *The belief of J_i at the kth iteration is $b^k_{J_i}(l) = 2t^k_{J_i}(l) + C$, where C is a constant depending on the initialization step of the algorithm.*

The proof is similar to that in [9] and is omitted here.

Remark 1. We only compute beliefs from the job side. If we do so from the machine side as $b^k_{M_j}(\mathcal{S}) = \sum_{q \in \mathcal{S}} w_{qj} + \sum_{p \in \mathcal{J}} m^k_{J_p \to M_j}(\mathcal{S})$, then when using the messages $M^k_{J_p \to M_j}$, we can not guarantee that the capacity constraints for the machines at the bottom of the computation tree are satisfied, which may lead to an infeasible tree assignment. This is since the capacity constraints are only incorporated in the messages $M^k_{M_j \to J_i}$, but not $M^k_{J_i \to M_j}$.

3   Simplified Algorithm

In this section, we will simplify the previous message passing algorithm to a pseudo-polynomial one. We first provide the resulting algorithm.

(1) Initialization:

$$\widetilde{m}^0_{J_i \to M_j} = \widetilde{m}^0_{M_j \to J_i} = 0$$

(2) At kth iteration:

$$\widetilde{m}^k_{J_i \to M_j} = w_{ij} - \min_{p \neq j} \left[\widetilde{m}^{k-1}_{M_p \to J_i} + w_{ip} \right]$$

$$\widetilde{m}^k_{M_j \to J_i} = \min_{\{\overline{S}, J_i\} \subseteq \mathcal{F}_j} \left[\sum_{p \in \overline{S}} (\widetilde{m}^{k-1}_{J_p \to M_j} + w_{pj}) \right] + w_{ij}$$

$$- \min_{\overline{S} \subseteq \mathcal{F}_j} \left[\sum_{p \in \overline{S}} (\widetilde{m}^{k-1}_{J_p \to M_j} + w_{pj}) \right] \qquad (3)$$

where $\overline{S}$ is the set of all the jobs except J_i. Note the two minimizations are knapsack problems (see Remark 2).

(3) Beliefs at kth iteration:

$$b^k_{J_i}(l) = w_{il} + \widetilde{m}^k_{M_l \to J_i}$$

(4) Assignment at the end of kth iteration:

$$a^k_{J_i} = \arg \min_{l \in \mathcal{M}} \{ b^k_{J_i}(l) \}$$

To prove the equivalence of the two algorithms, we need the following lemma.

Lemma 2. *In the message passing algorithm, subtracting a constant from all the coordinates of any particular message vector at any iteration will not influence the final assignment of each job.*

The intuition behind this lemma is as follows: the algorithm only performs minimization over the messages, so subtracting an equal amount from all coordinates of a vector will still maintain the same ordering of the coordinates and hence produce the exactly same results. The proof is obvious and therefore omitted here.

Lemma 3. *The message passing algorithm and the simplified algorithm compute the same assignment for each job.*

Proof. First, we show that for any particular message vector, there are only two distinct values for each entry. Consider $m^k_{J_i \to M_j}(S)$. If $J_i \notin S$, $m^k_{J_i \to M_j}(S) = \min_{l \neq j} [\sum_{p \neq j} m^{k-1}_{M_p \to J_i}(l) + w_{il}]$. The minimization does not include the case when $l = j$, because in the case $J_i \notin S$ and $l = j$, the compatibility function evaluates to $+\infty$, and thus cannot be the minimum. If $J_i \in S$, again due to the property of the compatibility function, $m^k_{J_i \to M_j}(S) = \sum_{p \neq j} m^{k-1}_{M_p \to J_i}(j) + w_{ij}$. As a result, in both cases, $m^k_{J_i \to M_j}(\mathcal{S})$ does not depend on $\mathcal{S}$ and therefore takes on only two different values. The same results hold for the message $m^k_{M_j \to J_i}(l)$. Consequently, if we only pass the difference (a scalar, not a vector) of the two values and if the receiver knows the message source, then the receiver can still recover the entire message vector which includes this difference and 0. According to *Lemma 2*, passing this new vector is equivalent to passing the original one.

However, recovering the vector is not necessary. Now we show by induction that the update rule (3) computes the difference of the two distinct values in the original message vector at each iteration. For the first iteration, it is trivially true. Suppose it is true for the $k - 1$th iteration. Then for the kth iteration,

$$\widetilde{m}^k_{J_i \to M_j} = \sum_{p \neq j} m^{k-1}_{M_p \to J_i}(j) + w_{ij}$$

$$- \min_{l \neq j} \left[\sum_{p \neq j} m^{k-1}_{M_p \to J_i}(l) + w_{il} \right]$$

$$= w_{ij} - \min_{l \neq j} \left[m^{k-1}_{M_l \to J_i}(l) + w_{il} \right]$$

$$= w_{ij} - \min_{l \neq j} \left[\widetilde{m}^{k-1}_{M_l \to J_i} + w_{il} \right]$$

Note in the deduction above, most of the messages in the kth iteration are 0, which can be removed. The equivalence of the updating rule for $\widetilde{m}^k_{M_j \to J_i}$ can be proved similarly.   □

Remark 2. In computing the message $\widetilde{m}^k_{M_j \to J_i}$, we are actually solving two knapsack problems for machine M_j: There are $n - 1$ items. Item p $(p \neq i)$ has value $\widetilde{m}^{k-1}_{J_p \to M_j} + w_{pj}$ and size w_{pj}. The capacity of bin j for the first knapsack is $c_j - w_{ij}$ and the second c_j. There are many efficient methods for the singe-bin problem. Using the dynamic programming solution [12], we get a pseudo-polynomial algorithm for each knapsack. Further note that the first knapsack problem is a subproblem of the second, so we can get its solution while solving the second. This means that computing the message $\widetilde{m}^k_{M_j \to J_i}$ is equivalent to solving one knapsack problem.

4   Simulation Results

In this section, we will compare our algorithm, henceforth denoted MPA, with other algorithms in different scenarios. We will use the results obtained by the MATLAB integer programming function *bintprog()* as the optimal solution. We will compare our algorithm with the efficient GAP algorithm (EGA) in [5]. We do not compare with the local search algorithm in [1], because it has the same approximation ratio as EGA, but is much slower. We do not compare with the LP-rounding algorithm in [1] by simulations, since its complexity is much higher.

We show two sets of experiments for comparison with EGA. For the first set, the parameters are as follows. The capacity of each machine is $c_j = 100$. The weights of the edges are drawn from a uniform distribution from 30 to 80. We run MPA with the number of iterations ranging from 0 to 9. The dimensions of the experiments range from 2×2 to 11×11, where $d \times d$ means d jobs are to be assigned to d machines. Each case is tested 1000 times. For the results returned by the two algorithms, we first verify if it is a feasible solution and then compare it with the optimum. Note that all the tests have feasible solutions, and so we define the *correct ratio* as the percentage of exactly correct solutions out of the 1000 tests.

The first 10 experiments are showed in Table 1. The first column indicates the number of iterations for MPA and the second row shows the dimension of the cost matrix. From the table we can see that MPA can reach an average correct ratio over 96.6% within 9 iterations. The smallest correct ratio for 9 iterations is 92.8% when the dimension is 11×11. The average correct ratio for EGA is 44.4% and the smallest correct ratio is 13.6%. When the dimension of the cost matrix is greater than 9×9, EGA can get 100% feasible solutions. However, the correctness is at most 21%.

Table 2 shows the case when the cost weights are drawn from a uniform distribution between 40 and 70. The average correct ratio is 91.7% for MPA and 42.1% for EGA, while the smallest correct ratio is 79.9% for MPA and 10.4% for EGA. The weights are closer now and the probability of two optima existing is therefore higher. Consequently, the correct ratio for MPA is lower than those in Table 1. Note for a particular dimension, the correct ratio will not always increase with the number of iterations. For instance, refer to the 7×7 case in Table 2; when the number of iterations increases from 8 to 9, the number of correct cases decreases by 1. This is because when the number of iterations is insufficient or when there are multiple optima, the decision of each job will oscillate; it is possible that the belief coordinate of the correct assignment is the largest at a particular iteration, but is no longer so at the next. For the cases where the MPA returns wrong solutions, we manually check them and find that either the number of iterations is insufficient or there are multiple optima.

To capture the key characteristics of the two algorithms, let us consider the following small example with cost matrix $W = \begin{pmatrix} 3 & 1 \\ 3 & 4 \end{pmatrix}$, where w_{ij} is the cost if J_i is assigned to M_j, and assume both machines have capacity 5. If we run EGA, it will first solve the knapsack problem for M_1. The following problem arises: both J_1 and J_2 have a cost of 3 if assigned to M_1, so the knapsack solution picks one at random. If it picks J_1, then the final assignment will not be optimal. However, our algorithm takes a more global view, and "knows" J_1 should wait for M_2.

In all of the experiments above, we did not change the capacity of the machines, because from the view of the jobs, it is equivalent to changing the distribution of the weights. Due to space limitations, we only show the full results from two sets of parameters for the uniform distribution. To summarize some other experiments, when the weights are drawn from uniform distributions with parameters $[0, 100]$, $[10, 90]$ and $[20, 80]$, and the problem dimension is 11×11, MPA achieves nearly 100% correctness at the first iteration. In those cases, even if each job greedily chooses their least-cost machines, the capacity constraint can

Table 1. Machine capacity = 100; Cost weights ∼ uniform(30, 80); Each case tested 1000 times; Feasible solutions always exist. For each entry (a, b) in the table, a is the number of cases the returned solution is feasible out of 1000 tests and b the number of correct solutions among the feasible ones.

	MPA									
Iter	2×2	3×3	4×4	5×5	6×6	7×7	8×8	9×9	10×10	11×11
0	857, 857	819, 819	775, 775	730, 730	686, 686	661, 661	644, 644	604, 604	620, 620	620, 620
1	857, 857	819, 819	775, 775	730, 730	686, 686	661, 661	644, 644	604, 604	620, 620	620, 620
2	860, 860	819, 819	775, 775	730, 730	686, 686	661, 661	644, 644	604, 604	620, 620	620, 620
3	994, 994	980, 975	979, 975	966, 956	953, 945	953, 945	942, 929	927, 914	928, 910	908, 889
4	994, 994	980, 975	979, 975	966, 956	953, 945	953, 945	942, 929	927, 914	928, 910	908, 889
5	994, 994	995, 990	994, 990	979, 969	976, 965	972, 964	973, 958	960, 944	958, 938	947, 926
6	994, 994	995, 990	994, 990	979, 969	976, 965	972, 964	973, 958	960, 944	958, 938	947, 926
7	994, 994	997, 992	994, 990	981, 971	981, 970	978, 970	975, 960	962, 946	963, 942	949, 927
8	994, 994	997, 992	994, 990	981, 971	981, 970	978, 970	975, 960	962, 946	963, 942	949, 927
9	994, 994	997, 992	994, 990	981, 971	981, 970	978, 969	975, 960	962, 946	963, 943	950, 928
EGA	904, 875	950, 790	980, 678	992, 552	997, 423	998, 338	999, 246	1000, 210	1000, 187	1000, 136

still be satisfied with high probability. We did not test dimensions larger than 11×11, since the MATLAB function *bintprog()* became unusably slow.

Consequently, we observe that MPA appears to converge towards the correct assignment. If the weights are closer together, the problem becomes more difficult for both algorithms, but MPA consistently outperforms EGA.

5   Optimum Uniqueness

According to our simulations, the message passing algorithm works well when the optimum is unique, but this may not be the case in general. For example, if all the weights are integers and their values are close, then with high probability, there will be more than one optimum. One way to rectify this situation is to add a small deterministic perturbation to each entry of the cost matrix so that we can ensure each assignment has a unique value. Namely, if we use the same indices for the jobs and machines as before, we will need to account for m^n possible configurations. Let $\tilde{w}_{ij} = w_{ij} + (j - 1)m^{-i}$, and $\tilde{c}_j = c_j + 1 - m^{-n}$. This can be viewed as appending to the value of an assignment the base-m representation of the assignment, i.e. adding the term $\sum_{i=1}^{n} m^{-i} J_i$, which is the base-$m$ number $0.J_1 J_2 \ldots J_n$. Recall that J_i is the machine assignment for job i. Since this additional value is in $[0, 1 - m^{-n}]$, and because the original capacities are integers, it follows that any assignment in the integer problem with weight matrix W and capacity vector c is valid if and only if the same assignment is valid in the modified, fractional problem with weight matrix $\tilde{W}$ and capacity vector $\tilde{c}$. Furthermore, the smallest gap between any two assignments is at least m^{-n}. As a result, the uniqueness of optimum is guaranteed.

Table 2. Cost weights $\sim$ uniform(40, 70); Other parameters are the same as in Table 1

Iter	2×2	3×3	4×4	5×5	6×6	7×7	8×8	9×9	10×10	11×11
					MPA					
0	803, 803	757, 757	709, 709	660, 660	593, 593	531, 531	511, 511	442, 442	411, 411	345, 345
1	803, 803	757, 757	709, 709	660, 660	593, 593	531, 531	511, 511	442, 442	411, 411	345, 345
2	803, 803	757, 757	709, 709	660, 660	593, 593	531, 531	511, 511	442, 442	411, 411	345, 345
3	992, 992	954, 950	964, 956	942, 934	914, 896	898, 877	882, 859	838, 812	809, 783	766, 722
4	992, 992	954, 950	964, 956	942, 934	914, 896	898, 877	882, 859	838, 812	809, 783	766, 722
5	992, 992	981, 975	986, 978	964, 955	944, 924	936, 911	934, 904	887, 857	870, 840	844, 787
6	992, 992	981, 975	986, 978	964, 955	944, 924	936, 911	934, 904	887, 857	870, 840	844, 787
7	992, 992	984, 978	986, 976	967, 958	953, 932	938, 912	938, 908	894, 863	881, 849	857, 799
8	992, 992	984, 978	986, 976	967, 958	953, 932	938, 912	938, 908	894, 863	881, 849	857, 799
9	992, 992	984, 978	987, 977	967, 958	953, 932	938, 911	937, 907	896, 865	885, 853	857, 799
EGA	900, 858	927, 743	972, 655	983, 542	994, 431	997, 321	998, 248	1000, 178	1000, 132	1000, 104

6   Strongly NP-Hardness

In this section, we will prove:

Theorem 1. *Given that there is a unique solution for the GAP, it is still impossible to develop a correct message passing algorithm which can terminate in pseudo-polynomial number of iterations, unless strongly NP-hard = weakly NP-hard.*

A description of strongly NP-hard can be found here [13]. For example, we know the single machine problem in our GAP can be solved in $O(Jc)$ time. Recall that J is the number of jobs and c the capacity of the single machine. If c is polynomial in J, the single machine problem can then be solved in $O(J^a)$, where a is some constant. This is an example of a weakly NP-hard problem. If the solution is still exponential in J even when c is polynomial in J, then it is called strongly NP-hard.

Now we are ready to prove the theorem.

Proof. 1) GAP is strongly NP-hard. GAP can be reduced from the 3-partition problem [14]. To see this, let each machine be a set in the 3-partition problem and let the jobs be the numbers to be partitioned. Further assume the capacities of the machines are *all equal* and the numbers are *very close* to each other. For example, consider this instance of the 3-partition problem. There are n (n is a multiple of 3) *negative integers* (since we need to do minimization for our GAP) with sum S, and each number is very close to S/n so that the sum of any two numbers is greater than $3S/n$ and any four is less than that. Set the number of machines to be $n/3$ and the capacity to be $3S/n$. At this point, the 3-partition problem is reduced to GAP. If the minimum assignment cost for GAP is S, there must be a feasible partition for the 3-partition problem. Note that S is the lowest possible cost we can reach, and we reach S only when we assign all of the jobs. Each machine would then have exactly 3 jobs due to the job size constraints.

If the minimum cost is not S, then there must not exist a feasible partition. GAP is therefore not easier than the 3-partition problem. Consequently, it is strongly NP-hard, since the 3-partition problem is strongly NP-hard [15].

2) GAP remains strongly NP-hard, even if there is one unique optimum. This can be shown by another reduction. Denote the GAP with a unique optimum as uGAP. By adding small deterministic perturbations to the GAP, as discussed in Section 5, GAP can be transformed to uGAP. This transformation takes $O(JM)$ time, which is polynomial in the input size. Clearly, a solution for uGAP is a solution for GAP, too. As a result, uGAP is not easier than GAP, and is therefore also strongly NP-hard.

3) It is not possible to develop a correct message passing algorithm which can terminate in pseudo-polynomial number of iterations, unless strongly NP-hard = weakly NP-hard. If we can have such an algorithm, we have a pseudo-polynomial algorithm for a strongly NP-hard problem, which would show strongly NP-hard = weakly NP-hard.   □

Finally, it is easy to develop a dynamic programming algorithm for GAP that runs in $O(Jc^M)$. However, it is almost impossible to have a solution with complexity $O(JcM)$. In our simulations, nonetheless, the message passing algorithm is able to produce correct solutions within a reasonable number of iterations for cases with sizes up to 11×11.

7   Conclusion and Future Work

In this paper, we proposed a message passing algorithm for GAP, which is strongly NP-hard. The basic algorithm passes an exponential number of real-valued messages in each iteration. We showed that the algorithm can be simplified so that only a linear number of real-valued messages are passed in each iteration. Through simulations, we observed that our algorithm is better than the well-known approximation algorithm EGA, when the optimum is unique. Future work will include improving the algorithm and investigating the relationship between the message passing algorithm and the LP relaxation.

References

1. Fleischer, L., Goemans, M.X., Mirrokni, V.S., Sviridenko, M.: Tight approximation algorithms for maximum separable assignment problems. Math. of Operations Research 36, 416–431 (2011)
2. Wikipedia, Generalized assignment problem,
   http://en.wikipedia.org/wiki/Generalized_assignment_problem
3. Shmoys, D.B., Tardos, E.: An approximation algorithm for the generalized assignment problem. Math. Program 62, 461–474 (1993)
4. Chekuri, C., Khanna, S.: A PTAS for the multiple knapsack problem. In: Proceedings of the 11th Annual ACM-SIAM Symposium on Discrete Algorithms, pp. 213–222 (2000)

5. Cohen, R., Katzir, L., Raz, D.: An efficient approximation for the generalized assignment problem. Info. Processing Letters 100, 162–166 (2006)
6. Koller, D., Friedman, N.: Probabilistic Graphical Models: Principles and Techniques. MIT Press, USA (2009)
7. Yuan, M., Li, S., Shen, W., Pavlidis, Y.: Belief propagation for minimax weight matching. University of Illinois, Tech. Rep (2013)
8. Yuan, M., Shen, W., Li, J., Pavlidis, Y., Li, S.: Auction/belief propagation algorithms for constrained assignment problem. Walmart Labs, Tech. Rep. (2013)
9. Bayati, M., Shah, D., Sharma, M.: Max-product for maximum weight matching: convergence, correctness, and LP duality. IEEE Trans. Info. Theory 54, 1241–1251 (2008)
10. Bayati, M., Borgs, C., Chayes, J., Zecchina, R.: Belief propagation for weighted b-matchings on arbitrary graphs and its relation to linear programs with integer solutions. SIAM J. Discrete Math. 25, 989–1011 (2011)
11. Sanghavi, S.: Equivalence of LP relaxation and max-product for weighted matching in general graphs. In: IEEE Info. Theory Workshop, pp. 242–247 (2007)
12. Wikipedia, Knapsack problem,
    http://en.wikipedia.org/wiki/Knapsack_problem
13. Strongly NP-hard, Website,
    http://en.wikipedia.org/wiki/Strongly_NP-complete
14. 3-partition problem, Website,
    http://en.wikipedia.org/wiki/3-partition_problem
15. Garey, M.R., Johnson, D.S.: Strong np-completeness results: Motivation, examples, and implications. Journal of the ACM 25, 499–508 (1978)

PPMS: A Peer to Peer Metadata Management Strategy for Distributed File Systems

Di Yang, Weigang Wu, Zhansong Li, Jiongyu Yu, and Yong Li

Department of Computer Science, Sun Yat-sen University
Guangzhou 510006, China
{yangdi5,lizhans,yujiongy,liyong36}@mail2.sysu.edu.cn,
wuweig@mail.sysu.edu.cn

Abstract. Distributed file system is one of the key blocks of cloud computing systems. With the fast increase of user scale and data amount, metadata management has become a crucial point affecting the overall performance of a distributed file system. In this paper, we design and implement PPMS, a novel metadata management strategy in a peer to peer way. Different from existing metadata management methods, we adopt a two layer structure to achieve high scalability and low latency. The upper layer is metadata index server, which is used to store metadata of directories, while the lower layer consists of metadata servers to store the metadata of files. More importantly, the lower layer is organized in a peer to peer way to further improve scalability. We implement a prototype file system based on PPMS and evaluate its performance via experiments. The results show that our design can achieve high performance with in terms of time latency and system throughput.

Keywords: Distributed File System, Metadata Management, Scalability, Low Latency, Peer-to-Peer.

1 Introduction

Distributed file system is one of the key enabling technologies for distributed computing, especially cloud computing [7][8][17]. Although metadata usually accounts for only a very small part of a distributed file system in terms of data size, more than half (50%~80%) of file operations are involved with metadata [1]. Metadata management has become one of key issues in distributed file system [13], and it can significantly affect the overall performance and scalability in large-scale distributed file system [2][17].

In most existing distributed file systems, such as HDFS of Hadoop [7] and GFS from Google [8], there is only one single metadata server (MDS for short), which is likely to become a bottleneck as users and the quantity of files increase. With the rapid increase of user scale, such metadata management is definitely not scalable enough.

Although there have been quite a number of distributed metadata management solutions proposed by researchers, including static subtree partitioning [1], dynamic

C.-H. Hsu et al. (Eds.): NPC 2014, LNCS 8707, pp. 435–445, 2014.

subtree partitioning [4], such tree-based metadata management strategies cannot scale well due to the tight coupling among metadata servers. To address this problem, peer to peer based metadata management strategies [5] have been recently proposed, which organize metadata servers in an ad hoc way. Such metadata management strategies are well scalable, but they cannot achieve fast metadata access due to the lack of connections among metadata servers and consideration of user behaviors.

In this paper, we propose a novel peer to peer based metadata management strategy, named PPMS (Peer-to-Peer Metadata Service), which also organizes metadata servers in a peer to peer way. However, different from existing peer to peer metadata management, we combine hierarchy structure with peer to peer way. More precisely, we propose the concept of metadata index server (MIS for short). Our design has two layers of servers, which are in charge of metadata of directories and files respectively. MIS is in the upper layer and takes charge of managing the metadata of directories. MDSs compose the lower layer and manage the metadata of files. The correspondence between a file metadata and its local MDS is established based on the location of the client that creates the file. Compared with existing metadata management strategies, PPMS can achieve a better tradeoff between scalability and latency.

To validate the correctness of PPMS and evaluate its performance, we have also developed a prototype file system, named PPFS. We test PPFS using the popular benchmark tool Postmark [16] and the RES trace. Various operations, including read, creation, are executed to measure access latency and system throughput. MooseFS [14] is also tested for comparison purpose. The results show that PPMS can outperform MooseFS in nearly all cases.

The rest of the paper is organized as follows. Section 2 briefly reviews existing solutions for metadata management, especially peer to peer based ones. We describe the design of PPMS and PPFS in Section 3. Section 4 presents the performance evaluation based on experiments. Finally, Section 5 concludes the paper and suggests future directions.

2   Related Works

With the emergency of large-scale distributed file systems that separate metadata from file read/write operations, metadata management strategies has become a hot research topic and quite a number of metadata management strategies have been proposed.

Static subtree partitioning [1] divides the whole file directory tree into non-overlapped partitions, which are assigned to different MDSs by the system administrator. The partitioning is static and can only be changed manually. This strategy is very simple and easy to implement. However, it is not flexible and may face the problem of workload imbalance among MDSs. Re-balancing will cause large overhead. Dynamic subtree partitioning [4] is proposed to solve the load imbalance problem of static partitioning. It divides the whole directory tree into overlapped partitions, each of which is assigned to one MDS dynamically. By migrating heavily workload metadata automatically and overlapping popular partitions, the workload among different MDSs can be well balanced [12]. However, such design requires additional mechanism to maintain consistency among different copies of the same piece of metadata.

Hash based partition [3] can also solve the imbalance problem of static partition. A hash function based on file identifier is used to distribute the workload among metadata servers. With a well designed hash function, load balance among MDSs is achieved easily. However, rename operations or change of MDSs may cause lots of metadata migrations crossing MDSs. Another drawback is that hashing inherently discards the advantage of locality.

All strategies above are based on portioning of the directory tree. Such strategies can achieve high performance in terms of access latency, but may suffer from poor scalability. On the other hand, with the increase of user scale and data scale, scalability is becoming more and more important. To achieve high scalability in metadata management, peer to peer based strategies have been proposed.

Hierarchical Bloom-Filter Array (HBA) [5] uses a two-tier probabilistic array, i.e. Bloom filter array, to calculate corresponding MDS to the file a user want to query. In the probabilistic array, the first layer has a higher accuracy ratio but only part of the metadata stored, and the second layer stores all the metadata about the files but has a lower accuracy ratio. When the number of files increases, HBA will have a demand of large memory space to ensure a certain degree of accuracy.

Grouped Hierarchical Bloom-Filter Array (G-HBA) [6] is an extension of HBA by introducing the concept of group of MDS. This scheme logically organizes MDSs into a multi-layered query hierarchy and exploits grouped Bloom filters to efficiently route metadata requests to desired MDS through the hierarchy.

Besides, there is some particular metadata management for special requiremnt including Spyglass and SmartStore [9] [10] .

Although peer to peer metadata management based on Bloom filter can scale easily due to the loose coupling among MDSs, such strategies are generally probabilistic in terms of locating a file, and consequently may suffer from long access latency [11] .

3   The Design and Implementation of PPMS

3.1   Overview of PPMS

Basically, we follow the idea of peer to peer file sharing, where each node can access data at other peers in a fully distributed way. Peer to peer approach can achieve high scalability easily and is also suitable for metadata management. However, to avoid long file access latency, we extend peer to peer based approach by introducing a two-tier hierarchy.

Metadata generally includes directory information and file information in distributed file system. And our proposed metadata strategy PPMS consists of two types of servers, i.e. metadata index server (MIS) and metadata server (MDS) correspondingly. MIS is mainly responsible for directory attributes, query and load balancing, while MDS is primarily responsible for the file attributes. MIS and MDS interact with each other, work together to complete the management of metadata, and accordingly handle a variety of user operations. In addition to the herein of metadata types, there is a classification for MDS logically, i.e. the local MDS and the related MDS. Local MDS is that a client mounts initially, while related MDSs represents MDSs that are binding with individual directories and most likely to store nonlocal file in that directory. The overall architecture of the PPMS is shown in Fig. 1.

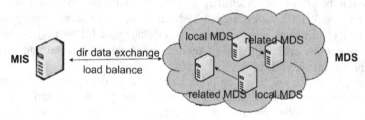

Fig. 1. Overview of PPMS. There are one MIS and multiple MDSs in PPMS, and MDSs are divided into local MDS and related MDS logically.

3.2   The Design of MIS

MIS manages the entire directory metadata information within PPMS, such as directory name, permissions, user name, group name, related MDS list and so on. MIS receives directory-related requests from MDS and provides directories operations, such as directory deletion, directory creation and so on. If a client queries for file metadata, the metadata that cannot be found in both the local MDS and related MDS or there is no related MDS for the file's parent directory, then the request will be forwarded to MIS to retrieve the corresponding metadata.

Although it hasn't had time to realize, MIS is a coordinator for load balancing among MDSs. MIS can monitor the workloads of MDSs via metadata requests received. If some MDSs have too much more workloads than others, MIS will invoke the migration procedure to migrate metadata from busy MDS to those with low workloads. With such mechanism, workloads balance is achieved in the scope of metadata service.

3.3   The Design of MDS

A MDS stores the metadata of files, including file name, permission, user name, user group, size, etc. Each client is associated with its local MDS. When a client creates a file, the file's metadata will be stored at the local MDS, and the metadata of its parent directory will be sent to the MIS.

One MDS becomes a local MDS once a client has mounted on it. As the local MDS for a client, it is directly responsible for the client's requests. Before mounting, the client configures the IP and port information of the local MDS. Then the client keeps contact with its local MDS. Also, the local MDS has become the only entrance for the client to the entire metadata management system. Compare to the other MDSs, the local MDS has a greater possibility to store the metadata that its corresponding clients requests.

Besides, every MDS also maintains a related MDS list for each directory of the files whose metadata is stored locally. A related MDS is designed for directory, and it is the node that has the file's attributes under the same directory. That is, a related MDS has metadata of files in the same directory. Related MDS also has a good possibility to have files under the same directory, and can be queried when the metadata requested is missed at the local MDS itself.

The design of related MDS is the core of PPMS. In the beginning, none of related MDS is defined in each MDS. When a client reads the metadata of given file, which is missing at the local MDS, MIS will be queried and the metadata of the file will be found at another MDS through MIS. Then, the requested MDS is defined as the related MDS for this file's parent directory in the local MDS. Since the number of MDS is uncertain, which the related MDS for a directory has one is not an effective solution when there is a very large number of MDS. For each directory, there may be more than one related MDSs. The number of MDS can be determined based on the availability of storage space and other factors.

3.4   Data Access

PPMS provides low latency and improves service quality continually through three layers of query structure after Related MDS appeared. The procedure of accessing a file is shown in Figure 2.

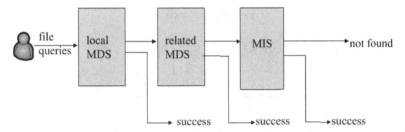

Fig. 2. The procedure of accessing a file. The query of a file involves three levels: looking up the storage of local MDS, looking up the related MDS and looking up MIS.

The first layer of the query structure is the local MDS, which has great probability to meet client needs by directly dealing with write and read requests. In general, files under the same directory have a great correlation and it is ordinary for a client who has interests in the same types. Therefore, the related MDS has also a high hit ratio as the second layer of the query structure. Moreover, the last layer of the query structure is MIS, which masters all the directory information to satisfy all client requests and avoid global broadcasting. As a result, PPMS has low latency to content clients' requests through hierarchical query structure after analyzing the user possible behavior.

3.5   PPFS -- A Prototype File System Using PPMS

In order to verify the feasibility and correctness of our strategy, we have implemented a prototype system, called PPFS, using C programming language. The system consists of three modules: metadata management module, chunk server (i.e. node storing file data) module, and client module. In addition, metadata management module, which is also called PPMS module, is responsible for managing allover metadata and namespace, and this module also includes MIS module and MDS module designed as stated above. And the job of chunk server module is to store actual file data. In addition, client can get file data in the distributed file system through client module on the mounted point. To simplify the implementation, client module is developed based on FUSE [15], a file system in user space included in the kernel of linux and widely used by many fields system, such as ZFS, glusterfs and lustre. Besides, we have also implemented client cache, MDS cache and chunk server cache to improve the performance of file access referring to other file system. Figure 3 shows the overall architecture of our PPFS prototype.

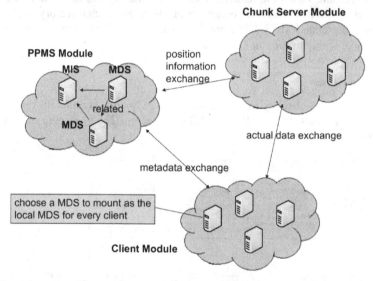

Fig. 3. Overview of PPFS. The system consists of three modules: PPMS module, chunk server module, and client module.

4   Performance Evaluation

In order to evaluate the performance of PPMS, we deploy the PPFS prototype. To make the experiment more persuasive, we did two experiments.

In the first experiment, this test was divided into two parts to show the advantage of PPMS. In the first part, we simply choose MooseFS to compare, because the first part just want to run PPFS with a MDS, and to look for a single MDS system to make a comprision. In addition, PPFS implementation refers to MooseFS, which has only one MDS, and MooseFS is a light weight distributed file system that has been widely used for research and testing [19] with a single MDS [14] . In the second part, we test the performance of the system by increasing the number of MDS isometric.

In the second experiments, we simulate the metadata operations using the RES traces and measure the performance in terms of hit ratio of the local MDS and the related MDS.

4.1 Testing Using Postmark

The testing is conducted using Postmark [16], a file system benchmarking software widely used. Postmark generates an initial pool of random text files ranging in a configurable size. Once this pool is created, a specified number of transactions, including create, delete, read and append, are performed on these files randomly. When all the transactions have completed, the remaining files and directories are deleted and statistics are done to compute the performance metric values. We use several metrics, including total time, number of operations per second, system throughput, etc.

We installed MooseFS on a computer equipped with 1G memory and running Ubuntu 11.10 and deployed PPFS on a machine with the same deployment. We use four performance metrics to measure performance of PPMS. These four metrics includes total time to complete all the transactions, number of transactions per second, number of creation per second and number of read per second.

When transaction is 2000 and number of files increase, the results of total execution time are plotted in Figure 4. First, we can see obviously the effect of number of files. More files are in the system, more time is needed. This is expected. Compared with MooseFS, PPFS can execute much faster in nearly all cases of file numbers. This clearly shows the advantage of our design. In PPFS, two-layer hierarchy helps much in locating a file.

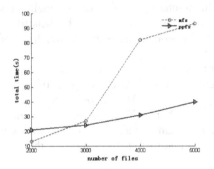
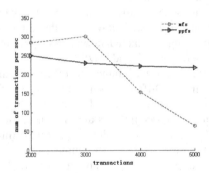

Fig. 4. Total execution time   **Fig. 5.** Number of transactions per second

Figure 5 demonstrates how many transactions can be completed per second. We test different numbers of transactions to show the performance under different cases. With the number of transaction increases from 2000 to 5000, the number of transactions processed by either system decreases. This is because that, with more transactions, there may be more conflicts in data update, and then fewer transactions can be completed per second.

Compared with MooseFS, PPFS performs much better since PPFS is not affected much by the increase of transaction number. With the help of MIS, which has a whole view of PPFS, PPFS can avoid conflicts in operations and consequently handle more transactions in the same time duration.

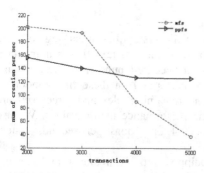

Fig. 6. Number of creations per second   **Fig. 7.** Number of read per second

Figure 6 and Figure 7 show the results of file creation and file read respectively. Comparing PPFS and MooseFS, we can see that PPFS can read/create files faster than MooseFS, in most cases. The difference increases with the increase of transaction number. This can be explained as follows. When a file is created in MooseFS, not only the metadata of the file need to be added, but also the hierarchical directory structure needs to be updated at the MDS. In PPFS, two different nodes are used to maintain the file metadata and directory metadata respectively, and obviously the task can be conducted faster. Of course, collaboration between MDS and MIS may cause addition overhead.

MooseFS is faster than PPFS only when the number of transactions is small. This because that, with few files, the directory structure is simple and the benefit of separating file metadata and directory metadata is counteracted by the overhead of cooperating MIS and MDS.

Finally, we examine the effect of number of MDSs in terms of total time by Postmark. Different from previous experiments, it has 14 machines, one of which running Windows 7 and others still running Ubuntu 12.04. The only one running Window 7 manipulates all Ubuntu machines using Xshell. Every client node creates 300 files and deletes all the files by Postmark at the same time. The results are plotted in Figure 8. We vary the number of MDSs from one to four. As expected, the total time decreases when the number of MDSs increases.

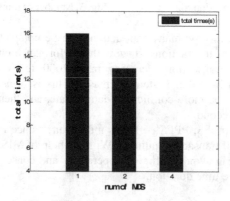

Fig. 8. Average latency of each request

4.2   Trace Simulation

To verify our system better, we simulate the metadata operations using RES trace and measure the performance in terms of hit ratio of the local MDS and the related MDS. RES trace was collected from 13 machines on the desktops of graduate students, faculty, and administrative staff of their research group project during one year at University of California Berkeley in 1996 and 1997 [18]. These hosts were used for a wide variety of tasks including document processing, program development, graphically displaying research results, email, and web browsing [18].

We downloaded part of data from official website and analyze data referring to the online prompts step. Since we only care about the metadata, operations that are not related was not extracted. Due to PPFS does not have directories and files at the beginning, we should create corresponding files and directories for replaying using a appropriate strategy and then replay RES trace on PPFS.

Limited by the experiment environment, we deploy a mini systems composed of 9 machine. Because real data is not involved in the replay, the chunk server module was not involved. In this system, there are one MIS, four MDSs, and four clients. After different machines running corresponding processes separately, the results are shown in Figure 9 and Figure 10.

Figure 9 and Figure 10 show hit ratio of MDSs by replaying RES trace on PPFS. We can clearly tell that the hit ratio of local MDSs are at a high level from the first figure. As time goes by and more traces are performed, the hit ratio of local MDSs are almost increasing gradually. This is because that design of local MDS in PPMS refers to the user's behavior, and it is directly responsible for user's write and read operations. At the same time, hit ratio of related MDSs has a common trend that the hit ratio is getting higher and higher in a long time. At the beginning, related MDSs need to establish and replace the antiquated, inefficient related MDSs, so the related MDSs were not efficient at that time. Due to the design of related MDS is based on user behavior in accessing files in the same directory with a high frequency and the files in the same directory is more likely in one MDS. Related MDSs has a high hit ratio overall with time increasing.

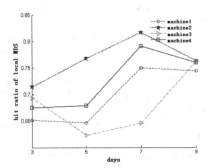
Fig. 9. Hit ratio of local MDS

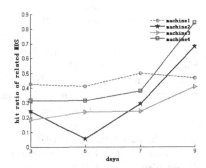
Fig. 10. Hit ratio of related MDS

5   Conclusion and Future Work

Distributed file system is one of the key blocks for distributed computing systems including cloud computing platforms. We focus on metadata management to achieve high scalability and low access latency simultaneously. With the novel concept of metadata index server, we divide metadata into two layers, i.e. file metadata and directory metadata, and propose a corresponding two layer metadata management strategy. In the lower layer, MDS servers are organized in a peer to peer way, so as to achieve high scalability. In the upper layer, MIS is used to achieve low latency. We have implemented a prototype file system and tested it using Postmark and RES. Compared with MooseFS, our design can achieves significant improvement.

Our design can be further improved and extended in many directions as the first stage. One extension may be multiple MISs. In the current design, there is only one MIS, which is prone to single point failure and may become a bottleneck in performance. A peer to peer MIS layer will be obviously more scalable and reliable. Another interesting work is metadata replication, which should be an effective way to reduce metadata access latency and improve reliability. Finally, the system implementation should be further improved.

Acknowledgments. This research is partially supported by National Natural Science Foundation of China (No. 61379157), Guangdong Natural Science Foundation (No. S2012010010670), and Pearl River Nova Program of Guangzhou (No. 2011J2200088).

References

1. Roselli, D.S., Lorch, J.R., Anderson, T.E.: A Comparison of File System Workloads. In: USENIX Annual Technical Conference, General Track, pp. 41–54 (2000)
2. Brandt, S.A., Xue, L., Miller, E.L., et al.: Efficient metadata management in large distributed storage systems. In: 2012 IEEE 9th International Conference on Mobile Ad-Hoc and Sensor Systems (MASS 2012), p. 290. IEEE Computer Society (2012)
3. Corbett, P.F., Feitelson, D.G.: The Vesta parallel file system. ACM Transactions on Computer Systems (TOCS) 14(3), 225–264 (1996)
4. Weil, S.A., Pollack, K.T., Brandt, S.A., et al.: Dynamic metadata management for petabyte-scale file systems. In: Proceedings of the 2004 ACM/IEEE Conference on Supercomputing, p. 4 (2004)
5. Zhu, Y., Jiang, H., Wang, J.: Hierarchical bloom filter arrays (hba): a novel, scalable metadata management system for large cluster-based storage. In: 2004 IEEE International Conference on Cluster Computing, pp. 165–174. IEEE (2004)
6. Hua, Y., Zhu, Y., Jiang, H., et al.: Scalable and adaptive metadata management in ultra large-scale file systems. In: ICDCS, pp. 403–410 (2008)
7. Borthakur, D.: The hadoop distributed file system: Architecture and design. Hadoop Project Website 11, 21 (2007)
8. Ghemawat, S., Gobioff, H., Leung, S.T.: The Google file system. ACM SIGOPS Operating Systems Review 37(5), 29–43 (2003)

 9. Leung, A.W., Shao, M., Bisson, T., et al.: Spyglass: Fast, Scalable Metadata Search for Large- Scale Storage Systems. FAST, pp.153-166 (2009)
10. Hua, Y., Jiang, H., Zhu, Y., et al.: SmartStore: A new metadata organization paradigm with semantic-awareness for next-generation file systems. In: Proceedings of the Conference on High Performance Computing Networking, Storage and Analysis, pp. 1–12. IEEE (2009)
11. Broder, A., Mitzenmacher, M.: Network applications of bloom filters: A survey. Internet mathematics 1(4), 485–509 (2004)
12. Weil, S.A., Brandt, S.A., Miller, E.L., et al.: Ceph: A scalable, high-performance distributed file system. In: OSDI, pp. 307–320 (2006)
13. Wang, J., Feng, D., Wang, F., et al.: MHS: A distributed metadata management strategy. Journal of Systems and Software 82(12), 2004–2011 (2009)
14. Moosefs, http://www.moosefs.org/
15. FUSE, http://fuse.sourceforge.net/
16. Katcher, J.: Postmark: A new file system benchmark. Technical Report TR3022, Network Appliance (1997), http://www.netapp.com/tech_library/3022.html
17. Patil, S., Gibson, G.A.: Scale and Concurrency of GIGA+: File System Directories with Millions of Files. In: FAST 2011, p. 13 (2011)
18. Trace,tracehost.cs.berkeley.edu
19. Yu, J., Wu, W., Li, H.: DMooseFS: Design and implementation of distributed files system with distributed metadata server. APCloudCC, pp.42-47 (2012)

Improving Log-Based Fault Diagnosis
by Log Classification

Deqing Zou, Hao Qin, Hai Jin, Weizhong Qiang, Zongfen Han, and Xueguang Chen

Services Computing Technology and System Lab
Cluster and Grid Computing Lab
School of Computer Science and Technology
Huazhong University of Science and Technology, Wuhan, 430074, China
deqingzou@hust.edu.cn

Abstract. In modern computer systems, system event logs have always been the primary source for checking the system status. As computer systems become more complex, such as cloud computing systems, the interaction among software and hardware is increasingly frequently. These components will generate enormous log information, including running reports and fault information. The massive data is a great challenge for analysis with manual method. In this paper, we implement a log management and analysis system, which can assist system administrators to understand the real-time status of the entire system, classify logs into different fault types, and determine the root cause of the faults. In addition, we improve the existing fault correlation analysis method based on the results of system log classification. We apply the log management and analysis system to cloud computing environment for evaluation. The results show that our system can classify fault logs effectively and automatically. By using the proposed system, administrators can easily detect the root cause of faults.

1 Introduction

With the widespread usage of cloud computing, computer systems are becoming increasingly complex and the components within the entire system also become diverse. Once some key parts failed, the whole system would be seriously implicated due to the frequent interactions and high coupling. Therefore, an effective fault detection and analysis method can help system administrators to locate the fault and identify the cause, which plays an essential role in large systems management.

System and software logs are important sources for diagnosing the system and software faults. However, for large systems, various components will generate amounts of log information in real time. If a fault occurs, it is difficult to extract useful information from the system efficiently and locate the fault accurately. Typically, we have to manually extract the useful information from vast amounts of data, which would seriously delay the response time of fault recovery. Therefore, an unified management system for fault log analysis is required, which can automatically identify the fault type and analyze the cause of the faults. It will provide a great help for system management.

A lot of studies have been proposed on log-based fault analysis, mainly falling in the following directions. The first is log collection and analysis, which investigate how to effectively and efficiently gather log information [1]. This information will be used to get profile information for analyzing the system situation [2] and extract the

C.-H. Hsu et al. (Eds.): NPC 2014, LNCS 8707, pp. 446–458, 2014.

feature [3]. The second part is fault location, which aims at determining the control flow of software through logs [4] and uses the source code [5] to locate the position of the faults occurred. The researches mentioned above use the log fault analysis in different scenarios. But few of them focus on the system administrator's perspective to design an integrated fault analysis system. The third part is fault correlation analysis. In the multi-node environment, the fault propagation is a critical problem for fault diagnosis. The area focuses on using log information to determine the connection between different faults. Researches use time and spatial correlation to find some connection, few of them consider the meaning of logs.

An integrated fault log analysis system will assist administrators to perform fault analysis, improving the administrator's ability to respond to the system fault and reduce the time consuming of fault processing. We implement a new fault classification method to assist manager to understand computer system and use fault correlation analysis to locate the root-cause of fault. In this paper, we propose an integrated fault log analysis platform (*UiLog*) to collect and manage various components logs, storing, filtering, and analyzing logs for administrators to quickly locate fault and analyze the cause of faults.

This platform consists of three components: 1) Fault log collection module is mainly used to collect log data from various components. 2) Fault log analysis module classifies log into the identifies fault type in real time. 3) Fault log correlation analysis module collects fault log caused by same root-fault as a tuple and tries to find the root cause of such faults. *UiLog* have deployed in a practical cloud environment, helping administrator to troubleshoot and find the root cause of fault. Our main contributions are:

We propose a novel classification method for fault logs, using fault keyword matrix to improve the accuracy. It reduces the time of determining the fault type and the workload of manual processing. Moreover, this method can be more convenient to add a new fault type without recalculated.

We improve the existing log correlation analysis. It combines the result of fault classification and time windows correlation analysis. Our method uses the fault type of logs as one factor in determining the size of the time window. It improves the accuracy of the log correlation and the location of the fault's root cause.

We illustrate a comprehensive log management system, which can help administrators to quickly grasp the operation status of the system and save troubleshooting time.

The remaining of this paper is organized as follows. Section 2 discusses background and related work. Section 3 outlines the structure of *UiLog* system and describes the implementation of the system. Section 4 describes the evaluation of our system whereas section 5 presents conclusions and future work.

2   Related Work

The aim of log information is to extract useful information from fault logs. The important techniques of previous work are mainly relied on regular expressions [5]. However, the rules of regular expressions require different knowledge from laborious and expert [6]. In addition, the deployment of new application and upgrading of system will change these templates of log frequency. It is difficult for designing these regular expressions [7].

Various studies are looking for how to understand the mean of logs, but it may be useful for detecting faults in cloud computing system [8]. Many interesting features are displayed by these studies. For instance, Stearley [9] has a new discovery that only through words cannot detect the fault type from logs. The position of each word is a powerful indicator to distinguish different messages.

Researchers have also looked at other way except system logs to diagnose system, such as application console logs [10]. However, this technique is limited to application specific anomalies and requires source code [11].

In addition, several techniques and algorithms for automatic log classification have been developed. [12] attempts to classify different raw logs into a set of categories. Moreover, in [13], the authors try to use the modified naive Bayesian model and *Hidden Markov Models* (HMM) to classify event logs based on the IBM CBE (*Common Base Event*) format. On the other hand, SLCT [14] and Loghound [15] are designed specifically to discover the format of logs and classify row log automatically. They use two similar algorithms, which are useful to extract the template from logs.

Similar to correlation analysis, time and spatial correlation techniques have been applied to a variety of large scale computing systems [16]. The current trend of this study is to use tuple with a fixed value for time window, such as 5 minutes [17].

Content-based correlation is also a hot topic. For example, [17] applies the lift data by mining operator to find frequent event patterns starting from log contents and try to isolate accidental patterns.

3   *UiLog* System

3.1   Overview of *UiLog*

The *Unify Log Analysis System* (*UiLog*) is a fault analysis and diagnosis system, which collects the system log information of each component and track logs for statistics.

Through the fault classification, *UiLog* learns the classification rules from training set of artificial classification. After that, the system determines the fault type in real time according the rule library. In addition, the fault correlation analysis can be deployed when system administrators need to diagnosis fault. Considering the propagation of the fault, *UiLog* can mining the association between faults generated by the same root-cause and collect these fault logs into the same cluster.

To implement the process, we apply three modules to represent the *UiLog*: fault log collection, fault log analysis, and fault log correlation analysis. As shown in Fig. 1, the fault log collection module collects logs from the entire target node. It collects software and system logs in all components. The analysis node is responsible for fault analysis and diagnose. In the analysis node, the fault log collection module stores all logs in log information database for analysing.

The process of fault log analysis module is shown in Fig. 1. The fault log collection module will be deployed respectively into Target Node for log collection and Analysis Node for storage. This module will gather software log and system log from Target Node and store log information into Log Information database. In the Analysis Node, the Fault log analysis module will extract log structure from fault log collection module. At first, these structures will be classified into different fault type by administrator. The Fault log analysis module will learn classification rules from administrator and store it into fault template database. After that, the fault log analysis module will automatic classify log for log diagnose.

The correlation analysis module will use the result of fault classification and expert knowledge to provide correlation analysis report from artificial analysis.

3.2   Fault Log Analysis

The fault log analysis module aims at classifying log into different log types. We adopt an example to illustrate the process: when an administrator analyzes the logs (Table 1) the first step is to determine whether the logs are fault record or not. The most commonly used method is finding keyword. The second step is the log analysis. The system administrator will weed out the details of log information to determine the cause of the fault. The first row in Table 1 shows that "Read socket failed", which indicates a socket problem when reading. The third step is the log classification. It is easily to determine that the first log belongs to the network fault and the subcategory is the remote network connection fault.

Through the above analysis, we can conclude that if we can deal with the semantic analysis of keywords and determine the fault type in advance, a large load of work can be automatically processed by the log analysis and classification.

As shown in Fig. 2, *UiLog* log classification method is divided into five steps. 1) Log Pretreatment. 2) Extracting Invariants. 3) Filtering Template Information. 4) Obtaining Fault Keyword Matrix. 5) Classifying Log Information. These steps will gradually extract log information for fault classification and remove irrelevant content.

The input of the whole algorithm is the log data flow obtained by fault log collection module. The output has two parts. One is the log classification rules (output at Step 4) based on the training set. The rules in our algorithm appear as the fault keyword matrix. The other is fault category of every log (output at Step 5). The following sub-sections describe each step of the algorithm in more detail.

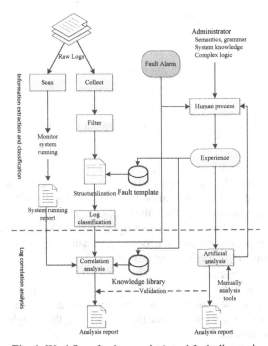

Fig. 1. Workflow for *log analysis* and fault diagnosis

Table 1. Example of log messages

Date	Host	Device	Message
2013-11-25 02:39:34	f1	sshd[18108]	fatal: Read from socket failed: Connection reset by peer
2013-11-23 16:57:13	f0	httpd[27807]	[error] [client 192.168.63.15 9] File does not exist: /var/www/html/favicon.ico

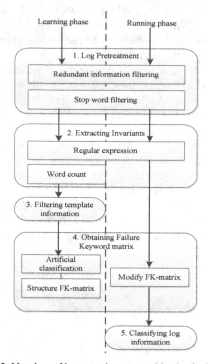

Fig. 2. Number of key words appeared in the fault logs

1) *Log Preprocessing*

Log preprocessing contains two parts. The first part is to filter repeated logs generated by the system. Many software faults are insufficient to cause the collapse in computer system and the component will persistent send fault message. We can choose an appropriate threshold to filter the duplicate logs.

The second part is the log filter of meaningless words. We use *English Stop Word Table* to filter meaningless words. In accessory, considering the special of logic, we also filter out the most of adjectives and adverbs.

2) *Extracting Invariants*

After preprocessing, the next step is to extract the template information. The template of log is used for classification. This step can reduce the solution space and compress the size of fault keyword matrix. In addition, the template will be used to match logs for fast classification.

3) Filtering Template Information

Before classification, we use automatic classification approach DBSCAN (*Density-Based Spatial Clustering of Applications with Noise*) [18] to classify the log for further reducing the manually determining space.

For a classification algorithm, based on *Levenshten Distance* (LD), we define our *Log Levenshten Distance* (LLD) to measure the distance between a log and a cluster. The distance between log *A* and log *B* is described in (1).

$$LLD(A,B) = \frac{2 \times LD(A,B)}{length(A) + length(B)} \tag{1}$$

wherein *LD(A, B)* is the original Levenshten distance, *length()* indicates the length of the log.

4) Obtaining Fault Keyword Matrix

When the system is in the learning stage, this step will learn the result of artificial classification. While in the running stage, this step will modify the classification's rules. Through the step of filter template information, the remaining numbers of raw logs have less than original.

For learning stage, the first requires administrator to classify logs manually. We pre-define a fault catalogue in the cloud environment. Through the last step, the classification has already marked a label to each fault cluster. Now the administrator will first modify the automatically label, then adjust the result of the classification. As shown in Table 2, after indicated the category, the result will be stored in the way of "Content: Mark". Label is a number that represents the fault type.

Table 2. Fault types

Content of Log	Label	Meaning
INFO: task * blocked * more * INUMI seconds.	14	Disk
udevd (INUMI): IDIRI is deprecated, please use IDIRI instead.	11	File
pam_succeed_if(*): error retrieving information about user *	7	Authenticate
Kernel reported iSCSI connection INUMI error * state	6	Drive
* received packet with * address * source	5	Network

Next, *UiLog* needs to learn the results of the artificial classification. Here we propose the *Fault Keyword Matrix* (FK-Matrix) for saving the learning result of artificial classification.

The FK-Matrix (matrix *A*) is a two-dimensional matrix constructed by the probability of each word appeared in each fault type in the template. It is an *m×n* matrix. *M* represents the different number of words in all the sample log, while *n* represents the number of fault types, $a_{i,j}$ denotes the probability of the *i*-th word belong to the *j*-th catalogue. (Note: $a_{i,j}$ is only a relative probability factor, not the true probability.)

$$A = \begin{pmatrix} a_{1,1} & a_{1,2} & \cdots & a_{1,n} \\ a_{2,1} & a_{2,2} & \cdots & a_{2,n} \\ \vdots & \vdots & \ddots & \vdots \\ a_{m,1} & a_{m,2} & \cdots & a_{m,n} \end{pmatrix} \tag{2}$$

The following describes how to calculate $a_{i,w}$. The value of $a_{i,w}$ is used to determine whether a word belongs to a certain type. As the value indicates the frequency of each word in a particular type of fault, we consider the probability of the word i in the fault type w as the ratio between the number of word i in type w and the total number of words in type w. The basic formula is described in (3). $P(i, w)$ represents the probability that the i-th word appears in the fault type w, $count(i, w)$ represents the times that the i-th word appears in the fault type w.

$$P(i,w) = \frac{count(i,w)}{\sum_{j=1}^{m} count(j,w)} \tag{3}$$

However, this formula only considers the distribution of different words in the same fault type, but it ignores the same word between different fault types in the log template. For example, if the word i only appears in the type w, then we believe that a log is very likely to belong to the fault type w as long as it contains the word i, even if how many time the word i appears in the type w. Therefore, we can amend the formula by adding a scale factor shown as (4).

$$K(i,w) = -\log\left(\frac{sum(i) - count(i,w)}{sum(i)}\right) + 1 \tag{4}$$

The $sum(i)$ represents the number of times that the word i appears in all the fault type of the template library, namely in (5).

$$sum(i) = \sum_{i=1}^{n} count(i,t) \tag{5}$$

$K(i, w)$ indicates the importance of the word i in the type w and it is in inverse proportion to the frequency of word i occurs in other types, i.e. if the occurrence that word i appears in the type w is more than in the other fault types, the word i is more important to determine whether the log is belong to type w.

Thereby, we can conclude that the probability coefficient $a_{i,w}$ is calculated as the product between the frequency of words in the fault type and the importance in the entire template, namely in (6).

$$a_{i,w} = P(i,w) \times K(i,w) \tag{6}$$

Importing the equations (3) and (4) can obtain equation (7).

$$a_{i,w} = \frac{count(i,w)}{\sum_{j=1}^{m} count(j,w)} \left[-\log\left(1 - \frac{count(i,w)}{sum(i)}\right) + 1 \right] \tag{7}$$

The following describes the learning process by using the FK-matrix. After obtaining the results of manual classification, according to the formula, we can calculate the matrix A by column. Next we will describe how to solve the w-th column as an example.

The program will count the total number of words in type w from the entire library template. The amount is named as $T(w)$, which is shown in (8).

$$T(w) = \sum_{j=1}^{m} count(j, w) \tag{8}$$

To facilitate revised and updated the FK-matrix, a new row will be added in the FK-matrix to store $T(w)$ for reducing the number of double counting.

For each word i in the fault type w, the program will calculate $sum(i)$. Similar to the $T(w)$, in order to reduce the number of calculations, the additional space will be used to store $sum(i)$. Thus, there is an expanded FK-matrix adding the additional row and column for storing statistical information. The final matrix A is shown in (9).

$$A = \begin{pmatrix} a_{1,1} & a_{1,2} & \cdots & a_{1,n} & sum(1) \\ a_{2,1} & a_{2,2} & \cdots & a_{2,n} & sum(2) \\ \vdots & \vdots & \ddots & \vdots & \vdots \\ a_{m,1} & a_{m,2} & \cdots & a_{m,n} & sum(m) \\ T(1) & T(2) & \cdots & T(n) & \end{pmatrix} \tag{9}$$

According to equation (7), we should calculate $count(i, w)$ before calculating $a_{i,w}$. Considering the value of $count(i, w)$ will be changed with updating of FK-matrix, $count(i, w)$ will be saved in the FX-matrix instead of $a_{i,w}$ in practice. *UiLog* will calculate $a_{i,w}$ until the occurrence probability of word is needed. Due to related variables has restored in the FK-matrix, it does not add any additional overhead.

After obtaining the FK-matrix through learning period, *UiLog* can classify log through FK-matrix. In the running period, administrators might modify or add new categories to different template for coping changes of system or software environment. At that moment, *UiLog* will modify FK-matrix.

5) Classifying Log Information

Through the fault keyword matrix, we can easily classify the fault log on the system. In the running period of the system, the *fault log collection module* will send fault logs to the *fault log analysis module* from various components. In this step, *UiLog* will scan every log message to compute the probability of different fault types of log, according the Fault Keyword matrix. Suppose the fault log L need to be classified, *UiLog* will compare each word in L with the FK-matrix. It will use an array (array s) to store the probability that every word in L belongs to different fault types. The Algorithm 1 gives the pseudo-code for calculating the probability.

Algorithm 1. Log classification
1 **function** *Classification*()
2   **for** *w* **in** counts of fault types
3   **for** *i* ← every word in *w*
4   **if** (*i* ∈ *L*) **then** *s[w]* ← *s[w]* + *A[w][i]*
5   **end for**
6   **if** (*maxpossible* < *s[w]*) **then**
7   *maxpossible* ← *s[w]*
8   *f* ← *w*
9   **end if**
10   **end for**
11   Inform administrator *L* belongs to fault type *f*
12   **for** *w* **in** counts of fault types
13   **if** ((*maxpossible*   *s[w]*) < threshold *t*) **then**
14   Inform *L* may belongs to fault type *w*
15   **end for**
16   **end function**

3.3   Fault Log Correlation Analysis

Fault log correlation analysis module diagnoses faults generated by different components of system and software through logs. It will use the result of log analysis to find connection between different fault logs.

In the *UiLog*, we use the results of our previous fault log classification to improve the traditional fault correlation method based on time. We note that different fault type has different time range to affect system. For example, a hardware fault has a relatively small range of time to affect the system, but it has a huge impact on the system within a short time. On the other hand, the time range of the influence of network fault is relatively wide. The associated component will produce a fault report after a long time. Thus, we can use different size of time windows to diagnose different fault types. It can improve the accuracy of judgment homologous fault.

As a practical application of the fault log classification, we collect log information generated by all hosts and virtual machines in *StrongCloud* within 10 months and analyze the fault happened in this time. Here we first use traditional fault correlation method based on time to diagnosis the fault. It uses the uniform window size. Then we manually analyze each log in the tuple to determine the different window size for every fault type.

In the specific process, the administrator will point out which log they want to diagnose. *UiLog* will query the *fault keyword matrix* for finding the appropriate time window after confirming the fault type of log. Then *UiLog* will use this time window to diagnose the fault.

4   Performance Evaluations

In this section, we test the main functions of *UiLog* system and evaluate the effect including fault log analysis. We construct a fault-tolerance testbed, *StrongCloud* [19], which is made up of five Inspur's NF5240M3 servers, each with 24 Intel Xeon E5-2420 1.90 GHz processors, 32 GB of RAM and four Gigabit Ethernet ports. Each host has a Domain0 with CentOS release 6.3 of kernel 3.7.1-xen.x86_64, and the hypervisor is Xen 4.2.1. *UiLog* is a sub-system of *StrongCloud*. The evaluations show the importance of log management.

4.1   Log Analysis

For log analysis module, the most important is to test the efficiency of log classification. In this test, *UiLog* classifies all the fault logs collected by log collection module. The sample data is derived from *StrongCloud* within one year. The details are shown in Table 3.

Table 3. Experimental environment

System	Beginning	Ending	Days	Size	Messages
CentOS	2012-12	2013-12	386	1.7GB	14450302

We first use the data of January and February to train *UiLog* to obtain the basic Fault Keyword matrix. The test is launched on the data from March 2013.

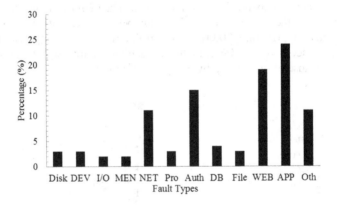

Fig. 3. Types of logs

To classify logs, we use trigger mechanism and *User Defined Function* (UDF) in database for analysis log timely. Whenever there is a log from the log collection module, the trigger is activated and UDF function will call log analysis module. The log analysis module will classify the fault log according to the described steps of running period by using the fault keyword matrix. If the type of log cannot be determined, this log will be saved in unprocessed database and *UiLog* will inform the administrator to manually classify this log. After dealing with this unsorted log artificially, *UiLog* will automatically learn from these new results and modify the *fault keyword matrix* to improve classification accuracy.

The bar chart (Fig. 3) shows the classification results for the one year fault log of *StrongCloud*. We divide fault log into 12 different types. Fig. 3 gives the ratio of each type. From the figure we can conclude that the main function of *StrongCloud* platform is network-related. The net error and web error are sum up to 43% of all faults. In addition, we can find that the platform has been subject to external attack, network authentication faults occupy 15%. The port SSL services or disable services are not commonly used.

From Fig. 3, we can demonstrate that through the fault log classification analysis, *UiLog* can help administrator to manage computer systems, finding problems and bottlenecks in the system to compensate the deficiencies in the system.

4.2   Learning Efficiency

The learning efficiency of artificial classification is a vary import indicator for evaluation the new fault classification method of *UiLog*. We use two months fault logs as a sample for learning period. When the system is running, we will classify those non-classification logs manually at the end of every month. *UiLog* will re-learn these new classification results to improve the Fault Key matrix for better automatic classification result.

Fig. 4 illustrates the number of classified fault logs and unclassified fault logs from March to October. It shows that there are only 568 fault log types cannot be judged in March after learning compared 2350 defined types. Then *UiLog* studies the results of new type rules by the end of March. The number of unclassified fault logs had dropped significantly, reaching 208 types on April. After that, the apparent decreasing tendency can be seen during March to June, reaching the lowest point (48 types) in June. That is because of re-learning by every end of month.

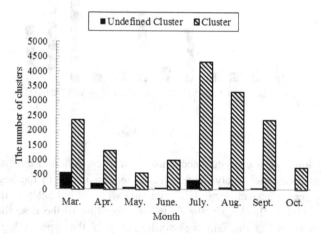

Fig. 4. Number of clusters

However, Fig. 4 also presents that the percentage of unclassified fault logs has a growth in July. According the previous analysis, it is due to the new application or software developed in July. This change generates a lot of new fault logs and leads to 324 new fault types. After finishing the re-learning step by the end of July, the percentage of unclassified logs has dropped dramatically and the system becomes gradually stabilizing. There are only 3 undefined log types.

Through the above experiments and analysis, our fault classification method is effective. It can be sufficiently carried out using the results of the automatic learning to automatically determine the type of fault log.

5   Conclusions and Future Work

With the development of cloud computing, the architecture of system and software are more complicated than before. This paper presents an integrated fault log analysis platform *UiLog* system, helping administrators to manage the log generated by the all the components of system, monitoring the running of the system and diagnosing the fault.

To effectively analyze the logs, we propose a new method to classify log into different catalogs according to the different fault types. We use *Fault Keyword matrix* to accelerate the speed of classification. In addition, we improve the fault correlation analysis. We use the result of fault classification to fix the time correlation window to reduce the truncation error and collision error.

Acknowledgments. This work is supported by National 973 Fundamental Basic Research Program under grant No. 2014CB340600 and National Science Foundation of China under grant No. 61272072.

References

1. Zawoad, S., Dutta, A.K., Hasan, R.: SecLaaS: secure logging-as-a-service for cloud forensics. In: Proceedings of the ACM Symposium on Information, Computer and Communications Security, pp. 219–230 (2013)
2. Rao, X., Wang, H., Shi, D., Chen, Z.: Identifying faults in large-scale distributed systems by filtering noisy error logs. In: Proceedings of the IEEE/IFIP International Conference on Dependable Systems and Networks, pp. 140–145 (2011)
3. Yuan, D., Mai, H., Xiong, W., Tan, L., Zhou, Y., Pasupathy, S.: SherLog: error diagnosis by connecting clues from run-time logs. Computer Architecture News 38, 143–154 (2010), doi:10.1145/1735971.1736038
4. Fu, Q., Lou, J., Wang, Y., Li, J.: Execution anomaly detection in distributed systems through unstructured log analysis. In: Proceedings of the IEEE International Conference on Data Mining, pp. 149–158 (2009)
5. Xu, W., Huang, L., Fox, A., Patterson, D., Jordan, M.: Detecting large-scale system problems by mining console logs. In: Proceedings of the ACM Symposium on Operating Systems Principles, pp. 117–132 (2009)
6. James, E.P.: Listening to your cluster with LoGS. In: Proceedings of the LCI International Conference on Linux Clusters: TheHPC Revolution, pp. 1–10 (2004)
7. Jain, S., Singh, I., Chandra, A., Zhang, Z., Bronevetsky, G.: Extracting the textual and temporal structure of supercomputing logs. In: Proceedings of the IEEE International Conference on High Performance Computing, pp. 254–263 (2009)
8. Stearley, J., Oliner, A.J.: Bad words: Finding faults in Spirit's syslogs. In: Proceedings of the IEEE International Symposium on Cluster Computing and the Grid, pp. 765–770 (2008)

9. Sandia, J.S., Stearley, J.: Towards informatic analysis of syslogs. In: Proceedings of the IEEE International Conference on Cluster Computing, pp. 309–318 (2004)
10. Xu, W., Huang, L., Fox, A., Patterson, D., Jordan, M.: Mining Console Logs for Large-Scale System Problem Detection. In: Proceedings of the IEEE Conference on Tackling Computer Systems Problems with Machine Learning Techniques, pp. 4–14 (2008)
11. Salfner, F., Tschirpke, S.: Error Log Processing for Accurate Failure Prediction. In: Proceedings of the USENIX Workshop on Analysis of System Logs, pp. 23–31 (2008)
12. Park, J., Yoo, G., Lee, E.: Proactive self-healing system based on multi-agent technologies. In: Proceedings of the ACIS International Conference on Software Engineering Research, Management and Applications, pp. 256–263 (2005)
13. Li, T., Liang, F., Ma, S., Peng, W.: An integrated framework on mining logs files for computing system management. In: Proceedings of the ACM International Conference on Knowledge Discovery in Data Mining, pp. 776–781 (2005)
14. Vaarandi, R.: A data clustering algorithm for mining patterns from event logs. In: Proceedings of the IEEE Workshop on IP Operations and Management, pp. 119–126 (2003)
15. Vaarandi, R.: A breadth-first algorithm for mining frequent patterns from event logs. In: Aagesen, F.A., Anutariya, C., Wuwongse, V. (eds.) INTELLCOMM 2004. LNCS, vol. 3283, pp. 293–308. Springer, Heidelberg (2004)
16. Oliner, A., Stearley, J.: What supercomputers say: A study of five system logs. In: Proceedings of the Annual IEEE/IFIP International Conference on Dependable Systems and Networks, pp. 575–584 (2007)
17. Pecchia, A., Cotroneo, D., Kalbarczyky, Z., Iyer, R.K.: Improving log-based field failure data analysis of multi-node computing systems. In: Proceedings of the IEEE/IFIP International Conference on Dependable Systems and Networks, pp. 97–108 (2011)
18. Ester, M., Kriegel, H., Sander, J., Xu, X.: A density-based algorithm for discovering clusters in large spatial databases with noise. In: Proceedings of the ACM International Conference on Knowledge Discovery in Data Mining, pp. 226–231 (1996)
19. StrongCloud, http://211.69.198.202:91

A Compilation and Run-Time Framework for Maximizing Performance of Self-scheduling Algorithms*

Yizhuo Wang[1], Laleh Aghababaie Beni[2],
Alexandru Nicolau[2], Alexander V. Veidenbaum[2], and Rosario Cammarota[3]

[1] Beijing Institute of Technology, Beijing 100081, P.R.China
frankwyz@bit.edu.cn
[2] University of California, Irvine CA 92697, USA
[3] Qualcomm Research, San Diego CA 92121, USA

Abstract. Ordinary programs contain many parallel loops which account for a significant portion of these programs' completion time. The parallel executions of such loops can significantly speedup performance of modern multi-core systems. We propose a new framework - Locality Aware Self-scheduling (LASS) - for scheduling parallel loops to multi-core systems and boost up performance of known self-scheduling algorithms in diverse execution conditions. LASS enforces data locality, by forcing the execution of consecutive chunks of iterations to the same core, and favours load balancing with the introduction of a work-stealing mechanism. LASS is evaluated on a set of kernels on a multi-core system with 16 cores. Two execution scenarios are considered. In the first scenario our application runs alone on top of the operating system. In the second scenario our application runs in conjunction with an interfering parallel job. The average speedup achieved by LASS for first execution scenario is 11% and for the second one is 31%.

Keywords: loop scheduling, self-scheduling, random forest.

1 Introduction

Multi-core, multi-socket systems offer a great potential for improving performance of ordinary programs, which are composed of many parallel loops and/or loops that can be auto-parallelized by the compiler or by the user. However, an effective exploitation of such a parallelism requires care in adapting chunks of parallel loops and allocating such chunks to the available cores - in order to balancing the load across cores and minimizing synchronization costs.

Loop scheduling algorithms and in particular self-scheduling algorithms (SS) addresses finding the correct trade-off between load balancing and synchronization costs to minimize the completion time of a parallel loop. However, the load

---

* This work was partially supported by the National Natural Science Foundation of China under grant NSFC-61300011.

C.-H. Hsu et al. (Eds.): NPC 2014, LNCS 8707, pp. 459–470, 2014.

imbalance which rises in modern multi-core systems - due to a deep and complex memory hierarchy organization and shared access to the main memory by multiple threads and processes, is such that self-scheduling algorithms deliver inconsistent performance across different parallel loops and in diverse execution conditions.

In this work we propose a new framework for scheduling parallel loops to multi-core systems - Locality Aware Self-scheduling (LASS). LASS has two main components: (a) a compilation environment which partitions the iterations of a parallel loops in batches and assigns each batch statically to one core. Each batch of iterations is subsequently partitioned in chunks of iterations according to one out of four widely adopted self-scheduling algorithms, a.k.a. SS [1], GSS [2], FSS [3], TSS [4] - these algorithms are customarily implemented in the GNU GCC compiler, the IBM XLC compiler and the Intel ICC compiler; (b) a runtime environment, which first selects the type of self-scheduling algorithm that is the most likely to speedup performance of a given parallel loop and second deploys LASS with the selected self-scheduling algorithm. A machine learning aided heuristic to select the self-scheduling algorithm and the number of cores to use is constructed offline. Experimental results show that LASS boosts up performance of known self-scheduling algorithms in diverse execution conditions.

The rest of the paper is organized as follows. Section 2 describes LASS. Experimental results are presented in Section 3. Section 4 provides a breakdown of prior work on self-scheduling and iteration scheduling in the presence of shared levels of memory hierarchy. Our conclusion is presented in Section 5.

2   Technique

In this section we present the LASS technique. To improve affinity, LASS assumes that each worker thread is assigned to a core, so the number of workers never exceeds the number of cores available on the system underneath.

2.1   Locality Aware Self-Scheduler

The Master thread spawns P Workers and pins each Worker to a core. Next, the Master produces a list of chunk sizes, $\mathbf{C}$, according to a given self-scheduling algorithm. In addition to the above, the LASS scheduler partitions the parallel loop in P batches and assigns one batch to each Worker. Subsequently, each Worker executes the Algorithm 1 during the execution of a parallel loop.

When the Worker T_i completes the execution of its current chunk, it first attempts to fetch the next available chunk size C_j in the list $\mathbf{C}$ and then attempts to fetch C_j iterations from its batch B_i. If C_j iterations are available in the batch B_i, then T_i fetches C_j iterations from B_i starting from the iteration # n_i. Toward the end of the batch, however, the number of iterations available in B_i may be less than C_j. In this circumstance, the chunk C_j is split in two parts at run-time. The iterations from n_i until u_i are fetched by T_i, whereas a new chunk $C' = C_j - (u_i - n_i)$ is inserted in the queue $\mathbf{C}$. Eventually, if no more

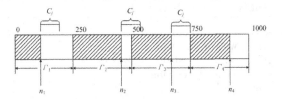

Fig. 1. LASS operations

iterations are available in the batch B_i, T_i can help other Workers completing their batches. In this case, multiple Workers will contend the access to the same batch of iterations, hence synchronization is required. This is the only scenario in which LASS requires synchronization. Indeed, with the exception of the last case mentioned above, a Worker can fetch C_j iterations from **C** without explicitly gain exclusive access to the queue of iterations. Once a Worker fetches a chunk size number from **C**, it moves the index of **C** to the next position. Because the index of **C** is shared by all the Workers, two or more Workers can access the same chunk size sometimes. Even if this happens, the algorithm can still run correctly because the termination of the loop is not detected by checking **C** and **C** just provides chunk sizes but not real chunks.

For clarity, we present the example in Figure 1. Let us assume the iterations space being composed of 1000 iterations, that is $\Gamma = \{I_1, I_2, \cdots, I_{1000}\}$, and that these iterations need to be scheduled to run on $P = 4$ cores. The iteration space is partitioned in four batches composed of 250 iterations, $\Gamma = \Gamma_1 \cup \Gamma_2 \cup \Gamma_3 \cup \Gamma_4$. Four Workers are spawn, T_1, T_2, T_3 and T_4. Each Worker is assigned to a different core, so that any time the Worker T_j processes a chunk, it will always run on the core P_j.

The Worker T_j is the owner of the batch Γ_j. When the parallel execution starts, the Worker T_j has exclusive access to its own batch. Before the Workers start, a self-scheduling algorithms is used to create a list of chunks, named **C**. Iterations are scheduled in chunks as indicated in **C**. Let n_i be the iterations index in Γ_i. At a scheduling step in Figure 1, $n_1 = 100$, $n_2 = 450$, and the upper bound for Γ_3 is $n_3 = 750$. There are three distinct possible scenarios:

- The Worker T_1 attempts to fetch C_j iterations from Γ_1. If $n_1 + C_j < u_1$, C_j consecutive iterations can be fetched from Γ_1. Next, the Worker T_1 fetches C_j consecutive iterations from Γ_1 starting from n_1 and executes them.
- The Worker T_2 attempts to fetch C_j from Γ_2. If $n_2 + C_j > u_2$, only $u_2 - n_2$ are fetched from Γ_2, and $C' = C_j - (u_2 - n_2)$ is a new chunk size which is appended to the list of chunk sizes.
- The Worker T_3 attempts to fetch C_j from Γ_3. If $n_3 + C_j = u_3$, all iterations in Γ_3 have already been processed. In this case, n_3 points to n_4. If the iterations in Γ_4 have also been consumed, both n_3 and n_4 point to n_1.

Algorithm 1. Locality aware self-scheduling

P : number of cores;
$\mathbf{T} = \{T_1, T_2, \cdots, T_P\}$: worker threads;
$\mathbf{C} = \{C_1, C_2, \cdots, C_{\#chunks}, 0\}$: list of chunk sizes;
$\varGamma = \{I_1, I_2, \cdots, I_N\}$: queue of iterations;
n_i : current index of the ith partition;
u_i : upper bound index of the ith partition;
f_i : set to 1 if P_i shares its partition;

t_exit=**FALSE**
while (**TRUE**) **do**
  if (f_i=**TRUE**) **then**
    lock($\varGamma$)
  end if
  get C_j iterations from $\varGamma$;
  $k = n_i + C_j$;
  if ($k < u_i$) **then**
    $lb = n_i$; $ub = n_i + C_j$; $n_i = n_i + C_j$;
  else
    if ($k - u_i > 0$) **then**
      Split the partition of the current chunk
      $C' = k - u_i$
      append C' to $\mathbf{C}$
    end if
    $lb = n_i$; $ub = u_i$; $n_i = u_i$; $k = i$;
    repeat
      $n_k = n_{(k+1)\%P}$; $u_k = u_{(k+1)\%P}$; $k = k + 1$;
      if ($i = k$) **then**
        t_exit=**TRUE**; break;
      end if
    until ($n_k \neq u_k$)
    f_k=**TRUE**
  end if
  if (f_i=**TRUE**) **then**
    unlock($\varGamma$)
  end if
  for $k = lb \rightarrow ub$ **do**
    Body of the parallel loop
  end for
  if (t_exit=**TRUE**) **then**
    exit
  end if
end while

2.2 Selection of the Iteration Scheduling Algorithm and the Number of Workers

LASS can work in combination with any self-scheduling algorithm and because there is no self-scheduling algorithm that enables optimal performance for any parallel loop, we propose a simple heuristic to the problem of selecting the most suitable self-scheduling algorithm, given a characterization of a parallel loop. Likewise, we propose a heuristic to select the number of Workers delivering best performance.

Note that the selection of a self-scheduling strategy and the number of threads to maximize performance depends on many factors on a real system, such as the dynamic availability of cores, their instant load, etc. Thus, accurate analytical models cannot be derived, and in any case, building such models is out of the scope of this paper.

The heuristic proposed in this section is based on classification trees [5]. We characterize the behavior of a parallel loop based on the features of its loop body, such as uniform vs. non-uniform loop body. Non-uniform loop bodies are further characterized in terms of the source of non-uniformity, such as multi-way loop, non-perfectly nested loop, presence of conditionals and nested conditionals, etc. To such features we associate - as a label - the most profitable self-scheduling algorithm which maximizes performance of these loops, e.g., G for GSS, F for FSS and T for TSS.

We build a predictor based on classification tree which learns from examples such as $\mathbf{f} \to \{G, F, T\}$, where $\mathbf{f}$ indicates the description of the loop. Given an unseen vector of features, our predictor is in charge to predict the most suitable self-scheduling algorithm to minimize the execution time of a parallel loop. Such a prediction, as we will see in the next section, can be performed independently from the number of Workers allocated for its execution.

Following the same principle, we build a second classification tree using as features as combination of loop's feature, the self-scheduling algorithm previously selected and the input size - which is expressed as the total number of instructions retired. The output of this second classifier is the number of Workers to use in order to maximize performance. Our predictor learns from examples such as $(\mathbf{f}, s, I) \to p$, where $s \in \{G, F, T\}$, I is the number of instructions retired, and p indicates the execution time (performance) of the parallel loop.

3 Experiments

In order to evaluate our locality aware self-scheduling technique, we selected three popular self-scheduling algorithms to run in combination with our technique. These algorithms are guided self-scheduling (GSS)[2], factoring self-scheduling (FSS) [3] and trapezoid self-scheduling (TSS) [4].

3.1 Experimental Setup

We extracted several kernels from the benchmark suites SPEC CPU2000/2006, SPEC OMP2001 and MiBenchII. The description of these kernels is provided

Table 1. List of kernels

Kernel	Benchmark suite	Benchmark	File, line
L1	SPEC CPU2000	179.art	scanner.c, 317
L2	MiBench	JPEG	jcdctmgr.c, 195
L3	SPEC CPU2000	183.equake	quake.c, 447
L4	SPEC CPU2006	470.lbm	lbm.c, 186
L5		matrix multiplication	mm.c
L6	MiBench	susan	susan.c, 738
L7	SPEC CPU2006	433.milc	quark_stuff.c, 1523
L8	SPEC CPU2006	462.libquantum	gates.c, 89
L9	SPEC CPU2006	462.libquantum	gates.c, 61
L10	SPEC CPU2006	464.h264ref	mv-search.c, 394
L11	SPEC CPU2006	482.sphnix3	vector.c, 512
L12	SPEC OMP2001	172.mgrid	mgrid.f, 189
L13		matrix transposition	mt.c

Table 2. System configurations

Processors	4 x Intel Xeon X7350 (Tigertown) @ 2.93GHz
L2	2 x 4MB
Main memory [GB]	8
Compilation	gcc4.5 -O3 -lpthread -lrt -lm
Thread library	NPTL 2.7
Operating system	Linux 2.6.22

in Table 1. We compiled and executed our kernels on the system configuration summarized in Table 2. Intel X7350 is a quad-core processor, which consists of two dual-core. This configuration accounts for a total of 16 cores. Each dual-core shares 4MB of shared L2 cache. We compiled the kernels listed in in Table 1 using GNU GCC v4.5 and the optimization level $-O3$ enabled.

Each performance result is the average of one hundred execution of each kernel to ensure dependability of the results. During each run we collect hardware performance counters using Perfmon2 [6].

3.2   Experimental Results

We implemented the Algorithm 1 presented in section 2. To produce the list of chunks we refer to three widely used self-scheduling strategies: GSS, FSS and TSS. These three self-scheduling algorithms differ in terms of their chunking strategy, thereby their synchronization costs are different [3].

In the presentation of the experimental results, we refer as LASS-G when LASS is applied in combination with GSS. Mutatis mutandis, we use the nomenclatures LASS-F and LASS-T to indicate that LASS is applied in combination with FSS and TSS respectively.

For each kernel, we compare completion time obtained with a given self-scheduling strategy with the completion time of LASS, say LASS-{G,F,T}. As indicator of performance we use the speedup as defined in equation 1. Such a speedup is relative to the completion time the parallel execution of a kernel subject to a given self-scheduling algorithm.

$$S_{\{G,F,T\}}^{\#Workers} = \frac{Completion\ time_{G,F,T}}{Completion\ time_{LASS-G,F,T}} \tag{1}$$

We conducted the experiments in two execution environments. In the first execution environment, named **free system**, our applications run alone, one by one, on the system. In the second execution environment, named **full system** our applications run in conjunction with an interfering parallel job influencing the load of multiple cores at random. For each execution environment we conducted our experiments for a variable number of Worker threads from 2 to 16.

Analysis of Performance and Locality. Results for the *free system* are reported in Figure 2. LASS improved performance in most cases. Our performance results are supported by the counters collected. In multi-cores, the cache miss count is the main reflection of the locality exploitation. Figure 3 shows the miss rate in the case of four threads running on the *free system*. This case is relevant given our hardware configuration. Figure 3 shows that L1 cache misses decreases, whereas L2 cache misses vary slightly or remains constant. The reduction of L1 cache misses is a direct effect of the adoption of LASS and does contribute to ameliorate performance. The slight variation in L2 misses is an artifact of the system we are running on.

For more than two workers, only couples of Workers share the second level of cache - because of the topology of the memory hierarchy on our system, limiting the benefit deriving from the enforcement of locality. Indeed, the kernels L10 and L11, whose working set size fits inside the last level of cache slightly benefit from the parallel execution with 2 Workers and their performance is severely compromised with the adoption a larger number of Workers.

On the other end, performance still improves because of the behavior of LASS toward the end of the parallel execution. Toward the completion of the parallel execution LASS creates additional chunks by splitting the last few chunks available. The availability of additional chunks increases the number of tasks to execute in parallel, the parallel execution still results profitable, thereby improves performance despite the obstacle imposed by our system configuration.

Moreover, kernels L7, L12 and L13 achieve the best speedups in most cases. Most likely reason is that the data in these kernels is much denser than other kernels. Therefore, LASS gains more benefits from the improvement of the data locality. However, it is hard to break down performance improvements attributed to various factors in a real machine.

Next, we considered another execution environment, the *full system*. In this execution scenario cores are not available for our applications at the same time. Nevertheless, LASS still enhances performance of classical self-scheduling strategies, as it is shown in Figure 4. Experimental results show that the average speedup is significantly higher when compared to those of system free. These results highlight that performance achieved because of the adaptivity of self-scheduling strategy is effectively amplified by LASS. Furthermore, these results show that there is opportunity to achieve higher speedups if, when applying a self-scheduling strategy in both free and full systems, we were able to select ad hoc the number of working threads.

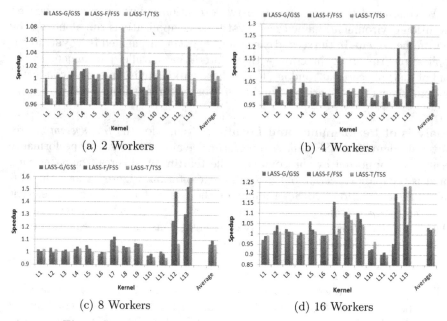

Fig. 2. Speedup w.r.t. self-scheduling algorithm on *free system*

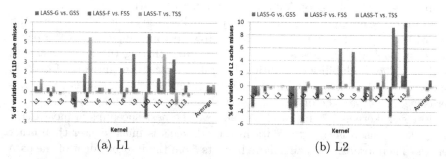

Fig. 3. L1 and L2 miss rates improvement for four threads on *free system*

Analysis of Synchronization Operations. Figure 5 shows the number of synchronization operations required to run LASS is significantly lower than the number of synchronization operations required by other non LASS self-scheduling strategies. This is a trend across the three GSS, FSS and TSS. The relative reduction of synchronization costs influences performance of each self-scheduling algorithms in a different way. For example, let us consider experiments using 16 worker threads. FSS is the self-scheduling strategy suffering from the highest synchronization costs because of the chunk sizes' distribution. When the threads involved in the computation start and progress simultaneously, the probability of having concurrent accesses is higher for FSS than GSS and TSS.

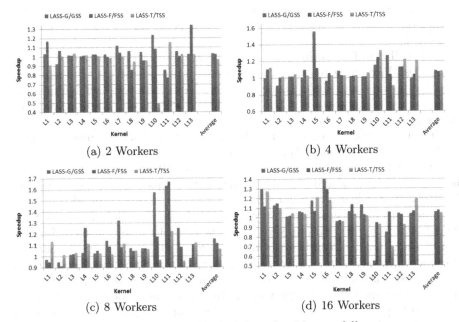

(a) 2 Workers

(b) 4 Workers

(c) 8 Workers

(d) 16 Workers

Fig. 4. Speedup w.r.t. self-scheduling algorithm on *full system*

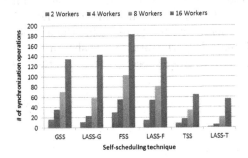

Fig. 5. Number of synchronization operations

Arguably, FSS is the self-scheduling strategy gaining the highest benefit from the elimination of the synchronization operations. Our experiments show an 3.42% average reduction in execution time. Also TSS shows an 1.83% average reduction in execution time and this number is 3.34% for GSS algorithm. The influence that the reduction of synchronization operations has on performance of a self-scheduling algorithm depends on the distribution of the chunk sizes.

Selection of the Self-scheduling Algorithm and of the Number of Workers. The analysis of the vectors of counters collected and the types of parallel loop adopted in our experiments suggest the adoption of two simple heuristics, based on decision trees [7], to cope with the following problems: (a)

Selecting the most beneficial self-scheduling algorithm for a given loop. (b) Selecting the number of Workers to achieve best performance from the parallel execution.

We classify our loops using the rules as follows: We refer as *uniform* such parallel loops which have constant cost per iteration. In this category fall loops with constant bounds and stride, containing inner loops with constant bounds and uniform strides, and containing function calls. We refer as *non uniform* such parallel loops containing conditionals, indirect references, variable bounds and/or strides. As first classification step we separate uniform from non uniform loops. Uniform loops containing other nested loops are labeled with an F, indicating FSS as the best candidate for this type of loops. Other uniform loops are labeled with G, which stands for GSS. Non uniform loops containing branches are labeled with F, which stands for FSS, whereas non uniform loops with indirect references or non constant loop body are labeled with T, which stands for TSS. This heuristic applied on our kernels is illustrated in Figure 6. Experimental results show that for both the execution environments, the *free system* and the *full system*, the selection of self-scheduling algorithm to apply can be performed visiting the decision tree in Figure 6 using the description of the parallel loop. This pass is done offline. We provide another offline heuristic which, given the features of a parallel loop and a self-scheduling algorithm, predicts the number of working threads needed to minimize its execution time. This second heuristic is based on the size of the input, represented by the number of instructions retired. This second heuristic is illustrated as an example in Figure 7.

The results of the experiments conducted using the heuristics described above are summarized in Table 3. Experimental results show an average speedup of 11% in the *free system*, and an average speedup of 31% in the *full system*.

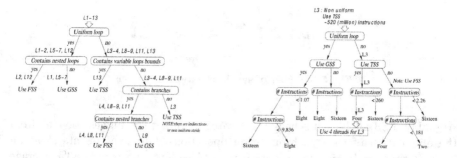

Fig. 6. Selection of self-scheduling per loop   **Fig. 7.** Selection of the number of threads

4   Related Work

Many iteration scheduling algorithms have been proposed in the literature. These algorithms leverage the presence of parallelism in a architecture to reduce execution time of ordinary programs. On one extreme, there is static scheduling which

Table 3. Selection of self-scheduling and # Workers on *free* and *full system*

Kernel	Free system			Full system		
	LASS	# Workers	Speedup	LASS	# Workers	Speedup
L1	G	8	1.02	G	16	1.30
L2	F	16	1.04	F	16	1.15
L3	T	4	1.08	T	16	1.05
L4	F	4	1.05	F	8	1.26
L5	G	8	1.06	G	2	1.56
L6	G	4	1.01	G	16	1.41
L7	G or F	16	1.16	G	8	1.32
L8	F	16	1.10	F	16	1.14
L9	G	16	1.10	G	16	1.13
L10	G	2	1.03	G	8	1.57
L11	F	2	1.01	F	8	1.67
L12	F	8	1.49	G	8	1.25
L13	T	16	1.24	T	8	1.21
Average			*1.11*			*1.31*

assigns even partitions of a loop iterations to multiple cores. Compared to other schemes, it has the lowest scheduling overhead but it may incur in the worst load balancing when scheduling irregular parallel loops. On the other extreme, there is the first self-scheduling [1]. It assigns one iteration to an idle core each time, to achieve best load balancing, but has the highest execution and synchronization overheads. For having a trade-off between execution overhead and load balancing, the adoption of fixed chunks was proposed by other authors [8]. However, The selection of the chunk size is challenging. In fact, small chunk sizes allow the exploitation of more parallelism, whereas larger chunk sizes reduce the run-time overhead. Rather than the use of fixed chunk sizes, Kruscal and Weiss in [9] proposed the adoption of chunk sizes with a decreasing profile down to chunks containing only one iteration. In the beginning, threads are allowed to fetch larger chunks, thus achieving low parallel execution overhead. Toward the end of the parallel loop the presence of smaller chunks allows to achieve better load balancing. Among the self-scheduling algorithms proposed in the literature, GSS [2], FSS [3] and TSS [4] are widely used and implemented in open source and commercial compilers.

In the other self-scheduling strategies technique in the literature [10,11], adjusted chunk sizes at run time or processor affinity is exploited. Markatos and LeBlanc in [12] propose affinity scheduling, which is locality aware, but it suffers of load balancing when dealing with irregular loops.

In the work stealing literature [13], the scheduling algorithms are all locality aware because of the use of per-processor work queues. Work stealing schedulers aim to tasks which are independent units of works that can be executed in parallel. In Cilk [14] and Intel TBB [15] which are popular frameworks using work stealing, a parallel loop is partitioned to fixed chunks. Then each chunk is viewed as a task. To the best of our knowledge, LASS technique combining self-scheduling with work stealing capabilities.

5   Conclusion

In this paper we proposed a new iteration scheduling technique - locality aware self-scheduling - which, in combination with any self-scheduling algorithm, systematically reduces the number of synchronization operations required to assign cores to chunks, enforces both spatial and temporal locality, enforces affinity and adapts the mapping of chunks onto iterations at run-time, therefore improves on load balancing and performance. As a part of our technique we propose a machine learning based heuristic, which is based on decision trees, to select the most suitable iteration scheduling algorithm and number of threads to minimize the completion time of a parallel loop.

References

1. Smith, B.J.: Architecture and applications of the HEP multiprocessor computer system. Real Time Signal Processing IV 298, 241–298 (1981)
2. Polychronopoulos, C.D., Kuck, D.J.: Guided self-scheduling: a practical scheduling scheme for parallel supercomputers. IEEE Trans on Computers 36(12), 1425–1439 (1987)
3. Flynn-Hummel, S., Schonberg, E., Flynn, L.E.: Factoring: A method for scheduling parallel loops. Communications of the ACM 35(8), 90–101 (1992)
4. Tzen, T.H., Ni, L.M.: Trapezoid self-scheduling: a practical scheduling scheme for parallel computers. IEEE Trans. on Parallel and Distributed Systems 4(1), 87–98 (1993)
5. Breiman, L., Friedman, J., et al.: Classification and Regression Trees. Chapman & Hall/CRC (1984)
6. Jarp, S., Jurga, R., Nowak, A.: Perfmon2: a leap forward in performance monitoring. J. Phys. Conf. Ser. 119, 042017 (2008)
7. Podgorelec, V., Kokol, P., et al.: Decision trees: An overview and their use in medicine. J. Med. Syst. 26, 445–463 (2002)
8. Tang, P., Yew, P.C.: Processor self-scheduling for multiple nested parallel loops. In: ICPP, pp. 528–535 (1986)
9. Kruskal, C.P., Weiss, A.: Allocating independent subtasks on parallel processors. IEEE Trans. Softw. Eng. SE-1 1(10), 1001–1016 (1985)
10. Cariño, R.L., Banicescu, I.: Dynamic load balancing with adaptive factoring methods in scientific applications. J. Supercomput 44(1), 41–63 (2008)
11. Tabirca, T., Freeman, L., et al.: Feedback guided dynamic loop scheduling: convergence of the continuous case. J. Supercomput. 30(2), 151–178 (2004)
12. Markatos, E.P., LeBlanc, T.J.: Using processor affinity in loop scheduling on shared-memory multiprocessors. IEEE Trans. Parallel Distrib. Syst. 5(4), 379–400 (1994)
13. Blumofe, R.D., Leiserson, C.E.: Scheduling multithreaded computations by work stealing. J. ACM 46(5), 720–748 (1999)
14. Blumofe, R.D., Joerg, C.F., et al.: Cilk: An efficient multithreaded runtime system. In: PPoPP, pp. 207–216 (1995)
15. Intel(R) Threading Building Blocks, Intel Corporation

PaxStore : A Distributed Key Value Storage System

Zhipeng Tan, Yongxing Dang, Jianliang Sun, Wei Zhou, and Dan Feng

Wuhan National Laboratory for Optoelectronics, School of Computer Science, Huazhong
University of Science and Technology, Wuhan, China

Abstract. Consistency, availability, scalability, and tolerance to the network
partition are four important problems in distributed systems. In this paper, we
have designed a consistent, highly available distributed key value storage system
that can run on lots of general devices and solve the four problems in distributed
systems, we call it as PaxStore. It uses zookeeper to complete leader election. It
uses a centralized Paxos-based protocol to guarantee the strong replica
consistency. The system node can automatically recover in case of failure.
Experiments show that PaxStore can guarantee the strong consistency and only
increases 20% overhead compared with local systems. By using log
optimization, such as the circular lock-free queue and Paxos protocol
optimization techniques, PaxStore has a high performance and recovery speed
than the older system which uses a basic Paxos protocol.

1   Introduction

With the rapid development of computer technology and Internet, especially the
emerging of Web 2.0 technology, information grows explosively. Therefore, it is
difficult to improve the system performance by using the scale-up[2] method (provide
larger and more powerful servers). The scale-out[2] method, in the form of clusters of
general machines, is a long-term solution to solve the bottlenecks of storage systems.
However, the problems in distributed systems are far more complex than problems in
a single machine. We have to solve various anomalies, such as node failure, disk
failure, network partition, message missing etc.. It is difficult to build a highly
available distributed storage system under complex conditions.

In distributed systems, consistency, availability and partition tolerance are three
important issues. However, no distributed systems can simultaneously achieve the
three goals according to Brew's CAP Theorem[3]. Stonebraker[4] argued that strong
consistency and availability may be a better design choice in a single datacenter
where network partitions are rare.

Replica consistency is an important issue of distributed systems. For some
application scenarios such as bank, military, and scientific experiment, any
inconsistency in replicas is intolerable. There are some popular replica consistency
protocols such as two phase commit protocol[5], and Paxos protocol[6] etc.
Unfortunately, in hostile system environments, two-phase commit may not guarantee
the strong consistency among multiple replicas and the high system availability. With

C.-H. Hsu et al. (Eds.): NPC 2014, LNCS 8707, pp. 471–484, 2014.

three or more replicas, the Paxos family of protocols is considered to be the only solution to guarantee the strong replica consistency. However it is not widely used in distributed systems due to its complexity and low efficiency.

Besides consistency, system availability is also one of the key principles in designing a distributed system. Many internet enterprises, like Google and eBay, often have to provide reliable service of 24×7 hours for their users. However, the node failure happens frequently in distributed systems when running on general servers. Therefore how to continuously provide service after a node is down is the problem that we should solve.

This paper presents a new distributed key-value storage system, called PaxStore, which can guarantee the strong replica consistency by using a centralized Paxos-based protocol. The protocol can significantly reduce the overhead compared with basic Paxos. In PaxStore, if the leader failed, PaxStore can automatically select a new leader to provide service uninterruptedly as long as the majority of its replicas are alive. Furthermore, the system node can automatically recover in case of node failure. Experiments show PaxStore can guarantee strong consistency among replicas and only increases 20% overhead compared with local systems. Furthermore, PaxStore is five times or more as fast as the older which also uses a basic Paxos protocol on write.

The rest of the paper is organized as follows. Section 2 provides a detailed survey of existing work and the related backgrounds. Section 3 presents the design of PaxStore. Section 4 is the implementation of PaxStore. Section 5 gives an experimental evaluation of PaxStore. Section 6 summarizes our work and draws conclusions.

2   Related Work

Brew's CAP theorem[3] is of great significance in the distributed systems, which shows that it is impossible for any distributed system to simultaneously provide all of the three following guarantees: consistency, availability and partition tolerance. Actually, many distributed storage systems choose two of the above goals based on their own application characteristics.

Many relational databases use the two-phase commit protocol, such as MySQL, which has very good C (strong consistency), but it's A (availability) & P (partition tolerance) are poor. For example, these systems can prevent data from being lost when facing with disk failures. But they may not provide service if a node fails or in the abnormal network conditions.

Dynamo[8], and Cassandra[9] provide high availability and partition tolerance by using eventual consistency. In CAP terminology, they are typical AP systems. Dynamo uses the Quorum mechanism to manage replicas, which is a decentralized system. When facing replicas inconsistency, applications must resolve the conflicts by using data update timestamp.

The Paxos algorithm was proposed by Leslie Lamport in 1990[7], which is a consistency algorithm based on message passing. At first, it didn't attract people's attention because it is difficult to understand. However, in recent years, the widespread use of Paxos algorithm proves its important role in distributed systems. The basic idea of the Paxos algorithm is that, the successful execution of each request needs the acceptance and execution of the vast majority of nodes in the systems; every Paxos instance has a sequence, which executes from small to large and all nodes have the same instance execution order; if a new node joins systems, it can recover data through catch-up mechanism to achieve the same status as the existing nodes. But the basic Paxos protocol is a decentralized protocol which requires multiple network communications, its efficiency is low. PaxStore uses a centralized Paxos-based protocol with small network overhead.

Zookeeper[10] uses basic Paxos to select the master node which controls data update. If the master goes down, it will select a new master. Zookeeper can guarantee strong consistency. But its design goal is to provide distributed lock service and high availability service for other distributed systems. It is not a dedicated distributed storage system, so its performance is poor. Google's Chubby[11] is also based on Paxos protocol, which is similar to zookeeper.

Megastore[12] is a distributed storage system based on Paxos protocol developed by Google, which relies on Bigtable. It has the advantages of both the scalability of a NoSQL datastore and the convenience of the traditional RDBMS, and provides both strong consistency guarantees and high availability. However, it uses the Paxos protocol without being fully optimized, its write performance is not good.

Rao et al designed a scalable, consistent, and highly available data store by using Paxos protocol, which is called Spinnaker[13]. But it doesn't analyze the situation that two leaders may appear in one system. Its read and write performance are not good.

Based on the above, we designed PaxStore by using zookeeper cluster and high performance Leveldb engine. In addition, we used a number of optimization techniques, such as log optimization, circular lock-free queue etc. It can not only guarantee strong consistency, but also improve the system performance, and keep the system scalability.

3   Design of PaxStore

3.1   Architecture

All data are divided into different ranges based on the key value of every record. The basic components of PaxStore include client, zookeeper cluster and storage server which include leader and follower. The architecture of PaxStore is depicted in Figure 3.1. The replica's number can be configured, here we set it to be 3. Every range has a leader and two followers. Client only sends write requests to the leader which synchronizes data to followers based on our Paxos-based protocol, but both of the leader and the followers can provide read service. In order to simplify the leader election process, we use Zookeeper for auxiliary election. At the same time, Zookeeper can also monitor the system state. PaxStore can elect a new leader automatically and records the times of leader election as epoch. Each write request is assigned a number (sequence) to indicate its execution order. When a new node joins in system, it will run a zookeeper client and connect with zookeeper server, and then upload its metadata such as epoch, IP, and LSN (the largest write request sequence in log), into zookeeper server. At last, PaxStore uses an improved and optimized Leveldb as local storage engine.

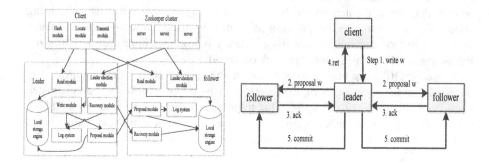

Fig. 3.1. PaxStore Architecture   **Fig. 3.2.** Protocol Flow Chart

3.2   Protocol Analysis

The basic process of the distributed replica protocol used by PaxStore is shown in Figure 3.2.

（1）Client sends write request (w) to the leader.

（2）After receiving W, leader firstly serializes W, appends W with epoch and sequence, then it writes the serialized W into log synchronously. In parallel with the log force, leader sends the serialized W to all of the followers.

（3）When the followers receive the proposal W message, they write it into log synchronously and send ACK message to leader.

（4）After writing W into the log and receiving more than 1 ACK message from followers, leader writes W into local storage engine, and send RET message to client.

（5）Furthermore, Leader periodically sends commit message to the followers to ask them to apply all pending write requests up to a certain sequence to their local storage engine.

Until now, the leader and followers have the same and the latest value of W.

From the above descriptions, it is obvious that under normal circumstances, the protocol overhead is extremely small, and only a RTT (Round-Trip Time) is needed to commit a write.

The client read protocol is also a Quorum-based protocol. As the follower may have an inconsistent state with leader for only a short time (leader periodically send COMMIT message to follower), we can choose either strong consistent read (read records from leader) or weak consistent read (read records from leader or followers). When choosing strong consistent read, the system needs first read record from leader and then read epoch message from a follower of this leader, if the follower has the same epoch message with leader, it shows that we read data successfully, otherwise the system errors occur.

4   Implementation

4.1   Component of Storage Node

The basic components of node are shown in Figure 4.1. It includes a log system, a storage engine and a zookeeper cluster. The replica consistency among multiple nodes is guaranteed by improved Paxos-base protocol which is described in Section 3.2. We choose Leveldb as our key-value storage engine, and replace its log module with our high available log system. The details of the log system and storage engine will be described in section 4.2.

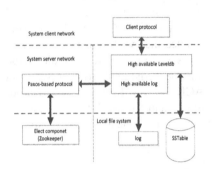

Fig. 4.1. Component of Storage Node Figure

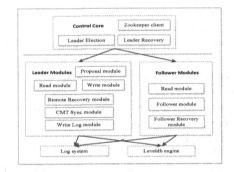

Fig. 4.2. The Software Modules of Node

4.1.1   Software Modules of Node

The software modules of node are depicted in Figure 4.2. Each node has five functional modules, that is, control core, leader modules, follower modules, log system and Leveldb storage engine. The control core includes zookeeper client module, Leader Election module and Leader Recovery module. Leader modules include Write module, Read module, Proposal module, Remote Recovery module (help followers to recover data), CMT Sync module and Write Log module. Follower modules include Read module, Follower module (used to response the proposal request and CMT request sent by leader) and Follower Recovery module. If a node is leader, the running modules include control core, leader modules, log system and storage engine. If it is a follower, the running modules include control core, follower modules, log system and storage engine.

If the leader goes down, system will elect a new leader from the remaining alive nodes by their leader election modules. The new elected leader should first stop its old follower modules, and deal with all of the data that have been written into log but have been written into leveldb engine. It will write these data into storage engine and send these data to at least one follower to write into follower's local storage engine. Finally, the new elected leader starts all of the leader modules to become a real leader. Now, system can continue to run normally.

4.1.2   Leader Logic

The basic implementation framework of leader, which handles the client requests by differentiating read and write.

(1) Leader execution logic

The design of read logic is simple. Read Worker thread manages the establishment and disconnection of read connection from the client. PaxStore can directly read the required data from local Leveldb engine. But in order to improve the read performance, we design a thread pool to use multi-core platform.

Write logic is the core part of the leader. The writing process is described in the following. First, Write Worker thread receives write request from client, then, it adds the request into Value Queue and sends a notify message to Proposal thread. Second, Proposal thread reads request from Value Queue, serializes it (i.e., adds epoch and sequence message) and then sends it to Proposal Round-robin Queue. The Proposal Queue is a circular lock-free queue which can reduce the synchronization overhead among threads. Third, PaxStore sends proposal message to follower, in parallel Write Log thread reads proposal message from Proposal Queue and then writes it into local log system. Once receiving at least half of the ACK message from followers (in our system, it needs to receive an ACK message), the system can write this request into local Leveldb engine and return Ret message to client. Periodically, Leader will also send CMT message to followers.

(2) Leader Election

The design principle of Leader election algorithm is to use a simple way to ensure that only one Leader can run normally at any time. The system cannot lose the committed write requests in leader election. If there is a majority of nodes alive, there must be the node containing all of the committed write requests. We only need to elect the node that has the largest LSN if it has the largest Epoch as leader.

The implementation of leader election needs the help of Zookeeper cluster. Every node will create an ephemeral file on the zookeeper server to save its metadata such as LSN, Epoch, and IP, when it joins system. If a node disconnects with zookeeper because of node failure, network partition or other reasons, its corresponding ephemeral file will disappear automatically. Once more than half of the nodes join system, they will compare their Epoch message and LSN message to elect a Leader. Leader will create an ephemeral Leader file on the zookeeper cluster to save its metadata. If Leader disconnect with zookeeper, this ephemeral Leader file will disappear automatically and system will elect a new leader.

In distributed systems, the case that there are two leaders may occur inevitably, as depicted in Figure 4.3, due to network reasons, A loses connect with zookeeper server, then system will do leader election again. B and C disconnect with A and C is elected as new Leader. But A may continue to run, so system has two leaders A and C at this time. PaxStore can ensure that only C can run normally. As no follower connects with A, even if it receives write requests, it can't execute these write requests successfully because it can't receive ACK. System will force to stop A until the client and zookeeper server find that A is in the isolate state. This can deal with the situation of the two leaders.

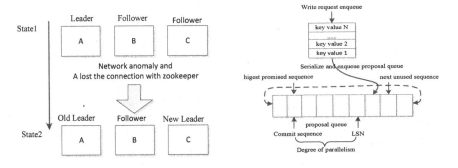

Fig. 4.3. Two Leaders appear   **Fig. 4.4.** The Proposed Round-robin Queue

(3)   Leader Design Optimization

Parallel processing optimization: firstly, leader executes the proposal sending and log writing in parallel, and then PaxStore executes multiple write requests in parallel. PaxStore can handle multiple proposal messages simultaneously. As shown in Figure 4.4, the commit sequence represents the largest committed request sequence, the highest promised sequence represents the largest request sequence that has receive ACK message, the LSN represents the largest request sequence that has been written into log system, the next unused sequence represents the smallest sequence number that has not been used. The requests between commit sequence and highest promised sequence are not written into Leveldb storage engine; the requests between highest promised sequence and next unused sequence are not proposed. The next unused sequence minus commit sequence is the current degree of parallelism. In order to control the system delays, we set an appropriate degree of proposal parallelism. To avoid proposal lost, as well as out-of-order problems, PaxStore uses TCP protocol and sets the TCP's sending buffer and receiving buffer to an appropriate value.

4.1.3   Follower Logic Design

The basic implementation framework in the follower is depicted in Figure 4.5. The basic implementation framework of follower is similar to Leader, but follower works relatively simpler than Leader. The design of read logic of follower is the same as leader. Follower does not have to deal with the client writes directly. It receives the proposal message sent by Leader, and then detects whether the sequence of proposal message is continuous or not; if it is, it receives this proposal and puts this proposal message into Fproposal Queue, follower writes this proposal into local log system and sends ACK to Leader. Because the communication between Leader and Follower uses TCP protocol, it ensures that the sequence of proposal message sent by Leader is continuous, if the proposal message sequence received by follower isn't continuous, Paxos-based protocol will not work normally; then follower will exit from system.

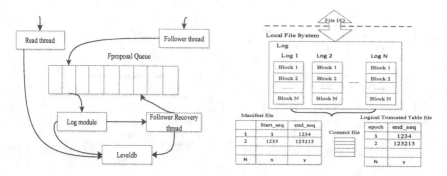

Fig. 4.5. Follower Execution Logic   **Fig. 4.6.** Log System Figure

If a new follower joins in system, it starts the follower recovery thread to finish recovery, which includes local recovery and remote recovery. The follower recovery mechanism will be depicted in section 4.4.

4.2   Implementation of Log and Storage Engine

The Log System is an important component of PaxStore. It stores both the data and metadata required by the normally running of PaxStore. Furthermore, log can also ensure that system can automatically complete the recovery.

The log structure is shown in Figure 4.6. The Log System is designed based on local file system. The threshold of each log file size can be configured. When reading data, we use block as a unit and the block size can be configured. The manifest file records the metadata of each log file and helps us to locate log file when reading data.

Logical Truncated Table file records the largest corresponding commit sequence of each Epoch, which can help determine which record can be read, and which record needs to be discarded when in recovery.

The above files constitute the basic log system. In order to meet the requirements of the strong system consistency, every write operation is synchronous, so the disk overhead is relatively large. In order to improve system performance, we use the overwrite method to optimize the log system, that is, we pre-allocate a fixed size of log file and clear all of the data content of the file, and then write all of the records into the file by using fdatasync() function instead of fsync. The fdatasync function has a much high performance than fsync because it needn't to update metadata of file. This method can improve log system performance.

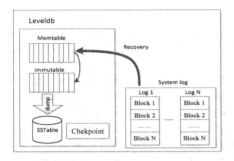

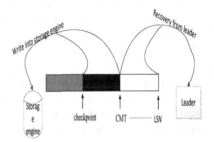

Fig. 4.7. Paxtore Storage Engine   **Fig. 4.8.** Log Layout

Leveldb log module is used to do local recovery for itself. PaxStore has its local log system, and Leveldb can get all of its needed data from PaxStore log system. So we modify Leveldb and remove its log module. As shown in Figure 4.7, Leveldb can get all of the data from PaxStore log system when in local recovery.

4.3   Recovery

4.3.1   Follower Recovery

Follower recovery is different from ordinary database recovery; it contains local recovery and remote recovery.

As shown in Figure 4.8, the records before checkpoint have been written to storage engine, so we need to recover these records. The records between checkpoint and CMT have been committed, so we can read them from local log system directly. The records between CMT and LSN are not yet confirmed, we need to do remote recovery, and they may have been committed and may be stale. In order to ensure complete recovery, follower should send remote recovery request to leader, receive recovery data and write these data into Leveldb (storage engine).

4.3.2   Leader Recovery

When the leader goes down, system will elect a new leader; then the new leader should do leader recovery work. New leader should re-propose the requests between CMT and LSN because these data may return to client already or haven't been committed. After at least one follower and new leader both write these data into storage engine, system can run normally.

5   Performance Evaluation

5.1   Write Latency

Write delay is an important parameter of evaluating our system and protocol. We optimize our log system, that is, we pre-allocate a fixed size of log file in order to use the overwrite method rather than append write method to write records. We inject 10,000 records with the same size into system. The size of write requests ranges from 512 Bytes to 8192 Bytes every time and all of the write log operations are synchronous. We compare the write latency of PaxStore between overwrite and append write method. As shown in Figure 5.1, the write latency increases with the increase of write requests size. In addition, the performance of overwrite method is much higher than append write method. This is because when it uses overwrite method, the log data block has been previously allocated, every write operation doesn't require the high overhead of disk seek operation, and every synchronous log write operation doesn't need to write metadata of log file by using fdatasync. The results show that our optimization of log can significantly improve PaxStore performance.

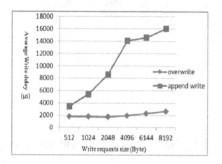

Fig. 5.1. Write Latency   **Fig. 5.2.** Protocol Overhead

5.2   Protocol Overhead

As shown in Figure 5.2, we firstly set the replica's number is1, that is, leader doesn't send any data to other nodes to measure the latency of local operations. The log uses asynchronous write mode. Then we set replica's number is 3 to measure the write latency of PaxStore, and the log uses the same write mode too. The figure shows that the overhead of our Paxos-based protocol is small which increases by about 20% overhead over the local operation. There are many reasons, for example, the execution of every write request only needs one RTT; write disk operation and network communication work in parallel when dealing with a write request; we use a circular lock-free queue which can reduce overhead caused by locking.

5.3   Comparison with Zookeeper

As shown in Figure 5.3, we compare the write performance of PaxStore with the older system which also uses a kind of Paxos-based protocol. Both of their logs use a synchronous write mode. When the size of write request is more than 2000 Bytes, PaxStore is five times or more as fast as the older. This is because the older is not a specialized storage system. Furthermore, we use a variety of methods to optimize PaxStore, such as overwrite log system, round-robin queue, disk and network works in parallel etc. The results show that PaxStore has a very high write performance.

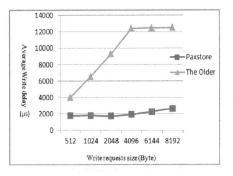 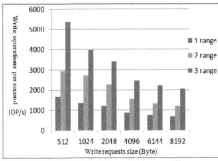

Fig. 5.3. Compare PaxStore with the older   **Fig. 5.4.** System Scalability

5.4   System Scalability

System can divide all of the data into some ranges based on the key, and each write request can only be written into one range. Every range has its own leader and followers. As shown in Figure 5.4, we test the system performance based on different data range number. In order to achieve optimal performance, every node runs only one PaxStore instance. Obviously, the system performance has a linear growth with the increase of data range number regardless of how much the size of write requests is. The results show that PaxStore has a linear scalability.

5.5   System Recovery

For distributed systems built on the commodity machine, node failure is frequent. In PaxStore, we set replica's number as 3, if one follower goes down, system can run normally, but if two nodes failure, system will stop service. System will elect a new leader from the remaining two nodes when the leader goes down. This process is very fast. The system can complete the leader election using less than 3s latency, which doesn't have a huge impact on the normal running of system. This is because once the leader goes down, zookeeper cluster will immediately perceive this situation and notify the other nodes, and system can elect a new leader by comparing the metadata of existing followers. Because zookeeper needs time to clean up obsolete information and receive new information, it may has 3s delay.

It is important to measure the recovery speed of our system when new follower joins in system and recovers to the current state of the system. As shown in Figure 5.5, we first write 10,000 records into system, and then new follower joins in system and recovers these 10,000 records. The size of write request is range from 512 to 8192 Bytes. The experiments show that the recovery of 10000*512 Bytes size records only needs 8s and 10000*8192 only needs 15s.

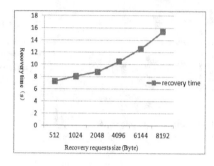
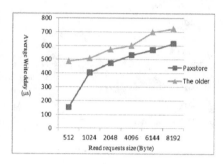

Fig. 5.5. Follower Recovery Time   **Fig. 5.6.** Read Latency

5.6   Read Latency

Because the read operation is not related to the complicated protocol, we only need to read data from local Leveldb engine, so the system read performance is basically the same as Leveldb. As shown in Figure 5.6, we firstly write 500,000 records into PaxStore, and then read the data based on random key. The records size ranges from 512 to 8192 Bytes. Results show that the read delay is only 150μs when records size is 512 Bytes, and the read delay increases as the records size increases. Besides, we test the read performance of the older. It is obvious that the read latency of PaxStore is much smaller than the older regardless of how much the size of request is.

5.7   Summary and Result

From the above testing, it is clear that PaxStore has a high performance. The log optimization technology improves the system performance significantly. Our protocol overhead is small which increases 20% overhead over local operation. The write performance is five times over Zookeeper. PaxStore also has a quick recovery speed.

6   Conclusion and Future Work

This paper designs and implements a consistency, high availability, distributed key value storage system, called PaxStore. In the PaxStore, we optimize its log system, circular lock-free queue and Paxos protocol. PaxStore has a high performance and lower protocol overhead. The results show that Paxos-based protocol is a good tool to implement this kind of system[15-16]. By using high available service module, including Chubby and Zookeeper, to do leader election, it can not only improve system performance and avoid a single point of failure, but also simplify the design of PaxStore. The practical experience of PaxStore has constructive value for other high-availability storage system designs.

In future work, we will use write batching method[17] to improve disk utilization and chained push method[18-19] to reduce the network overhead of leader.

Acknowledgments. This work is supported by 973 project 2011CB302301, the National Basic Research 973 Program of China under Grant by National University's Special Research Fee (C2009m052, 2011QN031, 2012QN099), Changjiang innovative group of Education of China No. IRT0725, is supported by Electronic Development Found of Information Industry Ministry.

References

[1] Bolosky, W.J., Bradshaw, D., Haagens, R.B.: Paxos replicated state machines as the basis of a high-performance data store. In: Proceedings of the 8th USENIX Conference on Networked Systems Design and Implementation, NSDI 2011, p. 11. USENIX Association, Berkeley (2011)

[2] Michael, M., Moreira, J.E., Shiloach, D.: Scale-up x Scale-out: A Case Study using Nutch/Lucene. In: IEEE International Parallel and Distributed Processing Symposium, IPDPS 2007, pp. 1–8 (March 2007)

[3] Brewer, E.A.: Towards Robust Distributed Systems. In: PODC, p. 7 (2000)

[4] DeWitt, D.J., Katz, R.H., Olken, F., Shapiro, L.D., Stonebraker, M.R., Wood, D.: Implementation Techniques for Main Memory Database Systems. In: SIGMOD, pp. 1–8 (1984)

[5] Raz, Y.: The Dynamic Two Phase Commitment (D2PC) protocol. In: Vardi, M.Y., Gottlob, G. (eds.) ICDT 1995. LNCS, vol. 893, pp. 162–176. Springer, Heidelberg (1995)

[6] Lamport, L.: Paxos Made Simple. ACM SIGACT News 32(4), 18–25 (2001)

[7] http://research.microsoft.com/users/lamport/pubs/pubs.html#lamport-Paxos

[8] DeCandia, G., Hastorun, D., Jampani, M., Kakulapati, G., Lakshman, A., Pilchin, A., Sivasubramanian, S., Vosshall, P., Vogels, W.: Dynamo: Amazon's Highly Available Key-Value Store. In: SOSP, pp. 205–220 (2007)

[9] Lakshman, A., Malik, P.: Cassandra: A decentralized structured storage system. ACM SIGOPS Operating Systems Review Archive 44(2), 35–40 (2010)

[10] Hunt, P., Konar, M., Junqueira, F.P., Reed, B.: Zookeeper: Wait-Free Coordination for Internet-scale Systems. In: USENIX (2010)

[11] Chandra, T.D., Griesemer, R., Redstone, J.: Paxos Made Live: An Engineering Perspective. In: PODC, pp. 398–407 (2007)

[12] Baker, J., et al.: Megastore: Providing Scalable, Highly Available Storage for Interactive Services. In: Conf. on Innovative Data Systems Research (2011)

[13] Rao, J., Shekita, E.J., Tata, S.: Using Paxos to Build a Scalable, Consistent, and Highly Available Datastore. In: VLDB (2011)

[14] Leveldb, A.: fast and lightweight key/value database library by Google, http://code.google.com/p/leveldb/

[15] Adya, A., Bolosky, W.J., Cermak, G., et al.: Farsite: federated, available, and reliable storage for an incompletely trusted environment. In: Proceedings of the 5th Symposium on Operating Systems Design and Implementation, OSDI 2002, pp. 1–14. ACM, New York (2002)

[16] Coulon, C., Pacitti, E., Valduriez, P.: Consistency management for partial replication in a high Performance database cluster. In: Proceedings of 11th International Conference on Parallel and Distributed Systems, ICPADS 2005, vol. 815. IEEE, USA (2005)

[17] Santos, N., Schiper, A.: Tuning Paxos for High-Throughput with Batching and Pipelining. In: Bononi, L., Datta, A.K., Devismes, S., Misra, A. (eds.) ICDCN 2012. LNCS, vol. 7129, pp. 153–167. Springer, Heidelberg (2012)

[18] Marandi, P., Primi, M., Schiper, N., et al.: Ring Paxos: A high-throughput atomic broadcast protocol. Dependable Systems and Networks 7129, 153–167 (2010)

[19] van Renesse, R., Schneider, F.B.: Chain replication for supporting high throughput and availability. In: Proceedings of the 6th Conference on Symposium on Opearting Systems Design and Implementation, OSDI 2004, vol. 8, USENIX Association, San Francisco (2004)

Semi-automatic Composition of Data Layout Transformations for Loop Vectorization[*]

Shixiong Xu[1,2] and David Gregg[1,2]

[1] Lero, The Irish Software Engineering Research Centre,
[2] Software Tools Group, Department of Computer Science,
University of Dublin, Trinity College,
Dublin, Ireland
{xush,dgregg}@scss.tcd.ie

Abstract. In this paper we put forward an annotation system for specifying a sequence of data layout transformations for loop vectorization. We propose four basic primitives for data layout transformations that programmers can compose to achieve complex data layout transformations. Our system automatically modifies all loops and other code operating on the transformed arrays. In addition, we propose data layout aware loop transformations to reduce the overhead of address computation and help vectorization. Taking the Scalar Penta-diagonal (SP) solver, from the NAS Parallel Benchmarks as a case study, we show that the programmer can achieve significant speedups using our annotations.

1 Introduction

Single instruction multiple data (SIMD) vector computational units are widely available in processors from large supercomputers to energy-efficient embedded systems. Programmers often depend on compilers to auto-vectorize key loops. However, some program features can hinder the compilers from fully unleashing the power of SIMD. One important feature is interleaved data access coming from the data organized in the manner of an array of structures (AoS). In order to efficiently deal with interleaved data access, vectorizing compilers generate a sequence of data shuffling instructions (e.g. *pshuffle*, *pblend* in Intel SSE) for data reorganization. As long as data is accessed in a non-linear pattern, there will always be a cost of shuffling or gathering data for vectorization.

We observe that for many scientific computing applications with data in AoS, different loops in the program often repeat the same patterns of data permutation. These patterns usually first do data permutations on a small portion of the whole data needed before the computation in each loop iteration, and apply data permutations on the results after the computation is done. One way of getting rid of these repeated data permutation operations is to transform the layout

---

[*] This work was supported, in part, by Science Foundation Ireland grant 10/CE/I185 to Lero - the Irish Software Engineering Research Centre (www.lero.ie).

C.-H. Hsu et al. (Eds.): NPC 2014, LNCS 8707, pp. 485–496, 2014.

of the data throughout the program. There are two main approaches to transforming array layouts in programs: automatic transformation by the compiler, or manual changes by the programmer.

Compilers face two major challenges when performing automatic data layout transformations for vectorization. First, the compiler needs a very sophisticated **whole-program** data dependency and pointer aliasing analysis to make sure that the transformation is safe. Secondly, it is difficult for the compiler to choose the best layout. It is perhaps easier for the programmer to determine whether modifying the data layout is safe. But it is tedious and error-prone for programmers to change their code by hand. They may have to change the type declarations and any code that operates on the array. This may involve modifications to many parts of the program, and may result in changes to array indexing, and even the introduction of new statements and loops.

To allow compositions of data layout transformations and evaluate the performance impact of data layout transformations on vectorization, in this paper we put forward a new program annotation (using C language pragma) to enable programmers to specify a sequence of data layout transformations. This data layout transformation pragma is implemented in the Cetus source-to-source compiler framework [1]. Our prototype implementation currently supports static arrays but can be easily extended to support dynamically allocated arrays using Sung et al.'s approach [2]. Our compiler changes data type declarations for all modified arrays, rewrites all functions that operate on modified arrays to change array indexing, and introduces additional loops and other code. Similar to other pragma annotation systems, such as OpenMP, we assume that where the programmer requests a transformation, that transformation is safe.

In this paper, we make the following contributions:

1. We put forward a new C language pragma to allow programmers to specify a sequence of data layout transformations. This language annotation serves as a script to control data layout transformations and thus can be integrated into a performance auto-tuning framework as an extra tuning dimension.
2. We implemented our proposed data layout transformation pragma in the Cetus source-to-source compiler. To reduce the overhead of address computation and help vectorization, we introduce data layout aware loop transformations along with the data layout transformations.
3. Manual tuning of data layout transformations on the SP in the NAS Parallel Benchmarks shows that with proper data layout transformations, significant speedups are possible from better vectorization.

2   Language Support for Data Layout Transformations

2.1   Motivating Examples

In this section, we take the kernel of tezar() in the SP (**S**calar **P**enta-diagonal), one of the benchmarks in the NAS Parallel Benchmarks (NPB) to demonstrate

```
1   double us      [KMAX][JMAXP][IMAXP];        20   r4 = rhs[k][j][i][3];
2   double vs      [KMAX][JMAXP][IMAXP];        21   r5 = rhs[k][j][i][4];
3   double ws      [KMAX][JMAXP][IMAXP];        22   uzik1 = u[k][j][i][0];
4   double speed   [KMAX][JMAXP][IMAXP];        23   btuz = bt * uzik1;
5   double qs      [KMAX][JMAXP][IMAXP];        24   t1 = btuz/ac * (r4 + r5);
6   double rhs     [KMAX][JMAXP][IMAXP][5];     25   t2 = r3 + t1;
7   double u       [KMAX][JMAXP][IMAXP][5];     26   t3 = btuz * (r4 - r5);
8                                               27   rhs[k][j][i][0] = t2;
9   for (k = 1; k <= nz2; k++) {                28   rhs[k][j][i][1] = -uzik1*r2 +
10    for (j = 1; j <= ny2; j++) {                        xvel*t2;
11      for (i = 1; i <= nx2; i++) {            29   rhs[k][j][i][2] = uzik1*r1 +
12        xvel = us[k][j][i];                             yvel*t2;
13        yvel = vs[k][j][i];                   30   rhs[k][j][i][3] = zvel*t2 + t3;
14        zvel = ws[k][j][i];                   31   rhs[k][j][i][4] =
15        ac   = speed[k][j][i];                          uzik1*(-xvel*r2 + yvel*r1)
16        ac2u = ac*ac;                                   + qs[k][j][i]*t2 +
17        r1 = rhs[k][j][i][0];                           c2iv*ac2u*t1 + zvel*t3;
18        r2 = rhs[k][j][i][1];                 32   } } }
19        r3 = rhs[k][j][i][2];
```

Fig. 1. The kernel of function tzetar() in the SP of NPB

the advantage of data layout transformations for efficient loop vectorization. This kernel conducts block-diagonal matrix-vector multiplication on the data.

There is a loop nest of depth three enclosing the main computations and all these loops are parallel, shown in Fig. 1. When vectorizing the innermost parallel loop i, compilers directly generate vector loads and stores for the data references to array us, vs, ws. On the contrary, the inter-leaved data access exposed by the references to array u and rhs may require compilers to apply suitable data reorganization. Compilers can treat these inter-leaved loads as gather operations. But the support for these gather operations in modern commodity processors is still not good enough [3]. Instead, the compiler may utilize available data permutation instructions to transform the inter-leaved data access into consecutive data access. On the other hand, the cost of data permutation instructions introduced by the data reorganization may not be well offset by the performance benefits gained by vectorization on the computations.

Table 1. Data layout schemes and vectorization strategies

Description	Declaration	Vectorization Strategy
Pure AoS	double u [KMAX][JMAXP][IMAXP][5];	Data permutation with stride 5
Split AoS (1:4)	double u1 [KMAX][JMAXP][IMAXP]; double u2 [KMAX][JMAXP][IMAXP][4];	Consecutive data accesses Data permutation with stride 4
Split AoS (4:1)	double u1 [KMAX][JMAXP][IMAXP][4]; double u2 [KMAX][JMAXP][IMAXP];	Data permutation with stride 4 Consecutive data accesses
Split AoS (1:2:2)	double u1 [KMAX][JMAXP][IMAXP]; double u2 [KMAX][JMAXP][IMAXP][2]; double u3 [KMAX][JMAXP][IMAXP][2];	Consecutive data accesses Data permutation with stride 2 Data permutation with stride 2
Split AoS (2:2:1)	double u1 [KMAX][JMAXP][IMAXP][2]; double u2 [KMAX][JMAXP][IMAXP][2]; double u3 [KMAX][JMAXP][IMAXP];	Data permutation with stride 2 Consecutive data accesses Consecutive data accesses
Pure SoA	double u [5][KMAX][JMAXP][IMAXP];	Consecutive data accesses
Hybrid SoA	double u [KMAX][JMAXP][IMAXP/4][5][4];	Consecutive data accesses

Instead of compilers generating data permutation instructions to reorganize data, programmers can change the data layout into a form amenable to vectorization. Table 1 gives several possible data layout schemes of array u and their related vectorizing strategies compilers may take. The vectorizing strategies shown in Table 1 illustrate that some data layout transformations may simplify the vectorization of interleaved data access. For instance, compilers deal with the inter-leaved data access with stride 2 in Split AoS instead of stride 5 in Pure AoS, demonstrated in Section 4. Similarly, since the data references to the array rhs are inter-leaved with stride 5, the array rhs could also have same data layout transformation schemes as the array u.

2.2   Data Layout Transformation Pragmas

In this paper, we put forward a program annotation, *array transform*, a C language pragma to express data layout transformations on the static arrays. The syntax of this new pragma is shown in Fig. 2.

⟨*pragma*⟩	::=	#pragma array_transform ⟨*array_name*⟩ ⟨*descriptor*⟩ ⟨*actions*⟩
⟨*descriptor*⟩	::=	[⟨*identifier*⟩] ⟨*descriptor_list*⟩
⟨*descriptor_list*⟩	::=	[⟨*identifier*⟩] ⟨*descriptor_list*⟩ | ⟨*empty*⟩
⟨*actions*⟩	::=	-> ⟨*pre_actions*⟩ ⟨*post_actions*⟩
⟨*pre_actions*⟩	::=	⟨*strip_mine*⟩ | ⟨*interchange*⟩ | ⟨*pad*⟩ | ⟨*pre_actions*⟩ | ⟨*empty*⟩
⟨*post_actions*⟩	::=	⟨*peel*⟩ | ⟨*empty*⟩ | ⟨*post_actions*⟩
⟨*strip_mine*⟩	::=	STRIP_MINE (⟨*identifier*⟩ , ⟨*stride_size*⟩ , ⟨*identifier*⟩)
⟨*interchange*⟩	::=	INTERCHANGE (⟨*identifier*⟩, ⟨*identifier*⟩)
⟨*pad*⟩	::=	PAD (⟨*identifier*⟩, ⟨*pad_size*⟩)
⟨*peel*⟩	::=	PEEL (⟨*identifier*⟩, ⟨*peel_size*⟩)

Fig. 2. Syntax of the data layout transformation pragma

The *array transform* pragma consists of *array descriptor* and *transform actions*. The *array descriptor* gives a name to each array dimension, and these names are used in the *transform actions* to record the related data layout transformations. The *transform actions* present the basic data layout transformations. In this paper, we define four basic data layout transformations, *strip-mining*, *interchange, pad*, and *peel*. These terms for data layout transformations are borrowed from the classic loop transformations [4].

The data storage of an array A can be viewed as a rectangular polyhedron. In [5], formal indices $\boldsymbol{\mathcal{I}}$ is introduced to describe the array index space

$$\boldsymbol{\mathcal{I}} = [i_1, i_2, \ldots, i_n]^T \tag{1}$$

where n is the dimension of the array A. The range of the formal indices $\mathcal{I}$ describes the size of the array, or index space, as follows:

$$\lambda \leq \mathcal{I} < \mu \tag{2}$$

where the lower bound vector $\lambda = [\lambda_1, \ldots, \lambda_n]^T$ and the upper bound vector $\mu = [\mu_1, \ldots, \mu_n]^T$ are $n \times 1$ vectors. The array index in C language can only start from 0, therefore, the lower bound vector λ in this paper is $\mathbf{0}$. As each array dimension is given a name by the *array descriptor*, these names can be treated as the formal indices to the arrays.

In contrast to the loop transformations which transform the loop iteration space formed by the loop indices, data layout transformations change the array index space. Since the array index space is changed, the subscripts in references to the array also have to be transformed accordingly.

The subscripts in a reference to an array in loops represent a function that maps the values of the loop iteration space to the array index space and this function is often expressed in the form of a memory access matrix [6]. Consider a data reference to an M dimensional array in the loop nest of depth D, where D and M do not need to match. The memory access pattern of the array in the loop is represented as a memory access vector, m, which is a column vector of size M starting from the index of the first dimension. The memory access vector is then decomposed as an affine form:

$$m = \mathbf{M}i + o \tag{3}$$

where $\mathbf{M}$ is a memory access matrix whose size is $M \times D$, i is an iteration vector of size D traversing from the outermost to the innermost loop, and o is an offset vector that is a column vector of size M and determines the starting access point in an array.

The semantics of the four data layout transformations are defined as follows:

Strip-mining: STRIP_MINE (id_1, *stride_size*, id_2)
  This transformation splits the array dimension i indicated by the id_1 into tiles of size *stride_size* and creates a new formal indices vector $\mathcal{I}'$ and two new dimension range vectors λ' which is $\mathbf{0}$ and μ'. Intuitively, the strip-mining splits the array dimension into two adjacent dimensions with dimension name id_1 and id_2, respectively. The new dimension id_1 takes the position of i and the new dimension id_2 takes the position of $i+1$ in the $\mathcal{I}'$. μ' is created by dividing μ_i into μ_h and μ_l, where $\mu_h = \lceil \mu_i / stride\_size \rceil$ and $\mu_l = stride\_size$. For each reference with subscripts s to the target array in the corresponding scope, new subscripts s' for each reference are created by dividing s_i into s_h and s_l, where $s_h = \lfloor s_i / stride\_size \rfloor$ and $s_l = s_i \bmod stride\_size$. Note that, when the original dimension size is not a multiple of block size *stride_size*, padding is introduced automatically at dimension i.

Interchange: INTERCHANGE (id_1, id_2)
  This transformation interchanges the array dimensions i, j indicated by id_1

and id_2 and creates a new formal indices vector $\mathcal{I}'$ and two new dimension range vectors $\boldsymbol{\lambda}'$ which is $\mathbf{0}$ and $\boldsymbol{\mu}'$. The upper bound vector $\boldsymbol{\mu}'$ is created by interchanging μ_i and μ_j. For each reference with subscripts $\boldsymbol{s}$ to the target array in the corresponding scope, new subscripts $\boldsymbol{s}'$ for each reference are created by interchange $\boldsymbol{s}_i$ and $\boldsymbol{s}_j$.

Pad: PAD $(id,\ pad\_size)$

This transformation pads the array dimension i indicated by id by the size of $|pad\_size|$ either from the beginning if the integer pad_size is negative or from the end if the integer pad_size is positive. Two new dimension range vectors $\boldsymbol{\lambda}'$ and $\boldsymbol{\mu}'$ are created, where $\boldsymbol{\lambda}'$ is $\mathbf{0}$ and $\boldsymbol{\mu}'$ is formed by increasing μ_i by $|pad\_size|$. If the pad_size is negative, for each reference with subscripts $\boldsymbol{s}$ to the target array in the corresponding scope, new subscripts $\boldsymbol{s}'$ for each reference are created, where $\boldsymbol{s}'_i = \boldsymbol{s}_i + |pad\_size|$.

Peel: PEEL $(id,\ peel\_size)$

This transformation peels the dimension i of an array $\mathcal{A}$ indicated by id by reducing the dimension size by $|peel\_size|$ and creates two arrays $\mathcal{A}_1, \mathcal{A}_2$. Two pairs of range vectors $(\boldsymbol{\lambda}'_h, \boldsymbol{\mu}'_h), (\boldsymbol{\lambda}'_l, \boldsymbol{\mu}'_l)$ are created for resulting arrays $\mathcal{A}_1, \mathcal{A}_2$, respectively, where $\boldsymbol{\lambda}'_h, \boldsymbol{\lambda}'_l$ are $\mathbf{0}$, and $\boldsymbol{\mu}'_h, \boldsymbol{\mu}'_l$ are as follows:

$$\boldsymbol{\mu}'_h = \begin{cases} |peel\_size| & \text{if } peel\_size > 0 \\ \mu_i - |peel\_size| & \text{otherwise} \end{cases}$$

$$\boldsymbol{\mu}'_l = \begin{cases} |peel\_size| & \text{if } peel\_size < 0 \\ \mu_i - |peel\_size| & \text{otherwise} \end{cases}$$

For each reference with subscripts $\boldsymbol{s}$ to the target array $\mathcal{A}$ in the corresponding scope, new subscripts $\boldsymbol{s}'$ are created by first choosing the right array, $\mathcal{A}_1$ if $\boldsymbol{s}_i$ is less than μ_i of array $\mathcal{A}_1$ or $\mathcal{A}_2$ otherwise; then new subscripts are calculated as follows:

$$\boldsymbol{s}'_i = \begin{cases} \boldsymbol{s}_i & \text{if refers to } \mathcal{A}_1 \\ \boldsymbol{s}_i - \boldsymbol{\mu}'_{hi} & \text{otherwise} \end{cases}$$

Note that, according to the semantics of array peeling, the subscripts in the dimension i of all the references to the array $\mathcal{A}$ should be compile-time constants. As the array peeling transformations can be chained together, in this case, all these chained array peeling actions should apply on the same array dimension. The input to the next array peeling transformation is decided by the current peeling size. If the current peeling size is positive, which means the target array dimension is peeled off from the beginning, the remaining array $\mathcal{A}_2$ will be the input for the next array peeling action. Otherwise, the target array dimension is peeled off from the end and thus the remaining array $\mathcal{A}_1$ will be the input for the next array peeling action, demonstrated by the Split AoS in Table 2.

The four data layout transformations are classified into two classes, *pre-action* and *post-action*. The *post-action* means all actions of this class can only be added after all the actions in the class of *pre-action*. We define *array peeling* as a member of the class *post-action* because we observe that for vectorization, array peeling is mainly used to split one array dimension for the data alignment or making the size of the array dimension power-of-two.

2.3   Composition of Data Layout Transformations

Our proposed *array transform* supports four primitive data layout transformations on static arrays. More complex data layout transformations can be achieved by composing these primitive transformations.

Array permutation permutes several array dimensions according to a given permutation command. It is more general than array interchange, which only swaps two array dimensions indicated by the dimension names. It is intuitive that array permutation can be decomposed as a sequence of array interchange actions. For example, given an array: `float A[SIZE_I][SIZE_J][SIZE_K]`, where i, j, k are the dimension names for each array dimension from the first to the last dimension, the permutation command (k, i, j), which rearranges the array dimensions indicated by i, j, k into a new order k, i, j, can be decomposed into a sequence of array interchange transformations, $(k, j)- > (i, k)$. Therefore, programmers can put the array transform pragma as `#pragma array_transform` `A[i][j][k] -> INTERCHANGE(k, j) -> INTERCHANGE(i, k)`

Rectangular array tiling blocks array dimensions into tiles, and thus decomposes the whole array into blocks which may help improve data locality. Array tiling is a process of choosing suitable hyperplanes according to certain conditions (e.g. data reuse distance) and partitioning the array data space with these hyperplanes. Here, *rectangular array tiling* means the determined tiling hyperplane for each array dimension is perpendicular to the axis of the array dimension to be tiled. Similar to the loop tiling which is a combination of loop strip-mining and loop interchange, *rectangular array tiling* can be decomposed into a sequence of array strip-mining, and array interchange, which are the primitive transformations defined in the *array transform* pragma.

As listed in Table 1 in Section 2.1, there are seven possible data layout transformation schemes for the motivating example. With our proposed *array transform* pragma, programmers can easily specify these data layout schemes by giving varying sequences of valid transformation actions, as shown in Table 2.

3   Data Layout Aware Loop Transformations

Array strip-mining introduces modulus operations to get offsets in the resulting tiles, illustrated in line 8 of Fig. 3. This kind of operation is not friendly to vectorization, because it might hinder the native compiler from detecting possible consecutive data access. Both the Intel C compiler and GCC are not able to identify that the data references to the transformed array are consecutive. We introduce data layout aware loop transformations to address this problem.

The modulus operations in the data references to the transformed arrays are from the array strip-mining. Therefore, if the data references to the target

Table 2. Data layout transformations assuming the array u is originally in the Pure AoS

Description	Declaration	Data Layout Transformation
Pure AoS	double u [KMAX][JMAXP][IMAXP][5];	NA

Split AoS (1:4)	double u1 [KMAX][JMAXP][IMAXP];
	double u2 [KMAX][JMAXP][IMAXP][4];
		#pragma array_transform u[i][j][k][m]->
		PEEL(m, 1)

Split AoS (4:1)	double u1 [KMAX][JMAXP][IMAXP][4];
	double u2 [KMAX][JMAXP][IMAXP];
		#pragma array_transform u[i][j][k][m]->
		PEEL(m, -1)

Split AoS (1:2:2)	double u1 [KMAX][JMAXP][IMAXP];
	double u2 [KMAX][JMAXP][IMAXP][2];
	double u3 [KMAX][JMAXP][IMAXP][2];
		#pragma array_transform u[i][j][k][m]->
		PEEL(m, 1) -> PEEL(m, 2)

Split AoS (2:2:1)	double u1 [KMAX][JMAXP][IMAXP][2];
	double u2 [KMAX][JMAXP][IMAXP][2];
	double u3 [KMAX][JMAXP][IMAXP];
		#pragma array_transform u[i][j][k][m]->
		PEEL(m, 2) -> PEEL(m, 2)

Pure SoA	double u [5][KMAX][JMAXP][IMAXP];	#pragma array_transform u[i][j][k][m]-> INTERCHANGE(m, k) -> INTERCHANGE(m, j) -> INTERCHANGE(m, i)
Hybrid AoS	double u [KMAX][JMAXP][IMAXP/4][5][4];	#pragma u[i][j][k][m]-> STRIP_MINE(k, 4, kk) -> INTERCHANGE(m, kk)

array to be transformed are enclosed in loops, one easy way to get rid of the modulus operations is to strip-mine the corresponding loops. In this paper we only consider the case where all the references to the arrays to be transformed have uniform effects to the surrounding loops. By which it means, if a loop is strip-mined with stride δ according to one data reference, there should be no other data references which require the same loop to be strip-mined with stride other than δ.

Data layout aware loop strip-mining according to the array strip-mining may include pre-loop peeling and post-loop peeling depending on whether the loop iteration space and the data index space are aligned, as shown in line 12-14, 20-22 of Fig. 3. If a loop starts from 0 and ends at SIZE-1 and the corresponding array dimension has a range from 0 to SIZE-1, in this case, the loop iteration space and the data index space are aligned, otherwise they are unaligned. Regarding the legality of these data layout aware loop peeling and loop strip-mining, they are always legal because these loop transformations inherently will not change the data dependencies across loop iterations.

In addition to the elimination of the modulus operations, the data layout ware loop strip-mining helps solve the alignment issue in vectorization. If the loop iteration space and the data index space are not aligned, pre-loop peeling and post-loop peeling are applied according to the boundaries of tiles from the array strip-mining. If the array starting address is aligned to 32 bytes and the tile size is 32 bytes, for instance, all the boundaries of tiles will be aligned to 32 bytes as well. As a result, all the loads from these boundaries are aligned to 32 bytes.

```
1   #pragma ary[i] -> STRIP_MINING(i, 4)
2     float ary[32];
3     /* before transformation: */
4     for (i = 1; i < 31; i++)
5       ... = ary[i];
6     /* after transformation: */
7     for (i = 1; i < 31; i++)
8       ... = ary[i/4][i%4];
9
10    /* data layout aware
             transformation:*/
11    /* from pre-loop peeling */
12    for (i = 0; i < 1; i++)
13      for (ii = 1; ii < 4; ii++)
14        ... = ary[i][ii];
15    /* from loop strip-mining */
16    for (i = 1; i < 7; i++)
17      for (ii = 0; ii < 4; ii++)
18        ... = ary[i][ii];
19    /* from post-loop peeling*/
20    for (i = 7; i < 8; i++)
21      for (ii = 0; ii < 3; ii++)
22        ... = ary[i][ii];
```

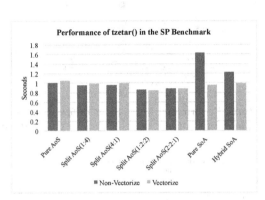

Fig. 3. Data layout aware loop trans-   **Fig. 4.** Performance of `tzetar()` with different
formation.   data layout transformations

4   Experimental Evaluation

4.1   Implementation

Our proposed array transform pragma is implemented in the Cetus source-to-source C compiler. All the *transform actions* are processed and collected in the pragma parsing phase. The actual data layout transformations and the data layout aware loop optimizations are done as transform passes in the Cetus compiler. The high-level internal presentation in the Cetus compiler keeps the array access close to the source code and thus simplifies the array transformation and the substitution of subscripts in array references.

4.2   A Case Study: Data Layout Tuning for Loop Vectorization

In this section, we use the SP in the NAS Parallel Benchmarks [7] as a case study to show the performance impact of data layout transformations upon loop vectorization. **SP** is one of the simulated CFD applications that solve the discretized compressible Navier-Stokes equations. We choose the data set of Class A in NPB, which has the size of $64 \times 64 \times 64$ with 400 iterations. All the experiments are conducted on an Intel Haswell platform (Intel Core i7-4770) running the Ubuntu Linux 13.04. We choose the Intel C compiler 13.1.3 to compile both the original and transformed code with the compiler option `-march=core-avx2 -O3 -fno-alias` for vectorization.

Performance of the Motivating Example. Fig. 4 gives the performance of the motivating example in different data layouts shown in Table 2. The results show that the best vectorization performance is given by the data layout

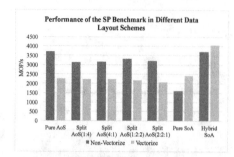

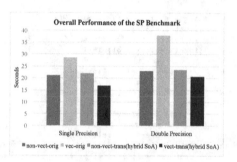

Fig. 5. Performance of the SP in different data layouts

Fig. 6. Performance of the SP of the NAS Parallel Benchmarks

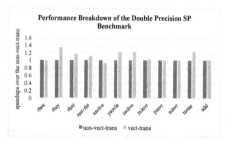

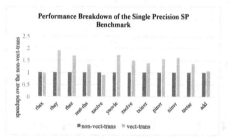

Fig. 7. Performance breakdown of the double precision SP of the NAS Parallel Benchmarks

Fig. 8. Performance breakdown of the single precision SP of the NAS Parallel Benchmarks

transformation `Split 1:2:2`. Splitting the last dimension of the array `u` (line 22 in Fig. 1) into three parts with sizes of 1, 2 and 2 helps the native compiler vectorize the load of array `u` with a contiguous vector load. In the mean time, data permutation instructions (e.g. `vperm2f128, vunpacklpd`) are used for the data reorganization of the array `rhs` (line 17 - 21 in Fig. 1) instead of gather instructions.

Overall Performance. We manually tune the data layout transformations for the SP and constrain the search space of data layout transformations to the ones mentioned in Table 2. Fig. 5 presents the overall performance of the SP in different data layouts. Among the seven data layouts, the `Hybrid SoA` gives the best overall performance. We also evaluated the performance of the single precision SP with the data layout `Hybrid SoA`, where the strip-mining size is 8. Compared to the double precision SP, the performance boost from vectorization for the single precision SP is more significant, as depicted in Fig. 6.

Fig. 7 and Fig. 8 give the performance breakdown of the single precision and double precision SP, respectively. With naive manual tuning of data layouts, for the SP, vectorization on the transformed data can outperform the vectorization on the untransformed data by a factor of 1.8. The experimental results demonstrate that it is necessary to introduce data layout tuning into existing performance auto-tuning systems, in particular, for the better performance of vectorization.

5   Related Work

Data layout transformations have primarily been applied to improving cache locality and localizing memory accesses in nonuniform memory architectures and clusters [8]. Maleki et al. [9] evaluated the vectorizing compilers and found that manually changing the data layout is a valuable way to help compilers to efficiently vectorize loops with non-unit stride accesses. However, compilers rarely automatically perform the memory layout transformations.

Our work is mainly inspired by the the work on semi-automatic composition of loop transformations for deep parallelism and memory hierarchies [10]. The main approach of previous work is introducing a script language to control the loop transformations upon the target loops. As far as we know, there are no such script languages available to control the data layout transformations. Similar language support for data layout transformations is designed mainly for optimizing data locality, such as the align and distribute directives in HPF [11].

Henretty et al. [12] propose a novel data layout transformation, dimension-lifted transposition, for stencil computations. This domain-specific technique solves the memory stream alignment issue. On the contrary, our work is a general solution to manual data layout transformations. Our work is greatly close to the work by Sung [2], which presents a framework that enables automatic data layout transformations for the structured grid codes in CUDA. Our work not only supports more data layout transformations but also presents data layout aware loop transformations for loop vectorization.

Jang et al.[6] optimize memory access into DRAM bursts (i.e. coalescing) by gaining unit-stride accesses with data layout transformations in the case of GPGPUs. Mey et al. [13] put forward a meta-data framework that allows both programmers and tuning experts to specify architecture specific and domain specific information for parallel-for loops of programs. The data layout transformations considered in this work are only AoS-to-SoA and SoA-to-AoS. Sinkarovs et al. [14] also present a compiler driven approach towards automatically transforming data layouts into a form that is suitable for vectorization. Their work is studied in the case of a first-order functional array programming language while our work focuses on the imperative C language.

6   Conclusion

In this paper, we put forward a new program annotation (using C language pragma) to enable programmers to specify data layout transformations and implemented it in the Cetus source-to-source compiler. In terms of loop vectorization, we introduce data layout ware loop transformations to help the native compilers to do better vectorization as well. The four primitive data layout transformations presented are suitable to be composed into more complex data layout transformations. The experimental results indicate that it is necessary to introduce semi- or fully automatic tuning of data layout transformations in order to help compilers to achieve better performance on vectorization.

References

1. Bae, H., Mustafa, D., et al.: The Cetus Source-to-Source Compiler Infrastructure: Overview and Evaluation. Int. J. Parallel Program. 41, 753–767 (2013)
2. Sung, I.-J., Stratton, J.A., Hwu, W.-M.W.: Data Layout Transformation Exploiting Memory-level Parallelism in Structured Grid Many-core Applications. In: Proceedings of the 19th International Conference on Parallel Architectures and Compilation Techniques, PACT 2010 (2010)
3. Ramachandran, A., Vienne, J., et al.: Performance Evaluation of NAS Parallel Benchmarks on Intel Xeon Phi. In: 2013 42nd International Conference onParallel Processing (ICPP), pp. 736–743 (2013)
4. Bacon, D.F., Graham, S.L., Sharp, O.J.: Compiler Transformations for High-performance Computing. ACM Comput. Surv. 26, 345–420 (1994)
5. O'Boyle, M.F.P., Knijnenburg, P.M.W.: Non-singular Data Transformations: Definition, Validity and Applications. In: Proceedings of the 11th International Conference on Supercomputing, ICS 1997 (1997)
6. Jang, B., Mistry, P., et al.: Data Transformations Enabling Loop Vectorization on Multithreaded Data Parallel Architectures. In: Proceedings of the 15th ACM SIGPLAN Symposium on Principles and Practice of Parallel Programming, PPoPP 2010 (2010)
7. Bailey, D.H., Barszcz, E., et al.: The NAS Parallel Benchmarks. Technical report, The International Journal of Supercomputer Applications (1991)
8. Kennedy, K., Kremer, U.: Automatic Data Layout for Distributed-memory Machines. ACM Trans. Program. Lang. Syst. 20, 869–916 (1998)
9. Maleki, S., Gao, Y., et al.: An Evaluation of Vectorizing Compilers. In: Proceedings of the 2011 International Conference on Parallel Architectures and Compilation Techniques, PACT 2011 (2011)
10. Girbal, S., Vasilache, N., et al.: Semi-automatic Composition of Loop Transformations for Deep Parallelism and Memory Hierarchies. Int. J. Parallel Program. 34, 261–317 (2006)
11. Rice University, CORPORATE:High Performance Fortran Language Specification. SIGPLAN Fortran Forum 12 (1993)
12. Henretty, T., Stock, K., Pouchet, L.-N., Franchetti, F., Ramanujam, J., Sadayappan, P.: Data Layout Transformation for Stencil Computations on Short-Vector SIMD Architectures. In: Knoop, J. (ed.) CC 2011. LNCS, vol. 6601, pp. 225–245. Springer, Heidelberg (2011)
13. Majeti, D., Barik, R., Zhao, J., Grossman, M., Sarkar, V.: Compiler-Driven Data Layout Transformation for Heterogeneous Platforms. In: an Mey, D., et al. (eds.) Euro-Par 2013. LNCS, vol. 8374, pp. 188–197. Springer, Heidelberg (2014)
14. Sinkarovs, A., Scholz, S.B.: Semantics-Preserving Data Layout Transformations for Improved Vectorisation. In: Proceedings of the 2nd ACM SIGPLAN Workshop on Functional High-performance Computing, FHPC 2013 (2013)

Dynamic Stripe Management Mechanism in Distributed File Systems

Jianwei Liao[1,2], Guoqiang Xiao[1], Xiaoyan Liu[1], and Lingyu Zhu[1]

[1] College of Computer and Information Science, Southwest University of China,
Beibei, Chongqing, P.R. China, 400715
[2] State Key Laboratory for Novel Software Technology, Nanjing University,
Nanjing, Jiangsu, P.R. China, 210023

Abstract. This paper presents a novel mechanism to dynamically re-size and re-distribute stripes on the storage servers in distributed file systems. To put this mechanism to work, the information about logical I/O access on the client side is piggybacked to physical I/O access on the storage server side, for building the relationship between the logical I/O access and physical I/O access. Moreover, this newly presented mechanism supports varying size of stripes on the storage servers to obtain finer concurrency granularity on accessing to data stripes. As a result, the mapping relationship can be utilized to direct stripe re-sizing and re-distributing on the storage servers dynamically for better system performance. Experimental results show that this stripe management mechanism can reduce I/O response time and boost I/O data through-put significantly for applications with complicated access patterns.

Keywords: Distributed/parallel file systems, Re-sizing and re-distributing stripes, Varying stripe size, I/O optimization.

1 Introduction

The progresses in computation, storage and communication technologies firmly speedup the development of complicated data processing applications that need to deal with big data in distributed computing environments. According to the EMC-IDC Digital Universe 2020 study, the amount of data created, replicated, and consumed in China may grow 24-fold over 2012 and 2020 [1]. Thus, one particularly difficult challenge in this context is to find the right approach to store and manage such huge amounts of data in a distributed or parallel computing environment. The traditional centralized client/server model file systems have been proven to be a barrier to scalable performance in distributed computing systems [4]. Therefore, the file system deployed in a distributed computing environment is called a distributed file system, which is always employed to be a backend storage system to offer I/O services for various sorts of data-intensive applications. Actually, the distributed file system leverages multiple distributed I/O devices by striping file data across the I/O nodes, and uses high aggregate bandwidth to meet the growing I/O requirements of distributed scientific applications. In other words, a distributed file system is responsible for distributing

C.-H. Hsu et al. (Eds.): NPC 2014, LNCS 8707, pp. 497–509, 2014.

files on top of the involved storage devices, as well as managing the created files and their attributes [5] and [6].

In general, the method describing the mapping from logical files to a physical layout of bytes on storage servers is called file data distribution function or stripe distribution function. The generally adopted stripe distribution function is able to divide one-dimensional logical files into a set of non-overlapping chunks of data, which are called stripes. To be specific, files are supposed to be separated into many stripes, and then stored on the I/O nodes with certain distribution methods. Normally, the stripes are stored in a round robin manner on data files on the storage nodes [8], certain advanced distributed file systems, such as GPFS [9], Lustre [10] and Google file system [11] employ this kind of stripe distribution mechanism. It is well-known that data striping performance is also influenced by the application's I/O behavior, however, stripe distribution does not adjust, even though the distribution goes against application's access modes [12]. For instance, the requirements of continuous media file servers differ from the requirements of scientific applications that needs to process multi-dimensional data but the traditional distributed file systems treat them without any distinction [13]. From certain previous studies, it seems that the static distribution mechanism and the fixed stripe size configuration may perform poorly in dealing with a substantial quantity of multi-dimensional data, which may be read/written concurrently by a large number of clients [14].

In this paper, we propose a dynamic stripe management mechanism for distributed file systems, which enables varying stripe sizes, and supports stripe re-sizing and re-distributing on the storage servers. As a result, the distributed file systems can adjust stripe sizes and distribute stripes dynamically on the basis of both applications' access patterns and their corresponding disk access patterns, to yield better I/O performance. This mechanism makes the following two contributions:

1. *Piggybacking applications' access information to disk access patterns.* Applications' logical access information reveals the applications' behavior on the client side, but only the stripe access information on the storage servers shows the real disk operations. In this stripe management mechanism, the logical access information is supposed to be piggybacked with client I/O requests for benefiting to mapping logical access to stripe access, but client file systems do not need to keeping logs for logical access. The mapping relationship can definitely do good to conduct I/O optimization strategies on the storage server sides in the distributed file systems.

2. *Re-sizing and re-distributing stripes dynamically on the storage servers.* Except for supporting varying size of stripes, the newly proposed mechanism is able to perform dynamic stripe re-sizing and re-distributing on the storage servers, according to the mapping relationship between logical access information and physical access information. This indicates that it can boost I/O data throughput, as well as reduce I/O response time through conducting relevant I/O optimization strategies according to both logical and physical access patterns.

The following paper is organized as follows: Section 2 describes certain background knowledge and related work that aims to improve I/O performance in distributed file systems by employing different I/O optimization strategies. We will demonstrate design details of the mechanism of dynamic stripe management on the storage servers in Section 3. The evaluation methodology and relevant results are illustrated in Section 4. Finally, we conclude this paper in Section 5.

2 Related Work

For the purpose of yielding attractive I/O performance in the distributed file systems, much current work focuses on I/O optimization strategies for better I/O performance by resorting to keeping and analyzing either logical I/O traces or disk I/O traces. This section discusses some typical approaches, which are mainly sorted as the following two categories:

I/O Optimization by using either logical I/O access information or physical I/O access information. T. Madhyastha et al. [15] presented two approaches to reveal various file access patterns and then employ these access patterns to carry out the appropriate caching and prefetching optimization for file systems. The main idea for characterizing access patterns is to use neural networks for short time scales and Hidden Markov models for long time scales. The project IOSig+ allows users to classify the I/O access patterns of an application in two steps: 1) obtain the trace of all the I/O operations of the application from the view point of clients; 2) through the offline analysis on the trace to yield the I/O Signature. Therefore, by using the I/O Signatures, which is the information about logical I/O access patterns, certain optimization on I/O systems, such as data pre-fetching, I/O scheduling, and cost model based data access optimization can be conducted [14]. Besides, J. He et al. [23] have explored and classified patterns of I/O within applications, thereby allowing powerful I/O optimization strategies including pattern-aware prefetching to enhance I/O performance.

There are also many studies about the analysis of access patterns on disk I/O traces. Z. Li and Y. Zhou first investigated the block correlation in the storage servers by employing data mine techniques, to benefit to I/O optimization in servers [16] and [17]. S. Narayan and J. Chandy [18] researched disk I/O traffics under different workloads and different file systems, and they declared the modeling information about physical I/O operations can contribute to I/O optimization tactics for better system performance [19]. In [20], an automatic locality-improving storage has been presented, which automatically reorganizes selected disk blocks based on the dynamic reference stream to boost effective storage performance. After that, *DiskSeen* has been presented that supports to perform prefetching directly at the level of disk layout [21]. H. Song et al [22] have presented a server-side I/O collection mechanism to coordinate file servers for serving one application at a time to decrease the completion time.

Intelligently setting stripe size in file systems. H. Simitci [24] proposed an adaptive mechanism to set the size of striping unit according to the system's state. To be specific, the size of stripes can be determined on the basis of some parameters including the request rate, the request size, the network flow, and disk speed. M. Medina et al. [13] proposed a self-tuning approach for automatically determining and refining the file system's striping parameters based on application access patterns. In other words, this technique relies on the monitoring of application I/O requests including their size, type, duration and inter-arrival times etc., and then a proper analytic model is used to decide file striping parameters to improve overall file system performance. Therefore, the self-tuning file systems usually operate correspondingly according to the principle that the behavior of the file system must change to match the application. B. Dong et al. [25] have proposed an analytic model to evaluate the performance of highly concurrent data access, and then they have described how to apply this model to determine the stripe size of a file. However, this adaptive disk striping approach does not allow change the size of file stripe dynamically and various sizes of stripes belonging to the file.

Besides, Triantafillou and Faloutsos [26] presented the mechanism of overlay striping, which is a novel data distribution scheme, it stores several copies of a file prior to its use, leveraging a number of different stripe widths. As a result, the relevant replica with the most beneficial stripe width will be accessed. N. Ali et al. have presented a fault-tolerant mechanism to distribute the parity computation for generalized Cartesian data distributions on the storage servers. Actually, in [12], we have proposed a self-tuning storage system that supports stripe movement among storage servers on the fly. But it requires the client file system to record the logical I/O events, and the stripe size is fixed all the time.

It is true that logical access patterns on the application side may affect the I/O performance on the storage server side, that is the reason certain file systems enable self-tuning functionality for determining stripe size and stripe location, according to logical access patterns. On the other hand, only the physical access patterns can disclose the disk behaviors corresponding to logical access. However, the fact is that none of the mentioned techniques and tools support the optimization strategy of supporting dynamic re-sizing and re-distributing stripes by analyzing both logical I/O access patterns and their corresponding physical access patterns in the distributed file systems. Therefore, our work addresses that it is able to build the connection between logical I/O access and physical I/O access; then help the storage servers to re-size and re-distribute the stripes, as well as enable varying size of stripes, for better I/O performance.

3   Dynamic Re-sizing and Re-distributing stripes

In Section 2, we depicted that a major part of I/O tracing approaches proposed by other researchers focus on the logical I/O access occurred on the client file system side, which might be useful for affirming application's I/O access patterns [14]. Nevertheless, without relevant information about physical I/O access, it is difficult to build the connection between the applications and the distributed file system for enhancing the I/O performance significantly through I/O

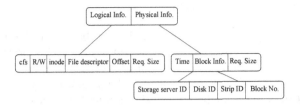

Fig. 1. Logged information about logical access and the corresponding physical access

optimization on the storage servers. Therefore, this section describes the details of the way to support varying size of stripes, and then enable dynamic re-sizing and re-distributing stripes on the storage servers to advance I/O system's performance.

3.1   Piggybacking Logical Access Information to Servers

In this newly presented stripe management mechanism, understanding the mapping relationship between logical access and physical access is a critical precondition to perform I/O optimization. Thus, for storage servers, it is necessary to know the information about client file systems and applications. Although we have proposed a mapping mechanism in our previous work [12], it requires the client file systems to keep the track of logical access information, and then send the tracing logs to the server side. To reduce the overhead resulted by client logging in our previous work, we leverage a piggybacking mechanism, to transfer related information from the client node to the storage servers for contributing to construct the mapping relationship between logical access and physical access. To put it from another angle, the client file system is responsible for keeping extra information about the application, client file system and the logical access information; after that, it piggybacks the extra information with relevant I/O request, and sends them to the corresponding storage server. On the other hand, the storage server is supposed to parse the request to separate piggybacked information and the real I/O request. Apart from forwarding the I/O request to the low level file system, the storage server has to record the disk I/O access with the information about the corresponding logical I/O access.

Briefly speaking, when sending a logical I/O request to the storage server, the client file system piggybacks information about the client file systems and the application. In this way, the storage servers can record disk I/O events with associated client information, which plays a critical role for modeling I/O access relationship, and then directing stripe optimization operations on the storage servers dynamically.

3.2 Mapping Access Patterns

As mentioned before, the client information is piggybacked to the storage servers, then the storage servers are possible to record the disk I/O operations accompanying with the information about relevant logical I/O events. Figure 1 demonstrates the structure of each piece of logged information, which is stored on the relevant storage server. The information about logical access includes *inode* information, *file descriptor*, *offset* and *requested size*. On the other hand, the information about the relevant physical access contains *storage server ID, stripe ID, block ID* and *requested size*.

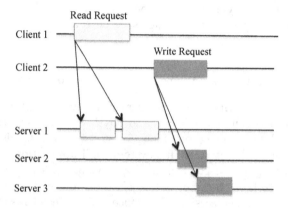

Fig. 2. Mapping Example of logical I/Os and physical I/Os

After analyzing the recorded logs for a series of I/O operations, we can easily to obtain the relations between logical access and physical access. Figure 2 illustrates an example case about I/O visualization of both kinds of I/O access information. In the figure, the *Read request* from *Client 1* is reflected to *Server 1*, so that the two relevant stripes on that server will be accessed sequentially, which may damage access concurrency. In addition, the *Write request* from *Client 2* is separately mapped to *Server 2* and *Server 3*. From the visualization illustration between logical access and physical access, it is not difficult to issue I/O optimization on the storage servers after understanding the shortcomings of the current stripes distribution. For example, the *Write request* from *Client 2* is mapped to *Server 2* and *Server 3*, which indicates that the two stripes should be updated, as well as the replicas corresponding to these two stripes. If this *Write request* is mapped to only one stripe (merging the involved two stripes), the number of replica synchronization can be reduced to a half. That is why we have done the work to support dynamically performing stripe optimization according to the access patterns.

3.3 Re-sizing and Re-distributing Functions

This paper presents a stripe management mechanism that allows varying size of stripes on storage servers on the basis of analysis of the mapping of access patterns. In other words, this newly introduced mechanism makes it possible that the stripes are possible to be re-sized and truncated dynamically for some reason. Figure 3 (a) and (b) illustrate two cases about re-distributing an existing stripe and creating a new stripe (i.e. truncating an existing stripe to generate a new stripe) respectively.

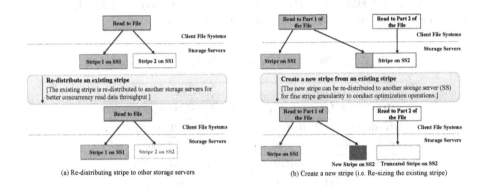

Fig. 3. Re-distributing and Re-sizing stripes on the storage servers

Let us take Figure 3(b) as an instance, the first read operation (i.e. *Read to Part 1 of the File*) is reflected to 2 stripes that stored in two different storage servers (i.e. *SS 1* and *SS 2*), the reason for this situation is due to application's specification and default round-robin stripe distribution function. In this case, the first read request does damage to the second read request (i.e. *Read to Part 2 of the File*) that might be issued by another client file system in our example. Because the first read needs to lock the whole stripe stored on *SS 2*, that means the second write or read request should wait until obtain the lock to that stripe, even though it does not read the contents that requested by the first read request. To overcome this problem, this paper introduces a novel stripe management approach, which supports varying size of stripe units, and enables dynamic re-sizing, re-distributing the existing stripes. Therefore, the conflicted stripe stored on the *SS2* can be divided into 2 stripes, and the first read request does not need to lock the stripe file, which is requested by the second read request. Without doubt, after re-sizing and re-distributing operations, the metadata server should be notified to update relevant metadata, e.g. stripe sizes and stripe locations.

4 Experiments and Evaluation

4.1 Experimental Setup

Experimental Platform. One cluster and two LANs are used for conducting the experiments, one active metadata server, 4 storage servers are deployed on the 5 nodes of the cluster. Moreover, for emulating a distributed computing environment, 6 client file systems are installed on a LAN that is connected with the cluster by a 1 GigE Ethernet; another 6 client file systems are installed on another LAN but with same node specifications, which is connected with the cluster by a 100M Ethernet, and both LANs equipped with MPICH2-1.4.1. Table 1 show the specifications of nodes on both of them.

Table 1. Specification of Nodes on the Cluster and the LANs

	Cluster	LANs
CPU	2xIntel(R) E5410 2.33G	Intel(R) E5800 3.20G
Memory	1x4GB 1066MHz/DDR3	4GB DDR3-SDRAM
Disk	6x114GB 7200rpm SATA	500GB 7200rpm SATA
Network	Intel 82598EB, 10GbE	1000Mb or 100 Mb
OS	Ubuntu 13.10	Debian 6.0.4

Evaluation Counterparts. To demonstrate the effectiveness of our proposed dynamic stripe management scheme, we have employed the conventional distributed file system and the self-tuning storage system, as comparison counterparts in our experiments:

- *Dynamic Re-sizing and Re-distributing Storage (D2RS).* The proposed mechanism has been implemented and applied in a prototype distributed file system, which enables varying stripe sizes and dynamic stripe re-sizing.
- *Conventional Self-Tuning Storage (CSTS).* We implemented a self-tuning storage system in our previous work [12], which supports certain preliminary optimized I/O strategies, such as stripe migration on storage servers, but without piggybacking mechanism and supporting for varying size stripes. As a matter of fact, this work is the most related scheme of our proposed *D2RS*.
- *Conventional Storage System (CSS).* The storage servers are responsible for all I/O operations normally, and the data stripes are distributed with the normal round-robin pattern. That indicates no I/O tracing and no dynamic stripe re-sizing and stripe re-distributing functionality.

Benchmarks. We selected two benchmarks to evaluate our proposed stripe management approach and its comparison counterparts.

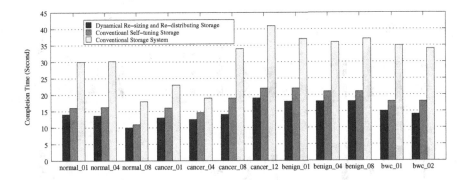

Fig. 4. Completion Times for Running *DDSM* Sampled Volumes

– *Digital Database for Screening Mammography (DDSM)*, which is a database of digitized film-screen mammograms with associated ground truth and other information. The purpose of this resource is to provide a large set of mammograms in a digital format that may be used by researchers to emulate medical image processing [2].
– *MADbench2*, which is an I/O benchmark derived from a real world application analyzing massive cosmic microwave background radiation in the sky from noisy pixelated datasets from satellites [3]. Since MADbench2 performs large, contiguous mixed read and write patterns, it has become a popular and often used benchmark in the parallel I/O community.

4.2   Experimental Results: Benefits and Overhead

In this section, we are expected to unveil the overhead brought by the scheme of dynamic re-sizing and re-distributing, as well as the benefits brought by this newly presented stripe management scheme. Thus, the following two sub-sections explore both positive and negative aspects of the proposed scheme respectively.

Improvement on I/O Performance We employed the aforementioned two application benchmarks to measure I/O responsiveness and data throughput respectively to show the merits brought by our proposed mechanism. First, we executed *DDSM* on the three storage systems, and recorded the time required for executing all sub-benchmarks in *DDSM*. The relevant results are reported in Figure 4, and it is not difficult to know that all sub-benchmarks of *DDSM* completed with the shortest times while it run on *D2RS*, because the computation times of the sub-benchmarks are the same, but *D2RS* caused the least times for I/O processing. For instance, when the sub-benchmark is *cancer_08*, *D2RS* yielded more than 30% execution accelerating, compared with *CSTS*, which means *D2RS* have better I/O responsiveness while processing multi-dimensional datasets.

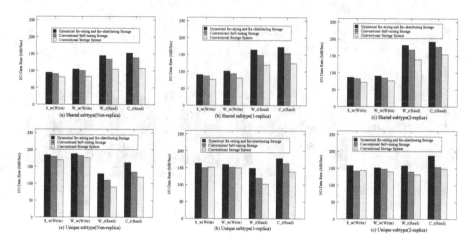

Fig. 5. MADbench2 Experimental Results (MPI, SYNC, 18KPIX, 16BIN)

Moreover, for the purpose of checking the improvement on data throughput by adopting our proposed mechanism, we run *MADbench2* benchmark, and set various number of replicas for each stripe to measure read/write data throughput. Actually, in *MADbench2*, the function S only writes, the function W both reads and writes, the function C only reads; so that, the sub-benchmarks are denoted as S_w, W_w, W_r, C_r to show the different I/O operations in the different functions. Figures 5 shows the experimental results of executing MADbench2 benchmark with *Shared* and *Unique* subtype when adopting different configuration of replicas. In all sub-figures, X axis shows the names of sub-benchmarks in *MADBench2*, while Y axis indicates I/O data rate, and the higher one is better. From the results shown in the figure, we can safely make a conclusion, compared with other two comparison counterparts, *D2RS* could potentially result in better overall data throughput. Especially, while the number of replicas is becoming larger, the improvement on data throughput is more attractive. This is because re-sizing stripes and creating new independent stripes may reduce the update synchronization overhead caused by write operations.

Overhead on Client and Storage Servers. After disclosing the positive effects brought by the newly proposed stripe management mechanism, it might be interesting to unveil the negative aspects on I/O performance caused by this mechanism. Table 2 shows the execution time and space overheads for performing stripe re-sizing and re-distributing dynamically on the storage servers, as well as keeping the track of physical I/O access. The results show that this newly proposed mechanism can effectively and practically guide re-sizing and re-distributing stripes on the storage servers for different workloads with acceptable overhead on CPU time and disk space. Because *MADbench2* is a typical I/O benchmark to test I/O performance of storage systems, more than 7.4%

time overhead on trace analyzing and re-sizing stripes on the storage servers. But, for the compute-intensive *DDSM* application, our proposed mechanism consumed not much time to yield preferable system performance. Namely, while the workload is *DDSM*, the time required for keeping disk traces and performing dynamic stripe management is around 3.7% of total processing time. This trend indicates that a major part of processing time can be used to tackle I/O processing; therefore, we can understand that this server-side, dynamic stripe management technique is practical for storage systems in distributed computing environments.

Table 2. Overhead on Dynamic Stripe Management Mechanism

Benchmarks	Consumed time (%)	Space for traces (MB)
DDSM (Overall)	3.7	588.4
Madbench (Shared, Non-replica)	7.4	332.7
Madbench (Unique, Non-replica)	8.6	443.8

Besides, we also recorded the disk space utilized to save the physical I/O traces, which are used to analyze access patterns for conducting potential optimization. The relevant results are reported in the table as well. It is clear that the space used for storing I/O traces is not so much, in contrast to the space used for storing the input and output data required by the benchmarks. For instance, *DDSM* benchmark deal with more than 60 GB data, but it uses less than 600 MB space for saving I/O trace data.

5   Concluding Remarks

This paper presents a novel stripe management technique in distributed file systems, in which the stripe size is varying from each other, and the data stripes can be re-sized and re-distributed dynamically according to the access patterns of target applications. The evaluation experiments have illustrated the effectiveness of this newly proposed mechanism, and the attractive experimental results demonstrated that our introduced stripe management mechanism is practical for storage systems in distributed computing environments. As a matter of fact, we have implemented this approach into a prototype distributed file system to verify the feasibility of the idea presented in this paper, it can be not only applied to other traditional distributed file systems, but also parallel file systems, such as the Lustre file system, the Google file system, the GPFS file system, or their extensions, as well.

Acknowledgment. This work was supported partially by "National Natural Science Foundation of China (No. 61303038)", "Natural Science Foundation Project of CQ CSTC (No. CSTC2013JCYJA40050)", and "the Opening Project of State Key Laboratory for Novel Software Technology (No. KFKT2014B17)".

References

1. Gantz, J., Reinsel, D.: The digital universe in 2020: Big Data, Bigger Digital Shadows, Biggest Growth in the Far East, United States (2013),
   http://www.emc.com/collateral/analyst-reports/
   idc-digital-universe-united-states.pdf (accessed on October 3, 2013)
2. Digital database for screening mammography,
   http://marathon.csee.usf.edu/Mammography/Database.html
   (accessed on December 12, 2011)
3. MADbench2. borrill/MADbench2/, http://crd.lbl.gov/
4. Weil, S.A., Pollack, K.T., Brandt, S.A., Miller, E.L.: Dynamic metadata management for petabyte-scale file systems. In: Proceedings of the 2004 ACM/IEEE Conference on Supercomputing, SC 2014, pp. 4–15. IEEE Computer Society, Washington, DC (2004)
5. Nieuwejaar, N., Kotz, D.: The galley parallel file system. Parallel Computing 23(4-5), 447–476 (1997)
6. Kunkel, J., Ludwig, T.: Performance evaluation of the pvfs2 architecture. In: Proceedings of 15th EUROMICRO International Conference on Parallel, Distributed and Network-Based Processing (PDP 200), pp. 509–516 (2007)
7. Liao, J., Ishikawa, Y.: Partial replication of metadata to achieve high metadata availability in parallel file systems. In: Proceedings of the 41st International Conference on Parallel Processing, ICPP 2012, pp. 168–177 (2012)
8. Latham, R., Miller, N., Ross, R., Carns, P.: A Next- Generation Parallel File System for Linux Clusters. Linux World 2(1) (2004)
9. Schmuck, F., Haskin, R.: Gpfs: A shared-disk file system for large computing clusters. In: Proceedings of the 1st USENIX Conference on File and Storage Technologies, FAST 2002. USENIX Association, Berkeley (2002)
10. Schwan, P.: Lustre: Building a file system for 1,000-node clusters. In: Proceedings of the Linux Symposium, p. 9 (2003)
11. Ghemawat, S., Gobioff, H., Leung, T.: The Google file system. ACM SIGOPS Operating Systems Review 37(5), 29–43 (2003)
12. Liao, J.: Self-tuning optimization on storage servers in parallel file system. Journal of Circuits, Systems and Computers 30(4), 21 pages (2014)
13. Medina, M.: A self-tuning disk striping system for parallel input/output. Dissertation. University of Illinois at Urbana-Champaign, USA (2007)
14. Byna, S., Chen, Y., Sun, X.-H., Thakur, R., Gropp, W.: Parallel i/o prefetching using mpi file caching and i/o signatures. In: SC 2008, pp. 44:1-44:12 (2008)
15. Madhyastha, T.: Automatic Classification of Input/Output Acess Patterns. Dissertation, Champaign, IL, USA (1997)
16. Li, Z., Chen, Z., Srinivasan, S., Zhou, Y.: C-Miner: Mining Block Correlations in Storage Systems. In: Proceedings of the 3rd Conference on File and Storage Technologies, FAST 2004 (2004)
17. Li, Z., Chen, Z., Zhou, Y.: Mining Block Correlations to Improve Storage Performance. ACM Transactions on Storage 1(1), 213–245 (2005)
18. Narayan, S., Chandy, J.: Trace Based Analysis of File System Effects on Disk I/O. In: Proceedings of 2004 International Symposium on Performance Evaluation of Computer and Telecommunication Systems, SPECTS 2004 (2004)
19. Narayan, S.: File System Optimization Using Block Reorganization Techniques. Master of Science Thesis, University of Connecticut (2004)

20. Hsu, W., Smith, A., Young, H.: The automatic improvement of locality in storage systems. ACM Trans. Comput. Syst. 23(4), 424–473 (2005)
21. Jiang, S., Ding, X., Xu, Y., Davis, K.: A Prefetching Scheme Exploiting both Data Layout and Access History on Disk. ACM Transaction on Storage 9(3), Article 10, 23 p. (2013)
22. Song, H., Yin, Y., Sun, X., Thakur, R., Lang, S.: Server-side I/O coordination for parallel file systems. In: Proceedings of 2011 International Conference for High Performance Computing, Networking, Storage and Analysis (SC 2011). ACM (2011)
23. He, J., Bent, J., Torres, A., Sun, X., et al.: I/O Acceleration with Pattern Detection. In: Proceedings of the 22nd International ACM Symposium on High Performance Parallel and Distributed Computing (HPDC 2013), pp. 26-35 (2013)
24. Simitci, H.: Adaptive Disk Striping for Parallel Input/Output. Dissertation, Champaign (2000)
25. Dong, B., Li, X., Xiao, L., et al.: A New File-Specific Stripe Size Selection Method for Highly Concurrent Data Access. In: Proceedings of 2012 ACM/IEEE 13th International Conference on Grid Computing (GRID), pp. 22-30 (2012)
26. Triantafillou, P., Faloutsos, C.: Overlay striping and optimal parallel I/O for modern applications. Parallel Computing 24(1), 21–43 (1998) Special Issue on Applications: Parallel Data Servers and Applications (1998)

Accelerating the Reconstruction Process in Network Coding Storage System by Leveraging Data Temperature

Kai Li and Yuhui Deng[*]

Department of Computer Science, Jinan University, Guangzhou 510632, P.R. China
likai328@gmail.com, tyhdeng@jnu.edu.cn

Abstract. Over the past few years, network coding has been employed in data reconstruction process of storage systems to minimize the recovery bandwidth. However, the time consumption of the decoding operations incurs a significant performance degradation. In this paper, we propose a data temperature-based reconstruction optimization algorithm and integrate it into the reconstruction process of a Network-Coding-Based File System (NCFS) which adopts regenerating code as its storage coding scheme. We conduct extensive experiments to evaluate the impacts on the data reconstruction process of regenerating codes. The experimental results demonstrate that our method outperforms the conventional approach both in reconstruction time, throughput and average response time with up to 33.17%, 60.61%, 37.77% improvement, respectively.

1   Introduction

Distributed storage systems have been widely deployed in industry to provide massive data storage service [1][2][3]. In such storage systems, data is allocated into a number of nodes in a stripe manner which enhances read/write performance in parallel ways. Since node failures are common [1], when a node storing encoded information fails, in order to maintain the same level of reliability we need to create encoded information at a new node. Therefore, redundancy must be introduced to reconstruct data. The simplest redundancy method is replication, which places several copies of same data in different nodes..

Erasure coding provides the same reliability as replication but requiring much less storage space [4][5]. This technique departs one piece of data into d pieces and then encodes them into n pieces $(n>d)$, then stripe encoded data. Such that any d of them are sufficient to reconstruct the original data. So, when we want to reconstruct a failed node, at least k times size data must be read from surviving nodes to participate in the decoding process, while in replication the repair of one replica needs that only one other replica is read.

Dimakis [6] proposed Regenerating Codes that stem from the concept of network coding [7] and minimize the repair traffic among storage nodes. They exploit the optimal trade-off between storage cost and repair traffic, and there are two optimal points. One optimal point refers to the minimum storage regenerating (MSR) codes, which minimize the repair bandwidth subject to the condition that each node stores

---

[*] Corresponding author.

C.-H. Hsu et al. (Eds.): NPC 2014, LNCS 8707, pp. 510–521, 2014.

the minimum amount of data as in Reed-Solomon codes. Another optimal point is the minimum bandwidth regenerating (MBR)codes, which allow each node to store more data to further minimize the repair bandwidth. The construction of MBR codes is found in [8], while that of MSR codes based on interference alignment is found in [9], [10]. We focus on MBR codes in this paper.

Therefore, using minimum bandwidth regenerating (MBR) codes can improve the performance of data recovery in case of node failure, while requiring less download bandwidth than traditional replication and erasure coding. However, recent work [12] has shown that regenerating codes takes too much computation overhead during data reconstruction which significantly increases the reconstruction time. Meanwhile, the time to rebuild a single disk has lengthened as the disk capacity far outpaces the disk bandwidth. Furthermore, the longer the period of single disk repair takes, the higher the possibility of a disk failure, which would probably lead to unrecoverable data loss. Hence, accelerating the data reconstruction process is becoming a pressing problem.

In this paper, we propose a data temperature-based reconstruction optimization algorithm in a network-coding-based file system, which uses data temperature to schedule reconstruction sequence in node recovery process. The frequently accessed data is called hot data, and the infrequently accessed data is determined as cold data. The hot data would be reconstructed prior to the cold data during the reconstruction process. Since the user request stream normally couple with the data rebuilding stream, we intend to reduce the disk seek time and disk head shuttling, so as to improve the rebuilding performance. The method is implemented atop network coding file system (NCFS) [11]. Extensive experiments indicate that our approach significantly outperforms the existing reconstruction schemes in terms of reconstruction time, throughput and average response time.

The rest of the paper proceeds as follows. Section 2 states background and motivation, and Section 3 describes the design and implementation issues. Section 4 presents our experimental results. Section 5 concludes this paper.

2   Background and Motivation

2.1   Definitions

Maximum-Distance Separable Codes(MDS Codes): An MDS code can be defined in the following way for storage: We can divide a file of size M into k blocks, each of size M/k, encode them into n $(n>k)$ encoded blocks and spread them to n nodes. Then, the original file can be reconstructed by any k coded blocks. This mechanism is optimal in terms of the redundancy–reliability tradeoff because k blocks, each of size M/k, provide the minimum data for reconstructing the file, which is of size M. The repair degree d is introduced for data repair, such that the repair for the lost blocks of one failed node are achieved by connecting to d nodes to recover the lost blocks. Both traditional storage codes RAID5 and RAID6 are MDS codes.

RAID5: In Fig. 1 (a), for special case $n = 4$, RAID5 is a (4,3) MDS code where $n = 4, k = d = 3$. RAID5 can tolerate at most a single node failure. In each segment, the sole code block is generated by the bitwise XOR-summing of the $k = n$ 1 native blocks. In reconstructing, the lost block can be rebuilt from the other $n - 1$ blocks in the same segment via bitwise XOR-summing.

RAID6: In Fig. 1 (b), RAID6 is a (4,2) MDS code where $n = 4$, $k = d = 2$. RAID-6 can tolerate at most two node failures with two code blocks known as the P and Q parities (corresponding to c1 and c2 in Fig.1). The P parity is generated by the bitwise XOR-summing of the $k = n - 2$ native blocks similar to RAID5, while the Q parity is generated by coefficient XOR-summing. In reconstruction, if single or double failures happen, then each lost block can be repaired from the blocks of the same segment in other surviving nodes.

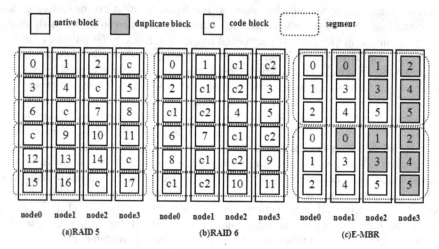

Fig. 1. The data layout of RAID5, RAID6, and E-MBR code for the case $n = 4$

2.2   MBR Codes

MBR is optimal repair bandwidth efficiency. It attains one of the two extreme points of the optimal Storage-Bandwidth Tradeoff curve [15] of regenerating codes. The tradeoff curve are given by [19], where $(\alpha_{MBR} , \beta_{MBR}) = (\dfrac{2Bd}{2kd - k^2 + k} , \dfrac{2B}{2kd - k^2 + k})$. When $\beta = 1$, we have $B = kd - \dfrac{k(k-1)}{2}$ and $\alpha = d$.

Table 1. Parameters of a regeneration code

Parameters	Descriptions
n	number of storage nodes
B	size of the source data to be stored, in terms of number of blocks
α	storage capacity of each node, in terms of number of blocks
k	the original file is recoverable from the data in any k nodes
d and β	on failure of a node, the replacement node connects to any d of the existing nodes, downloading at most β blocks from each of them
$d\beta$	reconstruct bandwidth, the total amount of data downloaded to reconstruct a failed node

2.3 E-MBR Codes

In regenerating codes, there are generally three data repair approaches [13]: (i) exact repair, which builds exactly the lost blocks in a new node, (ii) functional repair, simply reconstructs a new block that combined with the existing ones still forms an (n,k) MDS code, and (iii) a hybrid of both.

 Dimakis[6] proposed regenerating codes. However, they gave only a theoretical description of the codes without discussing implementation issues or computational costs. Recently, some practical MSR codes [16] and exact MBR codes [14][15] are proposed. Specifically, NCFS[11] implemented exact MBR (E-MBR) code [15] into its system, along with RAID5, RAID6 coding schemes. In this paper, we focus on a particular case where $d = k = n$ 1. For example, when n = 4 [Fig. 1 (c)2], specially, according to the formula $B = kd - \dfrac{k(k-1)}{2}$, the number of total native blocks is

$B = kd - \dfrac{k(k-1)}{2} = 6$. For each native block, we create a duplicate copy, so the number of duplicate blocks in each segment is also 6. According to formula $\alpha = d$, we have $\alpha = d = 3$, which means each node stores 3 blocks. When a node fails, each of living $d = 3$ contributes $\beta = 1$ block to reconstruct data on a new node.

Table 2. The Theoretical Overhead of RAID and E-MBR

Codes	Storage Cost	Reconstruction Traffic
RAID5	$B/(1-1/n)$	B
RAID6	$B/(1-2/n)$	B
E-MBR	$2B$	$2B/n$

 Block allocation mechanism is shown as Fig. 1. We consider a segment of B native blocks M_0, M_1,...M_{B-1} and their duplicate blocks $\overline{M}_0$, $\overline{M}_1$,...$\overline{M}_{B-1}$. Thus, the total number of blocks in one segment is $2B = n(n-1)$, which means each node stores $(n-1)$ blocks for each segment. There are $n(n-1)$ fields for allocating if we regard it as a matrix. For each block M_i, we search for a free field from top to bottom in a column-by-column manner, starting from the leftmost column; for duplicate block $\overline{M}_i$, we search for a free field from left to right in a rowby-row manner, starting from the topmost row. Until all blocks have been distributed.

 To reconstruct the data in failed node, we note that each native block has a duplicate copy, and the block and its copy are stored in two different nodes. Thus, for each lost block, we retrieve its duplicate copy from another survival node and write it to the new node. Note that based on the block allocation mechanism, each survival node contributes exactly one block for each segment. The theoretical comparison of storage cost and reconstruction traffic between RAID5, RAID6 and E-MBR is presented in Table 2.

2.4   Motivation

On the one hand, most of the distributed storage systems switch to a recovery mode after node failure to reconstruct data on a new node. On the other hand, systems continue to serve I/O requests. So we have reconstruction data stream and user request data stream contend the disk I/O simultaneously, which leads to frequent long seeks to and from the different separate data districts. Another problem is that regenerating codes take more computation than erasure codes [11][12], as a result, it needs more time to reconstruct data. Based on the test results in NCFS from our research, E-MBR suffers much more reconstruction time than either RAID5 or RAID6. They are 1.326s/MB, 0.133s/MB, 0.159s/MB respectively.

We believe that scheduling reconstruction sequence with user access patterns is a fundamental way to improve effectiveness of reconstruction process. The main idea is to reconstruct the hot data prior to the cold data so as to relieve disk I/O contentions. Tian et al. [17] proposed a popularity-based multi-threaded reconstruction optimization algorithm (PRO) to optimize the reconstruction process deployed in RAID-Structured Storage Systems by integrating the popularity and locality of workloads into the reconstruction process. To the best of our knowledge, our method is the first work that combines data temperature with the regenerating codes in reconstruction process.

3   Design and Implementation

3.1   System Architecture

The proposed idea has to track data temperature in the node so that reconstruct thread can conduct the repair sequence according to the temperature of each segment. In our architecture, there are four modules (Fig. 2.). Two of them, Scheduler and Taskexecuter, are inherent modules in NCFS. While the other two, Client and Tracker, are added by us for data temperature tracing. Data streams are represented by arrows with numbers in the Fig. 2. Streams 1,2 and 9,10 are user request data streams and reconstruction data streams respectively.

Client: It sends I/O requests to the NCFS with user access pattern, which implemented by using zipf distribution. Only read requests are considered in this paper. If the request falls on the failed segment on the failed node, reconstruct the data immediately and return it; otherwise, return the request data directly.

Tacker: Father process monitors I/O requests of Client to keeps track of access frequency of each segment, and maintain a segment number for next reconstruction. Child process communicates with Taskexecuter, conducts reconstruction sequence by using data temperature.

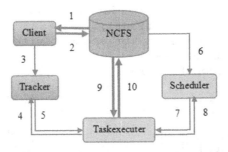

Fig. 2. System Architecture

Data Reconstruction Process: When node failure occurs, NCFS starts Scheduler and Taskexecuter. In the meantime, Client and Tracker begin to work. Scheduler receives reconstruction parameters and schedules reconstruction task, then sends task parameter struct to Taskexecuter telling it which task is going to be executed. Before task begins, Taskexecuter obtains data temperature characteristic from Tracker, then Taskexecuter launches reconstruction algorithm to rebuild data on the new node, until all the data have been reconstructed. The two major algorithms are detailed as below:

Algorithm of Client:
```
while (1) {
   initiate req_disk, recon[];
   offset = zipfDistribution() ;
   if ( req_disk != fail_disk ) {
      open(req_disk);
      read(offset);}
   else {if ( recon[offset] == 1 ) {
         open(req_disk);
         read(offset);
         good_req ++;}
       else if ( recon[offset] == 0 ) {
         recover_mbr(fail_disk, new_disk);
         open(req_disk);
         read(offset);
         bad_req ++;}}
   if finish reconstruction, break; }
```

Algorithm of Tracker:
```
while (1) {
   initiate hot_seg;
   fpid = fork();
   if (fpid == 0) {    //Child process
      while (1) {hot_seg = max (temp[]);
         listen( taskexecuter_sd );
         send ( hot_seg );
         if finish reconstruction, break;}}
```

```
else if (fpid > 0) {    //father process
    recv (req_disk, offset);
    segment = offset / mbr_segment_size;
    temp [segment] ++;}
if finish reconstruction, break;}
```

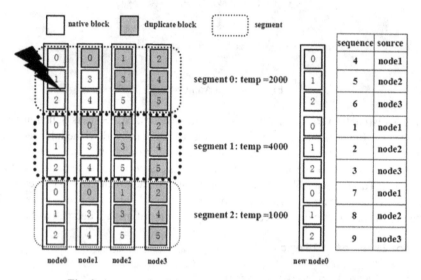

Fig. 3. An example of the reconstruction process of our method

Example: We describe our idea by Fig. 3, which shows a (4,3) E-MBR code and failures node 0. After node 0 failed, client continue to access data from node 0, the requests land up in different segments, which makes segment 1 the hottest zone, segment 0 and segment 2 in node 0 are relatively cold. When reconstruction thread starts, it selects segment 1 to rebuild data first. Inside segment 1, block rebuilding shall be at sequence order by finding corresponding duplicate blocks and copying them from other living nodes. In this case, reconstruction order should be segment 1:block 0 → segment 1:block 1 → segment 1:block 2 → segment 0:block 0 → segment 0:block 1 → segment 0:block 2 → segment 2:block 0 → segment 2:block 1 → segment 2:block 2.

3.2   Implementation Issues

Reconstruction Unit. Compare to the original approach reconstructing data block by block, our method use segment as a reconstruction unit. Considering that the data in the same segment are organized by the same allocation mechanism, it is more computational saving to recover all blocks in a segment once at a time than to recover each of them separately. On the other hand, spatial locality indicates that likelihood of referencing a resource is higher if a resource near it was just referenced. So blocks in the same segment would be very likely to be accessed by one request. Furthermore, preserving the inherent sequentiality inside segment is more conform to the disk drive

I/O pattern which is at many times the bandwidth of random accesses. This will lead to reduction of disk head rotations so as to save more reconstruction time.

4   System Evaluation

4.1   Experimental Settings

Our testbed is built on an open-source Network-Coding-Based Distributed File System (NCFS) [11], which supports a specific regenerating coding scheme called Exact Minimum Bandwidth Regenerating (E-MBR) codes [9]. We implement our approach DTemp on NCFS in the reconstruction process of E-MBR exploiting data temperature. The platform consists of 2.4GHz CPU, 2G DDR3 Memory, WDC WD5000AADS-00S9B0 disk, CentOS release 6.3 (Final), and NCFS 1.2.1.

4.2   Workloads

User access pattern is usually in accord with Pareto principle. Therefore, we use Zipf's law to imitate the distribution of workload characteristic from client. The Zipf-like distribution formula [18] depict this rule, given by $p_N(i) = \dfrac{\Omega}{i^\alpha}$, where $\Omega = (\sum_{i=1}^{N} \dfrac{1}{i^\alpha})^{-1}$, α is a constant, which is in the range $0 < \alpha \leq 1$. Let N be the total number of blocks in the node. So Ω is also a constant, while $P_N(i)$ should be the conditional probability of the ith block. For example, we have 10 blocks accessed by 10000 requests, then the Zipf-like distribution is shown in Figure 5. When $\alpha = 1$, block 0 and block 1 receive 7369 read requests while the other 8 blocks receive 2631 requests in total, which almost conform to the 80-20 rule.

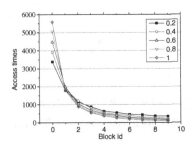

Fig. 4. Evaluate different alpha on Zipf-like access distribution

4.3   Performance Evaluation

We are mainly interested in the metric of reconstruction performance including Reconstruction time, throughput and average response time. We obtain the experimental results as follows. We write 100MB of data into each node via NCFS using E-MBR. We disable one of the nodes in the array to make a single node failure. We then perform the recovery operation by starting reconstruction thread, that is, reading data from surviving disks, reconstructing data, and writing data to a new node. In the meantime, client loads requests on the NCFS with the Zipf-like distribution workload mentioned above. Each result is the average value of at least three times experimental evaluation.

Impact of Alpha. The value of alpha indicates the dispersion degree of frequent access location. As we can see from Fig. 4. The lager the value of alpha is, the more centralized the hot data are. Apparently, the centralization of hot data is beneficial for data retrieval by reconstruction data stream and user access data stream simultaneously during the reconstruction process. The results show that DTemp perform over E-MBR at all alpha value in reconstruction time, throughput and average response time. As alpha value grows, the advantage expands.

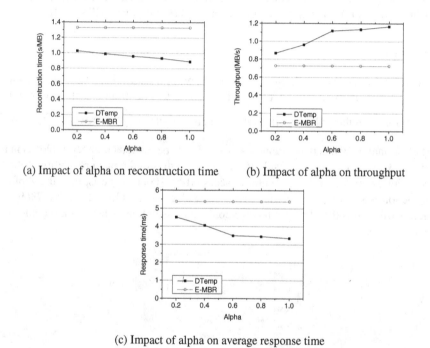

(a) Impact of alpha on reconstruction time   (b) Impact of alpha on throughput

(c) Impact of alpha on average response time

Fig. 5. Impact of alpha. E-MBR is not affected by alpha. The E-MBR curve on the graph just for comparison.

Impact of Block Size. We evaluate how different block sizes influence the reconstruction performance because block sizes directly affect I/O efficiency. Fig. 6 (a) shows the reconstruction time (s/MB) for different block sizes using conventional E-MBR and our method DTemp, respectively. We observe that as the block size increases, the reconstruction time decreases. The reason is that given the same amount of data, the block number decreases for a larger block size. In this way, the times of getting duplicate node and duplicate block are reduced greatly, which highly saves the computational cost. On the other side, average response time (Fig. 6 (c)) increase because reconstruction time of each block lengthened.

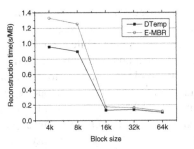
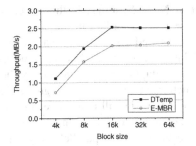

(a) Impact of block size on reconstruction time   (b) Impact of block size on throughput

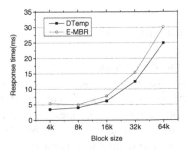

(c) Impact of block size on average response time

Fig. 6. Impact of block size

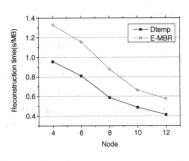
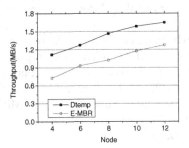

(a) Impact of node number on reconstruction time   (b) Impact of node number on throughput

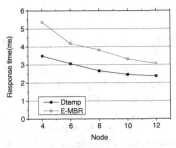

(c) Impact of node number on average response time

Fig. 7. Impact of node number

Impact of Node Number. In this paper, we only discuss E-MBR the case of (n,d) where $d = n-1$. According to the coding scheme of E-MBR, each segment contains $n(n-1)$ blocks, and every nodes own $n-1$ blocks of one segment while each of these $n-1$ has a duplicate in other $n-1$ nodes respectively. When a node corrupts, all need to do is to find the duplicate blocks and copy them to the replacement node to accomplish reconstruction. As node number grows, segment size grows as well, but segment number in one node will reduce. As a result, it leads to access reduction of duplicate block read operation on one single node but gain more nodes contributing duplicate blocks together in a parallel way. That's why with node quantity grows, reconstruction performance improves.

5   Conclusions and Future Work

In this paper, we exploit data temperature into the reconstruction process of regenerating codes, which reconstruct the hot data prior to the cold data. We implement our method, call DTemp, alongside with NCFS reconstruction mechanism. Our experimental results prove that DTemp does better performance than existing E-MBR reconstruction with up to with up to 33.17%, 60.61%, 37.77% improvement in terms of reconstruction time, throughput and average response time. We believe that there are still many directions for future research on our work. One direction is to include more regenerating code schemes to evaluate reconstruction performance using data temperature for horizontal comparison. Another idea is to investigate the impacts of DTemp in distributed storage system with real workload.

Acknowledgments. This work is supported by the National Natural Science Foundation (NSF) of China under grant (No.61272073, No. 61073064), the key program of Natural Science Foundation of Guangdong Province (no. S2013020012865), the Scientific Research Foundation for the Returned Overseas Chinese Scholars (State Education Ministry), the Educational Commission of Guangdong Province (No. 2012KJCX0013). The corresponding author of this paper is Yuhui Deng.

References

1. Ghemawat, S., Gobioff, H., Leung, S.: The Google File System. In: Proc. of ACM SOSP (December 2003)
2. DeCandia, G., Hastorun, D., Jampani, M., Kakulapati, G., Lakshman, A., Pilchin, A., Sivasubramanian, S., Vosshall, P., Vogels, W.: Dynamo: Amazon's Highly Available Key-Value Store. In: Proc. of ACM SOSP (2007)
3. Calder, B., Wang, J., Ogus, A., Nilakantan, N., Skjolsvold, A., McKelvie, S., Xu, Y., Srivastav, S., Wu, J., Simitci, H., et al.: Windows Azure Storage: A Highly Available Cloud Storage Service with Strong Consistency. In: Proc. of ACM SOSP (October 2011)
4. Rodrigues, R., Liskov, B.: High availability in DHTs: Erasure coding vs.replication. In: IPTPS (2005)

5. Weatherspoon, H., Kubiatowicz, J.D.: Erasure coding vs. replication: A quantitative comparison. In: IPTPS (2002)
6. Dimakis, A.G., Godfrey, P.B., Wu, Y., Wainwright, M., Ramchandran, K.: Network Coding for Distributed Storage Systems. IEEE Trans. on Information Theory 56(9), 4539–4551 (2010)
7. Ahlswede, R., Cai, N., Li, S.-Y.R., Yeung, R.W.: Network Information Flow. IEEE Trans. on Information Theory 46(4), 1204–1216 (2000)
8. Rashmi, K., Shah, N., Kumar, P.: Optimal Exact-Regenerating Codes for Distributed Storage at the MSR and MBR Points via a Product-Matrix Construction. IEEE Trans. on Information Theory 57(8), 5227–5239 (2011)
9. Rashmi, K.V., Shah, N.B., Kumar, P.V., Ramchandran, K.: Explicit Construction of Optimal Exact Regenerating Codes for Distributed Storage. In: Proc. of Allerton Conference (2009)
10. Suh, C., Ramchandran, K.: Exact-Repair MDS Code Construction using Interference Alignment. IEEE Trans. on Information Theory 57(3), 1425–1442 (2011)
11. Hu, Y., Yu, C.-M., Li, Y.-K., Lee, P.P.C., Lui, J.C.S.: NCFS: On the Practicality and Extensibility of a Network-Coding-Based Distributed File System. In: Proc. of NetCod (2011)
12. Duminuco, A., Biersack, E.: A Practical Study of Regenerating Codes for Peer-to-Peer Backup Systems. In: Proc. of IEEE ICDCS 2009 (2009)
13. Dimakis, A.G., Ramchandran, K., Wu, Y., Suh, C.: A survey on network codes for distributed storage. In: arXiv:1004.4438v1 [cs.IT] (2010)
14. Rashmi, K.V., Shah, N.B., Kumar, P.V.: Optimal exact-regenerating codes for distributed storage at the msr and mbr points via a productmatrix construction. In: arXiv:1005.4178v1 [cs.IT] (2010)
15. Rashmi, K.V., Shah, N.B., Kumar, P.V., Ramchandran, K.: Explicit construction of optimal exact regenerating codes for distributed storage. In: Proc. of Allerton Conference (2009)
16. Suh, C., Ramchandran, K.: Exact-repair mds codes for distributed storage using interference alignment. In: Proc. of IEEE ISIT (2010)
17. Tian, L., Feng, D., Jiang, H., Zhou, K., Zeng, L., Chen, J., Wang, Z., Song, Z.: PRO: A Popularity-based Multi-threaded Reconstruction Optimization for RAID-Structured Storage Systems. In: FAST 2007, San Jose, CA (February 2007)
18. Breslau, L.: Pei Cao, Li Fan, G. Phillips, S Shenker. Web Caching and Zipf-like Distributions: Evidence and Implications. In: Proc. of IEEE INFORCOM (March 1999)
19. Wu, Y., Dimakis, A.G., Ramchandran, K.: Deterministic Regenerating codes for distributed storage. In: Proc. Allerton Conference on Control, Computing and Communication, Urbana-Champaign, IL (September 2007)

Speedup Critical Stage of Machine Learning with Batch Scheduling in GPU

Yuan Gao, Rui Wang, Ning An, Yanjiang Wei, and Depei Qian

BeiHang University, XueYuan Road No.37 HaiDian District Beijing, China
`rui.wang@jsi.buaa.edu.cn`

Abstract. As a superior data analysis method, Machine Learning suffers the bottleneck from limited computing capability for many years. With the advent of numerous parallel computing hardwares, modern GPU is becoming a promising carrier for the tasks of Machine Learning. In this paper, we propose an efficient GPU execution framework to speedup the forward propagation process of convolution neural network. By extending the convolution unrolling method to fit this batch mode, we get a significant increase of throughput but very little overhead.

Keywords: convolution neural network, framework, GPU, batch process.

1 Introduction

With the fast-development of computer hardware, GPU has become a type of important computation carriers with dramatic speedup and better energy efficiency. More and more computing-intensive applications with natural data parallelism have been migrated to GPU environment. However, although the NVIDIA CUDA can help programmers to develop faster applications, programming on GPU is much more difficult than that on CPUs. Programmers need to determine the timing of copying the data from the host to the GPU, the number of blocks' or threads that should be divided reasonably to take full advantage of computing resources, and the size of data slice that should be allocated to each thread. It is quite difficult to develop a framework for a beginner to write efficient GPU programs in any purpose. However, research on high productivity method both in coding and in execution for special domains is promising.

2 CNN GPU Execution Framework

In this section, we take the image recognition application as an example to illustrate the operating mechanism of our framework.

2.1 Batch Process

Improving the GPU computing resource utilization is a good way to speed up the forward propagation since the computing hardware resource of GPU is quite

C.-H. Hsu et al. (Eds.): NPC 2014, LNCS 8707, pp. 522–525, 2014.

rich and forward propagation cannot take full advantage of GPU's ability if only handle one small size image at a time. What we can do, however, is to try to increase the throughput in a single task, which means the CNN processes several images in one forward propagation. The figure 1 presents the proposed framework which shows two of the most important modules: the input organization module and the convolution module. The input organization module automatically splices tiny input images into a larger one before CNN executes on GPU.

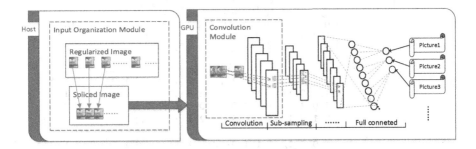

Fig. 1. Proposed GPU execution framework schematic

The convolution layer requires the most amount of the calculation and is also the optimization emphasis of our framework while the traditional convolution layer speeding up method involves unrolling convolution

In our framework, we extend the simple unfolding of a convolution technique to a batch mode which enables the convolution layer to process multiple images (input features) at the same time.

When the spliced image (input features) arrives at the convolution layer which came from the host or last layer a split operation is necessary at first. As we know, each layer of the neural network has its fixed input size that is obviously the processing layer's input size is 3×3 in the figure 2. According to this input size, the framework will split the spliced images (input features) into the standard size before unrolling convolution. The convolution operation works in a similar way except the unrolled input features from different images need to be added to the bottom of input feature matrix. As shown in the figure 2, the spliced image (input features) will be divided into nine 3×3 input features and be unrolled to a 12×12 input feature matrix and the kernel matrix is exactly same as the traditional unrolling convolution. After multiplying input features matrix by the kernel matrix, we get a 12×2 output feature matrix that is still able to find the boundary of different images. Instead of convoluting the three images in a row, the batch mode unrolls three images to one matrix and does only one multiplication to get the output features.

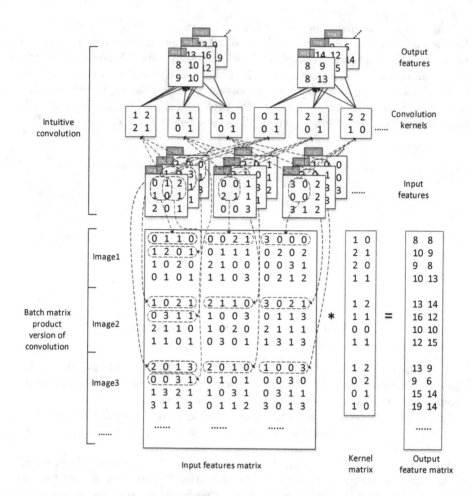

Fig. 2. Example batch mode unrolling convolution

3   Evaluation

Figure 3 and compared the execution time between the two methods, and in the experiment, the filter size is 5 and the number of output features is fixed by 10. We, however, still take the image dimension and the splicing number as variables.

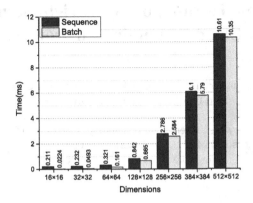

Fig. 3. Execution time for executing image convolution operations with varying image dimensions on the GPU and the splicing number is 10

4   Conclusion

In this paper, we propose an efficient neural network framework on GPU platforms. Our framework addresses the gap in abstraction between domain experts and current GPU programming frameworks, and accelerates the process of CNN forward propagation. The framework can organize the input data automatically to make use of GPU resources as much as possible for better performance. We demonstrate the advantage of our framework in each CNN phase with five experiments. According to the power of GPU, framework can extremely increasing the throughput of CNN. The optimization method that we adopt in the framework doesn't modify the structure of CNN or require training extra neurons, which can combine with other optimization method to achieve better performance.

Acknowledgment. This research is supported by 863 Program of China under grant 2012AA010902, and by the NSFC under grant 61133004, 61073011, 61202425, and Huawei company under grant No.YB2012120105.

The New Territory of Lightweight Security in a Cloud Computing Environment

Shu-Ching Wang[1], Shih-Chi Tseng[1], Hsin-Met Chuan[2],
Kuo-Qin Yan[1,*], and Szu-Hao Tsai[1]

[1] Chaoyang University of Technology, Taiwan, R.O.C.
{scwang,s10314901,kqyan,s9914603}@cyut.edu.tw
[2] Hsing-Kuo University, Taiwan, R.O.C.
hn88780752@yahoo.com.tw

Abstract. The cloud computing is an Internet-based resource sharing system in which virtualized resources are provided over the Internet. Cloud computing refers to a class of systems and applications that employ distributed resources for use in various applications; these computing resources are utilized over a network to facilitate the execution of tasks. However, cloud computing resources are heterogeneous and dynamic, connecting a broad range of resources. Thus, there are a large numbers of application and data center in the cloud computing environment. Therefore, the security issues of authentication and communication in application services and data center need to be considered in the cloud computing environment

Result

In this study, two security methods for client user are presented. (1) Group Key Authentication (GKA) is proposed for user to obtain the services from multiple servers quickly. And. (2) Authentication and Authorization within Two Factors (AATF) provides a more stringent authentication and authorization, and the security of cloud computing can be enhanced.

In a cloud-computing environment, each cloud service provider provides an authentication key to the user [3]. By using GKA, an authentication group key is generated by combining a set of authentication keys for different service providers at the same time. The generating steps of GKA are depicted in Fig. 1.

1. Group Key Req.: The user requests the Group Key.
2. ID Req.: AUTH Server requests the User's ID for identification when the server receives the Group Key Req.
3. ID Res.: User sends the account name and password to AUTH server to identify user.
4. Auth. ACK (Success/Failure): AUTH Server sends a message for User to notice the authentication is success or fail.
5. Services Sel.: If authentication is success, then User selects the services that user needed. In addition, a requirement is sent to AUTH server.

---

* Corresponding author.

C.-H. Hsu et al. (Eds.): NPC 2014, LNCS 8707, pp. 526–529, 2014.

6. Key Req.: After AUTH Server receives the service request, it will send the Key Request and ID to Service Servers.

7. Key Res.: When Service Server receives the request and ID, an authentication key is generated, and the key and ID are stored. In addition, Service Server sends the authentication key to AUTH Server. When AUTH Server receives the authentication key; then the Group Key will be assembled and stored.

When the user authentication group key is established, a one-time identity verification for several services is available to users. The format of Group Key = (SERVICE$_1$||SERVICE$_2$||... ||SERVICE$_n$||ID). If a new service requirement is presented by user, the key of the certification of the new service will be given, and the new authentication key is combined to the GK. Moreover, every authentication key is generated by Service Server randomly.

AATF security mechanism for the user during authentication and authorization process is used to strengthen the legitimacy of authenticating users and improve the security of user accounts. The execution flow of AATF is shown in Fig. 2.

Step 1. The user generates a set of random numbers, and then a random number RN with Request sent to the application server side.

Step 2. Application server-side receives a random number RN with Request, return the SC to the user, and will direct users to the authentication server-side.

Step 3. Users will send UN, PWD and SC to the authentication server-side for authenticating.

Step 4. When the authentication is successful, the authentication server-side will sent the AuT and S to the user, if authentication fails then return a failure message to the user.

Step 5. The receiving AuT and S by user will be retrieved in accordance with the number of RN to generate sRN, and then S and sRN are sent to the application server-side authentication.

Step 6. The compare action of authentication and authorization will be started when application server received the S and sRN; the ApT is returned to user when authentication and authorization is passing; if fail, the fail message is returned.

Step 7. When Users receive the ApT, ApT and AuT are combined into a Token, and then Token can be passed to the application for using the service.

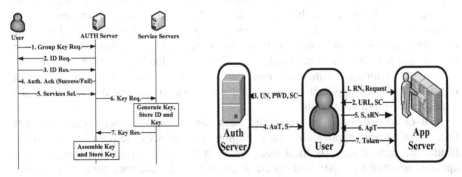

Fig. 1. Group Key generating   **Fig. 2.** The processes of AATF

There are a lot of services and users in the cloud computing environment, will be carried out to verify the identity through authentication and authorization protocol [4]. Therefore, the authentication and authorization are always making in cloud computing environments. When authentication and authorization requires a lot of steps and a large number of parameters, data exchange will be increased and the amount of resources needed to make authentication and authorization will be increased. Therefore, the number of steps, the total number of parameters and the amount of data exchanges will be used for comparison. Then, the authentication protocols proposed in this study can be verified as the lightweight computing security protocols. Form Table 1, the steps of certification, the total number of parameters and the amount of data exchange of GKA by AATF are less than OAuth [1] and the SAML[1].

Table 1. The comparisons with OAuth and SAML

	Step (times)	Parameter	Data Exchange
OAuth	10	11	30/time
SAML	8	12	14/time
GKA	7	4	8/time
AATF	7	11	13/time

Overall, our proposed lightweight security mechanisms can provide the security of information and communication and authentication, without wasting computing resources to enhance the security of cloud computing environment. Therefore, Group Key Authentication (GKA) is used to provide the services that users can quickly obtain multiple servers to improve security by reducing the transmission of secret information in the cloud computing environment. GKA also can reduced the number of users must be logged conversion services and waiting time. Authentication and Authorization within Two Factors (AATF) in the cloud computing environment at both ends of the server-side two-factor authentication through the authentication server-side services can provide more stringent authentication and authorization in order to verify the legitimacy of the identity of the user to enhance the cloud computing security.

Cloud computing is a concept in distributed systems. It is currently used mainly in business applications in which computers cooperate to perform a specific service together. In addition, the Internet applications are continuously enhanced with multimedia, and vigorous development of the device quickly occurs in the network system. As network bandwidth and quality outstrip computer performance, various communication and computing technologies previously regarded as being of different domains can now be integrated, such as telecommunication, multimedia, information technology, and construction simulation. Therefore, cloud computing is currently used many commodity computers that can cooperate to perform a specific service together [2]. Thus, applications associated with network integration have gradually attracted considerable attention.

In a cloud-computing environment, users can access the operational capability faster with Internet application, and the computer systems have the high stability to handle the service requests from many users in the environment [5]. Today, a new application service of operation system is emerged and it changes the user's usage in the past. Originally, the Internet infrastructure is continuous grow that many application services can be provided in the Internet. The reliability is improved in a cloud computing by using the low-power hosts. In addition, cloud computing has greatly encouraged distributed system design and application to support user-oriented service applications. Furthermore, there are a large number of cloud applications and data centers provided in the cloud computing environment, so the information and communications, and authentication is one of the important security issue that must be considered. In other words, the security is one of the most important aspects of cloud computing as it ensures overall reliability and fluency. To ensure the cloud computing is safety, a mechanism to ensure the security of information and communication is thus necessary.

Therefore, Group Key Authentication (GKA) is used to provide the services that users can quickly obtain multiple servers to improve security by reducing the transmission of secret information in the cloud computing environment. GKA also can reduced the number of users must be logged conversion services and waiting time. Authentication and Authorization within Two Factors (AATF) in the cloud computing environment at both ends of the server-side two-factor authentication through the authentication server-side services can provide more stringent authentication and authorization in order to verify the legitimacy of the identity of the user to enhance the cloud computing security.

Through the above description, the proposed method can enhance the security in the cloud-computing environment. According to the characteristics of cloud computing, by using the proposed methods, the cost of resources can be reduced and the quality of service can be improved. The proposed security mechanisms can meet the cloud computing security step to ensure that users and service providers to enjoy the security of cloud computing environment with the service provider.

Acknowledgments. This work was supported in part by the Ministry of Science and Technology MOST 102-2221-E-324-008 and MOST 103-2221-E-324-025.

References

1. Almulla, S.A., Chan, Y.Y.: Cloud computing security management. In: the 2nd International Engineering Systems Management and Its Application, pp. 1–7 (April 2010)
2. Bertram, S., Boniface, M., Surridge, M., Bricombe, N., Hall, M.M.: On-demand dynamic security for risk-based secure collaboration in clouds. In: the 3rd IEEE Cloud Computing, pp. 515–525 (July 2010)
3. Gong, Y., Ying, Z., Lin, M.: A survey of cloud computing. Lecture Notes in Electrical Engineering, vol. 225, pp. 79–84 (2013)
4. Jensen, M., Schwenk, J., Gruschka, N., Iacono, L.L.: On technical security issues in cloud computing. In: The IEEE International Conference on Cloud Computing, pp. 109–116 (2009)
5. Ramgovind, S., Eloff, M.M., Smith, E.: The management of security in cloud computing. In: The Information Security for South Africa (ISSA), pp. 1–7 (August 2010)

DP: Dynamic Prepage in Postcopy Migration for Fixed-Size Data Load

Shuang Wu, Ce Yang, Jianhai Chen, Qinming He, and Bei Wang

College of Computer Science, Zhejiang University, Zheda Rd. 38, Hangzhou 310027, China
{catting,yvxiang,chenjh919,hqm,wangbei}@zju.edu.cn

Abstract. Postcopy migration is a mature technology in virtualization. However the performance of postcopy is not stable. We find many memory intensive loads having a high proportion of independent fixed-size data (FSD) cases. To improve migration performance, we present DP: an algorithm which applies to intelligently tackle FSD load during postcopy migration. We implement DP as an online algorithm triggered by remote paging, and adjusting to prepage the most appropriate amount of pages related to recent page fault records. DP also has a threshold processing mechanism to prevent from noise which is derived from load size fluctuation. The experimental results show that DP algorithm can significantly reduce response time and implicit downtime in postcopy migration, with an high improvement on QoS.

1 Postcopy Migration

Postcopy migration[1,2] is one of the common methods in VM live migration. It forces to move the running VM to target side, then fetches pages from source side when page fault occurs, and pushes the remaining pages to target side at the same time.

In this paper we target to improve migration performance by reducing the response time for each page fault in postcopy migration, using a prepage method. Response time is bottleneck for migration. It is the time waiting for fetching pages from source side when page fault occurs. A proper prepage method can fetch a proper amount of pages in advance, and reduce the response time for each case.

2 Fixed-Size Data

We build up the model for FSD load. It has many independent cases and every case needs a certain amount of memory pages N to complete its work. If we fetch enough pages (more than N), page fault will not occur during the current case.

In practical situations, some cases in FSD-like load need a different amount of pages, which we called noises. Generalized FSD load should have a low *NoiseRate*.

There are many domains in real benchmark which can be magnified as fig.1. below. These domains show the characteristic of FSD with some noises.

C.-H. Hsu et al. (Eds.): NPC 2014, LNCS 8707, pp. 530–533, 2014.

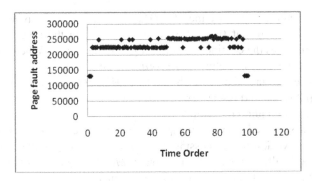

Fig. 1. The FSD-like domains. Page fault addresses are placed in a narrow range.

3   Dynamic Prepage

The purpose of DP is to fetch the most suitable amount of pages before next page fault in a noisy environment. We set a range for guessing from *NMin* to *NMax*, try to include the best amount *N*. Every time we try to fetch an estimated value which called *NTest*, we should decide which range it belongs to, and modify the limit value *NMin* and *NMax* cautiously.

Step 1: We divide the guess result into two situations. If the current page fault address is continuous with the pages we fetched the last time, then they belong to the same case, expressed as (1) below. And the opposite situation expressed as (2).

$$AddrsLast \pm NLast \begin{cases} = Addrs & (1) \\ \neq Addrs & (2) \end{cases}$$

A guessing result *NTest* is smaller than *N* or larger than *N*. The smaller one goes into step 2, and the larger one jump into step 3.

Step 2: From step 1 we get the conclusion $NTest < N$. But now we cannot trust this conclusion immediately. The modify of *NMin* should be very cautious, because we need a reliable value to make sure the subsequent guess is not out of range.

We introduce a new array *MinRecord[5]* to save the recent five *NTest*, and *MinHit* for the continuous times of going into step 2.

When *MinHit* reaches five, we choose the smallest value in *MinRecord[5]* as *NMin*. If noises in record is smaller than *N*, they will not affect the correct conclusion. Otherwise they must be larger than *N*. We avoid these noises by choosing the smallest one in record. Only noises are continuous for five times can lead us to wrong conclusion. Actually the rate of misguidance is related to *NoiseRate* and continuous times we choose to refresh *NMin* as expression 3.

$$Rate_{misguidance} = NoiseRate^{continuous\ times}. \tag{3}$$

When continuous times is 5, we can get a low rate of misguidance about 3.2%, even though *NoiseRate* is up to 50%. This makes the modify of *NMin* credible.

Then we jump into step 4.

Step 3: Similar to step 2, we modify *NMax* cautiously. An array *MaxRecord[5]* to keep records of the recent five *NTest* when it placed in the range between *N* and *NMax*. *MaxHit* saves the continuous times of going into step 3. When MaxHit reaches five we choose the largest one in *MaxRecord[5]* to be *NMax*.

Every time executing step 3, we should reset *MinHit* to zero. Similarly when starting from step 2 we should reset *MaxHit* to zero.

Then the program jump into step 5.

Step 4: Our purpose is to rapidly narrow the gap between *NMin* and *NMax*, and also correctly. So we adjust our guessing value *NTest* according to the current *MinHit*.

We fetch a smaller amount of pages when *MinHit* is close to the predetermined threshold. Otherwise a large adjustment as equation 4.

$$NLast = \frac{NMax - NTest_{last}}{2 \times MinHit}.$$ (4)

NLast is the amount we fetch this time and as a parameter transferred to the next round. *NTest_{last}* is the value last round we guessed. So that *NTest* can be calculated as equation 5.

$$NTest = NTest_{last} + NLast.$$ (5)

Then we get the amount of pages and return to Step 1.

Step 5: This time we try to rapidly narrow the gap from the NMax side.

We fetch the amount of pages closer to *NMax* when *MaxHit* is close to the predetermined threshold. Otherwise a further address from *NMax* as equation 6.

$$NTest = NTest_{last} - \frac{NTest_{last} - NMin}{2 \times MaxHit}.$$ (6)

Then set the *NLast* equal to *NTest* and return to Step 1.

Strategy of guessing process is as fig. 2. below. *MinHit* and *MaxHit* decide the next position of our guess. The purpose of recording hit times is to rapidly and reliably modify the limit both minimum side and maximum side. Each time going into Step 4 or Step 5, the opposite hit times will reset to zero.

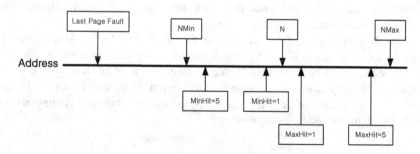

Fig. 2. The way adjusting *NTest* in both smaller side and larger side. Also the amount that we fetch is relating to *MinHit* or *MaxHit*. In this figure we see the different position of next guessing when *MinHit* = 1 and *MinHit* = 5. The same way that *MaxHit* works.

The complexity of DP algorithm is O(N), N is for the rounds of page fault in the whole migration.

4   Experimental Evaluation

We use simulation and benchmark ways to evaluate DP algorithm. In simulation experiment DP algorithm works well with the deviation below 0.05 when noisy rate is lower than 20 as fig.3. below.

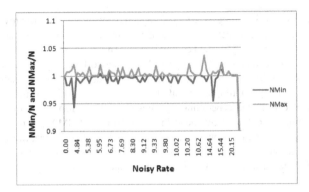

Fig. 3. Noisy rate and the result of *NMin*/N and *NMax*/N after DP algrithm in simulation experiment. Vertical axis shows the result of *NMin* and *NMax*, N is always set to be 1. Horizontal axis means the noisy rate for one case.

We add DP algorithm into postcopy migration and test the new migration on QEMU1.4 [3], Xeon CPU 2.13GHz, 16GB memory and gigabit network. In benchmark way we use STREAM [4] which is a FSD-like benchmark. And DP algorithm can reduce 33% response time in benchmark test.

Acknowledgments. This research is partly supported by the key Science and Technology Innovation Team Fund of Zhejiang under Grant~(No.\ 2010R50041).

References

1. Hines, M.R., Deshpande, U., Gopalan, K.: Post-copy live migration of virtual machines. ACM SIGOPS Operating Systems Review 43(3), 14–26 (2009)
2. Hirofuchi, T., Nakada, H., Itoh, S., et al.: Reactive consolidation of virtual machines enabled by postcopy live migration. In: Proceedings of the 5th International Workshop on Virtualization Technologies in Distributed Computing, pp. 11–18. ACM (2011)
3. McCalpin, J.D.: STREAM: Sustainable memory bandwidth in high performance computers. Silicon Graphics Inc. (1995)
4. QEMU, http://www.qemu.org/

Capacity Region of Wireless Network Coding

Jun Zhang and Shu-Tao Xia

Graduate School at Shenzhen, Tsinghua University, Shenzhen, China
zhangjun.zero@gmail.com, xiast@sz.tsinghua.edu.cn

Abstract. Network coding is a highly regarded technology for improving the capacity of wireless networks. COPE-sys network coding is an easily implemented and widely studied coding system. This paper studies the maximum throughput that can be supported by COPE-sys network coding over a practical CSMA/CA medium access control (MAC) protocol. Traditional method of analyzing capacity is multi-commodity flow (MCF) formulation, which assumes impractical centralized scheduling. We enhanced MCF formulation by taking into account the collision overhead in the distributed CSMA/CA protocol, to compute the maximum throughput. To the best of our knowledge, this paper is the first rigorous theoretical study of the achievable capacity over a multi-hop CSMA/CA based wireless network coding system.

1 Introduction

We develop a method to integrate CSMA/CA MAC analysis with the MCF formulation. We enhance traditional MCF clique constraints by utilizing the maximum normalized throughput. Our method can give a tighter upper bound of the network coding throughput over the CSMA/CA MAC. We also give an achievable lower bound of the network throughput by analyzing conflict within cliques and inter-cliques.

2 Capacity Region over CSMA/CA MAC

2.1 Throughput Analysis

The wireless network discussed in this paper is assumed to be a static, multihop wireless network where all nodes are single-channel single-radio and all antennas are omnidirectional. Let p_t denote the transmission probability for each node in any time slot. A time slot at the MAC layer could be an empty backoff time slot, a period associated with successful transmission, or a period associated with collision [1]. The length of a time slot equals to one physical time slot T_{idle} if the channel is idle, or the packet transmission time T_s if the channel is experiencing a successful transmission, or the packet collision time T_c if a collision happens. Let p_{idle}, p_s, and p_c denote the probabilities of seeing an idle slot, a successful transmission slot, and a collision slot, respectively. Let ε_i denote the number of native packets in an encoded transmission.

C.-H. Hsu et al. (Eds.): NPC 2014, LNCS 8707, pp. 534–537, 2014.
© IFIP International Federation for Information Processing 2014

Let L_p denote the payload size of a native packet and C the spectrum bandwidth. The normalized throughput S are expressed as

$$S = \frac{\sum_{i=1}^{N}[p_t(1-p_t)^{N-1} \times \varepsilon_i] \times L_p}{C \times (p_{idle} \times T_{idle} + p_s \times T_s + p_c \times T_c)} \qquad (1)$$

We use a Markov chain to compute ε_i. To obtain the maximum channel utilization and normalized throughput, we can determine p_t according to $\frac{d}{dp_t}R_s\Big|_{p_t=p_t^*} = 0$. The maximum normalized throughput can be computed as

$$S^* = \frac{\sum_{i=1}^{N}[p_t^*(1-p_t^*)^{N-1} \times \frac{n_i M}{M+1}] \times L_p}{C \times (p_{idle}^* \times T_{idle} + p_s^* \times T_s + p_c^* \times T_c)} \qquad (2)$$

2.2   Upper Bound

Suppose that there are k given commodities with pairs $\{s_x, t_x\}$, where $s_x, t_x \in V$ are source and destination for commodity x respectively. Let $\mathcal{F}_x$ denote the set of s_x-t_x flows. A k-flow is a sequence of flows $< f_1, f_2, ..., f_k >$ with $f_x \in \mathcal{F}_x$, x=1, 2, ... , k. The classic MCF formulation without considering the wireless interference is expressed as [2]

$$\max \sum_{i=1}^{k} val(f_x) \qquad (3)$$

$$f_x \in \mathcal{F}_x, x = 1,2, ..., k, \qquad (4)$$

$$(\sum_{x=1}^{k} f_x) \oslash \mathcal{B} \in \mathcal{P}, \qquad (5)$$

A clique in NC network in the conflict graph is a set of vertices that mutually conflict with each other. Note that a vertice in conflict graph in NC network may represent a hyperarc. In a clique at most one hyperarc can transmit at a time. Suppose that there are R maximal cliques in the conflict graph $\mathcal{G}$, denoted as $C_1, C_2, ..., C_R$, respectively. If a hyperarc (i, J) within a maximal clique is allocated the transmission time of t_{iJ} during the whole clique transmission interval T, the upper bound of the maximum network throughput can be solved by augmenting the basic MCF formulation with the clique constraint (6)

$$\sum_{(i,J)\in C_u} \sum_{(i,j)\in(i,J)} \frac{1}{B_{ij}} \sum_{1\le x\le k} f_{xij} \le |J| \quad u = 1, 2, ..., R \qquad (6)$$

Let $\hat{F}$ denote the upper bound of the MCF throughput based on the clique constraint. We have the following theorem about a tighter upper bound of the network throughput over the CSMA/CA MAC.

Theorem 1. A tighter upper bound of the optimal throughput of a wireless NC network based on a CSMA/CA MAC protocol is $\hat{X} = (S^*\hat{F})/|J|$.

Proof: Since simultaneous transmissions will not be successful under the CSMA/CA protocol within a clique, the maximum normalized throughput over a maximal clique is upper-bounded by S^*. Then the clique constraint under CSMA/CA MAC is now expressed as

$$\sum_{(i,j)\in C_u,} \sum_{(i,j)\in(i,j)} \frac{1}{B_{ij}} \sum_{1\leq x\leq k} x_{xij} \leq S^* \quad u = 1, 2, \dots, R \tag{7}$$

If we define $f_{xij} = \left(\frac{x_{xij}}{S^*}\right)|J|$, the new MCF formulation with the constraint of (7) is then transformed back to the original clique-based MCF formulation assuming a centralized scheduling (6). Therefore, the optimal throughput is $\hat{X} = (S^*\hat{F})/|J|$

2.3   CSMA/CA Area and CSMA/CA Clique

A circle with a diameter of X' is termed as a CSMA/CA area, where X' denote interference range. Considering that we adopt the protocol interference model, we define a CSMA/CA clique as follows: let $\mathcal{A}_C$ denote the CSMA/CA area and $i \in \mathcal{A}_C$ denote that node i is within the CSMA/CA area $\mathcal{A}_C$. The clique C consists of hyperarcs satisfying that source node of the hyperarc is within $\mathcal{A}_C$ or all the destination nodes of the hyperarc are within $\mathcal{A}_C$. We have the following lemma regarding the maximum normalized throughput over a CSMA/CA area and the associated CSMA/CA clique (the proof is ignored due to the limit of space).

Lemma 1. The total normalized throughput over a CSMA/CA clique can be transformed to that over the CSMA/CA area defining the clique, and vice versa. Thus, the maximum normalized throughput over a CSMA/CA clique is S^*

2.4   Lower Bound

The fundamental reason that the clique-based MCF formulation gives an upper bound, which may not be achievable, is that the interference among the cliques in the multihop context can not be described by the clique constraint. Considering inter-clique interference over each clique, we have the following theorem about a lower bound of the network throughput.

Theorem 2. For a uniform network, a lower bound of the optimal throughput over the CSMA/CA MAC is $\tilde{X} = \frac{\pi*(x')^2}{(\max\{\cup\{D_w\}\})*4}\hat{X}$, $w \in Nei\{i\}$, where X' denotes the interference range, D_i denotes the area of the circle center at node i, i can be any node in the network, and $\hat{X}$ is the upper bound given in Theorem 1. Thus, the lower bound is at least $\frac{\pi*(x')^2}{(\max\{\cup\{D_w\}\})*4}$ of the maximum capacity X^*.

Proof: From lemma 1, we can transform the total throughput over a CSMA/CA clique C to the associated CSMA/CA area $\mathcal{A}_C$. Let $D(\mathcal{A}_C)$ denotes the area of $\mathcal{A}_C$. If nodes are uniformly distributed with a density of ρ, the number of nodes contained in $\mathcal{A}_C$ is $\rho D(\mathcal{A}_C)$, each node $i \in \mathcal{A}_C$ can achieve the throughput of $S^*/\rho D(\mathcal{A}_C)$.

Suppose node A transmits to its neighbors. To ensure all destination nodes are free of conflict, all the circles centered at these destination nodes with radius of x' should be consider as one CSMA/CA area, as shown in Fig. 1. Then the number of nodes contained in this CSMS/CA area is $\rho * (D_B \cup D_C \cup D_D \cup D_E) = \rho * \cup \{D_w\}, w \in Nei\{A\}$, Then a lower bound of the achievable throughput of the tagged node A is $S^*/\rho * \cup \{D_w\}$. Considering all the nodes contained in $\mathcal{A}_C$, a lower bound of the achievable throughput of any node in $\mathcal{A}_C$ is $S^*/\rho * \max\{\cup \{D_w\}\}$.

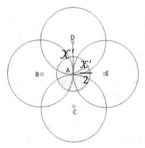

Fig. 1. Possible interference on a clique

In a uniform network, all nodes have the same stochastic behavior, therefore the same achievable throughput. Thus, the lower bound of the total achievable throughput over a CSMA/CA area, with inter-clique interference taken into account, is

$$\tilde{S} = \rho D(\mathcal{A}_C) \times \frac{S^*}{\rho * \max\{\cup \{D_w\}\}} = S^* \frac{\pi(\frac{x'}{2})^2}{\rho * \max\{\cup \{D_w\}\}} \tag{8}$$

$$= \frac{\pi * (x')^2}{(\max\{\cup \{D_w\}\}) * 4} S^*$$

Therefore, the total throughput S over a CSMA/CA clique C is achievable if $S \le \frac{\pi*(x')^2}{(\max\{\cup\{D_w\}\})*4} S^*, w \in Nei\{i\}, i \in C$. Regarding the total throughput over the whole network, we have theorem 2.

References

1. Bianchi, G.: Performance analysis of the IEEE 802.11 distributed coordination function. IEEE J. Sel. Areas Commun. 18(3), 535–547 (2000)
2. Zhou, J., Xia, S., Jiang, Y., Zheng, H., Cui, L.: Maximum Multiflow in Wireless Network Coding. IEICE Trans. Fundamental Theories for Communications E96-B(7), 1780–1790 (2013)

Tacked Link List - An Improved Linked List for Advance Resource Reservation

Li-bing Wu[1,2], Jing Fan[1], Lei Nie[1,2], and Bing-yi Liu[1]

[1] School of Computer, Wuhan University, Wuhan 430072, China
[2] State Key Laboratory of Software Engineering, Wuhan University, Wuhan, China
wu@whu.edu.cn

Abstract. Since advance resource reservation is a widely used mechanism in distributed systems and high-performance networks, the optimization of its performance has been greatly concerned. And the performance of the data structure plays an important role for the overall performance of the advance resource reservation. In this paper, the authors figured out the disadvantages in the existing data structures used in advance resource reservation and proposed an improved data structure called 'tacked list', to overcome these disadvantages. To demonstrate the performance of this improved data structure, the authors made mathematical analysis to explore the tradeoff between performance and cost. At last, the result of the simulation experiments show that the improved data structure can highly improve the performance of the whole reservation system at the starting up phase and still have a relatively good performance at the stable phase.

1 Model

Admittedly, the linked list could solve the problem that the query operation needs to traverse the data too many times in advance resource reservation. Based on the linked list, the indexed link list could improve the locating operation by introduce the index array and it has better performance than other data structures in advance resource reservation which has already been proved in previous article [3].

However, the index linked list still has some disadvantages. At the start phase, the index linked list needs to traverse backwards on each index to find the position of a certain value if the index has no value before. To solve this problem, we try to eliminate traversing from previous index point by adding a dummy node in the tacked link. The topology of these two structures is shown in figure 1.

2 Performance Analysis

The tacked list utilizes the index array to locate the target node, so the overall performance of tacked list is closely related to the size of the index array. Although a large index size can significantly promote the locating speed, it also increases the difficulty

C.-H. Hsu et al. (Eds.): NPC 2014, LNCS 8707, pp. 538–541, 2014.

of maintenance at the same time. We can figure out that the cost of each query operation match with formula 1.

$$Cost = C + D_{node} + \frac{2TR_{m1}}{t} + \frac{2d(R_{m2} + W_m)}{t} + \frac{tC_{release}}{2T} \qquad (1)$$

R_{m1} means the average time cost on traversal operation of each index node for locating the start point. R_{m2} and W_m mean the cost on traversing and modifying the value node. The $Cost_{release}$ means the time of the memory release operation. T means the interval between two index and t means the interval between two requests. d means the average duration of the requests.

We can minimum the cost of each query operation by set an optimal interval between two index nodes.

3   Simulation

The following experiments runs on the Intel(R) Pentium(R) CPU G2020 @ 2.90GHz dual-core CPU with 4GB memory. And the Operation System is Windows 7 Service Pack 1 64bit. The test programs is written by C++ and compiled with MinGW in eclipse. Since the main point of this paper is concentrated on the performance of the data structure, all of the reservation requests are pre-generate requests. And the reservation system will read them from the memory immediately to ignore the network influence. The other details will be described before each experiment.

The difference between tacked list and indexed list are analyzed in this section. the experiment contain the start-up performance test and the stable performance test. From the experiment, we notice that the mainly improvement of the tacked list is the performance during the start-up phase.

In the start-up performance test, we will record the processing time of the first 20 requests for these two data structures with different index size. From the analysis in the previous part, the processing time has no correlation with the time limited by reservation system, so the maximum of the reservation time is set to a relatively large value, 1048576 (220). In this way, we can make the parameter T to change precisely with the size of the index array. Furthermore, in order to get an accurate processing time, the system generated 20000 random requests at first and these requests were divided into 1000 groups. And the system also initialized 1000 instances of each data structure in advance. Then the system inserted the requests of each group into each instance of the data structure. After all the 1000 groups have been processed, the system will record the total processing time. The interval between two requests and the duration of every request are 4 time units. The results are shown in figure 2.

Since there is no backward search operation for the index nodes in the tacked list, the processing time is relatively stable along with index size growth. However in the indexed list, the processing time in the start-up phase increases linearly with the size growth of the index array.

In the stable performance test, the system generated 100 thousands requests at the beginning. To eliminate the influence of the start-up phase, the data structure will be fully filled before recording the processing time. To fill the data structure, the system will read a part of these requests until the time of the reservation system pass the reservation limit. After the data structure is fully filled, the system will process all of the 100 thousands requests again and record the processing time. The interval between two requests and the duration of them are the same as in the start-up performance test. The result is shown in figure 3.

Since the operations of these two data structures are highly similar in the stable phase, their performance with different index size is also highly similar. These are reflected in figure 3 and their average processing time are 297.3ms for tacked list and 297.0ms for indexed list.

After the comparison with the indexed list, the final test is the system capacity test. In this test we try to find the system capacity of the tacked list. In order to make the results more intuitive, there will be some comparison tests among indexed list, tacked list, time slot array and RRB+ tree. There are else some other data structures using for advance resource reservation, but they has already been researched comparatively [3].

In this test, the system will generate 1 million requests in advance. The duration range of these requests is from 30 seconds to 1800 seconds. The reservation time limit is 432000 seconds (5 days) after the received time. To make every request be accepted, the quantity of resource in every request is set to 1 unit and the max resource quantity is set to UINT_MAX. And the size of the index array is set to a relatively high value, 108000, to fit the high-traffic situation. During the test, the system will run two threads at the same time, one for reservation and one for recording.

From figure 4, we can find that the performance of the time slot array was very stable, because the only influential factor is the average duration of all requests. On the other hand, the performances of the other three data structures gradually decreased over time. This is because these data structures have very simple structures after the initialization. But with the requests filled in, their structures will become complex and the performances decrease. This will continue until it achieves the balance point that the old nodes become failed at the same speed of new nodes inserted.

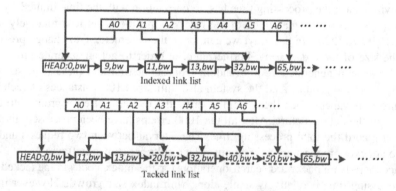

Fig. 1. Topology of indexed list and tacked list

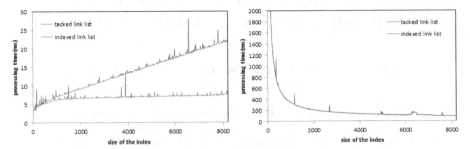

Fig. 2. Start-up performance   **Fig. 3.** Stable performance

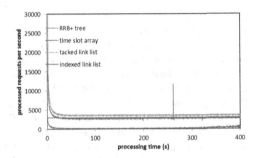

Fig. 4. System capacity test

4   Conclusion

After all of these analyses and experiment, we find that the tacked list has a much better performance at the start-up phase than indexed list. And in the stable phase the performance of tacked list is similar to the indexed list.

Acknowledgments. This work is supported by National Science Foundation of China (No. 61170017, 61272112), Science & Technology Plan of Wuhan city (No. 2013010501010146.) and the Fundamental Research Funds for the Central University (No. 2014211020202.)

References

1. Burchard, L.-O.: Analysis of data structures for admission control of advance reservation requests. IEEE Transactions on Knowledge and Data Engineering 17(3), 413–424 (2005)
2. Wu, L., Yu, T., He, Y., Li, F.: Index linked list suited for resource reservation. Journal of Wut (Information & Management Engineering) 33(6), 904–908 (2011) (in Chinese)
3. Yu, T.: Research of Data Structures and Algorithms on the Reservation of Grid Resource. M.Sc. Thesis. Wuhan University, China (2012)

CFIO2: Overlapping Communications and I/O with Computations Using RDMA Technology

Cheng Zhang, Xiaomeng Huang, Yong Hu, Shizhen Xu, Haohuan Fu, and Guangwen Yang

Ministry of Education Key Laboratory for Earth System Modeling, Center for Earth System Science, Tsinghua University, 100084, and Joint Center for Global Change Studies, Beijing, 100875, China zhangcheng12@mails.tsinghua.edu.cn

Abstract. The output data produced by numerical climate model simulations have increased greatly in complexity and size. The exploding volume of climate data is becoming a challenge for climate scientists. Our previous work, Climate Fast Input/Output (CFIO) library, implemented a two-phase I/O method to overlap I/O with computations, and achieved high throughput. In this paper, we present CFIO2, which can overlap communications with computations using Remote Direct Memory Access(RDMA) technology. We design a simple communication interactions model to implement asynchronous and concurrent data transfer. The experimental results show that CFIO2 can provide higher throughput than CFIO and can shorten the overall simulation time for climate model significantly.

1 System Architecture

CFIO [1] [2] utilizes a two-phase I/O method to offload its I/O tasks. MPI processes in CFIO are divided into two parts: I/O clients and I/O servers. When using CFIO in climate models, the clients are assigned for computation, and servers for I/O. After completion of several simulation steps, clients forward all output data to servers, and continue their next simulation step immediately. The I/O tasks are offload to servers, and servers execute I/O tasks by invoking PnetCDF interface separately. Thus, CFIO can overlap I/O with computations.

The data transfer between clients and servers, which is called communication phase as well in this paper, takes considerable time in overall simulation. The data transfer method of CFIO is to call MPI interfaces of send and receive correspondingly. It's obviously a synchronous way so this phase can not be overlapped. CFIO had also attempted to communicate asynchronously using multi-threads, but great impair is encountered due to competition of resources including CPU and network. In this work, our target is to overlap the communication phase with the computation phase as well.

To eliminate communication overhead on client side, we introduce a RDMA communication layer to CFIO, constructing CFIO2 as figure 1 illustrates. Using RDMA write/read operations, connected client and server could access the

C.-H. Hsu et al. (Eds.): NPC 2014, LNCS 8707, pp. 542–545, 2014.
© IFIP International Federation for Information Processing 2014

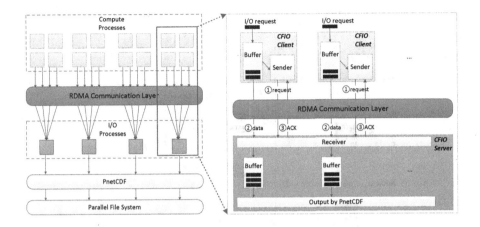

Fig. 1. The system architecture of CFIO2

memory of each other directly. What important is those access actions will not interrupt the process or occupy the CPU of the peer side. So asynchronous communication can be implemented.

Overlapping of communications and I/O with computations can be achieved via this asynchronous communication. Client just asynchronously posts I/O request by writing it's memory descriptor to server, and turns back to next computation phase immediately, without waiting for the completion of later communication and I/O. Server fetches output data from client's memory according to that descriptor, and acknowledges client about the completion of data transfer, both with asynchronous RDMA operations. Therefore, communication phase and I/O phase are both invisible at client's view.

2   Communication Interactions

To support RDMA communications, two kinds of memory region are registered at each process. One is used to buffer the output data, named data buffer. Another one is used to record key addresses of data buffer, start address as an example. We call this memory region as address buffer or descriptor of data buffer.

Figure 2 illustrates the scenario of communication interactions between one client and one server. Client (1) products some output data after one computation phase, which is stored in an area ranging from address *used* to address *free* of data buffer; (2) updates address buffer using the key addresses of data buffer, and importantly, changes flag to *1*; (3) copies the content of its address buffer to server's address buffer with RDMA write; and (4) turns to next computation phase immediately. Server (3) finds that flag of its address buffer is changed from *0* to *1*, recognizing that there are output data prepared for I/O. Then, it (5)

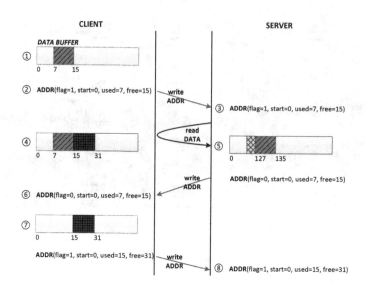

Fig. 2. An example of communication interactions between client and server

posts requests of RDMA read to get data from client according to the content of address buffer. Once all output data is fetched or local data buffer is full, (6) server updates its address buffer, changes its flag back to *0*, and writes content of address buffer to client. This address buffer describes which area of client's data buffer has been read. Client (7) updates its arguments of data buffer according to newly updated address buffer, noticed the change of flag. It then (8) updates address buffer and posts a write request again.

3   Results

We performed experiments on the *Explore*100 cluster of Tsinghua University. Each cluster node contains 2 2.93GHz Intel Xeon X5670 6-core processers, and 32G or 48G main memory. Those nodes are interconnect with InfiniBand, which provides a peak bandwidth of 40 Gb/s. The file system of *Explore*100 is Lustre, which consists of 1 Meta-Data server(MDS) and 40 Object Storage Targets(OST).

3.1   Write Performance

To measure the raw output performance, we tested CFIO2 with different proportions of client and server. This test case contains 20 iterations, and in each iteration the clients forward 3.2GB output data to servers. The number of clients is fixed to 256.

Figure 3 shows the write throughput of PnetCDF, CFIO, and CFIO2. The X-axis stands for the number of processes that call PnetCDF interface to execute parallel I/O. As expectation, write throughput of CFIO and CFIO2 are both lower than PnetCDF. CFIO2 reaches its peak throughput of 1.09 GB/s when running with 128 servers. CFIO2 Performs better than CFIO, because it takes advantage of event-driven method and achieve higher throughput of communication.

3.2   Overlapping Evaluation

To confirm the advantage of overlapping communication with computation, we imitated a climate model with typical I/O pattern. This experiment executes 20 iterations of computation and I/O. Each computation iteration costs 4.5 seconds and produce 3.2GB output data. The number of servers is 64.

The result is illustrated in figure 4. PnetCDF takes more total time than CFIO and CFIO2, because no overlapping occurs. CFIO can overlap I/O phase with computation phase, so it outperforms PnetCDF significantly. The iteration time of CFIO2 clients is about 91 seconds, which is very close to the pure computation time. And on the server side, the total time for communication and I/O of each iteration is less than 4.5 seconds. So, CFIO2 manages to overlap the communication phase with computation phase. As to both the CFIO and CFIO2, the gap of server and client is the data transfer time plus I/O time of the last iteration.

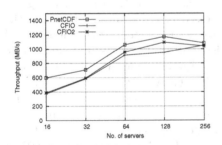
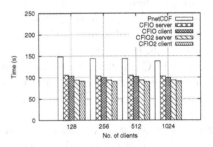

Fig. 3. I/O throughput   **Fig. 4.** Overall simulation time

References

1. Wang, W., Huang, X., Fu, H., et al.: CFIO: A Fast I/O Library for Climate Models. In: 2013 12th IEEE International Conference on Trust, Security and Privacy in Computing and Communications (TrustCom), pp. 911–918. IEEE (2013)
2. Huang, X., et al.: A fast input/output library for high resolution climate models. Geoscientific Model Development 7(1), 93–103 (2014)

Performance Analysis of End-to-End Services in Virtualized Computing Environments*

Guofeng Yan[1,2] and Yuxing Peng[2]

[1] School of Computer and Communication, Hunan Institute of Engineering, China
[2] Science and Technology on Parallel and Distributed Processing Laboratory,
National University of Defense Science and Technology, Changsha 410073, China
{gfyan,pengyuxing}@nudt.edu.cn

Abstract. In this paper, we present a novel stochastic analyzing model for e2e virtualized cloud services using hierarchical Quasi-Birth Death structures (QBDs). We divide the overall virtualized cloud services into three sub-hierarchies, and then, analyze each individual sub-hierarchy using QBDs. Our approach reduces the complexity of performance analysis. Our results are useful to prevent the cloud center from entering unsafe operation, and also reveal practical insights into load balancing and capacity planning for virtualized computing environments. ...

1 Introduction

Theoretical analyses on cloud services mostly rely on extensive research in performance evaluation of M/G/m queuing systems, as outlined in [1]. Using the distribution of response time, researchers discover the relationship among the maximal number of requests, the minimal service resources and the highest level of services [2]. However, as solutions for distribution of response time and queue length in M/G/m systems cannot be obtained in closed form, suitable approximations are sought. To ensure that the quality of service (QoS) perceived by end clients is acceptable, in [3], the performance of cloud server farms with general service time is analyzed. The researchers propose a general analytic model for e2e performance of cloud services. However, the proposed model is limited to the single arrival of requests and the start up delay of cold physical machines (PMs) has not been captured. The effect of virtualization on e2e cloud QoS need to be further studied based on these previous research.

2 System Model

We assume that L different servers, M distinct users, and N types of requests for each user. A type-k request, Req_k, is specified a type-k VM-*configuration*

---

* This work was supported by the National 973 Basic Research Program of China under Grant Number 2011CB302601, China Postdoctoral Science Foundation under Grant Number 2013M542561, and Scientific Research Fund of Hunan Provincial Education Department under Grant 14B040.

C.-H. Hsu et al. (Eds.): NPC 2014, LNCS 8707, pp. 546–549, 2014.

VM_k, and VM_k^i is the provisioning VM_k on server i. Assume that a global resource provisioning and deploying decision machine (RP&DDM) processes requests on a FCFS principle in our system and each request arrives stochastically at RP&DDM, and we define the size of the request Req_k as $|Req_k|$. Let $\mathbf{S} = \{active, passive\}$ be the state set of RP&DDM. In $active$, an arriving request can be served immediately; in $passive$, an arriving request can only be processed after PMs are redeployed. Assume that the requests of user k arrive according to a Poisson process with rate λ_k ($\lambda_1 = \cdots = \lambda_M$), each server maintains N different queues (i.e., $q_{i1}, q_{i2}, \cdots, q_{iN}$) for N different types of requests, and the processing time of Req_k on each server is exponentially distributed with parameter μ_k ($\mu_1 = \cdots = \mu_N = \mu$).

3   QBDs Stochastic Model for Cloud Computing System

Let $\lambda = \sum_{i=1}^{M} \lambda_i = M\lambda_i$ and Q_{req} denote the finite queue of all requests. We consider two state spaces: Λ and Λ_k^i. $\Lambda = \{Y(t), s_t\}$ describes the general characters of RP&DDM, where $Y(t) = 0, 1, 2, \cdots, Q$ denotes the number of requests in Q_{req}, and $s_t \in \mathbf{S}$ refers to the state of RP&DDM at time t. $\Lambda_k^i = \{(Y_k^i(t), r_{kj}^i, s_t^i) : j = 1, 2, \cdots, Q; r_{kj}^i \geqslant 0; s_t^i = 0, 1\}$ captures the characters of type-k request on server i, where r_{kj}^i, $Y_k^i(t)$ and s_t^i refer to the remaining size of the jth type-k request on server i, the the number of requests in q_{ik} at time t, and the current state of server i, respectively. Let $s_t = 0$ and $s_t = 1$ denote that s_t is $passive$ and $active$, respectively. Then, each state of Λ can be expressed as a combination $(Y(t), s_t)$. We compute the transition rates of the QBDs according to [4]. Let the probabilities of RP&DDM being in $active$, and $passive$ at time τ_i be $1 - e^{-p(\tau_i)}$, and $e^{-p(\tau_i)}$, respectively. Hence, we obtain the transition probabilities of RP&DDM from time τ_i to τ_{i+1} from $p_{00}^\Lambda = e^{-p(\tau_i)-p(\tau_{i+1})}$, $p_{01}^\Lambda = e^{-p(\tau_i)} - e^{-p(\tau_i)-p(\tau_{i+1})}$, $p_{11}^\Lambda = 1 - e^{-p(\tau_i)} - e^{-p(\tau_{i+1})} + e^{-p(\tau_i)-p(\tau_{i+1})}$, and $p_{10}^\Lambda = e^{-p(\tau_{i+1})} - e^{-p(\tau_i)-p(\tau_{i+1})}$.

For the state space Λ_k^i, let $r_{kj}^i(t)$ be the remaining request size of the jth type-k request on server i at time t, and $r_k^i(t)$ the queue state of type-k request on server i. Then, $Y_k^i(t) = \{r_k^i(t)\}_{k,i}$ is QBDs on Λ_k^i [1].

4   Performance Evaluation

Rejection Probability of Req_k. Let p_{reject}^{full} and $p_{reject}^{passive}$ be the rejection probabilities of Req_k due to Q_{req} full and no $active$ VM-$configuration$, respectively. Assume that s and $\pi_{(Q,s)}$ are the state of RP&DDM and the stationary state probability of the first hierarchical QBDs, respectively, $\frac{1}{\gamma_{passive}}$ is the mean searching delay to find a $passive$ server, $\pi_{ik}(n, passive)$ and λ_{ik} are the stationary state probability. We can obtain p_{reject}^{full} and $p_{reject}^{passive}$ from $p_{reject}^{full} = \frac{1}{N} \sum_{s \in \{active, passive\}} \pi_{(Q,s)}$ and

$$p_{reject}^{passive} = \sum_{i=0}^{L} \sum_{n=0}^{Q} \frac{\gamma_{passive} \cdot 1 - \pi_{passive}^{i} \cdot \pi_{ik}(n, passive)}{\lambda_{ik}}. \text{ Then, the rejection proba-}$$
bility p_{reject} is:

$$p_{reject} = \sum_{s \in \{active, passive\}} \pi_{(Q,s)} + \sum_{i=0}^{L} \sum_{n=0}^{Q} \frac{\gamma_{passive} \cdot p_{passive}^{i} \cdot \pi_{ik}(n, passive)}{\lambda_{ik}} \quad (1)$$

We use simulations to evaluate the acceptance probability (i.e., $1 - p_{reject}$). Let $L \in \{50, 100, 150, 200\}$ and $M \in [50, 600]$ users. We carry out our simulation with $\delta = 0.75$, $\lambda_k = 0.05$, $\mu = 0.5$, and $1/\gamma_{passive} = 5$. The experiment results and the calculative results are shown in Fig. 1. From Fig. 1, the calculating results of our analytical model and the simulation results are very similar. When $M > 350$, the acceptance probabilities seriously decrease with the increasing of M and it means that the system capacity of cloud computing is not enough for more than 350 users. Furthermore, we find that the acceptance probabilities for $L = 200$ are steady for all M and more than 0.95. These results show the benefits of adding more servers are reflected by having higher acceptance probabilities of user requests for a fixed μ and λ_k.

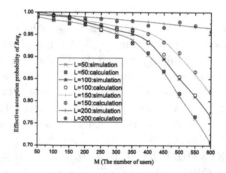

Fig. 1. Effective request acceptance probability of Req_k vs different number of users with $\mu = 0.5$ and $\lambda_k = 0.05$

E2e Response Delay. Let T_w denote the waiting time in the steady state, and $W(x)$ and $W^*(y)$ be the CDF of T_w and its LST, respectively. Let $f(z)$ be the generation function of Q_l, and we can obtain $f(z) = W^*(\lambda(1-z))$. Let $z = 1 - y/\lambda$ and we have $W^*(y) = \sum_{k=0}^{k=L-1} \pi_{(k,s)} + \sum_{k=L}^{k=2L} \pi_{(k,s)}(1 - y/\lambda)^{k-L}$ according to [1]. Hence, we get $E[T_w] = \sum_{k=L}^{k=2L} \frac{(k-L)\pi_{(k,s)}}{\lambda}$.

Similarity, let T_d and T_e be the resource deploying delay and the mean request executing time, respectively. Then, $E[T_d]$ and T_e can be calculated by $E[T_d] = \frac{1/\gamma_{active} + p_{passive}^{i}/\gamma_{passive}}{p_{accept}}$ and $T_e = \sum_{k=1}^{N} \frac{\lambda_{ik}(L\delta p_{11}^{t} + L(1-\delta)p_{01}^{t})}{\lambda \mu_k}$, respectively, where $1/\gamma_{active}$ and $1/\gamma_{passive}$ are the mean search delay when server i being in states *active* and *passive*. Therefore, the mean e2e delay of Req_k, T_{e2e}, is:

$$T_{e2e} = E[T_w] + E[T_d] + E[T_e] \quad (2)$$

The calculating results and simulation results in Fig. 2 show increasing the number of users will increase the response delay. For a small cloud server cluster (for example, $L < 50$), increasing the number of user will increase rapidly the response time of request. But for a large cloud server cluster (for example, $L > 200$), the response delay of request does not distinctly varies due to its enough capacity. Based on these information, cloud computing systems can achieve an more effective admission control policy to guarantee e2e cloud QoS.

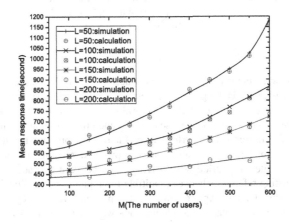

Fig. 2. Mean response time vs different number of users with $\mu = 0.5$ and $\lambda_k = 0.05$

5 Conclusion

We analyze the effect of virtualization on the IaaS cloud service quality. Our model is flexible in terms of scalability and diversity of requests and cloud computing clusters. However, we do not consider the remaining time of time slots when a request is finished before the given time slot terminates. Therefore, how to improve the precision of the analytical results is our further work.

References

1. Ma, B.N.W., Mark, J.W.: Approximation of the mean queue length of an M/G/c queueing system. Operations Research 43, 158–165 (1998)
2. Yang, Y., Zhang, Y., Wang, A., et al.: Quantitative survivability evaluation of three virtual machine-based server architectures. Journal of Network and Computer Applications 36, 781–790 (2013)
3. Khazaei, H., Mišić, J., MiMišić, V.B.: Performance analysis of cloud computing centers using M/G/m/m+r queueing systems. IEEE Transactions on Parallel and Distributed Systems 23(5), 936–943 (2012)
4. Yan, G.F., Wang, J.X., Chen, S.H.: Performance analysis for (X, S)-bottleneck cell in large-scale wireless networks. Information Processing Letters 111, 267–277 (2011)

Adopting Two Strategies to Ensure and Optimize the Quality of Service in Linux

Shaohua Wan

School of Information and Safety Engineering, Zhongnan University of Economics and Law,
430073 Wuhan, China
shwanhust@gmail.com

Abstract. This paper presents a new access-density-based prefetching strategy to improve prefetching for the access patterns, which have not been dealt with in the current Linux read-ahead algorithm. At the same time, motivated by the existing algorithms, we propose a hybrid and efficient replacement algorithm to improve buffer cache performance. Firstly, we propose the following three metrics to evaluate the above access patterns: reading file data backwards, reading files in a stride way (leaving holes between two adjacent references), alternating references between multiple file regions and reading files randomly. Secondly, having explored the eight representative recency/frequency-based buffer cache replacement algorithms, we carry on a hybrid replacement algorithm. Finally, these experimental results demonstrate the importance for buffer cache research to take both file system prefetching and replacement algorithm into consideration.

1 Results

Prefetching locates between page cache and disk buffer. According to [1], prefetching has significant impact on the performance of page cache replacement algorithms, while buffer cache replacement is critical to file system performance, so it worth to improve prefetching algorithm. The rationale of the design is that when pages in a region of a file are referenced, it is likely that pages around these pages may also be referenced. The entire file space is partitioned into a number of regions with the fixed size, and the number of pages which have been accessed, is tracked in a region. Once this number reaches a pre-determined threshold, prefetching makes all pages of the region resident in the buffer cache. So, further accesses of the pages in the same region can be hits. Moreover, to further overlap the computation time with I/O time, prefetching pages start in the adjacent regions when the number of accessed blocks in this region exceeds a higher pre-determined threshold. In this way, there can be no I/O stalls with the references to adjacent regions. This serves the same purpose as the operation of shifting two windows as references proceed in the Linux read-ahead. Only sequential access can be handled very well in a Linux kernel and can't handle random access and backward access. Figure 1(a) is sequential access, which can be handled very well in a Linux kernel. That is why there are so many fewer misses and so many more hits. Figure 1(b), however, is random access, so it shows no hits and all

C.-H. Hsu et al. (Eds.): NPC 2014, LNCS 8707, pp. 550–554, 2014.

misses. As can be seen in this figure, we can also notice that how far the curve that represents the number of misses blocks from X axis. the curve that represents "number of misses and number of prefetched" is very close to the curve that represents "number of hits and number of misses" in Fig. 1(a). Since the number of misses is very less (almost zero), the prefetched blocks are being used by user's requests, this means that the precision is good and the prefetching policy is performing very well. In Fig. 1(b) The curve that represents "number of misses and number of prefetched" is overlapping with the curve that represents "number of hits and number of misses", the reason for this can be explained by the fact that number of misses is used in both curves and the values of number of prefetched and hits are both zero. Again, the number of prefetched blocks is zero, so the prefetching policy in Fig. 1(b) is performing very badly. As for "Number of Prefetched but not yet Requested Blocks" metric, in Fig. 1 (a), almost all blocks that are prefetched are being used and this prefetching policy can guarantee cache buffer to have more spaces at its disposal for a higher hit ratio. On the contrary, the number of prefetched blocks is zero and the cache space does not function in Fig. 1(b). Therefore, from Fig. 1 (a) and (b), we draw a conclusion that the current Linux kernel cannot handle non-sequential workload access pattern.

As for backward access patterns, Linux kernel also can't handle it. So what is shown in the "linux-backward-stride1" curve, Figure 1(c) is all misses and no hits or prefetching. As for Figure 1(d), because of the region prefetching algorithm, all the blocks have been prefetched before being used. So it shows much more hits and fewer misses than Figure 1(c), which indicates the "My-backward-4-16-stride1" prefetching policy has much more accuracy and precision than Linux kernel. The comparison of space overheads in these two curves is similar to that in Fig. 1(a) and Fig. 1 (b).

For Figures 1(e) and 1(f), both two curves that represent the number of misses are approximately close to X axis, which shows there are extremely fewer misses and those two prefetching policies are able to predict user's future requests. In this case, we can say that both are equally accurate. But the upper line doesn't completely overlap the middle one. It means there are a few blocks prefetched which are useless. Figure 1(f) indicates the inability of the regional algorithm to handle the access pattern perfectly. That is why the number of missing blocks increases and the gap between the upper line and the middle line enlarges. It also means that only a small fraction of prefetched blocks are actually used later. In consequence, we can say that the "My-2streams-4-16-stride1" prefetching policy is much more precise than "My-2streams-4-16-stride2" policy. We also notice that almost all prefetched blocks are the same as the accessed blocks, in which the space overhead is low. While in Figure 1(f) we see that not all prefetched blocks are accessed, which means that the space overhead will be increased. The space overhead of the "My-2streams-4-16-stride1" prefetching policy is lower than the space overhead of the "My-2streams-4-16-stride2" policy.

Intuitively, there is no obvious difference between Figure 1(e) and Figure 1(g). The only difference of the algorithm in these two figures is the value of the high watermark that triggers the prefetching of pages in its adjacent regions and the low watermarks are same. However, zooming in on the two figures reveals the ".cuv" file directly; Figure 1(g) prefetches more aggressively than Figure 1(e). This can be demonstrated by the fact that the upper line is closer to the middle line in Figure 1(e). The fact that the gap between the upper line and the middle line becomes larger in Figure 1(g) shows that only a small fraction of prefetched blocks are actually used later. Thereby, the prefetching policy of "My-2streams-4-16-stride1" outperforms that of "My-2streams-4-2-stride1" in terms of the precision metric. We can also observe that the space overheads will be decreasing in both prefetching policies.

As for Figure 1(h) and Figure 1(i), the only difference is the size of the expand threshold. As can be seen in these figures, the curves that represent the number of misses are not overlapping with X axis, which indicates there are a few prefetched blocks that are not used. In terms of the accuracy metric, both prefetching policies don't perform perfectly. Because Figure 1(i) uses more aggressively prefetching, there are fewer misses at the cost of less precise prefetching. That is why the upper line in Figure 1(i) is further away from the middle one than that of Figure 1(h). Finally, both graphs show that, the whole file is prefetched in the beginning and all the blocks are occupying the cache space and need to wait sometime before they are requested by user's program. This means that the space overhead will be increasing and both prefetching policies are performing very badly in terms of space overhead.

We discuss the eight representative recency/frequency-based buffer cache replacement algorithms (OPT, LRU, LRFU, LRU-K, LIRS, 2Q, ARC, Hybrid) used in our evaluation of hit ratio,. For each replacement algorithm, we summarize the original algorithm followed by the adapted version that manages the blocks brought in by kernel. The motivation is simply to compare the different algorithms in a realistic scenario when implemented in the Linux buffer cache. A hybrid replacement algorithm is just that, when the cache is full it randomly implements the above-mentioned one replacement algorithm and picks which page will be replaced. In Figure 2 (a), this shows the hit ratios of the hybrid replacement algorithm and other algorithms mentioned before. Here I also include the OPT replacement, an off-line optimal replacement algorithm, which depends on the knowledge about the future accesses for its decision. In this hit ratio graph, X axis is for cache size, Y axis is for hit ratio. The hybrid hit ratio is very close to the optimal, much better than others. We can see that LRU hit ratios are very low before the cache reaches 400 blocks, the size of one of its locality scopes. LRU is not effective until this working set fully reside in the cache. The hybrid algorithm achieves as high hit ratio as LIRS algorithm in Figure 2(b). Figure 2(c) shows the easy case for all the replacement algorithms. All the curves are close to that of LRU. They all have high hit ratios. LIRS uses both IRR (or reuse distance) and recency for its replacement decision while 2Q uses only reuse distance. LIRS adapts to the locality changes when deciding which blocks have small IRRs. 2Q uses a fixed threshold in looking for blocks of small reuse distances. Both LIRS and 2Q are of low time overhead (as low as LRU). Their space overheads are acceptably larger.

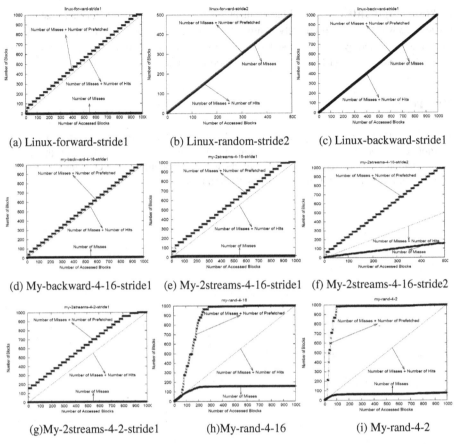

(a) Linux-forward-stride1   (b) Linux-random-stride2   (c) Linux-backward-stride1

(d) My-backward-4-16-stride1   (e) My-2streams-4-16-stride1   (f) My-2streams-4-16-stride2

(g)My-2streams-4-2-stride1   (h)My-rand-4-16   (i) My-rand-4-2

Fig. 1. The various curves of performance characteristics of the two prefetching policies

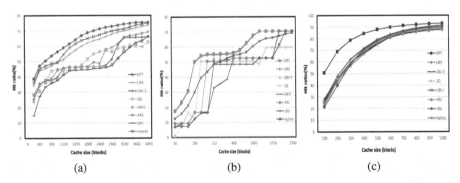

(a)   (b)   (c)

Fig. 2. Hit ratio curves by various replacement policies on various workloads: postgres, multi2 and sprite

Acknowledgments. We would like to thank the anonymous reviewers for their insight and suggestions which have substantially improved the content and presentation of this paper. This work was supported by the Fundamental Research Funds for the Central Universities of China under Grant No. 31141311303 and the Research Project Funds (32114113001).

Reference

1. Ali, R.: Butt,Chris Gniady, and Y. Charlie Hu: The Performance Impact of Kernel Prefetching on Buffer Cache Replacement Algorithms. In: Proceedings of the ACM International Conference on Measurement & Modeling of Computer Systems (SIGMETRICS), Banff, Canada, June 6-10 (2001)

Analysis of VMSS Schemes for Group Key Transfer Protocol

Ching-Fang Hsu[1] and Shan Wu[2,*]

[1] Computer School, Central China Normal University, Wuhan, 430079, China
[2] Wuhan Technology and Business University, Wuhan, 430065, China
cherryjingfang@gmail.com

Abstract. Known group key transfer protocols in group communications using classical secret sharing require that a t-degree interpolating polynomial be computed in order to encrypt and decrypt the secret group key. Secret sharing plays an important role in ensuring the group communications security. A verifiable multi-secret sharing (VMSS) scheme is a multi-secret sharing scheme with the verifiable property. Recently, Zhao et al. and Dehkordi et al. successively proposed two threshold VMSS schemes. Shortly, using the same verification mechanism, Dehkordi et al. presented another two VMSS schemes. In these schemes, authors claimed that the dealer was absolutely impossible to become a cheater. In this paper, we show that in both Zhao scheme and Dehkordi scheme, a dishonest dealer may distribute a fake share to a certain participant, and then that participant would subsequently never obtain the true secret. Indeed, verification mechanism should be improved in these schemes; and furthermore our results highlight that extra cautions still be exercised when constructing schemes in this direction.

Results

A verifiable multi-secret sharing (VMSS) scheme is a multi-secret sharing scheme with the verifiable property. Recently, Zhao et al. [3] and Dehkordi et al. [1] successively proposed two threshold VMSS schemes. Shortly, using the same verification mechanism, Dehkordi et al. presented another two VMSS schemes [2]. In these schemes, authors claimed that the dealer was absolutely impossible to become a cheater. In this paper, we show that in both Zhao scheme and Dehkordi scheme, a dishonest dealer may distribute a fake share to a certain participant, and then that participant would subsequently never obtain the true secret. Indeed, verification mechanism should be improved in these schemes; and furthermore our results highlight that extra cautions still be exercised when constructing schemes in this direction.

Cryptanalysis of Zhao Scheme

In Zhao scheme [3], we assume that D is a dishonest dealer. Let M_w ($w \in \{1.2, ..., n\}$) be a certain participant in M. The goal of D is to distribute a

---

** Corresponding author.

C.-H. Hsu et al. (Eds.): NPC 2014, LNCS 8707, pp. 555–558, 2014.

fake share to M_w and M_w will not detect this and, hence, M_w would subsequently never obtain the true secret. A more detailed description of the attack is as follows:

(1) As a preliminary step, D chooses an integer s_{n+1} from the interval $[2, N]$ and computes $I_{n+1} = R_0^{S_{n+1}} \bmod N$ such that $I_{n+1} \neq I_i$ for $i = 1.2, ..., n$;

(2) After polynomial $h(x) \bmod Q$ is constructed, D computes $y_i = h(I_i) \bmod Q$ for $i = 1.2, ..., n$, $i \neq w$ and specially computes $y_w = h(I_{n+1}) \bmod Q$ instead of $y_w = h(I_w) \bmod Q$. Afterwards, D publishs $(y_1, y_2, ..., y_n)$ or $(y_1, y_2, ..., y_n, h(1), h(2), ..., h(k-t))$;

(3) When any t participants include M_w want to recover the secrets $P_1, P_2, ..., P_k$ (without loss of generality, suppose participants $\{M_i\}_{i=1}^{t}$), it is easy to see that anybody can verify $I_i{}'$ is true or false but can not verify y_i is matched with I_i or not for $i = 1.2, ..., t$. Therefore, after the verifications are done, M_w is unable to detect any discrepancy on y_w (actually, $y_w = h(I_{n+1}) \bmod Q$ is not matched with I_w);

(4) By using Lagrange interpolation polynomial, these t participants include M_w will uniquely obtain another polynomial $h(x)' \bmod Q$ but not $h(x) \bmod Q$, since the complete share distributed to M_w, that is (I_w, y_w), is not correctly paired. As a consequence, M_w would never obtain the secrets $P_1, P_2, ..., P_k$.

Through the attack, the verification mechanism of Zhao scheme is completely compromised.

Cryptanalysis of Dehkordi Scheme

Indeed, the attack of Dehkordi scheme [1] is the same as that of Zhao scheme. In Dehkordi scheme [1], we assume that D is a dishonest dealer. Let $M_w (w \in \{1.2, ..., n\})$ be a certain participant in M. The goal of D is to distribute a fake share to M_w and M_w will not detect this and, hence, M_w would subsequently never obtain the true secret. A more detailed description of the attack is as follows:

(1) As a preliminary step, D chooses an integer $s_{n+1} \in \mathbb{Z}_N$ and computes $f(r, s_{n+1})$ such that $f(r, s_{n+1}) \neq f(r, s_i)$ for $i = 1.2, ..., n$;

(2) After $\{r, G_i = g^{f(r,s_i)}\}_{i=1}^{n}$ is published and polynomial $h(x) \bmod q$ is constructed, D computes $y_i = h(f(r, s_i)) \bmod q$ for $i = 1.2,...,n$, $i \neq w$ and specially computes $y_w = h(f(r, s_{n+1})) \bmod q$ instead of $y_w = h(f(r, s_w)) \bmod q$. Afterwards, D publishs $(y_1, y_2,..., y_n)$ or $(h(1), h(2),..., h(k-t), y_1, y_2,..., y_n)$;

(3) When any t participants include M_w want to recover the secrets $P_1, P_2,.., P_k$ (without loss of generality, suppose participants $\{M_i\}_{i=1}^{t}$), it is easy to see that anybody can verify $f(r, s_i)$ is true or false but can not verify y_i is matched with $f(r, s_i)$ or not for $i = 1.2,...,t$. Therefore, after the verifications are done, M_w is unable to detect any discrepancy on y_w (actually, $y_w = h(f(r, s_{n+1})) \bmod q$ is not matched with $f(r, s_w)$);

(4) By using Lagrange interpolation polynomial, these t participants include M_w will uniquely obtain another polynomial $h(x)' \bmod q$ but not $h(x) \bmod q$, since the complete share distributed to M_w, that is $(f(r, s_w), y_w)$, is not correctly paired. As a consequence, M_w would never obtain the secrets $P_1, P_2,.., P_k$.

Through this attack, the verification mechanism of Dehkordi scheme [1] is completely compromised. Furthermore, since the newer VMSS schemes proposed by Dehkordi et al. in [2] are based on the same verification mechanism, our attack equally applies to them.

Countermeasure

The main flaw in Zhao scheme and Dehkordi scheme is that there are no way for the participant to check whether I_i (or $f(r, s_i)$) chose by her/himself and y_i published by D are correctly paired or not. All participants can not be sure that y_i is matched with I_i (or $f(r, s_i)$) by only checking the correctness of I_i (or $f(r, s_i)$). This oversight allows the dishonest dealer in our attack to send the forged y_i without being detected by the participant.

The simplest way to resolve the security problems with Zhao scheme and Dehkordi scheme would be to change the verification equations. For Dehkordi scheme, instead of computing $G_i = g^{f(r,s_i)}$ for $i = 1.2, ..., n$, D need to compute $G_i = g^{P_{i+1}} \bmod p$ for $i = 0, 1, 2, ..., k-1$ and publish them. Through checking

$$g^{y_i} = \prod_{j=0}^{t-1} (G_j)^{f(r,s_i)^j} \bmod p \quad \text{(if } k \le t\text{)} \quad \text{or} \quad g^{y_i} = \prod_{j=0}^{k-1} (G_j)^{f(r,s_i)^j} \bmod p \quad \text{(if } k > t\text{)}$$

for $i = 1.2, ..., n$, the participants verify whether $f(r, s_i)$ and y_i are valid (i.e, correctly paired). After the secrets are recovered, the participants check $G_i = g^{P_{i+1}} \bmod p$ for $i = 0, 1, 2, ..., k-1$ to verify whether $P_1, P_2, .., P_k$ are valid. As a consequence, our attack will no longer be valid against the fixed scheme. In the same way, this verification mechanism equally applies to Zhao scheme and the newer VMSS schemes proposed by Dehkordi et al. in [2].

Conclusion

This paper has considered the security of Zhao scheme and Dehkordi scheme for verifiable multi-secret sharing. Although these schemes claimed the dealer was absolutely impossible to become a cheater, we have shown that the schemes are indeed completely insecure against a dishonest dealer. In addition, we have recommended a small change to the schemes that can address the identified security problem. Furthermore, our attack and security patch apply also to the newer VMSS schemes proposed by Dehkordi et al.

References

[1] Hadian Dehkordi, M., Mashhadi, S.: An efficient threshold verifiable multi-secret sharing. Computer Standards & Interfaces 30(3), 187–190 (2008)
[2] Hadian Dehkordi, M., Mashhadi, S.: New efficient and practical verifiable multi-secret sharing schemes. Information Sciences 178(9), 2262–2274 (2008)
[3] Zhao, J., Zhang, J., Zhao, R.: A practical verifiable multi-secret sharing scheme. Computer Standards & Interfaces 29(1), 138–141 (2007)

Resource Prediction for Inter-cloud Broker

Mohammad Aazam and Eui-Nam Huh

Department of Computer Engineering, Kyung Hee University,
Suwon, Republic of Korea
aazam@ieee.org, johnhuh@khu.ac.kr

Abstract. Media content over the Internet has massively been increasing, resulting in popularity gain of cloud computing. Cloud computing is the only solution in hand to handle rapidly increasing digital media content. Through cloud computing, digital media can be manipulated, stored, and communicated in a much better and easier way. But due to increase in user's demands and diversity of applications, it is, at times, not possible for a single cloud to fulfill all the requests. At that point, multiple clouds have to communicate and share resources through an intermediary, called cloud broker. To handle requests properly, broker has to predict the amount of resources required when a service is requested. This paper focuses on this particular issue. We present resource prediction part of our model here, along with its implementation and evaluation using CloudSim toolkit.

1   Introduction

The rapidly increasing digital media content has already surpassed traditional media, as a result of which long-term and vast changes are required for the contents shared over the Internet. In 2010, Internet video traffic had surpassed global peer-to-peer (P2P) traffic [1]. Excluding the amount of video exchanged through P2P file sharing, at the time being, Internet video is 40 percent of consumer Internet traffic. Since 2012, it has become over 50 percent and will reach 62 percent by the end of 2015. Counting all form of videos, the number will be approximately 90 percent by 2015 [2]. This media revolution not only brings great opportunities, but also bears some challenges. To meet those challenges, much better infrastructure, sophisticated technologies, and powerful capabilities are required to be incorporated.

Cloud computing still faces some open challenges, but to provide better reliability, availability, cost-efficiency, and QoS, inter-cloud computing has already been envisioned. Research on inter-cloud computing is still in its start, but its effectiveness cannot be denied by any means [3]. Cloud Service Providers (CSPs) have their customers dispersed all around the globe. To serve them optimally, CSPs have to setup many of their data centers at different geographical locations. Existing systems are not capable enough to coordinate dynamically the load distribution among data centers, to determine optimal location for hosting services to achieve desired

C.-H. Hsu et al. (Eds.): NPC 2014, LNCS 8707, pp. 559–562, 2014.

performance. Furthermore, users' geographical distribution cannot be predicted as well. Thus, load coordination and service distribution has to be done automatically. Inter-cloud computing is meant to counter this problem. It provides scalable provisioning of services with consistent performance, under variable workload and dynamically changing requirements. It supports dynamic expansion and contraction of resources, to handle abrupt variations in service demands [4]. In inter-cloud computing, an intermediary, broker, is responsible to identify appropriate CSP, according to the needs of its customer, through cloud exchange. Broker negotiates with the gateway to allocate resources, according to user and service requirements [4]. Resource management is a key attribute of broker. So far, the available literature addresses resource management issue in a trivial way.

In this paper, we present a part of our resource management model, in which we focus mainly on advanced reservation of resources, according to the type of customer and service. Implementation and simulation of our model was performed on CloudSim 3.0.3 toolkit.

2   Resource Prediction and Premium Amount Calculation

When a cloud service customer (CSC) [5] requests the broker [6] for a particular service, broker has to further contact cloud service provider (CSP) and negotiate the contract, including service level agreement (SLA) [7]. For some services, broker performs ad hoc allocation of resources, while for others; resources are required to be predicted. Based on the type of service, broker's resource prediction is formulated as under:

$$R_{res} = \sum_{i=0}^{n} \begin{cases} \left(C_{m_i} * n * P_i(L|H)\right) * \left(1 - P_i(L|H)\right) * (1 - \mu_i) * D_s \\ 0 \end{cases} \tag{1}$$

Where R_{res} is required service, C_m is the maximum cost a particular user can afford or willing to pay, n is the number of cloud customers, $P(L|H)$ is the probability of a particular customer of giving up the resource. For simplicity, we have categorized it into two, as low (L) or high (H) probability.

$$0 > L \leq 0.5, \ 0.5 > H \leq 1 \tag{2}$$

'μ' is User Characteristic, which represents the characteristic of the requesting user, based on its history. This value is assigned by the broker, on the basis of previous resource consumption log-file of a particular user. For an altogether new user, this characteristic is set to maximum positive value for the first time. After predicting the resources, broker asks its users to pay a particular premium amount, based on following formulation:

$$\rho_{prem} = C_m * P_L * \mu_L \tag{3}$$

Where, ρ_{prem} determines premium amount, P_L represents probability as "low". Actual and final price is paid once the resources are started to be consumed. Therefore, in equation 3, relinquish probability is set as low, instead of both low and high. Same is the case with user characteristic, which is set as positive for low relinquish probability customers.

The implementation and evaluation of this part of model was done on CloudSim 3.0.3 toolkit. Results are presented below.

Shown in figure 1, the unit is greater for L customers, having low relinquish probability, since they are more loyal, as compared to H customers. Prices for a total of 9 services have been shown, ranging from USD 100 to USD 500. On vertical axis, unit of resources to be reserved increase with the higher valued service. Better and costly service require more resources, hence, the unit of resources increase accordingly.

Figure 2 shows the premium amount to be paid, according to service type. Premium amount is shown on the top of the bars, in USD, while the values at the bottom represent the total price of services, in USD. Premium amount of each of the 9 services is shown.

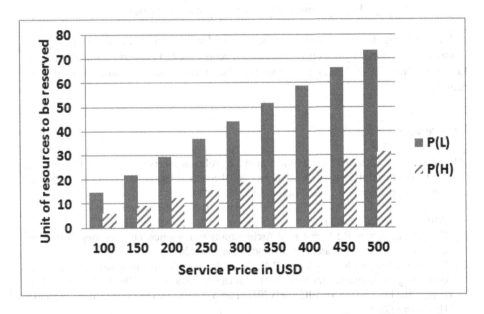

Fig. 1. Resource prediction for different types of customers, according to different services

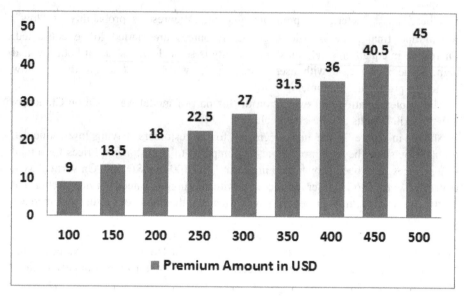

Fig. 2. Premium amount, according to service type

Acknowledgment. This research was supported by Basic Science Research Program through the National Research Foundation of Korea (NRF) funded by the Ministry of Education(No.NRF-2013R1A1A2013620). The corresponding author is Prof. Eui-Nam Huh.

References

[1] Tan, M., Su, X.: Media Cloud: When Media Revolution Meets Rise of Cloud Computing. In: Proceedings of The 6th IEEE International Symposium on Service Oriented System Engineering, Irvine, CA, USA, December 12-14 (2011)

[2] Cisco-White-Paper, Cisco Visual Networking Index – Forecast and Methodology, 2010–2015 (June 1, 2011)

[3] Grozev, N., Buyya, R.: Inter-Cloud Architectures and Application Brokering: Taxonomy and Survey. Wiley Software: Practice and Experience (2012)

[4] Buyya, R., Ranjan, R., Calheiros, R.N.: InterCloud: Utility-oriented federation of cloud computing environments for scaling of application services. In: Hsu, C.-H., Yang, L.T., Park, J.H., Yeo, S.-S. (eds.) ICA3PP 2010, Part I. LNCS, vol. 6081, pp. 13–31. Springer, Heidelberg (2010)

[5] Wenwu, Z., Chong, L., Jianfeng, W., Shipeng, L.: Multimedia Cloud Computing. IEEE Signal Processing Magazine 28, 59–69 (2011)

[6] Aazam, M., Huh, E.-N.: Inter-Cloud Architecture and Media Cloud Storage Design Considerations. In: The Proceedings of 7th IEEE CLOUD, Anchorage, Alaska, USA, June 27-July 2 (2014)

[7] Díaz-Sánchez, D., Almenarez, F., Marín, A., Proserpio, D., Cabarcos, P.A.: Media Cloud: An Open Cloud Computing Middleware for Content Management. IEEE Transactions on Consumer Electronics 57(2) (May 2011)

An Efficient Certificateless Blind Signature Scheme in the Random Oracle Model

Hao Xu, Baoyuan Kang, and Yongzheng Niu

School of Computer Science and Software Engineering,
Tianjin Polytechnic University, Tianjin, 300387, China
23880797@qq.com, baoyuankang@aliyun.com, niuer890214@163.com

Abstract. The blind signature schemes are useful in some applications where the anonymity is a thorny issue. The certificateless public key cryptography (CL-PKC) can eliminate the certificate management problem and solve the key escrow problem. In this paper, we put forward a secure and efficient CLBS scheme. We then illustrate that our new scheme is secure in the random oracle model. Also, we theoretically validate that our proposed scheme is more efficient than those existing ones in terms of computational complexity. We hope to transfer our scheme into applications.

Keywords: Certificateless blind signature, Certificateless public key cryptography, Random oracle model, Computational Diffie-Hellman problem.

1   Introduction

The blind signature was first proposed by Chaum [1], which can provide the anonymity of signed message. Informally, blind signature allows the message owner blind the message by the blind factors, and then lets the signer sign the blinded message. At last, the message owner eliminates the blind factors of signature to get the signer's signature of the original message. Blind signature is a special digital signature, it must also meet the property of blindness differing from other signatures. Therefore, blind signature schemes can used in order to eliminate the possible abuse of linkability.

Up to now, even if there have been a lot of researches for blind signature, most of works have been based on a traditional public key infrastructure (PKI) or an identity-based public key cryptography (ID-PKC). In the traditional PKI, the trusted Certificate Authority (CA) needs a large amount of storage and computing time to manage the certificates, which are signatures of CA on the public keys of users. This is called certificate management problem. In the ID-PKC, an inherent problem of ID-PKC is that a Key Generation Center (KGC) generates any user's private key with a master key of KGC. Obviously, a malicious KGC is able to forge the signature of any signer. This is key escrow problem. To tackle the problems above, Al-Riyami and Paterson [2] put forward a new paradigm named certificateless public key cryptography (CL-PKC) in 2003, which avoids the certificate management problem in traditional PKI and eliminates the key escrow problem in ID-PKC.

C.-H. Hsu et al. (Eds.): NPC 2014, LNCS 8707, pp. 563–566, 2014.

Blind signature and CL-PKC have gotten fruitful achievements since they were introduced. However, to our best knowledge, little attention has been paid to the design of provably secure blind signature scheme in CL-PKC [3]. In this paper, we propose an efficient CLBS scheme based on bilinear pairings, then show that our CLBS scheme is existentially unforgeable in the random oracle model under the Computational Diffie-Hellman (CDH) problem.

The remainder of this paper is organized as follows: In Section 2, we present the construction of our new CLBS scheme. We will show that our scheme is security in Section 3. Section 4 shows efficiency comparison with the existing schemes.

2　Certificateless Blind Signature Scheme

In this section, we propose a secure and efficient CLBS scheme. It consists of the following seven algorithms. The details are shown as follows:

- Setup: On the input of a security parameter k, the KGC firstly selects a cyclic additive group G_1 generated by a generator P of prime order q, a cyclic multiplicative group G_2 with the same order q and a bilinear map $e: G_1 \times G_1 \to G_2$, picks the master key master-key $s \in_R Z_q^*$ at random and keeps s secret, then sets $P_{pub} = sP$ as the public key. Choose three secure hash functions: $H_1: \{0,1\}^* \to G_1$, $H_2: \{0,1\}^* \to G_1$, $H_3: \{0,1\}^* \to Z_q^*$. The system parameters are params $= \{G_1, G_2, q, e, P, P_{pub}, H_1, H_2, H_3\}$.

- Partial-Private-Key-Extract: For a user with identity $ID_A \in \{0,1\}^*$, KGC computes $Q_A = H_1(ID_A)$ as the public identity of the user, and sends D_A to the user as his partial private key via a secure channel, where $D_A = sQ_A$.

- Set-Secret-Value: Given params, the user with identity ID_A selects a random $x_A \in_R Z_q^*$ as his secret value.

- Set-Public-Key: This algorithm accepts params, a user's identity ID_A and secret value x_A, then outputs the public key $P_A = x_A P$ of the user with identity ID_A.

- Set-Private-Key: This algorithm takes as input params, the signer's identity ID_A, partial private key D_A, public key P_A and secret value x_A to produce the signer's private key $SK_A = D_A + x_A T_A$, where $T_A = H_2(ID_A, P_A)$.

- Issue: To sign a message m, the signer with identity ID_A, public key P_A, private key SK_A, executes the following steps with the signature requester:

  (a) Request: The requester requests the signer for a CLBS. After receiving the request, the signer chooses $r \in_R Z_q^*$ at random and computes $R' = rP$, then sends R' to the requester.

(b) Blind: Upon receiving R', the requester randomly picks $\alpha, \beta \in {}_R Z_q^*$ as the blind factors, computes $R = \alpha R' + \beta P$, $h' = H_3(m, ID_A, P_A, R)$ and $h = \alpha^{-1} h'$, then sends h back to the signer.

(c) Sign: The signer sends S' to the requester, where $S' = h SK_A + r P_{pub}$.

(d) Unblind: The requester unblinds S' by computing $S = \alpha S' + \beta P_{pub}$, and outputs $\sigma = (R, S)$ as the CLBS on message m.

- Verify: For a message m, and the corresponding signature $\sigma = (R, S)$, the verifier computes the value $h' = H_3(m, ID_A, P_A, R)$, $T_A = H_2(ID_A, P_A)$, then check if the equation:

$$e(S, P) = \left(e(Q_A, P_{pub}) e(T_A, P_A)\right)^{h'} e(R, P_{pub})$$

holds. If the equation holds, the signature $\sigma = (R, S)$ is valid.

3   Security

About the security of our CLBS scheme, we have the following two theorems.

Theorem 1. The CLBS scheme is blindness.

Theorem 2. The CLBS scheme is existentially unforgeable under assuming that the CDH problem in a cyclic additive group G_1 is intractable.

4   Efficiency Analysis

We compare our scheme with other three available CLBS schemes [4-6] based on bilinear pairings in terms of secret key size and the required computational cost of signing and verifying. For our scheme, we omit the computation efforts which can be pre-computed by the verifier, for example, the computation of $e(Q_A, P_{pub})$ and $e(T_A, P_A)$. For convenient comparison, we include the following presentation, the notion $|G_1|$ denotes the bit length of an element in G_1, $|q|$ be the binary length of an element in Z_q, P_m be the scalar multiplication on the curve, P_{ex} be the exponentiation operator in G_2 and P_e be the bilinear pairing operation.

Table 1. Performance comparison of different schemes

Scheme	Sign	Verify	Secret key length
[4]	$3P_e + 4P_{ex} + 7P_m$	$1P_e + 1P_{ex} + 2P_m$	$|q| + |G_1|$
[5]	$2P_e + 1P_{ex} + 8P_m$	$3P_e + 1P_{ex} + 2P_m$	$|q| + |G_1|$
[6]	$3P_e + 2P_{ex} + 9P_m$	$2P_e + 1P_{ex}$	$|q| + |G_1|$
Our scheme	$7P_m$	$2P_e + 1P_{ex}$	$|G_1|$

From Table 1, we can clearly see that a prominent merit in our scheme is that no pairing operator is required in the whole signing process. To our best knowledge the computation of the pairing is the most time-consuming in pairing based cryptosystem. Besides, the length of the secret key is also shorter than other schemes. Thus, our scheme is more useful and efficient than the previous schemes.

5   Conclusion

In this paper, we put forward a new CLBS scheme on the bilinear pairings, and give some theorems of the security and efficiency analysis of our scheme, which show that the new proposed CLBS scheme is much more efficient and satisfy both blindness and unforgeability properties. Our CLBS scheme may have applications in areas such as electronic cash systems using CL-PKC.

References

1. Chaum, D.: Blind Signatures for Untraceable Payments. In: Crypto, pp. 199–203 (1982)
2. Al-Riyami, S.S., Paterson, K.G.: Certificateless Public Key Cryptography. In: Laih, C.-S. (ed.) ASIACRYPT 2003. LNCS, vol. 2894, pp. 452–473. Springer, Heidelberg (2003)
3. Zhang, L., Zhang, F.T., Qin, B., Liu, S.B.: Provably-secure Electronic Cash Based on Certificateless Partially-blind Signatures. Electronic Commerce Research and Applications 10(5), 545–552 (2011)
4. Zhang, L., Zhang, F.: Certificateless Signature and Blind Signature. Journal of Electronics (China) 25(5), 629–635 (2008)
5. Zhang, L., Zhang, F., Qin, B., et al.: Provably-secure Electronic Cash Based on Certificateless Partially-blind Signatures. Electronic Commerce Research and Applications 10(5), 545–552 (2011)
6. Liu, J., Zhang, Z., Sun, R., et al.: Certificateless Partially Blind Signature. In: 2012 26th International Conference on Advanced Information Networking and Applications Workshops (WAINA), pp. 128–133. IEEE (2012)

Increasing Multi-controller Parallelism for Hybrid-Mapped Flash Translation Layers

Hung-Yi Sung and Chin-Hsien Wu

Department of Electronic and Computer Engineering,
National Taiwan University of Science and Technology, Taiwan
{M10002137,chwu}@mail.ntust.edu.tw

Abstract. Nowadays, the architecture of solid-state drives (SSDs) is using multiple controllers to efficiently handle NAND flash memory chips. Several flash translation layers (FTLs) have been proposed to improve the overall performance of NAND flash memory. Therefore, the collaboration of FTLs and the multi-controller design of SSDs will become an important research topic. In this paper, we will propose a method to increase multi-controller parallelism for hybrid-mapped flash translation layers.

1   Problem Overview

In the paper, we explain the importance of handling read/write requests under a multi-controller design of SSDs. An SSD consists of a host interface, RAM buffer, a master controller, multiple slave controllers, and multiple NAND flash memory chips [1]. The master controller is responsible for the execution of a flash translation layer (FTL) which can handle read/write requests from the host interface. Each flash memory chip under a hybrid-mapped flash translation layer can be divided into data and log blocks. When a file system receives a read request, FTL will handle the read request and assign slave controllers to read data from the corresponding flash memory chips. When a file system receives a write request, FTL will allocate appropriate location (i.e., data and log blocks) in flash memory chips to write data.

Compared to hard-disk drives (HDDs), SSDs could provide faster read and write operation time in terms of sequential and random data access. Currently, SSDs use a fixed architecture, called the multi-controller design [2]. Under the architecture, one controller can access to flash memory chips on its own bus which could reduce execution parallelism of multiple controllers. Therefore, the performance will decrease while many I/O requests access those chips which belong to the same controller, and other idle controllers cannot perform the I/O requests in different buses.

2   Design Concept

As shown in Fig. 1, when a request is coming, it contains the information of *Start_LPA* and *Size* which means "read/write the pages of length *Size* from the logical

C.-H. Hsu et al. (Eds.): NPC 2014, LNCS 8707, pp. 567–570, 2014.
© IFIP International Federation for Information Processing 2014

page address of *Start_LPA*". If it is a write request, the request will be divided into sub-requests by the block striping technique. Assume that the maximum size of one sub-request is one block. Sub-requests may include data blocks {D1, D2, ..., Di}, or log blocks {L1, L2, ..., Lj}. If it is a read request, FTL will search its mapping table and translate the read request to sub-requests that could include data blocks {D1, D2, ..., Di}, or log blocks {L1, L2, ..., Lj}. Then, the read sub-requests will be performed by reading the data or log blocks from the corresponding flash memory chips.

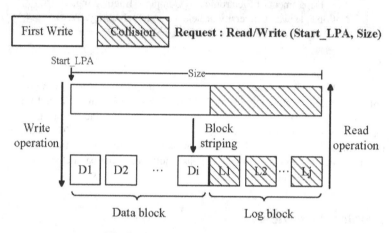

Fig. 1. Handling read/write operations

We show how to handle the first write request. As shown in Fig. 2.(a), when Request 1 is going to write data into data blocks, the write request is divided into sub-requests {D1, D2, D3, D4} by the block striping technique. The best case is to write the data blocks {D1, D2, D3, D4} into different buses by the page striping technique. The worst case of Fig. 2.(a) happens when that only one controller is involved and sub-requests are written into one bus. In order to effectively use multiple controllers and reduce the idle time of multiple controllers, we know that the allocation of data and log blocks for sub-requests is quite important because it can have impact on the multi-controller parallelism.

We show how to handle the request with overwritten data. Due to the out-of-place update of NAND flash memory, a write request could overwrite data and cause that some sub-requests write data to log blocks {L1, L2, ..., Lj}. As shown in Fig. 2.(b), Request 2 will write data to two log blocks {L1, L2}. Assume that the corresponding data blocks of L1 and L2 are D1 and D2, respectively. If partial valid data are stored in both {L1, D1} and {L2, D2}, the best case is to write the log block {L1} to Bus 2 and the log block {L2} to Bus 3, where the corresponding data blocks {D1, D2} are also not locating in Bus2 and Bus 3. If the log block is located in the same bus with the corresponding data block, when valid data in {L1, D1} or {L2, D2} are required, only one controller can be involved and reduce the multi-controller parallelism, as shown in Fig. 2.(b).

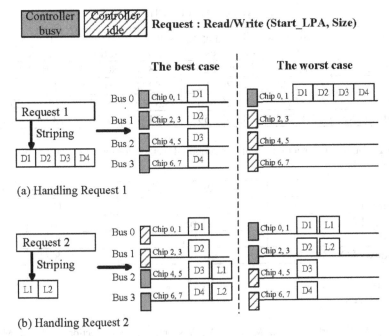

Fig. 2. Handling Request 1 and Request 2

Therefore, the allocation method of data and log blocks is to avoid a log block with its corresponding data blocks in the same bus. The allocation method can be implemented in the address translation function of FTL because FTL usually has a RAM-resident translation table, where each entry of the table contains the corresponding physical block addresses (i.e., data and log blocks) by indexing the logical block address. Assume that there are N buses and a write request can be translated to some sub-requests that could include data blocks {D1, D2, ..., Di}, or log blocks {L1, L2, ..., Lj}. For each data block Dx in {D1, D2, ..., Di}, it can be dispatched to the (x%N)-th bus in a block-striping way. For each log block Ly in {L1, L2, ..., Lj}, it can be dispatched to the bus where its corresponding data blocks are not locating. Therefore, if the number of corresponding data blocks is larger than the number of buses, a log block with the corresponding data blocks could co-exist in the same bus. In this case, the log block can be dispatched to the bus where its corresponding data blocks have the least number of valid pages. The design idea behind the allocation method is to distribute valid pages to different buses as much as possible. Thus, when read and write requests occur, we can increase the multi-controller parallelism to access flash memory chips efficiently.

3   Experimental Results

Four real traces are used in the experiments, as shown in Table 1. The improvement ratio with the proposed method for merge operations under 32 and 256 RW log blocks is shown in Table 2. According to the experimental results, we can utilize the execution parallelism to improve the execution time of partial and full merge operations.

Table 1. Four Real Traces

Trace	Total request Count	Total page accesses	Read ratio	Write ratio	Avg. read/write pages
Financial 1	5,334,987	6,967,821	19.23 %	80.77 %	1.08 / 1.37
Financial 2	3,699,194	4,479,959	79.52 %	20.48 %	1.17 / 1.40
AS SSD	246,957	8,925,678	33.37 %	66.63 %	69.96/ 29.10
Windows PC	2,398,728	8,532,159	55.24 %	44.76 %	3.54 / 3.58

Table 2. The improvement ratio with the proposed method for merge operations under 32 and 256 RW log blocks

Trace	32 RW log blocks	256 RW log blocks
Financial 1	15.52%	15.64%
Financial 2	15.68%	16.08%
AS SSD	3.9%	3.91%
Windows PC	8.34%	8.31%

References

1. Bez, R., Camerlenghi, E., Modelli, A., Visconti, A.: Introduction to Flash Memory. Proceedings of the IEEE 91(4) (April 2003)
2. Kang, J.U., Kim, J.S., Park, C., Park, H., Lee, J.: A multi-channel architecture for high-performance NAND flash-based storage system. Journal of Systems Architecture 53(9), 644–658 (2007)
3. Park, S.K., Park, Y., Shim, G., Park, K.H.: CAVE: channel-aware buffer management scheme for solid state disk. In: Proceedings of the 2011 ACM Symposium on Applied Computing, pp. 346–353 (May 2011)

An Estimation-Based Task Load Balancing Scheduling in Spot Clouds

Daeyong Jung[1], HeeSeok Choi[1], DaeWon Lee[2], Heonchang Yu[1], and Eunyoung Lee[3,*]

[1] Dept. of Computer Science Education, Korea University, Seoul, Korea
[2] Division of General Education, SeoKyeong University, Seoul, Korea
[3] Dept. of Computer Science, Dongduk Women's University, Seoul, Korea
{karat,hsrangken,yuhc}@korea.ac.kr, daelee@skuniv.ac.kr,
elee@dongduk.ac.kr

Abstract. Cloud computing is a computing paradigm in which users can rent computing resources from service providers according to their requirements. Cloud computing based on the spot market helps a user to obtain resources at a lower cost. However, these resources may be unreliable. In this paper, we propose an estimation-based distributed task workflow scheduling scheme that reduces the estimated generation compared to Genetic Algorithm (GA). Moreover, our scheme executes a user's job within selected instances and stretches the user's cost. The simulation results, based on a before-and-after estimation comparison, reveal that the task size is determined based on the performance of each instance and the task is distributed among the different instances. Therefore, our proposed estimation-based task load balancing scheduling technique achieves the task load balancing according to the performance of instances.

1 Introduction

In recent years, due to the increased interest in cloud computing, many cloud projects and commercial systems, such as the Amazon Elastic Compute Cloud (EC2) [1] and FlexiScale [2], have been implemented. Cloud computing provides high utilization and high flexibility for managing computing resources. In addition, cloud computing services provide a high level of scalability of computing resources combined with Internet technology that are distributed among several customers [3, 4]. In most cloud services, the concept of an instance unit is used to provide users with resources in a cost-efficient manner.

Spot-market-based cloud environment configures the spot instance. In the spot instance environment, spot prices changes depending on the supply and demand of spot instances. The environment affects the success or failure of task completion according to the changing spot prices. Spot prices have a market structure and follow the law of demand and supply. Therefore, cloud services (Amazon EC2) provide a spot instance when a user's bid is higher than the current spot price. Furthermore, a

---

* Corresponding author.

C.-H. Hsu et al. (Eds.): NPC 2014, LNCS 8707, pp. 571–574, 2014.

running instance stops when a user's bid becomes less than or equal to the current spot price. After a running instance stops, it restarts when a user's bid becomes greater than the current spot price.

We analyze the task and instance information from the price history data, and estimate the task size and instance availability from the analyzed data. A workflow is created using each available instance and the task size. However, the created workflow has a problem in that it does not consider the failure time of each instance. To solve this problem, we propose a scheme to change the task size of each instance using an estimation algorithm, such as Genetic Algorithm (GA).

2   Estimation Method

In this paper, using environment expands workflow scheduling scheme from our previous paper [5]. Our task distribution method determines the task size in order to allocate a task to a selected instance. Based on a compute-unit and an available state, the task size of an instance I_i (T_{I_i}) is calculated as

$$T_i = \left(\frac{U_i \times A_i}{\sum_{i=1}^{N} (U_i \times A_i)} \right) \times \frac{1}{U_i} \times T_{request} \times U_{baseline} \tag{1}$$

where $T_{request}$ represents the total size of tasks required for executing a user request. In an instance I_i, U_{I_i} and A_{I_i} represent the compute-unit and the available state, respectively. The available state A_{I_i} can be either 0 (unavailable) or 1 (available). The baseline represents the standard of the instance.

In our scheduling scheme, chromosome is defined as an assigned task to an instance. The length of chromosome composes the number of task. If available instances allocate the same length of chromosome, each instance is different task completion time. This reason, each instance has different the performance and the occurrence frequency of out-of-bid situation. The problem solution is the length of each chromosome varies to consider each instance condition (the performance, the occurrence frequency of out-of-bid situation, etc.). Therefore, we have designed a new crossover and mutation scheme for scheduling tasks that is based on the performance of each instance.

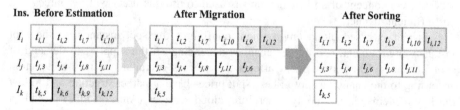

Fig. 1. Processing of migration and sorting

The scheduling scheme is depicted in Fig. 1. The instances I_i, I_j, and I_k have high, medium, and low performance, respectively. The instance I_k belongs to a positive group and the other two instances (I_i, I_j) belong to a negative group. In the crossover operation, we select an instance to find the target instances that belong to the positive group. Next, we calculate the size of tasks in the positive group that are to be sent to the negative group (e.g., I_k). Finally, the calculated tasks are distributed to instances in the negative group (e.g., I_i and I_j) according to the performance of each instance. In mutation, we perform the re-arrangement of tasks. The re-arrange method sorts tasks in the increasing order of their indices.

3   Performance Evaluation

The simulations were conducted using the history data obtained from Amazon EC2 spot instances [6]. The history data before 10-01-2010 was used to extract the expected execution time and failure occurrence probability for our checkpointing scheme. The applicability of our scheme was tested using the history data after 10-01-2010. Table 1 shows the parameters and values for the simulation.

Table 1. Simulation parameters and values for instances

Simulation parameter	Task time interval	Distribution time	Merge time	Checkpoint time	Recovery time
Value	43,200(s)	300(s)	300(s)	300(s)	300(s)

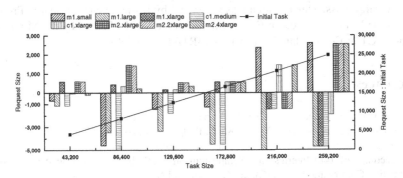

Fig. 2. Size variations in requested tasks

Fig. 2 shows the size variations of requested tasks in each instance before and after using the proposed estimation. Initial Task stands for the initial task size before using the estimation in all instances. The task size is determined based on the performance of each instance, and the task is distributed among the different instances. Each instance type (m1.small, m1.large, etc.) indicates the task size.

Fig. 3 shows the variation of the allocated task size in each instance I_i when task size is 86,400. In each instance, as the task size grows, the instance with high performance increased the task size, whereas the instance with low performance reduced the task size. It is due to the failure time of each instance. Therefore, we reduced the failure time of low performance instances in order to achieve similar estimated failure times across all instances.

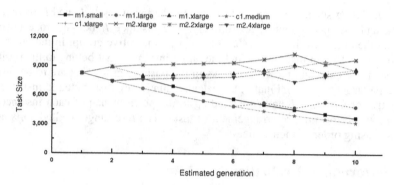

Fig. 3. Task size variation in each estimated generation

4   Conclusion

In this paper, we proposed an estimation-based task load balancing scheduling in unreliable cloud computing environments. The proposed scheduling technique achieves the task load balancing according to the performance of instances. In our scheme, we reduced the failure time of low performance instances in order to achieve similar estimated failure times across all instances.

Acknowledgments. This research was supported by Basic Science Research Program through the National Research Foundation of Korea (NRF) funded by the Ministry of Science, ICT & Future Planning (NRF-2013R1A1A3007940).

References

1. Elastic Compute Cloud (EC2) (2013), http://aws.amazon.com/ec2
2. Ferraris, F.L., Franceschelli, D., Gioiosa, M.P., Lucia, D., Ardagna, D., Di Nitto, E., Sharif, T.: Evaluating the Auto Scaling Performance of Flexiscale and Amazon EC2 Clouds. In: Proceedings of 14th International Symposium on Symbolic and Numeric Algorithms for Scientific Computing (SYNASC), pp. 423–429 (2012)
3. Van, H.N., Tran, F.D., Menaud, J.M.: SLA-Aware Virtual Resource Management for Cloud Infrastructures. In: Proceedings of the 2009 Ninth IEEE International Conference on Computer and Information Technology, vol. 2, pp. 357–362. IEEE Computer Society (2009)
4. Komal, M., Ansuyia, M., Deepak, D.: Round Robin with Server Affinity: A VM Load Balancing Algorithm for Cloud Based Infrastructure. Journal of Information Processing Systems 9(3), 379–394 (2013)
5. Jung, D., Lim, J., Yu, H., Gil, J., Lee, E.: A Workflow Scheduling Technique for Task Distribution in Spot Instance-Based Cloud. In: Jeong, Y.-S., Park, Y.-H., Hsu, C.-H(R.), Park, J.J(J.H.) (eds.) Ubiquitous Information Technologies and Applications. Lecture Notes in Electrical Engineering, vol. 280, pp. 409–416. Springer, Heidelberg (2014)
6. Cloud exchange (2013), http://cloudexchange.org

Distributed Ontology Integration Model for Cooperative Inference in Context Aware Computing

Soomi Yang

Department of Information Engineering, The University of Suwon
Hwangseong-si, Gyeonggi-do, Korea
smyang@suwon.ac.kr

Abstract. In this paper, an efficient ontology integration model for cooperative agent framework is proposed. Context aware computing with inference based on ontology investigates distributed entities on surveillance devices such as smart cameras or sensors which may carry heterogeneous data. However, even smart devices have small memory and power capacities which can only manage a portion of the ontology data. In the proposed ontology integration model, each of the agents that are built into devices get services not only from a region server, but also from peer agents with proper access control and data management.

1   Introduction

Context aware computing is indispensable for the construction of ubiquitous surveillance systems. Networked smart surveillance devices provide huge raw sensed data and inferred feature data. The available information is distributed over various information resources. The information resources are heterogeneous in their content, data format, organization, information management and the like. Heterogeneity of the information resources makes their integration difficult. Furthermore content within the information resources is changeable as it is continuously updated and modified. The agents installed in each smart device have constraints with regard to the memory and the power. Therefore the efficient management of their limited resources and the information is required.

2   Distributed Ontology Integration Model

Context aware computing regarding such as location trace requires the cooperation among the sensors[1]. For regional surveillance networks, a hierarchical tree infrastructure of the regional surveillance networks at the regional and administrative level similar to R-trees[2].

Ontology describes contexts such as concepts and relationships about target environment for the surveillance. None of single agent can accommodate the whole ontology. Each agent with a part of ontology forms a distributed graph structure. They can communicate each other freely within access control permission to perform their own intelligent distributed inference based on their own ontology[3]. We intend to refine

C.-H. Hsu et al. (Eds.): NPC 2014, LNCS 8707, pp. 575–578, 2014.

each of the local ontology groups and then develop knowledge bases by integrating several related neighboring ontologies. The regional surveillance network forms a hierarchical tree structure by administrative level. If the number of children that each non-leaf node is between m and M where $2 \leq m \leq M/2$, the height of the tree is bounded by $[\log_M N, \log_m N]$ when N is the number of ontology agents. Bandwidth between the agents is regulated by the tree level.

The data source agents need to carry out the indexing and retrieval of the information distributed across the agents in an efficient manner. To aid the task, a communication protocol is defined according to ONVIF standard[4]. As peers exchange information, they can negotiate and utilize caches based on the messages exchanged. For an adaptive cache management, weight of data is measured using $w = \lambda_{ki}^{f} \delta_{k}^{s} \mu_{i}^{r} h^{d}$ where λ is the access frequency, δ is the size of data, μ is the service interval and h is the distance between the agents similarly to [5]. As a result, better utilization of their limited cache space and higher system performance can be obtained.

3   Performance Evaluation

To evaluate the performance of the model, a simulation to count the number of packet transmissions for accomplishing context aware computing is carried out to inspect the effects on the average packet transmission. Fig. 1 shows the expected packet transmission by packet loss p and service interval μ. When the packet loss is small, the difference is small. However, as the packet loss gets bigger, it suffers more increasing packet transmission. When the packet loss is large, the performance can be managed by controlling the caching ratio q and adjusting the network structure.

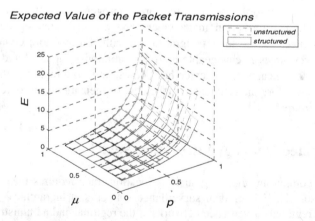

Fig. 1. A comparison of the expected packet transmissions

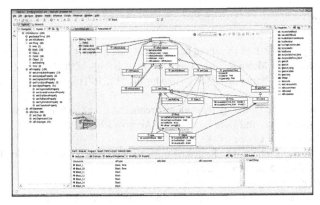

Fig. 2. An ontology description view

Several context ontologies reflecting various types of situation are under development, and the prototype system described in this paper is operated with inference based on ontology integration. Fig. 2 shows a portion of the ontology developed in TopBraid[6]. In the prototype system, surveillance environments are identified for context aware computing into knowledge bases. Final implementation of the proposed ontology integration model will be merged into wide area surveillance system named CUSST(Center for U-city Security and Surveillance Technology)[7].

4   Conclusion

In this paper, the distributed ontology integration model for cooperative inference in context aware computing is proposed. Data source agents exchange information with each other freely within access control in accordance to ONVIF standard. Agents perform their own integrated inference based on their own ontology knowledge base and others. The flexible cache scheme and scalable agent structure which is adaptive to the actual device demands and that of its neighbors help cooperative inference. Context inference including distributed multimedia data and biomedical feature data is widely used in surveillance environment including health surveillance[8]. In [8], biomedical ontologies are integrated in a graph approach. It can be combined with our ontology integration model.

The simulation and implementation are conducted to show the effectiveness of the proposed model. The expected packet transmission is inspected and the trend is analyzed. Realistic data is collected also to make the prototype system merge into wide area surveillance framework.

Acknowledgements. This work was supported by the GRRC program of Gyeonggi province. [GRRCSUWON2014-B1, Center for U-city Security and Surveillance Technology].

References

1. Sankaranarayanan, R.J.A., Veeraraghavan, A., Chellappa, R.: Object Detection, Tracking and Recognition for Multiple Smart Camaras. Proceedings of the IEEE 96(10) (2008)
2. Manolopoulos, Y., Nanopoulos, A., Theodoridis, Y.: R-Trees: Theory and Applications. Springer (2006)
3. Pan, J.Z.: A Flexible Ontology Reasoning Architecture for the Semantic Web. IEEE Transactions on Knowledge and Data Engineering Archive 19(2) (2007)
4. http://www.onvif.org/
5. Paknikar, A., Kankanhalli, M., Ramakrishnan, K.: A Caching and Streaming Framework for Multimedia. ACM Multimedia (2000)
6. http://www.topquadrant.com/
7. http://cusst.suwon.ac.kr/, http://grrc.suwon.ac.kr/
8. Shaban-Nejad, A., Haarslev, V.: An Enhanced Graph-Oriented Approach for Change Management in Distributed Biomedical Ontologies and Linked Data. In: Proceedings of the IEEE International Conferende on Bioinformatics and Biomedicine Workshops (2011)

Cross-Platform Parallel Programming
in PARRAY: A Case Study

Xiang Cui[1,2,4], Xiaowen Li[3], and Yifeng Chen[1,2]

[1] HCST Key Lab at School of EECS, Peking University, Beijing, China
[2] State Key Laboratory of Mathematical Engineering and Advanced Computing,
Wuxi, China
[3] Air Defense Forces Academy, Zhengzhou, China
[4] College of Computer & Information Engineering, Henan University, Kaifeng, China

Abstract. PARRAY (or Parallelizing ARRAYs) is an extension of C language that supports system-level succinct programming for heterogeneous parallel systems. PARRAY extends mainstream C programming with novel array types. This leads to shorter, more portable and maintainable parallel codes, while the programmer still has control over performance-related features necessary for deep manual optimization. This paper uses the case study on stepwise program refinement of matrix transposition to illustrate the basic techniques of PARRAY programming.

1   Introduction

PARRAY (or Parallelizing ARRAYs) is an extension of C language that supports system-level succinct programming for heterogeneous parallel systems [1,2]. PARRAY extends mainstream C programming with novel array types, which are then compiled to C code with machine-generated macros and vender-specific library calls. The programming style is unified for all forms of parallelism.

Matrix transposition, as a basic linear algebra algorithm, is implemented in PARRAY to demonstrate its *cross-platform* programming features. A unified PARRAY matrix-transposition code can run on hardware platforms like CPU, MIC and GPU with only memory types modified and achieve high performance.

2   Array Types of PARRAY

The following array type A in paged main memory has three dimensions:

$parray paged float[[n][n]][m] A

and consists of n*n*m elements. PARRAY supports various other memory types such as dmem for GPU device memory, micmem for MIC memory and so on. The following commands declare two type-A array objects x and y as pointers and allocate memory to the pointers using the corresponding library calls of the memory type. Note that the commands are the same as $create A(x,y) in shorthand.

C.-H. Hsu et al. (Eds.): NPC 2014, LNCS 8707, pp. 579–582, 2014.

```
float *x,*y;   $malloc A(x,y)
```

Unlike C language, type A nests its first two dimensions together, and is also a two-dimensional type. The size $size(A_0)$ of the column dimension A_0 is n*n, which is split into two sub-dimensions A_0_0 and A_0_1 of size n.

PARRAY allows array dimensions to refer to existing types. The following type B also consists of n*n*m elements:

```
$parray dmem float[[#A_0_1][#A_0_0]][#A_1] B
```

but is allocated in GPU's device memory. Its row dimension B_1 has the same offsets as A_1 (according to dimensional reference #A_1), but the sub-dimensions of the column dimension are swapped. The following PARRAY command $copy performed by a CPU thread duplicates n*n*m floats at address x in main memory to address y in GPU device memory :

```
$copy A(x) to B(y).
```

If we consider every m adjacent elements as a unit, the layout of y is exactly a matrix transposition of x. A simple way to map the elements of an array is to use for command like the following code of array initialization where the pointer y is moved to the address of each element for processing, and (*y) obtains the element:

```
$for B(y) {(*y)=0;}.
```

3   Case Study

The performance of matrix transposition on different hardware platforms highly depends on the underlying architecture and requires system-level programming. Unified cross-platform programming to achieve high performance is challenging. In this case study, we illustrate a simple algorithm, a cache-friendly block-wise algorithm and a tile-buffered algorithm with different levels of performance optimization. The programming style remains tidy and unified for these algorithms.

3.1   Simple Matrix Transposition

The following code performs a square matrix transposition in memory by CPU:

```
$parray {paged double [n][n]} C
$parray {paged double [#C_1][#C_0]} D
$main{......
    $for C(x),D(y){ *y=*x;}
    ......}
```

where type C is declared as a n*n double array in main memory. Type D also has two dimensions referred from C but swaped. The for command makes sure the pointer x is moved to the address of C's each element which is copied to corresponding pointer y whose offset is calculated according to type D. The square matrix is transposed as a result. By changing the memory type of C and D from paged to micmem or dmem, the code can be easily run on MIC or GPU.

3.2 Blocked Matrix Transposition

A more effective way to do the matrix transposition is the blocked transposition algorithm. The matrix is divided into a checkerboard of small blocks. Two blocks that are symmetrically distributed with respect to the leading diagonal are identified and their data is swapped with each other with the elements of every block also in transposed form. Data distribution is defined as follows:

```
$parray {paged double [[q][n/q]][[q][n/q]]} E
$parray {paged double [[#E_0_0][#E_1_0]][[#E_0_1][#E_1_1]]} F
$parray {paged double [[#E_1_0][#E_0_0]][[#E_1_1][#E_0_1]]} G
```

where type E partitions the initial square dimension of n*n into (q*(n/q)) * (q*(n/q)). F is declared by reordering E's dimensions to represent the initial array layout as q*q blocks of (n/q)*(n/q) doubles. Compared with F, type G represents the layout after transposition. The PARRAY code is as follows:

```
$main{......
   $for F_0(x),G_0(y){
      $for F_1(x),G_1(y) { *y=*x; }}
   ......}
```

where the outer for command moves the pointers x to the beginning addresses of each block before transposition and y after transposition respectively; then the inner for command handles each block.

3.3 Buffered Matrix Transposition

For different processors, data buffer could be used to further improve performance when transposing each block. Elements in one block could be fetched into a buffer and written back to memory in a more efficient way.

With MIC, in order to get higher memory bandwidth, array accesses should be vectorized. MIC has 512-bit vector registers and every 64 doubles can be fetched into one vector register. The data buffer is defined as follows:

```
$parray {vmem double [n/q][n/q]} H
```

where vector memory type H has the same size with one block and is used to describe the vector register buffer. The PARRAY code is as follows:

```
$main{......
   $for F_0(x),G_0(y){
      $for F_1(x) itile H, G_1(y) otile H {
         $for H(x,y) {*y=*x;}}}
   ......}
```

where itile/otile clause of PARRAY is used to specify the data buffer used. Actually, the above PARRAY code can be written in a more simply way:

```
$parray {paged double [n][n]} F
$parray {paged double [#F_1][#F_0]} G
$parray {vmem double [n/q][n/q]} H
$main{......
    $for G(x) itile H, H(y) otile H{
        $for H(x,y) {*y=*x;}}
    ......}
```

where the matrix will be divided to tiles automatically when doing transposition. Similarly, with GPU, shared memory can be used to avoid the large strides of accessing device memory when doing matrix transposition.

This code is tested for various matrix sizes and achieves about 78 and 88 GB/s on MIC and Nvidia K20 GPU respectively (which are about 70% peak bandwidths of contiguous data transfer on both accelerators).

Table 1. Matrix transposition v.s. peak bandwidth of contiguous data transfer

	Simple	Block-wise	Tile-buffered	Peak bandwidth
CPU	3.49	10.45	N/A	32.89
MIC(60 cores)	4.98	6.53	78.73	101.13
Nvidia K20 GPU	7.68	12.38	87.75	150.34

4   Conclusion

This paper uses a case study on stepwise program refinement of matrix transposition to illustrate the basic techniques of PARRAY programming and its *cross-platform* programming features. Layout patterns before and after transposition can be defined using PARRAY's *array types* easily and clearly. A unified PARRAY matrix-transposition code can run on hardware platforms like CPU, MIC and GPU with only memory types modified and achieve high performance.

Acknowledgement. This research is supported by the National HTRD 863 Plan of China under Grant No. 2012AA010902, 2012AA010903; the National Natural Science Foundation of China under Grant No. 61240045, 61170053, 61379048; the China Postdoctoral Science Foundation under Grant No. 2013M540821; the State Key Laboratory of Mathematical Engineering and Advanced Computing under Grant No. 2013A12; the Science and Technology Key Project of Education Department of Henan Province under Grant No. 13A520065.

References

1. Chen, Y., Cui, X., Mei, H.: PARRAY: A Unifying Array Representation for Heterogeneous Parallelism. In: PPoPP 2012 (2012)
2. PekingUniversityManycoreSoftwareResearchGroup (2014),
   http://code.google.com/p/parray-programming/

Different Solvers Evaluation for a Bucking Problem

Chau-Yi Chou[1], Jiunn-Horng Lee[1], Yu-Fen Cheng[1],
Chih-Wei Hsieh[1], and Weichung Wang[2]

[1] National Center for High-Performance Computing, Taiwan
[2] Institute of Applied Mathematical Sciences, National Taiwan University
cychou@nchc.narl.org.tw

Abstract. The linear system solver plays a key role in scientific computing. This paper evaluates the performances of PETSc (Portable, Extensible Toolkit for Scientific Computation) and HIPS (Portable, Extensible Toolkit for Scientific Computation) solving a singular matrix arising from a bucking problem from UF matrix collection. We employ preconditioned (Level-based ILU) iterative methods (GMRES) for PETSc while HIPS adopts the Schur complement method, named iterative or hybrid mode. Moreover, HIPS proposed HID (Hierarchical interface decomposition) to improve the parallel efficiency. We hope to transfer these results into industrial applications.

Results

These results were performed on ALPS in National Center for High-performance Computing (NCHC). The hardware of computing nodes on NCHC ALPS consists of 600 of Acer AR585 and are connected together with Qlogic InfiniBand in 4x QDR (40Gb). Each node contains 48 cores sharing 128 GB RAM in 4-memory-controller non-uniform memory access architecture.

The singular matrix was proposed by Arthur Raefsky for a buckling problem for container models in 1993. The id number in UF matrix collection [1] is 817. Table 1 presents the matrix characteristic. From Table 1, we know that this matrix is a singular matrix because of her dimension unequal to her rank.

Table 1. Matrix Characteristic

Name	N	NNZ	Condition Number	rank
raefsky4	19779	1316789	3.13E13	19771

The stopping criteria were used the scaled residual < 1E-7 [2]. This study first evaluated the performance of different k levels of ILU(k) preconditioned GMRES iterative method via PETSc. Table 2 depicted the results (the number of iterations, elapsed time in second, scaled residual, peak fill-in ratio) of different levels via PETSc. The "peak fill-in ratio" denoted the ratio of the memory to the original one in order to show the memory increment. It had to pay the penalties of the elapsed time and the memory for increasing levels. Because that the infinity norm [3] of the

C.-H. Hsu et al. (Eds.): NPC 2014, LNCS 8707, pp. 583–586, 2014.

computed solutions between 7 and 100 levels was near 7.55E-7, we adopted 7 levels for PETSc hereafter.

Table 2. Results of ILU(k) preconditioned GMRES iterative method via PETSc

ILU(k)	No. iter.	Elapsed time (Sec.)	Scaled residual	Peak fill-in ratio
7	37	2.75E1	8.30E-6	11.70
10	24	4.88E1	3.63E-6	15.89
100	2	1.80E2	4.38E-6	25.19

HIPS used the Schur complement method, HID, threshold ILUT preconditioned GMRES iterative method, named iterative or hybrid mode [4] to solve the linear system. Iterative mode used the ILUT preconditioned GMRES iterative method; however, hybrid mode first divided the linear system into the interior system and the Schur complement. Then, the direct method dealt with the interior system while the ILUT preconditioned GMRES iterative method dealt with the Schur complement. Therefore, the hybrid mode used both the direct and iterative methods to solve this linear system.

Take 100 Krylov subspaces and let the maximal number of iterations be 100. Use the scaled residual to check the accuracy of the computed solutions. Fig. 1 shows the breakdown of the iterative mode compared with PETSc_seq. HIPS outperforms because of HID. Fig. 2 illustrates the breakdown of the hybrid mode. From Fig. 1 and Fig. 2, the hybrid mode lightly outperforms iterative mode when MPI jobs are less than 16; however, the iterative mode shows lightly faster than the hybrid mode on 16 MPI jobs.

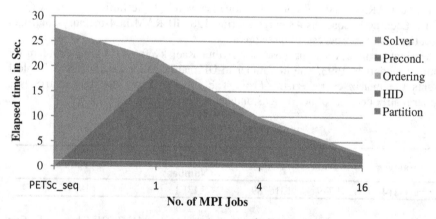

Fig. 1. Breakdown of PETSc and HIPS (iterative mode)

Fig. 3 shows the speedup of the iterative and hybrid modes via HIPS. Both modes via HIPS have near speedup because of problem size limit. Fig. 4 shows the number of iterations via HIPS. Parallel affects the accuracy in the iterative mode; however, the hybrid mode doesn't.

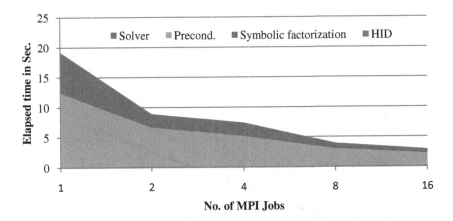

Fig. 2. Breakdown of HIPS hybrid mode

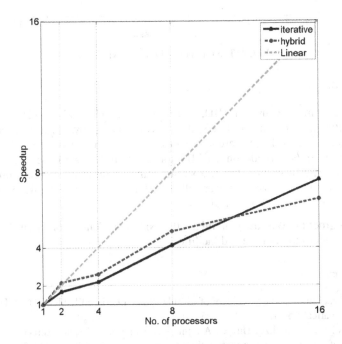

Fig. 3. HIPS Speedup

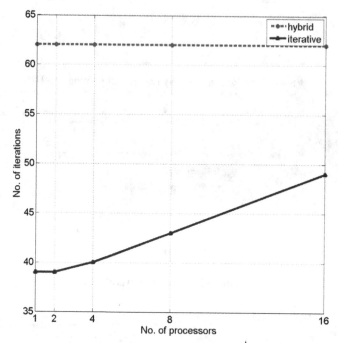

Fig. 4. The number of iterations via HIPS

Conclusion

HIPS outperforms because of HID. HIPS shows good parallel performance, too. Dealing with this problem via HIPS, the hybrid mode shows lightly faster than the iterative mode when MPI jobs are less than 16 while the iterative mode shows lightly faster than the hybrid mode on 16 MPI jobs. Our future work will focus on auto tuning via PETSc to suggest the best solution among these packages. Moreover, we will systematically analyze the linear solver performances for an application field, for example, solid and structural mechanics.

Acknowledgments. We are grateful to the National Center for High-Performance Computing for computer time and facilities.

References

1. Davis, T.A., Hu, Y.: The university of Florida sparse matrix collection. ACM Transactions on Mathematical Software 38(1), 1–25 (2011)
2. Gould, N.I.M., Scott, J.A., Hu, Y.: A numerical evaluation of sparse direct solvers for the solution of large sparse symmetric linear systems of equations. ACM Transactions on Mathematical Software 33(2), 10 (2007)
3. Golub, G.H., Loan, C.L.: Matrix computations, 3rd edn. Johns Hopkins University Press, Baltimore (1996)
4. Gaidamour, J., Hénon, P.: A parallel direct/iterative solver based on a Schur complement approach. In: Proceedings of the IEEE International Conference on Computational Science and Engineering, pp. 98–105 (2008)

Quality of Service Enhancement by Using an Integer Bloom Filter Based Data Deduplication Mechanism in the Cloud Storage Environment

Kuo-Qin Yan[1], Yung-Hsiang Su[1], Hsin-Met Chuan[2],
Shu-Ching Wang[1,*], and Bo-Wei Chen[1]

[1] Chaoyang University of Technology, Taiwan, R.O.C.
{kqyan,s10033905,scwang,s10114603}@cyut.edu.tw
[2] Hsing-Kuo University, Taiwan, R.O.C.
hn88780752@yahoo.com.tw

Abstract. Network bandwidth and hardware technology are developing rapidly, resulting in the vigorous development of the Internet. A concept, cloud computing, uses low-power hosts to achieve high quality service. According to the characteristics of cloud computing, the cloud service providers can support the service applications on the Internet. There are a lot of applications and data centers in the cloud-computing environment, then the loading of storage node is heavier than before. However, data deduplication techniques can greatly reduce the amount of data. Therefore, an integer Bloom Filter based Lightweight Deduplication Mechanism (LDM) under cloud storage is proposed. The proposed LDM can reduce the extra cost that traditional data deduplication technique needed.

Result

As network bandwidth and quality outstrip computer performance, various communication and computing technologies previously regarded as being of different domains can now be integrated, such as telecommunication, multimedia, information technology, and construction simulation. Thus, applications associated with network integration have gradually attracted considerable attention. Similarly, cloud computing facilitated through distributed applications over networks has also gained increased recognition. In a cloud-computing environment, users have access to faster operational capability on the Internet [2], and the computer systems must have high stability to keep pace with this level of activity.

In the data deduplication strategy, the block-level strategy is used. The block-level strategy has higher reduction ration than file-level but must consume more computing resource that is not suitable in cloud computing [3]. In this study, an integer Bloom Filter [4] based Lightweight Deduplication Mechanism (LDM) under cloud storage is presented to solve this problem. In the proposed LDM system architecture, several storage nodes are grouped into a cluster, each cluster has a storage node acts cluster are called Namenode, the other storage node are called Datanode. Namenode is responsible for perform LDM and placement data to Datanode, Namenode also

---

* Corresponding author.

C.-H. Hsu et al. (Eds.): NPC 2014, LNCS 8707, pp. 587–590, 2014.

provides the storage capacity. Each Namenode has two components, LDM and Metadata Table. The LDM is used to perform deduplication strategy, and Metadata Table is responsible for the metadata of stored data. The proposed system architecture is shown as Fig. 1. The main job of Transfer Agent System (TAS) is used to upload data when the requests of user are received. The data is partitioned into n chunks and translated into unique identifier by SHA-1. Then, the unique identifier of data chunks is delivered to cluster by TAS for comparison data.

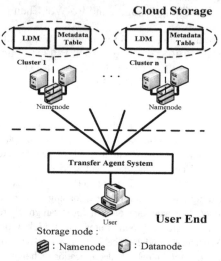

Fig. 1. The LDM System Architecture

In the proposed system architecture, each cluster executes LDM. The steps are described in below:

1. Set the number of hash function (k). For example, Cloud Service Provider (CSP) chooses seven hash functions.
2. Calculate the quantity of data that each cluster can store (n_{max}). For example, if the capacity of cluster is 40 GB and data chunk capacity is 64 MB, then this cluster can store 640 data (40 GB/64 MB).
3. Calculate the length of Bloom Filter (m) by using:

$$k=(m/n)\ln 2=m/n*0.69314 \tag{1}$$

   Through formula (1), Bloom Filter length (m) is 6463.
4. Calculate the probability of "Positive False" by using:

$$f'=(1-(1/m)^{kn})^k \tag{2}$$

   Through formula (2), the probability of "Positive False" is 0.0078 that means the average 1000 times query will occur 8 times "Positive False".
5. CSP chooses an accept probability of "Positive False", and then the initialization of Bloom Filter is completed. If CSP cannot accept an accept probability of "Positive False", then return to Step 1. In addition, a bigger k is chosen that can get smaller probability of "Positive False".

A linked structure is used by LDM to store the metadata. When a data is added, to calculate the unique identifier by k hash functions and mapping to Bloom Filter firstly, then the hash value is computed to decide the starting position of link. The calculator formula is shown in (3), where $val(h_i)$ is the i_{th} hash value, m is Bloom Filter length, % symbol is mod function.

$$Link(position) = (\sum_{i=1}^{k} val(h_i)) \% m \tag{3}$$

By formula (3), a position in Bloom Filter can be obtained, and then link to the metadata of data chunk. For example, if there are 4 hash functions, $val(h_1) = 6069$, $val(h_2) = 36$, $val(h_3) = 5$, $val(h_4) = 642$, and $m = 6463$, by using formula (3), the link start position is 289 [(6069+36+5+642) % 6463 = 289], therefore, this data will be linked to intBF index number 289. When the same result is gotten by different data through formula (3), then a links is generated by the last linked list. The progression of LDM is shown as Fig. 2.

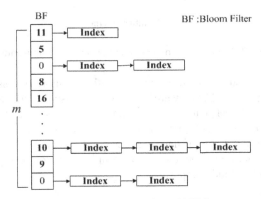

Fig. 2. The progression of LDM

In the data deduplication, the process of comparison is same as the process of data added. In the comparison process, the unique identifier is calculated by k hash functions firstly. Then, LDM judges the status of data existence by using intBF. If this data is not exist, do not perform the compare process, else if intBF judge this data is existence, to find the link position through formula (3), and search all link nodes to find the same data. However, the average comparison times in data duplication of our proposed LDM is compared with iBF (indexed Bloom Filter) proposed by Antichi et al. [1]. The capacity of storage node was generated by NS2, include current consume capacity and maximum capacity. The unique identifier was generated by md5-database [5], md5-database can transform data in to a unique identifier by MD5, SHA1, SHA256, and SHA512. However, SHA-1 was used in this experimental. There are 250 original data, include 150 movie data (2441 data chunk after partition), and 100 backup data (2518 data chunk after partition). Original data are partitioned by 64 MB, and there are 4959 data chunks totally. C++ is used to write the proposed mechanism. Finally, MS Excel 2010 is used to record experimental result. In addition, when a new data is uploaded, the unique identifier of data will be compared with storage system. In this experiment, data deduplication is performed in storage system which stored different number of data (25%, 50%, 75%, 100% of total data).

In this experiment, there are 20 data be uploaded in four kinds of situation and perform the data deduplication comparison processes. Fig. 3 is the results of average comparison times. X-axis is the different number of data; Y-axis is the average comparison times.

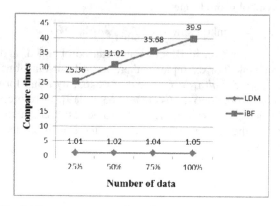

Fig. 3. The average comparison times in Data Duplication

According to the results shown in Fig. 3, whether in more or less number of data, the comparison times in LDM were keep in a constant time nearly. From the experiment results, LDM can use less computing resource to complete data deduplication process that is more suitable in cloud storage. In this study, LDM through rapid judge the status of data existence and compare the same data position can reduce the computing resource of data deduplication compare process, and then LDM more suitable in cloud computing.

Acknowledgments. This work was supported in part by the Ministry of Science and Technology MOST 102-2221-E-324-008 and MOST 103-2221-E-324-025.

References

1. Antichi, G., Pietro, A.D., Ficara, D., Giordano, S., Russo, F., Vitucci, F.: Achieving Perfect Hashing through an Improved Construction of Bloom Filters. In: The IEEE International Conference on Communications, pp. 1–5 (May 2010)
2. Aymerich, F.M., Fenu, G., Surcis, S.: An approach to a cloud computing network. In: The 1st International Conference on Applications of Digital Information and Web Technologies, pp. 113–118 (August 2008)
3. Tsuchiya, Y., Watanabe, T.: DBLK: Deduplication for Primary Block Storage. In: The of IEEE 27th Symposium on Mass Storage Systems and Technologies (MSST), pp. 1–5 (2011)
4. Wang, S.C., Wang, S.S., Yan, K.Q., Chen, B.W.: HDDS: Hybrid data DeDuplication Strategy over Cloud Storage. In: The International Conference on Innovation and Management, p. 103 (July 2012)
5. Unique Identifier Database, http://md5-database.org/sha1/

Fault-Tolerant Storage Servers for the Databases of Redundant Web Servers in a Computing Grid

MinHwan Ok

Korea Railroad Research Institute, Woulam, Uiwang, Gyeonggi, Korea
mhok@krri.re.kr

Abstract. Computing Grid in this paper is a Grid computing environment that supplies applications which run in a local computing site only, without any modification or adaptation for running globally in the Grid computing environment. Each stage of a running application is transcribed at all the management databases coupled with respective Web servers. The consistency is maintained by double-checking of every acknowledgement against a write to all the management databases and a circulated read response from either database. The storage spaces could be integrated into a single one by storage managers within a computing site. The modification of a file is broadcast to the storage managers sharing the storage space and their allocation tables are updated immediately. The system architecture is in a distributed control type, potentially the best match for Cloud computing.

Keywords: Scalable Web service, computing Grid, Fault-tolerant, Storage virtualization.

1 Constructing the Computing Grid

In the system model, the applications are provided to the users by Web service. A client computer connects to the Web server of the coordinator. Coordination Service is composed of user interfaces to log-on the computing Grid and to input parameters with user input/output data transfer. DB Organizer is the manager of information including parameters input, software title selected, and details concerned with user ID. It also selects appropriate computing site for the user. DB Connector is a client of DB Organizer and read/write information/report from/to the management database. Applications are launched, controlled and landed through Application Manager, which would be a kind of RFB Service. In Fig. 1, Application Manager delivers the commands included in the order, which is received via DB Connector, to the Application. When transferring the output data, Application Server should be re-authenticated for the security of user data.

On writing information to the management DB of the originator coordinator, the originator writes the same information to the management DBs of the other coordinator, if one or more coordinator does not respond to the writing, the coordinator is presumed crashed-down. This is broadcast to the remained coordinators. On reading information from the management DB of the originator coordinator, the originator

C.-H. Hsu et al. (Eds.): NPC 2014, LNCS 8707, pp. 591–594, 2014.

initiates reading from the management DB of the next coordinator, after reading the information from the its own management DB. The reading is relayed returning to the originator, thus it is named *Circulated Read Request*. If one or more coordinator does not respond to this reading, the coordinator is presumed crashed-down and this is also broadcast to the remained coordinators.

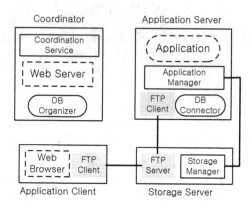

Fig. 1. System architecture of the computing Grid

Fig. 2 illustrates the circulated read request/response, the broadcast write is illustrated in Fig. 3. In both information writing and information circulated reading, the originator creates *Replay Roll* if it detects any crashed-down coordinator. Replay roll is the list of DB transactions from the point the crash-down is detected to the point the crashed-down coordinator broadcasts its restart. Then the coordinator updates its management DB following the replay roll the originator has sent. Keeping up the recorded information identical is the major issue in this follow-up scenario.

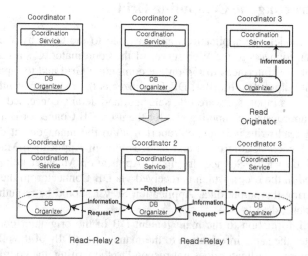

Fig. 2. Information reading from either management DB is relayed, which will be circulated to the originator and the originator responds with the information last

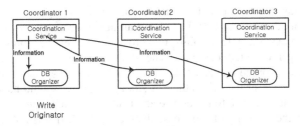

Fig. 3. Information writing to the management DB of the other coordinators are acknowledged later and the coordination service continues without these acknowledgements

2   Multiple Storage Servers

Ancillary to the selected one among local computing sites the software installed, one of storage servers is designated for sizable storage space to process large quantities of data with the storage farm. The storage space for application running is confined within the application server in the previous work[1]. It is also confined in the application server in this work, except that the whole data is partitioned and the partitions are replaced to be processed in the application server in the manner similar to the virtual memory. The application has restarted in the case of the storage server failure in the previous work, however the application rolls back to the previous phase of the current partition in this work. For active/standby failover, the allocation table is mirrored to the other storage server. A couple of storage servers are assigned to backups of each other, and the storage manager has dual modes between active/standby in normal status and active/active in abnormal status, of the other server. Coupling two storage servers is static and conducted by the administrator.

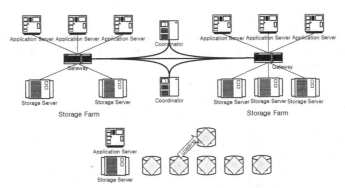

Fig. 4. Computing Grid Organization and storage management on partitioned data

Since multiple storage servers govern the storage farm, the write to a storage device is allowed while the storage manager has the token of the device that the token is traversing storage servers otherwise. Once the storage manager wrote to a storage device, it broadcasts allocation information of the written file to other storage managers so that storage managers sharing the storage space would update their allocation tables. The storage devices could constitute one single storage space spanned from one device to another, for availability losing an advantage of parallelized access of striping. When one storage device fails, it is broadcast among the storage managers by a storage manager detected the fault. The storage space of the device is marked 'missing' at all the storage managers, analogous to bad blocks, and access to files located at the space is restricted from then. A storage manager should have the token of a device when it has to write to the device and it waits for the token. The investigation protocol is described in Fig. 5 for the case the token of a device is not returned before the failure of a storage manager.

- The storage manager waited for a predefined duration broadcasts the request for the last use time of that token.
- If all the other managers responds the storage manager wait for another predefined duration. After the duration the storage manager queries the manager of the latest use whether the writing is done.

- On reply of 'In–Use' the storage manager waits for another predefined duration, and Repeat the querying/waiting. Otherwise, the storage manager creates other token and sends 'Alternative Token' to the manager it queried.
- If the manager it queried does not reply with 'Token Destroy', the storage server broadcasts the failure of the respective storage server.

Fig. 5. Investigation into the storage manager which is queried whether its writing is done

Reference

1. Ok, M.-H., Lee, K.-S.: A Consolidation Model of Web Application Servers toward a Simplified Computing Grid. In: International Conference on Multimedia and Ubiquitous Engineering, Seoul, Korea, pp. 757–761 (2007)

Scheduling Cloud Platform Managed Live-Migration Operations to Minimize the Makespan

Xiaoyong Yuan[1], Ying Li[1,2], Yanqi Wang[3], and Kewei Sun[3]

[1] School of Software and Microelectronics, Peking University, Beijing, China
[2] National Engineering Center of Software Engineering,
Peking University, Beijing, China
[3] IBM Research - China, Beijing, China

Abstract. Live-migration of virtual machines (VMs) has become an indispensable management operation of cloud platforms. The cloud platforms need to migrate multiple co-located and live VMs from one physical node to another for power saving, load balancing and maintenance. Such live-migration operations are critical to the running services, and thus should be completed as fast as possible. State-of-the-art live-migration techniques optimize the migration performance of single or multiple VMs by concentrating on Virtual Machine Monitor (VMM), little attention has been given to the cloud platforms which control and schedule the multiple migration operations. In this paper, we consider the problem of scheduling migration operations to minimize the makespan.

1   Cloud Platform Managed Migration Operations

Live-migration of VMs has become an indispensable management operation of cloud platforms. Cloud platforms present users the ability to deploy VMs over a cluster of physical machines on demand from a centralized management node, thus building what is usually referred to as a VM-based cloud, which can then be used to provide IaaS. At the current stage, however, several management issues still deserve additional investigation, such as performance of management operations. The research[1] reveals that the burst of management operations such as VM live-migration is the rule rather than the exception, in the VM-based cloud, and planning and orchestrating management operations is essential for efficient cloud operations. State-of-the-art live VM migration techniques optimize migration performance of single or multiple VMs performed by VMM, whereas the optimization of scheduling live-migrations centralized managed by cloud platform is still missing, especially for new platform(eg. OpenStack). For example, it will take more than 2 minutes for OpenStack to migrate 30 idle VMs (KVM driver), for that the applications within VMs suffer from degraded performance.

In cloud platform like OpenStack and CloudStack, live-migration as a management operation, is viewed as a transactional interaction between a controller node and two compute nodes which provide computation capability. The migration operation has 4 phases: 1) *checking* that the scheduler on controller node

C.-H. Hsu et al. (Eds.): NPC 2014, LNCS 8707, pp. 595–599, 2014.

finds a proper destination node; 2) *pre-migration* that the destination node builds a new idle instance for receiving contents; 3) *live-migration* that VMM (eg. Libvirt in OpenStack) is invoked to perform live-migration of VM from source to destination using pre-copy method[2]; 4) *post-migration* is a phase that the instance tears down network and updates its status on source node. In this paper, we consider optimizing migration operations of multiple co-located VMs from one physical node to another. Supposing we are given n VMs on the source node to be migrated, cloud platform will schedule and perform a set of n migration operations $\mathbf{M} = \{MO_1, MO_2, \ldots, MO_n\}$, as depicted in Figure 1. For each migration operation MO_i, T_{ij} is its processing time in phase j. Besides phase $1-4$, there is a phase 0 to indicate its waiting time for performing. The objective is to find a feasible schedule of minimum completion time of n migration operations; that is, to minimize the makespan $\mathbf{C}$:

$$\min_{\mathbf{M}} \mathbf{C}\left(\mathbf{M}\right), \tag{1}$$

where makespan $\mathbf{C}$ is the maximum completion time of n migration operations:

$$\mathbf{C}\left(\mathbf{M}\right) = \max_i \Sigma_{j=0}^{4} T_{ij}, \quad i = 1, 2, \ldots, n. \tag{2}$$

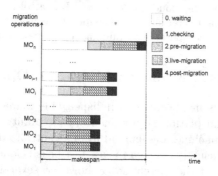

Fig. 1. Cloud platform managed VM migration operations

2   Scheduling

2.1   Multiple Migration Operations of Idle VM

In order to save physical resource and reduce operational cost, the cloud platform need to migrate idle or light workload VMs among servers for consolidation. When the cloud platform performs n migration operations of idle VMs between two nodes, the makespan varies with the number of migration operations m performed concurrently. If $m = 1$, n migration operations are performed sequentially, and with m increasing, more migration operations are executed simultaneously in one group. The migration operation in different phases is mainly performed on different node (i.e., phase 1 on controller node, phase 2 on destination node, phase 3 and 4 on source node). When $m = N_i$, the processing time of m migration operations in phase i will greatly exceed that of $m = N_i - 1$, because the nodes capacity can't afford that concurrency level. For example, in phase 1, controller node can't afford N_1 concurrent migration operations and the processing time would be extremely large compared with that of $N_1 - 1$ operations. The processing time of m concurrent migration operations in phase i is defined by

$$T_{ij}(m) = \begin{cases} (n - N_j)T_j^*, & n > N_j \\ T_j^*, & n \le N_j \end{cases} \quad (j = 1, 2, 4)$$

T_i^* is a constant coefficient of each equations. Here we perform m migration operations simultaneously by group. To complete n migration operations, $\frac{n}{m}$ groups are going to be migrated in all. Because the duration of live-migration phase of migration operations of idle VM is short compared with other phases, T_{3i} can be assumed as constant, and let $T_{3i} = T_3^*$. For there's no different in T_{i1}, T_{i2}, T_{i4} among VMs, for these phases are cloud management related, not VM related. We let $T_{i1} = T_1(m), T_{i2} = T_2(m), T_{i4} = T_4(m), m = 1, 2, \ldots, n$ for convenience. Waiting time in each group should be the maximum time among $\{T_1(m), T_2(m), T_4(m)\}$ (Figure 2), so that there is no overlap between different groups and won't affect each other. Hence the makespan of n migration operations is:

$$\mathbf{C}(\mathbf{M}) = T_{complete}(m) + T_{wait}(m)(\frac{n}{m} - 1), \tag{3}$$

where $T_{complete}$ is the complete time in one group: $T_{complete}(m) = T_1(m) + T_2(m) + T_3^* + T_4(m)$, and T_{wait} is the waiting time between groups: $T_{wait}(m) = \max\{T_1(m), T_2(m), T_4(m)\}$. The optimal number m in one group should be the minimum point of $\mathbf{C}(\mathbf{M})$.

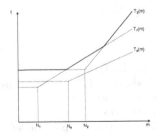 

Fig. 2. Waiting time function $T_{wait}(m)$

Fig. 3. Schedule for migration operations

2.2 Multiple Migration Operations of Busy VM

Sometimes, the cloud platform need to migrate busy VMs among servers for load balancing. For cloud platform managed migration operations of busy VM, the live-migration phase is the most influential one than others. We pay attention to migration operation in phase 3 this time. Supposing the migration operation MO_i with memory size VM_i, dirty page rate DR_i and bandwidth of each operation regulated as bm_i, we estimate processing time of live-migration phase T_{i3} by approximate algorithm[3]. As shown in Algorithm 1, once given input of MO_i: VM_i, bm_i, DR_i, the migration time T_{i3} can be estimated by simulating migration operation.

According to approximate algorithm, network bandwidth is the most influential parameter. As network bandwidth decreasing, migration performance starts to degrade rapidly especially for busy VM. We consider following network parameters: network bandwidth BD in cloud, bandwidth bm_i utilized in each operation, and bandwidth br_i reserved to maintain an acceptable quality of service in live-migration phase[5]. bd_i, sum of bm_i and br_i, is a necessity of network bandwidth for both migration performance and service quality during each migration. When migration operations are performed simultaneously, the number of migration operations m is limited so that the sum of m migration operations' bandwidth bd_i can't exceed network bandwidth BD. To minimize the makespan, our work is to arrange the order and waiting time for migration operations properly.

Now it is kind of strip-packing problem: pack items with various width and height into a big strip which has fixed width and variable height, and the objective is to minimize the height of strip. In Figure 3, we illustrate n migration

---

Algorithm 1. Performance Model for Migration

INPUT: $\qquad bm_i, VM_i, DR_i$
OUTPUT: T_{i3}
$v_o \leftarrow VM$, $v_{mig} \leftarrow 0$, $t_{mig} \leftarrow 0$; //Given $iter_{th}$, v_{th} as default values
for $i = 0$ **to** $iter_{th}$ **do**
$\quad t_i \leftarrow \frac{v_i}{bm_i}$;
$\quad v_{i+1} \leftarrow t_i \cdot DR_i$;
$\quad t_{mig} \leftarrow t_{mig} + t_i$;
$\quad v_{mig} \leftarrow v_{mig} + v_i$;
$\quad$**if** $v_{i+1} \leq v_{th}$ **or** $v_{mig} \geq VM_i$
$\quad$**then**
$\qquad$break;
$\quad$**end if**
end for
$T_{i3} \leftarrow t_{mig} + \frac{v_{i+1}}{bm_i}$

Algorithm 2. Scheduling of migration operations

INPUT: $BD, bm_i, br_i, VM_i, DR_i$ OUTPUT: $T_{i0}, \mathbf{C}$
for $i = 0$ **to** n **do**
$\quad T_{i3} = f(VM_i, bm_i, DR_i)$; //$f$ denotes Algorithm 1
end for
$bd_i = bm_i + br_i$;
$[bd_{k_1}, bd_{k_2}, \ldots, bd_{k_n}] = sort([bd_1, bd_2, \ldots, bd_n])$; //sort by non-increasing sequence
for $i = 0$ **to** n **do**
$\quad$//find lowest possible position left justified for operation k_i
$\quad (h_{k_i}, w_{k_i}) = lowleft(bd_{k_i}, T_{i3})$;
$\quad T_{k_i 0} \leftarrow h_{k_i}$;
end for
$\mathbf{C} \leftarrow \max(h_{k_i} + T_{k_i 3})$;

operations, each having live-migration time T_{i3} and waiting time T_{i0}. The width of strip is bandwidth of network. The height of strip shows the highest operation (the $(n-1)$th operation in Figure 3), the makespan in fact. After packing n migration operations into a 2-D strip composed by time and bandwidth, we will get an optimal schedule. Though strip packing problem is a NP problem, there are still some approximation algorithms such as Next-Fit Decreasing Height (NFDH), or metaheuristic algorithms like annealing and genetic algorithm[4]. Algorithm 2 uses the Bottom-Left (BL) algorithm to find an optimal schedule to minimize the makespan of cloud platform managed migration operations of busy VM.

References

1. Soundararajan, V., Anderson, J.M.: The impact of management operations on the virtualized datacenter. In: ACM SIGARCH Computer Architecture News, pp. 19–23 (June 2010)
2. Clark, C., Fraser, K., Hand, S., Hansen, J.G.: Live migration of virtual machines. In: Proceedings of the 2nd conference on Symposium on Networked Systems Design & Implementation, pp. 273–286 (2005)
3. Strunk, A.: Costs of virtual machine live migration: A survey. In: IEEE Eighth World Congress, pp. 323–329 (2012)
4. Lodi, A., Martello, S., Monaci, M.: Two-dimensional packing problems: A survey. European Journal of Operational Research, 241–252 (2002)
5. Breitgand, D., Kutiel, G., Raz, D.: Cost-aware live migration of services in the cloud. In: SYSTOR 2012 (2012)

Sequential Sensing and Transmission for Real-Time Traffic in Cognitive Networks

Show-Shiow Tzeng[1] and Ying-Jen Lin[2]

[1] Dept. of Optoelectronics and Communication Engineering,
National Kaohsiung Normal Univ., Kaohsiung, Taiwan
sstzeng@nknucc.nknu.edu.tw

[2] Dept. of Mathematics, National Kaohsiung Normal Univ., Kaohsiung, Taiwan

Abstract. This paper proposes a sequential sensing and transmission algorithm for real-time data in time-slotted multi-band cognitive networks. The proposed algorithm includes the backlog in a queue and the delay constraint of real-time data to select an appropriate band to send data such that more real-time data can be transmitted before being dropped. Simulation results show that the proposed algorithm reduces frames loss ratio and increases effective real-time throughput.

Keywords: sequential sensing, real-time traffic, frame loss ratio, multi-band, cognitive networks.

1 Introduction

Cognitive networks have been introduced to utilize the temporarily idle bands in licensed networks [1]. To access an idle spectrum band, the first step of a mobile user in cognitive networks (i.e. cognitive user) is to sense the band and determine whether the band is idle or busy. In a multi-band networks, a cognitive user can use sequential sensing to sense bands one by one. Once one idle band is found, the cognitive user can send out data on the band; otherwise, the user senses the next band. Sequential sensing allows cognitive users to sense two or more bands, which then leads to that cognitive users send out data more quickly in a cost-effective manner [2,3].

Previous sequential sensing algorithms implicitly assume that (i) frames are always available from an upper layer at any time and (ii) frames can tolerate long delay. Frames arriving from an upper layer are usually placed into a queue and then be transmitted latter. Due to the first assumption, the number of the frames in a queue is infinite and previous sequential sensing stops to send frames on the band which maximum throughput is the greatest among the sensing bands. However, the number of the frames in a queue is finite and is possibly variable. It is meaningless that a band which can transmit all the frames in a queue is found but we abandon the band and sense the next band due to the reason that the next band may have higher throughput. Therefore, we suggest that sequential sensing may stop on the band which can send out all the frames if the band is found, instead of the band which maximum throughput is the greatest;

C.-H. Hsu et al. (Eds.): NPC 2014, LNCS 8707, pp. 600–603, 2014.
© IFIP International Federation for Information Processing 2014

from this viewpoint, the frames can be sent more quickly. Under the second assumption, previous sequential sensing does not consider that real-time frames have the requirement of delay constraint; that is, frames are dropped when the frames suffer a specified delay time. Although sensing more bands may have more opportunity to find a throughput-maximum band, more frames may be also dropped. This paper designs a sequential sensing procedure for real-time traffic in a realistic network environment removing the two assumptions.

2   The Proposed Sensing and Transmission Algorithm

The radio environment herein is a licensed network in which radio spectrum is divided into spectrum bands and each band is further divided into time slots. M possible transmission rates are assumed to be available on a band; each rate is denoted by r_m, $1 \leq m \leq M$. The frames, consisting of header and payload, are real-time traffic with the constraint of delay time. The time that a frame stays in a queue is queuing time. The time that a frame is sent out is transmission time. For a frame, if the sum of queuing time and transmission time is greater than the delay requirement, the frame is dropped. Given a set of bands, the amount of real-time data successfully sent in a slot on the bands excludes sensing overhead, header overhead, and the failed data due to miss-detection and dropping. Then, the estimated real-time throughput (ERT) is defined as the ratio of the average amount of real-time data successfully sent in a slot on the bands to a slot time. In the proposed algorithm, a cognitive user starts to sense a time slot on band b_i, $i = 1$. If sensing result is busy, the user checks whether band b_{i+1} exists. If band b_{i+1} exists, the user senses the same slot on the next band b_{i+1}; otherwise, the user waits the beginning of the next slot and then repeats the proposed algorithm. If sensing result is idle, the user calculates (i) the ERT of band b_i and (ii) the ERT of the bands $\{b_{i+1}, b_{i+2}, ..., b_N\}$; then the user compares the values of the both ERTs. If the ERT of the bands $\{b_{i+1}, b_{i+2}, ..., b_N\}$ is higher, the user continues to sense the next band b_{i+1}; otherwise, the user sends frames in the residual time of the slot on band b_i.

In the following, we introduce the notation used in the equations to calculate the ERT, and then the equations are presented. The header length and payload length of a frame are denoted by L_h and L_d respectively. Let T_c, T_s, T_l, and T_p respectively denote the time of changing bands, sensing time, slot time, and the probing time of a band. Let T_q^j denote the queuing time of the q-th frame in a queue at the beginning of slot j. The probability that a slot is busy (or idle) is denoted by P_{busy} (or P_{idle}). The probability that a user correctly detects a busy slot is denoted by P_d. The probability that a user incorrectly identifies an idle slot as a busy slot is denoted by P_f. Let $E_{i,k}^j$ denote the ERT of slot j on bands $\{b_i, b_{i+1}, ..., b_N\}$, where $1 \leq i \leq N$ and k, $0 \leq k \leq i-1$, is the number of probing operations performed before band b_i. Let $e_{i,k}^j(x)$ represent the ERT of slot j on band b_i, where x is the transmission rate of band b_i and k is the number of probing operations performed before band b_i. We in turn derive $e_{i,k}^j(x)$ and $E_{i,k}^j$ as follows. When a cognitive user attempts to send frames in a queue in slot j

on band b_i, the user experiences i sensing times, $(i-1)$ times of changing bands, and at least one probing time. Since the user may have probed k bands before band b_i, the q-th frame can be sent at a rate x if (i) the frame is sent completely before the end of slot j, i.e. $iT_s + (i-1)T_c + (k+1)T_p + q(L_d + L_h)/x < T_l$ and (ii) the delay constraint D of the frame is satisfied, i.e. $T_q^j + iT_s + (i-1)T_c + (k+1)T_p + q(L_d+L_h)/x < D$, which can be expressed by an indicator function $\delta_q^j(x)$. The value of $\delta_q^j(x)$ is 1 if the frame is sent successfully; otherwise, the value is 0. The maximum number of frames which can be sent at a rate x in the remaining time of slot j is $\sum_{q\in Q} \delta_{i,k,q}^j(x)$, where Q is the set of frames in a queue at the beginning of slot j. Then, the ERT, $e_{i,k}^j(x)$, is calculated as follows:

$$e_{i,k}^j(x) = \frac{1}{T_l} \sum_{q\in Q} \delta_{i,k,q}^j(x)L_d. \tag{1}$$

When a user is in slot j on band b_i, the ERT of bands $\{b_i, b_{i+1}, ..., b_N\}$, $E_{i,k}^j$, is discussed into three cases: (i) the sensing result of idle band b_i is idle, which probability is $P_{idle}(1 - P_f)$, (ii) the sensing result of busy band b_i is idle, which probability is $P_{busy}(1 - P_d)$, and (iii) the sensing result of idle or busy band b_i is busy, which probability is $P_{busy}P_d + P_{idle}P_f$. In the first case, if the ERT, $e_{i,k}^j(x)$, of band b_i is greater than or equal to the ERT of bands $\{b_{i+1}, b_{i+2}, ..., b_N\}$, the user determines to send frames on band b_i; i.e., $E_{i,k}^j$ is $e_{i,k}^j(x)$. Otherwise, the user continues to sense the next band b_{i+1}; i.e., $E_{i,k}^j$ is $E_{i+1,k+1}^j$. Let $\delta_{i,k}^j(x)$ be an indicator function which value is 1 if the user sends frames in slot j on band b_i, i.e. $e_{i,k}^j(x) \geq E_{i+1,k+1}^j$, and which value is 0 if the user continues to sense. Let $\bar{\delta}_{i,k}^j(x)$ denote the complementary of the $\delta_{i,k}^j(x)$. The ERT of bands $\{b_i, b_{i+1}, ..., b_N\}$ in the first case is

$$\sum_{m=1}^M P_{r_m}[\delta_{i,k}^j(r_m)e_{i,k}^j(r_m) + \bar{\delta}_{i,k}^j(r_m)E_{i+1,k+1}^j], \tag{2}$$

where P_{r_m} denotes the probability that the transmission rate of band b_i is r_m, $m = 1, 2, ..., M$. In the second case, when a user probes the rate of band b_i, the user receives no response due to busy band b_i. The user continues to sense the next band b_{i+1}; then, the ERT, $E_{i,k}$, is $E_{i+1,k+1}^j$. In the third case, the user continues sensing from the next band b_{i+1}; then, the ERT, $E_{i,k}^j$, is $E_{i+1,k}^j$. The ERT of bands $\{b_i, b_{i+1}, ..., b_N\}$ is summarized in recursive Eq. (3) which can be solved by backward induction.

$$E_{i,k}^j = \begin{cases} P_{idle}(1 - P_f) \sum_{m=1}^M P_{r_m}[\delta_{i,k}^j(r_m)e_{i,k}^j(r_m) + \\ \bar{\delta}_{i,k}^j(r_m)E_{i+1,k+1}^j] + P_{busy}(1 - P_d)E_{i+1,k+1}^j + \\ (P_{busy}P_d + P_{idle}P_f)E_{i+1,k}^j \qquad 1 \leq i \leq N-1, \\ \\ P_{idle}(1 - P_f) \sum_{m=1}^M P_{r_m}e_{i,k}^j(r_m) \qquad\qquad i = N. \end{cases} \tag{3}$$

3   Simulation Results and Conclusions

Fig. 1 shows the ERT and frame loss ratio (the ratio of the number of loss frames to the total number of frames) of the proposed algorithm and the two other algorithms; one is the algorithm in [3], which produces maximal effective throughput (MET) without considering delay constraint and the backlog in a queue, and the other is the algorithm, called first-fit herein, which merely sends frames on a band which is first found on a slot and its bandwidth is sufficient to send all the frames in a queue. The unit of the ERT in Fig. 1 is the percentage of the load which can be successfully transmitted. From the figure, we observe that the proposed algorithm reduces frame loss ratio and increases effective real-time throughput because the proposed algorithm includes the backlog and the delay constraint to select an appropriate band to send frames as soon as possible.

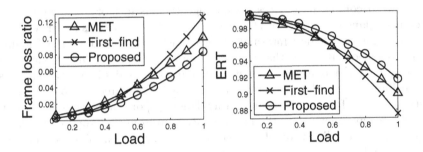

Fig. 1. Frame loss ratio and ERT

Acknowledgement. This research was partially supported by the National Science Council, Taiwan, under grants NSC 101-2221-E-017-011- and NSC 102-2221-E-017-006-.

References

1. Akyildiz, I.F., Lee, W.-Y., Vuran, M.C., Mohanty, S.: A survey on spectrum management in cognitive radio networks. IEEE Comms. Mag. 46(4), 40–48 (2008)
2. Shu, T., Krunz, M.: Throughput-efficient sequential channel sensing and probing in cognitive radio networks under sensing errors. ACM Mobicom 2009, 37–48 (2009)
3. Tzeng, S.-S., Lin, Y.-J.: Cross-layer sequential sensing with effective throughput maximization in time-slotted cognitive networks. Wireless Netw. 19(5), 591–606 (2013)

An Adaptive Heterogeneous Runtime for Irregular Applications in the Case of Ray-Tracing (Extended Abstract)

Chih-Chen Kao and Wei-Chung Hsu

Department of Computer Science, National Taiwan University, Roosevelt Road,
Taipei, 10617 Taiwan
hsuwc@csie.ntu.edu.tw

Heterogeneous architecture has been widely adopted in various computing systems, from mobile devices to servers. However, optimizing the performance for such platforms remains challenging in three aspects: the control flow divergence decreases the utilization of SIMD components, the significant memory copy overhead between computing devices consuming precious memory bandwidth and the load imbalance that degrades the overall performance. In this paper, we proposed three methodologies: Intermediate Feedback, Dynamic Task Partitioning and Heterogeneous Runtime that work collaboratively to overcome the aforesaid problems. We adopted and implemented these methodologies in a heterogeneous runtime library derived from Intel Embree[1] and compared the performance results of the two frameworks running Ray-Tracing[2] on various scenes. Experiment results have shown that the performance gain from the proposed methods is significant, especially in complex scenes with a large amount of objects or with large input data sizes the CPU cannot handle efficiently.

Due to the performance and power efficiency potentials of GPGPU and heterogeneous systems, a wide variety of applications, which include molecular simulation, fluid dynamics, biomedical image processing and computer vision, have been developed by leveraging the aforementioned programming models. However, for this type of heterogeneous configuration, many challenges remain before the performance potential can be fully unleashed. Despite significant advantages of GPU programming, writing high-performance heterogeneous programs still require programmers to be familiar with GPU architecture. The performance of a heterogeneous program is significantly influenced by how the computations are mapped into threads and how those threads are scheduled onto distinct cores, the usage of GPU registers and memory hierarchy, the synchronization among all threads and data access, the data transfer between host and GPU memories and the control flow branch divergence issue. In short, a program which benefits from GPGPU must contain explicit parallelism, high regularity and data reuse. The irregularities in an application may throttle the expected performance of the GPU by as much as an order of magnitude.

The terms regular and irregular are often used in compiler literature. For example, in regular code, control flow and data memory references are not data dependent. Dense matrix multiplication operations are good examples of regular code. On the other hand, in irregular code, both control flow and data memory references could be data dependent. For example, graph-based applications are

C.-H. Hsu et al. (Eds.): NPC 2014, LNCS 8707, pp. 604–607, 2014.

considered irregular, because the connectivity and values of the nodes in a graph are unknown before the input graph is available, and the connectivity and values of the nodes determine which graph elements are accessed[3]. Regular programs can often be efficiently mapped onto the GPGPU computing unit, and many of them have been ported to heterogeneous systems to benefit from increased performance and power efficiency. However, duplicating the success of heterogeneous computing from regular programs to irregular programs is a challenge. Irregular programs are often operated around pointer-based data structures such as graphs, trees or linked lists that are difficult to map to conventional regular GPU architecture or SIMD components. The execution paths of an irregular program are often unpredictable and could also vary dramatically during runtime[4]. Furthermore, in contrast to regular programs, the data dependencies in irregular programs can only be resolved dynamically at runtime, making it difficult to design a proper task scheduler[5][6].

The obstacles of efficiently adopting irregular programs to heterogeneous system can be categorized as follows: Firstly, the irregular memory access (e.g. indirect array references, sparse matrix references) could lead to low effective memory bandwidth, and there is no proper static solution to adaptively determine which type of memory should be used for irregular programs during execution. Secondly, the dynamically varying control flows create thread divergences, which reduces the level of parallelism and SIMD lane utilization in GPU. Thirdly, the chain of input dependencies often causes load imbalance among multiple cores, which degrades the overall throughput. Finally, memory-bound pointer chasing exhibits low data locality and exposes increased data access latency on GPGPU. Therefore, mapping irregular code efficiently onto a heterogeneous system remains difficult[7][8].

What type of heterogeneous computing model could handle irregular programs more efficiently is still debatable. For example, Ray-Tracing is an irregular program that is intensively used for global illumination in multimedia applications and has been adopted for implementation on different heterogeneous models. At the early stage of GPGPU computing, Ray-Tracing is designed to run on a GPGPU because a GPGPU is capable of handling a large number of rays in parallel. However, the potential irregularities of Ray-Tracing decrease the utilization of SIMD/SIMT components in GPU, and thereby offer little performance/power advantages[9].

Recently, Intel has announced a Ray-Tracing framework called Embree[1] with a different design philosophy that is optimized for traditional CPU architectures augmented with medium size (i.e. 512 bits) of SIMD capability. The Embree framework leverages CPU threads with wider SIMD units by using a compiler framework called Intel SPMD Program Compiler. (ISPC)[10]. The framework was originally designed for single ray traversal using SSE or AVX-enabled CPUs but has been extended to support Intel Xeon Phi architectures[11]. Embree features spatial acceleration structures and traversal algorithms and claim to support efficient Ray-Tracing with MIMD architectures and medium size SIMD capability. However, we believe that, with proper runtime and innovative methodologies, we could make traditional CPU/GPU type of heterogeneous system more competitive on irregular applications. In this work, we use Ray-Tracing as a case study to show the potential of our proposed approaches.

In this work, we address the forenamed problems of irregular programs and proposed a feedback tuning mechanism that can be used to model a specific category of heterogeneous program where the input data is recursively modified and added back to the commonly shared database for the next computation. Previous research applied a statistic approach and heuristic. Our method is based on analyzing and monitoring the communication protocol and behavior among all modules in a program. A new methodology is introduced in this research that encodes the representative feature of a heterogeneous program gathered at runtime and sends them to adjacent modules for adjusting iterative computation to fit the given platform configuration in order to gradually fine tune the system performance. We proposed a dynamic task partitioning mechanism and heterogeneous thread pool in order to resolve issues related to branch divergence and load imbalance. To demonstrate the effectiveness of our proposed schemes, we evaluate our performance gain by implementing the methodologies into a runtime library which is derived from the Intel Embree Ray-Tracing framework and compare the execution time with the original version.

In Conclusion, we explore the performance potential of mapping irregular programs onto heterogeneous systems by taking a Ray-Tracing algorithm as a case study. Three methodologies, Intermediate Feedback, Dynamic Task Partitioning and Heterogeneous Thread Pool, are introduced in this framework. The experiment results shows that our proposed methods could benefit heterogeneous computing resources and thereby increase the system performance, especially for handling complex scenes and for large input data sizes. We believe that the proposed methods could be applied to other heterogeneous frameworks to address the challenges of branch divergences, memory copy overhead and load imbalance when mapping irregular applications to GPGPU.

The benefit of the intermediate feedback is significant. Without this mechanism, the program must be built by pure heuristic approaches, which have limited success and are often effective for only certain specific configurations. The optimized execution setup will be lost if the system setting is changed. For instance, in the case of Embree, the hybrid packet/single-ray tracing algorithm is implemented by utilizing a specific type of BVH tree. However, determining the appropriate tracing method in the algorithm is based on heuristic. The process starts with a 16-wide packet traversal which performs 16-wide box tests. At any point in time, the bit in an active mask will be counted to indicate how many of the packet's rays are still active for a subtree. If this number falls below a given threshold, which is set to 7, the process leaves the packet traversal mode and sequentially traces all active rays in the single-ray mode[12]. The drawback of this method is that the threshold may need to change and the program will require recompilation if the system is moved to a machine with a shorter SIMD lane. Also, this method does not prevent any possible divergent execution that lowers the effectiveness of the SIMD engine. Our intermediate feedback differs from the above method by setting the correlation based on the actual activities and data analysis. It is effective for any kind of system configuration since the runtime would automatically adjust itself. If this method were moved to another platform, the program which utilized our runtime library could adapt and gradually arrives at an optimized setting.

References

1. Woop, S., Feng, L., Wald, I., Benthin, C.: Embree ray tracing kernels for cpus and the xeon phi architecture. In: ACM SIGGRAPH 2013 Talks, p. 44. ACM (2013)
2. Purcell, T.J., Buck, I., Mark, W.R., Hanrahan, P.: Ray tracing on programmable graphics hardware. In: Proceedings of the 29th Annual Conference on Computer Graphics and Interactive Techniques, SIGGRAPH 2002, pp. 703–712. ACM, New York (2002), http://doi.acm.org/10.1145/566570.566640
3. Burtscher, M., Nasre, R., Pingali, K.: A quantitative study of irregular programs on gpus. In: 2012 IEEE International Symposium on Workload Characterization (IISWC), pp. 141–151. IEEE (2012)
4. Zhang, E.Z., Jiang, Y., Guo, Z., Tian, K., Shen, X.: On-the-fly elimination of dynamic irregularities for gpu computing. In: ACM SIGARCH Computer Architecture News, vol. 39(1), pp. 369–380. ACM (2011)
5. Nasre, R., Burtscher, M., Pingali, K.: Data-driven versus topology-driven irregular computations on gpus. In: 2013 IEEE 27th International Symposium on Parallel & Distributed Processing (IPDPS), pp. 463–474. IEEE (2013)
6. Monteiro, P., Monteiro, M.P.: A pattern language for parallelizing irregular algorithms. In: Proceedings of the 2010 Workshop on Parallel Programming Patterns, ParaPLoP 2010, pp. 13:1–13:14. ACM, New York (2010), http://doi.acm.org/10.1145/1953611.1953624
7. Pingali, K., Nguyen, D., Kulkarni, M., Burtscher, M., Hassaan, M.A., Kaleem, R., Lee, T.-H., Lenharth, A., Manevich, R., Méndez-Lojo, M., et al.: The tao of parallelism in algorithms. ACM SIGPLAN Notices 46(6), 12–25 (2011)
8. Kulkarni, M., Burtscher, M., Inkulu, R., Pingali, K., Casçaval, C.: How much parallelism is there in irregular applications? SIGPLAN Not. 44(4), 3–14 (2009), http://doi.acm.org/10.1145/1594835.1504181
9. Aila, T., Laine, S.: Understanding the efficiency of ray traversal on gpus. In: Proceedings of the Conference on High Performance Graphics 2009, pp. 145–149. ACM (2009)
10. Pharr, M., Mark, W.R.: ispc: A spmd compiler for high-performance cpu programming. In: Innovative Parallel Computing (InPar), pp. 1–13. IEEE (2012)
11. Chrysos, G., Engineer, S.P.: Intel® xeon phi coprocessor (codename knights corner) (2012)
12. Benthin, C., Wald, I., Woop, S., Ernst, M., Mark, W.R.: Combining single and packet-ray tracing for arbitrary ray distributions on the intel mic architecture. IEEE Transactions on Visualization and Computer Graphics 18(9), 1438–1448 (2012)

DLBer: A Dynamic Load Balancing Algorithm for the Event-Driven Clusters

Mingming Sun, Changlong Li, Xuehai Zhou, Kun Lu, and Hang Zhuang

Computer Science University of Science and Technology of China, Hefei, China
{mmsun,liclong,local,zhuangh}@mail.ustc.edu.cn,
xhzhou@ustc.edu.cn

Abstract. The event-driven programming model has been proposed to efficiently process iterative applications and incremental applications. In clusters based the event-driven model, applications are structured as a series of triggers, each of which will be invoked when associate events are trigged. And framework assigns a newly submitted trigger to a node where the relevant datasets set. Unfortunately it may lead to load imbalance because associate events occur by chance. Numerous triggers in a node may be simultaneously invoked but other nodes have no triggers running. Jobs composed of short, sub-second triggers present a difficult balancing challenge. To the end, we design DLBer, a new dynamic load balancing algorithm for the event-driven clusters to maximize improve the utilization of node resources.

1 Introduction

The synchronous data-flow model such as MapReduce, Dryad and their variants is deficient for iterative applications since synchronous computation and lock-step across rounds. It also is not suitable for incremental applications because it processes total dataset for every increment, incurring a significant performance penalty. Therefore, the event-driven programming model is proposed as an asynchronous computation model such as Percolator[1], Oolongr[2] and Dominor[3] et al. This model follows the Event-Condition-Action (ECA) rule[4]. ECA rules are straightforward: when the event occurs, evaluate the condition; if the condition is fulfilled, execute the action automatically. Applications can be expressed in term of triggers, user-specified code blocks that can be invoked whenever the associated datasets modified. Each trigger completes a computation task. In iterative applications, the result of past iteration can be immediately used to determine the course of current execution. Incremental applications only need to process the updated dataset and some relevant data, which is affected by the updated dataset, instead, recalculates entire dataset.

In clusters based event-driven model, a newly submitted trigger is assigned to the node where the relevant datasets set. However triggers are not instantly executed after their submission, that is to say, specific events are needed to invoke triggers. This may lead to load imbalance because during execution time the cluster resource usage cannot be determined. Extreme case, a node has lots

C.-H. Hsu et al. (Eds.): NPC 2014, LNCS 8707, pp. 608–611, 2014.
© IFIP International Federation for Information Processing 2014

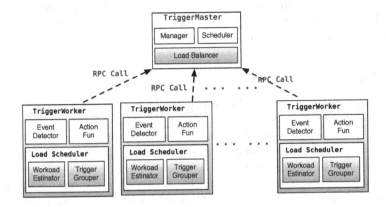

Fig. 1. The architecture of DLBer

of triggers invoked in the waiting queue, but other nodes are idle. So framework needs a load balancer to achieve better utilization of node resources and a high system throughout and quick response time of user requests. However, trigger may be short second or sub-second task. This presents a difficult balancing challenge. To address the above problems, we design DLBer, a new centralized dynamic load balancing algorithm for the event-driven clusters. Dynamic load balancing is essential for such systems since unpredictable load estimates. Our load balancer aims at maximize improve the utilization of node resources.

2   DLBer Design

As shown as Fig. 1, custer based event-driven model runs with a *TriggerMaster*, which assigns a newly coming trigger to workers where the relevant datasets of the trigger set, and multiple *TriggerWorkers*, each of which monitors the modification on dataset, and executes trigger tasks. Our DLBer consists of two main modules: a *LoadBalancer* in *TriggerMaster*, which coordinates and redistributes triggers invoked among *TriggerWorkers* according to their workloads, and *LocalScheduler* in each *TriggerWorker*. *LocalScheduler* contains *WorkloadEstimator*, which automatically predicts the execution time of trigger and evaluates current total workload, and *TriggerGrouper*, which picks out several suitable triggers to become a group as the basic unit of transfer. As trigger in the event-driven clusters may be short second or sub-second task, we divide triggers invoked into groups to avoid repeatedly network transmission and reduce pressure for *TriggerMaster*. Once the balancing decisions are made in *LoadBalancer*, a high-load *TriggerWorker* will receive transfer instructions and trigger *LocalScheduler* to transfer triggers. *LocalScheduler* first selects one or more trigger group, and then transfer trigger group to low-load destination

TriggerWorker according to transfer instructions. DLBer employs centralized load balancing policy because the accumulation of workoad information can be achieved by heartbeat message.

2.1 Trigger Group Policy

WorkloadEstimator calculates the mean completed time of same triggers, which have already completed, as the execution time of trigger. As triggers continue to complete, the execution time of trigger will be recalculated to get more precise time. Each *TriggerWorker* workload is the sum of the execution time of all triggers invoked in waiting queue.

The role of *TriggerGrouper* is to divide triggers invoked into groups as the basic unit of transfer. We define *TriGroup*, the size of trigger group, which depends on the worker computing capacity and network bandwith. Upon the arrival of a transfer request from *TriggerMaster*, *TriggerGrouper* sorts triggers in descending order of predicted execution time into trigger sequence. Then it selectes triggers from head of trigger sequence into a trigger group according to *TriGroup*. Then trigger group contains minimal triggers to reduce network transmission overhead.

2.2 Load Balancing Algorithm

DLBer focuses on *TriggerWorkers*, whose workload is lower than a threshold called *tunder*. *tunder* is greater than the sum of load balancing policy time, the heartbeat interval (default as 5 second) and transmission time of a trigger group. Then the low-load *TriggerWorker* can be still busy during the transfer triggers.

Algorithm 1 illustrates the process of load balancing algorithm. If workload of worker n is below the *tunder*, load balancing policy first considers the heaviest load worker a. Supposing worker a will transfer out a trigger group, the workload of worker a needs to exceed the load of worker n, otherwise it is not necessary to transfer tasks. When all nodes in cluster are busy, there is almost no extra scheduling overhead. At the other extreme, our method also avoid frequent task transfering since the defined *tunder*.

3   Evaluation

In order to test DLBer using a realistic workload, we ported Domino by writing a Domino load balancing plugin. Domino is an open-source trigger-based programming framework. We use application PageRank on a cluster, which has a master and 8 workers. PageRank in the event-driven model contains two triggers: *PageRankDist* and *PageRankSum*. Once pagerank value of a page is modified, *PageRankDist* will be invoked to change pagerank weights for all its relevant out-degree pages. Then the *PageRankSum* for such relevant out-degree pages will be invoked for these changes. The function of *PageRankSum* is to simply sum up all the rank values generated from different in-degree pages.

Algorithm 1. *Load Balancer*

Input:
    Array A: nodes queue by descending workload;
Iteration:
    while $n.load < tunder$ (n : *the tail of A*) **do**
        if $a.load > tunder$ & $a.load - TriGroup > n.load + TriGroup$ (a : *the head of A*) **then**
            $task\_fetch(a, n)$;
        else
            break;
        end if
        Reorder array by descending workers' workload;
    end while

PageRankDist will be invoked again. This continues until a tolerable error defined by user. Our results shows our load balancer outperforms default Domino about 100%.

Acknowledgment. Our work was supported by the National Science Foundation of China under grants No. 61272131 and No. 61202053, China Postdoctoral Science Foundation grant No. BH0110000014, Fundamental Research Funds for the Central Universities No. WK0110000034, and Jiangsu Provincial Natural Science Foundation grant No. SBK201240198.

References

1. Peng, D., Dabek, F.: Large-scale Incremental Processing Using Distributed Transactions and Notifications. In: OSDI, vol. 10 (2010)
2. Mitchell, C., Power, R., Li, J.: Oolong: asynchronous distributed applications made easy. In: Proceedings of the Asia-Pacific Workshop on Systems. ACM (2012)
3. Dai, D., et al.: Domino: an incremental computing framework in cloud with eventual synchronization. In: Proceedings of the 23rd International Symposium on High-Performance Parallel and Distributed Computing, ACM (2014)
4. McCarthy, D., Dayal, U.: The architecture of an active database management system. ACM Sigmod Record 18(2), 215–224 (1989)
5. Willebeek-LeMair, M.H., Reeves, A.P.: Strategies for dynamic load balancing on highly parallel computers. IEEE Transactions on Parallel and Distributed Systems 4(9), 979–993 (1993)

Performance Prediction Model and Analysis for Compute-Intensive Tasks on GPUs

Khondker S. Hasan, Amlan Chatterjee, Sridhar Radhakrishnan,
and John K. Antonio

School of Computer Science
University of Oklahoma
110 W. Boyd St., Norman
OK 73019, USA
{shajadul,amlan,sridhar,antonio}@ou.edu

Abstract. Using Graphics Processing Units (GPUs) to solve general purpose problems has received significant attention both in academia and industry. Harnessing the power of these devices however requires knowledge of the underlying architecture and the programming model. In this paper, we develop analytical models to predict the performance of GPUs for computationally intensive tasks. Our models are based on varying the relevant parameters - including total number of threads, number of blocks, and number of streaming multi-processors - and predicting the performance of a program for a specified instance of these parameters. The approach can be used in the context of heterogeneous environments where distinct types of GPU devices with different hardware configurations are employed.

Keywords: Compute-Intense Kernels, CUDA, GPU, Modeling and prediction.

1 Introduction

The availability of GPUs as commodity hardware and co-processors to CPUs, and the relative low cost-to-performance ratio has propelled these devices to the forefront or research in both academia and the industry. Compute Unified Device Architecture (CUDA), an extension to the C programming language, allows general-purpose problems to be solved using Nvidia GPUs. However, this paradigm shift has left developers striving for better performance from the available hardware. The general trend has been focusing on transferring compute intensive portions of tasks to the GPUs and exploiting parallelism in the existing code. Therefore, most of the research and studies relevant to GPUs focus on transferring the data from the CPU to the GPU and back, designing efficient data structures for the GPU, and utilizing available primitives to decrease memory latency [2, 4]. In reality, to exploit the full potential of these devices, understanding the underlying architecture and the basics of the programming model are required.

C.-H. Hsu et al. (Eds.): NPC 2014, LNCS 8707, pp. 612–617, 2014.

In this paper, we focus our research on optimally using the device at hand. We concentrate on deriving analytical models that can predict the *execution efficiency* of GPU programs i.e., GPU *kernels* based on certain parameters like the total number of resident blocks, number of threads in each block, the total number of blocks spawned in the device, the total number of streaming multi-processors available in the device, and others. The importance of our models are in the fact that it will help developers to unleash the full potential of the available hardware by predicting execution efficiency of thread blocks before placing them in the GPU run queue and also by providing suggestions to improve the efficiency by making arrangements for optimal execution time. The benchmark programs used for empirical analysis of our analytical model are professionally developed programs from the Nvidia CUDA GPU Computing SDK [8] for demonstrating the reliability and accuracy of our proposed model. The benchmark programs are tested in both Tesla C1060 and Kepler 20 devices, respectively and achieved very low prediction error with an error bound of 0.13-5.69%.

2   Analytical Models

An analytical framework for estimating the overall execution efficiency for batches of thread blocks is derived for GPU systems. The introduced prediction model incorporates the following three major observed categories while GPU executes several blocks of threads:

- When the number of blocks to be executed is more than the aggregate number of resident blocks for the GPU.
- When the number of warps to be executed is more than the aggregate number of resident warps for the GPU.
- When the total number of threads to be executed is more than the aggregate number of resident threads for the GPU.

Table 1 contains the notation and definitions of required parameters of the model. The execution time is ideal, denoted by τ, when the number of blocks and threads in each block is less than the aggregate resident blocks and threads for the GPU (this number varies by GPU architecture). The following model incorporates the effect for the case when the number of thread blocks spawned for execution is more than the aggregate resident blocks for all multi-core processors of the GPU; for measuring the execution time (ξ_{rb}):

$$\xi_{rb} = \begin{cases} \tau & \text{if } \beta \leq (\rho_b \times \rho_{sm}), \\ \text{Max}\left(1, \left\lceil \frac{\beta}{\rho_b \times \rho_{sm}} \right\rceil\right) \times \tau & \text{else} \end{cases} \tag{1}$$

A higher occupancy reduces processor idle time (SM may stall due to unavailability of data or busy functional units) and improves overall performance [9], [10]. The estimated execution time model can be derived as:

$$\xi_{rw} = \left\{ \frac{\beta \times \vartheta}{(\rho_w \times \sigma_w \times \rho_{sm})} \right\} \times \tau \tag{2}$$

Table 1. Terms and definitions of GPU efficiency prediction model parameters

Terms	Definition
ρ_{sm}	Number of Streaming Multi-core processors (SM) in the device.
ρ_w	Maximum number of resident warps in a streaming multi-core processor.
ρ_b	Maximum number of resident blocks in a streaming multi-core processor.
ρ_t	Maximum number of resident threads in a streaming multi-core processor.
σ_w	Size of warp. Size for both Tesla C1060 and Kepler 20 is 32.
σ_b	Maximum size (number of threads) of a block.
β	Number of blocks spawned in the GPU device.
ϑ	Number of threads per block (block size).

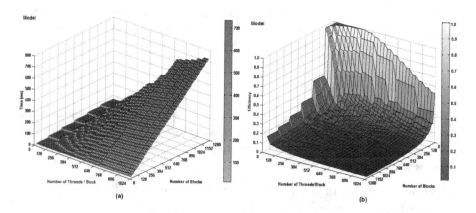

(a)   (b)

Fig. 1. Surface diagrams by deploying the introduced prediction model when ϑ is increased from 32 to 1024, β increased from 16 to 1248, and $\tau = 14.5$ (a) shows measured total execution time surface (b) shows measured efficiency surface diagram (associated with Eq. 3).

The composite prediction model which incorporates all major specified effects includes the input parameters: ideal thread execution time, execution efficiency when $\beta > (\rho_b \times \rho_{sm})$, and execution efficiency when threads in a SM $> (\rho_w \times \sigma_w)$. The model equation is derived from Eqs. 1 and 2 to reflect the observed effect in total thread execution time (κ).

$$\kappa = \begin{cases} \frac{\tau}{(\tau + \xi_{rw})}, & \text{when } (\beta \times \vartheta) \leq (\rho_w \times \sigma_w \times \rho_{sm}) \\ \frac{\tau}{(\xi_{rb} + \xi_{rw})}, & \text{when } (\beta \times \vartheta) > (\rho_w \times \sigma_w \times \rho_{sm}) \end{cases} \tag{3}$$

When the value of $(\beta \times \vartheta) \leq (\rho_w \times \sigma_w \times \rho_{sm})$, the τ is divided by an expression which incorporates the overhead of warp occupancy. Next, when $(\beta \times \vartheta) > (\rho_w \times \sigma_w \times \rho_{sm})$, the τ is divided by an expression which contains the overhead of both $\beta > \rho_b$ and $\vartheta > \rho_t$ expressed in Eqs. 1 and 2.

Figure 1 (a) shows the composite effect of increased blocks and threads in a block on total execution time of the GPU kernel. In this figure, two horizontal axes represents ϑ and β respectively and the vertical axis represents the total execution time in milliseconds. With careful observation, it can be seen that for each case when $\beta > (\rho_b \times \rho_{sm})$, the execution time jumps by the value of τ. Similarly, when $(\beta \times \vartheta) > (\rho_w \times \sigma_w \times \rho_{sm})$, for each $(\rho_w \times \sigma_w \times \rho_{sm})$, the execution time increases utilizing Eq. 2. The total execution time increases sharply for large number of blocks and its sizes. Figure 1 (b) depicts the execution efficiency surface measured by Eq. 3. The efficiency surface diagram clearly visualizes the composite effect of increased number of β and ϑ. The model depicts a sharp performance degradation as soon as the $\beta > \rho_b$.

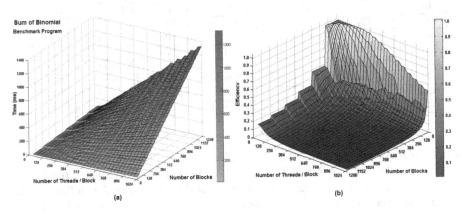

Fig. 2. Surface diagrams for the Sum of Binomial Series benchmark program (a) shows increasing run-time while ϑ increased from 32 to 1248 and β increased from 16 to 1024 (b) shows measured efficiency surface diagram with respect to τ

3 Empirical Studies

The purpose of this experimental study is to empirically measure the execution efficiency of kernels in GPUs as a function of aggregate blocks and threads in each block. The *Sum of binomial series* benchmark program is utilized from Nvidia CUDA SDK to conduct the empirical work to ensure real-world applications adaptability and accuracy. Two different GPU devices are used for evaluating the proposed efficiency prediction models for parallel thread execution. We have used Kepler 20 and Tesla C1060 GPU cards for empirical studies in heterogeneous environments.

It can be observed from Table 2 that for $\beta = 64$ and ϑ ranging from 32 to 320, as the $(\beta \times \vartheta) > \rho_t$, the execution time increases around $(2 \times \tau)$ depending on the number of warps. This behavior is modeled using Eq. 2. Next, when the total number of threads spawned $(\beta \times \vartheta)$ is more than the occupancy, $(\rho_w \times \sigma_w \times \rho_{sm} = 64 \times 32 \times 13 = 26,624$ for the Kepler 20 device), the specified series in Section 2

Table 2. Empirical results using **Kepler 20** GPU device for the Sum of Binomial Series benchmark program

β	Number of Threads per Block (ϑ)									
	32	**64**	**96**	**128**	**160**	**192**	**224**	**256**	**288**	**320**
16	14.61	14.61	14.62	14.63	14.62	14.62	14.62	14.62	14.63	14.64
64	14.61	14.60	14.63	14.62	15.42	15.91	16.90	17.73	21.34	22.57
112	14.60	14.53	15.20	16.69	21.38	24.35	27.93	42.31	42.74	41.72
160	14.54	15.19	17.84	22.47	40.29	40.58	44.35	45.28	52.16	65.71
208	14.55	15.83	20.80	27.64	43.00	45.12	52.69	55.23	70.21	77.90
224	29.02	30.36	35.30	42.16	42.97	46.65	56.08	69.69	75.50	78.63
272	29.05	30.37	35.47	43.40	50.60	66.41	70.39	79.28	84.12	95.45
320	29.07	30.54	36.56	45.43	67.23	71.02	80.39	98.46	102.9	117.3
368	29.08	31.60	39.95	51.77	69.03	78.60	96.55	103.4	123.5	127.1
416	29.02	31.63	41.58	55.38	75.08	93.54	102.2	110.4	129.7	147.5
432	43.45	46.13	56.03	69.73	78.60	94.69	105.3	124.9	134.9	147.9
480	43.50	46.15	56.19	70.99	93.14	99.24	124.6	134.3	153.7	170.8
528	43.51	46.32	58.16	74.42	94.91	117.8	132.6	152.3	164.8	178.4
576	43.50	46.75	60.69	79.36	101.6	120.7	139.1	161.9	181.4	199.4
624	43.51	47.41	62.39	83.10	105.8	130.2	152.4	165.5	192.9	209.2
640	57.87	61.91	76.75	97.30	118.9	131.1	156.4	180.1	203.4	222.6

can be observed in the Table 2. For $\beta = 208$ and $\vartheta = 128$, the number of threads spawned in the device is $208 \times 128 = 26,624$ (i.e., maximum occupancy reached)[1]. As soon as the ϑ or β increases, the execution time increases depending on the number of execution cycle. This observed behavior is modeled using Eq. 3.

Figure 2 (a) and (b) shows the complete measured *run time surface* and *efficiency surface* (using Eq. 3) diagram for the sum of binomial series benchmark program. Both surfaces depict the complete 2496 independent test run results to capture all possible scenarios by varying the values of β and ϑ. It can be observed from Figure 2 (a) that each time when $\beta \times \vartheta$ crosses ($\rho_w \times \sigma_w \times \rho_{sm}$), the execution time increases for new scheduling cycles. Similarly, when β crosses ($\rho_b \times \rho_{sm}$), the execution time increases by τ. It can be observed from Figure 2 (b)that the efficiency value decreases significantly when β and ϑ increases beyond the capacity of scheduling cycle. Both surface diagrams clearly depicts same behavior and shape as compared to the models' run-time and efficiency surfaces in Figure 1 respectively.

4   Conclusion

This paper has introduced prediction models to forecast the execution efficiency of GPUs for computationally intensive kernels. The key challenge was to determine the arrangement of blocks and threads in a block prior to placement of

---

[1] Maximum number of resident threads in a Kepler 20 SM is 2048 though a thread block can contain a maximum of 1024 threads.

threads into the run queue. The model has been validated with Nvidia CUDA GPU SDK benchmark program for accuracy. The provided surface diagrams depict clear visualization of measured efficiency based on variable number of blocks and size of blocks. The empirical studies performed on the prediction model show that the model surface follows the same shape and pattern of the real-world benchmark programs with only $0.13 - 5.69\%$ prediction error. The conducted study is highly useful for understanding and optimizing performance on GPUs and useful in the context of heterogeneous environment to choose the device with a better performance potential.

References

1. Sim, J., Dasgupta, A., Kim, H., Vuduc, R.: A Performance Analysis Framework for Identifying Potential Benefits in GPGPU Applications. In: 17th ACM SIGPLAN Symposium on Principles and Practice of Parallel Programming (PPoPP 2012), New Orleans, Louisiana, pp. 11–22 (2012)
2. Khondker, S., Hasan, J.K.: Antonio, and Sridhar Radhakrishnan, "A New Composite CPU/Memory Model for Predicting Efficiency of Multi-core Processing". In: The 20th IEEE International Symposium on High Performance Computer Architecture (HPCA 2014) Workshop, Orlando, FL, February 15-19 (2014)
3. Holmen, J.K., Foster, D.L.: Accelerating Single Iteration Performance of CUDA-Based 3D Reaction–Diffusion Simulations. International Journal of Parallel Programming 42(2), 343–363 (2014), doi:10.1007/s10766-013-0251-z
4. Chatterjee, A., Radhakrishnan, S., Antonio, J.K.: Data Structures and Algorithms for Counting Problems on Graphs using GPU. International Journal of Networking and Computing 3(2), 264–288 (2013)
5. Hasan, K.S., Radhakrishnan, S., Antonio, J.K.: Composite Prediction Model and Task Distribution on a Cloud of Multi-core Processors. In: IEEE International Conference on High Performance Computing (HiPC 2014) Workshop, Bangalore, India (December 2013)
6. Kepler Compute Architecture Technology in a Brief (2012), http://www.nvidia.com/content/PDF/kepler/ NV_DS_Tesla_KCompute_Arch_May_2012_LR.pdf
7. Zhang, Y., Owens, J.D.: A quantitative performance analysis model for GPU architectures. In: 2011 IEEE 17th International Symposium on High Performance Computer Architecture (HPCA), pp. 382–393 (2011)
8. Nvidia CUDA GPU SDK, Sample CUDA Toolkits, http://docs.nvidia.com/cuda/cuda-samples/
9. CUDA Warps and Occupancy. GPU Computing Webinar (July 2011), http://on-demand.gputechconf.com/gtc-express/2011/ presentations/cuda_webinars_WarpsAndOccupancy.pdf
10. Lam, S.K.: CUDA Performance: Maximizing Instruction-Level Parallelism (September 2013), http://continuum.io/blog/cudapy_ilp_opt

Interdomain Traffic Engineering Techniques to Overcome Undesirable Connectivity Incidents

Amer AlGhadhban, Ashraf Mahmoud, Marwan Abu-Amara,
Farag Azzedin, and Mohammed H. Sqalli

University of Hail, KFUPM
a.alghadhban@uoh.edu.sa,
{ashraf,marwan,fazzedin,sqalli}@kfupm.edu.sa

Abstract. The importance of Internet availability is supported by the overwhelming dependence of government services and financial institutions upon said availability. Unfortunately, the Internet is facing different level of undesirable connectivity incidents. So, it is imperative to take serious measures in order to increase Internet connectivity resilience. We consider a scenario where a concerned region is facing an undesirable connectivity incident by its primary Internet Service Provider (ISP) which still advertises reachability to the concerned region. Assuming that connectivity to a secondary ISP is available, software is designed to implement different traffic engineering techniques in order to enhance internet connectivity resilience and send the traffic through the secondary ISP. The work is characterized by the implementation of these traffic engineering techniques in the laboratory through a detailed set of experiments.

1 Introduction

Undesirable Internet connectivity incidents can occur due to many reasons that can be categorized into two main categories: intentional and unintentional. Unintentional reasons include router misconfiguration, hardware and software failures, and security violations of the ISP/BGP operations. On the other hand, intentional reasons may happen with malicious intent or for political reasons [1]. Traffic engineering techniques are used by Autonomous Systems (ASes) in order to optimize the utilization of network resources [2]. In this work software is designed to implement traffic engineering techniques in order to enhance internet connectivity resilience. The work is characterized by the implementation of different traffic engineering techniques in the laboratory through a detailed set of experiments. Performance figures for the different types of background traffic considered and the representative configurations are collected and compared with each other.

1.1 Problem Statement

This study focuses on the network configuration portrayed in Fig. 1 where the concerned region, represented by AS100, is connected to the Internet through the primary ISP and represented by AS300. AS100 is also connected through a secondary

C.-H. Hsu et al. (Eds.): NPC 2014, LNCS 8707, pp. 618–622, 2014.

ISP, called here the *good ISP* and represented by AS200. In this instance, AS100 faces undesirable connectivity incidents, such as significant bandwidth reduction and/or unacceptable delay by its primary ISP. Nevertheless, the primary ISP's border router continues to exchange BGP messages with the border router of the concerned region (AS100) and advertising its prefixes on the Internet.

1.2   Summary of Contributions

In this work we evaluate and prototype a different set of interdomain traffic engineering techniques that have the capability to control outgoing traffic and attract incoming traffic through a secondary ISP. The evaluation and prototyping is performed in a laboratory setting designed to mimic conventional deployment with support for two distinct topologies referred to by identical and non-identical topologies to symbolize the Internet's connectivity structure. In the identical scenario the *AS-Path* length from AS100 to AS600 over the two ISPs are the same. In the non-identical scenario the *AS-Path* from AS100 to AS600 through the two upstream ISPs are not the same, as shown in Fig. 1. For the sake of accurate and consistent testing procedures, software is created to detect the connectivity incident, deploy the prescribed solution, and to measure the network *convergence time*. When the connectivity incident, such as multiple packets drop, is detected the software forces the concerned region' border router to route the traffic via the good ISP.

2   Proposed Work

In this section, the proposed interdomain traffic engineering techniques are described. The proposed techniques are listed in Table 1. Some of the proposed BGP-based techniques can influence the incoming traffic to go through the *good ISP* while others can control the outgoing traffic.

Overlay Network is a virtual network that works over a real network such as the Internet. The most common type of overlay network is Virtual Private Network (VPN). VPN is usually used to build a secure network over an unsecure network like the Internet. *Overlay Network* methods can be used to overcome internet connectivity issues by establishing an overlay network between the region of concern AS and several cooperative ASes distributed around the world, e.g. IXPs, and route the traffic over a good ISP. Fig. 2 shows the effect of different overlay techniques on FTP and HTTP end-to-end delay. The FTP/HTTP applications are examined in our laboratory and tested under different background loads. Obviously, the end-to-end delay increases proportionally with the increase in the traffic load. The unencrypted overlay techniques show almost the same end-to-end delays when they are compared with no overlay technique.

The BGP methods tested in our labs that can influence incoming traffic, referred to as Attractors, are *AS-Path* Pre-pending, eBGP multihop, and Filtering outgoing advertisement. *AS-Path* Pre-pending [3] allows a router to advertise its prefixes with a longer *AS-Path* through one or more neighboring routers. Hence, this method advertises the prefixes through the primary ISP with a longer *AS-Path* and with a regular *AS-Path* through a *good ISP*. Consequently, the Internet ASes will prefer the shortest *AS-Path* which goes through the *good ISP*. The eBGP *multihop* scheme allows indirectly connected ASes to look as if they are directly connected. Consequently, the *AS-Path* length between the two eBGP *multihop* configured routers appears in the global routing table as one hop. This means that downstream ASes will prefer the path through the eBGP *multihop* routers over all other existing paths that might be physically shorter. Thirdly, filtering of outgoing advertisement method can control and filter the outgoing BGP routing advertisements of the local BGP *speaker*. This means that we can block the local prefixes from being advertised to the primary ISP and have them only advertised to the *good ISP*. Consequently, the local prefixes are not included in the advertisements of the primary ISP to the Internet, and the Internet routers learn about the local side prefixes only through the *good ISP*. The Outforwarders methods that can control the outgoing traffic are filtering of incoming advertisements, IP default/static, MED, Weight and Local Preference.

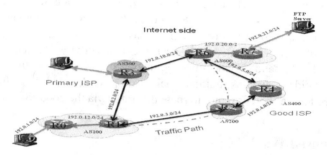

Fig. 1. Non-identical laboratory scenario

As seen in Table 1, some of the solutions have the ability to forward outgoing traffic via a *good ISP* and other solutions have the ability to attract incoming traffic. To overcome the undesirable connectivity incident we have to combine one solution from the Outforwarder list with another solution from the Attracter list. Then, configure the concerned region's BGP *speaker* with this combination.

Table 1. Classification of the proposed solutions

	BGP Solution Methods	Incoming	Outgoing
Attracter	*Overly Network*	Yes	No
	AS-Path pre-pending	Yes	Yes
	eBGP *multihop*	Yes	Yes
	Filter outgoing advertisements	Yes	No
Outforwarder	Filter incoming advertisement	No	Yes
	IP static/default route	No	Yes
	MED	No	Yes
	Weight	No	Yes
	Local Preference	No	Yes

2.1   Convergence Time Results

The traffic engineering techniques are examined under three different background traffic loads: 75%, 50% and 25% on the 1.544 Mbps inter-router links used in the laboratory implementation. The obtained *convergence time* of the evaluated solutions is between 0.1 and 0.3 second, as shown in Fig. 2. The *convergence time* exchanged messages are few in number and small in size. Thus, the effect of the background traffic load on the *convergence time* is very small. The combination of *Filter outgoing advertisements* + Weight always gives the fastest *convergence time* even with the different background traffic load. The *Filter outgoing advertisements* solution blocks the concerned region prefixes from being advertised to the Internet through the primary ISP. Also, it does not change or introduce any load on the BGP advertisements, unlike *AS-Path pre-pending* solutions.

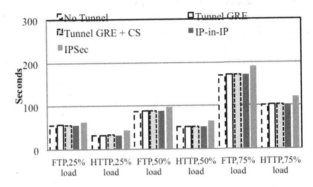

Fig. 2. Shows the end-to-end delay of the examined tunnelling techniques (CS=Checksum)

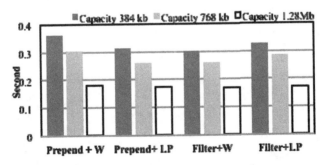

Fig. 3. Convergence time results (LP=Local-Preference W=Weight)

3   Conclusions

Government services and financial institution's dependence on Internet availability is sufficient proof of the importance of avoiding connectivity problems. The presented techniques address incidences wherein the primary ISP of the concerned region is showing unacceptable connectivity service. In this work we proposed multiple combinations of the interdomain traffic engineering techniques that can control outgoing traffic and influence incoming traffic. Based on the results, Internet Exchange Points (IXPs) and/or International ISPs can strengthen the Overlay Network and eBGP multihop solutions by agreeing to serve as remote cooperative ASes. The examined overlay techniques showed an acceptable overhead on the evaluated applications.

References

1. Arbor networks: Infrastructure security survey,
   http://www.arbornetworks.com/spsecurityreport.php
2. Secci, S., et al.: Efficient inter-domain traffic engineering with transit-edge hierarchical routing. Computer Networks 57, 976–989 (2013)
3. Rekhter, Y., Li, T., Hares, S.: IETF-A Border Gateway Protocol 4, BGP-4 (January 2006),
   http://www.ietf.org/rfc/rfc4271.txt

Author Index